A Companion
to Biblical Interpretation
in Early Judaism

A Companion
to Biblical Interpretation
in Early Judaism

Edited by

Matthias Henze

WILLIAM B. EERDMANS PUBLISHING COMPANY
GRAND RAPIDS, MICHIGAN / CAMBRIDGE, U.K.

© 2012 Wm. B. Eerdmans Publishing Co.

Published 2011 by
Wm. B. Eerdmans Publishing Co.
2140 Oak Industrial Drive N.E., Grand Rapids, Michigan 49505 /
P.O. Box 163, Cambridge CB3 9PU U.K.

Library of Congress Cataloging-in-Publication Data

A companion to biblical interpretation in early Judaism / edited by Matthias Henze.
    p.   cm.
Includes bibliographical references and index.
ISBN 978-0-8028-0388-7 (pbk.: alk. paper)
1. Bible. O.T. — Criticism, interpretation, etc., Jewish — History — To 1500.
I. Henze, Matthias.

BS1186.C66   2012
221.6 — dc23

2011023516

www.eerdmans.com

Contents

Preface

The idea to compile *A Companion to Biblical Interpretation in Early Judaism* came to me while editing another collection of essays, *Biblical Interpretation at Qumran* (Eerdmans, 2005). Working on the Qumran material, I was once again reminded that the multiple ways in which the biblical text was received and recited, copied and corrected, meditated and mediated at Qumran are all part of the much larger reception history of the biblical writings in Jewish antiquity. Biblical interpretation at Qumran constitutes but a small, albeit significant, part of biblical interpretation in late Second Temple Judaism, one piece in the larger mosaic of Judaisms and their diverse engagements with what was to become Scripture. To make sense of the former one needs to have at least some understanding of and appreciation for the latter.

It also became clear to me, on a more practical level, that contributions to a conference volume such as *Biblical Interpretation at Qumran* typically focus on a single text or specific topic and are often written without much consideration given to the larger picture. In recent decades the study of the Jewish literature of the Hellenistic and early Roman periods has matured to become an academic discipline in its own right. There are now several excellent introductions to this evolving field, including James C. VanderKam's *An Introduction to Early Judaism* (Grand Rapids: Eerdmans, 2001) and the second edition of George W. E. Nickelsburg's classic, *Jewish Literature Between the Bible and the Mishnah* (Minneapolis: Fortress, 2005). There are handbooks on the history of biblical interpretation, such as Magne Sæbø's multivolume *Hebrew Bible/Old Testament: The History of Its Interpretation* (Göttingen: Vandenhoeck & Ruprecht, 1996-), and now the *Blackwell Bible Commentaries* have begun to appear, a new commentary series devoted exclusively to the reception history of the books of the Hebrew Bible throughout the centuries. What does not exist, however, is a systematic introduction to biblical interpretation in the Jewish literature of antiquity. The present *Companion* seeks to fill that gap.

The *Companion* covers a period of about five hundred years, from the third century B.C.E. through the second century C.E., roughly the time from the end of the biblical period to the Mishnah. It was relatively easy to determine the parameters of the *Companion,* since the chronological borders largely suggest themselves. Few will dispute that biblical interpretation begins within the Jewish Bible itself and continues in its versions, and that the emergence of rabbinic literature on the other end of the chronological spectrum marks a major turning point in the history of Jewish biblical interpretation. The oldest text discussed in this volume, apart from the Hebrew Bible itself, is the Septuagint, and the last essay in the *Companion* looks forward and describes some lines of continuity, particularly in the field of legal exegesis, from Qumran to early rabbinic literature.

The selection and organization of the material, on the other hand, proved to be an altogether different and considerably more difficult issue. There simply are no organizational categories that emerge naturally from the texts themselves. One possible way of structuring this diverse group of writings would have been to arrange the texts according to the types of biblical interpretation they represent, such as legal/*halakhic* exegesis, narrative/*haggadic* exegesis, and prophetic/inspired exegesis. Such a division, however informative it might be, inevitably implies a somewhat arbitrary imposition of modern scholarly categories unto the ancient materials. Moreover, no matter how one divides up the texts, the result is bound to remain problematic, primarily because several books defy any such classification, as they fall under more than one rubric. Documents that include legal exegesis will also have narrative sections in them, and the same holds true for prophetically-inspired texts.

An alternative division would have been to line up the texts chronologically, in the hopes of reconstructing a history of biblical interpretation in early Judaism. The perhaps most obvious problem here is that biblical interpretation, like most other aspects in early Jewish thought, did not develop neatly in a linear fashion. Another problem with the chronological arrangement is that, while we know the compositional dates of some books, we do not know them for others. Moreover, some books, like Qumran's *Rule of the Community,* were subject to extensive rewriting and hence have multiple dates attached to them, while other books include significant portions of older materials, so that the date of their final composition is only of relative value.

In the end I decided to ask the contributors to the *Companion* to write on specific books of late Second Temple Judaism and to examine the extent to which the kind of biblical interpretation the reader finds in them is characteristic of exegetical techniques found elsewhere. I then organized the essays into six groups. The first group, called Hebrew Bible/Old Testament, contains three essays, on the Hebrew Bible, the Septuagint, and the Targums. The second group is called Rewritten Bible. Recently this label has fallen out of grace with many scholars. It retains its usefulness, however, when it is not understood as an absolute category but merely as a label that underscores parallel strategies of reading the Bible in these writings. The books chosen for the second group are *Jubilees,* the *Genesis Apocryphon,* and *Pseudo-Philo.* The third group, titled Qumran literature, looks at some of the most pertinent texts from the Dead Sea Scrolls, the *Community Rule,* the *Pesharim,* and the *Hodayot.* With the fourth group, Apocalyptic Literature and Testaments, we look at a different genre of early Jewish literature altogether that cuts across canonical lines, including writings from the Hebrew Bible, the Apocrypha, and the so-called Pseudepigrapha. The books here discussed are Daniel, *4 Ezra* and *2 Baruch,* and the *Testament of the Twelve Patriarchs.* The fifth group, Wisdom Literature, includes essays on two important apocryphal texts, Ben Sira and the *Wisdom of Solomon.* The sixth group, Hellenistic Judaism, includes an essay on Philo and one on Josephus. Each essay is followed by a pertinent bibliography. The volume ends with indices and a cumulative bibliography on biblical interpretation in Judaism of antiquity.

Perhaps more than other scholarly publications, a *Companion* of this sort is the product of a communal effort. I wish to thank my contributors, both for generously contributing their expertise to this project and for their patience throughout its preparation, which, I fear, I have tested to the limit. All authors very kindly agreed to revisions, both minor and substantial, and some went with me through several drafts. I remain in their debt. Heba Khan kindly helped with the cumulative bibliography at the end. I am grateful to Allen Myers, Senior Editor at Eerdmans Publishing Company, who expressed interest in this project when it was just an idea. Über allem aber steht, *Deo gratias.*

MATTHIAS HENZE

Abbreviations

AB	Anchor Bible
ABD	*Anchor Bible Dictionary*, ed. David Noel Freedman. New York, 1996
AbrN	*Abr-Nahrain*
AbrNSup	Abr-Nahrain: Supplement Series
AGJU	Arbeiten zur Geschichte des antiken Judentums und des Urchristentums
ALD	Aramaic Levi Document
ALGHJ	Arbeiten zur Literatur und Geschichte des hellenistischen Judentums
AnBib	Analecta biblica
ANRW	*Aufsteig und Niedergang der römischer Welt*, ed. Hildegard Temporini and Wolfgang Haase. Berlin, 1972–
APF	Archiv für Papyrusforschung und verwandte Gebiete
APOT	*The Apocrypha and Pseudepigrapha of the Old Testament*, ed. Robert H. Charles. Oxford, 1913
ArBib	The Aramaic Bible
ASP	American Studies in Papyrology
ATA	Alttestamentliche Abhandlungen
ATDan	Acta theologica danica
AUSS	*Andrews University Seminary Studies*
BBB	Bonner biblische Beiträge
BBR	*Bulletin for Biblical Research*
BEATAJ	Beiträge zur Erforschung des Alten Testaments und des antiken Judentum
BETL	Bibliotheca ephemeridum theologicarum lovaniensium
Bib	*Biblica*
BibOr	Biblica et orientalia
Bijdr	*Bijdragen: Tijdschrift voor filosofie en theologie*
BIOSCS	*Bulletin of the International Organization for Septuagint and Cognate Studies*

BJRL	*Bulletin of the John Rylands University Library of Manchester*
BJS	Brown Judaic Studies
BKAT	Biblischer Kommentar. Altes Testament
BN	*Biblische Notizen*
BRS	Biblical Resource Series
BWANT	Beiträge zur Wissenschaft vom Alten und Neuen Testament
BZ	*Biblische Zeitschrift*
BZAW	Beihefte zur Zeitschrift für die alttestamentliche Wissenschaft
CBET	Contributions to Biblical Exegesis and Theology
CBQ	*Catholic Biblical Quarterly*
CBQMS	Catholic Biblical Quarterly Monograph Series
CEJL	Commentaries on Early Jewish Literature
CHB	*Cambridge History of the Bible*
CHJ	*Cambridge History of Judaism,* ed. W. D. Davies and Louis Finkelstein. Cambridge, 1984–
ConBOT	Coniectanea biblica: Old Testament Series
CQS	Companion to the Qumran Scrolls
CRINT	Compendia rerum iudaicarum ad Novum Testamentum
CSCO	Corpus scriptorum christianorum orientalium
DBSup	*Dictionnaire de la Bible: Supplément,* ed. Louis Pirot and André Robert. Paris, 1928–
DJD	Discoveries in the Judaean Desert
DSD	*Dead Sea Discoveries*
DSSR	D. W. Parry and E. Tov, *Dead Sea Scrolls Reader.* 6 vols. Leiden: Brill, 2004-2005
EBib	Etudes bibliques
EDSS	*Encyclopedia of the Dead Sea Scrolls,* ed. Lawrence H. Schiffman and James C. Vanderkam. Oxford, 2002
EHAT	Exegetisches Handbuch zum Alten Testament
ErIsr	*Eretz-Israel*
EstBib	*Estudios biblicos*
ETL	*Ephemerides théologiques et religieuses*
ExpTim	*Expository Times*
FAT	Forschungen zum Alten Testament
FB	Forschung zur Bibel
FOTL	Forms of the Old Testament Literature
FRLANT	Forschungen zur Religion und Literatur des Alten und Neuen Testaments
FZPhTh	*Freiburger Zeitschrift für Philosophie und Theologie*
GAP	Guides to Apocrypha and Pseudepigrapha
GCS	Die griechischen christlichen Schriftsteller der ersten Jahrhunderte
GRBS	*Greek, Roman and Byzantine Studies*
HALOT	L. Koehler, W. Baumgartner, and J. J. Stamm, *The Hebrew and Aramaic Lexicon of the Old Testament.* 5 vols. Leiden: Brill, 1994-2000

HAR	*Hebrew Annual Review*
HDR	Harvard Dissertations in Religion
Hen	*Henoch*
HO	Handbuch der Orientalistik
HSB	Herder biblische Studien
HSM	Harvard Semitic Monographs
HTR	*Harvard Theological Review*
HTS	Harvard Theological Studies
HUCA	*Hebrew Union College Annual*
HUCM	Monographs of the Hebrew Union College
ICC	International Critical Commentary
Int	*Interpretation*
IOS	*Israel Oriental Studies*
JAC	Jahrbuch für Antike und Christentum
JAOS	*Journal of the American Oriental Society*
JBL	*Journal of Biblical Literature*
JBW	*Jahrbücher der biblischen Wissenschaft*
JEA	*Journal of Egyptian Archaeology*
JNES	*Journal of Near Eastern Studies*
JNSL	*Journal of Northwest Semitic Languages*
JPS	Jewish Publication Society TANAKH Translation
JQR	*Jewish Quarterly Review*
JSHRZ	Jüdische Schriften aus hellenistich-römischer Zeit
JSJ	*Journal for the Study of Judaism*
JSJSup	Journal for the Study of Judaism Supplement
JSNT	*Journal for the Study of the New Testament*
JSNTSup	Journal for the Study of the New Testament: Supplement Series
JSOT	*Journal for the Study of the Old Testament*
JSOTSup	Journal for the Study of the Old Testament: Supplement Series
JSP	*Journal for the Study of the Pseudepigrapha*
JSPSup	Journal for the Study of the Pseudepigrapha: Supplement Series
JSQ	*Jewish Studies Quarterly*
JSS	*Journal of Semitic Studies*
JSSSup	Journal of Semitic Studies Supplement
JTS	*Journal of Theological Studies*
L.A.B.	*Liber Antiquitatum Biblicarum*
LCL	Loeb Classical Library
LD	Lectio divina
LEC	Library of Early Christianity
LHB/OTS	Library of Hebrew Bible/Old Testament Studies
LSTS	Library of Second Temple Studies
LXX	Septuagint
MGWJ	Monattschrift für Geschichte und Wissenschaft des Judentums
MJS	Münsteraner judaistische Studien
MScRel	*Mélanges de science religieuse*

MSU	Mitteilungen des Septuaginta-Unternehmens
MT	Masoretic Text
NAWG	Nachrichten der Akademie der Wissenschaften in Göttingen
NETS	New English Translation of the Septuagint
NIV	New International Version
NovTSup	Supplements to Novum Testamentum
NRSV	New Revised Standard Version
NTL	New Testament Library
NTOA	Novum Testamentum et Orbis Antiquus
NTS	*New Testament Studies*
OBO	Orbis biblicus et orientalis
ÖBS	Österreichische biblische Studien
OLA	Orientalia lovaniensia analecta
OTL	Old Testament Library
OTP	*The Old Testament Pseudepigrapha,* ed. James H. Charlesworth. Garden City, 1983-85
OTS	Old Testament Studies
OtSt	*Oudtestamentische Studiën*
PAC	Philo of Alexandria Commentary Series
Phil	*Philologus*
Proof	*Prooftexts*
PTSDSSP	Princeton Theological Seminary Dead Sea Scrolls Project
PVTG	Pseudepigrapha Veteris Testamenti Graece
PW	A. F. Pauly, *Paulys Realencyclopädie der classischen Altertumswissenschaft.* New ed. Georg Wissowa. Munich, 1980
RB	*Revue biblique*
RBL	Review of Biblical Literature
RechBib	Recherches bibliques
REJ	*Revue des études juives*
RevistB	*Revista bíblica*
RevQ	*Revue de Qumran*
RRJ	*Review of Rabbinic Judaism*
RSR	*Recherches de science religieuse*
RStB	*Ricerche storico bibliche*
RTP	*Revue de théologie et de philosophie*
SamP	Samaritan Pentateuch
SBLEJL	Society of Biblical Literature Early Judaism and Its Literature
SBLMS	Society of Biblical Literature Monograph Series
SBLSCS	Society of Biblical Literature Septuagint and Cognate Studies
SBLSP	*Society of Biblical Literature Seminar Papers*
SBLSymS	Society of Biblical Literature Symposium Series
SBLTT	Society of Biblical Literature Texts and Translations
SBLWGRW	Society of Biblical Literature Writings from the Greco-Roman World
SC	Sources chrétiennes

ScrHier	*Scripta hierosolymitana*
SDSSRL	Studies in the Dead Sea Scrolls and Related Literature
SE	Studia evangelica
Sem	*Semitica*
SJ	Studia judaica
SJLA	Studies in Judaism in Late Antiquity
SJOT	*Scandinavian Journal of the Old Testament*
SNTSMS	Society for New Testament Studies Monograph Series
SPhA	*Studia philonica Annual*
SPhil	*Studia philonica*
SPhM	Studia philonica Monographs
SR	*Studies in Religion*
SSEJC	Studies in Early Judaism and Christianity
ST	*Studia theologica*
STDJ	Studies on the Texts of the Desert of Judah
StPB	Studia post-biblica
SUNT	Studien zur Umwelt des Neuen Testaments
SVTP	Studia in Veteris Testamenti pseudepigrapha
TANZ	Texte und Arbeiten zum neutestamentlichen Zeitalter
TBN	Themes in Biblical Narrative
TDOT	*Theological Dictionary of the Old Testament*, ed. G. Johannes Botterweck, Helmer Ringgren, and Heinz-Josef Fabry. Grand Rapids, 1974–
Text	*Textus*
TRE	*Theologische Realenzyklopädie*, ed. Gerhard Krause and Gerhard Müller. Berlin, 1977–
TS	*Theological Studies*
TSAJ	Texte und Studien zum antiken Judentum
TSK	*Theologische Studien und Kritiken*
TUGAL	Text und Untersuchungen zur Geschichte der altchristlichen Literatur
TZ	*Theologische Zeitschrift*
VC	*Vigiliae christianae*
VCSup	Vigiliae christianae Supplement
VT	*Vetus Testamentum*
VTSup	Supplements to Vetus Testamentum
WBC	Word Biblical Commentary
WMANT	Wissenschaftliche Monographien zum Alten und Neuen Testament
WUNT	Wissenschaftliche Untersuchungen zum Neuen Testament
ZAW	*Zeitschrift für die alttestamentliche Wissenschaft*
ZBK	Zürcher Bibelkommentare
ZNW	Zeitschrift für die neutestamentliche Wissenschaft und die Kunde der älteren Kirche
ZWT	*Zeitschrift für wissenschaftliche Theologie*

PART 1

INTRODUCTION

The Beginnings of Biblical Interpretation

James L. Kugel

What we call the Hebrew Bible is an anthology of texts that were composed over the course of several centuries.[1] How these texts ultimately came to be gathered together is still something of a mystery, but their various components were apparently preserved, at least at first, by different groups and institutions within Israel. These probably included the royal palace, the priestly establishment(s), prophetic guilds, courts of law, schools of various sorts, and perhaps yet other establishments. Many of the texts included in today's Bible no doubt originally played a role in the ongoing life of such institutions, preserving a record of past events and pronouncements as well as a precise formulation of how their affairs were to be conducted.

The fate of this store of texts was obviously influenced by two major political upheavals in the region, the conquest of the northern kingdom (Israel) by the Assyrians in 722 B.C.E. and the conquest of the southern kingdom (Judah) by the Babylonians in 586. These two catastrophes were similar, but not symmetrical: exiled by the Assyrians, many of the northerners simply disappeared from history and with them, no doubt, some (but not all) of their literary horde. The southerners' lot was somewhat different: exiled to Babylon, they held together long enough to see the Babylonian Empire taken over by the Persian king, Cyrus the Great, in 539.[2] Following the famous edict issued by Cyrus

---

1. "Hebrew Bible" itself is a somewhat slippery term; for purposes of this essay, it designates the Bible of rabbinic Judaism, that is, the Christian "Old Testament" without apocrypha/deuterocanonical writings.

2. On this: Richard N. Frye, *The History of Ancient Iran* (Munich: C. H. Beck, 1984); Ephraim Stern, "The Persian Empire and the Political and Social History of Palestine in the Persian Period," in *The Cambridge History of Judaism,* ed. W. D. Davies and Louis Finkelstein, vol. 1 (Cambridge: Cambridge University Press, 1984), 62-73; Edwin M. Yamauchi, *Persia and the Bible* (Grand Rapids: Baker, 1990), 85-92.

in 538, the Judeans began trooping back to their homeland and, once reestablished there, sought to rearrange their lives anew.[3] It was then that their collection of ancient writings — mostly Judean texts, but as well some northern writings that had presumably made their way south either before or just after the Assyrian conquest of Israel — suddenly came to assume a new importance in their lives.

This new importance of the ancestral writings is reflected within the Bible itself. Preexilic parts of the Bible rarely refer to Scripture as such; but the books compiled after the returnees began to trickle in from Babylon (such as Chronicles, Ezra-Nehemiah, Malachi, and others) mention, inter alia, the "Torah of Moses" or the "Torah of God," and they sometimes explicitly cite scriptural passages and their interpretation.[4]

Various factors combined to make for the new importance of Scripture within this group of returnees. The first was the fact of the Babylonian exile itself. In the harsh reality of exile, all that had been dear to the Jews was now a distant dream. The royal court, the Jerusalem temple, and other formerly crucial centers were no more; soon, the traditions and ways of thought associated with them began to fade. The exiles' heads were instead now filled with foreign institutions, a foreign language, and a way of thinking that hardly bothered to take account of the tiny nation from which they had come. Under such circumstances, Israel's ancient writings offered an island refuge. Here, the country's kings and heroes still lived in their full glory; here the God of Israel still reigned supreme, and his people and their history occupied center stage; and here was the exiles' old language, the Judean idiom, written down in the classical cadences of its greatest prophets and sages. It seems altogether likely that, during those years in Babylon, such writings as had accompanied the Judeans into exile only grew in importance — if not for all, then at least for some segment of the population. And once the exile was over, these same ancient texts continued in this role: they were the history of the nation and its pride, a national literature and more than that, a statement about the ongoing importance of the remnants of that kingdom, for its God and for the world.

---

3. The historicity of this edict has sometimes been questioned, but see Israel Eph'al, "Syria-Palestine under Achaemenid Rule," in *The Cambridge Ancient History*, vol. 4: *Persia, Greece, and the Western Mediterranean c. 525-479*, ed. John Boardman (Cambridge: Cambridge University Press, 1984), 139-64.

4. For the "Torah of God/the Lord" and "Torah of Moses," see, e.g., Dan 9:11, 13; Ezra 3:2; 7:6; Neh 8:1, 18; 9:3; 10:29; 1 Chr 16:40; 2 Chr 17:9; 23:18; 31:3-4; 34:14; 35:26. Apart from exact citation of earlier phrases and verses, postexilic writings often paraphrase earlier material; see, e.g., Ezra 9:11 and Neh 13:1-3, which apparently contain inexact citations of pentateuchal passages; compare with Lev 18:24-30; Deut 7:3; and Deut 23:3-5.

Beyond this was the whole *mode of return* in which the returnees found themselves. After all, they could have chosen (as others indeed did choose) to remain in Babylon. Returning to Zion was itself fraught with peril, and the life that awaited them was full of unknowns. Those who nevertheless resolved to go back were thus a self-selected group; for the most part, they did what they did out of a desire to reestablish what had been, or at least to start afresh the Jewish polity on its native soil. But what exactly *had* existed in years gone by? And how should the returning community go about reorganizing its collective existence? The body of ancient writings seemed to hold the answer to both questions. So it was that these texts were looked to now as a guide; they were concerned with events from the past, but what they said could be used as a model for the future. To be sure, the exiles were divided on many important questions: Should they settle into being obedient servants of their distant Persian masters, or should they harbor the hope of one day rebelling and reestablishing an independent Jewish state? Should they seek to be reunited with their northern neighbors, re-creating something like the great united monarchy of David and Solomon? Or were those inhabitants of the north mostly foreigners with whom Judea was to have no connection? Such questions were complex; there were good arguments on both sides. But precisely for that reason, exponents on either side sought to buttress their arguments with the ancient writings of prophets and sages and with examples from the people's history before the exile. In short, a new approach to Israel's ancient writings now emerged: They could tell you what to do *now*. This was a monumental change, and one that was to characterize the way Scripture was read for centuries and centuries to come.

The Importance of Laws

It is certainly no accident that so many of the postexilic evocations of Scripture found within the Hebrew Bible itself refer specifically to the "Torah of God" or the "Torah of Moses," both apparently appellations of the Pentateuch.[5] For the returning exiles, the laws of the Pentateuch seem to have played a more important role in their everyday lives than any of the other texts preserved from earlier days.

This circumstance in itself points up something significant about life in

---

5. See above, n. 4. It is not my intention here to discuss various recent theories that date the compilation of the Pentateuch itself to the Second Temple period, other than to say that I do not accept this view. I have discussed it, and my own views on the subject, in *How to Read the Bible: A Guide to Scripture, Then and Now* (New York: Free Press, 2007).

ancient Judea and how it differed from our own. Nowadays, a country's laws usually do not exercise a very great influence on people's day-to-day thoughts and actions — certainly not insofar as their religious lives are concerned. But such a mentality need not be assumed to exist in all societies at all times; there are some — and postexilic Judea seems to be one example — in which the subject of obedience to laws plays a somewhat more important role in people's everyday consciousness. In part, this may be due to the rather unique claim of the Pentateuch that its laws come from God rather than from merely human legislators. After all, someone who breaks the law in our society may have to pay a fine or even go to prison, but this in itself has no particular spiritual dimension. Likewise, someone who upholds the law may be proud to be a good citizen, but little more. In a society in which the laws are held to come from God, by contrast, to break the law is not merely to commit a crime; it is also to commit a sin. Likewise, observing the laws and doing what they say is not merely good citizenship, but a form of divine service, a way of actively seeking to do God's will. It is, of course, difficult to know how early, and to what extent, this view of things became normative in postexilic society, but it must at some point be factored into any attempt to explain the importance of law as reflected in Jewish writings of that period.

For the same reason, it is not difficult to imagine that the returnees' recent history may have further fostered an interest in biblical law in Second Temple Judaism. Scarcely a one of them could have failed to ask himself or herself why it was that God had ever allowed the Judean homeland to be conquered by the Babylonians and — a potentially related question — why the Babylonian Empire had in turn collapsed shortly thereafter. The answer to both questions doubtless was, for some, purely pragmatic: Babylonian military might had simply overwhelmed tiny Judah; by the same token, once the Medes and the Persians had combined forces, they easily overcame the Babylonians and took over their whole empire. But the Bible contains a different, more theological explanation: God *allowed* his people to be conquered as a punishment for their failure to keep his laws, the great covenant he had concluded with their ancestors. "Surely this came upon Judah at the command of the LORD" (2 Kgs 24:3). Then, lest anyone think it was by any merit of the Babylonians that Judah had been overcome, God subsequently dispatched the Persians to take over their country. If so, it was incumbent on the Judeans who had returned to their ancient homeland to avoid repeating their ancestors' misstep. This time they would scrupulously obey all of God's commandments; this time, everyone would be an expert in the application of divine law, so that there would be no mistakes (Jer 31:31-34).

There was probably another, more practical side to the importance attributed to these ancient laws. The Bible reports that the Persian administration actually adopted them as part of the Israelite legal system to be instituted in their new colony. The Persian emperor Artaxerxes I is thus reported to have written a letter to Ezra, a Jewish priest and sage who took over as a leader of the reestablished community:

> And you, Ezra, according to the God-given wisdom you possess, appoint magistrates and judges who may judge all the people in the province [of Judah] who know the *laws of your God;* and you shall teach those who do not know them. All who will not obey the law of your God and the law of the king, let judgment be strictly executed on them. (Ezra 7:25-26)

Of course, this account of the Persian promotion of Israel's laws may simply be the result of exaggeration or wishful thinking on the part of the biblical historian; all things considered, however, scepticism on this issue ought itself to be scrutinized carefully.[6] After all, other, extrabiblical sources have shown the Persians to have generally been enlightened rulers who sought to accommodate their subject peoples by, among other things, maintaining the local legal system; it would simply have been good sense to adopt such an approach with the Judeans as well.

The Rise of Biblical Interpreters

All the factors mentioned above — the role ancient texts may have played during the Babylonian exile itself, the implications they seemed to hold for the returning Judeans and the various uses to which they were put in consequence — combined to give this written legacy from the past an unusual relevance in Judea's present. But when texts from the past are granted such a role in any given society (as are, in our own time, various sorts of foundational documents — oaths, constitutions and bylaws, creeds and principles of faith, mission statements, and the like) they rarely speak for themselves; *interpreting* their words becomes in itself a major undertaking.

---

6. The idea was proposed by, among others, Elias Bickerman, *The Jews in the Greek Age* (Cambridge, Mass.: Harvard University Press, 1988), 30, and taken up by others. It was subjected to a careful reexamination in a series of essays edited by James W. Watts, *Persia and Torah: The Theory of Imperial Authorization of the Pentateuch.* SBLSymS 17 (Atlanta: SBL, 2001). On balance, the evidence presented contains arguments pro and con; in my opinion, while caution is warranted, I see no reason to reject the idea that Persian imperial policy was a strong factor in the final editing of the text.

In the case of the Hebrew Bible, the necessity for authoritative interpretation was obvious. On the most basic linguistic level, many words or expressions from the distant past were no longer understood. What is more, references to historical events, societal institutions, and the like often needed glossing, since many such things had long since passed from people's memories. But beyond such relatively straightforward matters, interpreters of Israel's Scripture came to play a more creative role. It was mentioned above that the resettled Judeans looked to ancient Scripture as a guide for re-creating their own new society; but of course there was no unanimity as to what sort of society that should be. Different sides in the debate thus sought to interpret Scripture in such a way as to bolster their arguments.

And then there was the matter of internal contradictions. If these ancient texts were to have an authoritative role in people's lives, they ought to speak with one voice — but often they did not. Take, for example, the matter of the sacrifice to be offered at the Passover festival. The instructions in the book of Exodus are rather clear:

> Tell the whole congregation of Israel that on the tenth of this month they are to take a lamb for each family, a lamb for each household. If a household is too small for a whole lamb, it shall join its closest neighbor in obtaining one; the lamb shall be divided in proportion to the number of people who eat of it. Your lamb shall be without blemish, a year-old male; you may take it from the sheep or from the goats. . . . They shall eat the lamb that same night; they shall eat it roasted over the fire with unleavened bread and bitter herbs. Do not eat any of it raw or boiled in water, but roasted over the fire, with its head, legs, and inner organs. (Exod 12:3-9)

The meat to be eaten at the Passover feast was to come "from the sheep or from the goats," and it was not to be boiled, but roasted. But if so, then how was an interpreter to explain this passage from Deuteronomy?

> You shall offer the passover sacrifice for the LORD your God, from the *flock and the herd,* at the place that the LORD will choose as a dwelling for his name. . . . You shall *boil it* and eat it at the place that the LORD your God will choose; the next morning you may go back to your tents. (Deut 16:2, 7)

"From the flock and from the herd" implies that a herd animal, such as a bull or cow, may also serve for the paschal meal, and "you shall boil it" seems to run completely counter to the instruction in Exodus, "Do not eat any of it raw or boiled in water." Which text was to be followed? This was hardly an isolated case; Scripture had quite a few apparent contradictions. Deuteronomy 23:3 said that an Ammonite or Moabite was not to be admitted "to the assembly of the LORD," yet the book of Ruth reported the marriage of Boaz to the Moabite Ruth without any censure, and the descendant of their union, David, was to be no less than the founder of the Judean royal dynasty — the bluest blood in Israel. The Ten Commandments present God as punishing children for their parents' sins, "to the third and the fourth generation" (Exod 20:5), whereas Deut 24:16 specifically forbade such vicarious punishment: "Only for their own crimes may persons be put to death." In all such cases, there was a felt need for authoritative interpretation to resolve the perceived difficulty.

It is therefore significant that, in the Bible's account of the events that followed the return from exile, the Judeans are said to have assembled to hear a lengthy public reading of "the book of the law of Moses" (Neh 8:1-8). Whether or not this passage from Nehemiah is a factual recital or an idealized happening, it is remarkable in several respects. The need to know what Scripture says comes here from the grass roots; that is, it is at the people's behest that Ezra undertakes this great public reading. Apparently, "all the people" knew that this great book of law (presumably our Pentateuch) existed, but they were still somewhat fuzzy about its contents. So they willingly stood for hours, "from early morning until midday," in order to hear its words firsthand. It is also noteworthy that this assembly included "both men and women and all who could hear with understanding," that is, children above a certain age: the Torah's words were, according to this passage, not reserved for some elite, or even for the adult males of the population, but were intended for the whole people to learn and apply. But — most significantly for our subject — this public reading is accompanied by a public *explanation* of the text. The Levites "helped the people to understand the law, while the people remained in their places"; thus, "they read from the book, from the law of God, *with interpretation.*"

Where Is Ancient Interpretation To Be Found?

We do not know what sort of interpretation was offered at Ezra's public reading, but scholars have naturally sought the earliest traces of interpretive activity within the Hebrew Bible itself.[7] This is no simple matter; what looks to some like interpretation (of a law or a story, for example) may seem to others to be merely a variant tradition of the same item.[8] Nor is there a great store of indis-

---

7. A number of examples are presented in Michael Fishbane, *Biblical Interpretation in Ancient Israel* (Oxford: Clarendon, 1985).

8. See my review of the foregoing, "The Bible's Earliest Interpreters," *Proof* 7 (1987): 269-83.

putable examples of such inner-biblical interpretation. But there certainly are some. For example, the contradiction mentioned above with regard to the preparation of the paschal sacrifice was apparently addressed in a passage in Chronicles:

> They [the Israelites] slaughtered the passover offering, and the priests dashed the blood that they received from them, while the Levites did the skinning. . . . Then they *boiled the passover offering in fire* according to the ordinance. . . . (2 Chr 35:11, 13)

"Boiled in fire" seems patently an attempt to reconcile the requirement of Exod 12:9 *not* to boil the sacrifice with "You *shall boil it* and eat it" in Deut 16:7. "Boiled in fire" (truly a contradiction in terms) was apparently coined by the Chronicler to suggest the roasting enjoined by Exod 12:9 while at the same time evoking the word "boiled" in Deut 16:7.

A similar harmonization of an apparent conflict occurs with regard to the legal status of Reuben, Jacob's eldest son. According to the law in Deut 21:15-17, a father is expressly forbidden to give the "birthright" — a special, double portion of his inheritance, which by law goes to his firstborn son — to any other son. But that is, according to the Genesis narrative, exactly what Jacob did with his firstborn son Reuben. After Reuben's sin with Bilhah (Gen 35:22), Jacob awarded the double portion that should have been Reuben's to Joseph, the son of his second wife, Rachel — as if Joseph were his firstborn. True, all this occurred before the great promulgation of laws at Mount Sinai. Still, it must have bothered interpreters to find Jacob guilty, even retroactively, of violating one of the Torah's laws. What is more, even after this disinheritance has taken place, Reuben continued to be referred to as the firstborn son (Exod 6:14, Num 1:20; 26:5, etc.). What was his true status? The Chronicler explains:

> The sons of Reuben, the firstborn of Israel [that is, Jacob]. (He *was* the firstborn, but because he defiled his father's bed, his birthright was given to the sons of Joseph son of Israel, so that he is not enrolled in the genealogy according to the birthright.) (1 Chr 5:1)

In Reuben's case, the Chronicler explains, an exception was made to the general rule because of Reuben's egregious sin with his father's concubine. He was still, in genealogical terms, the firstborn, but the firstborn's special inheritance was given instead to Joseph.

Such passages are a valuable witness to the ongoing interest in scriptural interpretation even within the biblical period. Yet they are, as noted, relatively few in number and often ambiguous in character. By comparison, the vast literature of the late Second Temple period that was not included in the Hebrew Bible offers a far richer store of ancient biblical interpretation. It is in these books — for the most part composed by Jews in Hebrew or Aramaic but preserved in secondary or tertiary translations by Christians — that one finds biblical interpretation in full flower. Indeed, essays in the present volume highlight nearly all of the most important writings from this period for the study of ancient biblical interpretation.

The Old Greek or Septuagint translation of the Bible, dating back to the third century B.C.E., is certainly one of the oldest repositories of such interpretation. As a translation it remains fairly close to its Hebrew original, but here and there it deliberately strays from a literal rendering in order to make an interpretive point. (For one example, see below.) From roughly the same period, *1 Enoch* contains a wealth of interpretive motifs focusing on the opening chapters of Genesis, in particular the deeds of the "fallen angels" that preceded Noah and the great flood. Moving into the early second century B.C.E., the book of *Jubilees* is perhaps the most impressive of all interpretive compositions of the period. Its anonymous author was an extremely creative exegete, whose clever solutions to problems in the biblical narrative still have the capacity to charm and astonish at a distance of more than two millennia; but he was also a deeply religious man whose book — in outward form, a retelling of the book of Genesis — constitutes a profound meditation on the religion of Israel and its ongoing covenant with its God.

Retelling, it should be said, was actually the preferred form of biblical commentary in this period. That is, instead of citing a particular verse and explaining its meaning (as our modern-day, and some ancient, commentators do), Second Temple writers preferred to *retell* the text, substituting for a problematic word or phrase one that would be understood by all readers. By the same token, biblical narratives that seemed to require comment — Why did Abraham do what he did in Egypt? How did Rebekah know what Esau thought? — would be retold in such a way as to address the perceived difficulty. This form of writing (*Jubilees* is only one example) has been termed the "Rewritten Bible," but it was almost never a rewriting for rewriting's sake; by retelling the text in their own words, commentators were able to explain things and eliminate any perceived inconsistencies or problems.

Ben Sira, a contemporary of the author of *Jubilees*, probably wrote his book of wisdom in the first two decades or so of the second century B.C.E. (It is included in many Christian Bibles under the rubric of biblical apocrypha or deuterocanonical works, where it is usually called "The Wisdom of Jesus, son of Sirach.") Its terse couplets, reminiscent in style of the biblical book of Proverbs, reflect here and there on the biblical narratives of Adam and Eve and various biblical laws, while its chapters 44–49 present a sustained survey of biblical heroes, beginning with Enoch and ending with Nehemiah. The book of Daniel is exceptional in the current volume in that it is actually part of the Hebrew Bible; chronologically, however, it (or at least part of it) belongs to the second century B.C.E. and fits with the general interest in biblical interpretation characteristic of this period.

The discovery of the Dead Sea Scrolls at Qumran, starting in 1947, has yielded a wealth of new texts, many of them of great interest to our subject. The *Temple Scroll*, of uncertain date, is an altogether unique composition, an interpretive recapitulation of numerous biblical laws. Another text, *Miqṣat Ma'aśê ha-Torah* ("some of the laws of the Torah," usually abbreviated as *MMT*) takes the form of a literary letter, in which the leader of the Qumran community (or perhaps some honored predecessor) spells out the community's halakic differences with the unnamed addressee. The *Genesis Apocryphon*, apparently from the late second or first century B.C.E., is, like *Jubilees*, a retelling of stories from Genesis with many interpretive details added in. Also from Qumran are the *Community Rule* and the *Hodayot* ("Thanksgiving Hymns"), which, while not specifically devoted to biblical interpretation, contain numerous passages that help reveal how specific biblical passages were understood in the closing centuries B.C.E. The Scrolls also contain a number of interpretive texts that follow our own form of biblical commentary today, in which successive verses or phrases are cited and explicated in turn. These texts, known as *pesharim*, often seek to apply scriptural passages from the distant past to the time of the Qumran community itself.

From the turn of the era come a number of other interpretive texts. The *Wisdom of Solomon* was originally composed in Greek, presumably by a Greek-speaking Jew who lived in Alexandria toward the end of the first century B.C.E. It refers to a great many different scriptural passages, bearing witness to numerous interpretive motifs; its main focus is, however, on the exodus from Egypt. The date and provenance of the *Testaments of the Twelve Patriarchs* is the subject of some dispute among scholars. It appears to be a multilayered text, in which older material was reused and supplemented by subsequent editors/authors. One opinion holds that it first appeared in its twelve-testament form in the first century B.C.E. (incorporating still older material) and was subsequently freely translated into Greek and supplemented, ultimately undergoing a Christian recension in perhaps the first or second century C.E., in which form it has come down to us today.

Two Jewish writers who composed their works in Greek in the first century of the Common Era are extremely important to any study of ancient biblical interpretation. Philo of Alexandria is the author of a lengthy series of commentaries on different parts of the Pentateuch. Many of his commentaries bear his unique stamp of allegorical exegesis; this notwithstanding, a considerable number of interpretive elements in his commentaries are shared with some of the works already mentioned; for all his uniqueness, he was undeniably part of the continuum of Jewish exegesis of this period. His slightly later contemporary, Flavius Josephus, was a Jerusalem priest and general who undertook to write a history of his people, the *Jewish Antiquities,* in Greek. The earlier portions consist of a retelling of biblical narrative full of interpretive details reflective, apparently, of the author's considerable religious education.

From the first century of the Common Era stem three final works. Pseudo-Philo's *Book of Biblical Antiquities* is a retelling of biblical narrative from Adam and Eve to the death of King Saul. In places its interpretive line bears a striking resemblance to that adopted by rabbinic Judaism in the centuries that followed. Pseudo-Philo makes no mention of the destruction of the second temple by the Romans in 70 C.E., an indication that its composition preceded that catastrophe. By contrast, *4 Ezra* and *2 Baruch* are both explicitly addressed to that upheaval, in the process drawing on a vast store of interpretive scriptural motifs as their authors seek to understand divine justice. From a still later period stem the various targums, Aramaic translations of the Bible (though their roots probably are to be sought in the first century or earlier), and along with these, the vast corpora of early Christian literature (including the New Testament) and of rabbinic writings.

If these are among the most important texts for the study of ancient biblical interpretation, they are far from the only ones. Indeed, it would be quite impossible, in the framework of the present volume, to survey everything. But apart from simply naming where ancient biblical interpretation is to be found, it is important to understand the overall approach to the task of exegesis that flourished in these closing centuries B.C.E. and how, in practical terms, interpreters went about doing what they did.

The Four Assumptions

In considering the works just listed, it might appear that they have little in common. After all, what could Ben Sira have in common with the biblical retellings of the book of *Jubilees* or the *Genesis Apocryphon?* Yet if one takes a step backward and surveys this variety from a distance, certain common elements — or rather, a common *attitude and approach* to the biblical text — emerge despite the obvious differences. It emerges that all ancient interpreters, whether they wrote in Hebrew or Aramaic or Greek and no matter what their particular political or societal allegiances may have been, shared a common set of four assumptions about *how* Scripture was to be read and interpreted. These four basic assumptions may be summarized as follows:

1. *The Bible is a fundamentally cryptic document.*[9] Often, when it seems to be saying X, what it really means is Y. Hence the necessity for careful interpretation: it was the interpreter's job to find the hidden meaning of the text and make it plain to others.

2. *The Bible is a great book of lessons.* Although most of its various parts talk about the distant past (a past that was distant even in the time of the ancient interpreters), its words are actually aimed at people today. Thus, the words spoken by Israel's prophets in the eighth or sixth century B.C.E. were interpreted so as to refer to events in the Roman-occupied Palestine of the interpreters' own day; laws that were attributed to Moses were explicated in such a way as to refer to situations and a way of life that existed in the interpreters' own time; the stories of heroes from the ancient past events were understood to contain lessons for proper conduct, the heroes themselves having been converted into moral exemplars through creative exegesis; and so forth.

3. *The Bible is perfectly consistent and free of error or internal contradiction.* Although its various texts were written in different periods and vastly different circumstances, penned by different authors representing different strata and institutions within society, nevertheless its words came to be held to be perfectly in harmony. Any apparent contradiction, or error of fact, or (eventually) any deviation for the interpreter's own ideology or school thus needed to be explained by clever exegesis in such a way as to make the contradiction or error disappear. Indeed, this approach was eventually carried to the point where even repetitions were ruled illusory: every word of Scripture was held to contain a necessary teaching.

4. *Every word of Scripture comes from God.* Certainly, sentences that began "And the Lord said to Moses" or "Thus says the Lord . . ." were two of Scripture's most common ways of designating divine speech. But what of the parts that are not so designated? Eventually, interpreters came to hold that

---

9. It is, of course, somewhat anachronistic to refer to a "Bible" when discussing these ancient writings, many of which were composed before any clearly delineated, *canonical* set of texts had been singled out as Israel's sacred library. Still, there is no doubt that the Pentateuch was, for all the sources listed, *the* sacred book par excellence and the one on which most interpretive attention was showered; the same four assumptions that applied to its interpretation seem to have applied equally to the still inchoate collection of prophetic writings, psalms, and other works that accompanied it.

every part of Scripture had been divinely dictated or divinely inspired or otherwise granted by God — the stories of Genesis or the court history of David no less than the laws given to Moses or the prophecies of Isaiah or Jeremiah. Even the psalms, whose words seemed to be directed *to* God, were nonetheless held to have come *from* God, indeed, to be a form of prophecy.[10]

Ancient interpreters rarely spoke of these assumptions as such; indeed, for most interpreters, they probably were *unconscious* assumptions (as assumptions usually are). Nevertheless, a careful reading will reveal that they underlie virtually everything that was written about Scripture during this crucial period and thus had a great deal to do with the "spin" that accompanied the Bible from antiquity through the Middle Ages, the Renaissance, and — to a great extent — even into our own day.

How Interpretation Worked

We can see some of these assumptions at work, as well as the way in which interpretations were passed on and modified in subsequent generations, by examining a concrete example, the Pentateuch's brief description of the life and death of Enoch:

> When Enoch had lived sixty-five years, he became the father of Methuselah. Enoch walked with God after the birth of Methuselah three hundred years, and had other sons and daughters. Thus all the days of Enoch were three hundred and sixty-five years. Enoch walked with God; and he was not, for God took him. (Gen 5:21-24)

It was this last phrase, "and he was not, for God took him," that fascinated ancient interpreters. A modern scholar would probably opine that this was merely a delicate way of referring to Enoch's death. Since his lifetime of 365 years was considerably shorter than that of the other antediluvian figures, one might think that Enoch's life had been cut short because he displeased God; the text is therefore careful to say — twice, in fact — that Enoch "walked with God" (meaning, presumably, that he acted in accordance with God's will) and that when he died, it was not because God had *killed* him out of anger, but rather that he had gently ended Enoch's life.

---

10. On this, see my "David the Prophet," in *Poetry and Prophecy: The Beginnings of a Literary Tradition* (Ithaca: Cornell University Press, 1990), 45-55.

But toward the end of the biblical period, the idea of the heavenly ascent — that certain flesh-and-blood human beings had actually ascended into heaven and communed there with God and the angels — had become a commonplace.[11] On the basis of various biblical texts themselves as well as certain exegetical motifs, Elijah (see 2 Kgs 2:11) and other prophets, indeed, Moses and Levi and other early biblical figures were held to have gone up to heaven during their lifetimes. At an early stage, Enoch had also been included in this company. After all, if the book of Genesis never actually said that he died but simply remarked that "he was not, for God took him," perhaps what it meant was that Enoch had ascended into heaven. This idea could only be strengthened by the preceding clause, which asserted that Enoch "walked with God." Did this not indicate that Enoch had physically walked about in God's heavenly abode?

> Before these things, Enoch was taken; and none of the sons of men knew where he had been taken or where he was or what had happened to him. But his deeds were with the Watchers [a class of angels], and his days were with the holy ones. (1 En. 12:1-2)

It may not be immediately obvious, but the first sentence above is actually a paraphrase of the last clause of Gen 5:24.[12] Enoch "was taken" was what the biblical text had said, but here "and he was not" is reinterpreted as if it really meant "and it was not known." The author then further explains that it was not known to any humans what had become of him, that is, "none of the sons of men knew where he had been taken or where he was or what had happened to him."[13] The reason for this was that Enoch had disappeared into heaven, where he communed with the angels: "his deeds were with the Watchers [a class of angels], and his days were with the holy ones."

It is impossible to know how far back the idea of Enoch's heavenly ascent goes, but it certainly seems to have preceded the compilation of the various parts of 1 Enoch. The very earliest part of this work, the "Book of the Luminaries" (1 Enoch 72-82), has been dated by some to the fourth or even fifth century B.C.E.; it presents scientific lore about the sun, the phases of the moon, the

---

11. On this subject there is a vast literature; see *inter alia* Martha Himmelfarb, *Ascent to Heaven in Jewish and Christian Apocalypses* (New York: Oxford University Press, 1993).

12. See on this, George W. E. Nickelsburg, *1 Enoch 1*. Hermeneia (Minneapolis: Fortress, 2001), 233.

13. As Nickelsburg notes, this understanding is uniquely echoed in Tg Neophyti to Gen 5:24, "And Enoch acted faithfully before God, *and it was not known where he was,* since he had been drawn away by the Memar that had come from God."

lunar year, and similar matters. Presumably, this lore had originated in Mesopotamia, which was then a major center for the study of astronomy and astrology. It seems likely that, at an early stage, this Mesopotamian material was repackaged for a Jewish audience as a conversation between Enoch and the angel Uriel, in which form it appears in our present book of Enoch. That is to say, Enoch "walked with God" in heaven in the sense that he conversed with God's angel Uriel, who informed him of all of what goes on amongst the stars.

On this basis, all sorts of other lore came to be attributed to Enoch. The rebellion in heaven that preceded the great flood of Genesis 6–8, the garden of Eden and its geography, the fate of the righteous and the wicked, and other subjects were all explored in works that were attributed to Enoch. No wonder that the book of Ben Sira says of Enoch:

> Enoch walked with the Lord and was taken, a sign of knowledge forever and ever. (Sir 44:16)[14]

He was a "sign of knowledge" by Ben Sira's time because he was now believed to be the author or tradent of the astronomical and other lore attributed to him in the growing Enochic corpus. He must have known a great deal!

Against this background, it is interesting to observe how the Septuagint translators rendered this same verse in Genesis:

> And Enoch *was pleasing to God;* and he was not found, for God *had transferred him.* (Gen 5:24)

This rendering actually seems to pull in opposite directions. The translators certainly could have translated "walked with God" literally; the fact that they did not indicates their discomfort with such an apparently anthropomorphic statement — "pleasing to God" was a more acceptable wording. This in turn tells us something about the state of Jewish belief by the third century B.C.E.: the corporeal, human-sized deity of numerous early passages in the Hebrew was already being reinterpreted as the incorporeal (or at least world-spanning) deity of the Bible's latest passages. At the same time, the idea that "walked with God" had once supported — namely, that Enoch had indeed ascended into heaven — is echoed by the wording "and he was not, for God *had transferred him.*" The Hebrew "for God took him" could easily have been rendered into Greek literally, but Enoch's reputation as one who lived on in heaven was apparently well established. The translators thus preferred the somewhat vague

---

14. On the textual history of this verse, see Patrick W. Skehan and Alexander A. Di Lella, *The Wisdom of Ben Sira.* AB 39 (New York: Doubleday, 1987), 499.

"transferred" *(metethēken)* in keeping with the traditions of Enoch's heavenly ascent.

Philo of Alexandria read and explicated the Bible in Greek. He rewords the Septuagint version of Gen 5:24 as follows:

> He [Enoch] was "transferred," that is, he changed his abode and journeyed as an immigrant from the mortal life to the immortal. (*Names* 38)

In keeping with his overall approach, Philo explains just before this sentence that Enoch actually represents both wisdom itself and "the lover of wisdom, the sage" (*Names* 37). Thus, if the Septuagint text said Enoch *was not found,* Philo explains that this is because wisdom is indeed a scarce commodity, "for where could one search and find this good thing?" As for "transferred," it is not clear in context whether Philo interprets this as indicating that Enoch had indeed ascended to heaven or that his soul (perhaps like *all* souls) had simply "journeyed as an immigrant from the mortal life to the immortal."[15]

Josephus's remark on the same verse is somewhat less ambiguous:

> Enoch . . . having lived three hundred and sixty-five years, withdrew to before God, for which reason no account of his death is recorded. (*Ant.* 1:85)

If no account of his death was recorded in Scripture, then what was recorded must be an account of something else, namely, his heavenly ascent. Similar is the assertion in the New Testament Letter to the Hebrews:

> By faith was Enoch taken up, *so that he should not see death;* "and he was not found, because God had taken him." Now before he was taken he was attested as having pleased God. (Heb 11:5)

The book of Ben Sira — like much of the biblical Apocrypha and Pseudepigrapha — was translated into Greek, and the Greek manuscripts bear witness to a slightly different version of the Hebrew verse cited above:

> Enoch pleased the Lord and was transferred, a sign of *repentance* for all generations. (Sir 44:16)

The first half of this translation follows the Septuagint's wording of Gen 5:24, but where did "sign of repentance" come from? (The Hebrew version cited earlier had "sign of knowledge.") A similar note is sounded in other texts:

---

15. See further the passages cited in David Winston, *The Contemplative Life; The Giants; and Selections: Philo of Alexandria* (New York: Paulist, 1981), 121-23.

> There was one [Enoch] who pleased God and was loved [by Him], and living among sinners he was transferred. He was snatched away lest evil change his understanding or trickery deceive his soul. . . . *Having been perfected in a short span,* he fulfilled long years; since his soul was pleasing to the Lord, He sped him off from the midst of wickedness. (Wis 4:10-14)

> What is the meaning of the words "Enoch was pleasing to God after he begot Methuselah"? [Scripture] legislates about the sources of all good things at the beginning of Genesis. . . . For not very long after the forgiving of Cain it introduces the fact that *Enoch repented,* informing us that forgiveness is wont to produce repentance. (Philo, *QG* 1.82)

In the second of these passages, Philo asserts outright that Enoch repented, but that seems to be the point of the first passage as well. If Enoch was "perfected in a short span," the text implies that he was not born perfect; apparently, it took him some time, if only a "short span," before reaching moral perfection. At some point he must have changed his ways for the better, that is, he repented. (It should also be noted that this passage contains a second idea, not seen until now: that if Enoch lived a short life in comparison to the antediluvian figures, it was not because he displeased God, but quite the contrary. Since Enoch was "living among sinners," God saved him by taking him; he was "snatched away lest evil change his understanding or trickery deceive his soul.")

To understand the origin of the motif of the penitent Enoch, it is necessary to look again at the original passage in Genesis:

> When Enoch had lived sixty-five years, he became the father of Methuselah. Enoch walked with God after the birth of Methuselah three hundred years, and had other sons and daughters. Thus all the days of Enoch were three hundred and sixty-five years. Enoch walked with God; and he was not, for God took him. (Gen 5:21-24)

If the text says that Enoch "walked with God *after* the birth of Methuselah," one possible implication is that before the birth of Methuselah he did *not* walk with God. He must have had a dissolute youth, complete with all the vices; but once he reached the age of sixty-five he settled down, started a family, and after that began to walk with God — the perfect model of a penitent soul.

Finally, it should be noted that later Jewish exegetes balked at the idea of a virtuous Enoch. Perhaps because his reputation as a heavenly traveler had caused others to go to extremes in their praise of him, or perhaps because of the overall rabbinic notion that the first ten generations of humanity were altogether wicked (*m. 'Abot* 5:2), these exegetes sought to puncture Enoch's postbiblical reputation.[16] Typical is the translation of our verse in the Aramaic Targum of Onqelos:

> And Enoch walked in the fear of the Lord, and he was not, for God *had killed him.* (Gen 5:24)

Here it may be worthwhile to spell out how these various understandings of Enoch embody the four assumptions listed above. There could hardly be a better illustration of the first — that the Bible often speaks cryptically — than the idea just seen above, that Enoch was actually a penitent sinner. After all, if that is what the Bible had wished to tell us, why did it not say so openly? But interpreters simply operated on the assumption that the Scripture often merely hinted at its full meaning, so that if it said "Enoch walked with God *after* the birth of Methuselah," perhaps indeed penitence was its deeper message. By the same token, if the text had wanted to tell us that Enoch had ascended bodily into heaven, why did it not simply say that? But again, subtle hints were taken to be sufficient: that Enoch "walked with God and he was not, for God took him" was all a wise interpreter needed to divine the half-hidden truth.

The second assumption, that the Bible is a great book of lessons, hardly needs glossing here. Enoch was someone who lived in the distant past, yet interpreters assumed that the story of his life was being told to teach us later readers something about our own lives. Thus, if Enoch had repented of his early sinfulness, was this not said in order that we ourselves do likewise? No doubt ancient preachers at some point began to connect that idea with the motif of Enoch's heavenly ascent: those who "please God" by abandoning their sinful ways may also hope that their souls will, after their death, ascend to heaven.

The third assumption, that the Bible is perfectly consistent, is not found explicit in the foregoing passages, but it certainly played a role in the overall scheme of things. To begin with, there is indeed another passage in the Bible dealing with the antediluvian Enoch, but there he is said to be the son of Cain: "Cain knew his wife and she conceived and bore Enoch; and he built a city and named it Enoch after his son" (Gen 4:17). Modern biblical scholars generally believe that this sentence derives from a somewhat different chronology, and genealogy, of the figures who lived before the flood — in short, that Gen 4:17-18 and 5:18-24 contradict each other. Such a thought of course would never occur to any ancient interpreter: the Enochs of these two passages may have shared the same first name (as, coincidentally, did the two Lamechs of Gen 4:18 and 5:25), but they had different fathers, so they were clearly different people.

---

16. See further *Gen. Rab.* 25:1.

On a deeper level, however, the third assumption came to mean not only that the various parts of Scripture itself were perfectly consistent, but also that there existed a perfect harmony between the biblical text and the interpreter's own ideology or creed. Thus, when the corporeal understanding of God began to fade, the idea that Enoch "walked with God" needed to be reinterpreted: as the Septuagint translators demonstrate, this came to be understood as "Enoch pleased God." For interpreters who held that the human soul is immortal, Enoch's "transfer" to heaven became a biblical assertion of this doctrine. And it was only when repentance was becoming a central doctrine of Judaism (which it was not in earlier times) that Enoch's brief story became an object lesson in this doctrine.

The fourth assumption, about the divine origin of all Scripture, plays no overt role in the passages examined above. It was generally assumed from an early period that the Pentateuch as a whole had been given by God to Moses, so the passage about Enoch, along with the rest of Genesis, was obviously the word of God. But ultimately this came to be extended to every part of Scripture; indeed, a famous verse from the New Testament restates this assumption, along with the second one, quite clearly: "All Scripture is inspired by God and is useful for teaching, for reproof, for correction, and for training in righteousness" (2 Tim 3:16).

Exegetical Motifs

Finally, it should be noted that ancient biblical interpretation is an interpretation of verses. Interpreters rarely lost sight of the larger units — they certainly knew that this or that verse was part of a longer story or prophetic oracle or legal code. But their comments are usually framed by a particular verse or even a phrase within a verse: "and he was not, for God took him" meant Enoch ascended to heaven; "walked with God after the birth of Methuselah" meant Enoch repented; and so forth.

These little explanations of phrases or verses are called exegetical motifs. Such motifs traveled. They were passed on by word of mouth or from one text to another, sometimes being modified on the way. When the authors of *Jubilees* or the *Genesis Apocryphon* or the *Book of Biblical Antiquities* set out to explain something from Scripture, they often combined more than one motif in their retelling. Since a well-known motif concerning verse X said such-and-such, while another motif concerning the adjacent verse Y said something else, it was only natural to join both motifs in their running retelling of the events. Thus, in studying ancient biblical interpretation, it is best to break down such a running text into its constituent motifs and say, for example, that the passage from the Wisdom of Solomon examined above actually contains two originally separate motifs, "Enoch the Penitent" and "Enoch Saved from Sinners." There have been many interpreters since these first generations. Later Jewish and Christian exegetes built on the interpretations they received from their forebears. Patristic exegetes, though they inherited the attitude to the text and a considerable body of interpretations from earlier times, created a highly developed set of typological and allegorical interpretations of their own; their writings ultimately led to the medieval doctrine of four levels of meaning in every biblical text. On the Jewish side, rabbinic interpretation further developed the same store of earlier exegetical motifs, and in the Middle Ages it too developed new forms of interpretation, philosophical, kabbalistic, and yet others. But all these later developments would not have been possible without the groundwork laid by the interpreters studied in the present volume — nor, despite the innovations of medieval times, were the four assumptions that shaped their approach seriously questioned until the modern period. Indeed, those assumptions, and many of the early interpreters' actual motifs, are to some extent still with us, having shaped the Bible's career for more than two millennia.

BIBLIOGRAPHY

Anderson, Gary A. "The Interpretation of Genesis 1:1 in the Targums." *CBQ* 52 (1990): 21-29.

————. "The Life of Adam and Eve." *HUCA* 63 (1992): 1-38.

Aptowitzer, Victor. "Asenath, the Wife of Joseph: A Haggadic Literary-Historical Study." *HUCA* 1 (1924): 239-306.

Baumgarten, Joseph M. *Studies in Qumran Law.* SJLA 24. Leiden: Brill, 1977.

Belkin, Samuel. *The Midrash of Philo.* New York: Yeshiva University Press, 1989. [Hebrew]

Bowker, John. *The Targums and Rabbinic Literature.* London: Cambridge University Press, 1969.

Brooke, George J., ed. *Temple Scroll Studies.* JSPSup 7. Sheffield: JSOT, 1989.

Enns, Peter. *Exodus Retold: Ancient Exegesis of the Departure from Egypt in Wis 10:15-21 and 19:1-9.* HSM 57. Atlanta: Scholars, 1997.

Feldman, Louis H. *Josephus's Interpretation of the Bible.* Berkeley: University of California Press, 1998.

Fraade, Steven D. *Enosh and His Generation: Pre-Israelite Hero and History in Postbiblical Interpretation.* SBLMS 30. Chico: Scholars, 1984.

Ginzberg, Louis. *Legends of the Jews.* 7 vols. Baltimore: Johns Hopkins University Press, 1998.

Hayward, C. T. Robert, trans. *Saint Jerome's Hebrew Questions on Genesis.* Oxford: Clarendon, 1995.

Hoek, Annewies van den. *Clement of Alexandria and His Use of Philo in the Stromateis: An Early Christian Reshaping of a Jewish Model.* VCSup 3. Leiden: Brill, 1988.

Japhet, Sara. *The Ideology of the Book of Chronicles and Its Place in Biblical Thought.* BEATAJ 9. Frankfurt: Lang, 1989.

Kister, Menachem. "Observations on Aspects of Exegesis, Tradition, and Theology in Midrash, Pseudepigrapha, and Other Writings." In Reeves, *Tracing the Threads,* 1-34.

Kugel, James L. "Two Introductions to Midrash." *Proof* 3 (1983): 131-55. Repr. *Midrash and Literature,* ed. Geoffrey H. Hartman and Sanford Budick. New Haven: Yale University Press, 1986, 77-103.

———. *In Potiphar's House: The Interpretive Life of Biblical Texts.* San Francisco: HarperSanFrancisco, 1990.

———. *Traditions of the Bible: A Guide to the Bible as It Was at the Start of the Common Era.* Cambridge, Mass.: Harvard University Press, 1998.

———. "Ancient Biblical Interpretation and the Biblical Sage." In *Studies in Ancient Midrash.* Cambridge, Mass.: Harvard University Press, 2001, 1-26.

———. *The Ladder of Jacob: Ancient Interpretations of the Biblical Story of Jacob and His Children.* Princeton: Princeton University Press, 2006.

Kugel, James L., and Rowan A. Greer. *Early Biblical Interpretation.* LEC 3. Philadelphia: Westminster, 1986.

Machiela, Daniel A. *The Dead Sea Scrolls Genesis Apocryphon: A New Text and Translation with Introduction and Special Treatment of Columns 13-17.* STDJ 79. Leiden: Brill, 2009).

Maori, Yeshayahu. *The Peshitta Version of the Pentateuch and Early Jewish Exegesis.* Jerusalem: Magnes, 1995. [Hebrew]

McNamara, Martin. *The New Testament and the Palestinian Targum to the Pentateuch.* AnBib 27. Rome: Pontifical Biblical Institute, 1966.

Najman, Hindy. *Seconding Sinai: The Development of Mosaic Discourse in Second Temple Judaism.* JSJSup 77. Leiden: Brill, 2003.

Newman, Judith. *Praying by the Book: The Scripturalization of Prayer in Second Temple Judaism.* SBLEJL 14. Atlanta: Scholars, 1999.

Reeves, John C. *Tracing the Threads: Studies in the Vitality of the Jewish Pseudepigrapha.* SBLEJL 6. Atlanta: Scholars, 1994.

Rofé, Alexander. "The End of the Book of Joshua according to the Septuagint." *Hen* 4 (1982): 17-36.

Runia, David T. *Exegesis and Philosophy: Studies on Philo of Alexandria.* Brookfield: Gower, 1990.

Schiffman, Lawrence H. *The Halakhah at Qumran.* SJLA 16. Leiden: Brill, 1975.

———. *Sectarian Law in the Dead Sea Scrolls: Courts, Testimony, and the Penal Code.* BJS 33. Chico: Scholars, 1983.

Vermes, Geza. *Scripture and Tradition in Judaism: Haggadic Studies.* StPB 4. 2nd rev. ed. Leiden: Brill, 1973.

———. *Post-Biblical Jewish Studies.* SJLA 8. Leiden: Brill, 1975.

PART 2

The Hebrew Bible/Old Testament

Inner-biblical Interpretation

Yair Zakovitch

Interpretation within the Biblical Text

Whoever wishes to know the history of biblical exegesis must begin his or her journey with inner-biblical interpretation: exegesis that appears within the Bible itself. By "inner-biblical interpretation" I refer to the light that one biblical text shines onto another — whether to solve some problem that has emerged in close or distant proximity or to adapt a verse to the beliefs and ideologies of the interpreter. The interpreting text may be far from the interpreted text, adjacent to it, or even within it. Moreover, the roles of "interpreting" and "interpreted" may not always be absolute: in some cases, two texts will mutually interpret one another.

In the Bible we find interpretation that is overt, i.e., explicitly directed at a known text — such as Chronicles' reworking of the historiographical narratives, the treatment of pentateuchal sources by writers of some historical psalms (e.g., Psalm 78), or the interpretation of laws from the Book of the Covenant (e.g., the Law of the Hebrew Slave in Exod 21:2-11) in Deuteronomy (15:12-18). Apart from this *overt* inner-biblical interpretation, there is also a *covert* type. Covert interpretation was planted by writers, editors, compilers, or interpolators who relied on alert and sensitive readers to perceive allusions they left when they introduced a literary unit into a particular context or incorporated within — or alongside — it something new that cast it in new light. The interpreter's enterprise is a creative one in every sense, making artificial the distinction between writers and editors, compilers and interpreters.

The Hebrew Bible is an interbranching network of relationships that connects distant texts and binds them to one another. Writings from different periods, representing a range of literary genres, read and interpret one another, being ultimately reflected back from a multitude of mirrors, which distort their original outlines. Poets interpret stories, narrators expound verses of poetry, prophets explain the Pentateuch. We do not exaggerate when we say that no literary unit in the Bible stands alone, isolated and independent, without another's drawing from its spring or casting new light upon it.[1]

The world of inner-biblical interpretation is not a recent discovery. That exegesis is embedded within the Bible was recognized by the last few generations of researchers, even when those scholars did not employ the term "inner-biblical interpretation" and though they were usually satisfied with making observations of one sort or another on only one aspect of the subject.[2] Biblical scholarship had to wait, therefore, for a daring and insightful architect to erect the edifice of inner-biblical interpretation in all its manifestations and to delineate its floor plan. Such an architect was found in Michael Fishbane, whose comprehensive *Biblical Interpretation in Ancient Israel* defined four broad categories of interpretation: Scribal Comments and Corrections; Legal Exegesis; Aggadic Exegesis; Mantological Exegesis (the interpretation of prophecies, dreams, omens, and oracles).[3] Each of the book's four sections deals with both overt and covert interpretation and identifies socio-historical factors that characterize exegesis in the different periods. Fishbane's book gave us tools for identifying typical forms of inner-biblical interpretation, lending a measure of ob-

---

1. When we investigate the exegetical connections between different literary units we are, in fact, dealing with the phenomenon of intertextuality, a much-discussed topic in modern literary criticism. Examples of scholarship on biblical intertexuality can be found, e.g., in Sipke Draisma, ed., *Intertexuality in Biblical Writings: Essays in Honour of Bas van Iersel* (Kampen: Kok, 1989); Danna N. Fewell, ed., *Reading between Texts: Intertextuality and the Hebrew Bible* (Louisville: Westminster John Knox, 1992); *Intertexuality and the Bible*, ed. George Aichele and Gary A. Phillips. Semeia 69-70 (Atlanta: SBL, 1995).

2. See, e.g., Hans Wilhelm Hertzberg, "Die Nachgeschichte alttestamentlicher Texte innerhalb des Alten Testaments," *BZAW* 66 (1936): 110-21; Nahum Sarna, "Psalm 89: A Study in Inner Biblical Exegesis," in *Biblical and Other Studies*, ed. Alexander Altmann (Cambridge, Mass.: Harvard University Press, 1963), 29-46; Frederick F. Bruce, "The Earliest Old Testament Interpretation," *OtSt* 17 (1972): 37-52; Jacob Weingreen, "Rabbinic-Type Glosses in the Old Testament," *JSS* 2 (1957): 149-62; "Exposition in the Old Testament and in Rabbinic Literature," in *Promise and Fulfillment: Essays Presented to Professor S. H. Hooke*, ed. Frederick F. Bruce (Edinburgh: T. & T. Clark, 1963), 187-201; "The Deuteronomic Legislator — A Proto Rabbinic Type," in *Proclamation and Presence: Old Testament Essays in Honour of Gwynne Henton Davies*, ed. John I. Durham and J. R. Porter (Richmond: John Knox, 1970; repr. 1983), 76-89; Isac Leo Seeligmann, "Voraussetzungen der Midraschexegese," *VTSup* 1 (1953): 150-81; "Anfänge der Midraschexegese in der Chronik," in *Gesammelte Studien zur Hebräischen Bibel/Isac Leo Seeligman*, ed. Erhard Blum. FAT 41 (Tübingen: Mohr Siebeck, 2004), 31-54; Harold Louis Ginsberg, "Daniel" (addition to entry), *Encyclopedia Mikra'it*, 2:949-52 [Hebrew]; Moshe Zvi Segal, *The Interpretation of the Bible*, 2nd ed. (Jerusalem, 1971), 5-7 [Hebrew].

3. Michael Fishbane, *Biblical Interpretation in Ancient Israel* (Oxford: Clarendon, 1985).

jectivity to our ability to isolate interpretative elements. He did not view this interpretative work as a literary phenomenon only but as one expression of a lively cultural tradition. Interpretation is always relevant; it is an ever-current indicator of a generation's contemporary concerns.[4] Others have broadened the discussion concerning the world of inner-biblical interpretation, e.g., in books written by myself, James Kugel and Rowan Greer, and the volume by Benjamin Sommer.[5]

The Indistinct Boundary between Inner-biblical and Extrabiblical Interpretation: The Fluid Boundaries of the Canon

The imprecision of the distinction between inner-biblical and extrabiblical interpretation is partially a consequence of the canon's fluid boundaries. Admittedly, our canon is now a well-defined, bound volume comprising twenty-four books that may be neither augmented nor — more seriously — decreased. But the process by which the canon took shape was a complex and drawn-out one.[6] Moreover, different groups of believers retained separate canons, some large, others less so. What was preserved by one group may have been excluded by another, yet the dimensions of each canon affect the manner in which its writings become interpreted. Let me demonstrate.

The most narrowly-defined version of the canon is the Samaritan Pentateuch. By separating the Pentateuch from the Former Prophets and holding it, alone, as canon, the Samaritans were able to claim the exclusive sanctity and singular status of Shechem, the city that enjoys unambiguous primacy in the Torah and the city in which God chose to dwell. Every verse in Deuteronomy that leaves an unanswered riddle awaiting resolution — "the place that the LORD God will choose amidst all your tribes to establish his name there" (Deut 12:5, just one of many similar examples) — riddles that were answered by the Former Prophets — for example, in 1 Kgs 14:21, "In Jerusalem, the city that the Lord chose to establish his name there from all the tribes of Israel" — were

4. For a review of Fishbane's book, see Yair Zakovitch, "The Varied Faces of Inner-biblical Interpretation," *Tarbiz* 56 (1986): 136-43 [Hebrew].

5. Yair Zakovitch, *An Introduction to Inner-biblical Interpretation* (Even Yehudah: Rekhes, 1992) [Hebrew]; James L. Kugel and Rowan A. Greer, *Early Biblical Interpretation*. LEC 3 (Philadelphia: Westminster, 1986); Benjamin D. Sommer, *A Prophet Reads Scripture: Allusion in Isaiah 40–66* (Stanford: Stanford University Press, 1998); and see further, note 66 below.

6. On the stages of the canon's formation, see, e.g., Sid Z. Leiman, *The Canonization of the Hebrew Scripture: The Talmudic and Midrashic Evidence* (Hamden: Archon, 1976; repr. 1991); James Barr, *Holy Scripture: Canon, Authority, Criticism* (Philadelphia: Westminster, 1983).

changed by the Samaritans from future tense to past: "who chose." And when? When did God choose? The Ten Commandments, as far as the Samaritans are concerned, are in fact nine commandments — a calculation made possible by their combining the first two commandments into one. To these they added their own, tenth commandment, which is entirely formed from verses in Deuteronomy about the sanctity of Shechem and Mount Gerizim:

> As soon as you have crossed the Jordan into the land of the Canaanites that you are about to enter and possess [see Deut 11:29] you shall set up large stones. Coat them with plaster and inscribe upon them all the words of the Teaching [see Deut 27:2-3]. Upon crossing the Jordan, you shall set up these stones, about which I charge you this day, on Mount Gerizim [see Deut 27:4].[7] There you shall build an altar to the Lord your God, an altar of stones. Do not wield an iron tool over them; you must build the altar of the Lord your God of unhewn stones. You shall offer on it burnt offerings to the Lord your God, and you shall sacrifice there offerings of well-being and eat them rejoicing before the Lord your God [Deut 27:5-7]. That mountain beyond the west road, that is in the land of the Canaanites who dwell in the Arabah — near Gilgal, by the terebinth of Moreh opposite Shechem [see Deut 11:30].

Such a modification in the Pentateuch makes possible — indeed, elicits — a different understanding of the verses in the Torah that have to do with Jerusalem. Thus "one of the mountains" that is in "the land of Moriah" (Gen 22:2) is identified, in Judaism, with the Mount of the Lord that is in Jerusalem, according to 2 Chr 3:1, the single verse in the Hebrew Bible in which that mountain is thus identified: "And Solomon began to build the house of the Lord in Jerusalem on Mount Moriah which had appeared to his father David at the place where David had designated, at the threshing floor of Ornan the Jebusite." Because the book of Chronicles is not included in the Samaritan canon, the Samaritans can claim that "one of the mountains" in "the land of Moriah" is Mount Gerizim in Shechem. They validate this claim with the phonetic similarity between "Moriah" and the name of the cultic site in Shechem, "the terebinth of *Moreh*" (Gen 12:6).

From the moment the books of the Later Prophets joined the historiographical treatise (which contained the Torah and Former Prophets), our perception of Jacob and Esau, to take just one example, was altered. It is generally recognized how the book of Genesis created well-balanced pictures of those

---

7. And note: the Masoretic Text reads "on Mt. Ebal," the mount of the Curse (Deut 11:29; 27:13). Indeed, the Samaritan version seems to be the original, which was changed in the Masoretic Text as part of the anti-Samaritan polemic.

brothers, using richly textured stories that employed neither pure black nor pure white in their depictions. The Esau of Genesis is a sympathetic character. True, his table manners may have been wanting ("Stuff me with that red stuff"; Gen 25:30) and he disdained the birthright even after he had satiated himself with food and drink (Gen 25:34), proving that he was undeserving, but the reader feels affection for Esau because of the birthright episode (Gen 25:27-34) and, even more, the blessing (Genesis 27) when he was deceived and misused by his brother.

When the stories are read in the light of the prophecies about Edom in the prophetic books, however, the balance that was maintained in Genesis is utterly broken. For example, the prophecy that opens the book of Malachi reads:

> I have shown you love, said the LORD. But you ask, "How have You shown us love?" After all — declares the LORD — Esau is Jacob's brother; yet I have loved Jacob and have hated Esau. I have made his hills a desolation, his territory a home for beasts of the desert. If Edom thinks, "Though crushed, we can build the ruins again," thus said the LORD of Hosts: They may build, but I will tear down. And so they shall be known as the region of wickedness, the people damned forever of the LORD. Your eyes shall behold it, and you shall declare, "Great is the LORD beyond the borders of Israel!" (1:2-5)

In Genesis it was Rebekah, Jacob's mother, who loved him (Gen 25:28), and Isaac, their father, loved Esau. Yet Malachi's prophecy does not speak of the parents' love but of God's love and hatred, and of God having unwaveringly and unambiguously chosen Jacob. In Genesis, Esau hates Jacob for stealing the blessing: "Now Esau loathed Jacob because of the blessing which his father had given him . . ." (Gen 27:41), while in Malachi God takes revenge on Esau's hate and hates him, in return.[8]

Although the biblical prophets portrayed Jacob in a thoroughly positive way in their prophecies concerning the relations between Jacob and Esau, in their prophecies about the moral character of the nation Jacob does not appear so innocent. The name change Jacob-Israel is alluded to in Isa 48:1: "Listen to this, O house of Jacob, *who are called by the name* Israel. . . . Who swear by the name of the LORD and invoke the God of Israel, though not in truth and sincerity." This verse returns to the tradition about the name change that is in Genesis, "*your name shall no longer be called* Jacob, but Israel will be your name"

---

8. For more on the interpretation of Genesis in the prophecies about Edom, see what I have written about Obadiah 2 in *An Introduction to Inner-biblical Interpretation*, 78; on Isa 63:1-6, see Yair Zakovitch, *Through the Looking Glass: Reflection Stories in the Bible* (Tel Aviv: ha-Kibuts ha-Me'uhad, 1995), 96-97 [Hebrew].

(Gen 35:10). The prophet's intention is clear: although the nation is already called "house of Israel," it is nonetheless still deserving the name "Jacob," *ya'aqov*, from the root *'-q-b*, "deceit," which continues to suit them, since they have yet to leave the path of corruption.

The expansion of the canon that occurred when the Writings became absorbed had similar exegetical consequences for our reading of the Torah and Former Prophets. The book of Chronicles, for example, casts new light onto David's reign: by omitting any element from David's biography that might dim the brilliance of the king's reputation, it affected the way in which we read the chapters of David's life when we return to the book of Samuel, too. David of Chronicles was also the undisputed founder of the cult in Jerusalem, the man who pushed forward the construction of the temple. In Chronicles, David was responsible for establishing the recitation of psalms in the temple and for the poets being installed there, making clear, therefore, the connection that exists between the book of Chronicles and the redaction of the book of Psalms and its attribution to David.[9] The relationship that is established by the titles of some of the psalms in the book of Psalms, between psalms and certain events in David's life, also changes entirely our perception of David's character.

One example of this is when David finds himself in danger in the court of King Achish and manages to escape through an act of cunning, though not, perhaps, in the most honorable fashion and without turning to God for help (1 Sam 21:11-16[Eng. 10-15]). But from the moment that Psalm 34 came to carry the subtitle "Of David, when he feigned madness in the presence of Abimelech,[10] who turned him out, and he left," the ordinary reader concludes that David did indeed pray to God when he found himself in trouble, and that God was the one who rescued him. David, therefore, gains a new dimension of piety, and the psalm to which this historiographical title was attached undergoes a process

9. The attribution of the psalmic poetry to David was encouraged by his depiction as a musician (1 Sam 16:14-23; 18:10-11; 19:9-10) and a poet (2 Sam 1:17-27; 3:33-34) already in the book of Samuel, and in the appendix to his biography (2 Samuel 22 [= Ps 18]; 23:1-7). Moreover, some of the psalms mention David in the body of the poems (Pss 78; 89; 132; 144). The book of Chronicles includes psalmic elements in a number of its chapters. To its account of the ark being brought to Jerusalem, the editor of Chronicles attached details about the establishment of the singing of the psalms there by David: "He appointed Levites to minister before the Ark of the LORD, to invoke, to praise, and to extol the LORD God of Israel . . . on that day, David first commissioned Asaph and his kinsmen to give praise to the Lord" (1 Chr 16:4-7), after which is included a psalm (vv. 8-36) that was constructed from segments taken from a number of different psalms: vv. 8-22 = Ps 105:1-15; vv. 23-33 = Ps 96:1-13; vv. 35-36 = Ps 106:47-48.

10. The replacement of the name Achish with Abimelech occurred under the influence of a story about another of the Bible's heroes — Abraham — who had found himself trapped in the palace of another Philistine king — Abimelech — and was rescued (Genesis 20).

of concretization: no longer the anonymously-written psalm that speaks generally of God's help to the righteous, it now speaks specifically of David's reverence, David's reliance on God in his moment of need when he found himself in the lion's den, the palace of Israel's enemy, the king of the Philistines.[11]

Until now I have discussed, albeit briefly, the exegetical implications resulting from the gradual canonization of the Hebrew Bible. Let us look now at other collections of sacred books, at other canons, and the effect they have on the interpretation of their constituent writings. We turn first to the collected sacred writings — the canon — at Qumran.

Because fragments from multiple copies of the book of *Jubilees* were found at Qumran, there is little doubt that that book was considered holy by the Qumran sect.[12] The book of *Jubilees* is a paraphrase of the Torah's stories, from the creation of the world until the giving of the Law, and the relationship between its stories and those in Genesis and Exodus is like that between Chronicles and the books of Samuel and Kings: the writer sifted through and selected materials that suited his beliefs and worldview. For instance, the writer of *Jubilees* — who took great interest in cultic, legal, and calendrical matters — wanted a historical anchor for Yom Kippur, the Day of Atonement, a day that is not explained by or linked to any historical event in the Bible (unlike, e.g., Passover). He found his anchor in the story of the selling of Joseph by his brothers, an event he assigns to a specific date, the tenth of Tishrei:

> This is why it is decreed that the sons of Israel should mortify themselves on the tenth of the seventh month (on the day that the news which made him weep for Joseph came to his father Jacob), *and* that on it they should make expiation for themselves with a young goat — on the tenth of the seventh month, once a year, for their sin (for they had resented their father's affection for his son Joseph). And this day has been set apart so that on it they should grieve for their sins and for all their transgressions and for all their misdeeds, *and* so cleanse themselves, once a year, on that day.[13] (*Jub.* 34:18-19)

---

11. Psalm 34 was chosen to illuminate and expound David's predicament with King Achish because of linguistic-associative proximity: the word with which v. 9 of the psalm opens, *ṭaʿămû* (the imperative "taste"), awakened the association with the story about David's having "changed his *sense*" ("sense, mind" is from the same root — *ṭaʿam*), an idiom meaning "to act crazily, to feign madness." It was for this reason that this particular detail is mentioned in the title, using the peculiar idiom that was employed in the telling of the story in 1 Sam 21:14.

12. Fragments from copies of *Jubilees* were found at Qumran; see James C. VanderKam, *The Book of Jubilees.* Guides to Apocrypha and Pseudepigrapha (Sheffield: Sheffield Academic, 2001), 143-44.

13. Translation by Robert H. Charles, rev. by Chaim Rabin, in *The Apocryphal Old Testa-*

Any reader who accepted the book of *Jubilees* as authoritative, as was the case, apparently, at Qumran, thus knew that the Yom Kippur fast marked the day of Joseph's being sold by his brothers.

Another canon is the Septuagint, which, alone among the different ancient witnesses, incorporates additional writings and books that represent a variety of literary genres including historiography, psalmic poetry, visions, and wisdom literature.

One such book which was almost included in the Hebrew Bible's canon — a fact we learn from a number of witnesses in rabbinic literature — is Ben Sira.[14] Indeed, it is possible that the exclusion of this patently Jewish book, which associates wisdom with Torah, stemmed from the publication of its author's identity: without the mystery and veil of antiquity, even if only a pretense of it, no piece of writing could assume the mantle of sanctity. People who accept Ben Sira as a holy book will read and interpret the Bible in its glow. I will demonstrate this with one example. Sandwiched between the final section of Ben Sira (called "In Praise of the Fathers," Sir 44:1–50:24) and the book's postscript there appears a numerical saying (50:25-26):

| Two nations my soul detests | and the third is a no-folk: |
| Those who live in Seir and the Philistines | and the evil nation who live in Shechem. |

The parallelism between "no-folk" and "evil nation" returns us to the Song of Moses: "I'll incense them with a no-folk, vex them with an evil nation" (Deut 32:21), making it clear that Ben Sira interpreted the verse in Deuteronomy as speaking about Shechem, i.e., the Samaritans who made their home there. The same interpretation is found in rabbinic sources, in *Midrash Tana'im*: "'I'll incense them with a no-folk,' these are the *kuthim* [Samaritans]."[15]

Ben Sira found support for his interpretation of Deut 32:21 in the expression "evil nation *(gôy nābāl)*," which is reminiscent of what is written about Shechem in the story of Dinah: "for he had committed an evilness *(nĕbālâ)* in Israel by lying with Jacob's daughter" (Gen 34:7). Note, too, the similarity between Ben Sira's words about Shechem and the explicit reference to Genesis 34

ment, ed. Hedley F. D. Sparks (Oxford: Oxford University Press, 1984). For further reading, see Isac Leo Seeligmann, "Äteiologische Elemente in der biblischen Geschichtsschreibung," in *Gesammelte Studien,* 92-93.

14. For rabbinic testimony concerning Ben Sira's inclusion or exclusion from the canon, see Patrick W. Skehan and Alexander A. Di Lella, *The Wisdom of Ben Sira.* AB 39 (New York: Doubleday, 1987), 20.

15. *Midrash Tana'im 'al Sefer Devarim* to Deut 32:21 (ed. David Tsevi Hoffmann, 196).

in *T. Levi* 7:2-3: "For from today Shechem will be called a city of imbeciles, for as a man mocks an imbecile so did we make a mockery of them, because they had indeed committed an evilness in Israel by defiling our sister." Reading the verse in the Song of Moses in the light of Ben Sira lends it a specificity it does not otherwise have, by identifying the enemy by name, and enlists Deuteronomy in the polemic against the Samaritans.

A much more comprehensive canon is the Christian one, which, containing also the New Testament, gave rise to a renewed interpretation of many of the Bible's verses. Thus, for instance, the writer of the Epistle to the Hebrews listed the revelations of faith that are worthy of praise, including the test successfully faced by Abraham when he was commanded to sacrifice Isaac. The terrible question of how to explain a father's readiness to sacrifice his son is also given an answer: "and he thought to himself that God is able to return even the dead to life" (11:19).

The Indistinct Boundary between Inner-biblical and Extrabiblical Interpretation: The Fluid State of the Canonical Books

The Masoretic Text is but one of the Bible's many versions, as attested by other Hebrew witnesses — e.g., copies of the biblical books among the Dead Sea Scrolls or the Samaritan Bible — and non-Hebrew witnesses, such as the ancient translations of the biblical books, primary among them the Septuagint. Is exegesis that is incorporated into these different versions inner-biblical or extrabiblical exegesis? We remind ourselves that the Masoretic version is not a more ancient or original one and that comparing it with other biblical witnesses helps us to discover interpretative additions also within it.

Thus, for example, the verses about the "man prophet" (*'îš nābî'*) who rebukes the Israelites in Judg 6:7-10 are absent from the copy of Judges that was found at Qumran. The appearance of the man prophet (pay attention to the end of verse 6: "and the Israelites cried out to the Lord") fills a gap by supplying an answer, in advance, to the question that will be posed by Gideon in verse 13, which the Qumran text leaves unanswered: "Please, my lord, if the LORD is with us, why has all this befallen us, and where are all his wondrous acts about which our fathers told us, saying, 'For truly the LORD brought us from Egypt.'" The answer is found in the interpolation, in the words of the prophet:

> Thus said the LORD the God of Israel, "I brought you up out of Egypt and took you out of the house of bondage. And I rescued you from the hand of the Egyptians and from the hand of all your oppressors and I drove them out

from before you and gave you their land. And I said to you, I am the LORD your God. You must not worship the gods of the Amorites in whose land you dwell, but you did not obey me." (Judg 6:8-10).

Because of their idol-worship, therefore, God does not save the Israelites as he had in the past.[16]

There are cases in which books differ significantly in one or another witness. The Greek versions of the tales of Daniel contain sizable additions: the prayer of Azariah and the song of the three youths in the fiery furnace, the stories of Susannah and of Bel and the Dragon. The scroll of Esther, too — a book in which God is never mentioned — was radically renovated in its Septuagint version, receiving seven additions: the first tells of Mordecai's dream, its solution being given in the seventh; the second, of Ahasuerus's command to kill the Jews, with the order's retraction given in the sixth; the third and fourth additions comprise Esther and Mordecai's prayers; the fifth expands the telling of the meeting between Esther and Ahasuerus when Esther, following Mordecai's direction, arrives at the palace. A look at one of these additions — Esther's prayer — will demonstrate its purpose. Esther's prayer serves to introduce the scroll's missing hero, the God of Israel, into the story. Esther turns to God, entreating him to save her and her people: "O my Lord, you only are our king; help me, who am alone and have no helper but you" (LXX Esth 14:3-4). The prayer even situates the entire story into the broader context of Israel's history: "Ever since I was born I have heard in the tribe of my family that you, O Lord, took Israel out of all the nations, and our ancestors from among all their forebears, for an everlasting inheritance, and that you did for them all that you promised" (14:5). The prayer, consistent with the general tendency of biblical historiography, finds grounds that justify the existential threat the Jews now face: "And now, we have sinned before you [. . .]" (14:6). Other difficulties that the reader finds in the Masoretic version are also resolved in Esther's prayer: readers who wonder how Esther could have had intimate relations with the uncircumcised king are happy to hear her testimony that "You know that I hate the splendor of the wicked and abhor the bed of the uncircumcised and any foreigner" (14:15). And if one questions whether Esther sinned by eating forbidden foods in the palace, she responds: "Your servant did not eat at Haman's table and the king's feast I did not honor and the wine of the libations I did not drink" (14:17).

The Esther of the Masoretic Text is thus quite different from the heroine of

16. For interpolation as an exegetical element, see Zakovitch, *An Introduction to Inner-biblical Interpretation*, 28-34.

the Septuagint's version. The exegetical spirit that is reflected in the Greek translation of Esther corresponds with what we find in the Aramaic Targums to Esther and with the book's exegesis in rabbinic literature.[17]

The Beginnings of Exegesis

It is often the case that traditions recorded in the Bible were not written *ex nihilo,* nor were they naively composed; instead, they represent deliberate manipulations of preexistent, popular — but problematic — traditions, whether in oral or written form, that were rejected by the biblical writers and not admitted into the sacred Scriptures. The stories they did write managed these troublesome traditions, reshaping them in order to make them admissible "to come before the Lord's community." This was accomplished by interpreting the popular traditions. Only minimal changes were introduced: on the one hand, the writer-editor sought to interpret and suit traditions to his religio-spiritual-ethical worldview; on the other, he made an effort to maintain as much resemblance to the original, popular tales as possible in order to win the trust of the people who were familiar with the more ancient version. This delicate balancing-act involved covert polemics with well-known traditions; it was an exegetical exercise that granted new meaning to traditions.

We can state, therefore, that the beginnings of the exegetical process occurred in the transition when traditions were poured from one container into another, from an oral to a written existence. Whoever wants to trace the lives of the rejected traditions, to reveal and reconstruct them, can do so by using the techniques of "literary archaeology," by identifying allusions to rejected elements that survived in the Bible's peripheral texts or even in extrabiblical literature. An element that was rejected by the Bible may have continued to exist in the tradition's oral version until, at some later period when it was no longer perceived as threatening to beliefs and ideologies, it found its way into a written text, in Second Temple or even rabbinic literature. Once again, therefore, we find the boundary between inner-biblical and extrabiblical interpretation blurred; the extrabiblical texts sometimes prove invaluable as repositories of ancient traditions, helping us reveal the roots of inner-biblical exegesis.

The scholar whose research in this field was ground-breaking was Umberto Cassuto. Cassuto successfully reconstructed the tradition of the mythological

---

17. Some of the Septuagint's additions are found, in Hebrew, in *Midrash Esther Rabbah.* Esther's prayer appears also in *Midrash Lekakh Tov.* Fragments from the additions are found also in the *Targum Rishon* and *Targum Sheni* to Esther.

sea battle prior to Creation — and thus the exegetical work of the biblical writers in their interpretation of that tradition — by using ancient Near Eastern texts (Mesopotamian and Ugaritic) and allusions within the Bible, which he found in prophetic books, Psalms, wisdom literature, and rabbinic literature.[18] Cassuto also revealed the exegetical nature of other biblical traditions when he reconstructed the mythological traditions against which the story about the "sons of God" and "daughters of man" (Gen 6:1-4) was written,[19] as well as the prebiblical tradition about Enoch ascending to heaven, with which he identified a number of obscure references in Gen 5:21-24.[20]

In a similar way, the story of Joshua's stopping the sun at Gibeon with his prayer (Josh 10:12-14) interpreted a mythological tradition that the Bible could not consent to, according to which Joshua enjoyed a particular relationship with the sun and was able to stop it by raising his arm. That tradition has many echoes in Jewish literature — in Ben Sira 46:4, rabbinic literature, and even in *Midrash Genesis Rabbati,* which is quoted by Rashi in his commentary on Josh 24:30.[21] Also, Judges 13 interprets a prebiblical tradition about Samson's birth, according to which he was the son of a sun-god and a human mother, a story similar to that told in Gen 6:1-4 about the "sons of God" and "daughters of man." The absence of a name etymology at his birth (Judg 13:24) is one piece of silent testimony concerning the Bible's uneasiness with admitting the obvious connection between Samson *(shimshōn)* and the sun *(shemesh).*[22]

The reconstruction of these and countless other traditions once again demonstrates the impossibility of separating biblical literature from extrabiblical literature, and reminds us of the power of extrabiblical literature to help us discover the more ancient stages in the exegetical process.[23]

18. Umberto Cassuto, "The Israelite Epic." In *Biblical and Oriental Studies,* 2 (Jerusalem: Magnes, 1975), 69-109.

19. Umberto Cassuto, "The Episode of the Sons of God and the Daughters of Man (Genesis 6:1-4)." In *Biblical and Oriental Studies,* 1 (Jerusalem: Magnes, 1973), 17-28.

20. Umberto Cassuto, *A Commentary on the Book of Genesis,* Part 1: *From Adam to Noah* (Jerusalem: Magnes, 1961; repr. 1978), 281-86.

21. See Yair Zakovitch, "Was It Not at His Hand the Sun Stopped? (Ben Sira 46:6): A Chapter in Literary Archaeology." In *Tehillah le-Moshe: Biblical and Judaic Studies in Honor of Moshe Greenberg,* ed. Mordechai Cogan, Barry L. Eichler, and Jeffrey H. Tigay (Winona Lake: Eisenbrauns, 1997), 107*-14*.

22. See Yair Zakovitch, *The Life of Samson (Judges 13–16): A Critical-Literary Analysis* (Jerusalem: Magnes, 1982), 74-84 [Hebrew].

23. See, e.g., Avigdor Shinan and Yair Zakovitch, *That's Not What the Good Book Says* (Tel Aviv: Yedi'ot aharonot: Sifre Hemed, 2004).

Modes of Interpretation

The importance of extrabiblical interpretation for understanding the types and history of inner-biblical interpretation stems not only from the unclear boundaries between "inner" and "extra." The various genres of extrabiblical interpretation from different periods help us identify modes of inner-biblical interpretation, since "there is nothing new under the sun." Familiarity with the various methods used in extrabiblical exegesis, many of which are explicitly expressed there, assist us in detecting those same methods within Scripture, even when their expressions are manifested there only implicitly. I do not mean to say that every mode of exegesis that we find in rabbinic literature will be found also in the Bible (e.g., *gematria*, the method of interpreting Scripture based on the numerical value of letters and words, entered the Jewish world from the Greek, after the biblical books had acquired their final forms), but the majority of forms were already known and were widely used by biblical writers.[24]

Lexical Interpretation

The need sometimes arises to elucidate the meaning of a difficult word or to replace a word whose use had dwindled with a more familiar one. In Song of Songs 4:2, for instance, there appears a *hapax legomenon*, the term *qĕṣûbôt:* "Your teeth are like a flock of *qĕṣûbôt* that have come up from bathing." We deduce the meaning of the word from the use of the same root (whose basic meaning is "to cut") in a verse from Kings, "The two cherubim had the same measure and same *extent*" (1 Kgs 6:25), i.e., they had been "cut" to the same measurements and given a unified shape (also 1 Kgs 7:37). *Qĕṣûbôt* in Song of Songs apparently referred to a flock of recently *shorn* sheep, but the word became obscure, and in the parallel verse in Song 6:6, it was replaced with "ewes [*rĕḥēlîm*]." Another example: in Obadiah, the prophet speaks about Esau (who is Edom), using the rare words, *niv'û maṣpunāyw,* "his treasures were searched out" (v. 6). In the later version of the prophecy in Jer 49:10, the difficult words are replaced with more common terms that explain them: *gillêtî et-mistārāyw,* "I have revealed his place of concealment."[25]

---

24. On gematria in rabbinic literature and its basis in Greek culture, see Saul Lieberman, *Hellenism in Jewish Palestine: Studies in the Literary Transmission, Beliefs and Manners of Palestine in the I Century B.C.E.–IV Century C.E.* (New York: Jewish Theological Seminary of America, 1950; repr. 1980), 69; Yonah Frenkel, *Darkhe ha-Aggadah veha-midrash* (Givataim: Yad la-talmud, 1991), 132-37.

25. Raphael Weiss, "Synonymous Variants in Divergences between the Samaritan and

This phenomenon of a word being explained by replacing it is commonplace in Chronicles. Instead of "*ḥayyat* of Philistines" (2 Sam 23:13), the Chronicler explained "*maḥănēh* ['a fighting force, a battalion'] of Philistines" (1 Chr 11:15). Instead of gold described as *mûpāz* (1 Kgs 10:18) — the only appearance of this expression in the Bible, perhaps related to "gold from *Ufaz*" (Jer 10:9; see also Dan 10:5) — in Chronicles the expression "*pure* gold" appears (2 Chr 9:17; it reappears also in 1 Chr 28:17; 2 Chr 3:4).[26]

Another phenomenon that can be identified is that of *etymological explanations,* which can be overt or covert, and which demonstrate one more hermeneutical tool of the biblical writers.[27] The first example is found in the words of Adam: "This one is bone of my bones, flesh of my flesh. And this one will be called woman [*'iššâ*] for from man [*'iš*] she was taken" (Gen 2:23).[28]

The etymology of the word *mān* ("manna") is another of the Bible's explicit etymologies, even though the etymology does not immediately follow the word: "And the Israelites saw it and said, each one to his brother, 'What is it? [*mān hû'*],' because they did not know. And Moses said to them, 'It is the bread that God gave you to eat.' . . . And the house of Israel named it *manna*" (Exod 16:15, 31).

There are cases where the overt etymology is an interpolation, a reader's comment that had been written in the margins and became incorporated into the biblical text. This is the case in the story about the first meeting between Samuel and Saul where Samuel is called a "seer" (*rō'eh;* 1 Sam 9:11, 18, 19). The comment, "Formerly in Israel, thus would say a man when he went to inquire of God, 'Come, let us go to the seer,' for a prophet of today was formerly called a seer" (v. 9), breaks the natural continuity of the conversation between Saul and his servant with an anticipatory etymology, since only from verse 11 is Samuel referred to with the rare term "seer."[29]

Masoretic Texts of the Pentateuch," in *Studies in the Text and Language of the Bible* (Jerusalem: Magnes, 1981), 121 [Hebrew].

26. Weiss, "Synonymous Variants," 174.

27. Word etymologies should not be confused with wordplays, another widespread phenomenon found, e.g., in Jonah: "By decree [lit., 'by the taste of,' i.e., by the judgment of] the king and his nobles, saying 'No man nor beast, no herd nor flock, will *taste* [i.e. eat] anything'" (3:7); "to make shade [*liḥyôt ṣēl*, lit., 'to be a shadow'] on his head and save [*lĕhaṣṣîl*, the phonetically similar verb 'rescue'] him . . ." 4:6); "And God provided *a worm* [*tôla'at*] at the *rise* [*ba'ălôt*] of dawn" (4:7). See Uriel Simon, *Jonah: Mikr'a le'Yisrael* (Tel Aviv: 'Am 'Oved, 1992), 24-25 [Hebrew].

28. The resemblance between the Hebrew words for "man" (*'iš*) and "woman" (*'iššâ*) was used by the rabbinic sages as proof that both the Torah and the world were created using Hebrew (*Gen. Rab.* 18:4).

29. See Isa 30:10. The term is used frequently in Chronicles, which tries to cloak itself in archaic language (1 Chr 9:22; 26:28; 29:29; 2 Chr 16:10).

Etymologies may be covert. The name given the seventh day, *Shabbat* ("Sabbath"), does not appear in the story of the creation that speaks of its distinct status. That said, the name is clearly interpreted there: "*And He ceased* [*wayyišbōt*] on the seventh day from all the work that he had done. And God blessed the seventh day and sanctified it because on it God *ceased* from all the work that he had created to do" (Gen 2:2-3). The term *shabbat* does not appear in the language of the law that appears in Exodus either: "Six days you will do your deeds and on the seventh day *you will cease* [*tišbōt*]" (Exod 23:12; also 34:21), nor, again, in the story of the manna: "And the people *will cease* [*wayišbĕtû*] on the seventh day" (Exod 16:30). The name *šabbāt* appears together with the corresponding verb, "to cease," in the directive to keep the Sabbath in Exodus 31, which returns to the story of the creation: "And the Israelites shall keep the Sabbath to do the Sabbath for their generations for an eternal covenant. Between me and the Israelites it is a sign for all time that six days God made the heavens and the earth and on the seventh day *he ceased* and was refreshed" (Exod 31:16-17).

Every so often a noun will appear in a literary unit along with the interpretation-explanation of its synonym. In the story of the expulsion from the garden of Eden, the serpent plays a central role, for which it is cursed-punished by God: "I will put enmity between you and the woman and between your offspring and her offspring. He *will bruise* [*yĕšûpkā*] your head, you *will bruise* [*tĕšûpennû*] his heel" (Gen 3:15). The terminology used in the curse interprets the synonym for "serpent" (called *nāḥāš* in this chapter): *šĕpîpōn*: "Dan shall be a serpent [*nāḥāš*] by the road, a viper [*šĕpîpōn*] on the path that bites the horse's heels and its rider topples backwards" (Gen 49:17).

Likewise, when Jonathan tastes from the forbidden honey, the verse reads: "He put out the stick he had with him, dipped it into the beehive of honey, and brought his hand back to his mouth, and his eyes *lit up* [*wattā'ōrnâ*]" (1 Sam 14:27), and Jonathan then confirms, "My father has brought trouble on the people. See for yourselves how my eyes *lit up* ['*ōrû*] when I tasted a bit of that honey" (1 Sam 14:29). These verses interpret another term for "honey" that has disappeared from Hebrew — *'ărî* — but survived in Arabic. An echo of it can be heard in the Hebrew root *'-r-h*: "I have come to my garden, My sister, my bride; I have *collected* [*'ārîtî*; a verb apparently related to the collection of honey] my myrrh and spice, eaten my honey and honeycomb . . ." (Song 5:1). The noun from the same root hovers behind the riddle that Samson poses about the honey that he collected from the lion's carcass: "Out of the eater came something to eat; and out of the strong came something sweet" (Judg 14:14). The answer that the townsmen offer, "What is sweeter than honey [*dĕbaš*] and what is stronger than a lion [*mē'ărî*]" (Judg 14:18), is formulated in such a way that recognizes the homonymic relationship between the word for "lion" (*'ărî*) and the synonym of *dĕbaš, 'ărî.* The verses about Jonathan, therefore, interpret the noun *'ărî,* "honey," as referring to a food that lights up the eyes, about which see also the description of the Torah that is in Psalm 19: "The commandment of the LORD is just, *lighting up* the eyes. . . . The judgments of the LORD are truth, . . . and sweeter *than honey,* than the drippings of the comb" (Ps 19:9-11).

Juxtaposition

The sages often asked the reason for the Bible's juxtaposition of different literary units — "Why was [. . .] juxtaposed to [. . .]?"[30] or "What is the business of [. . .] with [. . .]?"[31] — questions that are rooted in the assumption that it is in the power of textual proximity to provide additional meaning. As a consequence, for the rabbis each of the Bible's literary units carried more than one meaning: its meaning when read as an isolated unit and its meaning in the context of its neighboring texts.[32]

Striking evidence of the biblical writers' interest in the matter of juxtaposition is found in Chronicles' use of sources. In Kings we find the story of King Hezekiah's illness and miraculous recovery (2 Kgs 20:1-11) directly abutting the account of the Babylonian envoys' visit to the king's court (20:12-19). The writer of Kings joined the two events together under the pretext that the Babylonian king had sent "a letter and a gift to Hezekiah for he had heard that Hezekiah was ill" (20:12). The writer of Chronicles offered a different reason for the stories' juxtaposition: not Hezekiah's illness but the curiosity of the Babylonian king who had heard of God's miracle: "So, too, in the matter of the envoys of the princes of Babylon, who were sent to him to inquire about the sign that was in the land, when God forsook him in order to test him, to learn all that was in his mind" (2 Chr 32:31).

The story of Naboth's vineyard (1 Kings 21) made its way into two literary contexts, one in the Masoretic Text, another in the Septuagint. The different placements are evidence of distinct notions about the story's fundamental significance. In the Septuagint, the order of chapters 20 and 21 is reversed. Chapter 21, in which God sends Elijah to Ahab to announce his punishment, comes immediately after chapters 17–19, chapters about Elijah, and the two chapters that

---

30. E.g., *b. Sukkah* 2a. See Frenkel, *Darkhe ha-Aggadah,* 183-85.

31. E.g., *b. Ber.* 15b.

32. For the juxtaposition of episodes in biblical narrative, see Yair Zakovitch, "Juxtaposition in the Abraham Cycle," in *Pomegranates and Golden Bells: Studies in Biblical, Jewish, and Near Eastern Ritual, Law, and Literature in Honor of Jacob Milgrom,* ed. David P. Wright, David Noel Freedman, and Avi Hurvitz (Winona Lake: Eisenbrauns, 1995), 509-24.

tell of the wars against Aram, chapters 20 and 22, become similarly contiguous. The arrangement in the Septuagint has a further explanation: in chapter 21 Ahab commits a sin; when he repents of his actions, punishment becomes delayed until his son's lifetime (1 Kgs 21:29). In chapter 20 he again transgresses, and a prophet voices his punishment: "And he said to him, 'Thus said the Lord: Because you set free the man [the king of Aram] whom I doomed, your life will be forfeit for his life and your people for his people" (1 Kgs 20:42). In the Septuagint's adjacent chapter 22, that prophecy is realized with the death of Ahab in the war with Aram (LXX 1 Kgs 22:34-37).[33] The juxtaposition of chapters 17–19 with chapter 21 turns chapter 21 into an episode in the Elijah cycle, into a story whose chief figure is Elijah.

The arrangement of the chapters in the Masoretic Text serves its own exegetical logic: at the end of chapter 20, following the prophet's stern rebuke, we read that "the king of Israel went to his home dispirited and sullen" (1 Kgs 20:43); in the MT's next chapter, the king's response to Naboth's refusal is similar: "And Ahab came to his home dispirited and sullen" (1 Kgs 21:4). The close proximity between the two verses is doubly effective in light of the fact that this expression, "dispirited and sullen," appears nowhere else in the Bible except for these two, juxtaposed chapters.

The order of the chapters in the Masoretic Text has one more implication: "and the dogs lapped up his blood" (1 Kgs 22:38) is understood as the fulfillment of Ahab's prophesied punishment: "In the place where the dogs lapped up Naboth's blood, the dogs will lap up your own blood, too" (1 Kgs 21:19).[34] The juxtaposition between chapters 21 and 22 gives chapter 21 an aspect of being a preparatory and explanatory story for the subsequent account of the king's death in battle.

Analogy

Biblical narrative brims with analogies, parallels that are established between one event and another or between one character and another. In some instances

---

33. For rationale behind this order of the chapters, see David W. Gooding, "Ahab According to the Septuagint," *ZAW* 76 (1964): 270-71. Gooding does not view the Septuagint's sequence as original.

34. The verses 1 Kgs 22:35b, 38, added in order to create a tighter correspondence between chs. 21 and 22, is an example of the underlying assumption in Deuteronomistic historiography that every event was preceded by God's word and was pronounced by his prophets; Ahab is punished "in accordance with the word of the LORD that he spoke" (1 Kgs 22:38). On this principle, see Gerhard von Rad, *Studies in Deuteronomy* (Chicago: Regnery, 1953).

the biblical narrator shaped a situation or character and his actions as the antithesis of another. The newly created work triggers unmistakable associations with the source text; that said, the resemblance between the new story and its source is like that between a figure and its reflection, which reverses the contours of the original episode. Readers who recognize the deliberate relationship between the two stories — the original, source story and the reflection — will discern how the new situation or figure has been shaped as the antithesis of the source situation or figure and will evaluate the newer on the basis of a comparison with the older and the older on the basis of a comparison with the newer.[35]

Only a handful of the analogies are made explicitly.[36] This is the case in the words of the Philistines who are filled with fear at the appearance of the ark of the Lord in the battlefield: "'God has come to the camp.' And they cried, 'Woe to us! Nothing like this has ever happened before. Woe to us! Who will save us from the power of this mighty God? He is the same God who struck the Egyptians with every kind of plague in the wilderness'" (1 Sam 4:7-8).[37] The Philistines erroneously believed — as did the Hebrews — that the ark, which represents God's presence, was Israel's secret weapon and did not realize that God will not save Israel so long as he is not pleased with their actions and with the behavior of their leaders.

Another overt analogy: At the beginning of the tradition about the famine that was in the days of Isaac, the verse reads: "And there was famine in the land, apart from the first famine that was in the days of Abraham" (Gen 26:1), an allusion to the story of Abram and Sarai's descent to Egypt and to what happened to them there (12:10-20). The reader is indeed expected to compare the unflattering behavior of Abraham with that of Isaac, whom God forbade from descending to Egypt (Gen 26:2).

The Filling of Gaps

There are cases where readers were surprised or puzzled by a verse, and their attempt to explain caused them to fill in a narrative gap. A reader of Kings does not know why or how King Uzziah became leprous, all the more so since the verse attributes his affliction to an act of God: "The Lord struck the king with a plague, and he was a leper; until the day of his death he lived in isolated quar-

---

35. On this type of covert analogy, see my *An Introduction to Inner-biblical Interpretation*.

36. Galen Marquis, "Explicit Literary Allusions in Biblical Historiography (The Pentateuch and Former Prophets)" (Ph.D. diss., Hebrew University, 1999) [Hebrew].

37. In the story's continuation the ark indeed brought misfortune onto its captors, reminiscent of the plagues in Egypt (1 Sam 5:6-12).

ters" (2 Kgs 15:5). The Chronicler, in retelling the story, filled the gap by supplying a reason for Uzziah's leprosy: it was the sin of arrogance that had led the king to claim the authority of a priest: "When he was strong, he grew so arrogant he acted corruptly: he trespassed against his God by entering the temple of the LORD to offer incense on the incense altar" (2 Chr 26:16). After he did not heed the chief priest Azariah's warning, Uzziah's punishment was swift to arrive: "The leprosy broke out on his forehead in front of the priests in the house of the LORD beside the incense altar. When the chief priest Azariah and all the other priests looked at him, his forehead was leprous, so they rushed him out of there; he too made haste to get out, for the LORD had struck him with a plague" (2 Chr 26:19-20).

An example from the Samaritan Pentateuch: to the verse in Exod 6:9, "And Moses spoke thus to the Israelites but they did not listen to Moses, their spirits crushed by hard bondage," the Samaritan version adds: "and they said to Moses, 'Leave us alone and we will serve Egypt, for it is better for us to serve in Egypt than to die in the wilderness.'" The added words serve to answer our wonder at the verses in Exod 14:11-12, when the Israelites, fearing the Egyptian soldiers that pursued them, expressed regret at their decision to leave Egypt. They call out to Moses: "What have you done to us, taking us out of Egypt? Is this not the very thing we told you in Egypt, saying, 'Leave us alone and we will serve Egypt, for it is better for us to serve Egypt than to die in the wilderness'?"[38] Interestingly, Abraham Ibn Ezra referred to the same verse, Exod 6:9, in his commentary on Exod 14:12: "'Is this not the very thing' — this is not stated explicitly; we only know that it was so, for how could they say to his face something that had not occurred, and this thing was 'and they did not listen to Moses.'"

Resolving Contradictions

The sages disliked inconsistencies between verses and sought to resolve them, an inclination confirmed by the programmatic comment of Rabbi Eliezer: "Make sure to study Torah, and [learn] how to answer an *epikoros* [a heretic] about the words of the Torah [to show] that there are no contradictions."[39] But such efforts to resolve the Bible's inner contradictions (which stem from its be-

38. Exodus 14:12 is a flashback: consumed with their present suffering, it now seems to the Israelites that already back in Egypt they had understood that slavery was preferable over death in the wilderness; see Meir Weiss, "Weiteres über die Bauformen des Erzählens in der Bibel," *Bib* 46 (1965): 202-5.

39. *'Abot de Rabbi Nathan*, Recension B, 30 (Schechter ed., 33b). See Isaak Heinemann, *Darkhe Ha-Agadah* (Jerusalem: Magnes, 1954; repr. 1970).

ing a mosaic of sources from different periods, representing a variety of ideologies) can be found within the Bible itself.

The most famous of these contradictions concerns the identity of Goliath's killer. According to the main tradition in 1 Samuel 17, David slew the Philistine giant. In the appendix to David's life story, however, it is said that a different hero from Bethlehem, a man by the name of Elhanan, killed him (2 Sam 21:19). The writer of Chronicles solved the contradiction by claiming that Elhanan killed not Goliath but his brother: "And there was more fighting with the Philistines, and Elhanan son of Ya'ir killed Lahmi, the brother of Goliath the Gittite; his spear had a shaft like a weaver's beam" (1 Chr 20:5). A different harmonistic solution, the identification of anonymous or somewhat anonymous figures with famous ones, is found in the Aramaic translation (the Targum), which identified David with Elhanan,[40] and in *Midrash Ruth Rabbah*.[41]

There are cases where a contradiction is found between distant texts representing entirely different genres. In the census taken of all those who serve in Israel's army (Numbers 26), the writer enumerates the descendants of Reuben and mentions the unfortunate tale of Korah and his people: "and the sons of Eliab were Nemuel and Dathan and Abiram. These are Dathan and Abiram chosen in the assembly, who agitated against Moses and Aaron as part of Korah's band when they agitated against the Lord. And the earth opened its mouth and swallowed them and Korah when that band died [. . .]" (Num 26:9-10). This account, however, ends with the surprising words, "and the sons of Korah did not die" (Num 26:11), which ostensibly, at least, are in conflict with what was explicitly written in the story of that event back in chapter 16: "and the earth opened its mouth and swallowed them and their households and every person that was Korah's and all the possessions. And they descended, all that was with them, descended alive to Sheol, and the earth closed over them and they vanished from the midst of the congregation" (Num 16:32-33). The words "and the sons of Korah did not die" were apparently an exegetical comment meant to mediate the contradiction between what is told about Korah in Numbers 16 and the notification in chapter 26 that Korah's family still exists (see in the continuation there, 26:58, and particularly in the titles of certain psalms: e.g., 42:1; 44:1; cf., e.g., 1 Chr 6:17-22; 9:19). This resolution of one contradiction, however, created another problem, i.e., an inconsistency with chapter 16.[42]

40. Rashi, too, followed the Targum's lead.

41. *Ruth Rab.* 2:2.

42. For another comment of a similar nature, see: "Mephibosheth had a young son named Micah" (2 Sam 9:12a). That comment was incorporated into the story about David's generosity towards the last remnant of Saul's family, the cripple Mephibosheth son of Jonathan, in order to anticipate any possible disagreements when reading the genealogical list of the house of Saul,

In Josh 2:15 we are told about Rahab lowering the spies from her window: "And she lowered them with a rope through the window." The second part of the verse, "because her house was on the wall of the city fortifications and in the fortifications she dwelled," was omitted by the translator of the Septuagint in order to avoid a conflict with what is told in chapter 6 about the collapse of the city's fortifications, during which Rahab's house was preserved. But the verse in 2:15 makes no sense without its second half, since in it is found the explanation how the spies arrived outside the city after the city gates were shut.

The Identification of Anonymous Figures

Many of the Bible's secondary and marginal characters were not given a name within the Bible's pages. Extrabiblical literature freed many of these figures from anonymity by giving them names and identities.[43] In many cases, the anonymous figure was given the name of another biblical character — whether a marginal or principal one — thus collapsing the two and enriching both biographies, at once.

A further phenomenon, which brings similar results, is the identification between two figures whose names are identical, similar, or even entirely different.[44] The presumption to link figures with different names finds justification in the fact that a number of biblical figures indeed were referred to by two or more names, e.g., Esau/Edom/Seir (Gen 25:30; 36:8), Gideon/Jerubbaal (Judg 6:11, 32), or Jedidiah/Solomon (2 Sam 12:24-25).

Names Given to Anonymous Figures

The two stories in which David is first introduced to readers present him with his brothers. When Samuel arrives to anoint one of the sons of Jesse as king, David's seven brothers first pass before him: "And Jesse presented seven of his sons before Samuel, and Samuel said to Jesse, 'The Lord has not chosen any of these'" (1 Sam 16:10). Only then, after Samuel wonders, "Are these all of your boys?" (v. 11), is Jesse's youngest son, David — the chosen son — brought before Samuel. Although the numerical-literary pattern that stands behind this

---

according to which the line did not end with Mephibosheth: "and the son of Jonathan was Merib-baal; and Merib-baal begot Micah. The sons of Micah . . ." (1 Chr 8:34-35).

43. Heinemann, *Darkhe Ha-Agadah*, 28.

44. Heinemann, *Darkhe Ha-Agadah*, 27-32.

story is the seven-plus-one pattern (seven that are not chosen and the eighth that is), one cannot avoid feeling also the workings of another numerical pattern, the three-plus-one pattern.[45] The storyteller narrates the prophet's dismissal of only the eldest three of David's brothers: Eliab, Abinadab, and Shammah (1 Sam 16:6-9), while the names of the others, the fourth till the seventh, remain unmentioned. The storyteller jumps from the third son, Shammah, directly to the last: "And Jesse presented seven of his sons . . ." (v. 10). A similar picture emerges in the next chapter, the story of David and Goliath (1 Samuel 17) where, though the storyteller mentions the number of Jesse's sons — eight (v. 12) — he relates only the actions of the three eldest and David: "And Jesse's three eldest sons had followed Saul to the war and the name of the three sons who went to war were Eliab the firstborn, the second Abinadab, and the third Shammah. And David was the youngest and the three elder brothers followed Saul" (1 Sam 17:13-14).

The writer of Chronicles decided to supply the missing information and gave the anonymous sons names in the genealogical list of the clan of Judah: "Jesse begot Eliab his firstborn, Abinadab the second, Shimea the third, Nethanal the fourth, Raddai the fifth, Ozem the sixth, David the seventh" (1 Chr 2:13-15). The Chronicler didn't notice that he had replaced the seven-plus-one numerical pattern with the six-plus-one pattern, and that David was now the seventh.[46] The Peshitta to Chronicles sought to repair the damage and added another brother, changing David's position to eighth: "Elihu the seventh and David the eighth." The Syriac translator, or the writer of the Hebrew version from which he translated, had pulled the name Elihu from another verse in Chronicles: "to Judah, Elihu, of the brothers of David" (Pesh. 1 Chr 27:18).

The Conflation of Two Figures with the Same or Similar Names

It was the tendency to identify figures with similar names that caused Micaiah son of Imlah to be identified with Micah the Morashtite. Immediately after Micaiah son of Imlah's prophecy of Ahab's approaching trouble, "If you ever come home safe, the LORD has not spoken through me" (1 Kgs 22:28), the formula that introduces speech — *wayyōʾmer* ("and he said") — is repeated: "And he said, 'Listen, all you peoples!'" These words, missing from both Codex Vaticanus and the Lucianic recension of the Septuagint, are those with which

---

45. Yair Zakovitch, *For Three . . . and for Four* (Jerusalem: Makor, 1979) [Hebrew].
46. Zakovitch, *For Three . . . and for Four*, 47-49.

begins the prophecy of the prophet Micah: "Listen, all you peoples, Give heed, O earth, and all it holds [. . .]" (Mic 1:2). Whoever incorporated them into the book of Kings gave expression to the tendency to link the prophets of the prophetic stories with the classical prophets.

We find another brief example from the Minor Prophets in the title of the book of Zechariah, which identified the prophet as "Zechariah son of Berechiah son of the prophet Iddo" (Zech 1:1). Other verses do not mention Berechiah but list Iddo as the prophet's father (Ezra 5:1; 6:14). It seems that the words "son of Berechiah" in the first verse of Zechariah were an interpolation that was meant to identify the prophet Zechariah with another of the same name who was the son of Jeberechiah and who is mentioned in Isa 8:2: "and call reliable witnesses, the priest Uriah and Zechariah son of Jeberechiah, to witness for me."

Name Etymologies

Like isolated words, which may be interpreted or become the subject of exegesis, so, too, names in minimal textual units may trigger exegetical activity. Often, the original meaning of a name remains obscure, in that it derives from an ancient layer of the language that was no longer familiar to the Bible's writers and readers. Much has been written about biblical name etymologies, which, in both covert and overt form, occur frequently in the Bible[47] and persisted with particular intensity in postbiblical literature.[48]

The story of the daughter of Jephthah interprets Jephthah's name using the root *pê-ṣādê-hê*, a synonym of *pê-tāw-ḥêt* (the root of the name Jephthah).[49] In Judges 11 Jephthah tells his daughter: "I have *opened* [*pāṣîtî*] my mouth to the LORD [i.e., I have taken a vow] and I cannot retract" (Judg 11:35), to which she

---

47. Yair Zakovitch, "The Synonymous Word and Synonymous Name in Name-Midrashim," *Shnaton* 2 (1977): 100-115; "A Study of Precise and Partial Derivations in Biblical Etymology," *JSOT* 15 (1980): 31-50; "Explicit and Implicit Name-Derivations," *HAR* 4 (1980): 167-81; Andrzej Strus, *Nomen-Omen: La Stylistique Sonore des Noms Propres dans le Pentateuque.* AnBib 80 (Rome: Biblical Institute Press, 1978); Moshe Garsiel, *Biblical Names: A Literary Study of Midrashic Derivations and Puns* (Ramat Gan: Bar Ilan University, 1991) [Hebrew].

48. For a comprehensive listing of the name etymologies in rabbinic literature, see David Mendel Harduf, *Dictionary and Key to the Exegesis of Biblical Proper Names in the Talmud and Midrash* (Tel Aviv: Yizra'el, 1960) [Hebrew].

49. Compare "But if the Lord brings about something unheard-of, so that the ground opens up [from the root *pê-ṣādê-hê*] its mouth and swallows them" (Num 16:30), with "and the earth *opened* [from the root *pê-tāw-ḥêt*] its mouth and swallowed them up with their households . . ." (Num 16:32).

answers: "My father, you *opened* [*pāṣîtâ*] your mouth to God; do to me as you have vowed" (Judg 11:36). Jephthah, therefore, was the one who opened his mouth to make an unnecessary vow.

The Chronicler created an entire story in order to interpret the name of the king Jehoshophat, relating how he appointed judges and said to them: "Consider what you are doing, for you judge not on behalf of man, but on behalf of the LORD, and he is with you when you pass judgment" (2 Chr 19:6). With these words the Chronicler interpreted the two parts of the king's name as derived from the verb *š-p-ṭ*, "judge," joined with the name of God. In another case, he interpreted the name Asa according to the Aramaic *'asy'a*, "physician": "but ill as he was he still did not turn to the LORD but to physicians" (2 Chr 16:12).

The midrash, it seems, was aware of an implicit layer of the story of the garden of Eden when it interpreted the name of Eve, *hawwâ*, from the Aramaic *hiwyā'*, "snake."[50]

The Interpretation of Chronologies and Chronologies as Interpretation

There are cases where a length of time is the idea that is interpreted, and there are others in which the period of time is, itself, the interpretation. I will demonstrate the first phenomenon with the various appearances of the period of seventy years. The prophet Jeremiah prophesied a consolatory prophecy concerning the demise of Babylon and the return of the exiled to Israel after seventy years: "This whole land shall be a desolate ruin. And those nations shall serve the king of Babylon seventy years. When the seventy years are over, I will punish the king of Babylon and that nation and the land of the Chaldeans for their sins — declares the LORD — and I will make it a desolation for all time" (Jer 25:11-12); "For thus said the LORD: When Babylon's seventy years are over, I will take note of you, and I will fulfill to you my promise of favor — to bring you back to this place" (29:10). At the very end of the book of Chronicles, the prophecy of Jeremiah — which spoke of both the end to the Babylonian kingdom and the return of the exiled — and its realization are referred to: "Those who survived the sword he exiled to Babylon, and they became his and his sons' servants till the rise of the Persian kingdom, in fulfillment of the word of the LORD spoken by Jeremiah, until the land paid back its Sabbaths; as long as it lay desolate it kept Sabbath, till seventy years were completed" (2 Chr 36:20-21). In his forming this report of the prophecy's fulfillment, the Chronicler made clear use of the curses and threats that had been spoken by God in Leviticus: "And you

50. *Gen. Rab.* 20:11.

will scatter among the nations. . . . Then shall the land make up for its sabbath years throughout the time that it is desolate and you are in the land of your enemies; then shall the land rest and make up for its Sabbath years. Throughout the time that it is desolate, it shall observe the rest that it did not observe in your Sabbath years while you were dwelling upon it" (Lev 26:33-35). Not only Jeremiah's words but also those of the Torah, therefore, have been fulfilled, according to the Chronicler.

The writer of Daniel 9 wished to delay the prophecy's fulfillment until his own time, the period of Hasmonean rule (when the second, visionary section of the book of Daniel was written), and he put into Daniel's mouth words that bear explicit witness to the difficulty in negotiating the gap between the prophet's words and the somber reality in which the people lived: "I, Daniel, consulted the books concerning the number of years that, according to the word of the LORD that had come to Jeremiah the prophet, were to be the term of Jerusalem's desolation — seventy years I turned my face to the Lord God, devoting myself to prayer and supplication, in fasting, in sackcloth and ashes" (Dan 9:2-3). As a result of Daniel's entreaties and his confessions of Israel's sins, Gabriel appears to him and explains the prophecy's meaning: "Seventy weeks have been decreed for your people and your holy city until the measure of transgression is filled and that of sin complete, until iniquity is expiated, and eternal righteousness ushered in; and prophetic vision ratified, and the holy of holies anointed. You must know and understand . . ." (Dan 9:24-25). That bold thinker who interpreted Jeremiah's seventy years as "seventy weeks" (*šābu'îm šib'îm*) seems to have supported himself not only on the book of Jeremiah but also on the quotation of Jeremiah's prophecy in Chronicles and, especially, on Leviticus 26, which is alluded to and quoted from in Chronicles. The writer of Daniel 9 understood the seventy years as seventy Sabbaths, i.e., seventy *Sabbatical* Years (see Lev 25:3ff.) that the land was supposed to have observed, and since Sabbatical Years occur once every seven years, the period of the punishment reaches "seventy weeks," i.e., four hundred and ninety years.[51] The possibility cannot be excluded that the author of Daniel 9 based his interpretation on another verse in Leviticus 26, verse 18: "And if, for all that, you do not obey me, I will go on to discipline you sevenfold for your sins," meaning multiplying the seventy years by seven.[52]

Sometimes, the chronology itself is introduced in order to express a particular idea. The end of the Torah proclaims that Moses' age at his death was one

---

51. See further Avigdor Orr, "The Seventy Years of Babylon," *VT* 6 (1956): 304-6; Fishbane, *Biblical Interpretation in Ancient Israel*, 479-85.

52. For other references to Jeremiah's prophecy of seventy years, see Zech 1:12; 7:5.

hundred and twenty years: "And Moses was one hundred twenty years at his death. His eyes had not dimmed and his vigor was unabated" (Deut 34:7). One hundred twenty years is the limit God had placed on human life at the very beginning of the Pentateuch, in the story of the giants, the offspring born to the sons of God and the daughters of man: "And God said, 'My breath shall not abide in man forever, since he too is flesh; let the days allowed him be one hundred twenty years'" (Gen 6:3). The death of Moses at age one hundred twenty is meant as a firm reminder that Moses was a human being, flesh and blood, and not a god or the son of a god. True, until his last day, his "eyes had not dimmed and his vigor was unabated," and true, the number of his years was extreme; yet, still, he was but a man.

Genealogical Lists as Exegesis

Exegetical comments are embedded in the genealogies that are interspersed throughout the Bible. The first example I will bring is exegesis *ex silentio*. The genealogy of Terah reads: "Abram and Nahor took to themselves wives, the name of Abram's wife being Sarai and that of Nahor's wife Milcah, the daughter of Haran, the father of Milcah and Iscah" (Gen 11:29). The verse is notable for its lack of symmetry: nothing is said of Sarai's family while much is told about Milcah's. This silence, it seems, was deliberate. It makes room for Abraham's explanation of his relationship with Sarah. In Gen 20:12, "she is in truth my sister, my father's daughter though not my mother's, and she became my wife," which returns us to Abram's directive to Sarai back in 12:13, "Say you are my sister. . . ." Readers of chapter 12 suspect Abram of deceit, and the remark in 20:12 assures them that this was not, in fact, the case; the silence of chapter 11 provides confirmation.

At the beginning of the genealogy of the tribe of Reuben, the Chronicler explains:

> The sons of **Reuben** the firstborn of Israel, for he was the firstborn
> but when he defiled his father's bed, his birthright was given to the sons
>   of **Joseph** son
> of Israel so he is not reckoned as firstborn in the genealogy.
> Though **Judah** prevailed over his brothers and a leader came from him
> yet the birthright belonged to **Joseph.**
> The sons of **Reuben** the firstborn of Israel . . . (1 Chr 5:1-3).

In a perfect, pivotal structure, the genealogy opens and closes with Reuben, in a repetitive resumption in order to continue, afterwards, with the lineage of Reuben's sons. Also, Joseph is mentioned twice, following the first reference to Reuben and just before the second, a sign of the importance of that son who finally won the rights of the firstborn, an idea that fits well with the general view of the Chronicler. At the crux of the chiastic structure is Judah, the strongest of the brothers.

The Chronicler, who knew the book of Genesis in its entirety and that Joseph would come to occupy the primary place in that book, argued that it was due to Reuben's actions with Bilhah (Gen 35:22; 49:4) that Reuben lost the birthright to Joseph. It is possible that the Chronicler perceived Joseph as the inheritor of the birthright due to Joseph's having been allotted two portions of his father's inheritance — the legal right of the firstborn (Deut 21:17). His two sons, Manasseh and Ephraim, are counted among the tribes: "Now, your two sons, who were born to you in the land of Egypt . . . shall be mine; Ephraim and Manasseh shall be mine no less than Reuben and Simeon" (Gen 48:5). Perhaps this verse also teaches us that Ephraim and Manasseh took the places of Reuben and Simeon as first in line for the birthright.

At the same time, the Chronicler harbored reservations concerning the transfer of the firstborn rights to Joseph: "so he is not reckoned as firstborn in the genealogy," i.e., apart from the legal rights, Joseph did not take Reuben's primary position at the head of the lineage. With this the writer of Chronicles explained how, despite everything, Reuben remains at the head of the genealogy in Gen 35:23, the verse immediately following the story of his and Bilhah's misdeed, and is even referred to there as the firstborn (as also in Gen 49:3). The Chronicler's familiarity both with the Joseph stories, in which Judah plays a central role at the expense of Reuben, who is marginalized,[53] and with Genesis 49, which elevates Judah to the status of ruler, caused him to place Judah at the very center of the opening verses of his genealogy of Reuben's tribe.

In the Chronicler's genealogies, Samuel is counted among the descendants of Levi (1 Chr 6:13, 18[Eng. 28, 33]) in order to resolve any astonishment at his having served as a priest, "in the service of the Lord under Eli" (1 Sam 3:1), and even having "[slept] in the temple of the Lord where the Ark of God was" (3:3).

"Obed-edom" also becomes a Levite in the Chronicler's hands (1 Chr 26:4ff.) in order to put an end to readers' doubts over David's sending the ark of the Lord to the house of "Obed-edom the Gittite" (2 Sam 6:10 = 1 Chr 13:13), as well as to any doubts over how or why God had blessed that house (2 Sam 6:11 = 1 Chr 13:14). The Chronicler refers also to another Levite named "Obed-edom" in the days of Amaziah king of Judah (2 Chr 25:24).

---

53. Samuel E. Loewenstamm, "Reuben and Judah in the Joseph Cycle," *Fourth World Congress of Jewish Studies*, vol. 1 (Jerusalem: World Union of Jewish Studies, 1965), 67-70 [Hebrew].

The genealogy of Mordecai the Jew in the scroll of Esther unambiguously portrays him as a descendant of Saul: "In the fortress Shushan lived a Jew by the name of Mordecai, son of Jair son of Shimei son of Kish, a Benjaminite" (Esth 2:5). Mordecai was a member of Saul's tribe, Benjamin; Kish was the name of Saul's father (1 Sam 9:1); and Shimei was the name of one of Saul's relations, Shimei son of Gera (2 Sam 16:5). The name Jair, too — a name of a Gileadite family (e.g., Num 32:41) — appears in the lineage of Mordecai due to the relationship between the Benjaminites and the people of Gilead (Judg 21:6-14).[54] The exegetical effect of Mordecai's parentage is clear: it informs us that, with the tale of Esther, the house of Saul finally erased the mark that had stained it ever since Saul had avoided killing Agag king of Amalek (1 Samuel 15). Haman is called "Haman son of Hammedatha the Agagite" (Esth 3:1, 10; 8:3, 5; 9:24), bringing to a close the conflict that had raged between Saul and Agag, and making clear that the divine commandment to destroy Agag and his descendants had been carried out.

The Incorporation of Poetry into Narrative

The incorporation of a piece of poetry into a narrative context generates mutual interpretations: the poetic work is illuminated by its narrative context, and the narrative context is illuminated by the poetry. For instance, Hannah's song was inserted into the end of the story of Samuel's birth only after that story had already reached its final form. The absorption of a secondary element into the heart of an existing work often causes turbulence, minor earthquakes whose resulting tremors register at the edges of the receiving text in the various witnesses.[55] We see this in the case of Hannah's song, which did not find firm footing in 1 Samuel 2, as shown by various textual witnesses.[56]

54. See also Yair Zakovitch, "And Ira the Jairite Was Also David's Priest." *Beer-Sheva* 1 (1973): 132-34 [Hebrew].

55. On the incorporation of marginal comments into the wrong position, see my *An Introduction to Inner-biblical Interpretation*, 20-21.

56. In 1 Sam 1:28b the Masoretic Text reads: "and he/they bowed [*wayyištaḥû*] there to the LORD," with an unclear subject. The Samuel scroll from Qumran (4QSam[a]) reads: "and she left him there and she bowed to the Lord," i.e., Hannah is the subject and is, in fact, the speaker at the beginning of the verse. Other textual witnesses (the Lucianic recension of the Septuagint as well as the Vulgate and Peshitta) read: "and they bowed," i.e., Elkanah and Hannah together. The words "and he/they bowed there to the Lord" are not attested in Codex Vaticanus of the Septuagint. In that version, following v. 11 in ch. 2 the text reads: "and she left him [*watta'ăzbēhû*] there before the Lord." The Lucianic recension of the Septuagint reads in 2:11: "and they left him before the Lord there and they bowed down to the Lord."

It is generally acknowledged, and rightfully so, that the immediate pretext for ascribing the psalm to Hannah was the words "While the barren woman bears seven, the mother of many is forlorn" (1 Sam 2:5), a verse that is interpreted against the background of the rivalry between Peninnah, mother of many, and Hannah, the barren woman whom God remembered (1 Sam 1:2, 6). But Hannah's song plays a much more important role, which becomes clear from its frame, the expression with which it both begins and ends: ". . . My horn is raised by the LORD" (1 Sam 2:1); ". . . And he will raise the horn of his anointed on" (2:10). From this it is clear that, in its present context, the poem speaks about two topics: the fortunate reversal in Hannah's fate and the blessing that will rest on the future king-messiah. Just as Hannah overcomes her distress, "I gloat over my enemies" (v. 1), so, too, will the future king succeed with the help of God.

The poem's conclusion, ". . . He will give power to his king and he will raise the horn of his anointed one" (1 Sam 2:10), speaks of the future, of the life of King David. Also the story in which the psalm has been embedded addresses the future: the man of God who comes to Eli tells of his family and the ascent of another priest:

> And I will raise up for myself a faithful priest, who will act in accordance with my wishes and my purposes. I will build for him an enduring house, and he shall walk before my anointed evermore. And all the survivors of your house shall come and bow low to him for the sake of a money fee and a loaf of bread, and shall say, "Please, assign me to one of the priestly duties, that I may have a morsel of bread to eat" (1 Sam 2:35-36).[57]

The incorporation of Hannah's song at the beginning of Samuel makes possible — even invites — the interpretation of its verses in light of additional events that will take place in the book of Samuel, from the fall of the house of Eli and the rise of the prophet Samuel to the setting of Saul's sun and the dawning of the rule of David and his dynasty. It is thus clear that the psalm is viewed as a prophecy, a notion that receives explicit confirmation in *Targum Jonathan:* "And Hannah prayed with the spirit of prophecy. . . ." So, too, was the understanding of Rabbi David Kimhi (the twelfth-thirteenth century Jewish commentator known by the acronym RaDaK) in his commentary: "And Hannah said this as a prophecy."

---

57. The passage alludes to the future downfall of Abiathar, a descendant of the house of Eli (1 Kgs 2:26). As it is stated there: "And Solomon dismissed Abiathar from his office of priest of the LORD — thus fulfilling what the LORD had spoken at Shiloh regarding the house of Eli" (1 Kgs 2:27). Hannah's song thus proves to be a prophecy of that event.

The Interpretation of Narrative in Poetry

An example of the interpretation of narrative in poetry is found in the historical psalms in the book of Psalms (Pss 78; 105; 106), whose selection, presentation, and organization of traditions are guided by an exegetical conception about past events. The historiographic-didactic Psalm 78, for example, surveys the history of Israel, beginning with the plagues in Egypt and the crossing of the Sea of Reeds on dry land, until the choosing of Judah, Jerusalem, and David and the building of the temple by the God of Israel. Its guiding conception, however, is the tension between God's merciful acts towards his people and the ingratitude with which the people repaid him. As God's acts grow more and more extraordinary, so do the people's sins, and displays of unbelief mount until, when God reaches the ultimate act of magnanimity and endows Israel with its land and lodges the name of God in the temple at Shiloh, the people turn their backs to him, choosing idolatry. God's defeat of Israel's enemies in Egypt and Canaan does not stir the Israelites to return to him but, indeed, the opposite; in this way the inevitable moment arrives when Israel itself becomes God's enemy and was punished with the destruction of Shiloh, the banishment of God's name from there, and the capture of the ark.

The poet directs blame at Ephraim, the hegemonic tribe in the period. Ephraim had been defeated and had retreated in a battle in which the ark had fallen into enemy hands (Ps 78:9); God rejects Ephraim since it had not grasped the most important lesson, which the psalm's prologue states explicitly: God's blessing will not reside in a place or at a time when God's commandments are not obeyed, and compliance with the commandments hinges on the memory of God's wondrous acts, on recounting them and relaying their memory from generation to generation. Indeed, this interdependence between the transmission of the memory of God's wondrous acts and the keeping of the commandments encapsulates the entire teaching of the Torah; it even explains the essential meaning that stood behind the commandments having been incorporated into the context of the historiographical narrative that is the Torah.

Once God has turned his back on Ephraim and abandoned the temple in Shiloh, his anger at the people abates and he grants them another chance: God chooses David, the single person the psalm mentions by name. Having finally arrived at David, the psalm then draws to a close. David was chosen by God to shepherd the people in that God had failed in the role. The same expressions the psalm employs for describing God's leadership, God's shepherding of the Israelites (Ps 78:52-53), are used at the psalm's end in reference to David. The nation is in need of a human shepherd who will guide them — a shepherd and not king, a term that receives no mention in the psalm — in that they are incapable of grasping the nature of a divine leader.

The selection of Judah, Jerusalem, and David appears unconditional. An assessment of the psalm's end, however, in the context of the structure of the psalm as a whole, makes us aware of the connection between the psalm's end and its beginning. David's selection presents a wonderful opportunity, the ultimate manifestation of God's favor, but it forces the realization and recognition that Israel will flourish only when it keeps the Lord's commandments, and is not "like their fathers, a wayward and defiant generation, a generation whose heart was inconstant, whose spirit was not true to God" (Ps 78:8), and the people's faith in God is possible only if they remember the wonders he performed for them, the gracious acts God has shown Israel throughout their history. God has done his part — he selected Jerusalem and David; Israel is therefore commanded to do its part — to keep the Torah.

Poetry Creates Prose

Verses of poetry are sometimes interpreted in a way that triggers the writing of prose. The call to God of the lamenter in Lam 2:20 to gaze on the bitter fate of Zion — the malnourished mothers eating their own young, and priests and prophets, servants of the Lord, being murdered in God's temple — was used by the Chronicler to create a story about King Joash, who sent his messengers to kill a priest-prophet in the temple's courtyard:

> **See, O Lord**, and behold, to whom you have done this! Alas, women eat their own fruit, their newborn babes! Alas, **priest and prophet are slain** in the sanctuary of the Lord. (Lam 2:20)

> Then the spirit of God enveloped Zechariah son of Jehoiada the **priest**; he stood above the people and said to them, "Thus God said: Why do you transgress the commandments of the Lord when you cannot succeed? Since you have forsaken the Lord, he has forsaken you." They conspired against him and pelted him with stones in the court of the house of the Lord, by order of the king. And King Joash did not remember the loyalty that his father Jehoiada had shown him and **he killed** his son and as he was dying, he said, "**May the Lord see** and requite it." (2 Chr 24:20-22)

The Chronicler had need for a martyriological tale that would explain the death of King Joash at the hands of two conspirators: "His courtiers formed a conspiracy against Joash and assassinated him at Beth-millo that leads down to Silla" (2 Kgs 12:21[Eng. 20]). According to the Chronicler's concept of divine retribution, such a murder could not have taken place had the victim not previously committed some grave transgression; Joash's murder had to have been a measure-for-measure punishment. In Chronicles, the king's death comes as a result of and as retribution for the murder of Zechariah: "his courtiers conspired against him because of the murder of the sons of Jehoiada the priest, and they killed him in bed" (2 Chr 24:25). That a king would murder a prophet concurs with the Chronicler's interest in martyrdom (2 Chr 16:7-10; 25:15-16). This view was characteristic of the *zeitgeist* of the period, expressed, for example, in the prayer of Nehemiah: ". . . they killed your prophets who admonished them to turn them back to you" (Neh 9:26).[58]

A by-product of the martyr-story in Chronicles is the covert etymology of the name Zechariah: "And King Joash did not remember [*zākar*] the loyalty that his father Jehoiada had shown him" (2 Chr. 24:22), one more example of the Chronicler never missing an opportunity to create name etymologies (usually covert).

The story about Zechariah, which was based on the poetic Lam 2:20, elucidates the lament: while, in the lament, two tragedies — the eating of newborns and the violent deaths of priests and prophets — occur during Jerusalem's destruction at the hands of the Babylonians, for the Chronicler the eating of the children was Jerusalem's punishment for the killing of a priest and prophet — or a priest who was a prophet — Zechariah son of Jehoiada, in the sanctuary.

The Gospels, too, associated the temple's destruction (though they spoke of the second temple, and not the first) with the killing of prophets (including Zechariah): "that upon you may come all the righteous blood shed on earth, from the blood of innocent Abel to the blood of Zechariah son of Barachiah,[59] whom you murdered between the sanctuary and the altar. . . . 'O Jerusalem, Jerusalem, killing the prophets and stoning those who are sent to you!' . . . Behold, your house is forsaken and desolate" (Matt 23:35-38; see also Luke 11:50-51).

The sages, perceptive readers of the Bible's verses, realized the relationship between the verses in Chronicles and their source in Lamentations:

> They told him about Doeg, a son of Joseph who died and left a young son to his mother. She would measure him . . . every year and give his weight in gold [as an offering] to heaven, but when Jerusalem's citadel was surrounded she

---

58. Alexander Rofé, *The Prophetical Stories: The Narratives about the Prophets in the Hebrew Bible, Their Literary Types and History* (Jerusalem: Magnes, 1988), 197-213.

59. These verses from Matthew and Luke perhaps testify to a familiarity with the order of the biblical books from Genesis to Chronicles.

slaughtered him with her hand and ate him. About her lamented Jeremiah and said, "**My God**, 'women eat their own fruit, their new-born babes.'" The Holy Spirit answered, saying, "Alas, priest and prophet are killed in the sanctuary of the Lord." This is Zechariah son of Jehoiada the priest.[60]

Allegory

That the rabbis interpreted Song of Songs allegorically is well known; was the allegorical interpretation of Song a sophisticated rabbinic invention, however, the result of their desire to silence objections to the Song's inclusion in Scripture? That controversy was sealed by the famous argument of Rabbi Akiba: "Heaven forbid that any man ever disputed that the Song of Songs is holy. For the whole world is not worth the day on which the Song of Songs was given to Israel, for all the Writings are holy and the Song of Songs is holy of holies,"[61] with the conclusion found in the Tosefta: "Song of Songs is holy because it was said [under the influence] of the Holy Spirit."[62]

However, the supposition that the allegorical interpretation of Song of Songs originated with the rabbinic sages is misguided. Individual poems from Song of Songs were allegorically interpreted before the collection of poems existed, before the anthology had become Song of Songs; already in the First Temple period, Israel's prophets had granted a dimension of allegory to songs from the anthology. Two examples will suffice to demonstrate this.

The vineyard song, "Solomon had a vineyard in Baal-hamon . . ." (Song 8:11-12), is a poem that mocks Solomon, husband to a thousand wives (the fictional place name "Baal-hamon" means, literally, "husband to a multitude"). The poet compares his own relationship to his vineyard/wife, a passionate relationship that cannot be assigned monetary value, with the king's relationship to his vineyard, which was measured only by its monetary worth: "My vineyard is before me; the thousand are yours, Solomon" (8:12). Solomon, who could not tend to his own vineyard, has need of guards who will take care of his vines/women and even pays them for their work: "and two hundred for those who guard his fruit" (8:12).

It is clear that the prophet Isaiah knew the vineyard song; compare "A man will give for its fruit a thousand pieces of silver" (Song 8:11) with "a thousand vines for a thousand pieces of silver" (Isa 7:23). Isaiah, in his own vineyard song

---

60. *Sifra Beḥukotai* 6:3 (ed. Weiss, 102a). For this midrashic connection between Lamentations and Chronicles, see Avigdor Shinan, "The Development of a Rabbinic Aggadah: The Story of Doeg ben Yosef," *Maḥanaim* 7 (1984): 70-75 [Hebrew].

61. *M. Yad.* 3:5.

62. *T. Yad.* 2:14; see also *b. Meg.* 7a.

(Isa 5:1-7), makes skillful use of Song of Songs. His song opens exactly as does the one in Song of Songs, with the words *kerem hāyâ,* "A vineyard there was. . . ." Next, instead of Song's "to Solomon," there appears the designation *lîdîdî,* "to my beloved" — another of Solomon's names was *yĕdîdyāh* (2 Sam 12:25). Isaiah's vineyard song speaks of the special relationship a grape grower has with his vines: of the special relationship between God and Israel. It seems that the prophet, in his wish to capture his audience, opened his address with the words of a love poem familiar to his listeners, but the crowd that gathered to hear the popular song quickly discovered that it had been given new meaning, an allegorical one: God is the grape grower, and his vines, the source of his disappointment, are the house of Israel.[63]

A second example: In Song of Songs there are two dream poems that describe the dreams of the female lover (Song 3:1-5; 5:2–6:3). The poems are similar to one another in both language and content, both relating how the lover/dreamer sets out to find her beloved and finds him after a long search. Some version of this poem was used by the prophet Hosea to describe Israel's unfaithful, whom he likened to the adulterous woman who betrays God. The description of the woman's pursuit of her lovers, "She will pursue her lovers but will not overtake them, *she will seek them but will not find*" (Hos 2:9[Eng. 7]), returns to the dream poem: "I sought the one that my soul loved, I sought him but did not find him" (Song 3:1, 2; 5:6).[64] Hosea even tells of the revenge he thought to exact on the errant woman, "Lest I will strip her naked . . ." (Hos 2:5[3]), whereas in the dream poem in Song of Songs 5 it is told how the guards strip the woman who had taken to the streets in search of her lover: "They found me, the guards who patrol the city, they struck me and hurt me, they lifted my mantle from me, the guards of the walls" (5:7). These two examples are enough to suggest that, from a very early stage, love poems were simultaneously interpreted in two ways, following the *peshat* (the simple, original meaning of the text) and an allegorical meaning, which explained them as an expression of the relations between God and the congregation of Israel. It may have been the allegorical school of thought that was responsible for their being collected and included, ultimately, in Scripture.

*　　*　　*

Motives both ideological and contextual lay behind most of the exegetical efforts I have discussed in the various sections of this chapter. Ideological motives

---

63. The story of Naboth's vineyard (1 Kings 21) also opens with the topos "a vineyard there was to . . ." (1 Kgs 21:1).

64. Note the use of this topos also in the Wisdom literature (Prov 1:28).

are apparent at even the very beginning of the interpretative process, when writers first began to record traditions. Ideological motives guided various efforts to alter the images of certain figures, sometimes beyond recognition. Name etymologies were not simple word games. Nor were genealogies without ideological motivations. Practical motives, the need to solve objective difficulties in the biblical text, triggered lexical exegesis and were behind efforts to resolve contradictions or to "fill in" narrative gaps. It was for the purpose of concretizing the biblical text that writers worked to identify "unknown soldiers," to name anonymous and faceless characters. Finally, there was the desire to keep the text relevant, to keep it up-to-date, to connect the past with the ever-changing present. Needless to say, beyond these motives, the most powerful force driving the interpretative process was the creative one: an interpretation of a name has the power to create a new story, and verses of poetry can blossom into a completely new narrative.

In every section of this chapter we have observed how modes of interpretation that are typical of postbiblical literature are found also in the Bible itself and that the gap between inner-biblical and extrabiblical interpretation is a misconception. Postbiblical exegetes did not create new worlds *ex nihilo.* The Bible's textual witnesses, the Qumran literature, the Apocrypha, Pseudepigrapha, New Testament, and, above all, rabbinic literature and Jewish exegesis that fed from it all fastened themselves into the secure foundations of inner-biblical interpretation and proceeded along paths that had already been paved within the Bible.[65] Extrabiblical exegetical articulations are called *midrash,* the essence of which is a textual approach that allows, and even encourages, finding multiple — even contradicting — meanings in a text, out of the belief that all were planted in the text from its inception; there is no escape, therefore, from the determination that we should apply this term to the exegetical work that is present in the Bible as well.[66]

BIBLIOGRAPHY

Aichele, George, and Gary A. Phillips, eds. *Intertextuality and the Bible.* Semeia 69-70. Atlanta: SBL, 1995.
Barr, James. *Holy Scripture: Canon, Authority, Criticism.* Philadelphia: Westminster, 1983.
Bruce, Frederick F. "The Earliest Old Testament Interpretation." *OtSt* 17 (1972): 37-52.

---

65. I deal with this subject more thoroughly in my book *Inner-biblical and Extra-biblical Midrash and the Relationship between Them* (Tel Aviv: ʿAm ʿOved, 2009) [Hebrew].

66. Avigdor Shinan and Yair Zakovitch, "Midrash on Scripture and Midrash within Scripture," *ScrHier* 31 (1986): 257-77.

Draisma, Sipke, ed. *Intertexuality in Biblical Writings: Essays in Honour of Bas van Iersel.* Kampen: Kok, 1989.

Fewell, Danna N., ed. *Reading between Texts: Intertexuality and the Hebrew Bible.* Louisville: Westminster John Knox, 1992.

Fishbane, Michael. *Biblical Interpretation in Ancient Israel.* Oxford: Clarendon, 1985.

Frenkel, Yonah. *Darkhe ha-Aggadah veha-midrash.* Givataim: Yad la-talmud, 1991. [Hebrew]

Ginsberg, Harold Louis. "Daniel" (addition to entry). *Encyclopedia Mikra'it,* 2:949-52. [Hebrew]

Heinemann, Isaak. *Darkhe Ha-Agadah.* Jerusalem: Magnes, 1954; repr. 1970.

Hertzberg, Hans Wilhelm. "Die Nachgeschichte alttestamentlicher Texte innerhalb des Alten Testaments." *BZAW* 66 (1936): 110-21.

Kugel, James L., and Rowan A. Greer. *Early Biblical Interpretation.* LEC 3. Philadelphia: Westminster, 1986.

Leiman, Sid Z. *The Canonization of the Hebrew Scripture: The Talmudic and Midrashic Evidence.* Hamden: Archon, 1976; repr. 1991.

Marquis, Galen. "Explicit Literary Allusions in Biblical Historiography (The Pentateuch and Former Prophets)." Ph.D. diss., Hebrew University in Jerusalem, 1999. [Hebrew]

Sarna, Nahum. "Psalm 89: A Study in Inner Biblical Exegesis." In *Biblical and Other Studies,* ed. Alexander Altmann. Cambridge, Mass.: Harvard University Press, 1963, 29-46.

Seeligmann, Isac Leo. "Voraussetzungen der Midraschexegese." *VTSup* 1 (1953): 150-81.

———. "Anfänge der Midraschexegese in der Chronik." In *Gesammelte Studien zur Hebräischen Bibel/Isac Leo Seeligman,* ed. Erhard Blum. FAT 41. Tübingen: Mohr Siebeck, 2004, 31-54.

Shinan, Avigdor. "The Development of a Rabbinic Aggadah: The Story of Doeg ben Yosef." *Maḥanaim* 7 (1984): 70-75. [Hebrew]

———, and Yair Zakovitch. "Midrash on Scripture and Midrash within Scripture." *ScrHier* 31 (1986): 257-77.

Sommer, Benjamin D. *A Prophet Reads Scripture: Allusion in Isaiah 40–66.* Stanford: Stanford University Press, 1998.

Weingreen, Jacob. "Rabbinic-Type Glosses in the Old Testament." *JSS* 2 (1957): 149-62.

———. "Exposition in the Old Testament and in Rabbinic Literature." In *Promise and Fulfillment: Essays Presented to Professor S. H. Hooke,* ed. Frederick F. Bruce. Edinburgh: T. & T. Clark, 1963, 187-201.

———. "The Deuteronomic Legislator — A Proto Rabbinic Type." In *Proclamation and Presence: Old Testament Essays in Honour of Gwynne Henton Davies,* ed. John I. Durham and J. R. Porter. Richmond: John Knox, 1970; repr. 1983, 76-89.

Zakovitch, Yair. "The Synonymous Word and Synonymous Name in Name-Midrashim." *Shnaton: An Annual for Biblical and Ancient Near Eastern Studies* 2 (1977): 100-115.

———. "The Varied Faces of Inner-biblical Interpretation." *Tarbiz* 56 (1986): 136-43. [Hebrew]

———. *An Introduction to Inner-biblical Interpretation.* Even Yehudah: Rekhes, 1992. [Hebrew]

———. *Through the Looking Glass: Reflection Stories in the Bible.* Tel Aviv: ha-Kibuts ha-Me'uhad, 1995. [Hebrew]

————. "Juxtaposition in the Abraham Cycle." In *Pomegranates and Golden Bells: Studies in Biblical, Jewish, and Near Eastern Ritual, Law, and Literature in Honor of Jacob Milgrom*, ed. David P. Wright, David Noel Freedman, and Avi Hurvitz. Winona Lake: Eisenbrauns, 1995, 509-24.

————. "Was It Not at His Hand the Sun Stopped? (Ben Sira 46:6): A Chapter in Literary Archaeology." In *Tehillah le-Moshe: Biblical and Judaic Studies in Honor of Moshe Greenberg*, ed. Mordechai Cogan, Barry L. Eichler, Jeffrey H. Tigay. Winona Lake: Eisenbrauns, 1997, 107*-14*.

Translators as Interpreters:
Scriptural Interpretation in the Septuagint

Martin Rösel

Everyone who is taking a close look at the research on the Septuagint, the Greek translation of the Hebrew Bible, will most likely come across two sentences.[1] The first is the "truism that any translation is an interpretation."[2] The second is a quotation from the introduction to the Greek translation of the book of Jesus Sirach, written by his alleged grandson: "For what was originally expressed in Hebrew does not have exactly the same sense when translated into another language. Not only this book, but even the Law itself, the Prophecies, and the rest of the books differ not a little when read in the original."[3]

These two statements suggest that some changes were necessarily made when the Hebrew Bible was translated into Greek and that these changes can be attributed to certain acts of interpretation that inevitably belong to the process of translation. If so, several subsequent questions arise:

---

1. In this chapter, the term "Septuagint" (and its abbreviation in Roman digits "LXX") is used for the Greek Bible in general, although it was originally coined as a designation for the Greek Pentateuch only. Also, the content of the canon of the Septuagint can differ between the manuscripts. Cf. Jennifer M. Dines, *The Septuagint* (London: T. & T. Clark, 2004), 1-3, for the definition; Martin Hengel, *The Septuagint as Christian Scripture: Its Prehistory and the Problem of Its Canon.* OTS (London: T. & T. Clark, 2002); Mogens Müller, *The First Bible of the Church: A Plea for the Septuagint.* JSOTSup 206. Copenhagen International Seminar 1 (Sheffield: Sheffield Academic, 1996), for the problem of the canon.

2. See, e.g., John W. Wevers, "The Interpretative Character and Significance of the Septuagint Version," in *Hebrew Bible/Old Testament,* vol. 1.1: *Antiquity,* ed. Magne Sæbø (Göttingen: Vandenhoeck & Ruprecht, 1996), 84-107 (here p. 87). A very stimulating introduction into the problems of translation is Umberto Eco, *Mouse or Rat? Translation as Negotiation* (London: Weidenfeld & Nicolson, 2003). It is interesting that even the translated title of Eco's book shows a certain degree of interpretation, because the Italian original reads *"dire quasi la stessa cosa"* ("saying almost the same"). The English title is taken from one of the examples discussed in the book.

3. Vv. 21-26 NRSV.

(a) How is it possible to trace these acts of interpretation?
(b) Is it possible to make a distinction between different kinds or levels of interpretation?
(c) Are the reasons for and strategies of scriptural interpretation in the LXX discernable?
(d) Are there any differences between the translations of individual books of the Hebrew Bible, and, if so, are different attitudes towards Scripture perceptible?
(e) Finally, is it possible to discern some general principles of scriptural interpretation that can be detected in all or at least in most of the books of the Septuagint?

These five questions will serve to outline the problem. They are kept rather general here to give an impression of the topics that are discussed in Septuagint research.[4] Because of the limited space of this article, it will not be possible to answer them in detail; they will nevertheless prove helpful to provide the heuristic horizon for our dealing with these texts.

The Lawgiver in Psalm 9:21 as an Example

Following these general questions, I will begin with a textual example from the book of the Psalms in order to illustrate the complexity of LXX exegesis and to justify the differentiation just presented. Psalm 9:21 the Hebrew Bible (MT) reads:

שִׁיתָה יְהוָה מוֹרָה לָהֶם
יֵדְעוּ גוֹיִם אֱנוֹשׁ הֵמָּה

Put fear to them, O LORD;
nations shall know that they are (only) human.

In the Greek version of the Septuagint, the verse sounds quite different:

κατάστησον, κύριε, νομοθέτην ἐπ᾽ αὐτούς,
γνώτωσαν ἔθνη ὅτι ἄνθρωποί εἰσιν.

Appoint, O Lord, a lawgiver over them;
nations shall know that they are humans.

4. A very stimulation collection of articles describing the current state of research in Septuagint studies is Wolfgang Kraus and R. Glenn Wooden, eds., *Septuagint Research: Issues and Challenges in the Study of the Greek Jewish Scriptures.* SBLSCS 53 (Atlanta: SBL, 2005).

When comparing the texts, it is obvious that every element of the Hebrew (suffixes included) has a counterpart in the Greek version; the syntactical sequence of the words is the same. This is a characteristic of what one usually calls a "literal translation"; it is one of the typical features of most translations of the LXX.[5] It should be noticed that the plural ἄνθρωποι ("humans") is used to translate the singular אֱנוֹשׁ ("man"), but since this word can be understood as a collective ("mankind") and the plural is signaled by הֵמָּה ("they") and גּוֹיִם ("nations"), the translation only makes this fact explicit. This can be understood as a linguistic interpretation, but since acts like these necessarily belong to the process of reading and translation, it may be more appropriate to label it as *linguistic decoding*.[6]

The most interesting and important deviation in this verse is the translation of מוֹרָה ("fear") by νομοθέτης ("lawgiver"). When returning to the question (a) posed above (How is it possible to trace acts of interpretation?), the initial answer is quite clear: the meaning of the translated word is completely different from its *Vorlage*, and, moreover, it changes the meaning of the whole verse. The nations are able to discern their humanity not through an abstract act of fear of God but through his Torah.

Who was responsible for this interpretation? Since the LXX is a translation, it is always possible that it refers back to a different *Vorlage* so that it faithfully reproduces the meaning of a different Hebrew version. This means that, after an initial comparison of the texts, we need to employ the help of textual criticism in order to determine whether the text we read in the modern *Biblia Hebraica* does in fact represent the same or at least a similar version as the one which the translator had as his *Vorlage*. And, is the modern edition of the Septuagint reliable, so that one can safely assume that this is the text that comes from the hand of the translator, not from any kind of later redaction?[7]

---

5. It is important to notice that this use of the terms "free" and "literal" is approximate. For an exhaustive treatment of the problem, see James Barr, *The Typology of Literalism in Ancient Biblical Translations*. NAWG, Phil.-Hist. Kl. 11 (Göttingen: Vandenhoeck & Ruprecht, 1979), 294, for a list of six distinguishing features between literal and free translations.

6. See Folker Siegert, *Zwischen Hebräischer Bibel und Altem Testament: Eine Einführung in die Septuaginta*. MJS 9 (Münster: Lit, 2001), 121, for this distinction.

7. The problems associated with the use of the LXX for the reconstruction of its parent Hebrew text and the text-critical search for the original LXX, the history of its revisions and modern editions, cannot be discussed here. It may suffice to refer interested readers to the introductions by Karen H. Jobes and Moisés Silva, *Invitation to the Septuagint* (Grand Rapids: Baker, 2000); Emanuel Tov, *The Text-Critical Use of the Septuagint in Biblical Research*. 2nd rev. ed. Jerusalem Biblical Studies 8 (Jerusalem: Simor, 1997); and Natalio Fernández Marcos, *The Septuagint in Context: Introduction to the Greek Version of the Bible* (Leiden: Brill, 2000). It should be added that several scholars hold the opinion that in cases of larger divergences between MT and

In the case of Ps 9:21, there is in fact a variant in the Hebrew textual tradition concerning מוֹרָה ("fear"), the word in question. Several manuscripts read מוֹרָא, but this is only a orthographical variant that corrects the original, difficult reading to a more usual one. One can therefore conclude that the rendering "lawgiver" can be judged to be an interpretation as the result of the translation. Question (a) can thus be answered positively: Ps 9:21 is an example of scriptural interpretation.

The next question (b) concerns the kind of interpretation we can see in the current text. One should bear in mind that the translator read an unvocalized text (מורה). When decoding the verse, he obviously derived this word as a participle *Hiphil* from the root ירה III, which can mean "to instruct, to teach" (see *HALOT*). Thus the linguistic decoding would lead to the noun "instructor, teacher" (מוֹרָה). Moreover, it is also possible that he found an etymological connection to the word תּוֹרָה ("law"), which can also be derived from the root ירה.[8] Thus one can assume a combination of linguistic signals that has led the translator to amplify the meaning "instructor" to "lawgiver." This interpretation is clearly a kind of theologically motivated interpretation, because in other psalms one can find more "literal" renderings of the verb ירה ("teach, instruct").[9] Since the Lord is addressed in this verse, the new interpretation has consequences which go even further: it is not the Lord but his helpful law that brings fear to the nations.

However, question (b) can be answered in yet another way, which leads us directly to the problems that have to be discussed with respect to question (c): the reasons and strategies for interpretation. Although the word νομοθέτης ("lawgiver") in Ps 9:21 is a *hapax legomenon* in the LXX, one can find similar interpretations. According to the difficult text in Ps 84(LXX 83):7, the pious can go through a valley that has been covered by the early rain with blessings:

עֹבְרֵי בְּעֵמֶק הַבָּכָא מַעְיָן יְשִׁיתוּהוּ גַּם־בְּרָכוֹת יַעְטֶה מוֹרֶה

ἐν τῇ κοιλάδι τοῦ κλαυθμῶνος εἰς τὸν τόπον, ὃν ἔθετο·
καὶ γὰρ εὐλογίας δώσει ὁ νομοθετῶν.

LXX one has to assume the existence of a different *Vorlage* of the LXX, even if there is no witness for this text other than the translation itself. This position minimizes the possibility to attribute interpretations to the translators.

8. See Laurent Monsengwo Pasinya, *La notion de Nomos dans le Pentateuque Grec.* AnBib 52. Recherches Africaines de théologie 5 (Rome: Pontifical Biblical Institute, 1973), 131-35.

9. Ps 32(31):8; 45:4(5); 86:11; cf. Frank Austermann, *Von der Tora zum Nomos: Untersuchungen zur Übersetzungsweise und Interpretation im Septuaginta-Psalter.* MSU 27 (Göttingen: Vandenhoeck & Ruprecht, 2003), 177-78.

The MT reads מוֹרֶה ("early rain"). The translator of the LXX has chosen a similar linguistic and theological explanation of the Hebrew noun as in Ps 9:21, for we can read: "for the lawgiver (νομοθετῶν) will give blessings." Thus in Ps 84(83):7 the difficult metaphor of valley and rain has been avoided, and again the emphasis falls on the helpful, benevolent action of God and his law. Moreover, in other psalms one can also see that the verb ירה ("teach, instruct") has been translated by νομοθετήσει ("to be given the law").[10] Obviously the translator wanted to stress that the Torah is the only reliable base for instruction; therefore one can assume that he followed a particular strategy of interpretation when he translated a verse that speaks about instructions and teaching.[11]

This means that question (c) can be answered in the affirmative, too: in the book of Psalms there are strategies of interpretation concerning the idea of the Torah that affect individual renderings throughout the book.[12] But again, the question can be answered another way: the translation "lawgiver" in Ps 9:21 and elsewhere attests to the phenomenon of intertextuality.[13] By this I mean that a text can refer to other texts so that its meaning is enhanced. In the case of a translation, "intertextuality" can also mean that the translator has chosen his equivalents under the influence of other, previously translated texts. This can be due to the fact that in antiquity there has not been something like a lexicon;[14] it may be that he was not sure about the exact meaning of a Hebrew word, so that another translation served as an aid for orientation.[15] It is also possible that he wanted to create a connection between texts. In this case, the translation would refer to a wider horizon of thoughts and concepts than the original.

In the case of the "lawgiver" in Ps 9:21, the translation clearly depends on

10. Ps 25(24):8+12; 27(26):11, and esp. in the Torah psalm 119(118):33, 102, 104.

11. It is interesting to note that in the Psalms there are other interpretative translations that advance the idea of a divine education; cf. Ps 2:12; 90(89):10.

12. This is the most important result of the dissertation by Austermann, *Von der Tora zum Nomos*.

13. See Gilles Dorival, "Les phénomènes d'intertextualité dans le livre grec des Nombres," in *KATA TOYΣ O': Selon Les Septante. Festschrift Marguerite Harl*, ed. Dorival and Olivier Munnich (Paris: Cerf, 1995), 253-85, for an introduction to this field of research.

14. See for this problem Emanuel Tov, "The Impact of the LXX Translation of the Pentateuch on the Translation of the Other Books," in *The Greek and Hebrew Bible: Collected Essays on the Septuagint*. VTSup 72 (Leiden: Brill, 1999), 183-94; and the critical remarks by James Barr, "Did the Greek Pentateuch Really Serve as a Dictionary for the Translation of the Later Books?" in *Hamlet on a Hill: Semitic and Greek Studies Presented to Professor T. Muraoka*, ed. Martin F. J. Basten and W. Th. van Peursen. OLA 118 (Leuven: Peeters, 2003), 523-43.

15. Emanuel Tov, "Did the Septuagint Translators Always Understand Their Hebrew Text?," in *The Greek and Hebrew Bible*, 203-18.

Exod 24:12 and Deut 17:10, where the verb ירה ("teach, instruct") refers to the tablets of the commandments, which God has given to instruct his people. In both instances, the Greek translations were using νομοθετέω ("to give the law"), thus introducing this compound verb into the biblical language and emphasizing the special kind of divine teaching. The translator of the Psalms ties his references to the teaching of the Torah back to the revelation of this law at Mount Sinai (or Horeb in Deuteronomy).

The Greek Bible as a Collection of Scriptures and the Question of Overall Concepts

The discussion of Ps 9:21 has served to give some exemplary answers to three of the five questions posed above. Questions (d) and (e) cannot be settled on the base of the exegesis of one verse only but require more information. As for the individual books of the Septuagint and the different attitudes of their translators towards their task, it is now clear from the results of modern research that every book has to be treated as a separate unity. As a rule of thumb one can start with the assumption that each book has been translated by an individual translator (or perhaps by a group with the same working method). Only occasionally have scholars found sufficient reasons to reckon with more than one translator; the most important case is the tabernacle account in the book of Exodus.[16]

Although research on the question of the chronological setting and geographical origins of these individual translations has in most cases not led to unambiguous results, it is clear that the books of the Hebrew Bible were translated in the time from the third century b.c.e. until the first century c.e. During this period some of the existing translations were reworked or replaced by revisions or new translations. This explains why we have duplicate editions, for example in the case of the book of Daniel, Judges, or the book of Kingdoms. Presumably, most translations were carried out in Alexandria in Egypt, where the largest Jewish community outside of Israel flourished and where the needs to possess the Holy Scriptures in Greek had been urgent. But it is also possible that some of the books were translated in Israel, in Antiochia, or in Leontopolis, another important Jewish settlement in Egypt, where even a second Jewish temple besides the one in Jerusalem was built.[17]

16. Martha Lynn Wade, *Consistency of Translation Techniques in the Tabernacle Accounts of Exodus in the Old Greek*. SBLSCS 49 (Atlanta: SBL, 2003).

17. For an overview, see the tables in Gilles Dorival, Marguerite Harl, and Olivier Munnich, *La Bible Grecque des Septante: Du Judaïsme Hellénistique au Christianisme Ancien* (Paris: Cerf, 1988), 93, 107, 111.

When working on the books of the Septuagint it is important to bear these different chronological and geographical milieus in mind as the background for the translator's hermeneutic, because the way Scripture is interpreted always depends on theological tendencies and religious experiences (e.g., the Maccabean crisis) that are dominant at that time and in that social group.

The fact that the Septuagint has to be seen as a collection of Scriptures from different historical periods and geographical regions has important ramifications for our answer to question (e), the question whether or not we can detect some overall principles of scriptural interpretation in the whole of the Septuagint. The answer cannot be positive. The differences between some translations are so important — for example, between the book of Job on the one hand and Qohelet on the other, or between Exodus and Samuel — that common characteristics in scriptural interpretation that apply equally to all of them cannot be found. However, if individual translations are grouped according to their translational characteristics, then it is indeed possible to see some lines of interpretation that can be regarded as typical for these groups of books.[18]

To illustrate this approach one can refer to the enhanced importance of the concept of νόμος ("law"). This Greek word has been used very frequently, not only for Hebrew תּוֹרָה ("law"), but also for other words like חֻקָּה ("ordinance") or מִשְׁפָּט ("judgment"); moreover, the opposite ἀνομία ("lawlessness") was used to render a wide variety of Hebrew words, denoting acts of sin, lawlessness, or unjustness. Therefore the idea of νόμος and the negative results of deviating from this νόμος are much more present in the Greek than in the Hebrew Bible. Thus the importance of God's law for Israel is emphasized in most of the books of the Septuagint. A similar process can be seen when looking at the concept of תּוֹרָה in the late books of the Hebrew Bible or in Qumran.[19] It is obvious that the individual translations are influenced by an overall theological concept that was common in the Hellenistic age. This means that a positive answer for question (e) is possible, as long as we are dealing with a specific topic only and with a limited number of books.

---

18. A fuller methodological discussion of the possibilities and limitations of such a summarizing "theology" of several books of the Septuagint can be found in Martin Rösel, "Towards a 'Theology of the Septuagint,'"in Kraus and Wooden, *Septuagint Research*, 239-52.

19. For a fuller treatment of this problem, see Martin Rösel, "Nomothesie: Zum Gesetzesverständnis der Septuaginta," in *Im Brennpunkt: Die Septuaginta*, vol. 3: *Studien zur Theologie, Anthropologie, Ekklesiologie, Eschatologie und Liturgie der griechischen Bibel*, ed. Heinz-Josef Fabry and Dieter Böhler. BWANT 174 (Stuttgart: Kohlhammer, 2007), 132-50.

A Minimalistic Objection: The Paradigm of Interlinearity

The exegesis of Ps 9:21 and the five questions to classify elements of scriptural interpretation in the LXX are based on the assumption that most of the translators wanted to produce a text that could be read and understood independently of its Hebrew *Vorlage*. Obviously they were aware that they were translating and thereby producing a canonical text.[20] Moreover, they were also willing — although to a different extent — to correct obvious mistakes, clarify dubious passages, avoid misinterpretations, or bring the texts in line with its common interpretation in the religious community of the translator. While it is obvious that during the later *reception* history, especially in Christian communities, some new interpretations came to be associated with the texts (e.g., some messianic readings),[21] it is also clear that already the act of *producing* the translation involved several processes, some linguistically, and others culturally and theologically motivated (questions b, c + e).

The basic idea of how to approach the LXX is challenged by a new paradigm, which has been worked out by Albert Pietersma and his colleagues.[22] His concept has become very important, because the *New English Translation of the Septuagint* (NETS) is based on its principles. NETS is undoubtedly becoming very influential for the evaluation of the Septuagint in the English-speaking world. According to Pietersma, many of the translations in the LXX are not meant to be read independently. The Greek text was translated as a tool to understand the Hebrew, a "crib for the study of the Hebrew."[23] Only at a later stage in the history of reception were the Greek texts read independently. The paradigm is called "interlinear" because Pietersma compares the Septuagint with bilingual texts that were used in Hellenistic schools. These papyri originally had a Latin text (mostly by Vergil) in one column and its translation into Greek in the other.[24] The lines of these columns were very short, containing no more

20. Wevers, "Interpretative Character and Significance," 95.

21. For the necessary differentiation between production and reception, see Albert Pietersma, "Messianism and the Greek Psalter: In search of the Messiah," in *The Septuagint and Messianism*, ed. Michael A. Knibb. BETL 195 (Leuven: Peeters, 2006), 50-52. I disagree with his overall approach.

22. Albert Pietersma, "A New Paradigm for Addressing Old Questions: The Relevance of the Interlinear Model for the Study of the Septuagint," in *Bible and Computer: The Stellenbosch AIBI-6 Conference: Proceedings of the Association Internationale Bible et Informatique*, ed. Johann Cook (Leiden: Brill, 2002), 337-64.

23. Pietersma, "A New Paradigm," 360.

24. Robert Cavenaile, *Corpus papyrorum Latinarum*, 1 (Wiesbaden: Harrassowitz, 1958); Johannes Kramer, *Glossaria bilinguia altera (C. Gloss. biling. II)*. APF, Beiheft 8 (Leipzig: Saur, 2001), 28, and pp. 100-104 for a fable by Aesop.

than one up to a few words. According to this hypothesis it can easily be explained why in the LXX the Greek translation very often follows the word order of the Hebrew slavishly, which leads to a syntax that must have sounded very strange to Greek-speaking people. The hypothesis can also answer the question of why there are inconsistencies in the translations: if the translator was mainly thinking in small units as a short line of a column, it is understandable that he was not aiming for the same translation of one Hebrew word throughout the book. Furthermore, Pietersma argues that the connotations of the Greek words stay in the semantic range of the Hebrew. Even if a word like *psychē* or *kosmos* has a specific significance in the Greek-speaking world, only the meaning of its Hebrew counterpart can safely be applied in the translation. Applying its usual Greek meaning would mean that the reception overrules the original meaning of the text. Finally, Pietersma asserts that, like the parallel bilingual papyri, the origins of the Septuagint must also be seen in the educational goals of schools.[25]

This theory is the basis for one of the most significant features of the new translation of the LXX into English (NETS), which has been shaped under the editorial leadership of Albert Pietersma. It uses a translation of the Hebrew Bible, the NRSV, as the basic referential document, which is accepted also as the translation of the Greek Bible as long as its rendering can be seen as correct.[26] This means that the English translation of the LXX does not stand alone either but also refers back to the Hebrew text.[27]

Although this paradigm can in fact shed some light on obscure phenomena of the translational process, some serious problems remain. First, it should be stated that the bilingual Vergil papyri are not attested prior to the third century C.E. From the first century C.E. we have some comparable texts with verses by Homer in two columns, one in classic Greek and one in Koine. There is no proof that these aids existed as early as in the third century B.C.E. Moreover, those texts were not produced to learn basic Latin, but perhaps to give students an impression of the exemplary syntactical style of the poet. The Greek transla-

25. But see Raffaella Cribiore, *Writing, Teachers, and Students in Graeco-Roman Egypt.* ASP 36 (Atlanta: Scholars, 1996), 28, who argues against the view that these bilingual papyri were written for educational purposes in schools.

26. Cf. Albert Pietersma, "To the Reader of NETS," in *A New English Translation of the Septuagint and the Other Greek Translations Traditionally Included under That Title,* ed. Pietersma and Benjamin G. Wright (New York: Oxford University Press, 2007), xiii-xx.

27. For the problem of how to deal with books without a Hebrew original, see Joachim Schaper, "Translating 2 Maccabees for NETS," in *XII Congress of the International Organization for Septuagint and Cognate Studies, Leiden 2004,* ed. Melvin K. H. Peters. SBLSCS 54 (Atlanta: SBL, 2006), 225-32.

tions in these papyri are at times fragmented and nearly unintelligible. They are not coherent texts but lists of words and phrases that should be used as examples.[28] Second, when comparing different papyri in which the same text from Vergil is translated, one can see a high degree of variance between the translations. The aim of these texts has obviously not been to produce something like an authoritative Greek version of Vergil or Cicero. Therefore these bilingual papyri are not comparable to the LXX, because from the translation of Genesis legible and coherent texts were produced, even if their Hebraistic syntax may have sounded strange for Greek-speaking readers.

A third and even more important objection concerns Pietersma's focus on small translational units. According to his view, "the primary reason for a word's presence in such a translated text is to represent the Hebrew counterpart, rather than its appropriateness to the new context that is being created."[29] This does include, as mentioned earlier, the assumption that the Greek equivalents chosen by the translators have no other meaning than that of their Hebrew counterparts. Pietersma himself labels this position a kind of "linguistic heresy."[30] However, if this were a correct assumption, one could not explain why there are so many newly created Greek words *(neologisms)* in the Septuagint, for example, why the translators have carefully avoided words like βωμός ("altar") — except for heathen offerings — and only used θυσιαστήριον ("place of offering") for the true cult of the God of Israel (cf. Num 4:11 and 23:3).

Moreover, there is an overwhelming number of examples — some of them are given in the next sections — where the translators did not only look for a quantitative equation between the Hebrew text and the Greek version but were also trying hard to produce an appropriate meaning, as we have seen in the case of the "lawgiver." Finally, it should be stated that in the translations of the Septuagint numerous instances can be seen where a translation goes far beyond the level of the small unit of a single line. Mention has already been made of the phenomenon of intertextual translations. One can also refer to renderings in which the Greek text is stylistically improved over the Hebrew,[31] as well as to harmonizations between biblical texts, e.g., in the account of the creation in Genesis 1 or in the flood story in Genesis 6–8. One can add that the first known translation of the LXX, the book of Genesis, is of high quality and shows such lexical consistency as is hardly conceivable if we presume that it was produced

28. These arguments are based on Robert E. Gaebel, "The Greek Word-Lists to Vergil and Cicero," *BJRL* 52 (1969-70): 284-325, esp. 298-301.

29. Albert Pietersma, "Exegesis in the Septuagint: Possibilities and Limits (The Psalter as a Case in Point)," in Kraus and Wooden, *Septuagint Research*, 38.

30. Pietersma, "Exegesis in the Septuagint," 38.

31. See, e.g., Amos 1:13–2:6, and Gen 1:2, in Dines, *The Septuagint*, 54-57.

in a school.[32] It is therefore reasonable to conclude that the hermeneutical presuppositions that lie behind the paradigm of interlinearity do not fit the exegetical problems of the Greek Bible; the paradigm poses more questions than it is able to answer.

Examples of Interpretations in the Septuagint

Interpretations were introduced into the Greek text for different reasons. They were used *inter alia* because the translators wanted to clarify obscure passages, to harmonize or improve texts, or to avoid possible misunderstandings. In a number of cases they also wanted to refer to other biblical texts or to theological or cultural contexts. Moreover, one can also see that texts were applied to a new social or historical situation, mostly because of the fact that the translation was carried out in the Diaspora. The remainder of this article will illustrate these phenomena by collecting some striking examples and arranging them in a systematic order. The examples will be taken mainly from the books of the Greek Pentateuch and the Psalms, because a lot of important research on these books has been carried out. It is also interesting to see how the translators were interpreting in the context of narratives or liturgical texts. In the prophetic texts and in the book of Proverbs one can find an even higher degree of scriptural interpretation, because from the start prophecies were used for different applications, and educational texts were intended to be actualized.[33]

The following examples are related to questions (b) and (c) posed at the

32. See Arie van der Kooij, "Perspectives on the Study of the Septuagint: Who Are the Translators?" in *Perspectives in the Study of the Old Testament and Early Judaism. Festschrift Adam S. van der Woude,* ed. Florentino García Martínez and Edward Noort. VTSup 73 (Leiden: Brill, 1998), 214-29, for a more convincing theory that the translators must be seen as well-trained scribes. I for myself have proposed to see the origins of the Greek Pentateuch in an academic milieu like the *museion* of Alexandria; cf. Martin Rösel, *Übersetzung als Vollendung der Auslegung: Studien zur Genesis-Septuaginta.* BZAW 223 (Berlin: de Gruyter, 1994), 254-60. This theory was accepted and expanded by Siegfried Kreuzer, "Entstehung und Publikation der Septuaginta im Horizont frühptolemäischer Bildungs- und Kulturpolitik," in *Im Brennpunkt: Die Septuaginta,* vol. 2: *Studien zur Entstehung und Bedeutung der Griechischen Bibel,* ed. Kreuzer and Jürgen P. Lesch. BWANT 161 (Stuttgart: Kohlhammer, 2004), 61-75.

33. On Proverbs, see Johann Cook, "The Ideology of Septuagint Proverbs," in *X Congress of the International Organization for Septuagint and Cognate Studies, Oslo 1998,* ed. Bernard A. Taylor. SBLSCS 51 (Atlanta: SBL, 2001), 463-79; on Isaiah, see Arie van der Kooij, "The Septuagint of Isaiah: Translation and Interpretation," in *The Book of Isaiah — Le Livre d'Isaïe: Les Oracles et leurs Relectures, Unité et complexité de l'ouvrage,* ed. Jacques Vermeylen. BETL 81 (Leuven: Peeters, 1989), 127-33.

beginning of this article. It will be demonstrated what kinds or levels of interpretation one can find in the Septuagint and what reasons one can assume that have led the translators to produce the renderings in question. I have chosen a rough system of classification, which begins with cases in which the translators refused to interpret their text and thus created a version that called for an interpretation on the side of the readers. I then move to instances in which the interpretations are the result of linguistic problems. Finally, we will look at texts that prove that the translators were actively attempting to improve their text, to enhance it, or to give it a specific interpretation.[34]

No Interpretation Means: Interpreting Differently

First there are several instances in which the translators obviously avoided interpreting the text in order to provide their own interpretation.

Gen 6:14

קִנִּים תַּעֲשֶׂה אֶת־הַתֵּבָה

"make it an ark with compartments"

νοσσιὰς ποιήσεις τὴν κιβωτόν

"you shall make the ark with nests"

Well known is the translation νοσσιά ("brood, nest"; also "beehive") for קֵן ("nest") in Gen 6:14, where Noah is ordered to make the ark with compartments. According to James Barr, the translator was not able to understand this passage and transferred the problem to his readers by using a literal rendering.[35]

Another example of this type can be found in Gen 11:1.

Gen 11:1

וַיְהִי כָל־הָאָרֶץ שָׂפָה אֶחָת וּדְבָרִים אֲחָדִים

"And the whole earth had one language and the same words."

Καὶ ἦν πᾶσα ἡ γῆ χεῖλος ἕν, καὶ φωνὴ μία πᾶσιν.

"And the whole earth was one lip, and there was one speech for all."

---

34. Detailed discussions of the crucial texts can be found in Wevers on the individual books of the Pentateuch (e.g., *Notes on the Greek Text of Genesis*), and in the volumes of the *La Bible d'Alexandrie*: e.g., vol. 1: *La Genèse, Traduction du texte grec de la Septane: Introduction et Notes par Marguerite Harl* (Paris: Cerf, 1986).

35. Barr, *The Typology of Literalism*, 293; cf. Rösel, *Übersetzung als Vollendung der Auslegung*, 168.

According to the Hebrew text the whole earth had one language (שָׂפָה אֶחָת). In the LXX this has been translated quite literally by χεῖλος ἕν, "the earth was one lip,"[36] which sounds quite strange. The interesting fact is that in both contexts the translator has demonstrated his willingness to explain difficult passages by referring to other biblical texts (6:14) or by adding a word (11:1), so translating more freely.

This phenomenon occurs more often, also in other translations. In the book of Kingdoms, for example, one can find the tendency to transcribe obscure words (4 Kgs 20:12; 23:7).[37] In an important article on Ps 29(28):6, Adrian Schenker has demonstrated that in some cases the translator obviously wanted to keep the meaning of some passages obscure. The Greek text reads: "He will beat them small," instead of "He makes Lebanon skip."[38] It is possible that even this refusal to interpret is the expression of a certain theological assumption that the words of Scripture can transfer their meaning even if they are hardly comprehensible.[39]

Linguistic Decoding and Interpretation

As argued earlier, usually the act of vocalizing the Hebrew consonantal text can not be seen as an act of interpretation but as necessary linguistic decoding. But there are numerous instances where the boundaries between decoding and interpretation are porous. A specific decision how to vocalize or to deduce a word in its context can change the meaning of the passage in question.

Hab 3:5

לְפָנָיו יֵלֶךְ דָּבֶר וְיֵצֵא רֶשֶׁף לְרַגְלָיו

πρὸ προσώπου αὐτοῦ πορεύσεται λόγος,
καὶ ἐξελεύσεται, ἐν πεδίλοις οἱ πόδες αὐτοῦ.

One of the most striking examples is Hab 3:5. The MT reads, "Before him went pestilence." The translator has derived the word דָּבֶר ("pestilence") from דָּבָר

---

36. Perhaps the translator did not intend the meaning "lip" but "bank," referring to a primeval bank of the waters where all humans lived prior to their dispersion over the world; cf. Rösel, *Übersetzung als Vollendung der Auslegung*, 214.

37. See Siegert, *Zwischen Hebräischer Bibel und Altem Testament*, 284-86, for a more exhaustive discussion of these examples.

38. Adrian Schenker, "Gewollt dunkle Wiedergaben in LXX? Am Beispiel von Ps 28 (29)," *Bib* (1994): 546-55.

39. Jan Joosten, "Une théologie de la Septante? Réflexions méthodologiques sur l'interprétation de la version grecque," *RTP* 132 (2000): 31-46, esp. 42-44.

("word, speech") — perhaps because he wanted to avoid the notion of God's disease — and therefore translated: "Before his face a word will go." Since the second part of the verse now no longer fitted this statement, it was changed to: "and he will go out — his feet in sandals." The Hebrew text has: "and plague followed close behind."[40]

Even today, the exact meaning of שַׁדַּי אֵל (usually translated "God Almighty") remains unclear. Already in the oldest translations we can find this uncertainty: The translator of the Greek Genesis has used ὁ θεός σου ("your God"; Gen 17:1) or ὁ θεός μου ("my God"; 48:3), thus stressing the personal relation between God and the fathers. It is possible that this rendering is based on the linguistic derivation of שַׁדַּי from Aramaic דִּי (+ the relative particle שֶׁ or שֶׁל), a particle of relation that could be used to mark a genitive. Later translators have used a different strategy of decoding, because in the book of Ruth one can find ὁ ἱκανός ("he who is sufficient"; 1:20) for שַׁדַּי אֵל. Here the rendering is based on the Hebrew דַּי ("sufficiency"); the theological meaning of this designation of God has completely changed. Moreover, in the translation of Job, which is generally judged to be much less literal than others, one can find a third solution of the problem: שׁדי was translated παντοκράτωρ ("Almighty"; 5:17), which has in other books been used for צְבָאוֹת ("God of hosts"; e.g., Hab 2:13); the problem is solved by intertextuality.[41] It is reasonable that the translation παντοκράτωρ ("Almighty") reflects the attempt to accentuate God's power.

Num 24:7

יִזַּל־מַיִם מִדָּלְיָו וְזַרְעוֹ בְּמַיִם רַבִּים וְיָרֹם מֵאֲגַג מַלְכּוֹ וְתִנַּשֵּׂא מַלְכֻתוֹ

ἐξελεύσεται ἄνθρωπος ἐκ τοῦ σπέρματος αὐτοῦ
καὶ κυριεύσει ἐθνῶν πολλῶν,
καὶ ὑψωθήσεται ἡ Γὼγ βασιλεία αὐτοῦ,
καὶ αὐξηθήσεται ἡ βασιλεία αὐτοῦ.

Another interesting development from decoding to interpretation can be seen in Num 24:7. The Hebrew text starts with יִזַּל־מַיִם מִדָּלְיָו ("Water shall flow from his buckets"). In the Greek version the text reads: ἐξελεύσεται ἄνθρωπος ἐκ τοῦ σπέρματος αὐτοῦ ("A man shall come out of his seed"). The translator

---

40. The same confusion pestilence/word has happened in Ps 91(90):3, 6. For the difficulties in explaining the whole verse Hab 3:5, see pp. 289-90 in *La Bible d'Alexandrie*, vol. 23: *Les douze prophètes 4-9*, ed. Marguerite Harl et al. (Paris: Cerf, 1999).

41. On this problem, see Staffan Olofsson, *God Is My Rock: A Study of Translation Technique and Theological Exegesis in the Septuagint.* ConBOT 31 (Stockholm: Almqvist & Wiksell, 1990), 111-12; and Siegert, *Zwischen Hebräischer Bibel und Altem Testament*, 207-8.

has obviously derived the verbal form יָזֻל‎ I from Aramaic אֹזל‎ ("go, come").[42] This led him to parallel this verse with 24:17, where it is said that a star will come out of Jacob and a man from Israel. Therefore he also translated 24:7 in such a way that it is now the second important messianic announcement in the Balaam narrative.[43] Admittedly, one cannot say definitely whether the translator came from the Aramaic meaning of the verb to the messianic interpretation or from a preceding interpretation of the passage to this specific decoding and rendering.

Num 16:15

וַיִּחַר לְמֹשֶׁה מְאֹד וַיֹּאמֶר אֶל־יְהוָה אַל־תֵּפֶן אֶל־מִנְחָתָם
לֹא חֲמוֹר אֶחָד מֵהֶם נָשָׂאתִי וְלֹא הֲרֵעֹתִי אֶת־אַחַד מֵהֶם

καὶ ἐβαρυθύμησεν Μωυσῆς σφόδρα καὶ εἶπεν πρὸς κύριον μὴ πρόσχῃς εἰς, τὴν θυσίαν αὐτῶν· οὐκ ἐπιθύμημα οὐδενὸς αὐτῶν εἴληφα οὐδὲ ἐκάκωσα οὐδένα αὐτῶν.

The same insecurity can be observed in an interesting case of orthographical decoding. In Num 16:15 Moses states in the conflict with the group of Korah: "I have not taken one *donkey* from them!" The Greek version has: "I have not taken away the *desire* of any one of them." It is obvious that the translator has read חמוד‎ ("desire") instead of חמור‎ ("donkey"); the confusion of *daleth* and *resh* is quite frequent. But it is not clear whether this was mere accident or based on the translator's idea that the notion of Moses stealing things should be avoided.[44]

Ps 90(89):2b-3a

וּמֵעוֹלָם עַד־עוֹלָם אַתָּה אֵל
תָּשֵׁב אֱנוֹשׁ עַד־דַּכָּא

καὶ ἀπὸ τοῦ αἰῶνος ἕως τοῦ αἰῶνος σὺ εἶ.
μὴ ἀποστρέψῃς ἄνθρωπον εἰς ταπείνωσιν

---

42. The problem of the linguistic development from spoken late Hebrew to Aramaic in the Hellenistic period cannot be discussed here. See Tov, *Text-Critical Use of the Septuagint*, 105-16; Jan Joosten, "On Aramaising Renderings in the Septuagint," in Basten and van Peursen, *Hamlet on a Hill*, 587-600.

43. For a fuller discussion of Numbers 24, see Martin Rösel, "Jakob, Bileam und der Messias. Messianische Erwartungen in Gen 49 und Num 22-24," in Knibb, *The Septuagint and Messianism*, 151-75.

44. Tov, *Text-Critical Use of the Septuagint*, 101, who calls this phenomenon "tendentious paleographical exegesis."

Another phenomenon that can be discussed under the header of "decoding and interpretation" is the problem of word and verse divisions.[45] In Ps 90(89):2-3 the translator has seen the last word from v. 2, אֵל ("God") as the opening of the next verse. Moreover, he understood it as the negation אַל, which completely changed the meaning of v. 3. It now reads: "Do not turn man back to the state of humiliation." The Hebrew text has the contrary: "You return man to dust."

Deut 26:5

אֲרַמִּי אֹבֵד אָבִי וַיֵּרֶד מִצְרַיְמָה

Συρίαν ἀπέβαλεν ὁ πατήρ μου καὶ κατέβη εἰς Αἴγυπτον

A different division of two words can help to explain the deviation between LXX and MT in the confession Deut 26:5. While the MT has "A wandering Aramean was my ancestor," LXX reads "My father abandoned Syria." This can be seen as an improvement of the text because the narratives of the patriarchs do not state that the fathers, Abraham and Jacob, were Arameans but that they have come from Haran in Syria (Gen 11:31; 28:10). The rendering can easily be explained if one assumes that the translator has not read ארמי אבד ("a wandering Aramean") but ארם יאבד ("Aram, he left"), then modernizing "Aram" to "Syria" and taking it as an accusative. Again, it is hard to decide whether this was an accidental misreading or an intended act of interpretation on the side of the translator. But since in later rabbinic sources this method of enhancing the meaning of a text by using new divisons of words *(notarikon)* is used frequently, one can assume that it was a deliberate exegesis carried out by the translator.[46]

From these few examples it has become clear that interpretation can often be induced by linguistic or orthographical peculiarities in the Hebrew text, which then led the translator to find a less ambiguous rendering. In this process, his own religious or theological convictions could easily guide the process of translating the word in question adequately.[47] This means that there has not been a uniform and overall strategy of interpretation but an openness on the side of the translator to update the text where it seemed suitable or necessary.

45. See Tov, *Text-Critical Use of the Septuagint,* 117-21, for further examples.

46. See Siegfried Kreuzer, "Die Septuaginta im Kontext alexandrinischer Kultur und Bildung," in Fabry and Böhler, *Im Brennpunkt,* 3:49. The observation that some predecessors of the rabbinic rules stand behind some of the Septuagint translations goes back to the pioneering work of Zacharias Frankel, *Ueber den Einfluss der palästinischen Exegese auf die alexandrinische Hermeneutik* (Leipzig: Barth, 1851), where still a wealth of interesting examples can be found.

47. See also the different strategies to deal with unknown words, which Tov has systematized: contextual guesses and manipulations; reliance on parallelisms; employments of general words; or etymological renderings ("Did the Septuagint Translators Always Understand Their Hebrew Text?").

Improvements of the Text

As we have seen earlier, there is sometimes a tendency to keep literal translations, even if the text thus produced is hard to understand. On the other hand,
in some cases we notice an effort to improve the text. One of the most striking
phenomena of this kind is the frequently occurring harmonization. As an example, in Genesis 1 the translator has not only added several sentences that
seem to be missing in the clearly structured Hebrew text. Moreover, he tried to
smooth out the problem that there are two conflicting accounts of the creation.
Thus he translated 2:3: "God ceased from all his works which he *began to do,*"
instead of: "God rested from all the work that he had done in creation" (NRSV).
In 2:9, 19 he added ἔτι (*"further* God made . . .") over against his parent text,
thus emphasizing that there is only one act of creation. It should be added that
the translator not only harmonized the texts of Genesis 1 and 2; from his choice
of equivalents it is also clear that he used the platonic idea of a twofold creation
of the immaterial and material world as a paradigm to understand the sequence
of Genesis 1 and 2.[48]

Harmonizations can be found throughout the LXX. In some cases, as in
Genesis 1 or in the account of the flood (e.g., Gen 7:3), texts were added so that
different passages match each other. In Numbers 1 the list of tribes has been
standardized by additions and omissions. Moreover, it has been rearranged to
match the order of the sons of Jacob in Genesis 35 and 49. In other instances it
was sufficient to use only one Greek equivalent for different Hebrew words, or
to change the number of verbs or nouns. There are also cases in which one
translator harmonized his text with passages from other books.[49] For example,
Num 24:7, which we discussed above, obviously has been brought in line with
Gen 49:10.

Another way to improve a text was to translate some of the stylistic features
of the Hebrew into better Greek. The Hebrew narratives are characterized by
the use of a paratactic syntax: the sentences are mostly connected by "and,"
which led to a rather clumsy style. The easiest way was to translate the conjunc-
tive *waw* not only by καί ("and") but also by other particles like the adversative
δέ ("but"). This can be easily seen in Genesis 3. In Gen 3:1 δέ is used to signal the
new topic. In Gen 3:3 δέ stands to emphasize the central commandment, and in
3:17 one can find δέ in the final condemnation of Adam (this is also a harmoni-

48. For a detailed argumentation, see Rösel, *Übersetzung als Vollendung der Auslegung,* 28-
87.

49. See the instructive list in Gilles Dorival, *Les Nombres: La Bible d'Alexandrie 4* (Paris:
Cerf, 1994), 42-43, and the discussions of the texts in his commentary. It should be added that it
is not always easy to distinguish harmonizations from intertextual translations; see pp. 66-72.

zation with v. 11). The same attempt to bring a clearer structure into the narrative can be seen in Gen 4:1. Here the use of "but" marks the beginning of the story, and in 4:5 emphasis is laid on the main problem: *but* God did not accept Cain's offering.

The account of the flood begins in its Greek version (Gen 6:5-6) with another stylistic improvement. Here the paratactical structure of the sentence ("and . . . and . . . and") was rendered into a hypotactical, subordinate one, using a participle: "When Lord-God saw. . . ."[50] This rendering is quite frequent in the Balaam narrative in Numbers 22-24 (but not in the surrounding passages); the Greek version of this account gives a much more dynamic impression. In other cases sentences have been changed from a prospective to a retrospective view by using the future tense in the Greek text for an imperfect in the Hebrew (Gen 22:14). In Num 14:3 one can see that a question of the Hebrew has been changed to an affirmative sentence in the Greek version.

Num 8:9

וְהִקְהַלְתָּ אֶת־כָּל־עֲדַת בְּנֵי יִשְׂרָאֵל

καὶ συνάξεις πᾶσαν συναγωγὴν υἱῶν Ισραηλ

Although some of the improvements have the effect that the translated text sounds more like a Greek text, it is also possible to find the contrary. In Num 8:9 the Hebrew "assemble the whole congregation" is translated as "you shall assemble all the assembly." The Septuagint version has a *figura etymologica*, which is not very common in Greek literature.[51] But there are also instances where this figure has not been translated, for example, in Gen 2:16 or in 11:3.

Gen 11:3

הָבָה נִלְבְּנָה לְבֵנִים וְנִשְׂרְפָה לִשְׂרֵפָה

Δεῦτε πλινθεύσωμεν πλίνθους καὶ ὀπτήσωμεν αὐτὰς πυρί

50. There are also cases in which the use of participles to avoid the paratactical structure of the Hebrew cannot be seen as an improvement; see the striking example in Gen 22:9-10, where a chain of seven *waw*-consecutive clauses has been used in the Hebrew to intensify the drama of the story. The LXX has used three participles and sounds much less dramatic. John A. Beck, *Translators as Storytellers: A Study in Septuagint Translation Technique*. Studies in Biblical Literature 25 (New York: Lang, 2000), 30, offers a lot of interesting examples for the stylistic intentions of the translators.

51. See, e.g., Emanuel Tov, "Renderings of Combinations of the Infinitive Absolute and Finite Verbs in the Septuagint — Their Nature and Distribution," in *The Greek and Hebrew Bible*, 247-56; and Raija Sollamo, "The LXX Renderings of the Infinitive Absolute Used with a Paronymous Finite Verb in the Pentateuch," in *La Septuaginta en la Investigación Contemporánea (V. Congreso de la IOSCS)*, ed. Natalio Fernández Marcos (Madrid: Instituto "Arias Montano," C.S.I.C., 1985), 101-13.

Here the first *figura etymologica* has been translated "let us brick-makingly make bricks," the second not: "let us burn them in fire" (the translator also added αὐτάς ["them"] for the sake of clarification). There is no strategy discernable why the translators sometimes kept this Hebraism, sometimes skipped it, and occasionally imitated it.

Another characteristic feature of the Hebrew texts, especially from the Prophetic or the Wisdom literature, is the use of the *parallelismus membrorum*. Here the same multiplicity of approaches can be seen. Sometimes it is rendered quite literally, as in Gen 27:29: "accursed is who curses you, and blessed is who blesses you."

Num 27:17:

אֲשֶׁר־יֵצֵא לִפְנֵיהֶם וַאֲשֶׁר יָבֹא לִפְנֵיהֶם וַאֲשֶׁר יֹוצִיאֵם וַאֲשֶׁר יְבִיאֵם
וְלֹא תִהְיֶה עֲדַת יְהוָה כַּצֹּאן אֲשֶׁר אֵין־לָהֶם רֹעֶה

ὅστις ἐξελεύσεται πρὸ προσώπου αὐτῶν καὶ ὅστις εἰσελεύσεται πρὸ προσώπου αὐτῶν καὶ ὅστις ἐξάξει αὐτοὺς καὶ ὅστις εἰσάξει αὐτούς, καὶ οὐκ ἔσται ἡ συναγωγὴ κυρίου ὡσεὶ πρόβατα, οἷς οὐκ ἔστιν ποιμήν.

In other cases it is changed as if the translator wanted to play with words. See, for example, Num 27:17, where the Hebrew text has the verbs בוא ("come") and יצא ("go out"). In both parts of the parallelism, the translator has used ἔρχομαι ("go") in the first stichos and ἄγω ("go, lead") in the second, differentiating them by two different prefixes. Finally, sometimes one can find texts in which the translator is constructing a new parallelism; this phenomenon is frequent in the Psalms and in the book of Proverbs, and it can already be found in the book of Deuteronomy (32:23).[52]

There can be no doubt that in most cases there is no possibility to explain those improvements of the text with the assumption of a diverging *Vorlage*. Therefore these phenomena prove that some of the translators, especially those of the books which were translated first, wanted to produce a text that could stand on its own and does not refer back to the Hebrew original in any detail. Obviously they thought that some corrections or alterations might be in order, if these served to improve the persuasiveness of the Scriptures.

52. See Gerhardt Tauberschmidt, *Secondary Parallelism: A Study of Translation Technique in LXX Proverbs*. Academia Biblica 15 (Atlanta: SBL, 2004), for an extensive discussion of this phenomenon in the book of Proverbs.

Identifications and Actualizations

Another possibility to improve a translation and to bring it closer to the reader is to modernize the text. As we have already seen in Deut 26:5, the ancient "Aramean" has been rendered by "Syria," which was easily recognizable as the territory of the Seleucids. For Padan-Aram, where Jacob's relative Laban dwelled, Mesopotamia was used (Gen 28:5). Other actualized names include Idumea for Edom (Gen 36:16) and Heliopolis for On (41:45). And even the third river of paradise in Gen 2:14 has been explicitly identified with a well-known stream, the Euphrates.

Especially in the Joseph story one can find a lot of Hellenistic designations for professions. Most striking is the fact that in Gen 50:2 the word הָרֹפְאִים ("doctors") was translated ἐνταφιαστής, which means the "embalmer" well known in Egypt. According to the Greek book of Numbers, the tribes of Israel are not segmented into clans (מִשְׁפָּחֹת) but into *dēmous* (δήμους, 1:20), the usual designation for ethnic groups in Hellenistic Egypt. In the account of the wandering through the desert the Israelites' way of life has been accommodated to modern times. In the Hebrew text of Num 19:14 the Israelites live in tents, but according to the LXX they live in houses. The officials of the Israelites are now called σύγκλητοι βουλῆς ("councilors"); according to the Hebrew text they were only chosen from the assembly (קְרִאֵי מוֹעֵד, Num 16:2). It is obvious that outdated or unknown elements of the Scripture were identified with more modern terms. This is also true for God's blessing after the flood (Gen 8:22). In the Hebrew text God promises that "seedtime and harvest, summer and winter" shall not cease. The LXX has "summer and spring," which at first is quite astonishing. But in the Egyptian agricultural year there were only three seasons, the folding of the Nile in the winter, the heat of the summer, and sowing and harvesting in the spring. It is therefore easy to understand why the translator chose "spring" to designate the third season of the Egyptian year.

There are many other modernizations or actualisations like these.[53] Well known is the example of the Ibis in the list of unclean animals in the book of Leviticus, who replaces the owl (Lev 11:17). Because the Ibis was the holy bird of the Egyptian god Thot, it is clear that a pious Jewish translator wished to have

---

53. See, e.g., the path-breaking article by the Egyptologist Siegfried Morenz, "Ägyptische Spuren in der Septuaginta," in *Mullus. Festschrift Theodor Klauser,* ed. Alfred Stuidber and Alfred Hermann. JAC, Erg. 1 (Münster: Aschendorffsche, 1964), 250-58; Armin Schmitt, "Interpretation der Genesis aus hellenistischem Geist," *ZAW* 86 (1974): 137-63. See most recently Manfred Görg, "Die Septuaginta im Kontext spätägyptischer Kultur," in *Im Brennpunkt,* vol. 2: *Studien zur Entstehung und Bedeutung der griechischen Bibel,* ed. Heinz-Josef Fabry and Ulrich Offerhaus. BWANT 153 (Stuttgart: Kohlhammer, 2001), 115-30.

the bird of this pagan god in the official list of detestable animals and therefore skipped the owl. On the other hand the hare is missing in the Greek lists of unclean animals (Lev 11:6; Deut 14:7), because the usual Greek translation Λαγώς sounded too similar to the byname "Lagos" of the Ptolemaic king Ptolemy I.

One final example in this category will demonstrate that even a kind of demythologization could take place. In the account of the flood in Genesis 6–9, the Hebrew word מַבּוּל ("flood") has been translated by the Greek κατα-κλυσμός ("deluge"; e.g., Gen 7:6). Upon closer examination one can see that this word has a special meaning. According to a theory by the philosopher Eudoxos from Knidos, the term designates regular catastrophes when all the planets are properly aligned. This theory has also been accepted by Plato (*Timaeus* 22a-g; 39d). The Greek text brings the biblical tradition in accord with the philosophical knowledge of its time. Moreover, the flood is now a kind of a natural phenomenon rather than a punishment by an angry God.[54]

Besides this rendering there are many others which prove that the translators had a good knowledge of the philosophical and religious discussions in the cultures around them.[55] They are not hesitant to adopt those concepts. It is also interesting to see that the translator of Genesis corrected the whole chronology in Genesis 5 and 11, presumably to bring the biblical chronology in line with the Egyptian reckoning of dynasties.[56] But there are also limitations to this approach. One important line that is never crossed is the idea of God. This will be illustrated in the next section.

Corrections, Expansions, and Explanations: Theological Exegesis

The last example has already shown that the Greek version reveals aspects of a specific theology. Recent research has brought up numerous examples in which the Greek version shows distinctive deviations when it comes to anthropological, messianic, cultic, or theological topics.[57] Only a small selection of these can be given here, but they suffice to demonstrate that the translators were also theological thinkers.

---

54. See Rösel, *Übersetzung als Vollendung der Auslegung*, 169-70, for a fuller discussion of this topic.

55. See for the book of Proverbs, Cook, "The Ideology of Septuagint Proverbs."

56. Genesis has a "long" chronology that shows that the Second Temple was built in the year 5000 *anno mundi*; see Rösel, *Übersetzung als Vollendung der Auslegung*, 129-44.

57. See Emanuel Tov, "Theologically Motivated Exegesis Embedded in the Septuagint," in *The Greek and Hebrew Bible*, 257-69; and, for my own approach, Rösel, "Towards a 'Theology of the Septuagint.'"

Gen 2:2, 3

וַיְכַל אֱלֹהִים בַּיּוֹם הַשְּׁבִיעִי מְלַאכְתּוֹ אֲשֶׁר עָשָׂה

. . .

וַיְבָרֶךְ אֱלֹהִים אֶת־יוֹם הַשְּׁבִיעִי וַיְקַדֵּשׁ אֹתוֹ
כִּי בוֹ שָׁבַת מִכָּל־מְלַאכְתּוֹ אֲשֶׁר־בָּרָא אֱלֹהִים לַעֲשׂוֹת

καὶ συνετέλεσεν ὁ θεὸς ἐν τῇ ἡμέρᾳ τῇ ἕκτῃ τὰ ἔργα αὐτοῦ, ἃ ἐποίησεν . . .
καὶ ηὐλόγησεν ὁ θεὸς τὴν ἡμέραν τὴν ἑβδόμην καὶ ἡγίασεν αὐτήν, ὅτι ἐν
αὐτῇ κατέπαυσεν ἀπὸ πάντων τῶν ἔργων αὐτοῦ, ὧν ἤρξατο ὁ θεὸς ποιῆσαι.

Genesis 2:2-3 shows how translators were at the same time theologians. The Hebrew text reads: "And on the seventh day God ended his work which he had
made. . . . And God blessed the seventh day, and sanctified it: because on it he
had rested from all his work which God created and made." The Greek text is
rather different. "And God finished on the *sixth* day his works which he
made. . . . And God blessed the seventh day and sanctified it, because in it he
ceased from all his works which God began to do." Verse 3 has already been
cited to demonstrate that the translator wanted to bring the two accounts of the
creation into line with one another. Moreover, it was also important for him
that God did not perform any kind of work on the Sabbath, which is why he
had God finish work already on the sixth day.[58]

Gen 4:7

הֲלוֹא אִם־תֵּיטִיב שְׂאֵת וְאִם לֹא תֵיטִיב לַפֶּתַח חַטָּאת רֹבֵץ
וְאֵלֶיךָ תְּשׁוּקָתוֹ וְאַתָּה תִּמְשָׁל־בּוֹ

οὐκ, ἐὰν ὀρθῶς προσενέγκῃς, ὀρθῶς δὲ μὴ διέλῃς, ἥμαρτες; ἡσύχασον· πρὸς
σὲ ἡ ἀποστροφὴ αὐτοῦ, καὶ σὺ ἄρξεις αὐτοῦ.

Another important deviation can be seen in the crucial story of Cain and
Abel in Genesis 4. The Hebrew text of v. 7 is very difficult to understand, perhaps because it is damaged. "If you do well, will you not be accepted? And if
you do not do well, sin is lurking at the door; its desire is for you, but you
must master it" (NRSV). The translator tried to make sense out of his difficult *Vorlage* and was also driven by "a desire to understand why God should
be upset with Cain for bringing an offering that is approved in the Mosaic

58. This variant is also present in the Samaritan Pentateuch, in the Peshitta, and in *Jub.* 2:16,
25. Therefore the possibility cannot be ruled out that this deviation has already been in the
Vorlage, but most scholars now opt for an interpretation of the translator; see Jobes and Silva,
Invitation to the Septuagint, 98; Susan A. Brayford, *Genesis.* Septuagint Commentary Series
(Leiden: Brill, 2007), 225.

legislation."[59] Thus his rendering reads: "Have you sinned if you have [in fact] brought it [the offering] rightly, but not rightly divided it? Calm down, to you shall be its [the sin's] return, and you shall rule over it."[60] Although this version, too, is not easy to understand, the problem is solved: Cain has not divided the offering in a ritually correct way (the verb διαιρέω, "divide," is the same as in Gen 15:10); therefore God is not guilty of not accepting his offering without a reason.

The Greek version of Genesis 4 is revealing in yet another aspect. The Hebrew text is using the *tetragrammaton* YHWH to refer to God's actions throughout this section. The Septuagint distinguishes between two designations for God: It is ὁ θεός ("God") who is looking upon Abel and his offering; in verse 6 κύριος ὁ θεός ("Lord God") is speaking to Cain, and in verses 9-10 ὁ θεός ("God") is accusing the murderer, who in verse 16 is going forth from the presence of God (τοῦ θεοῦ; MT: יְהוָה מִלִּפְנֵי "Lord"/YHWH). It is interesting to see that in this section there are two verses, 3 and 13, in which the regular use of κύριος ("Lord") for the *tetragrammaton* can be seen. These texts speak about Cain's offering (v. 3) and Cain's prayer to the Lord (v. 13). Thus one has to conclude that κύριος is avoided when it is about the punishing or judging aspects of God. This view is confirmed by several other texts from the book of Genesis,[61] so that the translator of Genesis must have seen a theological differentiation between the two most used designations for God — YHWH/Lord on the one hand and *elohim*/God on the other. Moreover, he has made use of this differentiation to correct the text or to avoid a possible misunderstanding that God acts unjustly (see especially the translations in Gen 38:7, 10).

Again, this phenomenon can also be seen in other translations of the LXX.

Exod 15:3

יְהוָה אִישׁ מִלְחָמָה יְהוָה שְׁמוֹ

κύριος συντρίβων πολέμους, κύριος ὄνομα αὐτῷ.

According to Exod 15:3 the Lord is not a warrior, as the Hebrew text suggests, but someone who is breaking wars; the meaning has been reverted.[62] In Num 16:5, 11 and Deut 2:14 one can detect the same hesitation to say that the Lord has killed someone; therefore *elohim*/God is used although the *Vorlage* has had the

---

59. Jobes and Silva, *Invitation to the Septuagint*, 213.

60. For the translation, see Wevers, *Notes on the Greek Text of Genesis*, 104-7.

61. Cf. Martin Rösel, "The Reading and Translation of the Divine Name in the Masoretic Tradition and the Greek Pentateuch," *JSOT* 31 (2007): 411-28, for details.

62. See also Ps 9:21; God brings his law, not fear, to the people.

tetragrammaton.[63] Moreover, there are other texts where one can see that several aspects of the picture of God have been changed: it is no longer possible to see God, but only the *place* where God stood (Exod 24:10); not only blaspheming the name of the Lord carries the death penalty but already *naming* his name (Lev 24:16). Some of the translators seemed also to avoid anthropomorphic renderings.[64] Others avoided metaphorical designations, like God as a rock, as in Ps 78(77):35, where צוּר ("rock") has been translated by βοηθός ("helper"),[65] or in Ps 84(83):12, where God is no longer sun or shield (MT), but he loves mercy and truth.

Conclusion

Many more examples could be given to demonstrate different phenomena of interpretation in the Scriptures collected under the label "Septuagint," and many more topics like messianism or cultic terminology or the depiction of biblical persons like Moses could be treated.[66] One should also bear in mind that in this article I have separated the text examples from their contexts and arranged them in a systematic way. Usually one should clarify the specific profile of an individual translation as the first methodological step. But in spite of these — in the present context justifiable — shortcomings, it has become clear that the Greek translation of the Bible reflects the earliest stages of the history of interpretation of the Jewish Scriptures. Therefore it is good to see that in recent years the focus of scholarship has moved from text-critical to exegetical questions. Only after the different levels of linguistic and theological interpretation of a Greek translation have been described can it be used also for purposes of textual criticism.[67]

63. One could add that there is also a hesitation to use *kyrios* — the translation of the *name* of the God of Israel — together with foreigners, which can easily be seen in the Balaam story in Numbers 22–24; cf. John W. Wevers, "The Balaam Narrative According to the Septuagint," in *Lectures et Relectures de la Bible. Festschrift P.-M. Bogaert,* ed. J.-M. Auwers and André Wénin. BETL 144 (Leuven: Peeters, 1999), 133-44.

64. See, e.g., the classic study by Charles T. Fritsch, *The Anti-Anthropomorphisms of the Greek Pentateuch.* Princeton Oriental Texts 10 (Princeton: Princeton University Press, 1943).

65. Olofsson, *God Is My Rock.*

66. Moreover, much more secondary literature could have been cited. Instead, readers are referred to reference works like Jobes and Silva, *Invitation to the Septuagint;* Fernández Marcos, *The Septuagint in Context;* Dines, *The Septuagint;* or the systematically arranged bibliography by Cécile Dogniez, *Bibliography of the Septuagint — Bibliographie de la Septante (1970-1993).* VTSup 60 (Leiden: Brill, 1995).

67. Martin Rösel, "The Text-Critical Value of the Genesis-Septuagint," *BIOSCS* 31 (1998):

When comparing the individual profiles of scriptural interpretation in the books of the LXX with the Targumim[68] or with contemporary literature like the Hellenistic-Jewish texts or the texts from Qumran,[69] it becomes clear that the approach of the Greek translators was different. Their aim was not to rewrite the Bible[70] or to comment on it, but to produce an authoritative Greek version that was suitable for the needs of Jewish groups in the Hellenistic world. Because they were aware that they were translating and producing not an ordinary text but Scripture, they obviously felt restricted in how they could treat this text. It is interesting to see that those translations that were done first are less literal than later ones. One can assume that the circulation of the Greek Pentateuch has caused discussions about the question of the extent to which deviations from the original are acceptable. But even a more literal translation like the Greek Psalms shows a dynamic understanding of how to render these highly important texts. Even if cast in a new language, they will still be able to speak directly into the new situation and provide confidence in the God of Israel and his just government of the whole world. Thus scriptural interpretation in the LXX is not an end in and of itself or an academic exegetical game. Instead, it manifests the ways in which the translators and their community understood Scripture and how they thought it should be understood. Therefore, the Greek translation is a pivotal part of the earliest reception history of the Hebrew Bible.

BIBLIOGRAPHY

Aejmelaeus, Anneli. "Translation Technique and the Intention of the Translator." In *VII Congress of the International Organization for Septuagint and Cognate Studies, Leuven 1989*, ed. Claude E. Cox. SBLSCS 31. Atlanta: Scholars, 1991, 23-36.

Barr, James. *The Typology of Literalism in Ancient Biblical Translations.* NAWG, Phil.-Hist. Kl. 11. Göttingen: Vandenhoeck & Ruprecht, 1979.

62-70; and Theo A. W. van der Louw, *Transformations in the Septuagint: Towards an Interaction of Septuagint Studies and Translation Studies.* CBET 47 (Leuven: Peeters, 2007), 368-73.

68. Roger Le Déaut, "La Septante, un Targum?" in *Études sur le Judaïsme Hellénistique: Congrès de Strasbourg, 1983*, ed. Raymond Kuntzmann and Jacques Schlosser. LD 119 (Paris: Cerf, 1984), 147-95.

69. See the fine introduction by James C. VanderKam, "To What End? Functions of Scriptural Interpretation in Qumran Texts," in *Studies in the Hebrew Bible, Qumran, and the Septuagint: Essays Presented to Eugene Ulrich on the Occasion of His Sixty-Fifth Birthday*, ed. Peter W. Flint, Emanuel Tov, and VanderKam. VTSup 101 (Leiden: Brill, 2006), 302-20.

70. The Septuagint of Job can be seen as an exception; see C. E. Cox, "The Historical, Social, and Literary Context of Old Greek Job," in *XII Congress of the International Organization for Septuagint and Cognate Studies, Leiden, 2004*, ed. M. K. H. Peters. SBLSCS 54 (Atlanta: SBL, 2006), 105-16.

————. "Did the Greek Pentateuch Really Serve as a Dictionary for the Translation of the Later Books?" In *Hamlet on a Hill: Semitic and Greek Studies Presented to Professor T. Muraoka*, ed. Martin F. J. Basten and W. Th. van Peursen. OLA 118. Leuven: Peeters, 2003, 523-43.

Beck, John A. *Translators as Storytellers: A Study in Septuagint Translation Technique.* Studies in Biblical Literature 25. New York: Lang, 2000.

La Bible d'Alexandrie. Vol. 1: *La Genèse, Traduction du texte grec de la Septane: Introduction et Notes par Marguerite Harl.* Paris: Cerf, 1986.

Brayford, Susan. *Genesis.* Septuagint Commentary Series. Leiden: Brill, 2007.

Brock, Sebastian P. "The Phenomenon of the Septuagint." *OtSt* 17 (1972): 11-36.

————. "Aspects of Translation Technique in Antiquity." *GRBS* 20 (1979): 69-87.

Cook, Johann. "The Septuagint of Genesis: Text and/or Interpretation?" In *Studies in the Book of Genesis: Literature, Redaction and History*, ed. André Wénin. BETL 155. Leuven: Peeters, 2001, 315-29.

————. "Exegesis in the Septuagint." *JNSL* 30 (2004): 1-19.

Déaut, Roger Le. "La Septante, un Targum?" In *Études sur le Judaïsme Hellénistique: Congrès de Strasbourg 1983*, ed. Raymond Kuntzmann and Jacques Schlosser. LD 119. Paris: Cerf, 1984, 147-95.

Dines, Jennifer M. *The Septuagint.* London: T. & T. Clark, 2004.

Dorival, Gilles. "Les phénomènes d'intertextualité dans le livre grec des Nombres." In KATA TOΥΣ O': *Selon Les Septante. Festschrift Marguerite Harl*, ed. Dorival and Olivier Munnich. Paris: Cerf, 1995, 253-85.

————, Marguerite Harl, and Olivier Munnich. *La Bible Grecque des Septante: Du Judaïsme Hellénistique au Christianisme Ancient.* Paris: Cerf, 1988.

Fabry, Heinz-Josef, and Ulrich Offerhaus, eds. *Im Brennpunkt: Die Septuaginta.* Vols. 1-2: *Studien zur Entstehung und Bedeutung der griechischen Bibel.* BWANT 153-61. Stuttgart: Kohlhammer, 2001-2004.

Fabry, and Dieter Böhler, eds. *Im Brennpunkt: Die Septuaginta.* Vol. 3: *Studien zur Theologie, Anthropologie, Ekklesiologie, Eschatologie und Liturgie der griechischen Bibel.* BWANT 174. Stuttgart: Kohlhammer, 2007.

Fernández Marcos, Natalio. *The Septuagint in Context: Introduction to the Greek Version of the Bible.* Trans. Wilfred G. E. Watson. Leiden: Brill, 2000.

Gooding, David W. "Two Possible Examples of Midrashic Interpretation in the Septuagint Exodus." In *Wort, Lied und Gottesspruch.* Vol. 1: *Beiträge zur Septuaginta. Festschrift Joseph Ziegler*, ed. Josef Schreiner. FB 1. Würzburg: Echter, 1972, 39-48.

Hanhart, Robert. "Die Septuaginta als Interpretation und Aktualisierung: Jesaja 9:1(8:23)-7(6)." In *Isaac Leo Seeligmann Volume: Essays on the Bible and the Ancient World.* Vol. 3: *Non-Hebrew Section*, ed. Alexander Rofé and Yair Zakovitch. Jerusalem: Rubenstein, 1983, 331-46.

————. "The Translation of the Septuagint in the Light of Earlier Tradition and Subsequent Influences." In *Septuagint, Scrolls and Cognate Writings: Papers Presented to the International Symposium on the Septuagint and Its Relations to the Dead Sea Scrolls and Other Writings, Manchester, 1990*, ed. George J. Brooke and Barnabas Lindars. SBLSCS 33. Atlanta: SBL, 1992, 339-79.

Hengel, Martin. *The Septuagint as Christian Scripture: Its Prehistory and the Problem of Its Canon.* OTS. London: T. & T. Clark, 2002.

Honigman, Sylvie. *The Septuagint and Homeric Scholarship in Alexandria: A Study in the Narrative of the Letter of Aristeas.* London: Routledge, 2003.

Jobes, Karen H., and Moises Silva. *Invitation to the Septuagint.* Grand Rapids: Baker, 2000.

Knibb, Michael A., ed. *The Septuagint and Messianism.* BETL 195. Leuven: Peeters, 2006.

Kooij, Arie van der. "Perspectives on the Study of the Septuagint: Who Are the Translators?" In *Perspectives in the Study of the Old Testament and Early Judaism. Festschrift Adam S. van der Woude*, ed. Florentino García Martínez and Edward Noort. VTSup 73. Leiden: Brill, 1998, 214-29.

———. "The Septuagint of Isaiah: Translation and Interpretation." In *The Book of Isaiah — Le Livre d'Isaïe: Les Oracles et leurs Relectures, Unité et complexité de l'ouvrage*, ed. Jacques Vermeylen. BETL 81. Leuven: Peeters, 1989, 127-33.

Kraus, Wolfgang, and R. Glenn Wooden, eds. *Septuagint Research: Issues and Challenges in the Study of the Greek Jewish Scriptures.* SBLSCS 53. Atlanta: Society of Biblical Literature, 2006.

Louw, Theo A. W. van der. *Transformations in the Septuagint: Towards an Interaction of Septuagint Studies and Translation Studies.* CBET 47. Leuven: Peeters, 2007.

Müller, Mogens. *The First Bible of the Church: A Plea for the Septuagint.* JSOTSup 206. Copenhagen International Seminar 1. Sheffield: Sheffield Academic, 1996.

Olofsson, Staffan. *God Is My Rock: A Study of Translation Technique and Theological Exegesis in the Septuagint.* ConBOT 31. Stockholm: Almqvist & Wiksell, 1990.

Pietersma, Albert. "A New Paradigm for Addressing Old Questions: The Relevance of the Interlinear Model for the Study of the Septuagint." In *Bible and Computer: The Stellenbosch AIBI-6 Conference: Proceedings of the Association Internationale Bible et Informatique*, ed. Johann Cook. Leiden: Brill, 2002, 337-64.

Rösel, Martin. *Übersetzung als Vollendung der Auslegung: Studien zur Genesis-Septuaginta.* BZAW 223. Berlin: de Gruyter, 1994.

———. "The Text-Critical Value of the Genesis-Septuagint." *BIOSCS* 31 (1998): 62-70.

———. "The Septuagint-Version of the Book of Joshua." *SJOT* 16 (2002): 5-23.

———. "Towards a 'Theology of the Septuagint.'" In Kraus and Wooden, *Septuagint Research*, 239-52.

———. "The Reading and Translation of the Divine Name in the Masoretic Tradition and the Greek Pentateuch." *JSOT* 31 (2007): 411-28.

Schaper, Joachim. *Eschatology in the Greek Psalter.* WUNT ser. 2, 76. Tübingen: Mohr (Siebeck), 1995.

———. "Der Septuaginta-Psalter: Interpretation, Aktualisierung und liturgische Verwendung der biblischen Psalmen im hellenistischen Judentum." In *Der Psalter in Judentum und Christentum*, ed. Erich Zenger. HBS 18. Freiburg: Herder, 1998, 165-83.

Siegert, Folkert. *Zwischen Hebräischer Bibel und Altem Testament: Eine Einführung in die Septuaginta.* MJS 9. Münster: Lit, 2001.

Tauberschmidt, Gerhard. *Secondary Parallelism: A Study of Translation Technique in LXX Proverbs.* Academia Biblica 15. Atlanta: Society of Biblical Literature, 2004.

Tov, Emanuel. *The Text-Critical Use of the Septuagint in Biblical Research.* 2nd rev. ed. Jerusalem Biblical Studies 8. Jerusalem: Simor, 1997.

————. *The Greek and Hebrew Bible: Collected Essays on the Septuagint.* VTSup 72. Leiden: Brill, 1999.

Wevers, John W. *Notes on the Greek Text of Exodus.* SBLSCS 30. Atlanta: Society of Biblical Literature, 1990.

————. "The Interpretative Character and Significance of the Septuagint Version." In *Hebrew Bible/Old Testament: The History of Its Interpretation.* Vol. 1.1: *Antiquity,* ed. Magne Sæbø. Göttingen: Vandenhoeck & Ruprecht, 1996, 84-107.

For additional bibliography, see:

Brock, Sebastian P., Charles T. Fritsch, and Sidney Jellicoe, comp. *A Classified Bibliography of the Septuagint.* ALGHJ 6. Leiden: Brill, 1973.

Dogniez, Cécile. *Bibliography of the Septuagint — Bibliographie de la Septante (1970-1993).* VTSup 60. Leiden: Brill, 1995.

http://www.bts.edu/lxx/LXX%20Bibliography.htm (through 2002)

The Interpretation of the Hebrew Bible in the Targums

Edward M. Cook

The word "Targum" (תרגום) refers to any of several ancient Jewish Aramaic translations of the Hebrew Bible. Their renderings often strike readers as "free" or interpretive, and it is widely held that this is characteristic of them; but in fact almost all the extant Targums, even those noted for the freedom with which they treat the source text, have long stretches of "literal," unadorned translation. Nevertheless, it is the more interpretive parts that attract the most interest and that give the Targums a place within the history of biblical interpretation.

Since this volume is primarily concerned with *early* Judaism, it might well be asked why the Targums are included, since they — at least those transmitted within rabbinic Judaism — most likely are not "early" but come from later times. At least one of them (the Pseudo-Jonathan Targum to the Pentateuch) dates, in its final redaction, to the early Islamic period. Nevertheless, all of the rabbinic Targums contain some material that long predates their final written form; in a few cases, the interpretations are demonstrably contemporary with understandings found in Josephus, the Septuagint, or the New Testament. Hence the Targums are a repository of both early and late traditions.

And, of course, the earliest known Targums do come from the period of early Judaism. I refer to those found at Qumran, the Targum to Job (11QtgJob and 4Q157) and the Targum to Leviticus (4Q156). These date from the first century B.C.E., four to six centuries before the earliest attestation of the "classic" rabbinic Targums.[1]

---

1. The quotations from Targum Jonathan in the incantation bowl published by Stephen A. Kaufman are the oldest attested text of a rabbinic Targum; "A Unique Magic Bowl from Nippur," *JNES* 32 (1973): 170-74. Kaufman dates the magic bowls to 350-500 C.E. (p. 173).

The Origins of the Targums

The practice of writing Targums, then, did belong to early Judaism. In later Jewish tradition, the origin of Targumic reading was sought in the time of Ezra. "So they read from the book, from the law of God, with interpretation (מְפֹרָשׁ). They gave the sense, so that the people understood the reading" (Neh 8:8 NRSV). The Babylonian Talmud (b. *Meg.* 3a; cf. y. *Meg.* 74d) says, "מְפֹרָשׁ — this is the Targum." Here, no doubt, the rabbis understood the biblical period in the light of their own later synagogue practice, in which the Targum was recited (or chanted) after the lections from the Hebrew Bible. Few today would place the extant Targums quite so early. It is more common to trace their origin to a time when an Aramaic translation was thought to be needed, that is, to a period when Hebrew was on the decline and Aramaic was widely known. This is usually said to be "the postexilic period";[2] some scholars try to be more specific, like Klaus Beyer, who specifies a date of ca. 400 B.C.E., when Hebrew was no longer spoken.[3] Sometime within this period, it is said, the practice of translating the Bible into Aramaic, either orally or in writing, must have originated. "It was ignorance of Hebrew which called the Targum into existence."[4]

Despite its popularity, this view is almost certainly incorrect. Even before the discoveries at Qumran, it was known that composition of original works in Hebrew, such as Ben Sira, continued throughout the Second Temple period; M. H. Segal argued that, on the evidence of Mishnaic Hebrew, some form of Hebrew was continually spoken within Jewish circles in Palestine till around 400 C.E.[5] The discoveries in the last century of Hebrew documents, including both literary and religious works and documentary texts, at Qumran, Murabbaʿat, Masada, and Nahal Ḥever, dating from the second century B.C.E. to the early second century C.E., demonstrated to the satisfaction of most scholars that Hebrew was a viable language in the Second Temple period and after, although the areas where it principally flourished are still a matter of some debate.[6]

---

2. Philip S. Alexander, "Targum, Targumim," in *ABD*, 6:329.

3. Klaus Beyer, *Die aramäischen Texte vom Toten Meer* (Göttingen: Vandenhoeck & Ruprecht, 1984), 58.

4. William O. E. Oesterley and George H. Box, *A Short Survey of the Literature of Rabbinical and Mediaeval Judaism* (1920; repr. London: SPCK, 1973), 45-46.

5. Moses H. Segal, *A Grammar of Mishnaic Hebrew* (1927; repr. Oxford: Oxford University Press, 1980), 1, 9-10.

6. James Barr, "Hebrew, Aramaic and Greek in the Hellenistic Age," in *CHJ*, vol. 2: *The Hellenistic Age* (Cambridge: Cambridge University Press, 1989), 83. For a different perspective, see Seth Schwartz, "Language, Power and Identity in Ancient Palestine," *Past and Present* 148 (1995): 3-47.

It is true that Hebrew was not used to the exclusion of Aramaic, which was also widely used in the Second Temple period. All indications point to a bilingual society, and probably Greek too was used when necessary. Hence Targums existed in the same times and places where Hebrew was known. The Qumran Job Targum and Leviticus Targum were preserved in libraries of predominantly Hebrew documents, including Bible manuscripts, and therefore were used by those who knew Hebrew well. The existence of written Targums at a later period is also presupposed by *m. Yad.* 4:5, where עברית שכבו תרגום, "Hebrew [biblical text] written as [Aramaic] Targum," is named among the kinds of biblical texts that do not "render the hands unclean."

If Hebrew was known, then whence the Targum? Aramaic translations of Scripture offered the advantage of clarity when the original Hebrew was ambiguous or unclear. An example lies ready to hand in 4QtgLev, the oldest surviving written Targum.

Lev 16:14, Hebrew:	he shall sprinkle it [the blood] on the *kapporet* and before the *kapporet*
4QtgLev:	[he shall sprinkle it o]n the cover and before the cover[7]

The word *kapporet* has been understood as "place of propitiation," agreeing with the principal use of the root כפר (hence *hilastērion* of the Septuagint); but it could be construed with the more prosaic sense "to cover" (as, for instance, JPS: "over the cover and in front of the cover"). The ancient targumist chose the second option. (This example is not trivial, since all of the later Targums simply Aramaized the word as *kaphurta*.) The usefulness of the Targum lay in providing semantic specificity where the original was ambiguous. A commentary would have done the same thing, but the commentaries of Qumran were not devoted to such matters.

A Hebrew paraphrase would have served the same purpose; but towards the end of the Second Temple period, the text and canon of the Hebrew Bible were in the process of being fixed. Any rendition of the Hebrew into simpler or less ambiguous words would have risked encroaching on the increasing sanctity of the original text and might even have generated a kind of rival or substitute Bible. Therefore, I believe, after a certain point, Jewish interpreters had to incorporate their exegetical or interpretive insights into learned works or else shunt them into the Targums, which were the only outlet for "rewriting" large

---

7. 4Q156 (4QtgLev) is quoted from *Qumrân grotte 4.II: I. Archéologie, II. Tefillin, Mezuzot et Targums (4Q128-4Q157)*, ed. Roland de Vaux and Jósef T. Milik. DJD 6. Oxford: Clarendon, 1977, 86-89.

portions of Bible text. The extant rabbinic Targums are the surviving written deposit of that process.

If the Targums did originate in this way, as I believe, then they are both less and more than translations of the Bible. *Less,* because a translation is meant to be a kind of substitute for the original text. A Bible translation is a surrogate Bible for those who do not know the original language, and so we find the Vulgate, Septuagint, and Peshitta, as well as various modern translations, becoming simply "the Bible" for the communities that used them. But, as Moshe Bernstein has recently emphasized,[8] the Targums never became "the Bible" for Aramaic-speaking Jews, even when at last the knowledge of Hebrew was reduced to a few. In fact, many of the regulations about the Targums in rabbinic literature — that it should be recited, not read, or that the *meturgeman* (the reciter of the Targum) should not speak louder than the one reading the Torah — are meant to emphasize that they are not and should not be confused with Scripture.

But this also liberates the Targums to be *more* than just translations. As James Barr has noted, the coexistence of the Targum with the Hebrew original enabled the Targum to add to its literal renderings various amplifications and expansions that were "easily recognized as such," since the Hebrew, not the Aramaic, was the "acknowledged source of ultimate authority."[9]

Hence, the Targum was "always a bridesmaid, never a bride" — but this liberated it from the necessity to stick close to the text and enabled it to range far and wide in its renderings, in some cases coming close to out-and-out commentary. It now remains to show the different ways in which the Targums used this freedom.

The Extant Targums

The Targums to be considered in this essay may be divided into four main groups:

1. Early Targums from Qumran, consisting of the Job Targum (11Q10 and 4Q157) and the Leviticus Targum (4Q156)[10]

---

8. Moshe J. Bernstein, "The Aramaic Targumim: The Many Faces of the Jewish Biblical Experience," in *Jewish Ways of Reading the Bible*, ed. George J. Brooke. JSSSup 11 (Oxford: Oxford University Press, 2000), 137-38.

9. James Barr, *The Typology of Literalism in Ancient Biblical Translations.* MSU 15 (Göttingen: Vandenhoeck & Ruprecht, 1979), 305.

10. Translation of the Qumran Targums are mine, based on the text published in DJD.

2. The "Babylonian" Targums, Targum Onkelos to the Pentateuch and Targum Jonathan to the Prophets[11]

3. The Palestinian Targum to the Pentateuch, which is preserved as a whole only in (a) Targum Neofiti, and in part in (b) the Fragment-Targum, and (c) fragmentary manuscripts from the Cairo Geniza.[12] The Palestinian Targum (PT) was also used as a source by Targum Pseudo-Jonathan, which preserves many old and alternate renderings

4. Later Targums, including Pseudo-Jonathan to the Pentateuch and the Targums to the Writings: Psalms, Job, Proverbs, Chronicles, and the Five Megilloth: Kohelet, Lamentations, Ruth, Song of Songs, and Esther[13]

All of these texts present complicated problems of date, provenance, language, and mutual influence that cannot be investigated here. For our purposes, it must suffice to say that the order just given is approximately chronological, without excluding the possibility of older material appearing in later texts. Onkelos and Jonathan appear to be earlier than the Palestinian tradition, based on their language, and a date in the late second or early third century C.E. for them would not be far wrong. The Palestinian group, which probably goes back to a single text or text family, must be later by at least a century (again because of the Aramaic dialect used). Pseudo-Jonathan,[14] despite recurrent efforts to date it in the Second Temple period, is self-evidently a composite text incorporating elements of Onkelos, the Palestinian Targum, rabbinic midrashim, Talmudic law, and other sources. Its language, which is an artificial amalgam of all the Jewish Aramaic dialects, cannot be earlier than the completion of the Babylonian Talmud, and unmistakable historical references place its final redaction in the early Islamic period (seventh century C.E.). The Targums to Psalms, Job, and Chronicles all have affinities with it in text and language. The other Targums to the Writings are similarly late.

The rabbinic Targums (2-4 above) are the principal focus of this essay. De-

---

11. Translations of Onkelos and Jonathan are mine, on the basis of Alexander Sperber, ed., *The Bible in Aramaic Based on Old Manuscripts and Printed Texts* (Leiden: Brill, 1959-1973).

12. Translations from the Palestinian Targums are mine, on the basis of the texts available at the website of the Comprehensive Aramaic Lexicon (http://cal1.cn.huc.edu/).

13. Except where otherwise noted, translations are mine, on the basis of the texts available at the website of the Comprehensive Aramaic Lexicon (http://cal1.cn.huc.edu).

14. The name Pseudo-Jonathan originates in a confusion of the abbreviation ת״י, which is meant to stand for תרגום ירושלמי, Targum Yerushalmi, but was sometimes wrongly taken to stand for תרגום יונתן, Targum Yonatan. In older scholarship, Pseudo-Jonathan was known as Targum Yerushalmi I and the Fragment-Targum as Targum Yerushalmi II. In this essay it is abbreviated Ps-J.

spite their different times of origin, they all share similarities of approach, of which the following short survey can do no more than give the reader a taste. Their translation technique can generally be understood as a tendency to make explicit in the translation what is implicit in the text. The targumists, as we will see, might find implicit information where we do not. But I will begin with some examples in which we would likely agree with the targumists.[15]

Implicit Information: Resolving Figurative Speech

One major trait of the Targums is that they tend to resolve biblical metaphors into nonmetaphorical speech; they rewrite the figurative as the literal. An example is the following from Num 14:9.

Hebrew text:	Do not fear the people of the land, for *they are our bread*
Onkelos, Ps.-J.:	for they are delivered into our hands
Neofiti:	for, just as it is easy for us to eat bread, so it is easy in our sight to destroy them

Here, two different approaches are taken to resolving the simple metaphor "the people of the land are our bread." Onkelos takes the phrase to mean simply that the hostile people will be delivered by God into the power of the Israelites. There is no attempt to refashion the metaphor into a simile or to highlight any property of bread as the reason for the image; instead, the targumist resorts to straight paraphrase, possibly harking back to the wording of Exod 23:31 ("I will deliver the inhabitants of the land into your hands").[16] Neofiti, on the other hand, truly resolves the metaphor into a simile, explaining why the biblical text uses the image of bread in the first place.

Another example is in Deut 28:13.

Hebrew:	the Lord will make you the head and not the tail
Onkelos:	the Lord will make you strong and not weak
Neofiti:	the Lord will make you kings and not commoners

---

15. To save space, I will not treat other techniques in which implicit information is made explicit, e.g., the tendency of the Targums to rewrite rhetorical questions as declarative sentences; see Michael L. Klein, "Converse Translation: A Targumic Technique," *Bib* 57 (1976): 515-37.

16. This may be an example of what Michael Klein calls associative translation, in which the Targum of one verse is assimilated to that of an earlier verse that expressed the same idea; Michael L. Klein, "Associative and Complementary Translation in the Targumim," *ErIsr* 16 (1982): 134*-40*.

In this instance both Onkelos and Neofiti simply substitute literal equivalents for the metaphorical words "head" and "tail."

One final example, from Ezek 18:2 (= Jer 31:29).

Hebrew: the fathers eat sour grapes and the children's teeth are set on edge
Jonathan: the fathers sin and the children are punished

In thus returning the metaphorical speech to its presumed semantic kernel, the targumists are not, in principle, going beyond the proper job of a translator. Of course, the examples just given are of speech that we, in common with the targumists, would recognize as metaphorical. But the targumists saw figurative language in many places that we would not, as in the next category.

Implicit Information: Anthropomorphisms

One striking characteristic of the Targums is their treatment of anthropomorphic language in speaking of God. It is important to note that this is simply part of the Targumic approach to figurative language in general. We are not sure whether the biblical writers believed their language about God to be figurative, but it is certain that the targumists thought it was.[17] Examples are ready at hand.

For instance, when the biblical text says that God "sees," the targumists often substitute some form of the root גלי, "to reveal, be manifest."

Exod 3:7, Hebrew: I have indeed seen the affliction of my people
Onkelos: the affliction of my people is indeed manifest (גלי) unto me

The targumists treat the hearing of God somewhat differently. Sometimes they cast the verb into the passive.

Ps 6:10, Hebrew: the Lord heard my plea
Targum: my plea was heard before the Lord

In other cases, the verb "receive, accept" (קבל) is used as a substitute, especially when the idea of "listening to" someone is uppermost.

---

17. Some anti-anthropomorphism is implicit in Israelite religion (Exod 20:4) but becomes programmatic only in the late Second Temple period. For earlier manifestations of the tendency, see, e.g., Charles T. Fritsch, *The Anti-Anthropomorphisms of the Greek Pentateuch* (Princeton: Princeton University Press, 1943).

Deut 26:7, Hebrew   the Lord heard our voice
Onkelos, Ps.-J.:   the Lord accepted (קבל) our prayer
Neofiti: the sound of our prayer was heard (שמיע) before the
                     Lord

As the Neofiti rendering above shows, the Targums are not uniform in the ways they avoid figurative speech about God. Nor do they always agree on which instances call for paraphrase.[18]

The parts of God's "body" are also resolved into more literal speech. The "hand of the Lord" becomes his "power" or a "smiting."

Isa 25:10, Hebrew: the hand of the Lord shall rest on this mountain
Jonathan: the power of the Lord shall be revealed on this
                     mountain

1 Sam 5:6, Hebrew: the hand of the Lord was heavy against the
                     Ashdodites
Jonathan: the smiting of the Lord was strong against the men of
                     Ashdod

This tendency, too, is not carried out consistently (compare Exod 13:9 in the various Targums).

Much more could be said on this topic; let it suffice to say that the general, but not universal, tendency in the Targums is to avoid attributing bodily actions to God by recasting the words of Scripture at a higher level of abstraction. But when God is the object, not the subject, of bodily actions, the targumists were faced with a problem. It was obvious that the human actions themselves could not be metaphorical; but the object of them had to be understood in a different way.

For instance, when the Bible says that someone saw God, it is clear that they saw something, and that something had to be identifiable as God, without suggesting that God himself was visible in bodily form. One solution to this is to introduce God's "glory" (יקר), understood as a visible bright light.

1 Kgs 22:19, Hebrew: I saw the Lord sitting on his throne
Jonathan: I saw the glory of the Lord resting on his throne

The concept of the visible "glory" of God had already been introduced in the Bible itself: "You shall see the glory of God" (Exod 16:7), "the appearance of the

18. E.g., in Gen 1:4, Onkelos and Ps.-J. translate the Hebrew literally as "God saw the light," while Neofiti says that it was "manifest before him."

glory of the Lord was like a consuming fire" (Exod 24:17), "the glory of the Lord will appear to you" (Lev 9:6), and so on; compare also *1 En.* 14:20: "The great glory sat on the throne" (see also *T. Levi* 3:4). It also appeared previously in other translations; compare the Septuagint rendering to the Targum in the following verse:

Isa 6:1, Hebrew:	I saw the Lord . . . and his skirts filled the temple
Septuagint:	I saw the Lord . . . and the house was full of his glory
Jonathan:	I saw the glory of the Lord . . . and the temple was filled with the brightness of his glory[19]

Hence, the concept of the visible glory of God as a substitute for speech about the visible God was well known before the Targums were written, and the targumists follow in the steps of that tradition.[20]

"Glory" can also be used wherever the targumist wished to render any biblical text that suggested God was spatially located in a place, as in Gen 28:16 (Onkelos, Neofiti) or in the following:

Gen 17:22, Hebrew:	God went up from Abraham
Onkelos:	the glory of the Lord was removed from where Abraham was

Usually, however, God's local manifestation was denoted by the term "presence" (שכינה):

Exod 29:45, Hebrew:	I will dwell in the midst of the children of Israel
Onkelos:	I will make my Presence rest among the children of Israel
Deut 23:15, Hebrew:	the Lord your God walks in the midst of your camp
Onkelos:	the Lord your God, his Presence walks in the midst of your camp

Unlike the term "glory," the term *Shekhinah* did not already have a long tradition behind it in Jewish theology, but the concept goes back to the biblical use of the verb שכן, used to denote the "dwelling" or local manifestation of God (e.g, Exod 40:35; Deut 33:16). שכינה is a Hebrew *nomen actionis* from that verb

---

19. Compare also the Septuagint and Onkelos at Num 12:8.

20. See Jarl E. Fossum, "Glory," in *Dictionary of Deities and Demons in the Bible*, ed. Karel van der Toorn, Bob Becking, and P. W. van der Horst. 2nd rev. ed. (Leiden: Brill and Grand Rapids: Eerdmans, 1999), 348-52.

and means "dwelling" or "residing," but is used exclusively for the divine presence. The targumists borrowed the Hebrew term to render texts that suggested that God was bodily present in a place.

Exod 17:7, Hebrew: is the Lord among us, or not?
Onkelos: is the Presence of the Lord among us, or not?

The Palestinian Targum tradition prefers to combine the two terms "glory" and "presence":

Neofiti, Ps.-J.:   is the glory of the Lord's presence truly resting among us, or not?

Again, as with "glory," the targumists use the "Presence" of God as a way of accounting for the wording of the Hebrew text, without the suggestion that God is visible or limited to one place; the *Shekhinah* both is and is not God.

Besides "glory" and "presence," the targumists use "word," "command," or "utterance" (*Memra,* מימרא) to render speech by and about God. The use of *Memra* across the Targums is unsystematic, but the core of its meaning seems to be that God acts in and through his powerful commands, so that in any context of God's speech or action the *Memra,* like "glory" and "presence," can stand for God himself.

Gen 20:3, Hebrew: God came to Abimelech in a dream
Onkelos, Ps.-J.:   An utterance (מימר) from before the Lord came to Abimelech in a dream
Neofiti: The utterance of the Lord was revealed to Abimelech in a dream

Gen 21:22, Hebrew: God is with you
Onkelos, Ps.-J.:   the Word of the Lord is your help[21]

Isa 1:14, Hebrew: my soul hates your months and festivals
Jonathan: my Word has rejected your months and festivals

The literature on the use of *Memra* in the Targums is massive, largely because, for many years, many interested parties have wished to assert (or deny) its rele-

---

21. In this frequent Targumic idiom (מימרי בסעדך *et sim.*) I take the *beth* as a *beth essentiae:* "my word is your help," not, e.g., "my Memra will be at your aid" (Daniel J. Harrington and Anthony J. Saldarini, *Targum Jonathan of the Former Prophets.* ArBib 10 [Wilmington: Glazier, 1987], 19, at Josh 1:5). The wording has antecedents in Biblical Hebrew (Exod 18:4; Ps 146:5; and elsewhere).

vance as background for the Logos concept found in Philo and in the Gospel of
John. The discussion has been ongoing for a long time. When Joseph Priestley
summarized the positions in 1782, it was already an old topic:

> We find that the Chaldee Paraphrasts of the Old Testament often render the
> *Word of God,* as if it was a being distinct from God, or some angel who bore
> the name of God, and acted by deputation from him. So, however, it has been
> interpreted, though with them it might be no more than an idiom of speech.[22]

The two positions, that the *Memra* is a being somehow independent from God
or that it is only an "idiom of speech," remain with us today. In favor of the former is the fact that the *Memra* in the Targums does more work than would be
expected if it were simply a way of talking about God's speaking or command-
ing. And, as with "glory" and "presence," there is biblical precedent for the personification of the Word.[23]

Nevertheless, the term *Memra* as a periphrasis for God or his action is confined to the Targums. This fact alone implies that it is a phenomenon of translation, invented by the *meturgemanim* to render anthropomorphic words and
expressions in Scripture, and not a theological category indicating subsidiary
divine beings or division of persons in the Godhead. This position is further
strengthened when we see different Targums using different terms (or no term)
in the same verse.

Deut 1:30, Hebrew: the Lord your God who goes/walks before you, he
will fight for you

Onkelos: the Lord your God who guides before you, *his Word*
will fight for you

Neofiti: the Lord your God, he in the *Glory* of his *Presence*
guides before you, he will fight your victorious
battles

---

22. Joseph Priestley, *A History of the Corruptions of Christianity,* 1782, quoted in John
Jamieson, *A Vindication of the Doctrine of Scripture, and of the Primitive Faith: Concerning the
Deity of Christ* (Edinburgh: Neill, 1794), 1:48. More recent publications on this topic include
George Foot Moore, "Intermediaries in Jewish Theology," *HTR* 15 (1922): 41-85; D. Muñoz León,
Dios-palabra: Memrá en los Targumím del Pentateuco. Institución San Jeronimo 4 (Granada:
Santa Rita, 1974); Robert Hayward, *Divine Name and Presence: The Memra* (Totowa: Allanheld,
Osmun, 1981); Andrew Chester, *Divine Revelation and Divine Titles in the Pentateuchal
Targumim.* TSAJ 14 (Tübingen: Mohr (Siebeck), 1986).

23. Note also this saying from Ben Sira 37:16: "At the beginning of every deed is מאמר"
(other witnesses: דבר), which seems to broaden the idea of "word" to "thought, plan," as in the
parallel stich (the Greek translator used λόγος).

Ps.-J.: the *Word* of the Lord your God who guides before you, he will fight for you

There are two anthropomorphic expressions in this verse: God is said to "go/walk (הלך) before you" and also to "fight for you." All the Targums change "go/walk" to "guide," but only Onkelos introduces *Memra* before "fight." In Neofiti, the "Glory of his Presence" guides, but it is the Lord who fights. Only in Ps.-J. does the *Memra* both guide and fight.

It is clear from these and other instances that the targumists could and did vary their anti-anthropomorphic expressions as they saw fit, and that to some degree these expressions were considered synonyms.[24] In the course of time, the *Memra* came to predominate over the older expressions, so that in the later Pentateuchal Targums it is used more often than any other, but this is not a theological change.[25] *Memra* simply became the "default" anti-anthropomorphic expression; in some Targums it is added in verses where the other Targums see no need for paraphrase (e.g., Exod 12:27, Ps.-J.).

The expressions "glory," "presence," and "word," then, are special modes of speech developed to talk about God's actions in the world. There was no highly developed theology behind this strategy. It has been asserted that a heightened awareness of God's transcendence, of his infinite distance from the world, led to these circumlocutions. Although this assertion is normally deployed to the disadvantage of Judaism, there is a kernel of truth to it, in that the idea of God continued to develop after the close of the canon, and it became normal to stress his invisibility, his holiness, and his difference from human beings. All of these attributes were described in the Bible: "No man shall see me and live" (Exod 33:20); "To whom will you liken me?" (Isa 40:25); "I am God and not man" (Hos 11:9). A reverent attentiveness to them meant that biblical expressions that seemed to contradict them were felt to be figurative speech, and ways had to be found to translate these figures into less misleading terms. Even then, as we have seen, the Targums were far from consistent and left many anthropomorphic expressions unchanged. The targumists were not the first, nor would they be the last, to have difficulty in speaking simultaneously of God's immanence and his transcendence.

---

24. Cf., e.g., the texts of Exod 19:17; many like examples can be found.
25. In Onkelos, the term מימר occurs 213 times, in Neofiti 330 times, in Ps.-J. 368 times.

Excursus: Anti-Anthropomorphism in the Qumran Job Targum?

Michael Klein has argued that the Job Targum from Qumran (11QtgJob) does not employ any circumlocutions in speaking of God.[26] It is true that several anthropomorphic expressions are left unchanged in this Targum, and none of the later terms such as "Glory," "Presence," and "Word" described above are employed. Nevertheless, there are at least two verses where the targumist has not translated literally, probably because God's honor or abilities would be impugned by doing so.

The first is an expression found twice, in Job 38:3 and 40:7. God is speaking.

Hebrew: I will question you and you instruct me (וְהוֹדִיעֵנִי)
11QtgJob: I will question you and give me an answer (והתיבני פתגם)

The Septuagint Job gives a similar rendering: "I will ask you and you answer me." Since it would have been easy to translate literally (as the later rabbinic Job Targum would do), it is likely that the targumist simply shrunk from the idea that Job could actually instruct or inform the all-knowing God about anything.

Another example is found in Job 42:2. Job is speaking.

Hebrew: no scheme (מְזִמָּה) is impossible for you
11QtgJob: no strength or wisdom is withheld from you

Here, too, the Septuagint paraphrases: "Nothing is impossible for you." What difficulty did the ancient translators see? It is possible that the Hebrew word מְזִמָּה, which is frequently used *in malem partem* in the Bible, had negative overtones for the targumist. He did not want to impugn God's holiness by attributing to him an evil "plot" or "scheme" and therefore put "strength and wisdom" in its place.

Therefore, although anthropomorphic speech in itself posed no problems for the Qumran targumist, he still was sometimes aware that there were pitfalls involved in speech about God. This awareness would blossom into the marked anti-anthropomorphic tendencies of the later Targums.

Not only did the targumists wish to make explicit the textual and stylistic meanings implicit in the text, they also allowed themselves to make various additions, expansions, and rewritings in order to display the understandings of

26. Michael Klein, *Hagshamat ha-El ba-Targumim ha-Aramiyyim la-Torah* [*Anthropomorphisms and Anthropopathisms in the Targumim of the Pentateuch*] (Jerusalem: Makor, 1972), 135-39.

the text that were current in Jewish tradition. The categories of midrashic exegesis described by Geza Vermes[27] have proved their usefulness as heuristic tools, and I will employ them below in describing Targumic exegesis.

Exegesis: Obscure Words

This category, for the Targums, is on the border between translation and interpretation. Every translator, even one committed to a "literal" rendering of the text, must sometimes guess at the meaning of a difficult word or simply translate according to the context, or, as a last resort, simply transliterate. Leviticus 16:14, quoted above, is an example of two different approaches to the problem, and both of them are still in the realm of the *sensus literalis*. But at a certain point, the Targums begin to weave larger structures of meaning into their informed guesswork.

An example is in Ps 68:7: the obscure phrase, "he brings out the prisoners to prosperity (?)" (בַּכּוֹשָׁרוֹת), appears in Targum Psalms as "[he] brought out the house of Israel, who was bound in Egypt, for the proper (כשרין) deeds of their fathers." The targumist comes at the verse from three directions, only one of which is philological. The *hapax legomenon* כשרין calls to mind the common root כשר, and the targumist thought the Hebrew word meant something like "proper, fitting things." His theological framework suggested that the "proper things" that entailed a freeing of prisoners were the merits of the patriarchs; and then he identified this liberation with the Exodus, which forms the first of a series of historical correspondences the Targum reads out of the Psalm.

The targumist thus does not stop with a solution of the philological problem. He could have acted as the translator of the Syriac Old Testament did, who rendered the phrase "he brings out the prisoners with skill" and left it at that. But the history of Israel and the rabbinic understanding of it was a curriculum that the targumists were always teaching.

Another example is in Judg 5:21. The phrase נַחַל קְדוּמִים, today translated as "ancient torrent" or "onrushing torrent," puzzled the ancient translators. LXX[a], Vulgate, and Syriac all transliterated קְדוּמִים in their various ways, taking it as a proper name, while LXX[b] has "stream of the ancients," connecting the word, reasonably enough, with the root קדם. Targum Jonathan also makes the same connection, but with a difference, rendering the phrase as "the stream by which signs and miracles were performed for Israel in ancient times (מלקדמין)" —

---

27. Geza Vermes, "Bible and Midrash: Early Old Testament Exegesis," in *The Cambridge History of the Bible*, vol. 1: *From the Beginnings to Jerome*, ed. P. R. Ackroyd (Cambridge: Cambridge University Press, 1970), 199-231.

presumably a reference to the miracles of Elijah at Carmel (1 Kgs 18:20-40). Again, the targumist could have followed the same tack as one of the other translations, but he wanted to make an edifying connection between two points of the history of Israel.

Exegesis: Adding Detail

Vermes's second category comes into play when the biblical text "lacks sufficient detail."[28] One Targumic example, out of many, must suffice here. According to Num 12:1, Moses had married a Cushite (Ethiopian) woman; however, this wife is not mentioned in any other passage, and the wife of Moses is otherwise said to be the Midianite woman Zipporah. The Targums fill in this gap in different ways. Onkelos is the most succinct.

Num 12:1, Hebrew: Miriam and Aaron spoke against Moses on account of the Cushite woman he had married, for he had married a Cushite woman

Onkelos: Miriam and Aaron spoke against Moses on account of the beautiful woman he had married, for the beautiful woman he married he kept at a distance

The "Cushite woman" is apparently Zipporah, and "Cushite" is taken to be a symbolic synonym for "beautiful."[29] But why would they object to Moses' marrying a beautiful woman? Because he "kept her at a distance." This may denote that he abstained from sexual relations with her,[30] or it may refer to the idea that Moses had divorced her before returning to Egypt (Exod 18:2).

Targum Pseudo-Jonathan fills in the gaps in a completely different way:

Ps.-J.: Miriam and Aaron were saying words that were not proper against Moses on account of the Cushite woman that the Cushites gave to him in marriage when he fled from Pharaoh; and he kept her at a distance, for the Cushites gave him in marriage the queen of Cush; but he kept her at a distance.

28. Vermes, "Bible and Midrash," 205ff.

29. Roger Le Déaut cites an opinion that the equation "Cushite" = "beautiful" is based on *gematria:* the numerical value of כושית (736) is the same as that of יפת מראה, "beautiful of appearance." Cf. Roger Le Déaut, *Targum du Pentateuque,* vol. 3: *Nombres.* SC 261 (Paris: Cerf, 1979), 115 n. 1. But see the discussion below.

30. See the discussion by Bernard Grossfeld, *The Targum Onqelos to Leviticus and the Targum Onqelos to Numbers.* ArBib 8 (Wilmington: Glazier, 1988), 103.

The targumist sets aside the idea that the woman was Zipporah, or that "Cushite" meant "beautiful," and draws on an extrabiblical legend that Moses had married a queen or princess of the Ethiopians, as Josephus relates[31] (*Ant.* 2.251-53). There was in fact a wife prior to Zipporah, says the targumist, but she was wife in name only and Moses had no relations with her.[32]

Neofiti offers a third take on the situation:

> Neofiti: Miriam and Aaron spoke against Moses on account of the Cushite woman he married. Now it is not that Zipporah, the wife of Moses, was a Cushite woman! But that just as a Cushite is different in body from all other people, so was Zipporah, wife of Moses, comely in countenance and beautiful in appearance, and different in good deeds from all other women of that generation.

Neofiti's perspective is like that of Onkelos, but the targumist explicitly states why the word "Cushite" can be applied to Zipporah. But he avoids the implication that anything unusual was going on in the marriage.

The targumists, it should be noted, all get help from outside the text to explain the text. Onkelos and Neofiti both draw on a rabbinic tradition that understands the term "Cushite" in symbolic terms, although only Neofiti spells out one possible rationale of the tradition.[33] Pseudo-Jonathan draws on a variant of an even older tradition. Again, their purpose is not purely exegetical; rather, their goal is to mediate to the academy and synagogue as many of the resources of Jewish tradition as possible.

---

31. The Targum's concept of the legend is somewhat different than Josephus's. In the *Antiquities,* Moses marries the Ethiopian *princess* while he is still a prince of Egypt, while in the Targum he marries the *queen* of Ethiopia *after* he fled from Pharaoh. Josephus also explicitly states that Moses consummated the marriage, while the Targum suggests that he never did.

32. For the relationship of Ps.-J.'s portrayal of Moses to extra-Targumic sources, see Michael Maher, "Targum Pseudo-Jonathan of Exodus 2.21," in *Targumic and Cognate Studies: Essays in Honour of Martin McNamara,* ed. Kevin J. Cathcart and Maher. JSOTSup 230 (Sheffield: Sheffield Academic, 1996), 81-99.

33. One manuscript of the Fragment-Targum (Paris Bibliothèque nationale Hébr. 110) goes even further in spelling out the source of tradition; see the text and translation *ad loc.* in Michael L. Klein, *The Fragment-Targums of the Pentateuch: According to Their Extant Sources.* 2 vols. AnBib 76 (Rome: Biblical Institute Press, 1980).

Exegesis: Harmonization

The targumists assumed the Bible as a whole was a noncontradictive unity. For example, Ps.-J. translates Exod 16:13-14, in part, as follows:

Hebrew: In the morning there was a layer of dew; and the layer of dew ascended; and behold, on the surface of the desert [was manna].

Ps.-J.:   In the morning there was a layer of dew, solidified, fixed like tables around the camp; and the clouds went up and brought down manna upon the layer of dew.

There are two occasions for harmonization in the Hebrew verses. The text might seem to imply, for one thing, that the manna came first and then the dew, and that the manna was only visible when the dew evaporated. But this is in clear contradiction to Num 11:9: "When the dew came down at night, the manna would come down on it." The verses in Exodus must therefore be construed to mean that the dew came first.[34] Ps.-J. accomplishes this by introducing "clouds" to ascend in place of the dew, which remains fixed in place on the ground. These "clouds" then bring down the manna upon the solidified dew.[35] This has the additional benefit of linking the story with Ps 78:19 ("Can God prepare a table in the wilderness?") and Ps 23:5 ("You prepare a table before me in the presence of my enemies"; Targum Psalms translates as "a table *of manna*").

A theological example involves the harmonization of Exod 20:5, which states that God will punish the children of those who hate him for three and four generations, with Deut 24:16, which says that children will not be slain for the sins of their fathers, but that everyone is slain for their own sin.

Exod 20:5, Hebrew: [I] visit the iniquity of the fathers on the children unto the third and fourth generations of those who hate me.

Onkelos: [I] visit the sins of the fathers on rebellious children unto the third generation and the fourth generation of those who hate me, when the children follow their fathers in sinning.

---

34. Note that the Vulgate in Num 11:9 translates so as to imply that the dew and manna came down together: *cumque descenderet nocte super castra ros descendebat pariter et man.*

35. For this tradition, see Louis Ginzberg, *Legends of the Jews*, vol. 3: *Moses in the Wilderness* (Baltimore: Johns Hopkins University Press, 1998), 44, and the literature cited; see also *Exod. Rab.* 25:7.

Neofiti:	[I] punish the wicked zealously on rebellious children to the third generation and the fourth generation of those who hate me; when the children follow their fathers in sin, I call them "those who hate me."

Both Onkelos and Neofiti stress that the children of the wicked are not being punished for sin that is merely imputed to them, but for acts they have wholeheartedly imitated. Neofiti stresses that the expression "those who hate me" refers to the children, not to the parents.[36]

Exegesis: Avoidance of Disrespect

The Targums wished to avoid the appearance of disrespect for the patriarchs and matriarchs and other heroes of the faith, even in biblical expressions. Hence a body of interpretation grew up around certain problematic verses that insulated the patriarchs and others from disrespectful ideas and expressions.

For instance, in Gen 27:13, after Jacob expresses some fear that Rebecca's plan to deceive Jacob will garner him execration instead of blessing, Rebecca uses an expression that had an air of ill-omen about it, and the Targums go to some lengths to expunge or soften it.

Hebrew:	Unto me is your curse, my son.
Onkelos:	It has been told unto me in prophecy that curses shall not come upon you, my son.
Ps.-J.:	If he blesses you with blessings, they will be upon you and your children; if he curses you with curses, they will be upon me and upon my soul.

Onkelos simply inserts a paraphrase that is only remotely motivated by the words of the text; but it avoids the unpropitious expression "your curse" and contributes to a sense of the story's unity by harking back to the revelation that Rebecca received at Gen 25:23. Ps.-J., on the other hand, displays a greater attachment to the *sensus literalis,* but balances the worrying possibility of cursing with the equal possibility (a certainty, from the reader's or auditor's perspective) of blessing. It also converts the perfomative nuance of the original Hebrew into a comfortingly hypothetical proposition.

36. See Solomon Schechter, *Aspects of Rabbinic Theology* (1909; repr. New York: Schocken, 1961), 186.

In the story of the golden calf in Exodus 32, it is easy to get the impression that Aaron, the priestly ancestor *par excellence,* participated in and approved of the deed, a conclusion the ancient exegetes were reluctant to draw. To help solve the problem, they made use of the fact that in Exod 32:5 the verb meaning "and he saw" (וירא) could be revocalized to mean "he was afraid."

Hebrew: And Aaron saw and built an altar before it [the calf]; and he called out and said, "A feast to the Lord tomorrow."

Neofiti: And Aaron saw Hur slaughtered[37] before it and was afraid; and he built an altar before it; and he proclaimed and said, "A feast before the Lord tomorrow."

Ps.-J.:   And Aaron saw Hur slaughtered before it and was afraid; and he built an altar before it. And Aaron called out in a sad voice and said, "A feast before the Lord tomorrow for the death by slaughter of his enemies, those who deny their master and have exchanged the glory of his Presence for this calf."

Ancient interpreters had noticed that Hur, who forms a third with Moses and Aaron up to Exod 24:14, disappears from the narrative thereafter, and the story arose that the Israelites had originally asked him to make the golden calf; when he refused, they killed him.[38] To avoid death, Aaron had to pretend to go along with them. Both Neofiti and Ps.-J. (Onkelos translates literally) allude to this background story without narrating it. Ps.-J. adds to this Targumic tradition a unique expansion that has Aaron explicitly identifying the feast of the Lord with the slaughter of the idolaters by the Levites after Moses returns. (The targumist had evidently forgotten that Aaron had to be pretending to cooperate with the idolaters.)

In the following section, instead of Vermes's term "applied exegesis,"[39] I prefer to use the term *contemporization* for the Targums, since they attempt to bring the text into conformity with the synagogue's cultural, geographical, and historical milieu. The Targums were always interested in making the Bible, in Le Déaut's words, "une Écriture actualisée."[40]

---

37. Reading נכיס, as in Fragment-Targum, the Neofiti marginalia, and Ps.-J., for נביא.
38. See James L. Kugel, *The Bible as It Was* (Cambridge, Mass.: Belknap, 1997), 425-26.
39. Vermes, "Bible and Midrash," 221ff.
40. Roger Le Déaut, *Targum du Pentateuque.* Vol. 1: *Genèse* SC 245 (Paris: Cerf, 1978), 57ff.

Geographic Contemporization

This is most evident in the translation of *geographic terms*. In all the Targums, for instance, "Argob" (Deut 3:4) is translated by "Trachonitis," "Ararat" (Gen 8:4) by "Kardu" (Cordyene; this translation is also found in the Peshitta), "Zoan" (Num 13:22) by "Tanis" (an interpretation also found in the Septuagint), and "Caphtorim" (Gen 10:14) by "Cappadocians" (also found in the Septuagint). In this respect, the Targums, as is evident, are in step with the translation technique of late antiquity, and many cities and provinces of the time are identified, with varying degrees of plausibility, with biblical locations in the Targums (e.g., Edessa [Neofiti/Ps.-J. Gen 10:10], Nisibis [Tg. Ezek. 27:23], Ctesiphon [Neofiti/Ps.-J. Gen 10:10], Antioch [Tg. 1 Chr 1:16], Apamea [Neofiti/Ps.-J. Num 34:10], Alexandria [Tg. Jer 46:25], Caesarea Philippi [Neofiti Gen 14:14], Seleucia [Neofiti/Ps.-J. Deut 3:10], Cyrene [Tg. Amos 9:7], etc.). They do not always agree in the identifications, however; for instance, in Gen 10:10, Onkelos and Neofiti translate "Shinar" as "Babylon," while Ps.-J. and one manuscript of the Fragment-Targum translate it as "Pontus." The literature on this subject, as might be expected, is large.[41]

Halakic Contemporization

The same drive towards "relevance" is visible in passages that bring biblical texts in line with rabbinic halakah. This is most apparent in the Targums of the Pentateuch; in some cases, it can overwhelm the translation, as in this example from Pseudo-Jonathan:

Lev 23:42, Hebrew:	You shall dwell in booths seven days; all the native born of Israel shall dwell in booths.
Ps.-J.:	In booths of two walls according to their rule and the third (wall) up to a handbreadth (higher); and whose shade is greater than its sunlight [m. *Sukkah* 1:1]; made for shade for the purpose of the festival [m. *Sukkah* 1:1] from kinds that grow from the earth [m. *Sukkah* 1:4]; and the space of the height

41. See Philip S. Alexander, *The Toponymy of the Targumim With Special Reference to the Table of the Nations and the Boundaries of the Land of Israel* (Boston Spa: British Library Document Supply Centre, 1974); Martin McNamara, "Geography of Neofiti," in *Targum and Testament: Aramaic Paraphrases of the Hebrew Bible: A Light on the New Testament* (Grand Rapids: Eerdmans, 1972), 190-205; Dov Rafel, "Shemot geografiyyim ve-shemot 'ammim be-Targum Onqelos [Geographic and Ethnic Names in Targum Onqelos]," *Beth Miqra* 29 (1983-84): 67-84.

(within) is ten handbreadths [m. *Sukkah* 1:9]. All
the males in Israel shall dwell in it seven days, even
the minors who do not need their mother
[m. *Sukkah* 2:8] shall dwell in the booths, blessing
their creator every time they enter there.

The targumist has put into this verse several of the rules relating to the Sukkah
found in the mishnaic tractate of the same name. None of the additions are
motivated by anything within the text but are derived from rabbinic elaborations of the pentateuchal law.

Not all examples are this blatant, however. Sometimes the accommodation
to halakah is simply a matter of substituting specific words for vague words,
when the tradition has become more particular than the words of the text. For
instance, in Lev 23:40, the text mentions four kinds of tree branches to be used in
the Feast of Booths: "the fruit of beautiful trees, palm branches and boughs of
leafy trees and willows of the brook." All of the Targums translate these four
kinds, in accordance with tradition of long standing, as "citrons *(ethrogin),* palm
branches *(lulavin),* myrtles and willows of the brook" (see, e.g., m. *Sukkah* 3:4).

Sometimes these translation choices betray an understanding of halakah
that seems to be at variance with the tradition. One famous example occurs in
Exod 22:4(Eng. 5).

Hebrew: When someone causes a field or vineyard to be grazed over, or
          lets livestock loose to graze in someone else's field. . . .
          (NRSV)
Onkelos: When a man uses up a field or vineyard and he lets loose his
          livestock to eat in the field of another. . . .
Neofiti: If a man burns a field or vineyard and he allows the burning
          to kindle in the field of another. . . .

The rendering of Onkelos is in line with what seems to be the literal sense of the
verse, that the root בער refers to destruction of crops by grazing. Neofiti follows a different tack and translates in accordance with a homonymous root
meaning "to burn." But by doing this, Neofiti seems to reduce the four "fathers
of damages" — "the ox and the pit and the crop-destroying beast and the outbreak of fire" (m. *B. Qam.* 1:1) — to three, eliminating the scriptural basis for
the crop-destroying beast. Since this is clearly counter to the Mishnah, some
have claimed that Neofiti's interpretation comes from a time before the
mishnaic tradition was fully accepted.[42]

42. The claim of antiquity based on this verse was first made by Paul Kahle, *The Cairo*

Historical Contemporization

A third area of contemporization is the mention of historical events, especially as a fulfillment of prophecy.[43] This is comparatively rare in the Targums. Although the targumists did not hesitate to read the religious ideas and practices of their own times back into the biblical text, they were apparently more reluctant to do this with history and politics. Hence the few references in the Targums to extrabiblical people and occurrences gain added importance for what they might tell us about the time of the Targums' composition and redaction. But even these texts present problems of interpretation; as Robert Gordon notes, "'historical' references in the Targums can be extremely difficult to pin down in a precise chronological way."[44]

For instance, Deut 33:11 contains a blessing on the tribe of Levi, which ends, "Let his enemies rise no more." The Targums generally translate this clause literally; however, Ps.-J. translates as follows: "Let there be for the enemies of Yohanan the high priest no foot on which to stand." This clearly refers in a positive way to John Hyrcanus, the Hasmonean high priest of the Jewish state from 135 to 104 B.C.E. This rendering, according to some, points to the high antiquity of this portion of the Targum.[45] Still, "Yohanan the high priest" is known in the rabbinic literature (e.g., m. *Yad.* 4:6) and is a heroic figure in the post-Talmudic *Scroll of Antiochus*. Therefore, according to others, this rendering is not necessarily contemporary with Hyrcanus.[46]

An example with a greater claim to contemporaneity can be found in Targum Lamentations 4:21-22.

Hebrew: 21Rejoice and be glad, O Daughter of Edom, you who live in the land of Uz. But to you also the cup will be passed; you will be drunk and stripped naked. 22O Daughter of Zion,

---

Geniza (Oxford: Oxford University Press, 1947), 124 (one of the Palestinian Geniza fragments shares the reading of Neofiti); see also Alejandro Díez Macho, "The Recently Discovered Palestinian Targum: Its Antiquity and Relationship with the Other Targums," in *International Organization for the Study of the Old Testament, Congress Volume, Oxford 1959.* VTSup 7 (Leiden: Brill, 1960), 222-26.

43. Vermes, "Bible and Midrash," 225.

44. Robert P. Gordon, *Studies in the Targum to the Twelve Prophets: From Nahum to Malachi.* VTSup 51 (Leiden: Brill, 1994), 61.

45. First noted by Abraham Geiger, *Urschrift und Übersetzungen der Bibel in ihrer Abhängigkeit von der innern Entwickelung des Judenthums* (Breslau: Hainauer, 1857), 479.

46. The arguments B. Schaller advances against the probability of a Hasmonean date for Ps.-J. Deut 33:11 seem to me to be conclusive, while leaving the possibility open; "Targum Jeruschalmi I zu Deuteronomium 33,11: Ein Relikt aus hasmonäischer Zeit?" *JSJ* 3 (1972): 52-60.

                your punishment will end; he will not prolong your exile.
                But, O Daughter of Edom, he will punish your sin and
                expose your wickedness (NIV).

Targum: 21Rejoice and be of good cheer, Constantinople, city of wicked
                Edom, which is built in the land of Armenia with crowds
                from the people of Edom. Retribution is about to come
                upon even you, and the Persians[47] will destroy you and the
                accursed cup shall pass to you and you shall become drunk
                and exposed. 22And after this your iniquity will be finished,
                O Congregation of Zion. But you will be freed by the hands
                of the King Messiah and Elijah the High Priest and the lord
                will no longer exile you. And at that time I will punish your
                iniquities, wicked Rome, built in Italy and filled with
                crowds of Edomites. And the Persians will come and
                oppress you and destroy you for your sins have been made
                known before the Lord.[48]

This Targum contemporizes the Hebrew text to refer to a time when both Constantinople in "Armenia" and Rome in Italy were threatened by Persians and expresses the targumist's hope that deliverance, and the appearance of the Messiah, were close at hand. The most likely historical setting for such a conflict is the prolonged war between the Byzantine Empire under Heraclius and the Sassanian Empire in the early seventh century C.E.; and in fact, apocalyptic speculation was rife in Jewish literature of this period.[49] But the reference to Persians oppressing and destroying Rome in Italy is puzzling, since the western Roman Empire was already defunct by the time of the Byzantine-Sassanian war. It is possible that the text of the Targum was revised and updated over a long period and that an original reference to the fall of the Western empire was assimilated to the conflict that threatened the Eastern empire. It is impossible to be sure.

Whatever the original historical setting of the translation, the Targumic method of reframing the biblical text to speak to the times of the audience is

47. The reading "Persians" is found in some manuscripts; the text of MS. Urb. 1, from which the rest of the translation is taken, reads "Parkewai." For a discussion of the reading, see Christian M. M. Brady, *The Rabbinic Targum of Lamentations: Vindicating God*. Studies in the Aramaic Interpretation of Scripture 3 (Leiden: Brill, 2003), 128-30.

48. The translation is that of Brady, *The Rabbinic Targum of Lamentations*, 127, except for the correction to "Persians" in v. 21.

49. W. J. van Bekkum, "Jewish Messianic Expectations in the Age of Heraclius," in *The Reign of Heraclius (610-641): Crisis and Confrontation*, ed. Gerrit J. Reinink and Bernard H. Stolte. Groningen Studies in Cultural Change 2 (Leuven: Peeters, 2002), 95-112.

clear. Throughout rabbinic literature "Edom" is an allegorical equivalent of "Rome," and judgment on "Edom" coupled with deliverance for Zion was a welcome thought for Judaism throughout the period of Roman dominance.

Ultimately, however, historical exegesis of this type was generally unproductive and uncharacteristic of the Targums. The rabbinic Targums at their most typical read the Bible with minds transformed by the Judaism of the synagogue and the *beth midrash,* and then recited that text, changed and often enriched, back to hearers who shared the same perspective. History was rarely allowed to interrupt or add to this circle of mutual influence.

BIBLIOGRAPHY

Text Editions

Clarke, Ernest G. *Targum Pseudo-Jonathan of the Pentateuch: Text and Concordance.* Hoboken: Ktav, 1984.

Díez Macho, Alejandro. *Targum palestinense Ms. de la Biblioteca vaticana.* 6 vols. Madrid and Barcelona: Consejo Superior de Investigaciones Cientificas, 1968-1979. [Targum Neofiti]

García Martínez, Florentino, Eibert J. C. Tigchelaar, and Adam S. van der Woude. "11QtargumJob." In *Qumran Cave 11: II, 11Q2-18, 11Q20-31.* DJD 23. Oxford: Clarendon, 1998, 79-180.

Klein, Michael L. *Genizah Manuscripts of Palestinian Targums to the Pentateuch.* 2 vols. Cincinnati: Hebrew Union College Press, 1986.

Lagarde, Paul de. *Hagiographa Chaldaice.* Leipzig, 1872; repr. Osnabruck: Zeller, 1967. [Targums to Psalms, Proverbs, Job, Ruth, Esther, Qoheleth, Lamentations, Song of Songs, I-II Chronicles]

―――. "Targum du Lévitique," "Targum du Job." In *Qumrân grotte 4.II: I. Archéologie, II. Tefillin, Mezuzot et Targums (4Q128-4Q157),* ed. Roland de Vaux and Jósef T. Milik. DJD 6. Oxford: Clarendon, 1977, 86-90.

Sperber, Alexander. *The Bible in Aramaic Based on Old Manuscripts and Printed Texts.* Vol. 1: *Targum Onkelos;* vol. 2: *Targum Jonathan to the Former Prophets;* vol. 3: *Targum Jonathan to the Latter Prophets;* vol. 4A: *Targums to Chronicles, Ruth, Song of Songs, Lamentations, Qoheleth, and Esther [first targum]).* Leiden: Brill, 1959.

Translations (Books Listed in Canonical Order)

The Aramaic Bible Series (Wilmington: Glazier and Collegeville: Liturgical Press).

McNamara, Martin. *Targum Neofiti: Genesis.* ArBib 1A. Wilmington: Glazier, 1992.

Maher, Michael. *Targum Pseudo-Jonathan: Genesis.* ArBib 1B. Collegeville: Liturgical, 1992.

McNamara, Martin, and Michael Maher. *Targums Neofiti 1 and Pseudo-Jonathan: Exodus.* ArBib 2. Collegeville: Liturgical, 1994.

McNamara and Maher. *Targums Neofiti 1 and Pseudo-Jonathan: Leviticus.* ArBib 3. Collegeville: Liturgical, 1994.

McNamara and Ernest G. Clarke, *Targums Neofiti 1 and Pseudo-Jonathan: Numbers*. ArBib 4. Collegeville: Liturgical, 1995.

McNamara. *Targum Neofiti 1: Deuteronomy*. ArBib 5A. Collegeville: Liturgical, 1997.

Clarke, Ernest G. *Targum Pseudo-Jonathan: Deuteronomy*. ArBib 5B. Collegeville: Liturgical, 1995.

Grossfeld, Bernard. *The Targum Onqelos to Genesis*. ArBib 6. Wilmington: Glazier, 1988.

———. *The Targum Onqelos to Exodus*. ArBib 7. Wilmington: Glazier, 1988.

———. *The Targum Onqelos to Leviticus and the Targum Onqelos to Numbers*. ArBib 8. Wilmington: Glazier, 1988.

———. *The Targum Onqelos to Deuteronomy*. ArBib 9. Wilmington: Glazier, 1988.

Le Déaut, Roger. *Targum du Pentateuque: Traduction des Deux Recensions Palestiniennes Complètes*. Vol. 1: *Genèse*. 2: *Exode et Lévitique*. 3: *Nombres*. 4: *Deutéronome*. SC. Paris: Cerf, 1978-1980. [Neofiti and Pseudo-Jonathan]

Harrington, Daniel J., and Anthony J. Saldarini. *Targum Jonathan of the Former Prophets*. ArBib 10. Wilmington: Glazier, 1987.

Chilton, Bruce D. *The Isaiah Targum*. ArBib 11. Wilmington: Glazier, 1987.

Hayward, Robert. *The Targum of Jeremiah*. ArBib 12. Wilmington: Glazier, 1987.

Levey, Samson H. *The Targum of Ezekiel*. ArBib 13. Wilmington: Glazier, 1987.

Cathcart, Kevin J., and Robert P. Gordon. *The Targum of the Minor Prophets*. ArBib 14. Wilmington: Glazier, 1989.

Mangan, Celine, John F. Healey, and Peter S. Knobel. *The Targum of Job, The Targum of Proverbs, The Targum of Qoheleth*. ArBib 15. Collegeville: Liturgical, 1991.

Stec, David M. *The Targum of Psalms*. ArBib 16. Collegeville: Liturgical, 2004.

Alexander, Philip S. *The Targum of Canticles*. ArBib 17A. Collegeville: Liturgical, 2003.

Grossfeld, Bernard. *The Two Targums of Esther*. ArBib 18. Collegeville: Liturgical, 1991.

Beattie, D. R. G., and J. Stanley McIvor. *The Targum of Ruth and The Targum of Chronicles*. ArBib 19. Collegeville: Liturgical, 1993.

Aramaic Dictionaries

Cook, Edward. *A Glossary of Targum Onkelos: According to Alexander Sperber's Edition*. Studies in the Aramaic Interpretation of Scripture 6. Leiden: Brill, 2008.

Dalman, Gustaf. *Aramäisch-Neuhebräisches Handwörterbuch zu Targum, Talmud und Midrasch*. 1901; 2nd ed., Frankfurt: Kauffmann, 1922.

Levy, Jacob. *Chaldäisches Wörterbuch über die Targumim und einen grossen Theil des rabbinischen Schriftthums*. Leipzig: Baumgärtner, 1866-67; repr. Darmstadt: Melzer, 1966.

Sokoloff, Michael. *A Dictionary of Jewish Palestinian Aramaic of the Byzantine Period*. 1990; 2nd ed. Ramat-Gan: Bar-Ilan University Press and Baltimore: Johns Hopkins University Press, 2002.

Bibliographies

Forestell, J. Terence. *Targumic Traditions and the New Testament: An Annotated Bibliography with a New Testament Index*. Aramaic Studies 4. Chico: Scholars, 1979.

Grossfeld, Bernard. *A Bibliography of Targum Literature*. Vols. 1-2: Cincinnati: Hebrew Union College Press, 1972-77; vol. 3: New York: Sepher-Hermon, 1990.

Internet Resources

The Comprehensive Aramaic Lexicon: Targumic Studies Module (http://cal1.cn.huc.edu/
    Targumstartpage.html).

Newsletter for Targumic and Cognate Studies (http://www.Targum.info).

General Articles

Alexander, Philip S. "Targum, Targumim." *ABD* 6:320-31.

Le Déaut. Roger. "The Targumim." In *CHJ* 2:563-90.

McNamara, Martin. "Interpretation of Scripture in the Targumim." In *A History of Biblical
    Interpretation,* vol. 1: *The Ancient Period,* ed. Alan J. Hauser and Duane F. Watson.
    Grand Rapids: Eerdmans, 2003, 167-97.

PART 3

Rewritten Bible

Biblical Interpretation in the Book of *Jubilees:* The Case of the Early Abram (*Jub.* 11:14–12:15)

Jacques van Ruiten

The book of *Jubilees* consists of a rewriting and interpretation of the biblical narrative from the creation until the arrival of the children of Israel at Mount Sinai.[1] *Jubilees* is closely related to the biblical material that it represents. One can find the biblical material in chapters 2–50. First the primaeval history of Genesis 1–11 is retold in *Jubilees* 1-10,[2] then the history of the patriarchs Abraham, Isaac, and Jacob of Genesis 12–50 in *Jubilees* 11–45, mainly concentrating on Abraham in *Jubilees* 11–23 and Jacob in chapters 23–45.[3] After Jacob's death

---

1. We may assume that there was no fixed and closed canon of sacred Scriptures at the time the book of *Jubilees* was written. Because of the textual and canonical fluidity, it is somewhat anachronistic to speak about the rewriting of the biblical narrative. There is enough evidence, however, that in the last centuries before the Common Era there should have been several books that were considered divinely inspired works by Jewish groups, especially the five books of Moses. For the sake of convenience I therefore speak about rewriting the biblical narrative. See, e.g., James C. VanderKam, "Questions of Canon Viewed through the Dead Sea Scrolls," *BBR* 11 (2001): 269-92; Edward D. Herbert and Emanuel Tov, eds., *The Bible as Book: The Hebrew Bible and the Judean Desert Discoveries* (London: British Library, 2002); Michael Segal, "Between Bible and Rewritten Bible," in *Biblical Interpretation at Qumran,* ed. Matthias Henze. SDSSRL (Grand Rapids: Eerdmans, 2005), 10-28.

2. Cf. Jacques T. A. G. M. van Ruiten, *Primaeval History Interpreted: The Rewriting of Genesis 1–11 in the Book of* Jubilees. JSJSup 66 (Leiden: Brill, 2000); Michael Segal, *The Book of Jubilees: Rewritten Bible, Redaction, Ideology and Theology.* JSJSup 117 (Leiden: Brill, 2007), 47-58, 103-87.

3. For the rewriting of the Abraham stories in the book of *Jubilees,* see James C. VanderKam, "The *Aqedah, Jubilees,* and PseudoJubilees," in *The Quest for Context and Meaning: Studies in Biblical Intertextuality in Honor of James A. Sanders,* ed. Craig A. Evans and Shemaryahu Talmon. Biblical Interpretation 28 (Leiden: Brill, 1997), 241-61; Jacques T. A. G. M. van Ruiten, "Abraham, Job and the Book of Jubilees: The Intertextual Relationship of Genesis 22:1-19, Job 1:1–2:13 and Jubilees 17:15–18:19," in *The Sacrifice of Isaac: The Aqedah (Genesis 22) and Its Interpretations,* ed. Ed Noort and Eibert J. C. Tigchelaar. TBN 7 (Leiden: Brill, 2002), 58-

in *Jubilees* 45, the author seems to be in a hurry to tell in chapters 46–50 the rest of the narrative, the welfare of the children of Israel in Egypt, the change from prosperity to open hostility from the side of the Egyptians, the subsequent exodus, and the first part of the journey in the wilderness until the arrival at Mount Sinai.[4]

The most important older material that is incorporated in the book of *Jubilees* is the material that can be found in the biblical text from Genesis 1 until Exodus 19. However, this material is put in a new setting. The author presents the book as a revelation that Moses received at Mount Sinai. Both in the prologue and in the first chapter, *Jubilees* claims that the book is set in the situation described in Exod 24:12, 15-18. The author wants to situate the work at the historical point in which the Sinaitic covenant had just been concluded on the previous day and when Moses had ascended the mountain to receive additional information from God.[5] This circumstance is not only mentioned at the

---

85; and "Lot versus Abraham: The Interpretation of Genesis 18:1–19:38 in *Jubilees* 16:1-9," in *Sodom's Sin: Genesis 18–19 and Its Interpretation*, ed. Ed Noort and Eibert Tigchelaar. TBN 7 (Leiden: Brill, 2004), 29-46; Segal, *The Book of Jubilees*, 189-202, 229-61.

For the rewriting of the Jacob stories in *Jubilees*, see John C. Endres, *Biblical Interpretation in the Book of Jubilees*. CBQMS 18 (Washington: Catholic Biblical Association, 1987); Segal, *The Book of Jubilees*, 59-91.

4. Betsy Halpern-Amaru, "Burying the Fathers: Exegetical Strategies and Source Traditions in Jubilees 46," in *Reworking the Bible: Apocryphal and Related Texts at Qumran. Proceedings of a Joint Symposium by the Orion Center for the Study of the Dead Sea Scrolls and Associated Literature and the Hebrew University Institute for Advanced Studies Research Group on Qumran, 15-17 January, 2002*, ed. Esther G. Chazon, Devora Dimant, and Ruth A. Clements. STDJ 58 (Leiden: Brill, 2005), 135-52; Jacques T. A. G. M. van Ruiten, "The Birth of Moses in Egypt according to the Book of *Jubilees* (*Jub* 47.1-9)," in *The Wisdom of Egypt: Jewish, Early Christian, and Gnostic Essays in Honour of Gerard P. Luttikhuizen*, ed. George H. van Kooten and Anthony Hilhorst. AGJU 59 (Leiden: Brill, 2005), 43-66; and "Between Jacob's Death and Moses' Birth: The Intertextual Relationship between Genesis 50:15–Exodus 1:14 and *Jubilees* 46:1-16," in *Flores Florentino: Dead Sea Scrolls and Other Early Jewish Studies in Honour of Florentino García Martínez*, ed. Anthony Hilhorst, Émile Puech, and Eibert J. C. Tigchelaar. JSJSup 122 (Leiden: Brill, 2007), 467-89; Segal, *The Book of Jubilees*, 203-28.

5. James C. VanderKam, "The Scriptural Setting of the Book of Jubilees," *DSD* 13 (2006): 61-72 (esp. 64). See also Jacques T. A. G. M. van Ruiten, "The Rewriting of Exodus 24:12-18 in *Jubilees* 1:1-4," *BN* 79 (1995): 25-29. For the first chapter of *Jubilees*, see Gene L. Davenport, *The Eschatology of the Book of Jubilees*. StPB 20 (Leiden: Brill, 1971), 19-31; Betsy Halpern-Amaru, "Exile and Return in Jubilees," in *Exile: Old Testament, Jewish and Christian Conceptions*, ed. James M. Scott. JSJSup 56 (Leiden: Brill, 1997), 127-44; Michael A. Knibb, "*Jubilees* and the Origins of the Qumran Community" (Inaugural Lecture; London, 1989; repr. in *Essays on the Book of Jubilees and Other Early Jewish Texts and Translations*. SVTP 22 [Leiden: Brill, 2009], 232-54); Ben Zion Wacholder, "*Jubilees* as the Super Canon: Torah-Admonition versus Torah-Commandment," in *Legal Texts and Legal Issues: Proceedings of the Second Meeting of the International Organization*

beginning of the book, but there are many direct and indirect reminders that the angel is dictating to Moses.[6] In fact, the book ends where it began, with the arrival of Moses at Mount Sinai (*Jub.* 50:2).

The material is presented mostly in the same sequential order as in the Bible, and nearly all pericopes can be discerned in the new composition. Nevertheless, a superficial reading of the book of *Jubilees* is sufficient to observe that there are many differences between the (older) scriptural text and the new composition. There are passages that run (almost) complete parallel in both texts. However, most passages in *Jubilees* that run parallel to the text of Genesis are not verbatim quotations from Genesis. Not only are there changes in the sequence of events and other variations within the pericopes, there are also additions and omissions. Material is left out or added for exegetical reasons (such as the removal of contradictions, doublets, and other inconsistencies). Many variations and additions have a basis in the biblical text, but the material can also come from *other* biblical passages or even nonbiblical texts and traditions (especially with regard to halakic matters). Usually *Jubilees* is considered a polemic writing with a clearly priestly orientation. It adapts biblical texts and introduces other theological traditions. The clear goal is to confirm the authenticity and authority of its version of the revelation to Moses.[7]

With regard to the other sources and traditions that are also incorporated in the book, one can point, in the first place, to the addition of material originating from the Enochic traditions (4:15-26; 5:1-12; 7:20-39; 10:1-17).[8] Some

---

for Qumran Studies, Cambridge 1995, Published in Honour of Joseph M. Baumgarten, ed. Moshe Bernstein, Florentino García Martínez, and John Kampen. STDJ 23 (Leiden: Brill, 1997), 195-211.

6. See James C. VanderKam, *The Book of* Jubilees. Guides to Apocrypha and Pseudepigrapha (Sheffield: Sheffield Academic, 2001), 24-25.

7. Hindy Najman, "Interpretation as Primordial Writing: Jubilees and Its Authority Conferring Strategies," *JSJ* 30 (1999): 379-410; and *Seconding Sinai: The Development of Mosaic Discourse in Second Temple Judaism.* JSJSup 77 (Leiden: Brill, 2003).

8. See esp. James C. VanderKam, "Enoch Traditions in Jubilees and Other Second-Century Sources," *SBLSP* 1 (1978) 229-51; repr. *From Revelation to Canon: Studies in the Hebrew Bible and Second Temple Literature.* JSJSup 62 (Leiden: Brill, 2000), 305-31. This essay influenced his *Enoch and the Growth of an Apocalyptic Tradition.* CBQMS 16 (Washington: Catholic Biblical Association, 1984), 179-88, and formed the basis of a chapter in *Enoch, A Man for All Generations.* Studies on Personalities of the Old Testament (Columbia: University of South Carolina Press, 1995), 110-21. See also Robert H. Charles, *The Book of Jubilees, or the Little Genesis* (London: SPCK, 1917), xliv, 36-39, 43-44; Pierre Grelot, "La légende d'Henoch dans les apocryphes et dans la Bible: Origine et signification," *RSR* 46 (1958): 5-26, 181-210; Jósef T. Milik, *The Books of Enoch: Aramaic Fragments of Qumrân Cave 4* (Oxford: Clarendon, 1976). VanderKam is followed by, e.g., George W. E. Nickelsburg, *1 Enoch: A Commentary on the Book of 1 Enoch, Chapters 1–36; 81–108.* Hermeneia (Minneapolis: Fortress, 2001), 71-76.

scholars opt for a common source for *1 Enoch, Jubilees,* and some of the Qumran texts (the so-called *Book of Noah*).[9] Others even consider *Jubilees* to be an Enochic document in which the so-called Zadokite Torah (i.e., Genesis and Exodus) was incorporated and digested into the Enochic revelation.[10] However, most scholars do not go that far and instead speak of the incorporation of other traditions into the rendering and explanation of the biblical text, or of the fusion and reconciliation of different Jewish streams in the second century B.C.E. With respect to the latter, one can also point to the influence of other works. It is likely that the author of *Jubilees* also knew and used the traditions on which the *Aramaic Levi Document* is based (see, e.g., *Jubilees* 31-32).[11] One can also point to the influence of 4QVisions of Amram (see *Jubilees* 46).[12]

Recently the thesis has been put forward that the book of *Jubilees* is not a

9. See, e.g., Florentino García Martínez, *Qumran and Apocalyptic: Studies on the Aramaic Texts from Qumran.* STDJ 9 (Leiden: Brill, 1992), 1-44; Michael E. Stone, "The Book(s) Attributed to Noah," *DSD* 13 (2006): 4-23.

10. See Gabriele Boccaccini, *Beyond the Essene Hypothesis: The Parting of the Ways Between Qumran and Enochic Judaism* (Grand Rapids: Eerdmans, 1998), 86-98. See also Paolo Sacchi, "Libro dei Giubilei," *Apocrifi dell'Antico Testamento,* 1 (Turin: Unione tipografico-editrice torinese, 1981), 179-411.

11. Pierre Grelot and others opt for a dependency of *Jubilees* on the *Testament of Levi.* See Grelot, "Le coutumier sacerdotal ancien dans le Testament araméen de Lévi," *RevQ* 15 (1991): 253-63 (esp. 255); and "Le livre des Jubilés et le Testament de Levi," in *Mélanges Dominiques Barthélemy: Études bibliques offertes à l'occasion de son 60ᵉ anniversaire,* ed. Pierre Casetti, Othmar Keel, and Adrian Schenker. OBO 38 (Fribourg: Éditions universitaires and Göttingen: Vandenhoeck & Ruprecht, 1981), 109-31. So also, e.g., Michael E. Stone, "Ideal Figures and Social Context: Priest and Sage in the Early Second Temple Age," in *Ancient Israelite Religion: Essays in Honor of Frank Moore Cross,* ed. Patrick D. Miller et al. (Philadelphia: Fortress, 1987), 575-86. See also Grelot, "Quatre cents trente ans (Ex 12,40)," in *Homenaje a Juan Prado: Miscelánea de estudios biblicos y hebráicos,* ed. Lorenzo Avarez Verdes and E. Javier Alonso Hernandez (Madrid: Consejo Superior de Investigaciones Científicas, 1975), 559-70; Émile Puech, *Qumrân grotte 4:XXII: Textes araméens 1: 4Q529-549.* DJD 31 (Oxford: Clarendon, 2001), 285-86; Henryk Drawnel, *An Aramaic Wisdom Text from Qumran: A New Interpretation of the Levi Document.* JSJSup 86 (Leiden: Brill, 2004), 63-75; Jonas C. Greenfield, Michael E. Stone, and Esther Eshel, eds., *The Aramaic Levi Document: Edition, Translation, Commentary.* SVTP 19 (Leiden: Brill, 2004), 19-22; Marinus de Jonge, "The Testament of Levi and 'Aramaic Levi,'" *RevQ* 13 (1988): 367-85 (esp. 373-76); repr. *Jewish Eschatology, Early Christian Christology and the Testaments of the Twelve Patriarchs.* NovTSup 63 (Leiden: Brill, 1991), 244-62. According to Robert A. Kugler, a so-called "Levi-apocryphon" was the source for both the *Aramaic Levi Document* and *Jubilees;* see Kugler, *From Patriarch to Priest: The Levi-Priestly Tradition from Aramaic Levi to Testament of Levi.* SBLEJL 9 (Atlanta: Scholars, 1996), 138. According to Jürgen Becker, both the *Aramaic Levi Document* and *Jubilees* go back to common oral traditions; see Becker, *Untersuchungen zur Entstehungsgeschichte der Testamente der zwölf Patriarchen.* AGJU 8 (Leiden: Brill, 1970), 86.

12. Cf. Jósef T. Milik, "4Q Visions de Amram et une citation d'Origèn," *RB* (1972): 77-97 (esp. 97); Puech, DJD 31, 285-86, 322-24; Halpern-Amaru, "Burying the Fathers," 146-52.

uniform and homogeneous work, composed by one single author.[13] There are internal contradictions, doublets, tensions and discrepancies, both in detail as well as with regard to the biblical stories in general. These contradictions are the result of the literary development of *Jubilees*. Rewritten biblical stories and extant exegetical texts were adopted and assimilated into the new composition. The tensions and contrasts within the book result, therefore, from the integration of this existing material into a new framework.[14]

One of the main characteristics of the rewriting of *Jubilees* when compared to Genesis and Exodus is the continuous chronological system in which the biblical narrative is put, from the creation of the world unto the entrance into the promised land.[15] According to *Jubilees,* this entrance took place in the year 2450, calculated from the creation *(anno mundi).* In his chronological system, the author sometimes uses years and dates that occur in Genesis and Exodus, but these are far from complete. In *Jubilees* all events are dated, whether this is the stay of Adam and Eve in the garden of Eden, the flood, the births of the patriarchs before and after the flood, the covenant with Abraham, etc. Characteristic of the chronological system of *Jubilees* is the heptadic structure. The history is periodised by means of Jubilees. Every Jubilee consists of seven weeks of years, that is to say, seven times seven years. The author dates the events nearly always with the number of the Jubilee, the week of Years, and the Year in which the event took place. Most probably, the concept of the Jubilee is borrowed from Leviticus 25, but the author of *Jubilees* interprets the concept in a different way. In Leviticus, the Jubilee is the fiftieth year, in which the individual Hebrew could get liberation from slavery and could return to one's own property. For the author of *Jubilees,* the Jubilee is a period of forty-nine years. The total chronology of 2,450 years is divided in fifty of these periods of forty-nine years. The fiftieth Jubilee is the climax of the chronology, because the Israelites were liber-

13. Segal, *The Book of Jubilees.* Earlier, Davenport argued that *Jubilees* is a composite work, consisting of an original text and two subsequent revisions of it; see *The Eschatology of the Book of Jubilees.* Ernest Wiesenberg argued that chronological inconsistencies point to the activity of more than one writer; see Wiesenberg, "The Jubilee of Jubilees," *RevQ* 3 (1961): 3-40.

14. Segal, *The Book of Jubilees,* 29. According to Segal, a redactor adopted already existing rewritten stories and incorporated them into his book, but he added new material as well, mainly in the chronological framework and the law passages. The redactional strand is consistent in style, language, and theological view, whereas adopted stories are not consistent. In this way, Segal is able to distinguish between an editorial layer and the sources included therein.

15. For a study of the chronology in the book of *Jubilees,* see James C. VanderKam, "Studies in the Chronology of the Book of Jubilees," *From Revelation to Canon: Studies in the Hebrew Bible and Second Temple Literature.* JSJSup 62 (Leiden: Brill, 2000), 522-44. See also James M. Scott, *On Earth as in Heaven: The Restoration of Sacred Time and Sacred Space in the Book of Jubilees.* JSJSup 91 (Leiden: Brill, 2005).

ated from the Egyptian slavery, after which they could enter the land of their ancestors. What in Leviticus is applied to each individual in *Jubilees* is applied to the whole people in the fiftieth Jubilee.

Another aspect of the chronological system is the emphasis on the calendar.[16] The author of *Jubilees* attributes the beginning of calendrical knowledge to Enoch (cf. *Jub.* 4:17-18). Details about the calendar are disclosed in connection with the story of the flood (*Jub.* 5:20-38). The author omits much of this story, but he does take up and elaborate on the chronology. Noah ordained the beginning of each quarter as festivals because they were a reminder for him of the important events of the flood. On the first of the first month he was told to make the ark, and on the same day the earth became dry; on the first of the fourth month the openings of the depths of the abyss below were closed; on the first of the seventh month, all the openings of the earth's depths were opened; on the first of the tenth month, the summits of the mountains became visible. These four memorial festivals, celebrated on the first day of each three-month period, are closely related to the solar calendar of 364 days, which are four quarters of 91 days, or 52 weeks. In this calendar, each year has four intercalary days (12 months of 30 days, plus 4 days), which must be celebrated as annual festivals. Within this arrangement each festival has an exact time when it is to be celebrated. The weekly rhythm is marked with the Sabbath, which is very important for the author of *Jubilees*, and which should be observed very consciously. By referring to the flood, the solar calendar is thus given greater authority. Noah had already inaugurated it, and it therefore was put on the heavenly tablets. On this ground, it has authority for Israel. It is interesting that not only the solar calendar but also the prophecy that not all Israelites will follow this calendar is recorded on the heavenly tablets. This points to the conclusion that *Jubilees* was written in a period when the solar calendar was neglected. The followers of the lunar calendar would be punished.

Another point is that *Jubilees* stresses the priesthood. The patriarchs, even the antediluvian patriarchs, are acting as priests. Adam, Noah, and Abraham offer sacrifices, whereas Enoch is burning incense of the sanctuary. The priestly line continues from Adam until Levi, the third son of Leah and Jacob. Levi is presented more favorably in *Jubilees* than in Genesis. The sacred writings are transmitted within the priestly line. "Jacob gave all his books and the books of

16. See Annie Jaubert, *The Date of the Last Supper* (Staten Island: Alba House, 1965), 31-52; James C. VanderKam, "The Origin, Character, and Early History of the 364-Day Calendar: A Reassessment of Jaubert's Hypothesis," *CBQ* 41 (1979): 390-411; and *Calendars in the Dead Sea Scrolls: Measuring Time*. The Literature of the Dead Sea Scrolls (London: Routledge, 1998); and *The Book of Jubilees* (2001), 94-101.

his fathers to his son Levi so that he could preserve them and renew them for his sons until today" (*Jub.* 45:15).[17]

An important number of extensive additions to the text of Genesis deal with the laws and the correct application of them. According to the biblical texts, the divine laws were revealed only in postpatriarchal times. According to the author of *Jubilees*, the patriarchs also kept these laws and Noah kept the festival of weeks. The emphasis on the keeping of the commandments and the insertions of several laws (keeping the Sabbath; prohibition of consuming blood; firstfruits) by the patriarchs might reflect a certain opinion in the days of the author that there had once been a time when the laws (that separate the Jewish people from others) were not yet in existence. His point is that there was never such a time. The patriarchs Adam and Noah have already kept them or inaugurated them. Mosaic law is simply a renewing of the law of the patriarchs.

The chosen people have always been distinguished from other nations by special laws that they observed from the earliest days. There is a sharp dividing line between the elect ones and the impure nations. Both groups have to be kept separate. This separation brings about a prohibition of mixed marriages.[18]

A Case Study: The Early Abram

Within the framework of this *Companion*, I will concentrate here on the first pericopes about the life of Abram,[19] namely the passage from his birth until his departure from Ur (*Jub.* 11:14–12:15). The aim is to investigate the way Gen 11:26-31 is rewritten in this passage. In order to achieve this goal, I compare Gen 11:26-31 and *Jub.* 11:14–12:15 with each other. Questions as to what the author of *Jubilees* has adopted from Genesis, and the way in which he adopted it, are important. Only after this should one consider the function of the rewriting.

In view of the argument that *Jubilees* is not a uniform and coherent work, and in view of some inconsistencies in *Jub.* 11:14–12:15, I will also address the question of coherence and tradition of this passage. There are some tensions and incoherencies within this passage. For example, Abram first separates from his father (11:16-17) and later goes back to him and tries to persuade him to

17. Cf. James L. Kugel, "Levi's Election to the Priesthood in Second Temple Writings," *HTR* 86 (1993): 1-64.

18. See, e.g., Eberhard Schwarz, *Identität durch Abgrenzung: Abgrenzungsprozesse in Israel im 2. vorchristlichen Jahrhundert und ihre traditionsgeschichtliche Voraussetzungen: Zugleich ein Beitrag zur Erforschung des Jubiläenbuches.* Europäische Hochschulschriften, ser. 23, 162 (Frankfurt am Main: Lang, 1982).

19. I will speak consistently about Abram, since his name is changed to Abraham only in Gen 17:5 (*Jub.* 15:7).

abandon idolatry (12:1-8). Several motifs seem to cause Abram's recognition of the one God, creator of all things. First he realizes the mistakes of mankind, after which he prays to God (11:16-17). In 12:1-8 he shows his father again that the God of heaven, the creator, is the only one, and that idols have no *raison d'être*. With regard to the etymology of the city of Ur of the Chaldeans, on the one hand, the naming of the city is connected to the founder of that city, Ur, son of Kesed, father of Ara, the wife of Ragew (11:3), whereas, on the other hand, legends about "fire" in relation to Ur also seem to play a role (12:12-14). There seems to be no coherence between the passages about the ravens and the passages about idolatry. There is no causal connection between the departure of Terah and his sons from Ur of the Chaldeans and the temple burning, although both events are put adjacent to each other. These tensions and incoherencies not only question the unity of the passage, they also point to the use of already existing traditions. The allusions to several situations and events also contribute to this suggestion. I would point out in this regard the allusion to Terah as a priest (12:6), the tensions between Terah and the Chaldeans (12:7), and the motif of the negative interaction of Abram and his brothers (12:8).[20]

In order to be able to address the question of coherency within *Jub.* 11:14–12:15, I will distinguish the smaller pericopes from each other within this passage on the basis of their use of words and themes. I will then try to show how they are interrelated. Finally, I will investigate the way Genesis is rewritten.

The Rewriting of Genesis 11:26-31 in *Jubilees* 11:14–12:15

An Overall Comparison of the Pericopes

Jubilees 11:14–12:15 deals with the first stages in Abram's life, from his birth until his departure from Ur. The theme of this passage can be summarized as follows: at an early age Abram renounces the services of the many gods and their idols and testifies to his belief in the one true God.[21] The genealogical elements (*Jub.* 11:14-15; 12:9-11) can be considered a rewriting of Gen 11:26-30. The additions in *Jub.* 11:16–12:8 have no counterpart in Gen 11:10-26, whereas the additions in *Jub.* 12:12-15 are partly based on Gen 11:28, 31. In the following overall comparison, not only the common framework for both texts should become evident but also the numerous deviations of *Jubilees* from this model text.

---

20. Cf. also the search for Abram by the Chaldeans (*Jub.* 12:21).

21. See, e.g., George W. E. Nickelsburg, "Abraham the Convert: A Jewish Tradition and Its Use by the Apostle Paul," in *Biblical Figures Outside the Bible,* ed. Michael E. Stone and Theodore A. Bergren (Harrisburg: Trinity Press International, 1998), 151-75 (esp. 156).

Genesis 11:27b-31	Jubilees 11:14–12:15
Birth of Abram, Nahor, and Haran (11:27b; cf. 11:26)	1. Marriage of Terah and Edna, *birth of Abram* (11:14-15)
	2. ABRAM'S SEPARATION FROM HIS FATHER (11:16-17)
	3. ABRAM AND THE RAVENS (11:18-22)
	4. ABRAM INVENTS A SOWING-MACHINE (11:23-24)
	5. CONVERSATION OF ABRAM WITH HIS FATHER (12:1-8)
Birth of Lot (11:27c)	
Death of Haran (11:28)	
Marriages of Abram <u>and Nahor</u> (11:29)	6a. *Marriage of Abram* (12:9)
BARRENNESS OF SARAI (11:30)	
	6b. Marriage of Haran and <u>birth of Lot</u> (12:10)
	6c. <u>Marriage of Nahor</u> (12:11)
	7. Story around <u>the death of Haran</u> (12:12-14)
Departure of Terah with Abram, Lot, and Sarai from Ur and arrival in Haran (11:31)	8. *Departure from Ur of the Chaldeans and arrival in Haran* (12:15)

Jubilees 11:14–12:15 is part of a larger text, *Jub.* 8:1–23:8, which can be considered a genealogy interrupted by narrative additions. This larger text incorporates all the genealogical entries of Gen 11:12-32.[22] It not only mentions the birth of the patriarchs but also gives names to the wives of the patriarchs and includes a marriage report.[23] The structure of the genealogies in *Jub.* 8:1–12:8 differs greatly from that of Genesis. The two texts have only the name of the father and

---

22. Genesis 11:10-11 is combined with Gen 10:22 and can be found in *Jub.* 7:18. Also included is the birth of Kainan (*Jub.* 8:1-4), which is otherwise only found in LXX, Old Latin, and Eth Gen 11:13 but not in MT, Peshitta, Syriac, and the Targums. They all say that Arpachsad is the father of Shelah. In MT and SamP Gen 11:12-13, there is no mention of Kainan (Kenan). The addition of Kenan should probably be considered as secondary. First, the name is missing in the genealogy of 1 Chr 1:18, 24. Second, the same name does occur in Gen 5:9-14. Third, the age of Kenan when his first child was born, the duration of the rest of his life, and his total age are identical with those of Shelah. Cf. John Skinner, *A Critical and Exegetical Commentary on Genesis*. ICC (Edinburgh: T. & T. Clark, 1930 [1910]), 231; Martin Rösel, *Übersetzung als Vollendung der Auslegung: Studien zur Genesis-Septuaginta*. BZAW 223 (Berlin: de Gruyter, 1994), 133-34, 224.

23. Cf. *Jub.* 4:1-33.

the son in common. Otherwise, the genealogy in *Jubilees* is a complete transformation of the genealogy of Genesis.

Abram's Birth (Jubilees 11:14-15)

Jubilees 11:14-15 can be considered the rewriting of Gen 11:26-27b. *Jubilees* reads the twofold entry (Gen 11:26; 11:27b) for the birth of Terah's children as one entry, whereas the heading (Gen 11:27a) is not taken over. As can be seen in the synoptic overview, the content and form of the reports of Abram's birth are completely different in both texts:[24]

Genesis 11:26-27b	Jubilees 11:14-15
	14a DURING THE THIRTY-NINTH JUBILEE, IN THE SECOND WEEK, IN THE FIRST YEAR, Terah MARRIED A WOMAN WHOSE NAME WAS EDNA, THE DAUGHTER OF ABRAM, THE DAUGHTER OF HIS FATHER'S SISTER.
[ ]	

24. All translations of *Jubilees* are based on James C. VanderKam, *The Book of Jubilees: A Critical Text*, vol. 2. CSCO 511. Scriptores Aethiopici 88 (Leuven: Peeters, 1989), and all translations of the biblical text on the Revised Standard Version. However, I feel free to deviate from these translations in order to do justice to the repetition of words. In the synoptic overview, I have tried to present a classification of the similarities and dissimilarities between Genesis and *Jubilees*. I have used small caps to highlight those elements of Genesis that do not occur in *Jubilees*, and vice versa, i.e., the omissions and additions. I have used "normal script" for the corresponding elements between both texts, i.e., the verbatim quotations of one or more words from the source text in *Jubilees*. I put in italics all variations between Genesis and *Jubilees* other than addition or omission. Sometimes there is a rearrangement of words and sentences. I have underlined those elements. When a passage in *Jubilees* deviates from the parallel passage in MT Genesis, it is not always possible to ascertain whether the deviation reflects the hand of the author or the text of his *Vorlage*. The comparison of Genesis and *Jubilees* is complicated by the fact that one should establish which Hebrew biblical text the author had in front of him when he composed his book. VanderKam compared *Jubilees* with all the extent versions of Genesis and Exodus and concluded that the biblical text of *Jubilees* should have been an early Palestinian text. It agrees more often with LXX and SamP than with MT, but it is independent of them. Often I will point to significant textual variations. Sometimes the text reflects several textual traditions at the same time. Cf. VanderKam, *Textual and Historical Studies in the Book of Jubilees*. HSM 14 (Missoula: Scholars, 1977), 136-38; and "Jubilees and Hebrew Texts of Genesis-Exodus," *Text* 14 (1988): 71-85.

Genesis 11:26-27b	Jubilees 11:14-15
26a WHEN Terah *had lived seventy years,*	15a *In the seventh year of this week she gave birth to* A SON FOR HIM,
b *he became the father of* Abram, NAHOR AND HARAN.	
	b AND HE CALLED HIM Abram AFTER THE NAME OF HIS MOTHER'S FATHER
	c BECAUSE HE HAD DIED BEFORE HIS DAUGHTER'S SON WAS CONCEIVED.
27a NOW THESE ARE THE DESCENDANTS OF TERAH.	[ ]
b TERAH WAS THE FATHER OF ABRAM, NAHOR AND HARAN.	

As with the other genealogical entries, the report of the birth is reworked into a combined marriage and birth report. The dating of the birth of the first son fits into the absolute dating system.[25] It is striking that Abram's mother Edna is mentioned with reference both to her father ("Abram") and her mother ("his father's sister"). Abram is named after his grandfather, because he died before the conception of Abram. The purport of the naming of Abram after his grandfather could be that the author wants to stress that the influence of Abram's grandfather, who is not from the genealogical line of Shem, is confined to giving his name.[26] It is possibly also influenced by the fact that, in the biblical text, Nahor, Abram's brother, is named after the other grandfather, Terah's father. However, the most important element in the rewriting is the fact that Abram's mother Edna originates from the genealogical line of Shem.[27] She is the sister of Terah's father Nahor, the son of Serug, who himself married a woman outside the genealogical line of Shem ("Iyaseka, the daughter of Nestag of the Chal-

25. The author uses a system of years, weeks, and Jubilees for the dating of the events. He gives an absolute chronology, whereas the chronology of Genesis is related to the age of the father. Abram is born in the seventh year of the second week of the thirty-ninth Jubilee, which is the year 1876.

26. Cf. Betsy Halpern-Amaru, *The Empowerment of Women in the Book of Jubilees.* JSJSup 60 (Leiden: Brill, 1999), 26-27.

27. Davenport, *The Eschatology of the Book of Jubilees,* 82, note 1, states that the names of the wives and fathers-in-law have no relevance for the concerns that occupied the attention of the author of *Jubilees:* "They hardly seem relevant for his interest in the purity of Israel." See, however, John Rook, "The Names of the Wives from Adam to Abraham in the Book of Jubilees," *JSP* 7 (1990): 105-17; Halpern-Amaru, *The Empowerment of Women,* 9-31 *et passim.*

deans").[28] Terah originates from his father's side, and Edna, even more importantly, on her mother's side from the genealogical line of Shem. Finally, it is striking that the reports of the birth of Nahor and Haran are omitted in *Jubilees*,
despite the fact that both brothers play a part in the continuation of the narrative.

From Abram's Birth until His Marriage (Jubilees 11:16–12:8)

The passage 11:16–12:8, which describes events in Abram's life after his birth but
before his marriage with Sarai, can be divided into four pericopes on the basis of
the content: (a) Abram separates from his father (11:16-17); (b) Abram and the
ravens (11:18-22); (c) Abram invents a sowing machine (11:23-24); (d) conversation of Abram and his father (12:1-8). The four pericopes are distinguished from
each other by subject and the use of words, especially by the occurrence of word
repetition. Because of the length of the passage as a whole, I will present first the
text of the smaller pericopes, followed by a short description of its literary unity.
After this, I will treat the coherence of the passage as a whole.

Jubilees 11:16-17: Abram separates from his father

16a   The child began to realize the strayings of the land
b   — that everyone was going astray after the statues and after impurity.
c   His father taught him (the art of) writing.
d   When he was two weeks of years, he separated from his father
        in order not to prostrate himself before idols with him.
17a   He began to pray to the creator of all
b   that he would save him from the strayings of mankind
c   and that it might not fall to his share to go astray after impurity and
        wickedness.

The first pericope of the addition shows the following repetition of words:
"strayings," "going astray" (11:16a, 16b, 17a, 17b), "after impurity" (11:16b, 17c),
and "his father" (11:16c, 16d). Moreover, there is affinity between the verbs "to
prostrate oneself" (11:16d) and "to pray" (11:17a). The unity of this small passage
is strengthened by the structure, in that the first two lines (11:16ab: the child realizes the strayings) is balanced by the last two lines (11:17bc: the child wants to
be saved from the strayings).[29] Within this framework there is also a balance

---

28. Rook states incorrectly that Edna is "the grand-daughter of the second, but unnamed,
son of Seroh and Melka"; "The Names of the Wives," 117.

29. In this text, the strayings of the land are worked out in "statues," "impurity," and "wickedness."

between 11:16c (his father teaches him to write)[30] and the first part of 11:16d (he separates from his father) in which the relationship of father and son is the central issue.[31] The second part of 11:16d (the non-worshipping of the idols) is balanced with 11:17a (the praying to the creator of all).

Jubilees 11:18-22: Abram and the ravens

18a   When the time of the seed arrived for sowing in the land,

b   all of them went out together to guard the seed from the ravens.

c   Abram — a child of fourteen years — went out with those who were going out.

19a   As a cloud of ravens came to eat the seed,

b   Abram would run at them before they could settle on the land.

c   He would shout at them before they could settle on the land to eat the seed

d   and would say:

e   "Do not come down;

f   return to the place from which you came!"

g   And they returned.

20a   That day he did (this) to the cloud of ravens seventy times.

b   Not a single raven remained in any of the fields where Abram was.

---

30. It is not said in which language his father taught Abram to write. *Jubilees* 12:25-27 relates that Hebrew, forgotten after the collapse of Babel, was revived in the days of Abram *through the revelation of an angel.* This revelation allowed Abram to learn the writings of his forefathers like Enoch and Noah (cf. 21:10). The first thing Abram did after he learned Hebrew was to copy his father's books and study them for six months. This means that Abram, according to *Jubilees*, is to have access to esoteric knowledge inherited from the age before Babel, which is often revealed by the angels (e.g., 3:15; 4:15, 18, 21; 10:10-12; cf. also 8:3-4). Cf. Steve Weitzman, "Why Did the Qumran Community Write in Hebrew?" *JAOS* 119 (1999): 35-45. This would mean that Abram's father did not teach him Hebrew, and that he had no access to the knowledge of his forefathers before the revelation of the angel. This would also mean that the books he got from his father (*Jub.* 12:27) are just mechanically handed down after the collapse from father to son. It was not part of his father's instruction, which was related to idolatry. See also 11:8 ("His father [= Serug] taught him [= Nahor] the studies of Chaldeans: to practice divination and to augur by the signs of the sky"). And *Jub.* 8:2: "And his father taught him writing," which cannot be anything else than writing Hebrew. After this, Kainan was able to read the inscriptions of the watchers with regard to astrology, which were apparently written in Hebrew.

31. The statement that Abram separated from his father seems to be in contradiction with 12:1-8, where Abram tries to persuade his father to abolish idolatry; with 12:15, where Abram departs from Ur of the Chaldeans together with his father and subsequently lives with his father for fourteen years in Haran; and with 12:28-31, where Abram asks permission from his father to depart for Canaan.

21a   All who were with him in any of the fields would see him shouting:

b   then all of the ravens returned.

c   His name became great throughout the entire land of the Chaldeans.

22a   All who would sow came to him in this year,

b   and he kept going with them until the seedtime came to an end.

c   They sowed their land

d   and that year brought in enough food.

e   So they ate

f   and were filled.

This pericope also shows repetition of words: "raven" (11:18b, 19a, 20a, 20b, 21b; twice in collocation with "cloud": "cloud of ravens": 11:19a, 20a); "to sow/seed" (11:18a [2x], b, 19c, 22a, 22b, 22c); "land" (11:18a, 19b, 19c, 21c, 22c);[32] "to go out" (11:18b, 18c, 22b) and "to return" (11:19g, 21b); "fields" (11:20b, 21a); "to shout" (11:19c, 21a). With regard to the indications of time, this passage can be subdivided into two parts: 11:18-21 and 11:22. The events described in 11:18-21 took place in one day,[33] whereas the events of 11:22 took place during the rest of the year up until the end of seedtime. Moreover, one can point to the story line in 11:18-21: exposition (18a-c); complication (19a); climax (19b-f); and *dénouement* (19g-21). The problem in the exposition is the coming of the ravens, which finds its solution in the chasing away of them (11:21). *Jubilees* 11:22 seems to be a secondary expansion of 11:18-21.

Jubilees 11:23-24: Abram invents a sowing machine

23a   In the first year of the fifth week Abram taught the people who made implements for bulls — the skillful woodworkers —

b   and they made an implement above the land, opposite the plow beam, so that one could place seed on it.

c   The seed would then drop down from it onto the end of the plow and be hidden in the land;

d   and they would no longer be afraid of the ravens.

24a   They made (something) like this above the land on every plow beam.

b   They sowed,

c   and all the land did as Abram told them.

d   So they were no longer afraid of the birds.

---

32. The Ethiopic word *medr*, as Hebrew אֶרֶץ, could mean "earth," "land," and "ground." In order to be able to show the repetition of words in the translation, I have translated this word everywhere by "land."

33. Cf. 11:18a ("When the time . . . arrived") and 11:20a ("That day").

In this small passage, Abram is involved in the construction of a plow. One can point to the following repetition of words: "implement" (11:23a, 23b); "plow beam" (11:23b, 24a; cf. also "plow" in 11:23c); and "not being afraid" (11:23e, 24d). See too words that occur also in 11:18-22: "land" (11:23b, 23d, 24a, 24d) and "seed/to sow" (11:23b, 23c, 24b).

Jubilees 12:1-8: Conversation of Abram and his father

12:1a	During the sixth week, in its seventh year, Abram said to his father Terah:
b	"My father."
c	He said:
d	"Yes, my son?"
2a	He said:
b	"What help and advantage do we get from these idols before which you worship and prostrate yourself?
3a	For there is no spirit in them
b	because they are dumb.
c	They are a straying of the heart.
d	Do not worship them.
4a	Worship the God of heaven
b	who makes the rain and dew fall on the land and makes everything on the land.
c	He created everything by his word;
d	and all life (comes) from his presence.
5a	Why do you worship those things that have no spirit in them?
b	For they are works of the hands
c	and you carry them on your shoulders.
d	You receive no help from them,
e	but instead they are a great shame for those who make them
f	and a straying of the heart for those who worship them.
g	Do not worship them."
6a	And he said to him:
b	"I, too, know (this), my son.
c	What shall I do with the people who have ordered me to serve in their presence?
7a	If I tell them what is right,
b	they will kill me
c	because they themselves are attached to them
d	so that they worship and praise them.
e	Be quiet, my son, so that they do not kill you."
8a	When he told these things to his two brothers

b   and they became angry at him,

c   he remained silent.

This passage can be isolated from its context by the dialogue between father and son, which does not occur in the preceding passage (11:18-24) nor in the following one (12:9-11). One can point to the repetition of words: "father" (12:1a, 1b); "son" (12:1d, 6b, 7e); "to worship," which is mostly used in reference to the worshipping of idols (12:2b, 3d, 5a, 5f, 5g, 7d), but is used once for the worshipping of the God of heaven (12:4a);[34] "no spirit" (12:3a, 5a); "straying of the heart" (12:3c, 5f); and "land" (12:4b, 4c). In this passage, Abram tries to convince his father Terah to renounce idolatry. This implies that Terah is a priest of the idols. Both of his brothers are also characterized as idolatrous (12:8b: "and they became angry at him"). The scene can be characterized as a family affair in which for the first time in *Jubilees* Abram's brothers are also mentioned.

These four pericopes (11:16-17; 11:18-22; 11:23-24; 12:1-8) are distinguished from each other by subject and the use of words. However, they are not isolated from each other, but are in one way or another connected. With regard to the indications of time, both the first and second pericopes speak about the fourteenth year of Abram (11:16d: "When he was two weeks of years"; 11:18c: "a child of fourteen years"). In the absolute dating system of the book, this is the year 1890. The third passage takes place "in the first year of the fifth week," which is 1891. The fourth passage, finally, is dated "the sixth week, in its seventh year," which is 1904, when Abram was twenty-eight years old. With regard to content and use of words, it is evident that especially the first and the fourth passages and the second and third are closely connected. The central issue in the first and fourth passages is Abram's aversion to idols and his wish to worship the creator of all. The father-son relationship plays an important part in both passages. There is also common use of words: "idols" (11:16d; 12:2b); "straying/going astray" (11:16a, 16b, 17b, 17c; 12:3c, 5f); "to prostrate" (11:16d; 12:2b); and the "creation of all" (11:17a; 12:4d). The second and third passages are closely connected by the common theme of Abram who saves the seed from the ravens.[35]

---

34. Note that the word *malaka* ("to worship") is different from *sagada* in 11:16 ("to bow; to prostrate oneself") and *sallaya* in 11:17a ("to pray"; cf. 12:19a, 22a). Note, however, that in 12:2b *malaka* is used in parallelism with *sagada*, and in 12:7d with *sabběha* ("to praise").

35. According to Sebastian P. Brock, "Abraham and the Ravens: A Syriac Counterpart to Jubilees 11-12 and Its Implications," *JSJ* 9 (1978): 135-52 (esp. 140), the purpose of the story in *Jubilees* is to introduce Abram as the inventor of the seed-plow. Erkki Koskenniemi, *The Old Testament Miracle-Workers in Early Judaism.* WUNT ser. 2, 206 (Tübingen: Mohr Siebeck, 2005), 53, stresses the fact that Abram is presented as the first inventor of the useful technique of adapting a plow to hide seed in the earth. The topos of the first inventor was common in Greek literature.

In these passages, the relationship between Abram and his family seems not to play an important part. Instead, the relation between Abram and the rest of the land is prominent (cf. 11:21c: "His name became great throughout the entire land of the Chaldeans"; 11:24c: "and all the land did as Abram told them").

A   11:16-17:   aversion of idols (father and son, going astray, to prostrate)
B   11:18-22:   saving of the seed from the threat of the ravens
B′ 11:23-24:   invention of sowing-machine against the threat of the ravens
A′ 12:1-8:   aversion of idols (father and son, going astray, to prostrate)

The coherence between the passages about the ravens and those about idolatry is not clear at first sight. Abram's struggle with the ravens seems to have no clear connection with the pericopes in which Abram distances himself from idolatry. One could point to the pericope in which Abram observes the stars (12:16-18). He does this with respect to the rains. Both pericopes share an agricultural character. However, this correspondence seems to be too superficial to explain the incorporation of the raven pericopes.[36] There is, in point of fact, a stronger connection between the passages about the ravens (11:18-24) and the passage about the ravens before Abram's birth (11:11-13). In this passage the relationship between the ravens and idolatry is more obvious. The text of 11:11-13 runs as follows:

Jubilees 11:11-13

11a   Prince Mastema sent ravens and birds to eat the seed that was being sown in the land and to destroy the land in order to rob mankind of their labors.
b   Before they plowed in the seed,
c   the ravens would pick (it) from the surface of the land.
12a   For this reason he named him Terah:
b   because the ravens and birds reduced them to poverty
c   and ate their seed.
13a   The years began to be unfruitful due to their birds.
b   They would eat all of the fruit of the trees from the orchards.
c   During their time, if they were able to save a little of all the fruit of the earth, it was a great effort.

There are many similarities between 11:18-24 and 11:11-13. Also in 11:11-13 the word "ravens" occurs (11:11a, 11b, 12b), as well as "birds" (11a, 12b, 13a). The par-

---

36. Michael P. Knowles, "Abram and the Birds in Jubilees 11: A Subtext for the Parable of the Sower?" *NTS* 41 (1995): 145-51 (esp. 146), points to the fact that the interruption of the agricultural cycle by the ravens is a contravention of the Noahic covenant (cf. *Jub.* 6:4), and Abram restores the divine order promised to Noah.

allelism between "ravens" and "birds" also occurs in 11:23-24. In 11:11-13 the sowing in the land (11:11a) is also mentioned, as well as the eating of the seed by the ravens (11:11a, 12c). Elements in 11:11-13 that do not occur in 11:18-24 are the motifs of the destruction of the land, the people being robbed of their labors, the poverty, the eating of the fruit of the trees, and the setting aside of the fruit with great effort.[37] One can point to the relationship between the mention of the famine (11:13) and the remark that after Abram's actions the people could eat and were filled (11:22d-f). The text of 11:18-24 does not go explicitly into the destruction of the land,[38] the robbery of mankind, and the poverty. However, the fact that Abram chases away the ravens and invents a sowing machine can be understood as an answer to these threats.

The episodes of the ravens very strongly link prince Mastema, the leader of the evil spirits who sent the ravens, and Abram, who chases the ravens away. By the way he acts, Abram shows that he can save the land from the results of the actions of Mastema. By keeping the ravens away from the fields and by inventing a sowing machine, Abram is able to cancel at least part of the influence Mastema has over mankind.[39]

Elsewhere in the book, Mastema and the evil spirits are held responsible for the strayings of the people, for idolatry, and impurity (10:1-14; 11:4-5; 12:20-21). As a result, there exists a connection between the passages of the ravens (11:18-22; 11:23-24) and the passages about idolatry (11:16-17; 12:1-8), which also speak about the strayings of the people and impurity (11:16-17; 12:2-3, 5).

Finally, I would like to point to some similarities between the passages about the ravens and God's answer to Abram's prayer (12:19-24). After Abram's first actions with regard to the ravens, it is said: "His name became great throughout the entire land of the Chaldeans" (11:21c). In his answer to Abram's prayer to save him from the evil spirits, God says: "and I will make your name great, and you will be blessed in the land" (12:23). After Abram has invented the sowing machine, it is stated twice that the people were no longer afraid of the ravens and the birds (11:23e, 24d). In God's answer to Abram's prayer, he says that Abram

---

37. The description in 11:13c looks like an antithesis of the description of the paradisiacal situation after the angels taught Adam how to till the land. Cf. 3:16: "He would keep the garden against birds, animals, and cattle. He would gather its fruit and eat it and would store its surplus for himself and his wife. He would store what was being kept." In paradise, the temptation of the serpent ends this situation. In 11:11-13 it is Mastema who sends the ravens and the birds.

38. For the destruction of the land by the evil spirits, see 10:3, 5.

39. Compare this to the angels' teaching Noah about medicine so that he will be able to cure the people of the influence of the evil spirits (10:10, 12-13). According to Koskenniemi, *The Old Testament Miracle-Workers*, 53, agricultural knowledge is here combined with the wisdom to control Mastema and his demons.

will be blessed in the land and he will be his God, and then summons them not to be afraid (12:24b). Another interesting point of comparison is the use of the image of sowing the seed in the land in 11:18-24 and Abram's question about establishing his seed (12:20c), along with God's assurance that Abram and his seed will be established in the land, growing into a large and populous people (12:22), and that he will be the God of Abram and his seed (12:24). It is true, of course, that the seed is used literally in 11:18-24, whereas in 12:19-24 it is used in the sense of progeny. However, the use of the same word *(zera')*, apart from the other similarities, strengthens the connection between these passages and shows that the passages of the ravens are integrated into their literary context. One could also point to the use of the verb "to return" in both pericopes (11:19f, g, 21b; 12:21b). I refer especially to the similarity between 11:19f ("return to the place from which you came") and 12:21b ("Shall I return to Ur of the Chaldeans who are seeking me to return to them?"). The frequent use of the word "land" also strengthens the similarity between both passages. The most important element in the similarities between both passages is keeping the demonic ravens away, along with the request to be saved from the demons (12:20). It is remarkable that Abram enters into battle with the ravens without begging for God's help. Later on in his prayer he begs for God's help to save him from the evil spirits (12:20), just as Noah does in his prayer (10:3-6). In this way, one could consider the episode of the ravens as an anticipation of a narrative form of Abram's prayer.[40]

From Abram's Marriage until the Arrival in Haran (Jubilees 12:9-15)

Unlike *Jub.* 11:16–12:8, there are connections between 12:9-15 and the biblical text. *Jubilees* 12:9-15 can be considered as a rewriting of Gen 11:27c-31. On the basis of the content, this passage can be subdivided into three smaller passages: (a) marriage reports of Abram, Haran, and Nahor (12:9-11); (b) Abram burns the house of idols (12:12-14); and (c) departure from Ur and settling in Haran (12:15).

Jubilees 12:9-11: Marriages of Abram, Haran, and Nahor

12:9a During the fortieth Jubilee, in the second week, in its seventh year, Abram took a wife.

b And her name was Sarai, the daughter of his father,

c and she became his wife.

10a His brother Haran took a wife in the third year of the third week,

---

40. Cf. Knowles, "Abram and the Birds," 146. Todd Russell Hanneken, "Angels and Demons in the Book of Jubilees and Contemporary Apocalypses," *Hen* 28 (2006): 11-25 (esp. 21), speaks about the invention of agricultural equipment as a type of rediscovering monotheism.

b   and she gave birth to a son for him in the seventh year of this week.

c   He named him Lot.

11a   And his brother Nahor took a wife.

Jubilees 12:12-14: Story around the death of Haran

12a   In the sixtieth year of Abram's life (which was the fourth week, in its
      fourth year), Abram got up at night

b   and burned the house of the idols.

c   He burned everything in the house

d   but no one knew (about it).

13a   They got up at night

b   and wanted to save their gods from the fire.

14a   Haran dashed in to save them,

b   but the fire raged over him.

c   He was burned in the fire

d   and he died in Ur of the Chaldeans before his father Terah.

e   They buried him in Ur of the Chaldeans.

Jubilees 12:15: Departure from Ur of the Chaldeans and arrival in Haran

15a   And Terah went forth from Ur of the Chaldeans — he and his sons — to
      go to the land of Lebanon and the land of Canaan.

b   He settled in Haran,

c   and Abram settled with his father in Haran for two weeks of years.

The smaller pericopes are distinguished from each other by subject and the use of words. In the first pericope, which contains the genealogy with the marriage reports of Abram, Haran, and Nahor, the expression "to take a wife" occurs three times (12:9a, 10a, 11a). Moreover, there are several proper names (Abram, Sarai, Haran, Lot, and Nahor). Repetitions of words that are characteristic for the second pericope are "to burn" (12:12b, 12c, 14c; also compared with "to rage" in 12:14b); "fire" (12:13b, 14b, 14c); "house" (12:12b, 12c); "to save" (12:13b, 13c); and "Ur of the Chaldeans" (12:14d, 14e). Compare also "idols" (12:12b) with "their gods" (12:13b). The repetition in the third passage is restricted to the words "to settle" (12:15b, 15c); "land" (12:15a); and Haran (12:15b, 15c).

The events in the first passage take place between the years 1925 (12:9a: "During the fortieth Jubilee, in the second week, in its seventh year"), when Abram gets married; 1928 (12:10a: "In the third year of the third week"), when Haran gets married; and 1932 (12:10b: "In the seventh year of this week"), when Lot is born. The event of the second passage takes place in the sixtieth year of Abram's life (12:12a), which is the year 1936 (12:12a: "The fourth week, in its fourth year"), whereas the events in the short third passage take place over a period of fourteen years, beginning at an unspecified moment after the burning of the house of idols, probably between the years 1936 and 1950, because the next passage, in which Abram is observing the stars (12:16-18), is dated to the year 1951.

The three pericopes are interrelated. As far as the spatial aspects are concerned, the first two passages are located in Ur of the Chaldeans, while in the third passage Terah and his children depart from Ur of the Chaldeans and arrive in Haran. One can also point to the characters involved. In 12:9-11 there are Abram, Sarai, Haran, Lot, and Nahor; in 12:12-14 "Abram" (12:12a), "Haran" (12:14a), and "his father Terah" (12:14d); and in 12:15 "Terah" (12:15a), "he and his sons" (12:15a), and "his father" (12:15c). The following passage (12:16-27) concentrates on Abram as the only acting person.

The fact that 12:9-15 can be considered a rewriting of Gen 11:27c-31 proves the unity and coherence of the three passages. Apart from verbatim quotations with variations (cf. *Jub.* 12:9a, 15), omissions (Gen 11:29c-31a), and additions (11:12-14c, 14e, 15c), there is a striking rearrangement of some words and phrases (compare Gen 11:27c-28 with *Jub.* 12:10, 14d). In the following synoptic overview I have put both texts side by side.

Genesis 11:27c-31	Jubilees 12:9-15
27c *And Haran was the father of Lot.*	[Jub 12:10b]
28a And *Haran* died before his father Terah IN THE LAND OF HIS birth, in Ur of the Chaldeans.	[Jub 12:14cd]
[ ]	9a DURING THE FORTIETH JUBILEE, IN THE SECOND WEEK, IN ITS SEVENTH YEAR,
29a Abram <u>and Nahor</u> *took wives;*	Abram *took a wife*
b the name *of Abram's wife* was Sarai,	AND *her* name was Sarai,
[ ]	THE DAUGHTER OF HIS FATHER,
	b AND SHE BECAME HIS WIFE.
[Gen 11:27c]	10a HIS BROTHER HARAN TOOK A WIFE IN THE THIRD YEAR OF THE THIRD WEEK,
	b *and she gave birth to a son for him*
[cf. Gen 11:29a]	IN THE SEVENTH YEAR OF THIS week.
	c HE NAMED HIM Lot.

c AND THE NAME OF NAHOR'S
   WIFE,
   Milcah, the daughter of Haran
   the father of Milcah and Iscah.
30a NOW SARAI WAS BARREN;
b SHE HAD NO CHILD.

11a AND HIS BROTHER Nahor *took a
    wife.*
    [ ]

Genesis 11:27c-31

[ ]

Jubilees 12:9-15

12a IN THE SIXTIETH YEAR OF
    ABRAM'S LIFE (WHICH WAS THE
    FOURTH WEEK, IN ITS FOURTH
    YEAR), ABRAM GOT UP AT NIGHT
b   AND BURNED THE HOUSE OF THE
    IDOLS.
c   HE BURNED EVERYTHING IN THE
    HOUSE
d   BUT NO ONE KNEW (ABOUT IT).
13a THEY GOT UP AT NIGHT
b   AND WANTED TO SAVE THEIR
    GODS FROM THE FIRE.
14a HARAN DASHED IN TO SAVE THEM,
b   BUT THE FIRE RAGED OVER HIM.
c   HE WAS BURNED IN THE FIRE

[Gen 11:28]

d   and *he* died [ ] in UR OF THE
    Chaldeans before his father Terah.
e   THEY BURIED HIM IN UR OF THE
    CHALDEANS.
    [ ]

31a Terah TOOK ABRAM HIS SON
    AND LOT THE SON OF HARAN,
    HIS GRANDSON, AND SARAI HIS
    DAUGHTER-IN-LAW, HIS SON
    ABRAM'S WIFE,
b   and *they* went forth WITH THEM
    from Ur of the Chaldeans [ ] to
    go to [ ] the land of Canaan;

15a And *Terah* went forth [ ] from
    Ur of the Chaldeans — HE AND
    HIS SONS — to go to THE LAND
    OF LEBANON and the land of
    Canaan.
b   *He settled in* Haran,

c   *they came to* Haran,
d   *and they* settled *there.*

c   *and Abram* settled *with his father
    in Haran*
    FOR TWO WEEKS OF YEARS.

[ ]

The rearrangement of the genealogical details in *Jubilees* results in a sequence of three marriages, that of Abram and Sarai (in the year 1925), of Haran with an unidentified woman (in 1928), and of Nahor, for whom neither the name of the woman nor the date is given. Only the marriage of Haran is followed by a report of the eldest son, Lot. This genealogical report, therefore, closely resembles the genealogical entries in *Jub.* 8:1–12:8, with the difference that the name of Haran's wife and her origin are not mentioned.

As far as the report of Abram and Sarai's marriage is concerned (*Jub.* 12:9), *Jubilees* fails to mention that Sarai was barren (Gen 11:30).[41] However, the information about their marriage is considerably expanded. In Genesis the reference is quite brief. In *Jubilees* a date is provided ("During the fortieth Jubilee, in the second week, in its seventh year"). Their marriage is described in greater detail ("Abram married a woman whose name was Sarai . . . and she became his wife"), and her descent is mentioned ("the daughter of his father"). In other words, Sarai was Abram's sister. This addition could have been prompted, on the one hand, by the fact that Abram called Sarai "his sister" elsewhere in Genesis, namely, when he visited Pharaoh (Gen 12:10-20) and the king of Gerar (20:1-18).[42] On the other hand, it is not impossible to imagine that the author of *Jubilees* would have wanted to stress Sarai's excellent provenance. She came from the right family. In the mind of the author she could not have been the daughter of Haran, as can be concluded on the basis of the biblical text: "Abram and Nahor took wives; the name of Abram's wife was Sarai, and the name of Nahor's wife, Milcah, the daughter of Haran the father of Milcah and Iscah" (Gen 11:29). Sarai's father was not mentioned, however, although Milcah's was, and it could be inferred that Sarai was also a daughter of Haran. In early Jewish literature, there are several examples of the identification of Sarai and Iscah.[43] This was not the case for the author of *Jubilees*, however.

41. The author does not establish her barrenness but rather her *descent* as a central issue. This aspect of *Jubilees* is stressed emphatically by Halpern-Amaru, *The Empowerment of Women*, 34-35. Halpern-Amaru underlines that Sarai is the "dominant bride," that she is the only woman named and the only one with "genealogical credentials."

42. It is interesting to note, however, that the author of *Jubilees* does not refer to Sarai as Abram's sister when they encounter the pharaoh (*Jub.* 13:13-15), and the visit with the king of Gerar is also omitted altogether.

43. See Pseudo-Philo, *L.A.B.* 23:4; Josephus, *Ant.* 1:151; *Tg. Ps.-J.* on Gen 11:29; *b. Meg.* 14a; *b. Sanh.* 69b; *Gen. Rab.* 38:14. Cf. Dirk U. Rottzoll, *Rabbinischer Kommentar zum Buch Genesis: Darstellung der Rezeption des Buches Genesis in Mischna und Talmud unter Angabe Targumischer und Midraschischer Paralleltexte.* SJ 14 (Berlin: de Gruyter, 1994), 201-2; Halpern-Amaru, *The Empowerment of Women*, 35, n. 4.

Further changes in the text support the author of *Jubilees*'s opinion that Sarai could not have been Haran's daughter. This is a reference to the fact that in Genesis most information concerning Haran is given before the marriages of Abram and Nahor: his birth, his fathering of Lot, and his death (Gen 11:26-28). In *Jubilees,* however, the information concerning the marriage of Abram with Sarai is placed before the marriage of Haran (*Jub.* 12:9-10).[44]

The marriage of Abram and Sarai does not result immediately in the birth of a son. The postponement of the birth of their first son forms the main clue to the story line in Genesis. *Jubilees* cannot continue with the birth of a son and an elaboration on events during the life of this child. Instead, a second marriage report is inserted, that of Abram's brother Haran (12:10), whose birth is not stated in *Jubilees.* Haran's marriage is not recounted in Genesis. In *Jubilees* it is described in a manner comparable to the marriage of Abram and Sarai. In conformity with Genesis, a son is born from this marriage. With the relocation of the mention of Lot's birth closely after the marriage of Abram and Sarai, the author seems to suggest that Lot is going to play the role of the not (yet) born son of Abram and Sarai.[45] Although Lot plays a part in the continuation of the story in Genesis and in its rewriting in *Jubilees,* it gradually becomes clear that he cannot take the place of the son of Abram and Sarai. It is possibly for this reason that the name of Haran's wife is not recorded, nor is her origin. *Jubilees* betrays a somewhat ambivalent attitude towards Lot. On the one hand, the genealogy points to a positive appreciation. On the other hand, disapproval is shown by the fact that the derivation of his mother is not mentioned and his father is depicted as an idolator.[46]

The marriage report of Nahor (*Jub.* 12:11), which is quite extensive in Gen 11:29 where the name of the wife and her origin are mentioned, is very cursorily presented in *Jubilees:* "His brother Nahor also got married." It is not clear why the author does not mention the name of Haran's wife. Possibly he had a need to push her origin, being a daughter of Haran, into the background. Much later in the story, Milcah is mentioned as the grandmother of Rebecca, the wife of Isaac. In *Jub.* 19:10 the story of Gen 24:1-67 is condensed into a genealogical remark, one verse in length, about Isaac's wife, a remark that is at the same time a genealogy of Nahor. Three times Rebecca is called the daughter of Bethuel. And of this Bethuel it is said that he is the son of Abram's brother Nahor and of

---

44. Halpern-Amaru, *The Empowerment of Women,* 35.

45. In 12:30 Terah says to Abram: "Take Lot, the son of your brother Haran, with you as your son." In 13:18, after the separation from Lot, it is said of Abram: "He was brokenhearted that his brother's son had separated from him for he had no children."

46. On the ambivalent attitude of *Jubilees* with regard to Lot, see van Ruiten, "Lot versus Abraham."

Milcah, "who was the wife of Abram's brother Nahor." The text does not put forward the fact that she is a daughter of Haran, whereas when mentioning the origin of the women of the patriarchs the father is always mentioned.

Finally, in Genesis the report of the death of Haran, the father of Lot, is quite neutral (Gen 11:28). In *Jubilees,* however, his death is connected to the fact that he tried to save from fire the idols that Abram tried to burn (*Jub.* 12:12-14). The addition of the burning of the house of idols fits in with the context of *Jub.* 11:14–12:15, which shows Abram as someone who gradually turns away from idolatry. First, he breaks with his father in order not to worship idols (*Jub.* 11:16-17) and, subsequently, he tries to persuade his father to give up idolatry (*Jub.* 12:1-8).[47] The burning of the house of idols can be seen as a climax in this story line.

Genesis does not mention idolatry or the burning of the idols.[48] However, there are some clues in the biblical text. Haran, who is mentioned as the third son of Terah, becomes the father of a son (11:27c). However, there is no marriage report for him, as is the case for both his brothers (11:29a). Immediately after the birth of Lot, it is mentioned that Haran dies (11:28). With regard to Haran's death, Genesis mentions some striking details: "and Haran died before Terah (עַל־פְּנֵי תֶּרַח; Gen 11:28)"; "in the land of his birth." One can easily deduce from the death of Haran, on the one hand, and the departure of Terah, on the other, that something irregular must have happened. The mention of a burning could be motivated by the mention of the name of the city of Ur. The root אור ("become light"), and in particular the noun אוֹר ("brightness; light"), can be related to fire.[49] Moreover, one can point to a tradition found in Josh 24:2-3, 14-15, which states that Terah and his fathers "lived of old beyond the Euphrates," and there "they served other gods" (Josh 24:2). Therefore, God has led Abram from there (Josh 24:3).[50]

The extensive description of the events surrounding the death of Haran does serve one clear function. It characterizes Haran as the prototype of the unfaithful one, in opposition to the faithful and righteous Abram. Although both

---

47. I have already pointed out the contradiction between both passages. Other places in *Jubilees* dealing with idolatry are 11:4 and 20:6-10. In 11:4, the worshipping of the idols is connected with the straying of the evil spirits. In 20:6-10, Abraham summons his children to follow God, to keep his commandments, and not to follow the idols.

48. The burning of idols does not occur elsewhere in *Jubilees,* with the exception of *Jub.* 31:1-2, which is a rewriting of Gen 35:1-4. In Genesis, Jacob hides the idols beneath the oak, which is in the land of Shechem. *Jubilees* adds not only that Rachel had stolen them from her father Laban, but also that Jacob, before hiding them, first burned the foreign gods.

49. For the tradition that Abram was saved from the fire, see James L. Kugel, *The Bible As It Was* (Cambridge, Mass.: Belknap, 1997), 143-44.

50. For this tradition see, e.g., Kugel, *The Bible As It Was,* 133-38.

derive from Terah and in that sense are in the line of Shem, the line of the chosen people will only continue through Abram. This is why it is significant that Sarai should not be defiled by the faithless Haran either, that she should come straight from Terah. According to *Jubilees,* it is important that a pure line can be drawn from Abram and Sarai back to the forefathers, via Terah, Shem, Noah, and the other antediluvians, back to Seth and Azura and with them to Adam and Eve. The election of Israel is built into the creation of the world, as can also be illustrated using other passages from the book of *Jubilees.*[51] The marriage of Abram and Sarai is considered to be in the same line as that of the forefathers. In this case, this is done through the establishment of a sibling relationship between Abram and Sarai. This harkens back to the first generations after Adam and Eve, which were, in the eyes of *Jubilees,* also brother-sister unions.[52]

The main focus of *Jub.* 12:9-14 is on the marriage of Abram and Sarai. The author of *Jubilees* was not really interested in Abram's brothers. Only Haran is mentioned at any length in order to provide a contrast to a holy Abram and in order to make clear that Sarai was not his daughter. Sarai's infertility was not stressed by the author of *Jubilees;* rather, it was her origin that carried weight, that of going straight back to the creation of the first man and woman. With these few changes to the Genesis text, the author of *Jubilees* has completely changed the plot of the story. It is no longer the story of the continuously threatened promise of numerous offspring; it is a story of a pure lineage. By setting the marriage of Abram and Sarai in the same line as the forefathers, the nature of the miracle, i.e., the conception of children in old age, becomes much less important.

The last part of this passage describes the family's departure from Ur and their arrival in Haran (Gen 11:31; *Jub.* 12:15). There is some disagreement among the ancient versions of Gen 11:31. The Samaritan Pentateuch adds to the enumeration of the family of Terah that went forth from Haran (11:31a) Nahor and his wife: "and Sarai his daughter-in-law, *and Milcah his daughter-in-law,* the wife of his son Abram, *and his brother Nahor.*" This addition can be considered a harmonization. It is somewhat odd that Nahor would remain in Ur, whereas the rest of the family departs for Haran. Moreover, much later in the narrative the biblical text itself shows that Nahor and Milcah left Ur as well (cf. Gen 24:10). The construction וַיֵּצְאוּ אִתָּם ("they went forth with them") is somewhat

---

51. See, e.g., *Jub.* 2:20. Cf. Berndt Schaller, "Gen. 1.2 im antiken Judentum: Untersuchungen über Verwendung und Deutung der Schöpfungsaussagen von Gen 1.2 im antiken Judentum" (Diss., Göttingen, 1961), 63; James C. VanderKam, "Genesis 1 in Jubilees 2," *DSD* 1 (1994): 300-321 (esp. 318); Lutz Doering, "The Concept of the Sabbath in the Book of Jubilees," in *Studies in the Book of Jubilees,* ed. Matthias Albani, Jörg Frey, and Armin Lange. TSAJ 65 (Tübingen: Mohr Siebeck, 1997), 179-205 (esp. 185-88); van Ruiten, *Primaeval History Interpreted,* 49, 57-65.

52. Cf. Halpern-Amaru, *The Empowerment of Women,* 36-37.

peculiar. The text changes from singular (11:31a: "Terah took") to plural, and the addition of "with them" seems unusual. The Samaritan Pentateuch and the Septuagint read this as a singular form of the *hipʿil* ("he brought forth") instead of plural *qal* ("they went forth") and אֹתָם (*nota accusativi*: "them") instead of אִתָּם (preposition: "with them"): "he brought them forth."

The first omission in *Jubilees* concerns Gen 11:31a. Instead of two verbs, "to take" (singular) and "to go forth" (plural) in the Masoretic Text, along with "to bring forth" (singular) in the Samaritan Pentateuch and the Septuagint, *Jubilees* reads only one ("to go forth," singular). Moreover, *Jubilees* omits the enumeration of Gen 11:31a. One could argue here that the enumeration of Gen 11:31a is being summarized in the prepositional construction אִתָּם ("with them") in Gen 11:31b. In that case, *Jub.* 12:15 puts both the enumeration and its summary together in the words "he and his sons."

The first addition ("to the land of Lebanon") can be considered a harmonization. In the biblical text there is some disagreement between the statement that it was Terah who initiated the journey from Ur to Canaan and the view that the journey to Canaan was Abram's response to God's call.[53] The biblical text gives no answer to the question of why Terah gave up his intention of reaching the land of Canaan. Once he arrived in Haran, he settled there instead. By adding "to the land of Lebanon," the author shows that a twofold trip, first to Lebanon and thereafter to Canaan, was in fact foreseen. This harmonization is then continued in 12:28-31: his father gives Abram permission to go to Canaan but asks him to come back and take him with him, if Abram finds a pleasant land to live in. Only his death prevents Terah from settling in Canaan.

The second addition gives the period of time Abram stays in Haran ("two weeks of years"). The departure from Ur of the Chaldeans is not dated by the author, although he is fond of dating all the important events in history. It seems reasonable, then, to suggest that the departure most likely took place in the same year as the burning down of the house of idols. This incident brings with it the flight of Abram's family. The text suggests tensions between Abram's family and a group of people, who are not identified, but to whom reference is made implicitly (e.g., 12:7: "If I tell them what is right, they will kill me because they themselves are attached to them so that they worship and praise them. Be quiet, my son, so that they do not kill you"). Later on, Abram refers implicitly to certain tensions in his prayer: "Shall I return to Ur of the Chaldeans who are looking for

---

53. Cf. Yair Zakovitch, "The Exodus from Ur of the Chaldeans: A Chapter in Literary Archaelogy," in *Ki Baruch Hu: Ancient Near Eastern, Biblical, and Judaic Studies in Honor of Baruch A. Levine,* ed. Robert Chazan, William W. Hallo, and Lawrence H. Schiffman (Winona Lake: Eisenbrauns, 1999), 429-39 (esp. 431).

me to return to them?" (12:22c). After the flight from Ur, the settling in Haran lasts fourteen years. It seems obvious to suppose that these fourteen years must cover the period between the burning down of the house of idols (1936), the observation of the stars, and the call to depart for Canaan (*Jub.* 12:16-24; 1951).

It is not completely clear why the period in Haran is noted as a period of fourteen years. The data points to the suggestion that the author of *Jubilees* has his own dating system, in which the unit of seven years plays an important part. In the early life of Abram the events that take place in multiples of the seventh year play an important part.[54] One can point to the age of 70 years of Terah (10 × 7) when Abram was born (11:14-15), to the age of 14 years (2 × 7) at which Abram separates from his father (11:16-17) and chases the ravens (11:18-22), to the age of 28 years (4 × 7) in which he has a conversation with his father to persuade him to abandon the idols (12:1-8), to the age of 49 years (7 × 7) in which he marries (12:9), to his age of 56 years (8 × 7) in which Lot is born (12:10), and to his age of 77 years when he leaves Haran (12:28).[55] Some data do not fit in with this system: the invention of the equipment (11:23-24), the marriage of Haran (12:10), and the burning of the temple (12:12: Abram: 60 years). One event does not receive an explicit date, the departure from Ur of the Chaldeans for Haran (12:15).[56] As far as the invention of the equipment is concerned, one could argue that this follows naturally from the events in the fourteenth year. Further, the dating of Haran's marriage is a result of the wish of the author to put Haran's marriage after the marriage of Abram and Sarai. He could have dated Haran's marriage so that it was in the same year as Lot's birth, but he did not do so.

Abram's incendiary efforts, which are set in his sixtieth year, do not fit in with the system of dating vis-à-vis the seventh year of a year-week. According to Sebastian Brock, *Jubilees* is dependent here on an older tradition, which is later attested to in Syriac sources (Jacob of Edessa, the Catena Severi, Michael the Syrian, Bar Hebraeus) and in Jerome. Brock argues that *Jubilees* took over certain elements from this chronological framework (the numbers 60 and 14) and reused them without comprehending the rationale that lay behind them.[57] According to this tradition, Abram leaves Haran 14 years after the burning of the house of idols. When Terah died at the age of 145 (Samaritan Pentateuch), Abram had time to bury his father before he left Haran at the age of 75. Jerome preserves the reasoning that resulted in dating the temple incident to Abram's sixtieth year. Jerome refers to a Jewish tradition stating that Abram left Haran

---

54. In fact, many events are dated in the seventh year of a year-week. See VanderKam, "Studies in the Chronology," esp. 530, 534-38.

55. Abram dies at the age of 175 years (25 × 7).

56. Note that Terah's death is not mentioned at all (Gen 11:32).

57. Brock, "Abraham and the Ravens," 144-49, 151.

75 years after leaving Ur and the destruction of the idols in the temple. Since Abram was born when Terah was 70 years of age, and Terah died at the age of 205 (according to the Masoretic Text), 75 years after Abram's "conversion" must have been in his sixtieth year of age.[58] This is precisely the figure given in *Jubilees*. This number determined that the length of the subsequent stay in Haran would be 14 years.

The family's departure from Ur does not get a new date. It is possible that this, too, took place in Abram's sixtieth year. Although *Jubilees* does not make any causal relationship between both events, the adjacent position of both events makes it natural to suppose that the incident with the temple causes the family to flee from Haran. The text shows tensions between the Chaldeans and Abram's family (*Jub.* 12:7). However, Abram and his family leave Ur and settle in Haran for two weeks of years (*Jub.* 12:15). From Abram's departure from Haran at the age of 77 (*Jub.* 12:28), one can infer that the beginning of the period of fourteen years must have been at the age of 63, which would fit in nicely with his predilection for dating the events in the seventh year (9×7). However, this would mean a gap of three years between the burning of the house of idols and the departure of the family.[59] According to James VanderKam, it is somewhat forced to say that *Jubilees* does not connect the temple burning with the departure from Ur.[60] In his opinion *Jub.* 12:15 does not refer to the entire time that Abram spent with Terah in Haran, but only to the period from their arrival to the next event narrated.

Conclusion

The passage about the early life of Abram until his arrival in Haran can be divided into eight semantic pericopes (*Jub.* 11:14-15; 11:16-18; 11:19-22; 11:23-24; 12:1-8; 12:9-11; 12:12-14; 12:15). These pericopes are tied together in three textual subunits (*Jub.* 11:14-15; 11:16–12:8; 12:9-15). The subunits are tied together on the basis that Abram at an early age renounces the services of the many gods and their idols and testifies instead to his belief in the one and true God.

The analysis of 11:14–12:15 has shown that the text of *Jubilees* is guided to a large extent by Gen 11:26-31, as far as content and sequence are concerned. As far

58. See Brock, "Abraham and the Ravens," 144; also VanderKam, "Studies in the Chronology," 535-36.

59. See Brock, "Abraham and the Ravens," 141-42. Cf. William Adler, "Abraham and the Burning of the Temple of Idols: Jubilees' Traditions in Christian Chronography," *JQR* 77 (1986-87): 95-117.

60. VanderKam, "Studies in the Chronology," 537.

as the wording is concerned, one can point to the fact that 12:9-11, 14d, 15 are based on the biblical text (Gen 11:27c-31). Moreover, the main sequence of the events is the same in both texts: Abram's birth, the marriages of Abram and his brothers, the departure from Ur, and the arrival in Haran. These events form the basic framework for both texts. At certain places, the sequence deviates in *Jubilees*. I indicated as one example the marriage of Haran, which is put later than that of Abram. This seems to be a conscious adaptation of the biblical text in order to make clear that Sarai is not Haran's daughter. Moreover, this rearrangement brings out Lot's birth after the marriage of Abram and Sarai, as well as Haran's death after this marriage. Both aspects make it easier to view Lot as the surrogate son of Abram and Sarai. In this way, the author lessens the emphasis on the biblical notion of Sarai's infertility, which is after all in contradiction to Isaac's birth. These alterations of the framework can be attributed to the author of *Jubilees*.

Apart from the change in the framework of the passage, the author changes drastically the structure of the genealogical entries. This is the case with the marriage-report of Terah, which is the birth-report of Abram (Gen 11:26, 27b; *Jub.* 11:14-15) and is in line with the rewriting of all the genealogical entries in the book (*Jub.* 4:1-33; 8:1–11:14). In the end, this is what can be considered the real task of the author of the book. The mentioning of the wives of the patriarchs and their identification is an appropriate touch for an author who is so concerned with the sacred line of inheritance. It is possible, therefore, that the author of *Jubilees* added the wives independently. However, it is also possible that he was influenced by certain traditional elements from nonbiblical sources.[61]

It is clear that one cannot trace back a large portion of the text of *Jub.* 11:14–12:15 to the biblical text. One should consider this, then, to be an addition. There are, however, some clues in the biblical text (gaps, etymologies), which can still explain some portion of this addition. It is, for example, not clear why Terah decides to leave Ur of the Chaldeans and to set out for Canaan. The text

---

61. According to Davenport, *The Eschatology of the Book of Jubilees*, 82, n. 1, the names of the wives and fathers-in-law were added even before the author received the list. In support of this view, one can point to the *Genesis Apocryphon*. In what remains of this work, it is clear that in cols. 2 and 6 the names of two of the wives do occur: Bitenos and Amzara. Moreover, Noah says in col. 6: ". . . for my sons I took wives from my brother's daughters, and my daughters I gave to my brother's sons, according to the eternal law." Since the *Genesis Apocryphon* is only partially preserved, one cannot be sure that the names of the wives of the other patriarchs were also originally mentioned. Since the structure and wording of the book of *Jubilees* and the *Genesis Apocryphon* are quite different, it is reasonable to suppose that both texts borrowed their material from a common tradition.

does not make clear either why Haran died during his father's life. Both gaps in the text are combined in the history of interpretation, as well as in the book of *Jubilees.* Moreover, it is not clear why Terah gives up his original intention to go to Canaan and why it is Abram who goes instead.[62] Some characteristics in *Jub.* 11:14–12:15 (contradictions, irregularities in the plot of the story, allusions to known details, and presentation of some events in a very short form) suggest the influence of older traditions on the text.[63]

The polemic against foreign gods is deeply rooted in the Hebrew Bible.[64] One can point to Deuteronomy, but also to the prophetic literature, such as Second Isaiah and Jeremiah. The renouncing of idolatry is no invention of *Jubilees.* What is striking, however, is the fact that *Jubilees* connects these anti-idol polemics with Abram.[65] This characteristic, too, seems to be a traditional one. In any case, one can see that Josh 24:2-3 refers to the idolatry of the fathers on the other side of the river (also 24:14-15). Unlike Genesis, Ur of the Chaldeans is here the point of departure for Abram's journey to Canaan. Moreover, the departure from Ur is on God's initiative and not on Terah's. It is not completely clear whether it is meant in Josh 24:2-3 that Abram also served other gods or only that Terah and Nahor did. *Jubilees* does not follow the account in Joshua that on God's initiative Abram departed from Ur without his family. Instead, it follows Genesis. *Jubilees* does follow Joshua in the connection that is made between Abram and the renouncement of idolatry, however. Judith 5:6-9 speaks of Abram's early life and connects Abram with the anti-idol polemic.[66] Comparable to *Jubilees,* the departure from Ur is related to the renouncing of the foreign gods ("they would not follow the gods of their fathers"). They left the way of their parents and "worshipped the God of heaven, a god whom they had come to know" (cf. Jdt 5:8). Because of this, they were driven out of Ur. This tradition concerning Abram's transition from idolatry to monotheism is quite similar to that of *Jubilees.* Even though *Jubilees* does not say that the family is expelled from Ur, there are some traces of the tensions between Abram's family and the Chaldeans (*Jub.* 12:6-8).[67] Also the fact

---

62. Zakovitch, "The Exodus from Ur of the Chaldeans"; Kugel, *The Bible As It Was,* 133-48.

63. Cf. also Nickelsburg, "Abraham the Convert," 157.

64. See, e.g., Edward M. Curtis, "Idol, Idolatry," *ABD,* 3:376-81.

65. Apart from his early years, one can point to Abraham's testamentary speeches (20:7-9; 21:3-5, 21-23; 22:16-22).

66. Adolfo Roitman, "The Traditions about Abraham's Early Life in the Book of Judith (5:6-9)," in *Things Revealed: Studies in Early Jewish and Christian Literature in Honor of Michael E. Stone,* ed. Esther G. Chazon, David Satran, and Ruth A. Clemens. JSJSup 89 (Leiden: Brill, 2004), 73-87.

67. Cf. also *Jub.* 12:21.

that the departure from Ur is put immediately after the fire of the house of idols points in the direction of a flight.[68]

The specific linkage of the story of the ravens with the polemic against the religion of the Chaldeans has possibly been implemented by the author. The struggle against the ravens can be related to the fight against the evil spirits. However, it is possible too that this linkage is also a traditional one. In the *Letter of Jeremiah* the struggle against idols plays a prominent role. They cannot save themselves from war or calamity. They cannot set up a king over a country or give rain to men (Ep Jer 29–51; cf. *Jub.* 12:1-8). Moreover, the text speaks about a fire that breaks out in a temple, and about their priests who will flee and escape (Ep Jer 54; cf. *Jub.* 12:12-14). Sun and moon and stars are sent forth for service and are obedient. Only when God commands the clouds to cover the whole world do they carry out his command (Ep Jer 59–61; cf. *Jub.* 12:16-18). It is in this context of anti-idol polemics that ravens are also mentioned: "for they have no power; they are like *ravens* between heaven and earth." The powerless idols are compared to the ravens, who have no power when they are flying in the air. Although the Letter of Jeremiah does not speak about Abram, the connection is easily made, since the letter describes the situation of Babel and the Chaldeans.[69]

To sum up, it can be said that the rewriting of Genesis in the book of *Jubilees* can be seen in terms of the principle that the author of *Jubilees* omits those elements of Genesis that he considers redundant, adds what he thinks is missing in the biblical text, and varies and rearranges what he thinks he has to. The omissions either do not add anything to the story line (e.g., doublets) or they create tensions in the story (e.g., inconsistencies) with other biblical stories or with certain interpretations of a story. The variations and rearrangement also solve tensions and inconsistencies. The additions can be a consequence of gaps in Genesis, or of tensions and inconsistencies in the biblical story, or between several biblical stories, between a story and a certain interpretation of it. However, by making these additions the author is also able to interpret and actualize the text of Genesis in a way that might have its basis in the biblical text, but

---

68. For the development of this tradition, mostly from somewhat later sources, see Pseudo-Eupolemus (*Praeparatio Evangelica* 9.17.2-9; 9.18.2); *Orphica* (25-31; long recension); Philo, *Abraham* 68-88; *Migration* 176ff.; *Dreams* 1.44ff., etc.; Josephus, *Ant.* 1.7.1-2; Pseudo-Philo, *L.A.B.* 6–7; *Apoc. Abr.* 1–8; Acts 7:2-4; *Tg. Neof.* on Gen 11:28, 31; 15:7; and *Tg. Ps.-J. (passim)*. Cf. Roitman, "The Traditions about Abraham's Early Life," 74; Nickelsburg, "Abraham the Convert," 159-71; Kugel, *The Bible As It Was*, 133-48.

69. Cory D. Crawford, "On the Exegetical Function of the Abraham/Ravens Tradition in Jubilees 11," *HTR* 97 (2004): 91-97 (esp. 96), suggests that the raven tradition, before it was integrated into *Jubilees*, served as an explanation for the odd use of the word "raven" in Ep Jer 53.

which is independent of it. I would tend to conclude that the author of *Jubilees* was a careful reader of Genesis, and that he tried to reproduce the story of Genesis as faithfully as possible, though without the tensions and inconsistencies that are in the biblical story. At the same time, he weaves elements into the main story line that are not available in Genesis but that have been derived from early Judaic circles and which can sometimes be traced to other sources.

BIBLIOGRAPHY

Adler, William. "Abraham and the Burning of the Temple of Idols: Jubilees' Traditions in Christian Chronography." *JQR* 77 (1986-87): 95-11.

Albani, Matthias, Jörg Frey, and Armin Lange, eds. *Studies in the Book of Jubilees.* TSAJ 65. Tübingen: Mohr Siebeck, 1997.

Albeck, Chanoch. *Das Buch der Jubiläen und die Halacha.* Berlin: Scholem, 1930.

Alexander, Philip S. "Retelling the Old Testament." In *It Is Written — Scripture Citing Scripture: Essays in Honour of Barnabas Lindars,* ed. D. A. Carson and H. G. M. Williamson. Cambridge: Cambridge University Press, 1988, 99-121.

Berger, Klaus. *Das Buch der Jubiläen.* JSHRZ, V. 3. Gütersloh: Gütersloher, 1981.

Brock, Sebastian P. "Abraham and the Ravens: A Syriac Counterpart to Jubilees 11–12 and Its Implications." *JSJ* 9 (1978): 135-52.

Charles, Robert H. *The Ethiopic Version of the Hebrew Book of Jubilees.* Anecdota Oxoniensia 8. Oxford: Clarendon, 1895.

———. *The Book of Jubilees, or the Little Genesis: Translated from the Ethiopic Text.* London: SPCK, 1917.

Crawford, Cory D. "On the Exegetical Function of the Abraham/Ravens Tradition in Jubilees 11." *HTR* 97 (2004): 91-97.

Davenport, Gene L. *The Eschatology of the Book of Jubilees.* StPB 20. Leiden: Brill, 1971.

Dillmann, August. "Das Buch der Jubiläen oder die kleine Genesis." *JBW* 2 (1850): 230-56; 3 (1851): 1-96.

Endres, John C. *Biblical Interpretation in the Book of Jubilees.* CBQMS 18. Washington: Catholic Biblical Association, 1987.

Grelot, Pierre. "Le Livre des Jubilés et le Testament de Lévi." In *Mélanges Dominiques Barthélemy: Études bibliques offertes à l'occasion de son 60ᵉ anniversaire,* ed. Pierre Casetti, Othmar Keel, and Adrian Schenker, 109-31. OBO 38. Göttingen, 1981.

Halpern-Amaru, Betsy. *Rewriting the Bible: Land and Covenant in Post-biblical Jewish Literature.* Valley Forge: Trinity Press International, 1994.

———. *The Empowerment of Women in the Book of Jubilees.* JSJSup 60. Leiden: Brill, 1999.

———. "Burying the Fathers: Exegetical Strategies and Source Traditions in Jubilees 46." In *Reworking the Bible: Apocryphal and Related Texts at Qumran. Proceedings of a Joint Symposium by the Orion Center for the Study of the Dead Sea Scrolls and Associated Literature and the Hebrew University Institute for Advanced Studies Research Group on Qumran, 15-17 January 2002,* ed. Esther G. Chazon, Devora Dimant, and Ronald E. Clements, 135-52. STDJ 58. Leiden: Brill, 2005.

Hanneken, Todd Russell. "Angels and Demons in the Book of Jubilees and Contemporary Apocalypses." *Hen* 28 (2006): 11-25.

Knibb, Michael A. "Jubilees and the Origins of the Qumran Community." Inaugural Lecture, King's College. London, 1989.

Knowles, Michael P. "Abram and the Birds in Jubilees 11: A Subtext for the Parable of the Sower?" *NTS* 41 (1995): 145-51.

Koskenniemi, Erkki. *The Old Testament Miracle-Workers in Early Judaism*. WUNT ser. 2, 206. Tübingen: Mohr Siebeck, 2005.

Kugel, James L. "Levi's Election to the Priesthood in Second Temple Writings." *HTR* 86 (1993): 1-64.

Littmann, Enno. "Das Buch der Jubiläen." In *Die Apokryphen und Pseudepigraphen des Alten Testaments*, ed. Emil F. Kautzsch. Tübingen: Mohr, 1900, 2:31-119. Repr. Darmstadt, 1975.

Milik, Jósef T. "4Q Visions de Amram et une citation d'Origèn." *RB* (1972): 77-97.

Müller, Karlheinz. "Die hebräische Sprache der Halacha als Textur der Schöpfung: Beobachtungen zum Verhältnis von Tora und Halacha im Buch der Jubiläen." In *Bibel in jüdischer und christlicher Tradition: Festschrift für Johann Maier zum 60. Geburtstag*, ed. Helmut Merklein, Müller, and Günter Stemberger. BBB 38. Frankfurt a/M: Hain, 1993, 157-76.

Najman, Hindy. "Interpretation as Primordial Writing: Jubilees and Its Authority Conferring Strategies." *JSJ* 30 (1999): 379-410.

———. *Seconding Sinai: The Development of Mosaic Discourse in Second Temple Judaism*. JSJSup 77. Leiden: Brill, 2003.

Nickelsburg, George W. E. "Abraham the Convert: A Jewish Tradition and Its Use by the Apostle Paul." In *Biblical Figures Outside the Bible*, ed. Michael E. Stone and Theodore A. Bergren. Harrisburg: Trinity Press International, 1998, 151-75.

Roitman, Adolfo. "The Traditions about Abraham's Early Life in the Book of Judith (5:6-9)." In *Things Revealed: Studies in Early Jewish and Christian Literature in Honor of Michael E. Stone*, ed. Esther G. Chazon, David Satran, and Ruth A. Clements. JSJSup 89. Leiden: Brill, 2004, 73-87.

Rönsch, Hermann. *Das Buch der Jubiläen: oder, Die kleine Genesis; unter Beifügung des revidierten Textes der in der Ambrosiana aufgefundenen lateinischen Fragmente*. Leipzig: Fues, 1874. Repr. Amsterdam: Rodopi, 1970.

Rook, John. "The Names of the Wives from Adam to Abraham in the Book of Jubilees." *JSP* 7 (1990): 105-17.

Ruiten, Jacques T. A. G. M. van. *Primaeval History Interpreted: The Rewriting of Genesis 1–11 in the Book of Jubilees*. JSJSup 66. Leiden: Brill, 2000.

———. "Abraham, Job and the Book of Jubilees: The Intertextual Relationship of Genesis 22:1-19, Job 1:1–2:13, and Jubilees 17:15–18:19." In *The Sacrifice of Isaac: The Aqedah (Genesis 22) and Its Interpretations*, ed. Ed Noort and Eibert Tigchelaar. TBN 7. Leiden: Brill, 2002, 58-85.

———. "Lot versus Abraham: The Interpretation of Genesis 18:1–19:38 in Jubilees 16:1-9." In *Sodom's Sin: Genesis 18–19 and Its Interpretation*, ed. Ed Noort and Eibert J. C. Tigchelaar. TBN 7. Leiden: Brill, 2004, 29-46.

———. "The Birth of Moses in Egypt according to the *Book of Jubilees* (*Jub* 47.1-9)." In *The*

Wisdom of Egypt: Jewish, Early Christian, and Gnostic Essays in Honour of Gerard P. Luttikhuizen, ed. George H. van Kooten and Anthony Hilhorst. AGJU 59. Leiden: Brill, 2005, 43-66.

———. "Between Jacob's Death and Moses' Birth: The Intertextual Relationship between Genesis 50:15–Exodus 1:14 and *Jubilees* 46:1-16." In *Flores Florentino: Dead Sea Scrolls and Other Early Jewish Studies in Honour of Florentino García Martínez,* ed. Anthony Hilhorst, Émile Puech, and Eibert J. C. Tigchelaar. JSJSup 122. Leiden: Brill, 2007, 467-89.

Sacchi, Paolo. "Libro dei Giubilei." In *Apocrifi dell'Antico Testamento,* 1. Turin: Unione tipografico-editrice torinese, 1981, 179-411.

Schaller, Berndt. "Gen. 1.2 im antiken Judentum: Untersuchungen über Verwendung und Deutung der Schöpfungsaussagen von Gen 1.2 im antiken Judentum." Diss., Göttingen, 1961.

Schwarz, Eberhard. *Identität durch Abgrenzung: Abgrenzungsprozesse in Israel im 2. Vor-christlichen Jahrhundert und ihre traditionsgeschichtliche Voraussetzungen: Zugleich ein Beitrag zur Erforschung des Jubiläenbuches.* Europäische Hochschulschriften, ser. 23, 162. Frankfurt am Main: Lang, 1982.

Scott, James M. *Geography in Early Judaism and Christianity: The Book of Jubilees.* SNTSMS 113. Cambridge: Cambridge University Press, 2002.

———. *On Earth as in Heaven: The Restoration of Sacred Time and Sacred Space in the Book of Jubilees.* JSJSup 91. Leiden: Brill, 2005.

Segal, Michael. *The Book of Jubilees: Rewritten Bible, Redaction, Ideology and Theology.* JSJSup 117. Leiden: Brill, 2007.

Stone, Michael E. "The Book(s) Attributed to Noah." *DSD* 13 (2006): 4-23.

VanderKam, James C. "Enoch Traditions in Jubilees and Other Second-Century Sources." *SBLSP* 1 (1978): 229-51. Repr. in *From Revelation to Canon: Studies in the Hebrew Bible and Second Temple Literature.* JSJSup 62. Leiden: Brill, 2000, 305-31.

———. *The Book of Jubilees: A Critical Text.* 2 vols. CSCO 510-11. Scriptores Aethiopici 87-88. Leuven: Peeters, 1989.

———. "Biblical Interpretation in 1 Enoch and Jubilees." In *The Pseudepigrapha and Early Biblical Interpretation,* ed. James H. Charlesworth and Craig A. Evans. JSPSup 14. Sheffield: Sheffield Academic, 1993, 96-125.

———. "Genesis 1 in Jubilees 2." *DSD* 1 (1994): 300-321.

———. "The *Aqedah,* Jubilees, and PseudoJubilees." In *The Quest for Context and Meaning: Studies in Biblical Intertextuality in Honor of James A. Sanders,* ed. Craig A. Evans and Shemaryahu Talmon. Biblical Interpretation 28 (Leiden: Brill, 1997), 241-61.

———. *Calendars in the Dead Sea Scrolls: Measuring Time.* The Literature of the Dead Sea Scrolls. London: Routledge, 1998.

———. "Studies in the Chronology of the Book of Jubilees." In *From Revelation to Canon: Studies in the Hebrew Bible and Second Temple Literature.* JSJSup 62. Leiden: Brill, 2000, 522-44.

———. *The Book of Jubilees.* Guides to Apocrypha and Pseudepigrapha. Sheffield: Sheffield Academic, 2001.

———. "Questions of Canon Viewed through the Dead Sea Scrolls." *BBR* 11 (2001): 269-92.

————. "The Scriptural Setting of the Book of Jubilees." *DSD* 13 (2006): 61-72.

Wacholder, Ben Zion. "Jubilees as the Super Canon: Torah-Admonition versus Torah-Commandment." In *Legal Texts and Legal Issues: Proceedings of the Second Meeting of the International Organization for Qumran Studies, Cambridge 1995, Published in Honour of Joseph M. Baumgarten,* ed. Moshe Bernstein, Florentino García Martínez, and John Kampen. STDJ 23. Leiden: Brill, 1997, 195-211.

Weitzman, Steve. "Why Did the Qumran Community Write in Hebrew?" *JAOS* 119 (1999): 35-45.

Wiesenberg, Ernest. "The Jubilee of Jubilees." *RevQ* 3 (1961): 3-40.

Zakovitch, Yair. "The Exodus from Ur of the Chaldeans: A Chapter in Literary Archaelogy." In *Ki Baruch Hu: Ancient Near Eastern, Biblical, and Judaic Studies in Honor of Baruch A. Levine,* ed. Robert Chazan, William W. Hallo, and Lawrence H. Schiffman. Winona Lake: Eisenbrauns, 1999, 429-39.

The *Genesis Apocryphon:*
Compositional and Interpretive Perspectives

Moshe J. Bernstein

The *Genesis Apocryphon,* one of the first seven scrolls to be discovered in Cave 1 at Qumran and the last of them to be unrolled and published, is an Aramaic text surviving in a single fragmentary copy whose broad framework is the narratives of Genesis 5–15.[1] It is composed of several segments that were probably derived from originally discrete sources (see below, "Sources") and that have been shaped, with little attempt to conceal their diverse natures, into a composition that retells the stories in that portion of the Hebrew Bible. Despite the consecutive nature of the material, it is not all cut from the same cloth, and the nature and type of the biblical interpretation that it contains varies from section to section. It was already clear when only columns 2 and 19-22 were published that column 2, a scene between Lamech and his wife Bitenosh following the birth of Noah, was related to the Bible in a way very different from columns 19-22 that described the adventures of Abram from his entry to Egypt with Sarai (Gen 12:10) through the beginning of his vision following the war of the four kings vs. the five (Gen 15:4). The former material was largely extrabiblical, while the latter adhered closely to the biblical narrative with the insertion of a variety of expansions, some large and some small.[2] The very fragmentary portions of the text which could not be read

---

1. The *editio princeps,* containing the Aramaic text of cols. 2 and 19-22 with English and Modern Hebrew translation, photographs, and introductory material, some of which deals with the unpublished columns, is Nahman Avigad and Yigael Yadin, *A Genesis Apocryphon: A Scroll from the Wilderness of Judaea* (Jerusalem: Magnes and Heikhal ha-Sefer, 1956). The currently regnant commentary is Joseph A. Fitzmyer, *The Genesis Apocryphon of Qumran Cave 1 (1Q20): A Commentary.* 3rd ed. BibOr 18B (Rome: Pontifical Biblical Institute, 2004).

2. The original editors actually wrote (38), "The work is evidently a literary unit in style and structure, though for the reasons referred to above, it may perhaps be divisible into books — a Book of Lamech, a Book of Enoch, a Book of Noah, a Book of Abraham."

and presented by its original editors were deciphered and published in the 1990s.[3]

Structure

It would appear that the surviving material of the *Apocryphon* can be divided into at least three sections, 0–5:25 (Lamech);[4] 5:26–18:24 (Noah);[5] 18:25–22:34 (Abram), with the only doubtful segmentation pertaining to the first one: Was there only a single section before the "book of the words of Noah" in column 5? Might there have been a division within columns 0-5 or what preceded them? How should we characterize that first section, even as it stands now? We can surely understand why Nahman Avigad and Yigael Yadin referred to it as the "book of Lamech," even though that name might not be appropriate for the earlier section that involved the Watchers, or for the significant portion where Enoch plays a major role. Esther Eshel has suggested that the whole first section should be associated specifically with Enoch as its hero,[6] but it is not at all clear

3. Jonas C. Greenfield and Elisha Qimron, "The Genesis Apocryphon Col. XII," in *Studies in Qumran Aramaic*, ed. Takamitsu Muraoka. AbrNSup 3 (Leuven: Peeters, 1992), 70-77; and Matthew Morgenstern, Elisha Qimron, and Daniel Sivan, "The Hitherto Unpublished Columns of the Genesis Apocryphon," *AbrN* 33 (1995): 30-54. From the recent work on the Apocryphon, Daniel A. Machiela, *The Dead Sea Scrolls Genesis Apocryphon: A New Text and Translation with Introduction and Special Treatment of Columns 13-17.* STDJ 79 (Leiden: Brill, 2009); and the chapters on the *Apocryphon* in Daniel K. Falk, *Parabiblical Texts: Strategies for Extending the Scriptures among the Dead Sea Scrolls.* CQS 8. LSTS 63 (London: T. & T. Clark, 2007); and Sidnie White Crawford, *Rewriting Scripture in Second Temple Times.* SDSSRL (Grand Rapids: Eerdmans, 2008) are worthy of special mention.

4. The rather unusual label column 0 is employed for the fragments of the *Apocryphon* that extend to the right of what had been referred to as column 1 since the initial publication, based on the arrangement of the pieces of 1Q20. This designation, which has been adopted by all current students of the *Apocryphon,* was suggested by Michael Wise and Bruce Zuckerman when they presented this data at the 1991 SBL meeting.

5. Armin Lange has pointed out ("1QGenAp XIX 10–XX 32 as Paradigm of the Wisdom Didactic Narrative," in *Qumranstudien: Vorträge und Beiträge der Teilnehmer des Qumranseminars auf dem internationalen Treffen der Society of Biblical Literature, Münster, 25.-26. Juli 1993*, ed. Heinz-Josef Fabry, Lange, and Hermann Lichtenberger [Göttingen: Vandenhoeck & Ruprecht, 1996], 192, n. 10) that there is a one-and-a-half line *vacat* before 18:25 that very likely marks the beginning of the Abram material. Unfortunately we do not have any idea whether or not the section began with a heading such as "book of the words of Abram."

6. Most recently in "The Genesis Apocryphon: A Chain of Traditions," *The Dead Sea Scrolls and Contemporary Culture: Proceedings of the International Conference held at the Israel Museum, Jerusalem (July 6-8, 2008),* ed. Adolfo D. Roitman, Lawrence H. Schiffman, and Shani L. (Berrin) Tzoref. STDJ 93 (Leiden: Brill, 2010), 184.

to me that Enoch is the main figure in the surviving material, and I believe that we must exercise a good deal of caution when making assertions about a text that is as fragmentary as columns 0-5. Daniel Falk's position is also a bit too certain, in my judgment: "it is preferable to view the *Genesis Apocryphon* — at least as preserved for us — as structured around two stories: a Noah cycle and an Abram cycle. The Lamech section is best seen as part of the Noah cycle, and its purpose is to more fully place the story of Noah in the context of the sons of God myth from Gen. 6.1-5."[7] The presence of the clear marker, "the book of the words of Noah,"[8] however, seems to suggest that the composer saw that which preceded it as belonging to a different unit.

The way in which the author tells the story is quite striking.[9] The largest portion of 0-21 is told in the first person by whoever is the major character "on-stage" at a given moment, although there is some material, particularly in the section of the division of the earth among Noah's children, which is fairly clearly third person narrative.[10] The last column and a fraction, beginning with the equivalent of Gen 14:1, are completely in the third person, probably because Abram, the narrator at that point, is "off-stage" for the initial portion of that section.

Despite the fact that we can see lines of demarcation between the three segments, there is no question that the *Apocryphon* is intended by its final author/composer to be read as a unified whole; it is not a "collection" of stories placed side by side. By employing language that is borrowed from the Abram narrative for God's address to Noah, there is a clear attempt to link their stories.[11] Certain motifs, furthermore, recur in more than one section and may owe their presence to the interests of the final author/composer: The married couples Bitenosh and Lamech and Sarai and Abram engage in extrabiblical dialogue.[12] Revelatory vi-

---

7. Falk, *Parabiblical Texts*, 30.

8. Cf. Richard C. Steiner, "The Heading of the *Book of the Words of Noah* on a Fragment of the Genesis Apocryphon: New Light on a 'Lost' Work," *DSD* 2 (1995): 66-71.

9. The use of the term "author" is for the sake of convenience, in order not to have to write constantly "author/editor/compiler/redactor/scribe"; it is not by any means intended to imply a single hand.

10. 16:12, 21; 17:15 and 22. Falk, *Parabiblical Texts*, 30, is among several to point out that 5:24-25 indicates an "impersonal narrator" as well.

11. See below, pp. 174-75 and n. 61.

12. Cf. George W. E. Nickelsburg, "Patriarchs Who Worry About Their Wives: A Haggadic Tendency in the Genesis Apocryphon," in *Biblical Perspectives: Early Use and Interpretation of the Bible in the Light of the Dead Sea Scrolls: Proceedings of the First International Symposium of the Orion Center for the Study of the Dead Sea Scrolls and Associated Literature, 12-14 May 1996*, ed. Michael E. Stone and Esther G. Chazon. STDJ 28 (Leiden: Brill, 1998), 137-58; repr. in *George W. E. Nickelsburg in Perspective: An Ongoing Dialogue of Learning*, ed. Jacob Neusner and Alan J.

sions are vouchsafed to both Noah and Abram. Geography plays a significant role in both the Noah and Abram segments. Whereas these commonalities are not sufficient, in my view, to obliterate the very clear lines of demarcation that we have observed between the segments, they do serve to give the reader a perspective of continuity and sequentiality, indicating that the work was conceived of as a unified whole, meant to be read from beginning to end.[13]

Sources and Relationship with Other Second Temple Literature

It is clear that the *Genesis Apocryphon* was not composed by its author without resource to earlier material or compositions. What are debatable, however, are the identity, nature, and number of the earlier sources, whether they were written or oral, and how much of the final product we can attribute to the final "author" of the *Apocryphon* as opposed to his sources. Some of the time, furthermore, we cannot even be certain whether the *Apocryphon* derives from another ancient work or whether it is the source for it.

The two most prominent extant works that have been linked to the *Apocryphon* are *1 Enoch* and *Jubilees*.[14] These links were noted already by the initial editors: "We may confidently emphasize the close connection between the scroll and many parts of the *Book of Enoch* and the *Book of Jubilees,* leading at times to the conclusion that *the scroll may have served as a source for a number of stories told more concisely in those two books*" [emphasis in the original].[15] Current scholarship on the book of *Enoch* would not allow for such a sequence, and, although most scholars would date *Jubilees* earlier than the *Apocryphon,* the question of which of those documents has chronological priority is currently being debated once again. Falk writes that on the whole "in comparison with *Jubilees,* the version in the *Genesis Apocryphon* looks secondary. We can

Avery-Peck. JSJSup 80 (Leiden: Brill, 2003), 1:177-99, with a response by Eileen M. Schuller (200-212), to which Nickelsburg then offered a rejoinder (213-15).

13. Cf. Moshe J. Bernstein, "Is the Genesis Apocryphon a Unity? What Sort of Unity Were You Looking For?" *Aramaic Studies* 8 (2010): 107-34.

14. See Falk, *Parabiblical Texts,* 96-100, for lists of parallels with both works and brief discussion regarding "whether these are to be explained by direct textual relations, use of common textual sources, or more general common traditions" (96). For parallels with *Enoch,* see further, George W. E. Nickelsburg, *Jewish Literature Between the Bible and the Mishnah: A Historical and Literary Introduction.* 2nd ed. (Minneapolis: Fortress, 2005), 174-76.

15. Avigad and Yadin, *A Genesis Apocryphon,* 38. One of the best examples of shared material is the story of Noah's birth in col. 2 of the *Apocryphon* and in *1 Enoch* 106-7. Nickelsburg writes, *Jewish Literature,* 174, "As to the relationship between the two stories, it is likely that the Genesis Apocryphon represents a rewriting of the story in 1 Enoch 106-107."

thus safely rule out the possibility that the *Genesis Apocryphon* was a source for *Jubilees*."[16] Scholars such as Cana Werman and Esther Eshel, among others, maintain the view that the *Apocryphon* is earlier than *Jubilees*.[17] On the other hand, there are scholars who adopt a middle position, claiming that since we are dealing with traditions which may very well have been orally transmitted, it is impossible to assert literary precedence for one of the works or the other.[18]

Daniel Machiela, in the introductory section of his book, presents the most comprehensive recent survey of the *status quaestionis* of the *Enoch-Apocryphon* and *Jubilees-Apocryphon* relationships (with either work influencing the other or both drawing from common sources), being careful to separate the *Enoch* and *Jubilees* questions from one another.[19] There he concludes regarding *Enoch*, "the relationship between these texts remains highly debatable,"[20] while about *Jubilees* he writes, "the current evidence appears to point toward the priority of the Apocryphon or to the common source theory."[21] Returning to this issue in his conclusion, however, he goes a step further, asserting that "the most logical conclusion seems to be that the Genesis Apocryphon preserves the stories [of the birth of Noah and geographical material, MJB] in their original setting, while Jubilees and 1 Enoch do not. If this is to be judged the case, we have perhaps the strongest argument yet for the preliminary suggestion of Avigad and Yadin that the Apocryphon is an earlier witness to these accounts than other known works."[22]

16. Falk, *Parabiblical Texts*, 99.

17. Cana Werman, "Qumran and the Book of Noah," in *Pseudepigraphic Perspectives: The Apocrypha and Pseudepigrapha in Light of the Dead Sea Scrolls: Proceedings of the Second International Symposium of the Orion Center for the Study of the Dead Sea Scrolls and Associated Literature, 12-14 January, 1997*, ed. Esther G. Chazon and Michael E. Stone. STDJ 31 (Leiden: Brill, 1999), 172, writes: "the author of Jubilees was acquainted with the Genesis Apocryphon and even made use of it." Cf. also 173-77. Eshel has made this claim most recently in "Chain of Traditions," 185-86, 190.

18. Loren T. Stuckenbruck, "The Lamech Narrative in the Genesis Apocryphon (1QapGen) and Birth of Noah (4QEnoch[c] ar): A Tradition-Historical Study," in *Aramaica Qumranica: The Aix-en-Provence Colloquium on the Aramaic Dead Sea Scrolls*, ed. Katell Berthelot and Daniel Stökl Ben Ezra. STDJ 94 (Leiden: Brill, 2010), 253-71, adopts this view regarding the Noah material in *Enoch* and the *Apocryphon*, modifying the position that he had adopted in *1 Enoch 91-108*. CEJL (Berlin: de Gruyter, 2007), 613.

19. Machiela, *The Genesis Apocryphon*, 8-17.

20. Machiela, *The Genesis Apocryphon*, 13.

21. Machiela, *The Genesis Apocryphon*, 16-17. At the conclusion of his discussion of the geographical material in the *Apocryphon* and *Jubilees*, he reaffirms that view, "the nature of the parallel passages treated in this chapter points toward the Apocryphon as the earlier of our two works."

22. Machiela, *The Genesis Apocryphon*, 141.

An even more vexed question is the one regarding the "Book of Noah": Did it ever exist, and, if it did, was it a source for the *Apocryphon*?[23] Florentino García Martínez, acknowledging that most scholars assume that the *Apocryphon* is dependent on *Jubilees*, claims that "the text of the *Genesis Apocryphon* cols. I-XVII contains a summary of the lost *Book of Noah* which is independent of *Jubilees*."[24] If the heading in column 5 of the *Apocryphon* is an indication that such a work existed, we should be careful to recall that the critical story of Noah's birth and the predictions about his future did not belong to that work.[25]

I have shown in a recent article that the ways in which the *Apocryphon* refers to God in Part I (cols. 0-17) and Part II (cols. 19-22) differ, with the former section being similar to *Enoch* and the latter to *Jubilees*, and this dichotomous behavior leads me to see the *Apocryphon* as subsequent to both *Enoch* and *Jubilees*.[26] James L. Kugel, moreover, has recently argued convincingly (in my view), based on comparative exegetical motifs in the two works, that the *Apocryphon* represents, in each and every one of about ten cases, a more developed and expansive way of working the biblical story than does *Jubilees*.[27] I therefore believe that Falk is justified in writing, "There is no definitive evidence, however, that the *Genesis Apocryphon* was dependent on a textual Noah source beyond

---

23. Regarding this work, see Florentino García Martínez, "4QMess Ar and the Book of Noah," in *Qumran and Apocalyptic: Studies on the Aramaic Texts from Qumran*. STDJ 9 (Leiden: Brill, 1992), 1-44; Devorah Dimant, "Noah in Early Jewish Literature," in *Biblical Figures Outside the Bible*, ed. Michael E. Stone and Theodore A. Bergren (Harrisburg: Trinity Press International, 1998), 123-50; Werman, "Qumran and the Book of Noah," 171-81; Moshe J. Bernstein, "Noah and the Flood at Qumran," in *The Provo International Conference on the Dead Sea Scrolls: New Texts, Reformulated Issues and Technological Innovations*, ed. Donald W. Parry and Eugene Ulrich. STDJ 30 (Leiden: Brill, 1999), 199-231 (esp. 226-31); Michael E. Stone, "The Book(s) Attributed to Noah," *DSD* 13 (2006): 4-23; and Dimant, "Two 'Scientific' Fictions: The So-called Book of Noah and the Alleged Quotation of Jubilees in CD 16:3-4," in *Studies in the Hebrew Bible, Qumran, and the Septuagint presented to Eugene Ulrich*, ed. Peter W. Flint, Emanuel Tov, and James C. VanderKam. VTSup 101 (Leiden: Brill, 2006), 230-49 (231-42).

24. García Martínez, "4QMess Ar and the Book of Noah," 40.

25. Cf. Steiner, "The Heading of the *Book of the Words of Noah*," 69. Falk, *Parabiblical Texts*, 100, follows this reasoning as well. García Martínez, 40-41, explicitly insists that Noah's birth story belongs to the "Book of Noah."

26. Moshe J. Bernstein, "Divine Titles and Epithets and the Sources of the Genesis Apocryphon," *JBL* 128 (2009): 291-310.

27. James L. Kugel, "Which Is Older, Jubilees or the Genesis Apocryphon? An Exegetical Approach," in Roitman, Schiffman, and Tzoref, *The Dead Sea Scrolls and Contemporary Culture*, 257-94. My thanks to Professor Kugel for allowing me to see his full paper in prepublication form. His conclusions dovetail well with a remark by Fitzmyer, *The Genesis Apocryphon*, 21: "One gets the impression that scanty details in Genesis, 1 *Enoch*, or *Jubilees* are here utilized in an independent way and filled out with imaginative additions."

1 Enoch (primarily 106–107 for the birth of Noah) and a *Jubilees* narrative, supplemented with the author's own interpretation and haggadic expansion of Genesis."[28] We should recall, however, that the absence of definitive evidence does not imply that we can assert that there were no other sources employed.

Genre[29]

The initial editors of this text, Avigad and Yadin, correctly saw it as being associated with the rest of Second Temple literature.[30] But many, if not most, of the scholars who studied the text attempted to classify it, despite its earlier date, against the background of the later rabbinic Jewish literature that was more familiar to them. The two categories into which the *Apocryphon* was most commonly placed were targum,[31] since after all it contains some biblical text translated into Aramaic, and midrash,[32] since after all it expands and interprets the

28. Falk, *Parabiblical Texts,* 101. I should not go as far as Falk, however, in suggesting that the author of the *Apocryphon* knew a "proto-*Jubilees* narrative without the laws."

29. Broad discussions of the genre of the *Apocryphon* can be found in Fitzmyer, *The Genesis Apocryphon,* 16-25; Craig A. Evans, "The Genesis Apocryphon and the Rewritten Bible," *RevQ* 13 (1988): 153-65; Falk, *Parabiblical Texts,* 41-42; Machiela, "The Genesis Apocryphon," 5-13. My own most recent treatment appears in "The Genre(s) of the Genesis Apocryphon," in Berthelot and Stökl Ben Ezra, *Aramaica Qumranica,* 317-38, to which this section is heavily indebted.

30. Avigad and Yadin, *A Genesis Apocryphon,* 38.

31. E.g., Manfred R. Lehmann, "1Q Genesis Apocryphon in the Light of the Targumim and Midrashim," *RevQ* 1 (1958-59): 249-63; Gerald J. Kuiper, "A Study of the Relationship between A Genesis Apocryphon and the Pentateuchal Targumim in Genesis 14₁-₁₂," in *In memoriam Paul Kahle,* ed. Matthew Black and Georg Fohrer. BZAW 103 (Berlin: Töpelmann, 1968), 149-61; Pierre Grelot, "De *l'Apocryphe de la Genèse* aux *Targoums:* sur Genèse 14,18-20," in *Intertestamental Essays in Honour of Józef Tadeusz Milik,* ed. Zdzislaw J. Kapera (Kraków: Enigma, 1992), 77-90. Matthew Black (although initially referring to the *Apocryphon* as "targum" [Kuiper, 149]) later favored "midrash" over "targum" for the *Apocryphon* in *An Aramaic Approach to the Gospels and Acts,* 3rd ed. (Oxford: Clarendon, 1967), 40. My views on the larger question of the *Apocryphon* and the targumim will appear in "The Genesis Apocryphon and the Aramaic *Targumim* Revisited: A View from Both Perspectives," in *The Dead Sea Scrolls in Context: Integrating the Dead Sea Scrolls in the Study of Ancient Texts, Languages, and Cultures,* ed. Armin Lange, Emanuel Tov, and Matthias Weigold. VTSup 140 (Leiden: Brill, 2011), 2:651-71. Cf. also Thierry Legrand, "Exégèses targumiques et techniques de réécriture dans l'Apocryphe de la Genèse (1QapGen ar)," in Berthelot and Stökl Ben Ezra, *Aramaica Qumranica,* 225-48.

32. E.g., André Dupont-Sommer, *Les Écrits Esséniens Découverts près de la Mer Morte,* 3rd ed. (Paris: Payot, 1968), 293; Eng. trans. *The Essene Writings from Qumran* (Oxford: Blackwell, 1961), 280; Hubert Lignée, trans. and comm., "L'Apocryphe de la Genèse," in *Les Textes de Qumran traduits et annotés,* ed. Jean Carmignac et al. (Paris: Létouzey et Ané, 1963), 2:210-15; Addison G. Wright, "The Literary Genre Midrash (Part Two)," *CBQ* 28 (1966): 425-26.

biblical text in ways similar to that later rabbinic form. Joseph Fitzmyer, however, dismisses both of these potential categories, writing, "It is not simply a *midrash,* just as it is not simply a *targum.*"[33]

When it became clear that those preexisting generic rubrics did not fit the *Apocryphon,* new ones were sought. Many scholars have adopted, and some still retain, Geza Vermes's assignment of the *Apocryphon* to the genre "rewritten Bible," described as "a substantial narrative where the midrashist inserts haggadic development into the biblical narrative — an exegetical process which is probably as ancient as scriptural interpretation itself."[34] More recently, there has been a growing reluctance among some scholars to employ the terms "Bible" or "biblical" in descriptions of works from the Second Temple period, and looser terms such as "parabiblical" have been suggested.[35] My own preference is for generic descriptions to be as tight as possible, and I believe that "parabiblical" is best used for works that are less tightly bound to the Bible than are *Jubilees* or the *Genesis Apocryphon.*[36]

My own difficulty with categorizing the *Apocryphon* as "rewritten Bible," however, has nothing to do with my dissatisfaction with the term as a generic classification, but derives rather from the fact that the *Apocryphon* is a composite work. It therefore must be acknowledged to be a very different sort of "rewritten Bible" from a work like *Jubilees,* or Pseudo-Philo's *Liber Antiquitatum Biblicarum,* or Josephus's *Jewish Antiquities,* each of which appears to have been composed by a single hand. As noted above, Part I and Part II appear related to two different sources, *Enoch* and *Jubilees* respectively, which themselves have very different relationships to the biblical text.[37] The second part conforms to my conception of "rewritten Bible," while the first is what I should call "parabiblical." As a result,

33. Fitzmyer, *The Genesis Apocryphon,* 19.

34. Geza Vermes, *Scripture and Tradition in Judaism: Haggadic Studies,* 2nd rev. ed. StPB 4. (Leiden: Brill, 1973), 95. I have discussed (and decried) the growing tendency to employ this term, if it is employed at all, much too broadly in "'Rewritten Bible': A Generic Category Which Has Outlived Its Usefulness?" *Text* 22 (2005): 169-96.

35. First suggested by Harold L. Ginsberg, in his review of Fitzmyer, *The Genesis Apocryphon,* in *TS* 28 (1967): 574. Falk, *Parabiblical Texts,* 41-42, also prefers this term, although with some hesitation, conceding that it "is even less suitable [than 'rewritten Bible'] as the name of a literary genre . . . and is best used as an umbrella for a wide range of texts of various genres generated centrifugally from Scripture." He concludes, "But it seems best not to regard either of these as specific literary genres."

36. This view is shared by White Crawford, *Rewriting Scripture,* 14, who excludes from "rewritten Scripture" (my "rewritten Bible") such "parabiblical" texts as *1 Enoch* or *Pseudo-Ezekiel,* which "use a passage, event, or character from a scriptural work as a 'jumping off' point to create a new narrative or work."

37. Cf. Bernstein, "Divine Titles and Epithets."

neither of those terms, in my view, is appropriate for the whole, and we need to search for a more suitable overarching category.[38] Esther Eshel has recently suggested the term "narrative midrash" for the *Apocryphon's* genre,[39] and the employment of the term "narrative" for this category may indeed be a step forward, but I remain among those who are reluctant to use the term "midrash" for prerabbinic material. Fortunately, the lack of an agreed-upon generic designation for the *Apocryphon* is only a minor obstacle to its analysis.

Language and Date

The date most frequently assigned to the language of the *Genesis Apocryphon* is the first century B.C.E., following the analysis of E. Y. Kutscher, with the manuscript itself being assigned to the late first century B.C.E. or early first century C.E.[40] Fitzmyer, agreeing with Kutscher's conclusions, on the whole, concludes, "the Aramaic of this scroll is a representative of Middle Aramaic [200 B.C.E.– 200 C.E., MJB] and forms a transition between Daniel and later Western Aramaic."[41] Machiela has recently resurveyed the evidence and suggested the possibility of a date of composition in the second century B.C.E.[42] The question whether the *Genesis Apocryphon* depends on *Jubilees* or vice versa, for example, adds a literary-historical dimension to the paleographical and linguistic issues, thus creating a problem with perhaps too many variables to be solved easily.[43]

38. At the Aix-en-Provence conference in 2008 I actually suggested referring to the *Apocryphon* as a *Mischgattung*.

39. "Chain of Traditions," 182. Her model is Rachel Adelman's proposal of that term for the later rabbinic text *Pirqe Rabbi Eliezer*.

40. Edward Y. Kutscher, "Dating the Language of the Genesis Apocryphon," *JBL* 76 (1957): 288-92; "The Language of the Genesis Apocryphon: A Preliminary Study," in *Aspects of the Dead Sea Scrolls*, ed. Chaim Rabin and Yigael Yadin. ScrHier 4 (Jerusalem: Magnes, 1958), 1-35. See the discussions in Fitzmyer, *The Genesis Apocryphon*, 26-37, and Machiela, *The Genesis Apocryphon*, 137-40. Scholars are careful, on the whole, to distinguish between the date of the manuscript and the date of composition.

41. Fitzmyer, *The Genesis Apocryphon*, 36.

42. Machiela, *The Genesis Apocryphon*, 140. On 142, he goes a step further, "A safe range would be 200-150 B.C.E., although an earlier date should not be ruled out absolutely."

43. So, e.g., White Crawford, *Rewriting Scripture*, 106, believing that the *Apocryphon* draws on *Enoch* and *Jubilees*, writes, "If we are correct, the Genesis Apocryphon's date of composition must be later than those for the earlier books of Enoch (third century B.C.E.) and Jubilees (mid-second century B.C.E.), which certainly accords with a date of composition for the Genesis Apocryphon in the early first century B.C.E." Machiela, *The Genesis Apocryphon*, 17, shows how closely the dating of the Apocryphon by modern scholars is tied to their assumptions about its relationship with *Enoch* and *Jubilees*, and it is notable that his own suggestion regarding an ear-

The *Genesis Apocryphon* and the Biblical Narrative

Macrostructure: Rewriting and Interpretation in Broad Focus

We shall begin our discussion with the ways in which the *Apocryphon* handles the larger elements of the structure of the biblical story and then proceed to the smaller details. We surely are not surprised when the author of the *Apocryphon* follows the sequence of the biblical narrative or includes its details since that is what we "expect." Not infrequently, however, the *Apocryphon* is willing to re-arrange and even to omit details of the biblical narrative. Sometimes the reasons for the deviation from biblical sequence appear clear either for exegetical or literary reasons, but on occasion the motivation is not so obvious. Omissions, likewise, cannot always be explained easily. What is significant is that both of these techniques indicate that the biblical order and contents are not always the most compelling factor for the *Apocryphon's* composer and that he feels free to manipulate the story as he chooses.

Rearrangement and Omission Although in Genesis the birth of Noah is de-scribed at the end of chapter 5, just before the verses which give rise to the stories of the "fallen angels," the *Apocryphon* locates the story of the Watchers before the birth of Noah.[44] The narrative logic of the presentation in the *Apocryphon* does not introduce Noah, who will be the savior of mankind, until after the Watchers, who are the threat to man, have appeared on the scene. The effect is to highlight Noah even more strongly than in the biblical story. Similarly, there are two major deviations from the biblical sequence of events in the narrative following the flood. In the Bible, Noah exits from the ark (Gen 8:15-19) and only then offers sacrifices (8:20-21). In the *Apocryphon,* he offers sacrifices after the ark rests on the mountaintop (10:12) while he is still on the ark (10:13); in the opening line of column 11, Noah is still at the entrance of the ark.[45] Perhaps the sacrifices are dis-

---

lier redating for the *Apocryphon* coincides with his claim regarding the chronological prece-dence of the *Apocryphon* to *Jubilees.*

44. This arrangement is found elsewhere in the works from the Second Temple period that expand the story of the Watchers (*Jub* 4:15 [in the days of Jared], *1 En.* 6:6 [= 4QEn^a ar 1 iii 4] and 106:13 [= 4QEn^c ar 5 ii 17-18]). The reordering could be "supported" exegetically by the reading of the verb of Gen 6:4, הנפלים היו בארץ בימים ההם, as a pluperfect.

45. Our inference is predicated on the ark's resting on the mountain being described for the first time in 10:12, and not somewhere earlier in the lost portion of the text. The possibility that these sacrifices on the ark are not parallel to the ones in Genesis, and that those took place later in the *Apocryphon,* is precluded by the fact that there is no room for the sacrifices of Gene-sis 8 in col. 11, which is parallel to Genesis 9.

placed so that the purification of the earth takes place before Noah leaves the ark, so that he and his fellow survivors would not immediately be rendered impure upon exit by their contact with the impure earth.[46] The *Apocryphon* also seems to have omitted (or to have displaced to later in column 10) the contents of Gen 8:5-14, including the sending out of the birds to see whether the earth has dried up. The motivation for this omission (or displacement) is not obvious.[47]

Finally for Part I of the *Apocryphon,* in Genesis the descendants of Noah are listed in chapter 10, but the *Apocryphon* shifts the position of that section to column 12 before presenting the story of Noah's vineyard that appears in Gen 9:20-27. Although due to the fragmentary nature of the manuscript we cannot tell how much more information the *Apocryphon* supplied about later generations of Noah's family, it is likely that this change is made to create a smoother narrative.[48] It appears, moreover, that the whole story of Noah's drunkenness followed by the blessing of Shem and Japhet and cursing of Canaan is omitted. The story of Noah's drinking followed by his sleep is transformed into a visionary event by the *Apocryphon,* and the result of the omission and alteration is the removal of the major blot on the character of Noah from the narrative.

Whereas we could not write a fairly close and *detailed* summary of the story in Genesis 5–10 on the basis of Part I of the *Apocryphon,* one could do so for Genesis 12–14 on the basis of Part II.[49] Almost all the details of the Genesis 12–14 narrative are significant for the retelling in Part II of the *Apocryphon,* except perhaps the treatment of the separation between Abram and Lot (Gen 13:5-12). The quarrel between the shepherds is reduced to an "incident" (21:5, עובד רעותנא), and the wickedness of Lot's new neighbors, the Sodomites (Gen 13:13), is omitted. Abram adds to Lot's possessions (21:6) and regrets their separation (21:7). The net result is to minimize the significance of the incident and to leave the reader with a higher opinion of Lot than is held by the reader of the biblical text.[50]

---

46. Cf. my "From the Watchers to the Flood: Story and Exegesis in the Early Columns of the *Genesis Apocryphon,*" in *Reworking the Bible: Apocryphal and Related Texts at Qumran,* ed. Esther G. Chazon, Devorah Dimant, and Ruth A. Clements. STDJ 58 (Leiden: Brill, 2005), 59-60.

47. *Jubilees* omits this element of the story as well, while 4Q252, Genesis Commentary A, includes the dove but omits the raven.

48. I analyze this rearrangement in "Re-Arrangement, Anticipation and Harmonization as Exegetical Features in the Genesis Apocryphon," *DSD* 3 (1996): 40-44, suggesting a number of ways in which it might have made the story flow better.

49. This point, of course, must acknowledge the very fragmentary nature of cols. 0-17.

50. Note that Lot is also given a significant, if minor, role in the liberation of Sarai from Pharaoh in col. 20, as opposed to the biblical narrative, where his presence is virtually unnoticed.

Addition and Supplementation   Located at the analytical pole opposite to omissions from the biblical story are the large supplements to the narrative found in the *Apocryphon*. Here we must distinguish between those supplements, even substantial ones, for which we can find a strong literary or exegetical motivation in the Bible and therefore refer to as "triggered," and those whose link to the biblical narrative is far more tenuous ("untriggered"). It will become clear in the course of this section that there is a dichotomy in the nature of the additions between Parts I and II of the *Apocryphon*.

In its surviving form, a very large fraction of Part I of the *Apocryphon* is devoted to material that is not found in the biblical narrative and that has only minimal connections to it. Thus the very fragmentary textual remains before column 2, which are linked to the "fallen angels" traditions that were so prominent in Second Temple literature, are tethered to the biblical text only through creative reading of Gen 6:1-4. The details of those stories, whether found in *1 Enoch, Jubilees,* or the *Apocryphon,* are fundamentally extraneous to the biblical narrative.[51] Likewise, the emotional scene between Lamech and his wife Bitenosh focusing on the parentage of their newborn son in column 2, the only fairly well-preserved one in Part I, is fundamentally unattached to the text of Genesis. It must be conceded that the vignette probably has as its springboard the word זֶה in Gen 5:29; the Hebrew demonstrative, "this one," is taken to mean a child of such miraculous or supernatural qualities that his father was led to suspect his mother's infidelity with one of the Watchers.[52] But once that textual stimulus has done its job, the dialogue as a whole, as well as the ensuing three columns (3-5) of very fragmentary conversation between Methuselah and Enoch, bears no real connection to the biblical text.[53]

---

51. Toward the end of col. 1, in the "Trever fragment" (so-called because it had been detached from the scroll in the late 1940s and remained in the possession of John Trever), the *Apocryphon* does use vocabulary that reminds us of the language used by Genesis to describe the antediluvian period: e.g., כול בשרא, "all flesh," appears twice, as does ארצא, "earth" or "land"; the equivalent Hebrew terms appear (the latter frequently) in Genesis 6 in the context of the depravity of man. But the occasional use of biblical language cannot conceal the fundamentally unbiblical nature of the story line.

52. Cf. James L. Kugel, *Traditions of the Bible: A Guide to the Bible as It Was at the Start of the Common Era* (Cambridge, Mass.: Harvard University Press, 1998), 218-19. The same impetus probably generates the depiction of the room being filled with light at Noah's birth in a very fragmentary Qumran Hebrew text (1Q19 3 4-5). Note that the dialogue of Lamech and Bitenosh is unparalleled in *1 Enoch* 106–7, which tells the same story, and is therefore likely to be a product of the creativity of the author of the *Apocryphon* (or of an intermediate source between *1 Enoch* and him).

53. If Enoch predicts to Methuselah in this section the imminent destruction of most of life on earth, it would be another significant departure in sequence from the biblical story, but the state of the manuscript makes the drawing of an inference too hazardous to venture.

Although the beginning of the Noah section of Part I (beginning with the words כתב מלי נוח, 5:29) moves the story briefly closer to the narrative of Genesis through its use of biblically influenced language, the surviving contents of column 6 (after Noah tells of the birth of his children and their marriages) through column 7 are also largely extrabiblical. They describe Noah's receipt of one or more visions that have no biblical parallel, and, if the *Apocryphon* did relate the story of Noah's building and loading of the ark, virtually no traces of it seem to remain.[54] Likewise, the narrative at the conclusion of the flood, columns 10-11, is also largely nonbiblical and untriggered by the biblical text, although the description of the sacrifices offered by Noah at the end of column 10 is modeled on material in Leviticus, and the food regulations at the end of column 11 derive from Genesis 9. What is significant is that even these brief biblical allusions have been fitted into a story line which does not depend closely on the Bible.

The biblical story of the covenant with Noah must have been contained in the now unreadable second half of column 11, since 12:1 begins with the sign (of the rainbow) in the cloud. Most of the remainder of column 12 is biblical in origin, but it expands the single biblical verse about Noah's planting a vineyard into a story about his observing the laws regarding the drinking of the first wine, found in Lev 19:23-25, and celebrating with his family in a fashion reminiscent of *Jub.* 7:3: "On that day he made a feast with rejoicing." The story of Noah's drunkenness, however, is altered by the *Apocryphon* into a positive event, his lying down after the feast and sleeping (reading ושכבת על משכבי, [ת]ודמכ "I lay down on my bed and slep[t]" in 12:19), and then being the recipient of a divine revelation.[55] His waking afterward is partially preserved in the text ואתעירת אנא [נוח מן שנתי], "[I,] Noah [awoke] from my sleep," (15:21) and is probably based on Gen 9:24 "Noah woke from his sleep." The revelation itself, which covers columns 13-15, is completely untriggered despite the clever exegesis that links it to the text, and the detailed description of the division of the earth among Noah's sons (16-17) is also completely independent of the narrative of Genesis. Thus, all the material in the last five surviving columns of Noah material consists of extrabiblical additions, and we are thus hard-pressed to find a substantial supplement in Part I of the *Apocryphon* that we can characterize as "triggered."

---

54. With the possible exception of 7:19, למבנה "to build," and the opening words of col. 8, אנתתה בתרה, which should be rendered "his wife after him" rather than "after him a woman" (as in DSSR). Even granting the fragmentary remains of the manuscript, is it fortuitous that only nonbiblical material survives from these columns?

55. That reading is very likely produced by a creative piece of exegesis, interpreting Gen 9:21 ויתגל, literally, "he was uncovered," as "he was revealed," i.e., he received a revelation, as first suggested by Machiela.

Part II differs starkly from Part I in terms of the nature of its major additions to the biblical story; most of them find an impetus in the biblical text, while few of them are completely "untriggered" in nature. The events following Sarai's abduction to Pharaoh's palace in 20:10-32 furnish a good example of the two sorts of expansions side by side. The Bible moves from the abduction to Pharaoh's punishment with no comment at all about Abram's reaction to the events. The *Apocryphon* adds to the biblical narrative a lengthy prayer by Abram entreating God to punish Pharaoh and to preserve Sarai's purity. There is nothing in the text that stimulates it directly, although it is natural and appropriate to the narrative at this point. The description of God's plaguing Pharaoh, on the other hand, is an expansion and interpretation of the biblical verse, "and the Lord smote Pharaoh," with the addition of clarificatory details, such as Pharaoh's inability to approach Sarai, the length of time that she spent in his house, and the failure of the Egyptian physicians and wise men to cure him because they too were suffering from the same affliction.[56]

This is followed by another gap-filling expansion that is also likely to be "triggered." The story in Genesis omits any explanation of how Pharaoh learned of the relationship between Abram and Sarai; the *Apocryphon* fills the informational vacuum by having Lot inform Hirqanosh of it when the latter comes to ask Abram to pray on behalf of Pharaoh.[57] The latter two "triggered" additions differ slightly in the nature of their triggers since the information in the first instance is not as critical to the story as it is in the second, but they are both characteristic of "rewritten Bible" as we define it, following Vermes. They respond to real or perceived omissions of information or clarification in the biblical text, even though they cannot be said to be derived exegetically from the text.

There are several other substantial supplements of this sort in Part II of the *Apocryphon*. When Abram and Sarai are about to enter Egypt, Abram has a dream about a palm tree and a cedar in which the palm saves the cedar from being cut down by crying out that they stem from one root (19:14-17). He interprets the dream as foretelling an impending threat to him and Sarai, with an attempt on his life that only she can avert by declaring that he is her brother. This creativity on the part of the author of the *Apocryphon* is most likely directed at

56. For the approaches of other early biblical interpreters to these details, cf. Geza Vermes, "Bible and Midrash: Early Old Testament Exegesis," in *Post-Biblical Jewish Studies*. SJLA 8 (Leiden: Brill, 1975), 67-68 (originally in *CHB*, vol. 1: *From the Beginnings to Jerome*, ed. P. R. Ackroyd [Cambridge: Cambridge University Press, 1970], 207-8); and Kugel, "Sarah's Virtue Intact," in *Traditions of the Bible*, 272-73.

57. For other ancient solutions to the problem "how did Pharaoh find out," see Vermes, "Bible and Midrash," 68 (*CHB* 1:208).

resolving one or more "perceived" gaps in the biblical story: first, how does Abram know that the Egyptians will seize Sarai, and second, why does he adopt the amoral solution of lying in order to save the situation?[58] The interpretation is not derived from the text, but is consonant with the method of rewritten Bible to tell the story in such a fashion as to avoid questions that could arise from a reading of the biblical text itself.

Sometimes the trigger for the expansion is more subtle. The description of Sarai's beauty in column 20, which appears extraneous to the narrative, is an expansion of Gen 12:14-15, "The Egyptians saw that the woman was very beautiful; when the nobles of Pharaoh saw her, they recited her praises to Pharaoh." It is indeed something of a poetic *tour de force*, but can realistically be said to be triggered by the biblical text. Similarly, Abram's circumambulation of the land in 21:15-19 is also unparalleled in the biblical text and is a different sort of gap-filler. If God commanded Abram, "Arise and walk through the land, by its length and breadth, for I shall give it to you," certainly Abram fulfilled God's command. The *Genesis Apocryphon* makes such fulfillment explicit, perhaps impelled as well by the interest in geography that it shares with other Second Temple works such as *Jubilees*.

Microstructure: Rewriting and Interpretation in Narrow Focus

In the preceding section we have examined the broad strokes with which the *Apocryphon* approaches the retelling and interpretation of the biblical story, the large elements in its composition. We now turn our attention to the smaller exegetical and stylistic units out of which the *Apocryphon* is built. Because Part II of the *Apocryphon*, as we have demonstrated, stands in closer proximity to the biblical story, we are not surprised to find more actual "interpretation" of the biblical narrative in it.

"Translation" of the Hebrew Text   One of the features of the *Apocryphon* that played a role in the early debate about its genre was the appearance within it of passages that appear to render the Hebrew text of Genesis into Aramaic, leading some scholars to misidentify the *Apocryphon* as a targum. I do not believe that the author/composer of the *Apocryphon* was ever attempting to present his readers/listeners with a rendition of the Hebrew text of Genesis into Aramaic, but that his knowledge of that text and of other biblical material led him con-

---

58. For a discussion of this and other ancient "solutions" to these problems, cf. Vermes, "Bible and Midrash," 67 (*CHB* 1:207); and Kugel, *Traditions of the Bible*, 255-56 and 271-72.

sciously or subconsciously to employ biblical models in writing his story. In Part I there are very few instances of more than a couple of words that clearly reflect the underlying biblical text: 10:12 (Gen 8:4), 11:17 (Gen 9:2-4), 12:1 (Gen 9:13), 12:10-12 (Gen 10:22, 6, 2). The absence of any systematic use of translated biblical material makes it extremely unlikely that what appear to us to be translations of the Hebrew should be analyzed as such under normal circumstances. This is not to say that the writer is not influenced in choice of language by the biblical original. Thus Noah's initial appearance on the scene, mid-poetic-speech, at the top of column 6, echoes the biblical language that first describes him. His characterization as צדיק in the Hebrew of Gen 6:9 reflects itself in the multiple occurrences of the root קשט, "truth," in GenAp 6:1-6, and the description מהלך בשבילי אמת עלמא, "walking in the paths of eternal truth" (and other terms such as נת]יב], מסל and אורחא, all of which indicate "paths") probably derives from את־האלהים התהלך־נח, "Noah walked with God" (Gen 6:9).

In Part II the presence of translations of phrases and clauses of the biblical text is commoner than it is in Part I, but the text as a whole still never approaches being a translation of Genesis. The goal of the author is to tell his story, not render the Hebrew text into Aramaic. Even in the following lengthy citation, where the italicized words represent a substantial fraction of the Hebrew text of Gen 14:13-19 in order, it is clear that not all of the Hebrew is to be found in the Aramaic, only as much as the author chooses to employ as the frame for the *Apocryphon's* expanded narrative (22:1-14):

There came to Abram one of the shepherds whom Abram had given to Lot *who had escaped from the captivity, and Abram was then dwelling in* Hebron, *and he told him that Lot his nephew had been captured* with all his flocks, but had not been killed, and that the kings had set forth by way of the Great Valley to their country, taking captives, plundering, destroying, and killing, and that they were on their way to the city of Damascus. Abram then wept for Lot his nephew, and summoned up his courage, and arose *and chose from his servants three hundred eighteen* selected for war. Arnem, Eshkol, and Mamre set forth with him. *And he was pursuing them until he reached Dan,* and he found them camped in the valley of Dan. *And he attacked them at night from four sides, and he was killing among them by night; and he smashed them and was pursuing them,* and all of them were fleeing from him *until they reached Helbon which is north of Damascus. And he retrieved from them* everything that they had captured, and everything that they had plundered, and *all their goods; and also Lot his nephew he saved* and all his flocks. *And he brought back all the captives whom they had captured. And the king of Sodom* heard that

Abram had brought back all the captives and all the booty, and he *went up to meet him* and came to Shalem which is Jerusalem while Abram was encamped in *Emeq Shaveh, which is the Valley of the King,* the Valley of Bet Ha-Kerem. *And Melchizedek, king of Salem, being priest to God Most High, brought out food and drink* for Abram and all his men. *And he blessed Abram and said, "Blessed is Abram to God Most High* Lord *of heaven and earth."*

Note that the biblical text does not suffice for the author of the *Apocryphon,* and that he intersperses within the "translated" material a considerable amount of nontranslated material with which he fleshes out his version of the story.

Reading and Writing Intertextually   A very different and particularly interesting employment of "translated" biblical text occurs when the *Apocryphon* "borrows" language from other parts of the Pentateuch and introduces them into the narrative. Although it is difficult to be certain of the author's intention, we are left with the feeling, at times, that such material is not utilized merely formally, but that it may have exegetical and literary significance. An outstanding example is 20:16-23:

> On that night, God Most High *sent against him [Pharaoh] a pestilential spirit to afflict him and all the men of his household* [cf. Gen 12:17], an evil spirit, and it continued to afflict him and all the men of his household, so that *he was unable to approach her* [cf. Gen 20:4], and did not know her, although he was with her for two years. And at the end of two years, the afflictions and plagues against him and all the men of his household grew more intense, and *he sent and called all the wise men of Egypt and all the magicians* [cf. Gen 41:8 and Exod 7:11] with all the doctors of Egypt, thinking that they might cure him and the men of his household from this affliction. *And* all the doctors and *the magicians* and wise men *were unable to stand* to heal him *because* [cf. Exod 9:11] the spirit was afflicting all of them, and they ran away.
>
> Then Hirqanosh came to me and begged me that I should come and pray for the king and lean my hands upon him so that he might live, for he had see[n me] in a d[r]eam. Lot then said to him, "My uncle Abram cannot pray for the king while his wife Sarai is with him. So go now and tell the king that he should send his wife back to her husband, *so that he will pray for him and he will live* [cf. Gen 20:7]."

There are two intertextualities at play in the *Apocryphon*'s composition here, one relating the story of Abram and Sarai in Egypt to the similar incident in Genesis 20 involving Abimelech, and the other referring to later interactions between Abram's descendants and later Egyptian kings (Genesis 41 and Exodus

7 and 9). Their possible functions need to be considered independently. The former could very well be only an unconscious harmonization on the part of the author of the two wife-sister stories, were it not for the fact that the biblical Pharaoh narrative omits the crucial point that Sarai remained untouched by his advances that is critical to the rewriting in the *Apocryphon*. The author is more likely drawing this analogy between the two incidents intentionally in order to make this significant point. The use of the language of Gen 20:7 by Lot may also serve to create an analogy between the two passages, emphasizing Abram's role in the saving of the kings who appropriated his wife.

If the language that is drawn from the stories of the two later Pharaohs, in the time of Joseph and the time of the exodus, was employed consciously by the composer of the *Apocryphon*, then we have evidence of a sort of theological sophistication that goes well beyond the drawing of analogies between historical incidents. The linguistic suggestion that the behavior and fates of the three Egyptian kings are linked would indicate a way of reading the Pentateuch that we might not have expected in this period.

In at least one case, the intertextuality evinced by the *Apocryphon* seems to serve an exegetical function responding to a gap in the biblical narrative, an "omission" in the biblical text of the sort that texts like the Samaritan Pentateuch (and 4QRP) and exegetes like the rabbis noticed frequently, but which in this instance seems not to have been noticed and responded to except by the author of the *Apocryphon*.[59] Genesis 20:13 reads, "And it was when God made me wander from my ancestral home that I said to her 'This be the kindness that you do with me, wherever we arrive, say regarding me "He is my brother."'" Nowhere earlier in the adventures of Abra(ha)m and Sarai/Sarah, however, do we find this quotation. How could that be? The author of the *Apocryphon* therefore skillfully integrates this verse into his rewriting of Gen 12:12-13, "When the Egyptians see you, they will say, 'She is his wife,' and they will kill me and let you live. Please say that you are my sister so that it will go well with me on your account, and my soul will live because of you," as follows: "They will seek to kill me and leave you alone. *But let this be the whole kindness that you shall do with me, wherever we are, say regarding me that 'he is my brother.'* And I shall live because of you and my soul shall escape for your sake" (19:19-20). Now the subsequent statement by Abraham is vindicated by a passage earlier in Genesis.

Finally, in 11:11 of the *Apocryphon*, Noah declares that he went out (presumably from the ark) and "walked upon the earth, by its length and by its breadth,"

---

59. I discuss this example in detail in "Re-Arrangement, Anticipation and Harmonization," 51-54, where I refer to it as a "constructive harmonization." Cf. Emanuel Tov, "The Nature and Background of Harmonizations in Biblical Manuscripts," *JSOT* 31 (1985): 3-29.

perhaps in response to a divine command for him to do so that does not survive in legible form. A few lines later, in 11:15, God appears to Noah and says אל תדחל יא נוח עמך אנה ועם בניך די להון כואתך לעלמים, "Do not fear, O Noah, I am with you and with your sons who will be like you forever." Each of these passages is a virtual citation of material referring to Abram later in Genesis, 13:17: "Arise and walk through the land by its length and by its breadth,"[60] and 15:1: "Do not fear, O Abram; I am your shield." The latter passage, indeed, actually appears, with an expansion that resembles those in the later targumim, in the Aramaic of the *Apocryphon* at 22:30-31: אל תדחל אנה עמך, "Do not fear; I am with you (and I shall be for you support and strength, and I am a shield over you and your buckler against anyone stronger than you)." I have suggested that the employment of the language of the Abram material in a Noah context is part of an effort to acknowledge Noah as another "patriarch" in the chain of tradition.[61]

Concluding Observations

We have focused on a variety of the features that reflect the ways in which the *Apocryphon* rewrites and interprets the biblical text: translation of the Hebrew on a small or large scale; rearrangement and omission of details; triggered and untriggered additions to the narrative. When reflecting on the *Apocryphon,* however, or on any of the other members of the genre "rewritten Bible," as biblical interpretation, we must always keep in mind that we are reading and thinking about those works very differently from the way that the ancient reader (or listener) did. The ancient reader read (or heard) a narrative that he may or may not have been able to compare with its biblical original as he read it; we can sit with a copy of Genesis in one hand and the *Apocryphon* in the other and go back and forth between them at our leisure, looking for those implicit interpretive details that characterize this genre.[62] We are also *looking* for the interpretation embedded in the narrative, while the ancient reader may simply have been listening to a good story derived from the Bible. And at the same time, the primary goal of the author(s)/composer(s) of that story may

60. In the Noah passage, ארצא probably means "earth," while in the Abram one it means "land."

61. "Noah and the Flood at Qumran," 209, and 220-21; "From the Watchers to the Flood," 60-61.

62. Vermes, *Scripture and Tradition,* 95, stresses that one of the points of the rewriting is "to anticipate questions, and to solve problems in advance." For this purpose, I do not distinguish between the two parts of the *Apocryphon* as I did earlier.

very well have been to tell the story well, and that may have affected the way that he told it; we cannot always tell what takes precedence, the interpretation of the underlying scriptural narrative by the author or the story that he is telling. He certainly was an interpreter of the Bible, but he may have seen himself simultaneously as something else as well. We conclude our limited analysis of the *Apocryphon*, therefore, with the *caveat* that, despite the wealth of interpretations to be found in it, we should remember not to treat it only as a commentary in narrative form, but also as the literary artifact that it was undoubtedly intended to be.

BIBLIOGRAPHY

Amihay, Aryeh, and Daniel A. Machiela. "Traditions of the Birth of Noah." In Stone, Amihay, and Hillel, *Noah and His Book(s)*, 53-69.

Avigad, Nahman, and Yigael Yadin. *A Genesis Apocryphon: A Scroll from the Wilderness of Judaea*. Jerusalem: Magnes and Heikhal ha-Sefer, 1956.

Bernstein, Moshe J. "Re-arrangement, Anticipation and Harmonization as Exegetical Features in the Genesis Apocryphon." *DSD* 3 (1996): 37-57.

———. "Noah and the Flood at Qumran." In *The Provo International Conference on the Dead Sea Scrolls: Technological Innovations, New Texts, and Reformulated Issues*, ed. Donald W. Parry and Eugene Ulrich. STDJ 30. Leiden: Brill, 1999, 199-231.

———. "From the Watchers to the Flood: Story and Exegesis in the Early Columns of the Genesis Apocryphon." In *Reworking the Bible: Apocryphal and Related Texts at Qumran*, ed. Esther G. Chazon, Devorah Dimant, and Ruth A. Clements. STDJ 58. Leiden: Brill, 2005, 39-63.

———. " 'Rewritten Bible': A Generic Category Which Has Outlived Its Usefulness?" *Textus* 22 (2005): 169-96.

———. "Divine Titles and Epithets and the Sources of the Genesis Apocryphon." *JBL* 128 (2009): 291-310.

———. "The Genesis Apocryphon and the Aramaic Targumim Revisited." In *The Dead Sea Scrolls in Context: Integrating the Dead Sea Scrolls in the Study of Ancient Texts, Languages, and Cultures*, ed. Armin Lange, Emanuel Tov, and Matthias Weigold. VTSup 140. Leiden: Brill, 2011, 2:651-71.

———. "The Genre(s) of the Genesis Apocryphon." In Berthelot and Stökl Ben Ezra, *Aramaica Qumranica*, 317-38.

———. "Is the Genesis Apocryphon a Unity? What Sort of Unity Were You Looking For?" *Aramaic Studies* 8 (2010): 107-34.

Berthelot, Katell, and Daniel Stökl Ben Ezra, eds. *Aramaica Qumranica: The Aix-en-Provence Colloquium on the Aramaic Dead Sea Scrolls*. STDJ 94. Leiden: Brill, 2010.

Cohen, Shaye J. D. "The Beauty of Flora and the Beauty of Sarai." *Helios* 8 (1981): 41-53.

Crawford, Sidnie White. *Rewriting Scripture in Second Temple Times*. SDSSRL. Grand Rapids: Eerdmans, 2008.

Dehandschutter, Boudewijn. "Le rêve dans l'Apocryphe de la Genèse." In *La littérature juive entre Tenach et Mischna: Quelques problèmes,* ed. Willem Cornelis van Unnik. RechBib 9. Leiden: Brill, 1974, 48-55.

Eshel, Esther. "Isaiah 11:15: A New Interpretation based on the Genesis Apocryphon." *DSD* 13 (2006): 38-45.

———. "The *imago mundi* of the *Genesis Apocryphon.*" In *Heavenly Tablets: Interpretation, Identity and Tradition in Ancient Judaism,* ed. Lynn LiDonnici and Andrea Lieber. JSJSup 119. Leiden: Brill, 2007, 111-31.

———. "The Genesis Apocryphon: A Chain of Traditions." In Roitman, Schiffman, and Tzoref, *The Dead Sea Scrolls and Contemporary Culture,* 181-93.

———. "The Aramaic Levi Document, the Genesis Apocryphon, and Jubilees: A Study of Shared Traditions." In *Enoch and the Mosaic Torah: The Evidence of Jubilees,* ed. Gabriele Boccaccini and Giovanni Ibba. Grand Rapids: Eerdmans, 2009, 82-98.

———. "The Dream Visions in the Noah Story of the Genesis Apocryphon and Related Texts." In *Northern Lights on the Dead Sea Scrolls: Proceedings of the Nordic Qumran Network 2003-2006,* ed. Anders Klostergaard Petersen et al. STDJ 80. Leiden: Brill, 2009, 41-61.

———. "The *Genesis Apocryphon* and Other Related Aramaic Texts from Qumran: The Birth of Noah." In Berthelot and Stökl Ben Ezra, *Aramaica Qumranica,* 277-97.

———. "The Noah Cycle in the Genesis Apocryphon." In Stone, Amihay, and Hillel, *Noah and His Book(s),* 77-95.

Evans, Craig E. "The Genesis Apocryphon and the Rewritten Bible." *RevQ* 13 (1988): 153-65.

Falk, Daniel K. *The Parabiblical Texts: Strategies for Extending the Scriptures in the Dead Sea Scrolls.* CQS 8. LSTS 63. London: T. & T. Clark, 2007.

———. "Divergence from Genesis in the *Genesis Apocryphon.*" In Parry et al., *Qumran Cave 1 Revisited,* 193-204.

Fitzmyer, Joseph A. *The Genesis Apocryphon of Qumran Cave 1 (1Q20): A Commentary.* 3rd ed. BibOr 18B. Rome: Pontifical Biblical Institute, 2004.

Gevirtz, Marianne Luijken. "Abram's Dream in the Genesis Apocryphon: Its Motifs and Their Function." *Maarav* 8 (1992): 229-43.

Greenfield, Jonas C., and Elisha Qimron. "The Genesis Apocryphon Col. XII." In *Studies in Qumran Aramaic,* ed. Takamitsu Muraoka. AbrNSup 3. Leuven: Peeters, 1992, 70-77.

Grelot, Pierre. "De *l'Apocryphe de la Genèse* aux *Targoums:* sur Genèse 14,18-20." In *Intertestamental Essays in Honour of Józef Tadeusz Milik,* ed. Zdzisław J. Kapera (Kraków: Enigma, 1992), 77-90.

Kugel, James L. "Which Is Older, Jubilees or the Genesis Apocryphon? An Exegetical Approach." In Roitman, Schiffman, and Tzoref, *The Dead Sea Scrolls and Contemporary Culture,* 257-94.

Kuiper, Gerald J. "A Study of the Relationship between A Genesis Apocryphon and the Pentateuchal Targumim in Genesis 14_{1-12}." In *In Memoriam Paul Kahle,* ed. Matthew Black and Georg Fohrer. BZAW 103. Berlin: Töpelmann, 1968, 149-61.

Kutscher, Edward Y. "The Language of the Genesis Apocryphon: A Preliminary Study." In *Aspects of the Dead Sea Scrolls,* ed. Chaim Rabin and Yigael Yadin. ScrHier 4. Jerusalem: Magnes, 1958, 1-35.

Lange, Armin. "1QGenAp XIX_{10}–XX_{32} as Paradigm of the Wisdom Didactic Narrative." In *Qumranstudien: Vorträge und Beiträge der Teilnehmer des Qumranseminars auf dem* internationalen Treffen der Society of Biblical Literature, Münster, 25.-26. Juli 1993, ed. Heinz-Josef Fabry, Lange, and Hermann Lichtenberger. Göttingen: Vandenhoeck & Ruprecht, 1996, 191-204.

Legrand, Thierry. "Exégèses targumiques et Techniques de Réécriture dans *l'Apocryphe de la Genèse* (1Qap Gen ar)." In Berthelot and Stökl Ben Ezra, *Aramaica Qumranica*, 225-52.

Lehmann, Manfred R. "1Q Genesis Apocryphon in the Light of the Targumim and Midrashim." *RevQ* 1 (1958-59): 249-63.

Machiela, Daniel A. "'Each to his own inheritance': Geography as an Evaluative Tool in the Genesis Apocryphon." *DSD* 15 (2008): 50-66.

———. *The Dead Sea Genesis Apocryphon: A New Text and Translation with Introduction and Special Treatment of Columns 13-17.* STDJ 79. Leiden: Brill, 2009.

———. "Genesis Revealed: The Apocalyptic Apocryphon from Qumran Cave 1." In Parry et al., *Qumran Cave I Revisited*, 205-22.

Morgenstern, Matthew. "A New Clue to the Original Length of the Genesis Apocryphon." *JJS* 47 (1996): 345-47.

———, Elisha Qimron, and Daniel Sivan. "The Hitherto Unpublished Columns of the Genesis Apocryphon." *AbrN* 33 (1995): 30-54.

Muraoka, Takamitsu. "Notes on the Aramaic of the Genesis Apocryphon." *RevQ* 8 (1972): 7-51.

———. "Further Notes on the Aramaic of the 'Genesis Apocryphon.'" *RevQ* 16 (1993-95): 39-48.

Nickelsburg, George W. E. "Patriarchs Who Worry about Their Wives: A Haggadic Tendency in the Genesis Apocryphon." In *Biblical Perspectives: Early Use and Interpretation of the Bible in the Light of the Dead Sea Scrolls: Proceedings of the First International Symposium of the Orion Center for the Study of the Dead Sea Scrolls and Associated Literature, 12-14 May, 1996,* ed. Michael E. Stone and Esther G. Chazon. STDJ 28. Leiden: Brill, 1998, 137-58.

Parry, Donald W., et al. *Qumran Cave 1 Revisited: Texts from Cave 1 Sixty Years after Their Discovery. Proceedings of the Sixth Meeting of the IOQS in Ljubljana.* STDJ 91. Leiden: Brill, 2010.

Peters, Dorothy. "The Recombination and Evolution of Noah Traditions as Found in the *Genesis Apocryphon* and *Jubilees:* The DNA of Fraternal Twins." In Parry et al., *Qumran Cave I Revisited*, 223-32.

Reed, Stephen A. "The Use of the First Person in the 'Genesis Apocryphon.'" In *Aramaic in Postbiblical Judaism and Early Christianity,* ed. Eric M. Meyers and Paul V. M. Flesher. Winona Lake: Eisenbrauns, 2010, 193-215.

Roitman, Adolfo D., Lawrence H. Schiffman, and Shani L. (Berrin) Tzoref, eds. *The Dead Sea Scrolls and Contemporary Culture: Proceedings of the International Conference held at the Israel Museum, Jerusalem (July 6-8, 2008).* STDJ 93. Leiden: Brill, 2010.

Steiner, Richard C. "The Mountains of Ararat, Mount Lubar, and הר הקדם." *JJS* 42 (1991): 247-49.

———. "The Heading of the *Book of the Words of Noah* on a Fragment of the Genesis Apocryphon: New Light on a 'Lost' Work." *DSD* 2 (1995): 66-71.

Stone, Michael E., Aryeh Amihay, and Vered Hillel, eds. *Noah and His Book(s)*. SBLEJL 28. Atlanta: Society of Biblical Literature, 2010.

Stuckenbruck, Loren T. "The Lamech Narrative in the Genesis Apocryphon (1QapGen) and Birth of Noah (4QEnoch^c ar): A Tradition-Historical Study." In Berthelot and Stökl Ben Ezra, *Aramaica Qumranica*, 253-71.

VanderKam, James C. "Textual Affinities of the Biblical Citations in the Genesis Apocryphon." *JBL* 97 (1978): 45-55.

———. "The Poetry of 1QApGen, xx,2-8a." *RevQ* 10 (1979-1981): 57-66.

———. "The Birth of Noah." In *Intertestamental Essays in Honour of Józef Tadeusz Milik*, ed. Zdzislaw J. Kapera. Qumranica Mogilanensia 6. Kraków: Enigma, 1992, 213-31.

———. "The Granddaughters and Grandsons of Noah." *RevQ* 16 (1994): 457-61.

Weigold, Matthias. "Aramaic *Wunderkind:* The Birth of Noah in the Aramaic Texts from Qumran." In Berthelot and Stökl Ben Ezra, *Aramaica Qumranica*, 299-315.

———. "One Voice or Many? The Identity of the Narrators in Noah's Birth Story (1QapGen 1-5.27) and in the 'Book of the Words of Noah' (1QapGen 5.29–18.23)." *Aramaic Studies* 8 (2010): 89-105.

Werman, Cana. "Qumran and the Book of Noah." In *Pseudepigraphic Perspectives: The Apocrypha and Pseudepigrapha in Light of the Dead Sea Scrolls: Proceedings of the Second International Symposium of the Orion Center for the Study of the Dead Sea Scrolls and Associated Literature, 12-14 January, 1997*, ed. Esther G. Chazon and Michael E. Stone. STDJ 31. Leiden: Brill, 1999, 171-81.

Biblical Interpretation in Pseudo-Philo's
Liber Antiquitatum Biblicarum

Howard Jacobson

The very opening words of *Liber Antiquitatum Biblicarum* will bring up short the reader who is familiar with the Bible. Adam, we are told, begat three sons and one daughter, the latter's name being Noaba. Then, Pseudo-Philo informs us, after the birth of Seth Adam begat twelve sons and seven daughters, who are then named. But the Bible reports that Adam first had three sons (no daughters), Cain, Abel, and Seth, and afterwards (5:4) "sons and daughters." Immediately we see *L.A.B.*'s propensity for detail, especially details of name and number. The Bible is spare, *L.A.B.* is expansive. The Bible is minimalist, *L.A.B.* is obsessive. But on other occasions the opposite is the case. Where the Bible is detailed and lengthy, *L.A.B.* will be terse and sketchy. This much is obvious. We will return to it later.

Before the biblical canon had been completed, readers and authors were already interacting with the texts they possessed in creative ways. Thus, later books of the biblical canon clearly react to earlier ones. Only after the close of the canon did "independent" works of understanding and explanation arise. Of course, these must have started as oral discussions and only after some time emerged as written "works" in their own right. And these works will have differed in their structure and format. Thus, some will have looked like works of scholarship in which the biblical text received almost line by line explanation, clarification, and expansion, almost in the fashion of the Hellenistic Alexandrian scholars. But others will have been fashioned in the image of the texts they were responding to, that is to say, they will look like they are in competition, so to speak, with the original biblical texts as literary works in their own right. *L.A.B.* falls into the latter category. It is a narrative midrash that mimics the biblical narrative; it is not a midrash like the *Mekhilta* or *Sifra* or *Genesis Rabba*, which reads and runs, elucidating as it moves.

L.A.B., like much other midrash, is interpretive, is problem-solving, and is literarily creative. It fills gaps, clarifies ambiguities, resolves difficulties and contradictions, provides connections, responds to the reader's curiosity, expands or subtracts for tendentious purposes, makes changes to enhance the reputation of a biblical hero or worsen that of a villain, and answers questions that are implicitly raised by the Bible's narrative. We will look at some of these aspects.

An ancient reader of *L.A.B.* would have been struck and impressed at how similar his narrative was to the narrative books of the Bible, in its style, vocabulary, and flow. Indeed, many readers probably could not have distinguished between *L.A.B.'s* narrative style and that of the Bible. If confronted by a passage from *L.A.B.*, unless the reader virtually knew the Bible by heart, he might well have thought it quoted from the Bible. *L.A.B.'s* knowledge of the Bible is truly profound. He regularly quotes from or echoes it. Quotations are seamlessly woven into and integrated in the author's narrative to an even greater degree than in Qumran texts like *The Words of Moses* and the *Genesis Apocryphon*. This familiarity with the Bible has a significant effect on the construction and substance of the narrative. Speeches, episodes, descriptions are generated by the intermingling or conflating of different (and often unrelated) passages. This, one might justifiably assert, is the predominant creative narrative technique in *L.A.B.* This is *L.A.B.'s* own version of intertextuality.

Innovation by Way of Analogy

In this respect, it is fair to say that *L.A.B.'s* major creative narrative-exegetical technique is governed by analogy — or at least by what he saw as analogous narratives. *L.A.B.* routinely contains themes, language, and elements of plot that are not present in the source biblical narrative, but which he has taken from "analogous" biblical contexts. I note here several examples. In his account of the flood, *L.A.B.* has God declare that he will destroy the earth's vegetation (3:3). There is no explicit mention of the destruction of vegetation in the Bible's account of the flood. There is, however, such mention in Genesis's other account of vast destruction, that of Sodom and Gomorrah (19:25). *L.A.B.* has transferred it here. Similarly, after the sin of the golden calf, God, intent on destroying the people, responds to Moses' pleas with the words, "I forgive, in accord with your request" (11:10). No such statement is made in the Exodus narrative of this event. But the words are in fact God's response to Moses' pleas in an analogous context, God's plan to destroy the people after the sin of the spies (Num 14:20).

When *L.A.B.'s* spies return with their report, the people protest and complain about God's promise to them of a land of milk and honey (15:4). No such complaint is found in the biblical narrative. But it is present in a different biblical story of rebellion, that of Korah (Num 16:14), and *L.A.B.* has moved it here. When *L.A.B.*'s Moses then pleads with God on behalf of the people, he disclaims personal responsibility (15:7). No such disclaimer is present in the Bible's account of this episode. *L.A.B.* has adopted here Moses' disclaimer on another occasion (Num 11:12), when the people complain bitterly about the lack of meat.

In chapter 11 *L.A.B.* recounts Moses' first ascent on Mount Sinai. A number of elements of his account are not in the relevant biblical passage. They in fact come from the Bible's report of Moses' *second* ascent (to which *L.A.B.* gives short shrift). These include God's explicit commands to Moses to prepare himself and to make the ascent, as well as the illumination of Moses' face (12:1).

Before his death, *L.A.B.*'s Moses entreats God to tell him how much time remains (19:14). He prefaces his request with the words *si adhuc potero petere.* Moses, in his many entreaties of God in the Bible, never says anything like this. But *L.A.B.* is borrowing Abraham's words at Gen 18:32, in the latter's famous pleading with God.

In *L.A.B.*'s treatment of Deborah's war against the Midianites, he uses material from the Exodus account of the Jews' victory over the Egyptians (Exodus 14-15), e.g., the divine impeding of the enemy chariots (31:1), the boasting of the enemy army (31:1), the role of the entire people in the song of triumph (32:1).

The biblical recounting of the divine selection of Gideon (Judg 6:11-27) tells of Gideon's being in hiding from the Midianites when an angel appears to commission him. Gideon expresses skepticism about God's interest in the Jewish people, asserts his own inadequacy, and requests divine signs. These are present in *L.A.B.*'s narrative (ch. 35). But there are several added elements. Thus, there is a mountain setting; God is justified and the people condemned; Gideon indicates a death wish. These novel elements are introduced by *L.A.B.* from another story that involves a despairing hero who flees and is encouraged by an angel, namely Elijah at 1 Kgs 19:3-11. We might note also that when *L.A.B.*'s Gideon greets the angel's call with reluctance (as in the Bible), he says *quis ego sum* (35:5), words not spoken by the Bible's Gideon. *L.A.B.* has taken this theme from another biblical figure who is reluctant to accept God's call (Moses at Exod 3:11).

When Jephthah returns victorious, the women come out to greet him dancing (40:1). At Judg 11:34 only his daughter does. *L.A.B.* is here influenced by the nearly identical language of Judg 11:34 and Exod 15:20 (also in a context of postvictory celebration). The former has "she came out with drums and dancing," the latter "all the women came out with drums and dancing." The plurality of women from the Exodus context has infiltrated *L.A.B.*'s language here.

At 42:3 the angel tells Eluma that she will have a son (Samson). This is based on Judg 13:3-5. But the angel's assertion that God has heard her and his instructions as to how to name the baby are *L.A.B.*'s additions. They come from another biblical episode where an angel tells a woman that she will have a son (Genesis 16).

Samson later goes to Gerar, where he meets Delilah (43:5). This episode is pieced together by *L.A.B.* out of several Samson episodes in Judges, one of which takes place at Timna. When *L.A.B.* begins the narrative with the phrases "He went down, he saw . . . he took" (phrasing not found in any of the Bible's Samson-episodes), he is — quite remarkably — borrowing the language from a different biblical tale that is located in the same place, Timna (Gen 38:1-2).

L.A.B. recounts the tale of the concubine from Judges 19 (ch. 45). The local residents surround the house, as in the Bible. They make hostile remarks to the homeowner and begin to use force (45:3). Neither of these themes is in the Judges narrative. They both come from another tale of inhospitality toward visitors (Gen 19:9).

To be sure, *L.A.B.*'s familiarity with the biblical text is so deep and wide that "alien" material will become part of a narrative even when there is but a small sense of analogy — and sometimes virtually none at all. Thus, for example, in *L.A.B.* Moses' mother hides him in a wooden basket. But in the Bible the basket is made of bulrushes (Exod 2:3). It seems clear that the reason here was the word for "basket," namely *tēbâ*. This noun only occurs one other time in the Bible; it is Noah's ark. Both "arks" are the means through which an outstanding figure is saved. Thus, Moses' basket is assimilated to Noah's ark and becomes wooden.

When Sisera comes to Jael's tent and requests water "for I am weary" (31:4), he is probably quoting Esau at Gen 25:30, who requests food "for I am weary." When she responds by concocting a test that she will hold to reflect God's support (31:5), she does so in a way that clearly mimics the sign fashioned by Abraham's servant at Genesis 24. *L.A.B.* has apparently been led to make this association by the mere fact that both in the Genesis passage (24:17) and the Judges one (4:19) the man says to the woman, "Give me a little water to drink."

When Hannah brings the child Samuel to Eli, she presents the boy with pretty much the same words as does the biblical Hannah (51:2; cf. 1 Sam 1:27). But the exact language seems to come from another woman who has made a request, Esther (Esth 5:6; 7:2). When Hannah later sings her song of triumph, she calls upon Elkanah to rise up (51:6). This is taken by *L.A.B.* from Deborah's similar call to a man to "rise up" in the middle of her song (Judg 5:12). Eli later recalls his words to Hannah, "what will be born from you will be a son for me" (53:12). Eli never says anything like this in the Bible. Rather, *L.A.B.* is putting in his mouth God's words to David about his future son Solomon (2 Sam 7:12-14).

Samuel anoints David in the presence of his brothers, and then David sings a psalm. In it he says, "My brothers were envious of me" (59:4). This is almost a quotation of Gen 37:11, with reference to Joseph and his brothers. *L.A.B.* presumably associated David and Joseph as young men destined for leadership and greatness in preference to their brothers.

In a recent book (and several articles), Bruce Fisk has taken the above argument and expanded it. Fisk believes that not only are there out-of-context biblical quotations and allusions present in *L.A.B.*'s narrative, but that they are often tendentious, set in alien places for specific purposes, sometimes purposes that are different from or even alien to the original biblical narrative. Thus, for example, *L.A.B.*'s account of the golden calf episode contains allusions that have the effect of turning the biblical story with its emphasis on the sin of the people into a tale that emphasizes God's faithfulness and the long-term viability of the people.[1] Similarly, the tale of the twelve spies is transformed by the presence of secondary allusions from a story of rebellion and sin into a defense of the covenant.[2]

These are illuminating interpretations. Still, words of caution must be made. Rather than seeing this as a pervasive technique, it is closer to the truth to say that it is occasional. More often than not, it is not possible to tell whether the secondary allusion is serving any particular purpose. Often indeed it is quite clear that there is no further purpose and the presence of the allusion is no more than a reflexive reaction on *L.A.B.*'s part derived from his powerful memory of and familiarity with the biblical text. It is not impossible that such allusions were sometimes entirely unconscious.

Expansion of Characters

We noted at the outset that *L.A.B.* is sometimes spare, sometimes expansive. Both features are easily illustrated. Indeed, one sometimes sees both in one and the same passage. Thus, for example, *L.A.B.* cruises through the life of Jacob that occupies the Bible's attention for more than twenty chapters in about a page, noting little more than the episode of the rape of his daughter Dinah and his son Joseph's success in Egypt. Even in such a passage, wherein the biblical narrative is severely truncated, *L.A.B.* chooses to expand one aspect of the narrative. After the rescue of Dinah, the Bible tells us nothing of her subsequent

---

1. Bruce N. Fisk, *Do You Not Remember? Scripture, Story and Exegesis in the Rewritten Bible of Pseudo-Philo.* JSPSup 37 (Sheffield: Sheffield Academic, 2001), 136-90.
2. Fisk, *Do You Not Remember?* 191-227.

fate and life. *L.A.B.* felt the lack. Here was a gap that needed to be filled. And so, *L.A.B.* reports (8:8), with no biblical authority, that even after her checkered sexual history Dinah married no less a figure than the famous Job and had many children by him. Thus, *L.A.B.* provides a happy ending for the story. How *L.A.B.* managed to see Job and Dinah as contemporaries is easy to understand. He identified Iobab of Gen 36:33 with Job.

Indeed, *L.A.B.* has a particular propensity for filling gaps with respect to characters of the biblical narrative. Sometimes we can reasonably surmise why he did so in a particular case, but often his motivation is not apparent. Any number of persons whose role, like Dinah's, is very limited and about whom we learn next to nothing in the Bible are fleshed out and occasionally made of serious importance. Thus, for example, Moses' father Amram. In the Bible he is a nullity, aside from the simple fact that he fathers three major figures. In contrast to his wife and daughter, he does nothing in the face of catastrophe. Indeed, beyond his fathering of Miriam, Aaron, and Moses, we hear nothing of him. *L.A.B.* turns him into the great leader of his generation, a communal activist who is truly heroic (9:3-14). When the elders despair in the face of Pharaoh's genocide, Amram recommends renewed resistance and abiding faith. What motivated *L.A.B.*? Perhaps the near-total absence of Amram from the biblical narrative spurred him to filling in this lacuna. Perhaps he could not tolerate the idea that Moses' father was a nobody. At all events, in *L.A.B.* Amram becomes a central figure.

Another father whose role and stature in the Bible are limited, though not to the degree that Amram's are, is Elkanah the father of the great prophet and leader Samuel. In the Bible Elkanah is essentially an appendage to his wife Hannah. He is seen throughout in terms of his relationship to her (1 Samuel 1 and 2). He has, it is fair to say, no existence without her. In contrast, *L.A.B.'s* Elkanah has nearly an entire chapter devoted to him before we even hear of the existence of his spouse. We learn that the people have chosen him to be their leader, but he refuses the position. However, God reveals that his as-yet unborn son will lead the people in due course. As with Amram, *L.A.B.* turns the great man's father into a man of importance with leadership potential.

Sometimes *L.A.B.* will adopt a biblical character about whom the Bible tells us little other than his existence and turn him into a fairly significant person with important accomplishments. Such is Jair (ch. 38), of whom we learn in the Bible (Judg 10:3-5) that he was a judge for twenty-two years, had thirty sons and thirty cities, and was buried in Kamon. That is it. In contrast, Jair in *L.A.B.* becomes a rather major figure, a judge who became corrupt, promoted the worship of Baal, and in the end was chastised and mortally punished by an angel of the Lord.

Lesser instances are those of Abdon and Elon (ch. 41). Biblical Elon (Judg 12:11-12) had a ten-year tenure as judge and was buried in the land of Zebulun. *L.A.B.* credits him with victories over the Philistines and the capture of twelve cities. Of Abdon we learn some family information, his burial place, and that he was judge for eight years (Judg 12:13-15). *L.A.B.* makes him a significant warrior who fights against and routs the Moabite enemy.

Other significant figures in *L.A.B.* seem to be created whole cloth out of names in the Bible. For example, in the book of Judges, after the death of the judge Gideon, there is a civil war over the succession (ch. 9). An important ally of Gideon's son Abimelech is named Zebul. *L.A.B.* also presents an important character named Zebul in the time of the judges. But rather than being an elaborated biblical Zebul, it is a completely different — invented — person of the same name. *L.A.B.*'s Zebul is himself a judge, who distributes inherited property to daughters, who preaches against idolatry, and establishes a treasury for God.

Of course, many important biblical characters are given added adventures or characteristics. A character with a small (she doesn't even have a name) but significant role in the Bible is the daughter of Jephthah (Judges 11). When Jephthah vows to offer up to God whatever first comes out to him on his return from a successful battle, he does not anticipate that his daughter will be the one. She accepts her fate, requests two months to mourn in the mountains with her comrades, then returns, and the vow is fulfilled. *L.A.B.* much expands this. The daughter has a name (Seila). In addition, she apparently seeks to have the elders nullify her father's vow, but to no avail. While the Bible simply reports that she mourns for two months in the mountains, *L.A.B.* puts in her mouth a substantial and moving lamentation (40:5-7). Enhancing her status further, *L.A.B.* reports that the women of Israel set up an annual memorial celebration for Seila.

Another figure, Jael, is of real import in the Bible (Judges 4), but her role is expanded significantly in *L.A.B.* The biblical figure seals the victory of the Jews over the Canaanites by killing the general Sisera. The Bible describes her brief interaction with Sisera, how she deceives him and then kills him. This structure is maintained by *L.A.B.*, who also adds much else that is in tune with *L.A.B.*'s general thematics. *L.A.B.*'s Jael effectively seduces Sisera. Then *L.A.B.* puts into her mouth a substantial prayer to God that focuses on the chosenness of Israel. The killing itself has an element of the dramatic that is absent in the Bible.

In the case of David, it is interesting to note one technique *L.A.B.* utilizes to expand his information about David. At 59:4 David sings, "my brothers were envious of me." Now, it is fair to say that there is nothing in the books of Samuel that suggests that David's brothers envied him. But at Ps 69:8, the Psalmist sings, "I have become a stranger to my brothers, an alien to my mother's sons." Assuming, as was widely held, that the Psalmist was none other than David, *L.A.B.* takes this statement and incorporates it into David's biography. The same thing occurs immediately thereafter (59:4). "My father and my mother abandoned me," David sings. Once again, *L.A.B.* uses material from the Psalms as biography for David. Here the source is Ps 27:10, "My father and my mother have forsaken me."

Joshua is a fairly significant figure in *L.A.B.*, as he is, of course, in the Bible. But *L.A.B.* appears to have found one flaw in the Bible's narrative. Surprisingly, the Bible says nothing about the people's mourning for Joshua on the occasion of his death. This was apparently too much for *L.A.B.* He added an entire paragraph on the mourning: "All Israel gathered together to bury him. They made a great lamentation for him and they said this in their lamentation." This is followed by a keening of four lines. The whole is, by the way, to some extent modeled on nothing less than the mourning for Jacob in Genesis 50.

Certainly the most mysterious and baffling figure in *L.A.B.* is Cenaz, the leader of the people who succeeds Joshua and to whom are attributed numerous and significant actions that occupy more than a tenth of the entire *L.A.B.* narrative and that therefore make him, from at least a quantitative angle, the most important character in *L.A.B.* after Moses. But who exactly is this Cenaz? In the Bible there is one person by this name, and he occupies pretty much the same chronological time slot as does *L.A.B.'s* Cenaz, coming right after Joshua. But of the Bible's Cenaz we know only one thing — that he is the father of the first-mentioned of the "judges." The latter is "Othniel the son of Cenaz." Othniel, the Bible tells us (Judg 1:11-15), conquered Kiriath-sepher and thereby won the hand of Achsah, Caleb's daughter; he became the savior of Israel and their "judge," defeating the king of Mesopotamia and bringing peace to Israel for forty years (Judg 3:7-11). That is all we hear of Othniel. Some have argued that *L.A.B.* (like Josephus) has simply substituted Cenaz for his son, but no one has offered a good explanation for his so doing; in addition, there is no correlation between the deeds of *L.A.B.'s* Cenaz and those of the biblical Othniel. Further, the actions of *L.A.B.'s* Cenaz are a strange collection, including some that do not bear even a remote similarity to any episodes in the entire Bible (e.g., the elaborate story of the stones, ch. 26). *L.A.B.'s* plot-creativity and ingenuity are nowhere more in evidence than in his lengthy recounting of the leadership of Cenaz, but no one has satisfactorily expounded the unity — if there is any — and *Tendenz* of the Cenaz narrative nor why *L.A.B.* has chosen to delegate so important a role to a character who in the Bible has virtually no importance.

Clearing Up Difficulties and Ambiguities

Many changes or elaborations or abbreviations in *L.A.B.* serve the purpose of clarification, that is, to take a biblical original that was, at least at some level, not perfectly clear and to render it clear. Here are several instances.

Genesis's story of the tower of Babel is terse and to the point. God declares of the tower-builders, "let us confuse their language so they don't understand each other's speech." God so acts, and they are then scattered across all the earth (Gen 11:7-9). *L.A.B.* (7:5) does four things with this tale. First, he adds to it: God changes the appearances of the builders. Second, he "clarifies" what may not be crystal clear; namely, "confuse the language" becomes "God divided up their languages." Third, he uses the material for etiological purposes. Thus, God's actions here become the source for the varying languages and the disparate physical appearances of the peoples of the earth. Fourth, he adds narrative dramatic detail to the Bible's tale. Thus, we learn of particular incidents that plague the builders after God's actions and that in the end ruin the whole project.

The Bible tells us (Exod 2:2) that when Amram's wife gave birth, she hid her baby for three months. The text does not tell us why this particular mother with this particular baby ventured so risky an action. But *L.A.B.* apparently offers us something of an explanation. Jochebed will have recognized that her son was special, for he was born circumcised (9:13).

When Moses makes his first descent from Mount Sinai (Exod 32:19), he sees the idolatry in the Israelite camp and angrily takes the two tablets of the law and throws them down, smashing them. *L.A.B.* provides an interesting variation (12:5): "Moses descended in haste and saw the calf. He looked at the tablets and saw that they were not written upon, and agitated he smashed them." It is clear what is going on here. In the Bible, Moses receives the two tablets (31:18), "tablets that were written by the finger of God." A reader may well be shocked. How does Moses smash the tablets when they contain the words of God written by the finger of God? *L.A.B.* explains. When Moses reached the camp, the words on the tablets had vanished and so they were blank. When he noticed that, he was at liberty to smash them.

In some cases, *L.A.B.* will clarify an ambiguous biblical text, or rather, turn an ambiguous text into a transparent one. In Genesis the mysterious character Lamech utters some cryptic autobiographical remarks (4:23-24). It is difficult to tell whether they are meant to put him in a fundamentally positive light or to show him as a villain. But in *L.A.B.*'s version of Lamech's remarks (2:10), there can be no doubt that Lamech's remarks are self-condemnatory. He is an evil man.

Shortly thereafter (3:2), *L.A.B.* refers to God's angry statement at Gen 6:3,

"My spirit shall not abide in man for ever, for he is flesh, and his days shall be 120 years." The sense of this verse is by no means clear. What does the last part ("his days shall be 120 years") mean? *L.A.B.* again removes the ambiguity and turns the words into a clear-cut assertion through expansion (3:2). He too writes, "his days shall be 120 years," but then appends "at which I have set the limit of the world." So we see that *L.A.B.'s* words have nothing to do with the life span of an individual human, but rather with the period that mankind has remaining on the earth before God brings the flood.

In Genesis 6–7, God instructs Noah as to how many of each species to bring on board the ark. But the biblical instructions are by no means crystal clear. Modern scholars attribute the difficulties to the use of variant documentary sources. *L.A.B.* (3:4) rearranges, conflates, and simplifies so as to remove any appearance of inconsistency or confusion and produces a clear and straightforward text.

Another such instance begins with Genesis 10. That chapter reports the genealogies of the Noachite families with indications about their distribution across the world and concludes with the statement that the Noachite families lived all over the world after the flood. But the beginning of chapter 11 appears to contradict this by saying that all humanity dwelt in a valley called Shinar. *L.A.B.* reconciles Genesis 10 and 11 by filling in a "gap" between the two chapters. *L.A.B.* indicates that the Noachite families will indeed have scattered all over the earth, but will then have reassembled for the purpose of a census and stayed together. Later, after the episode of the tower of Babel, they will have again — and finally — dispersed.

Occasionally the biblical narrative will seem incomplete or at least fails to provide details or explanations that would seem helpful or desirable. *L.A.B.* will then provide them. For example, Genesis 11 presents genealogies that end with Abram. Genesis 12 begins straight off by reporting that God chose Abram. No explanation for God's choice is indicated. L.A.B. fills this gap (chs. 6–7) by making Abram the pious hero of the tower of Babel story (with which he had no connection in the Bible).

L.A.B.'s Agenda and His Exegesis

Deviations from the Bible in *L.A.B.* often find their motive in the author's pursuit of his agenda, be they matters of theology, philosophy, politics, history, religion, or proper behavior. We note here a few cases.

In the Bible the story of David and Goliath is presented largely as a battle between Israel and its enemy. It is true that David repeatedly declares his faith in God and sees himself as a representative of the Lord (1 Sam 17:26, 36, 45-47), but Goliath is never represented as anything other than the hero of the Philistine enemy. *L.A.B.* turns this story into a battle between the God of Israel and the gods of the Philistines, for not only does David see himself as fighting for God (61:3-6), but Goliath is presented as the representative of the pagan deities. Thus, whereas the biblical Goliath declares, "if I prevail . . . you will be our servants and serve us" (17:9), *L.A.B.*'s Goliath asserts, "I will make your people serve our gods" (61:2). In addition, in a speech with no foundation in the biblical narrative, David rehearses before Goliath their common family history, pointing out that his mother chose the ways of the Lord, while her sister, Goliath's mother, chose the gods of the Philistines. Thus, even speaking genealogically, the battle between David and Goliath is a battle between the true God and the pagan deities. This is of course a recurring theme in *L.A.B.* *L.A.B.*'s introduction here of an angel who aids David (61:5, 8-9) also enhances the divine character of the duel.

Important theological matters that *L.A.B.* holds dear will sometimes find themselves interpolated into a piece of biblical narrative where they have no presence in the Bible. If *L.A.B.* sees a handle to latch onto, he will grab it. An excellent illustration is at 3:9-10. Following the Bible's lead (Gen 8:21-22; 9:11-15), *L.A.B.* has God, after the destruction of the flood, promise that he will never again destroy the world by a flood. Using the precise words of the Bible, *L.A.B.* declares, "For all the days of the earth, seedtime and harvest, cold and heat, summer and winter will not cease day and night." But to this quote he immediately adds these nonbiblical words: "as long as I remember those who inhabit the earth, until time is fulfilled," built upon a hint in the Bible's words, "for all the days of the earth." And with the expression "until time is fulfilled" *L.A.B.* is off and running, telling us exactly what will happen when "time is fulfilled." *L.A.B.* can now speak of eschatological cosmic developments, the resurrection of the dead, the ultimate judgment of humankind, the fate of the underworld, and a new heaven and earth, themes of particular importance for him.

At 39:9, also in the interest of his theological views, *L.A.B.* acts differently, denying in his narrative what was explicit in the Bible. Thus, at Judg 11:24 Jephthah sends a message to the Ammonite king, warning him to be satisfied with the territory that the god Chemosh has given the Ammonites. *L.A.B.* counters this explicitly and declares (39:9) that the Ammonite claim to land that their god has given them is without foundation, for their "gods" are not gods.

Sometimes *L.A.B.* will make a subtle change in the biblical text in order to make a theological or philosophical point. Thus, at 7:4 God asserts his choice of Abram and his intent to bring him to the land of Israel, "the land upon which my eye has looked from the beginning." Now the latter words are in fact a quotation of Deut 11:12, wherein God is said to keep his eye upon the land of Israel from the beginning of the year to the end of the year. By this slight change in wording, *L.A.B.* has altered a statement of the blessedness (i.e., fertility) of the land to an assertion of its eternal historical significance, that God chose the land of Israel from the beginning of time, with the presumption that it was intended as home for Abraham and his descendants from the beginning. Along these lines is also the (nonbiblical, indeed counterbiblical) statement (7:4) that the land of Israel was not affected by the great flood of Noah's time.

The Bible presents the story of Korah's rebellion (Numbers 16). Korah the Levite, two prominent Reubenites (descendants of Jacob's oldest son), and their followers protest against the power held by Moses and Aaron. The situation degenerates from there, ending in catastrophe. *L.A.B.* makes the conflict much more than a struggle between Moses and Korah, and thereby makes the catastrophic denouement more understandable. His narrative begins (16:1) with Korah's complaint about the imposition on the people of the law of fringes: "Why is an unbearable law imposed upon us in this way?" Thus, Korah's rebellion is not against Moses' authority but rather against the law imposed on the people by God and consequently against God himself. The grave destruction that follows is more readily understood.

L.A.B. is not averse to re-creating characters and entire narrative elements in his pursuit of his agenda. Thus, for example, in chapter 44 (part of *L.A.B.*'s remaking of the book of Judges) we learn that Delilah had a son by the name of Micah. In the book of Judges there is no indication that the seductress Delilah has any children. But beyond this, the whole episode that *L.A.B.* presents surrounding the characters Delilah and Micah is a drastic revision of the story in Judges 17-18, which is a small story embedded in a larger and more important one, that of the conquest of the Danites. In brief, Delilah persuades her son to create several icons for idolatry and to make himself their priest. He does so and leads the people astray. God is furious and punishes horribly both Micah and his mother and the people as well. In this admonitory tale, *L.A.B.* spells out in concrete detail the practice of idolatry and the terrible consequences thereof, themes that he mentions often but usually does not describe in such graphic and detailed light. The biblical narrative contains some of these elements but underplays them. Most significantly, in the Bible's narrative God plays no role whatsoever, there is no inveighing against idolatry, and there is no punishment for the idolatry. *L.A.B.* transforms this into a mainline-*L.A.B.* tale of the evils of idolatry. Indeed, *L.A.B.*'s narrative associates Micah's actions with those of the worshippers of the golden calf.

Another such deviating narrative is found in chapter 22, where we read of the building of an altar in Transjordan by the two and one-half tribes who have settled there. This is grounded in the narrative of Joshua 22, wherein we learn that the two and one-half tribes, on permanently settling in Transjordan, build themselves there a large altar. The Israelites chastise them and prepare for war. The tribes defend themselves and assert that the altar was merely a symbol to connect themselves to their brethren in Israel, but was neither intended nor used for worship and sacrifice. Reconciliation is effected. *L.A.B.*'s narrative is very similar but differs in one key way. While the tribes in *L.A.B.* do defend themselves in a fashion similar to the Bible's, asserting that their building of the altar was a means to connect themselves more closely to their brethren in the worship of God, they have been offering sacrifices and readily admit it. Since they do so, the response of the Israelites is totally different than in the Bible. Joshua explains to the tribes that sacrifices are not of great importance and that the altar can and should even be destroyed. What is important, he expounds, is the study of God's law. It seems apparent that *L.A.B.*'s serious revision of the Bible's story is to afford Joshua the opportunity to belittle sacrifice and magnify the import of study. This is clearly a theme of great significance for *L.A.B.* at a point when, with the temple destroyed, the Jews had no possibility of sacrifice and had to find, as they did, a new focus of their energies and devotion, namely, the study of the law.

L.A.B. will adapt the meaning of biblical verses. For instance, in the eschatological passage at 23:13, God declares that in the end time "I will restore you to your fathers and your fathers to you." This is clearly based on the famous verse at Mal 3:23-24 (4:5-6), wherein God declares, "I will send you Elijah the prophet before the coming of the great and awesome day of the LORD. And he will restore the hearts of fathers to their children and the hearts of children to their fathers." What in the Bible is some sort of spiritual reconciliation between fathers and children, *L.A.B.* has transformed into a kind of physical resurrection and reunion of fathers and children after death.

L.A.B. has a strong affection for the principle of "measure for measure." In particular, he uses it frequently in the context of meting out punishment. Thus, for example, at 12:7 those who willingly and sincerely participated in the sin of the golden calf lost their tongues. This is apparently punishment for their tongues' declaration that "this calf is the god who took us out of Egypt." Similar is Doeg's punishment at 63:4. A worm will attack his tongue and cause him to rot away. Doeg the informer has sinned with his tongue and is punished through his tongue. At 31:1 the enemy general is given a threefold measure-for-measure punishment. Because he boasted of his mighty arm, he is defeated by the arm of a woman; because he boasted of taking spoils for his young men, young women take spoils from him; because he boasted of taking captive women as concubines, he will die at the hands of a woman. But "measure for measure" is not limited to punishment. The Bible spells out the Decalogue as a series of injunctions, some positive, some negative. In most of the cases it does not indicate either explanations or goals (but see Exod 20:5, 11, 12). In contrast, *L.A.B.* provides such explanation for nearly all the commandments, and the explanations mostly follow a single principle, that of (so to speak) measure for measure (11:6-13). Thus, for example, do not commit adultery because your enemies committed adultery against you; do not covet, lest others covet your possessions.

L.A.B. has a special interest in the course of Jewish history. The Bible occasionally presents reviews of Jewish history. *L.A.B.* will start with them and elaborate in various ways (23-24; 32:1-10). On occasion in the biblical narrative the history of the Jews is reviewed. Thus, for example, in his valedictory address (Joshua 24) Joshua starts with Terah and ends with the recent conquest of the land of Israel, recounting in substantial detail and touching on highlights like the drowning of the Egyptians at the Red Sea and the transforming of Balaam's expected curses into blessings. What is most notable, perhaps, is how closely the review adheres to the biblical narrative of the Hexateuch, with virtually no elaboration beyond the straightforward recounting of facts. Contrast *L.A.B.* (23:4-14). He, too, puts a review of Jewish history into Joshua's mouth that begins with Abraham's birth and goes up to the present. But *L.A.B.* introduces symbolic or mystical language that is not in the book of Joshua and stresses the covenant of the pieces and the giving of the law at Sinai, neither of which is mentioned by Joshua in the Bible. At one and the same time *L.A.B.* adheres to the Bible, yet also pursues his own agenda.

Similar is *L.A.B.*'s version of the Song of Deborah. In the Bible (Judges 5) the latter is a famous and familiar episode. In it Deborah celebrates the recent victory over the Canaanites. In glorious poetic language she sings in detail (after a brief allusion to the revelation at Sinai) of the events of the victory. That is the sum and substance of the song. *L.A.B.* follows suit by giving his Deborah a celebratory song as well. But in this lengthy song just a few lines are devoted to an account of the victory (32:11, 12, 15). Most of the song is devoted to yet another review of Jewish history from Abraham to the present, with an emphasis this time on the themes of sterile women giving birth, the binding of Jacob, and the revelation at Sinai. Much detail that is not in the Bible is provided.

Embellishments

There are numerous other ways in which *L.A.B.* turns the biblical narrative into his own. I end here by noting just a few. *L.A.B.* often adds details and twists to the biblical events, sometimes increasing dramatic tension. A good example is in his description of the crossing of the Red Sea (10:3). In the Bible (Exodus 14) the Egyptians pursue the fleeing Jews and corner them at the Sea. The Jews in fear cry out to Moses, complaining that they would prefer to be slaves back in Egypt. *L.A.B.* has a dramatically different version. After the initial complaints of the people at their impending doom, they divide up into three factions, each with its own plan of action. Some tribes want to drown themselves in the sea; others to return to their former lives as slaves in Egypt; and a third group to take up arms and fight the Egyptians. Another nonbiblical element in *L.A.B.*'s version of the crossing of the Sea may also be attributable to his interest in increasing the drama. This is his having Moses strike the sea (10:5). In the Bible Moses merely stretches his hand out over the sea.

A similar "dramatic" escalation can be found in the account of the revelation at Sinai. Exodus's description is impressive and awe-striking (19:16-19; 20:18). There are thunder and lightning, a dense cloud, a trumpet's blast, fire and smoke. Yet, all this was not enough for *L.A.B.*, who apparently thought that by adding further cosmic phenomena he could make the scene even more impressive. Thus, at 11:4-5 we are told not only that the revelation involved thunder, lightning, trumpet blasts, and fire, but also that "the earth trembled, the hills shook, the mountains tottered, the depths bubbled, all the habitable world was shaken, the heavens folded up, the clouds dripped water . . . winds and storms roared, the stars assembled, and angels ran ahead" — in other words, that not only did the region of Sinai partake in the experience, but the entire earth, indeed the entire cosmos, earthly and divine, did.

Dreams, indeed meaningful dreams, play a substantial and important role in the biblical narrative. Think of the dreams of Abraham and Jacob, of Joseph and Pharaoh. *L.A.B.* invents nonbiblical dreams to enhance his narrative and to magnify the reputation of the figure. Thus, Miriam has a dream that forecasts the greatness of her as-yet unborn brother, Moses (9:10). Cassandra-like, she is not believed. In that same narrative, the daughter of Pharaoh is stimulated by a dream to go down to the river and thereby becomes the discoverer and the adoptive mother of Moses (9:15).

Sometimes *L.A.B.* is motivated by a desire to avoid something unpleasant in the Bible. For instance, L.A.B. reports Joseph's ascendancy to power in Egypt and mentions his brothers' visit to Egypt and their failure to recognize Joseph (8:10). *L.A.B.*'s "he was not recognized by them" calls to mind a fascinating complex of events, which are, frustratingly for the reader familiar with Genesis, totally ignored. It seems likely that *L.A.B.* leaves out the elaborate interactions between Joseph and his brothers in Egypt because they tend to put Joseph in a bad light, as he manipulates and abuses his brothers. So the story is touched on and then passed over.

Reading Backward

A common technique *L.A.B.* uses that accords with the Bible is what I would call "reading backward." That is, often in the Bible a reference within a particular narrative will be made to an earlier action that was not explicitly mentioned in its chronological place. *L.A.B.* will jump on this kind of reference and exploit it by re-creating that earlier moment in light of this reference. Thus, for example, when the Jews appear trapped at the Red Sea, Moses "cries out" to God and prays for help (10:4). But there is no such "crying out" to God by Moses at the Red Sea in the Bible (Exodus 14). However, *L.A.B.* has not invented this *ex nihilo*. For at the Red Sea God says to Moses, "Why do you cry out to me?" (Exod 14:15). *L.A.B.* then proceeds (reasonably) to portray such a "crying out" for Moses.

L.A.B. reports a gathering of the people in the time of Deborah for the purpose of confession, repentance, and prayer (30:4). There is no such episode in the Bible. But when Samuel reviews Jewish history at 1 Samuel 12 he alludes *inter alia* to the period of Deborah and mentions the people's confession and prayer. It is out of this brief recollection that *L.A.B.* has concocted this episode.

When the angel appears to Manoah's wife a second time in *L.A.B.*, he instructs her to run and summon her husband (42:6). But in the Bible the angel says nothing (Judg 13:9). *L.A.B.* has concocted the angel's words from the following verses in the Bible, which reports that she runs and tells her husband, who then returns with her to the place. Thus, *L.A.B.* assumes that her actions were precipitated by the command of the angel and so sets it out explicitly.

At 64:4, when Saul asks the witch of Endor to bring up Samuel, she responds, "I fear Saul." She does not say this explicitly in the Bible. This is of course a reasonable inference, but *L.A.B.* is also reading backward the biblical narrative. For Saul later says to her, "Do not be afraid" (1 Sam 28:13).

Brief Survey of *L.A.B.* Scholarship, with Some Recent Trends

Johannes Sichardt published the editio princeps of *L.A.B.* in 1527.[3] There is no evidence that *L.A.B.* was much read or studied thereafter for nearly four centuries. The work almost seems to have vanished: "Its existence had been forgotten."[4] Then, in 1898, Leopold Cohn published a lengthy article in *JQR* in which

---

3. Johannes Sichardt, *Philonis Iudaei Alexandrini Libri Antiquitatum. Quaestionum et Solutionum in Genesin* (Basel: Adamus Petrus, 1527).

4. Leopold Cohn, "An Apocryphal Work Ascribed to Philo of Alexandria," *JQR* 10 (1898): 277-332 (278).

he, so to speak, unearthed the *L.A.B.* and brought it to the attention of the scholarly world.[5] Cohn's primary focus was to show that the *L.A.B.* was in fact part of the corpus of midrashic (Cohn himself used the term "Hagadic") literature, even though its form and structure were different from the usual midrashic text. His learned piece notices many points of contact between *L.A.B.* and midrashic exegetical traditions.[6]

Two decades later, Montague R. James published a translation of *L.A.B.* into English, with a valuable introduction and sparse notes.[7] Unlike Cohn, James's interest was not so much in *L.A.B.*'s role in the world of midrash as in matters like the manuscript tradition of the work, its title and attribution, the original language, date, themes, relationship to works such as *4 Esdras* and *Jubilees,* and its quotations from the Bible.

Amazingly, neither Cohn nor James provided their readers with the text of *L.A.B.* Guido Kisch's edition of 1949 represents the first attempt to provide readers with a critical edition of the work and is, not surprisingly, interested in little other than the relationship of the manuscripts to each other and the establishment of the "correct" text.[8] But the *Sources Chrétiennes* volumes of *L.A.B.* by Daniel Harrington et al. are something else, seeking to provide not merely a critical edition of the text (and one very different from Kisch's), but also, by virtue of containing a lengthy introduction and an ample commentary, providing illumination on many fronts.[9] Aside from the edition's discussion of the textual transmission, its largest contribution is the discussion of themes in *L.A.B.* and its identification of additional biblical quotations.

In 1971 James's *L.A.B.* volume was republished with a very long prolegomenon by Louis Feldman.[10] It amplified James's discussion on all points, but its most striking and important contribution was the recognition of many more correspondences to midrashic texts than previously noticed.

In 1996 Howard Jacobson published his commentary on *L.A.B.*[11] Therein, virtually every aspect of *L.A.B.* is discussed in greater detail than had been pre-

---

5. Cohn, "An Apocryphal Work."

6. "An Apocryphal Work," 314-24.

7. Montague R. James, *The Biblical Antiquities of Philo* (London: SPCK, 1917; repr. New York: Ktav, 1971).

8. Guido Kisch, *Pseudo-Philo's Liber Antiquitatum Biblicarum* (Notre Dame: University of Notre Dame Press, 1949).

9. Daniel J. Harrington, Jacques Cazeaux, Charles Perrot, and Pierre-Maurice Bogaert, *Pseudo-Philon: Les Antiquités Bibliques.* 2 vols. SC 229-30 (Paris: Cerf, 1976).

10. Louis H. Feldman, "Prolegomenon," in James, *The Biblical Antiquities of Philo,* lviii-lx.

11. Howard Jacobson, *A Commentary on Pseudo-Philo's Liber Antiquitatum Biblicarum, with Latin Text and English Translation.* 2 vols. AGJU 31 (Leiden: Brill, 1996).

viously done. It is worth noting two aspects. First, whereas previous commentators had noted numerous biblical quotations and echoes in *L.A.B.*, they had been seriously limited by focusing on quotations in context. Jacobson showed that hundreds of biblical quotations are found in *L.A.B.* that are out of context, even alien to context. This provided groundwork for understanding *L.A.B.'s* exegetical and literary techniques. Second, by detailed reconstruction of the Hebrew original, Jacobson's translation is closer than previous translations to *L.A.B.'s* actual text in hundreds of places.

Several scholars have recently sought to study *L.A.B.* from what we might call a more literary perspective. In particular, we may single out the work of Eckart Reinmuth, Frederick Murphy, D. C. Polaski, and Bruce Fisk.[12] Thus, Murphy focuses on an elaborate discussion of the important themes of *L.A.B.*, Reinmuth on hermeneutics and discourse, and Polaski on gender discourse, while Fisk is primarily concerned with *L.A.B.'s* hermeneutical strategies (some of which have been noted above).

Other scholars, especially Feldman and Christopher Begg, have studied *L.A.B.'s* adaptations of biblical episodes and biblical personages by comparing and contrasting them to other postbiblical rewritings of the Bible. Thus, for example, Feldman has studied the views of Philo, Josephus, and Pseudo-Philo on Sodom and Gomorrah, on Sihon and Og, and on the tenth Egyptian plague,[13] while Begg has analyzed *L.A.B.'s* and Josephus's versions of the story of the priests of Nob from 1 Samuel.[14]

Some have recently argued that *L.A.B.* tends toward being a feminist and have reasonably pointed to the important roles given to several women, e.g., Deborah, Jael, Hannah, Jephthah's daughter.[15] While this is true — and it is perfectly clear, for example, that L.A.B. is not hostile to women to the degree that, say, Josephus was — the fact is that most of the positive material about women in *L.A.B.* is taken from the biblical text and so does not necessarily tell us anything about *L.A.B.* himself.

---

12. Eckart Reinmuth, *Pseudo-Philo und Lukas.* WUNT 74 (Tübingen: Mohr Siebeck, 1994); Frederick J. Murphy, *Pseudo-Philo: Rewriting the Bible* (New York: Oxford University Press, 1993); D. C. Polaski, "On Taming Tamar: Amram's Rhetoric and Women's Roles in Pseudo-Philo's *Liber Antiquitatum Biblicarum* 9," *JSP* 13 (1995): 79-99; and Fisk, *Do You Not Remember?*

13. Louis H. Feldman, "The Destruction of Sodom and Gomorrah According to Philo, Pseudo-Philo and Josephus," *Hen* 23 (2001): 185-98; "The Portrayal of Sihon and Og in Philo, Pseudo-Philo and Josephus," *JJS* 53 (2002): 264-72; "The Plague of the First-Born Egyptians in Rabbinic Tradition, Philo, Pseudo-Philo and Josephus," *RB* 109 (2002): 403-21.

14. Christopher T. Begg, "The Massacre of the Priests of Nob in Josephus and Pseudo-Philo," *EstBib* 55 (1997): 171-98.

15. For a qualified view of feminist tendencies in *L.A.B.* with respect to the character of Tamar, see Polaski, "On Taming Tamar."

BIBLIOGRAPHY

Baker, Cynthia. "Pseudo-Philo and the Transformation of Jephthah's Daughter." In *Anti-Covenant*, ed. Mieke Bal. JSOTSup 81. Sheffield: Almond, 1989, 195-209.

Bauckham, Richard. "The Liber Antiquitatum Biblicarum of Pseudo-Philo and the Gospels as 'Midrash.'" In *Gospel Perspectives*, vol. 3: *Studies in Midrash and Historiography*, ed. R. T. France and David Wenham. Sheffield: JSOT, 1983, 33-76.

Begg, Christopher T. "The Massacre of the Priests of Nob in Josephus and Pseudo-Philo." *EstBib* 55 (1997): 171-98.

Burnette-Bletsch, Rhonda. "At the Hands of a Woman: Rewriting Jael in Pseudo-Philo." *JSP* 17 (1998): 53-64.

Cohn, Leopold. "An Apocryphal Work Ascribed to Philo of Alexandria." *JQR* 10 (1898): 277-332.

———. "Pseudo-Philo und Jerachmeel." In *Festschrift zum siebzigsten Geburtstage Jakob Guttmanns*, ed. Martin Philippson. Leipzig: Fock, 1915; repr. New York: Arno, 1980, 173-85.

Dietzfelbinger, Christian. *Pseudo-Philo: Antiquitates Biblicae*. JSHRZ 2.2. Gütersloh: Gütersloher, 1975.

Feldman, Louis H. "Prolegomenon." In James, *The Biblical Antiquities of Philo*, lviii-lx.

———. "The Destruction of Sodom and Gomorrah According to Philo, Pseudo-Philo and Josephus." *Hen* 23 (2001): 185-98.

———. "The Portrayal of Sihon and Og in Philo, Pseudo-Philo and Josephus." *JJS* 53 (2002): 264-72.

———. "The Plague of the First-Born Egyptians in Rabbinic Tradition, Philo, Pseudo-Philo and Josephus." *RB* 109 (2002): 403-21.

———. "The Portrayal of Phinehas by Philo, Pseudo-Philo, and Josephus." *JQR* 92 (2002): 315-45.

Fisk, Bruce N. *Do You Not Remember? Scripture, Story and Exegesis in the Rewritten Bible of Pseudo-Philo*. JSPSup 37. Sheffield: Sheffield Academic, 2001.

Harrington, Daniel J. "The Original Language of Pseudo-Philo's Liber Antiquitatum Biblicarum." *HTR* 63 (1970): 503-14.

———. "Pseudo-Philo." In *OTP*, 2:297-377.

———, Jacques Cazeaux, Charles Perrot, and Pierre-Maurice Bogaert. *Pseudo-Philon: Les Antiquités Bibliques*. 2 vols. SC 229-30. Paris: Cerf, 1976.

Hayward, C. T. Robert. "The Figure of Adam in Pseudo-Philo's Liber Antiquitatum Biblicarum." *JSJ* 23 (1992): 1-20.

Horst, Pieter W. van der. *Essays on the Jewish World of Early Christianity*. NTOA 14. Freiburg: Universitätsverlag, 1990.

Jacobson, Howard. "Marginalia to Pseudo-Philo Liber Antiquitatum Biblicarum and to the Chronicles of Jerahmeel." *REJ* 142 (1983): 455-59.

———. *A Commentary on Pseudo-Philo's Liber Antiquitatum Biblicarum, with Latin Text and English Translation*. AGJU 31. 2 vols. Leiden: Brill, 1996.

James, Montague R. *The Biblical Antiquities of Philo*. London: SPCK, 1917. Repr. New York: Ktav, 1971.

Kisch, Guido. *Pseudo-Philo's Liber Antiquitatum Biblicarum*. Notre Dame: University of Notre Dame Press, 1949.

Lewis, Jack P. *A Study of the Interpretation of Noah and the Flood in Jewish and Christian Literature*. Leiden: Brill, 1968.

Murphy, Frederick J. *Pseudo-Philo: Rewriting the Bible*. New York: Oxford University Press, 1993.

Polaski, D. C. "On Taming Tamar: Amram's Rhetoric and Women's Roles in Pseudo-Philo's *Liber Antiquitatum Biblicarum* 9." *JSP* 13 (1995): 79-99.

Reinmuth, Eckart. *Pseudo-Philo und Lukas*. WUNT 74. Tübingen: Mohr Siebeck, 1994.

Riessler, Paul, *Altjüdisches Schrifttum ausserhalb der Bibel*. Augsburg: Filser, 1928.

Sichardt, Johannes. *Philonis Iudaei Alexandrini Libri Antiquitatum, Quaestionum et Solutionum in Genesin*. Basel: Adamus Petrus, 1527.

Smits, Esmé R. "A Contribution to the History of Pseudo-Philo's Liber Antiquitatum Biblicarum in the Middle Ages." *JSJ* 23 (1992): 197-216.

Vermes, Geza. *Scripture and Tradition in Judaism: Haggadic Studies*. StPB 4. Leiden: Brill, 1961; 2nd rev. ed. 1973.

Wadsworth, Michael. "Making and Interpreting Scripture." In *Ways of Reading the Bible*. Brighton: Harvester, 1981, 7-22.

PART 4

The Qumran Literature

The Use of Scripture in the *Community Rule*

Shani Tzoref

Introduction to the Texts

The category of "Rules" encompasses those compositions that outline the beliefs and behaviors required of members of the *Yahad* Community and that describe processes and rituals of induction and affirmation of commitment. The most prominent and best-preserved of these works is the *Community Rule (Serekh Hayahad)*, which will serve as the basis of our current discussion.[1] This composition has survived, in various recensions in about a dozen manuscripts: 1QS; ten copies from Cave 4;[2] 5Q11; and possibly 11Q29.[3] The Cave 1 manuscript tends to be used as the primary text, since it is the most complete and was the first copy discovered in modern times.[4]

---

1. For an overview of the composition, see Sarianna Metso, *The Serekh Texts*. CQS 9. LSTS 62 (London: T. & T. Clark, 2007).

2. Philip Alexander and Geza Vermes, *Qumran Cave 4. XIX: 4QSerekh Ha-Yahad and Two Related Texts*. DJD 26 (Oxford: Clarendon, 1998).

3. Cf. Eibert J. C. Tigchelaar, "A Newly Identified 11QSerekh ha-Yahad Fragment (11Q29)?" in *The Dead Sea Scrolls: Fifty Years after Their Discovery: Proceedings of the Jerusalem Congress, July 20-25, 1997*, ed. Lawrence H. Schiffman, Emanuel Tov, and James C. VanderKam (Jerusalem: Israel Exploration Society and Shrine of the Book, 2000), 285-92.

4. This despite the fact that it is not considered the most reliable witness. The scroll containing 1QS was one of the first seven scrolls found in Qumran Cave 1 in 1947 and was initially published in 1951 under the title "Manual of Discipline," in Millar Burrows, John C. Trever, and William H. Brownlee, *The Dead Sea Scrolls of St. Mark's Monastery* (New Haven: American Schools of Oriental Research, 1951), 2.2. The current siglum reflects the ancient title, "Serekh

---

An early version of this paper was delivered at a seminar of the Department of Bible at Haifa University in April 2008. I would like to thank Jonathan Ben-Dov for inviting me to address the seminar group, and to thank the participants for their helpful feedback.

Related texts include the *Rule of the Congregation* (1QS[a]) and the *Rule of Blessings* (1QS[b]), which are preserved on the same scroll as 1QS, as well as the *Sectarian Rule* (5Q13), which includes parallel material to parts of the *Community Rule*.[5] The *Damascus Document* is a composition of more complex genre than the *Community Rule* but also contains regulatory material with important parallels to 1QS.[6]

The generally accepted outline of the composition is as follows:[7]

1QS I, 1-15 Introduction

- 1QS I, 16–III, 12 Liturgy for the Renewal of the Covenant
- 1QS III, 13–IV, 26 Treatise on the Two Spirits
- 1QS V, 1–VII, 25 Rules for Community Life (with the Penal Code at VI, 24– VII, 25)
- 1QS VIII, 1–IX, 26a "Manifesto" (with the *Maskil* section at IX, 12-26)

1QS IX, 26b–XI, 22 Concluding Psalm

The *Serekh* texts have received much scholarly attention in recent years, mostly from a redaction-critical perspective.[8] Our own focus here will be on the use of the Hebrew Bible in 1QS. It is helpful to discuss biblical interpretation with respect to characteristics of content, motive, and form. As far as con-

---

haYahad," which is preserved in the opening lines of the manuscript and which has been translated into English as the "Community Rule."

5. Cf. Lawrence H. Schiffman, "Sectarian Rule (5Q13)," in *Rule of the Community and Related Documents*, ed. James H. Charlesworth. PTSDSSP 1 (Tübingen: Mohr Siebeck and Louisville: Westminster John Knox, 1994), 132-43. Additional related works are 4Q265 Miscellaneous Rules (formerly *Serekh Dameseq*); 4Q477 Rebukes of the Overseer (formerly Decrees); 4Q275 Communal Ceremony; 4Q279 Four Lots; 4Q502 Ritual of Marriage (frg. 16), as well as the compositions classified as "Ordinances": 4Q159 (4QOrd[a]), 4Q513 (4QOrd[b]), and 4Q514 (4QOrd[c]); and the Berakhot texts (4Q286-290).

6. A citation of 1QS col. VII is found in two copies of the *Damascus Document*, 4Q266 frag 10 col. II and 4Q270 frag 7 col. I (J. M. Baumgarten et al., *Qumran Cave 4: XIII, The Damascus Document (4Q266-274/3)*. DJD 18 [Oxford: Clarendon, 1996], 74, 162-63).

7. With some minor variation; see Pierre Guilbert, "Le plan de la 'Règle de la Communauté,'" *RevQ* 1 (1959): 323-44, 327; Jacob Licht, *The Rule Scroll — A Scroll from the Wilderness of Judaea — 1QS, 1QSa, 1QSb: Text, Introduction and Commentary* (Jerusalem: Mosad Biyalik, 1965) [Hebrew], 19; Metso, *The Serekh Texts*, 7-14; and "Constitutional Rules at Qumran," in *The Dead Sea Scrolls After Fifty Years: A Comprehensive Assessment*, ed. Peter W. Flint and James C. VanderKam (Leiden: Brill, 1998), 1:186-210.

8. The work of Sarianna Metso has been particularly influential. See esp. *The Textual Development of the Qumran Community Rule*. STDJ 21 (Leiden: Brill, 1997). See also Philip S. Alexander, "The Redaction-History of Serekh ha-Yahad: A Proposal," *RevQ* 17 (1996): 437-56. Charlotte Hempel has employed similar methodology in her analysis of the *Damascus Document*; see, *inter alia, The Damascus Texts*. CQS 1 (Sheffield: Sheffield Academic 2000); and more recently, "The Literary Development of the S-Tradition: A New Paradigm," *RevQ* 22 (2006): 389-401; "Sources and Redaction in the Dead Sea Scrolls: The Growth of Ancient Texts," in *Redis-*

tent — unlike exegetical compositions, the *Rules* do not feature systematic halakic, haggadic, or eschatological interpretation, but rather selectively use a range of scriptural texts for the justification of sectarian practices and beliefs and for exhortation towards these.[9] This characteristic is directly related to motive — the author of 1QS recasts biblical language and concepts for his sectarian purposes, especially to present the Community as the righteous remnant of Israel, destined for salvation through proper observance of God's Torah. The current discussion is structured with respect to a particular aspect of form — the use of biblical language in 1QS can be effectively scaled along a spectrum of explicitness, in keeping with recent models for analyzing how nonexegetical works from Qumran reuse the Bible.[10] Thus, in her examination of *Hodayot*, Julie Hughes follows trends in biblical and literary studies to delineate the categories of "quotation," "allusion" and "idiom."[11] Esther Chazon similarly desig-

---

covering the Dead Sea Scrolls: An Assessment of Old and New Approaches and Methods, ed. Maxine Grossman (Grand Rapids: Eerdmans, 2010), 162-81.

9. See Sarianna Metso, "The Use of Old Testament Quotations in the Qumran Community Rule," in *Qumran Between the Old and New Testaments*, ed. Frederick H. Cryer and Thomas L. Thompson. JSOTSup 290 (Sheffield: Sheffield Academic, 1998), 219.

10. Earlier descriptions tended to distinguish more simply between "explicit" and "implicit" exegesis; see Joseph A. Fitzmyer, "The Use of Explicit Old Testament Quotations in Qumran Literature and in the New Testament," *NTS* 7 (1960-61): 297-333; repr. in *Essays on the Semitic Background of the New Testament* (London: Chapman, 1971), 3-58; Geza Vermes, "Biblical Proof-Texts in Qumran Literature," *JSS* 34 (1989) 493-508; Jean Carmignac, "Les citations de l'Ancien Testament dans 'La Guerre des Fils de Lumière contre les Fils de Ténèbres,'" *RB* 63 (1956): 234-60, 375-90. Despite his use of binary language in his taxonomic discussions, Vermes was aware of greater complexity in the use of the Bible at Qumran. E.g., he wrote of CD, "The work includes every shade in the spectrum from the pale simplicity of an implicit biblical inference to the variegated intricacies of a multi-level exegetical construct"; "Biblical Proof-texts," 497. Devorah Dimant's comprehensive overviews in the 1980s featured the broad headings "implicit" and "explicit," but also introduced categories and methodologies for more nuanced distinctions. Thus, e.g., Dimant distinguished "reminiscence" alongside allusion and implicit and explicit citation; "Use, Authority and Interpretation of Mikra at Qumran," in *Mikra: Text, Translation, Reading and Interpretation of the Hebrew Bible in Ancient Judaism and Early Christianity*, ed. Martin Jan Mulder. CRINT 2.1 (Assen: Van Gorcum and Philadelphia: Fortress, 1988), 401 n. 84. See also Dimant, "Qumran Sectarian Literature," in *Jewish Writings of the Second Temple Period: Apocrypha, Pseudepigrapha, Qumran Sectarian Writings, Philo, Josephus*, ed. Michael E. Stone. CRINT 2.2 (Assen: Van Gorcum and Minneapolis: Fortress, 1984), 483-550, esp. 504.

11. Julie A. Hughes, *Scriptural Allusions and Exegesis in the Hodayot*. STDJ 59 (Leiden: Brill, 2006), 41-55. See Jonathan G. Campbell, *The Use of Scripture in the Damascus Document 1-8, 1-20*. BZAW 228 (Berlin: de Gruyter, 1995), 11-32. For discussions of this issue in biblical studies, see Michael Fishbane, *Biblical Interpretation in Ancient Israel* (Oxford: Clarendon, 1985), 285-87; Richard B. Hays, *Echoes of Scripture in the Letters of Paul* (New Haven: Yale University Press, 1989); Stanley E. Porter, "The Use of the Old Testament in the New Testament: A Brief Com-

nates "quotation," "allusion," and "free use" as three "manners of borrowing" in 4Q505-507 (4QWords of the Luminaries).[12]

Adapting these approaches, I will examine some of the ways in which Scripture is employed in 1QS through: (1) explicit citation using a formulaic marker; (2) allusion by means of verbal parallel; (3) "free use" of biblical idiom; and (4) implicit reworking of biblical language. In each of these forms, it may be shown that the author relies upon exegetical traditions associated with the biblical base text. This survey does not aim to provide an exhaustive account of references to the Bible in 1QS but rather to put forth representative examples of the ways in which Scripture is used in the composition.

Explicit Citation

The use of Scripture is easiest to spot when it is introduced by a citation formula.[13] In this section, I discuss the three instances in which full citation formulas appear in 1QS:

- 1QS V, 15, "for thus it is written," preceding a citation of Exod 23:7

---

ment on Method and Terminology," in *Early Christian Interpretation of the Scriptures of Israel: Investigations and Proposals,* ed. Craig A. Evans and James A. Sanders. JSNTSup 148 (Sheffield: Sheffield Academic, 1997), 79-96; Benjamin D. Sommer, *A Prophet Reads Scripture: Allusion in Isaiah 40–66* (Stanford: Stanford University Press, 1998); Richard L. Schultz, *The Search for Quotation: Verbal Parallels in the Prophets.* JSOTSup 180 (Sheffield: Sheffield Academic, 1999).

12. "Scripture and Prayer in 'The Words of the Luminaries,'" in *Prayers That Cite Scripture,* ed. James L. Kugel (Cambridge, Mass.: Harvard University Press, 2007), 25-41. See also "The Use of the Bible as a Key to Meaning in Psalms from Qumran," in *Emanuel: Studies in the Hebrew Bible, Septuagint and Dead Sea Scrolls in Honor of Emanuel Tov,* ed. Shalom M. Paul, Robert A. Kraft, Lawrence H. Schiffman, and Weston W. Fields. VTSup 94 (Leiden: Brill, 2003), 85-96. Chazon (28) further outlines four "modes of composition," scaling relative proportions of direct borrowing and independent expression in a given pericope. These four are: "modeling a new literary unit upon a biblical passage"; "linking a chain of complete biblical quotations into a florilegium"; "patching biblical quotations, allusions, and expressions together with new material into a pastiche"; and "free composition using isolated biblical expressions, motifs, and formulas." Cf. Dimant, "Use, Authority," 409-19; Michael Fishbane, "Use, Authority and Interpretation of Mikra at Qumran," in Mulder, *Mikra,* 339-77, esp. 356-60. He examines the use of Mikra as "model for language," "model for composition," and "model for practices or procedures."

13. See the classic treatment by Fitzmyer, cited above, "The Use of Explicit Old Testament Quotations"; Vermes, "Biblical Proof-Texts." Now with the availability of the extant corpus in its entirety, we can confirm that explicit citation is rare in the scrolls, appearing mostly in the pesharim and CD, with some occurrences in 1QM and 4QMMT and here in 1QS (see Steven D. Fraade, "Interpretive Authority in the Studying Community of Qumran," *JJS* 144 [1993]: 46-69, esp. 48 n. 6).

- 1QS V, 17, "as it is written," preceding a citation of Isa 2:22
- 1QS VIII, 14, "as it is written," preceding a citation of Isa 40:3. In a related additional case, at 1QS IX, 19, a revised re-citation of Isa 40:3 is flagged by a pronominal identifying formula.

In this discussion it will be necessary to recapitulate much of Sarianna Metso's thorough analysis of these texts in order to build upon her observations.[14] The novum in my presentation is my emphasis upon the exegetical significance of sectarian terminology and of prior traditions for explaining the function of these citations.[15]

1QS col. V. Exod 23:7 and Isa 2:22: Explicit Citation with Introductory Formula

The first two explicit citations in 1QS are both brought as textual supports for communal regulations that restrict association with nonmembers of the Community. 1QS V, 13-18 reads:

> 13. . . for one is not cleansed 14unless one turns away from one's wickedness, for he is unclean among all the transgressors of his word. No-one should associate with him in his work or in his possessions lest he burden him with 15iniquity [and] guilt; rather he should remain at a distance from him in every "matter" (כיא ירחק ממנו בכול דבר) for thus it is written (כיא כן כתוב) <Exod 23:7>: "You shall remain at a distance from every matter of falsehood"

---

14. Sarianna Metso, "The Use of Old Testament Quotations"; and "Biblical Quotations in the Community Rule," in *The Bible as Book: The Hebrew Bible and the Judaean Desert Discoveries*, ed. Edward D. Herbert and Emanuel Tov (London: British Library, 2002), 81-92; *The Serekh Texts*, 41-50 (ch. 5: "The Community Rule and the Bible"); *Textual Development*, 81-86. Metso, in turn, relied heavily upon Fitzmyer's analysis in "The Use of Explicit Old Testament Quotations," 33-36.

15. Fishbane ostensibly stresses the exegetical nature of the use of proof-texts in Qumran literature. He emphasizes that these explicit citations "can almost never be read according to their plain-sense. Due to their recontextualization, they must each be construed according to the point which precedes them" ("Use, Authority," 348). However, for Fishbane, and more so for subsequent scholars relying on his work, such "recontextualization" tends to be associated with claims that the sectarian author ignores the original context and plain sense of the cited verse, and that the ties between the citation and application are tenuous and superficial. I aim to show that the relationship between the cited text and its sectarian application is tighter than is generally assumed. See my similar arguments regarding the importance of the biblical base text of *pesher* in Shani L. Berrin, *The Pesher Nahum Scroll from Qumran: An Exegetical Study of 4Q169*. STDJ 53 (Leiden: Brill 2004), 12-18.

(מכול דבר שקר תרחק).[16] None of the men 16of the Community should acquiesce to his authority in any law or regulation. No one should eat of any of their possessions, or drink or accept anything from their hands, 17unless at its price, as it is written (כאשר כתוב) <Isa 2:22> *"Shun the man whose breath is in his nostrils, for how much is he worth?"* (במה נחשב הוא). For 18all those not numbered in his covenant (כול אשר לוא נחשבו בבריתו) will be segregated, they and all that belongs to them. No holy man should support himself on any deed of 19futility, for futile are all those who do not know the covenant.

The citation of Exodus serves as a proof-text for the prohibition against business dealings with people outside the community.[17] The basis for the citation is the function of the verb רחק in 1QS as a technical term to denote exclusion from the Community. It is the opposite of קרב, which denotes acceptance and inclusion of members.[18] The word דבר regularly denotes "formal matter" in 1QS and in CD, particularly in the legal cases outlined in CD column IX. See especially the use of the word in the descriptions of the gradual initiation process in 1QS VI, 14-23 and 1QS VII, 21.[19] It is true, as others have observed, that the citation is em-

---

16. The evidence of LXX παντὸς ῥήματος indicates that this textual variant (כול) was likely to have been found in the author's Vorlage, rather than having been created for 1QS. There may be some resonance here with Deut 23:10, "When you go forth [as] a camp against your enemies, guard yourself against all matter of evil" (כי תצא מחנה על איביך ונשמרת מכל דבר רע). Cf. 1QM VII, 7, which seems to apply this verse to the need for purity and exclusivity among the troops fighting the eschatological war against the sons of darkness.

17. Fishbane views the mandated activity as "separation from persons who can transmit impurity to a covenanter" ("Use, Authority," 349). Similarly, Fitzmyer states, "the member must avoid all contact with the impure, wicked outsider" ("The Use of Explicit Old Testament Quotations," 33). However, the specific nature of the "nonrelations" in this portion of the text pertains to "labor and property," not ritual purity. This is significant because it links the sense of the word דבר in the biblical text to the application in 1QS. See n. 20 below. This rule is thus similar to that in 1QS IX, 7-11, ". . . their goods must not be mixed with the goods of the men of deceit" (*pace* Catherine Murphy's contrast between the two passages, in *Wealth in the Dead Sea Scrolls and in the Qumran Community.* STDJ 40 [Leiden: Brill, 2002], 150). See also 1QS VI, 24-25, "if one is found among them who has lied concerning possessions knowingly, he shall be excluded. . . ."

18. See 1QS VI, 16: "Depending on the outcome of the lot he shall be included or excluded (יקרב או ירחק). When he is included in the Council of the Community (ובקורבו לעצת היחד), he shall not touch the pure food of the Many until they test him . . ." (Thus also in VI, 19, 22; VII, 21; VIII, 18; IX, 15).

19. VII, 20-21 reads: "When he has completed two years, the Many shall be asked concerning his affairs (דבריו). If they allow him to draw near, he shall be enlisted in his place, and afterwards he may be asked concerning judgment." At times, the use of דבר in Classical Hebrew seems as though it may be related to the verbal nature of legal proceedings, but this is not always the case. See Werner H. Schmidt, *TDOT,* 3:104, 108, s.v. דָּבָר; *HALOT,* 1:211, def. 2, "matter." See

ployed in a manner that differs from its sense in the original biblical context of jurisprudence.[20] But it is noteworthy that the recontextualization is firmly grounded in sectarian terminology, and that this terminology reflects a technical use of דבר that is within a similar semantic field to that of the biblical context.[21]

The citation of Isa 2:22 in the above passage is similarly grounded in the special sectarian use of the root חשב in 1QS and CD, as indicating membership in the Community.[22] Metso observes that "in Isaiah, this verse counsels the

---

Preben Wernberg-Møller on 1QS VI, 1, "Some Reflections on the Biblical Material in the Manual of Discipline," *ST* 9 (1955): 40-66 (here 49).

The technical use of דבר throughout the *Rules* texts offers sufficient explanation for the use of Exod 23:7 as a proof-text for the prohibition against business dealings with outsiders. It does not seem necessary to posit more complex exegetical grounds, such as the suggestion of Moshe J. Bernstein and Shlomo Koyfman that Exod 23:7 was "perhaps interpreted as 'from every speaker (דובר) of falsehood stay away'" ("The Interpretation of Biblical Law in the Dead Sea Scrolls: Forms and Methods," in Matthias Henze, ed., *Biblical Interpretation at Qumran*. SDSSRL [Grand Rapids: Eerdmans, 2005], 72).

20. As noted already by Vermes, "Biblical Proof-Texts," 503; Fitzmyer, "The Use of Explicit Old Testament Quotations," 33-34; Alfred R. C. Leaney, *The Rule of Qumran and Its Meaning: Introduction, Translation, and Commentary*. NTL (Philadelphia: Westminster, 1966), 174. Vermes explains that the original sense is a prohibition against "the laying of false charges." See also Metso, *Textual Development*, 82; "Use of Old Testament Quotations," 221. Fitzmyer states that the word דבר "also has the generic meaning of 'thing' and so the Manual of Discipline was able to quote the phrase without any regard for its original judicial context and apply it to the question of contact with wicked outsiders." Where Fitzmyer sees a vague, almost sloppy reapplication of a "generic" term, I propose a specific exegesis that depends upon the technical use of the term, both in its original biblical context and in sectarian terminology, not a "disregarding" of the original verse, but a close, sectarian, re-rereading of it.

21. Vermes picks up on the use of רחק and דבר in our passage; "Biblical Proof-Texts," 503. He considers this citation as an example of a "direct proof" that "is convincing because it contains the correct sounds." Metso also notes the significance of the verbal resonance for 1QS. She observes that "the catchwords here are רחק and דבר." However, whereas she points to the formal significance of the internal lexical echo, noting the occurrence of דבר both before the citation formula here in line 15 and in the previous line, I would like to emphasize the semantic significance of this technical term in the document as a whole. Licht (*The Rule Scroll*, 133 ad loc.) states that the locution "remain at a distance from him in every task" in line 15 was employed in order to enable the use of Exod 23:7. Fishbane seems to suppose a reverse process — that the selection of the verse emerged from the terminology already employed in the text. However, he says of the "transformed reuse" of Exod 23:7 "to serve an entirely new purpose" in 1QS, that it was generated "simply on the basis of similar terms!"; "Use, Authority," 349. Whether the expression in line 15 reinforces the language of the biblical citation or the reverse, the quotation of the verse is surely due to the resonances of דבר and רחק *throughout* 1QS. In turn, the sectarian connotations of these terms will have derived from biblical usage, including that of Exod 23:7.

22. Qimron and Charlesworth point to "the paronomasia with *ḥšb* in 5:11, 5:17, and 5:18"; "Rule of the Community (1QS)," in *Rule of the Community and Related Documents*, 23, n. 114.

people to cease trusting in the proud man, for on the day of God's judgment human pride will be humbled. Isaiah's prophecy has been given a totally different point of reference [in 1QS]."[23] As in the citation of Exod 23:7, this reuse is not arbitrary but reflects a specific, established, sectarian frame of reference. This includes not only the technical connotation of חשב, but also the tradition of identifying nonmembers of the Yahad as arrogant, in contrast to the "humble" members of the Community. Preben Wernberg-Møller points out the wordplay between "breath in his nostrils" in the citation and "futility/futile" (הבל, also meaning "breath") in line 19. Moreover, the broader context of the biblical source is relevant to the process of recontextualization. Although the function of the citation does not explicitly relate to the original biblical context of eschatological humbling, this concept is entirely pertinent to the devaluation of a nonmember, or lapsed member, of a Community that locates itself in the eschaton.

1QS cols VIII-IX. Isa 40:3: Explicit Citation with Introductory Formula; Citation with Pronominal Identifier

Two references to Isa 40:3 — with an explicit citation formula at 1QS VIII, 14 and with a pronominal identification at IX, 19 — are intended to validate an over-arching principle, or principles, of the Community, rather than to support specific rules of conduct as did the earlier citations of Exodus and Isaiah.[24]

The prophetic exhortation to "prepare the way" is cited as proof of the necessity for proper (sectarian) instruction in Torah, in isolation from the wider Jewish population. In VIII, 14 the verse is sandwiched by citation indicators. It

---

They focus on the formal isolexism within the pericope, as does Metso (similarly to her discussion of the previous citation of Exod 23:7; cf. nn. 19 and 21 above). We would add, with Licht (*The Rule Scroll*, 134), the semantic significance of the term in 1QS. Similar use of the root in the passive to indicate belonging to the Community is found in III, 1, 4 as well as in CD XIX, 35 לא יחשבו בסוד עם.

23. *Textual Development*, 82-83; see also "Biblical Quotations," 84; "Use of Old Testament Quotations," 223. Again, I accept the main point of Metso's observation but with a significant difference in nuance. She states that "the writer made a word-play on the verb נחשב, 'to be accounted, be esteemed' and twisted its sense so as to make it bear the meaning 'being reckoned in the community' as in 1QS 5:11," adopting Fitzmyer's use of the term "twists" ("The Use of Explicit Old Testament Quotations," 34). Exegetically speaking, rather than viewing the author as having "twisted" the sense of the word חשב, it is more helpful to note that he has recast it in accordance with standard sectarian usage.

24. For a view of this passage as a key foundational statement of the Community, see the sources cited by Metso, "Biblical Quotations," 91, n. 11.

is cited as support for a general assertion concerning segregation and then explicated in a manner identifying the separation as pertaining to Torah study.[25]

> When these become the Community in Israel they shall separate themselves from the session of the men of deceit in order to depart into the wilderness to prepare there the Way of the Lord (?);[26] as it is written:[27] "In the wilderness prepare the way of • • • •,[28] make level in the desert a highway for our God." This (alludes to) the study of the Torah wh[ic]h he commanded through Moses to do, according to everything which has been revealed (from) time to time, and according to that which the prophets have revealed by his Holy Spirit.

In IX, 19, the double application of the verse to both Torah instruction and isolation is repeated. A lengthy description of the role of the *Maskil* concludes.

> This is the time *for preparing the path to the wilderness.* And he will teach them about all that has been discovered so that they can carry it out in this moment so they will be detached from anyone who has not withdrawn his path from all injustice.

In this case, the "citation" is actually a paraphrase, which presupposes the full citation in col. VIII. It uses a modified form of the verb, "to prepare," in contrast to the original imperative, as is characteristic of indirect quotation. The citation is flagged by the identifying pronoun, "this." In our spectrum of explicit-

---

25. Translation of Qimron and Charlesworth, "Rule of the Community," 35. On the structure of the passage, cf. Vermes, "Biblical Proof-Texts," 497; Fishbane, "Use, Authority," 349; George J. Brooke, "Thematic Commentaries on Prophetic Scriptures," in Henze, *Biblical Interpretation at Qumran,* 136-37. Brooke notes that the author cites only this one verse, rather than gathering a variety of proof-texts, in contrast to the style found in the thematic *pesharim* from Qumran. As we indicate below, the use of the citation nonetheless implies a well-developed exegetical tradition. Fishbane views the twofold application of the verse, for isolation and study, as reflecting biblical justification and reinterpretation respectively ("Use, Authority," 349). These roughly approximate Fitzmyer's categories of "literal/historical" application and "accommodation." Fitzmyer himself categorizes the use of Isa 40:3 in 1QS as "accommodation," i.e., a case "in which the Old Testament text was obviously wrested from its original context, modified or deliberately changed by the new writer in order to adapt it to a new situation or purpose" ("The Use of Explicit Old Testament Quotations," 16). His other two categories are "modernization" and "eschatological" adaptation.

26. דרך הואה in 1QS; 4QS[e] reads דרך האמת.

27. כאשר כתוב, like the formula preceding the citation of Isa 2:22 at 1QS V, 17.

28. I.e., the Lord. Transcription of the Tetragrammaton is avoided, and the divine name is represented by four dots.

ness of citation, this biblical reference is less explicitly identified than the previous examples and is less precisely cited.

It is clear that the author of 1QS interprets Isaiah's preparation of the "way" as representing instruction in Torah. There has been some debate as to whether the advocacy of retreat to the desert to facilitate this instruction is intended literally, referring specifically to residence at the site of Qumran, or signifies a metaphorical withdrawal from society.[29] In either case, once again, the author has removed a biblical verse from its original biblical context for use as a prooftext for a sectarian teaching. Nonetheless, I would again suggest that there is an exegetical connection between the verse and its application, with respect to both context and language. As in our earlier examples in column V, the cited biblical terminology is construed with regard to sectarian exegetical tradition, and reflects isolexism within the pericope, and with key words throughout 1QS, specifically דרך and הלך. The original biblical context of divine eschatological salvation is relevant to the sectarian adaptation of preparing the way for ultimate redemption.[30]

Moreover, this adaptation reflects and reinforces broad sectarian traditions concerning the centrality of proper teaching of Torah for the formation of the Community and for maintaining ongoing right conduct with the aim of meriting salvation. Specifically, the images of "walking," "watering," and "building" recur in Qumran literature in depictions of desirable or undesirable behavior associated with proper vs. distorted or insufficient knowledge of Torah law.

29. On the significance of "the desert" in the self-understanding of the Community, see Shemaryahu Talmon, "The 'Desert Motif' in the Bible and in Qumran Literature," in *Biblical Motifs: Origins and Transformations,* ed. Alexander Altmann (Cambridge, Mass.: Harvard University Press, 1966), 31-66. Most recently, Devorah Dimant has argued for an exclusively metaphorical interpretation, in "Not Exile in the Desert but Exile in Spirit: The Pesher of Isa. 40:3 in the Rule of the Community," *Meghillot* 2 (2004): 21-36 [Hebrew]; see Norman Golb, *Who Wrote the Dead Sea Scrolls: The Search for the Secret of Qumran* (New York: Scribner, 1995), 75. George J. Brooke supports both the literal and figurative reading, in "Isaiah 40:3 and the Wilderness Community," in *New Qumran Texts and Studies: Proceedings of the First Meeting of the International Organization for Qumran Studies, Paris 1992,* ed. Brooke and Florentino García-Martínez. STDJ 15 (Leiden: Brill, 1994), 117-32. The prepositional *lamed* in both passages, "to the wilderness," seems to point to a physical relocation, in addition to the metaphorical message.

30. Metso notes that "in the book of Isaiah this verse belongs to the Deuteroisaianic Book of Consolation of Israel. Yahweh intends to place himself at the head of his people and lead them to freedom from exile across the desert, as he did at the Exodus from Egypt into the Promised Land. But the Qumran writer disregards the historical context, and uses the verse to provide a motive for the community's withdrawal into the desert to live a life of perfection in accordance with the Law" (*Textual Development,* 86). Cf. Fitzmyer, "The Use of Explicit Old Testament Quotations," 35-36. As stated above, I do not see a disregard for the eschatological biblical context, but an exegetical adaptation of it.

Walking   The "clearing of a path" as a metaphor for the propagation of sectarian teaching is a natural extension of biblical references to walking in the way of the Lord.[31] Instruction in the law establishes the proper "way" along which leaders direct the members of the Community, leading ultimately to salvation.[32] Uwe Glessmer summarizes his insightful explanation of how the citation of Isa 40:3 encapsulates a "complex theological idea," stating that it evokes "already established pictures given in Isaiah[33] and Maleachi[34] concerning an eschatological meaning of 'preparation of the way' as well as the scheme of the 'two ways' and the 'desert situation' in Dtn and the separation from the 'counsel of the wicked' in Ps 1."[35] Glessmer further notes that "time" is a central concern in 1QS IX.[36] In Qumran texts, the "wilderness" is associated with a period of testing at the eve of the eschaton.[37]

Watering   It is significant that the correct path is cleared in the wilderness. The desert is not only a region of unmarked terrain where one can easily get

31. For the biblical phrases, and Akkadian background, see Moshe Weinfeld, *Deuteronomy and the Deuteronomic School* (Oxford: Clarendon, 1972), 76-77, 333-34.

32. Cf. Catherine Murphy, *Wealth in the Dead Sea Scrolls*, 126, esp. n. 9. For the significance of "the Way" in Qumran literature, see Richard Bauckham, "The Early Jerusalem Church, Qumran, and the Essenes," in *The Dead Sea Scrolls as Background to Postbiblical Judaism and Early Christianity: Papers from an International Conference at St. Andrews in 2001*, ed. James R. Davila. STDJ 46 (Leiden: Brill, 2003), 63-89 (here 75-78). Menahem Kister has associated the use of Isa 40:3 here in 1QS with CD I, 11, God "raised up for them a Teacher of Righteousness, in order to direct them in the path of his heart." He discerns an implicit exegesis of Isa 57:17; "Biblical Phrases and Hidden Biblical Interpretations and Pesharim,"in *The Dead Sea Scrolls: Forty Years of Research*, ed. Devorah Dimant and Uriel Rappaport. STDJ 10 (Leiden: Brill, 1992), 27-39 (here 33-34).

33. "Preparing the way" occurs also at Isa 57:14 and 62:10.

34. Mal 3:1; cf. 3:18, 22-23.

35. Uwe Glessmer, "The Otot-texts (4Q319) and the Problem of Intercalations in the Context of the 364-day Calendar," in Heinz-Josef Fabry, Armin Lange, and Hermann Lichtenberger, eds., *Qumranstudien: Vorträge und Beiträge der Teilnehmer des Qumranseminars auf dem internationalen Treffen der Society of Biblical Literature. Münster 1993* (Göttingen: Vandenhoeck & Ruprecht, 1996), 140-41.

36. Glessmer, The Otot-texts," 134-38.

37. On the forty-year typology in CD, see Hanan Eshel, *The Dead Sea Scrolls and the Hasmonean State*. SDSSRL (Grand Rapids: Eerdmans and Jerusalem: Yad Ben-Zvi, 2008), 58-59. It has been noted that 4QpPs 37 also reflects a well-developed typological tradition contextualizing the community in the wilderness, in association with Torah and repentance. Thus, שבי המדבר (III 1) and שבים לתורה (II 2-3) and the perishing of the wicked "at the end of forty years." Steven Fraade observes that "the ritualized discipline of study . . . also served to construct a self-conception of that society in continuity with the biblical 'camp', with the heavenly 'sanctuary', and with the eschatalogical order"; "Interpretive Authority." Cf. Talmon. "The 'Desert Motif.'"

lost and where, historically (and typologically), the generation of the Exodus did indeed go astray on their way to full redemption. It is also a region without water. The "wilderness" represents a time and place in which metaphorical "water," i.e., knowledge, is lacking and must be introduced. The metaphor of water for instruction at Qumran is most evident in the antithetical epithets מורה הצדק (Teacher/Rain of Righteous)[38] and מטיף הכזב (Spouter/Dripper of Lies) and in the extended exegesis of the diggers of the "well" of Num 21:18 in CD VI, 3-11.[39] It may also be evident in the use of Deut 29:18 in 1QS and CD.[40]

Building[41]   Somewhat more tentatively, I would suggest that 1QS may additionally employ Isa 40:3 to present inspired sectarian Torah study as a cornerstone for the foundation of the Community, through paronomasia with פנה. This section of 1QS follows immediately upon a section in which the Community is depicted as a true temple. 1QS 8:7 reads:

> This [the community] is that tried wall, the "precious cornerstone" פנת יקר, whose foundations shall neither rock nor sway in their place.[42]

The collocation פנת יקר points to Isa 28:16,

הִנְנִי יִסַּד בְּצִיּוֹן אָבֶן אֶבֶן בֹּחַן פִּנַּת יִקְרַת מוּסָד מוּסָד הַמַּאֲמִין לֹא יָחִישׁ

---

38. See Joel 2:23. On this figure, see Michael A. Knibb, "Teacher of Righteousness," in *EDDS*, 2:918-20.

39. See Yonah Frenkel, *Darkhei ha-Aggadah ve-ha-Midrash* (Masada: Yad la-Talmud, 1991), 2:478-80 [Hebrew].

40. The biblical verse also combines the imagery of walking and watering. See also 1QH XVI, 17-21. The poet thanks God: "you have put (words) in my mouth as showers of rain . . . ," leading to a revelatory emergence of greenery and planting of trees. I am grateful to Deborah Bedolla for bringing the *Hodayot* reference to my attention. For this same image of teaching as water, and conflicting assessments of the wilderness generation, in rabbinic literature, see Daniel Boyarin, "Inner Biblical Ambiguity, Intertextuality and the Dialectic of Midrash: The Waters of Marah," *Proof* 10 (1990): 29-48.

41. For the use of building imagery to depict community formation in Qumran writings, see Bilha Nitzan, *Pesher Habakkuk: A Scroll from the Wilderness of Judaea (1QpHab)* (Jerusalem: Bialik, 1986), 45-46 [Hebrew]; Licht, *The Rule Scroll*, 171-72, and his *Megillat ha-Hodayot — The Thankgiving Scroll — A Scroll from the Wilderness of Judaea: Text, Introduction, Commentary and Glossary* (Jerusalem: Bialik, 1957), 117, on the use of Isa 28:16-17 in 1QH XIV, 26-27 (Licht's 6:26). For the significance of "house" in 1QS cols. 8 and 9, see Devorah Dimant, "The Volunteers in the 'Rule of the Community': A Biblical Notion in Sectarian Garb," *RevQ* 23 (2007): 233-45 (here 238-42).

42. Wernberg-Møller discusses the building imagery in 1QS ("Some Reflections," 52-53).

פנה is not common in Qumran literature, either in the sense of "corner" or "turning."[43] The relative rarity of the form indicates that the isolexism of the allusion to Isa 28:16 פנת יקר (VIII, 7) and to Isa 40:3 פנות דרך (VIII, 14) is unlikely to be mere coincidence. The preparation of the way is akin to the laying of a cornerstone.[44]

Lastly, although 1QS omits the words "a voice calls" in its citation, we might consider the possibility that the tradition underlying the association of Torah interpretation and instruction with Isa 40:3 may have been rooted in the word קורא in the prophetic verse. The word קרא in the sense "to read," is associated with the acquisition of proper knowledge of Torah law in 1QS VI, 7 ("to read in the book and expound the regulation") and CD V, 2 ("David did not read in the sealed book") and with revelation in 1QpHab VII, 3.[45] Despite the omission of

43. The noun פנה appears in Qumran literature primarily in a literal physical sense, in the *Copper Scroll* and *Temple Scroll* as well as in 4Q365 and 4Q365a and the *Songs of Sabbath Sacrifice*. Manfred Oeming, "פָּנָה," *TDOT*, 11:589, writes that 1QS VIII, 7 is the only "figurative theological usage" of the term in the Dead Sea Scrolls. In fact, there is one additional, and probably related occurrence (besides the restored parallel to 1QS at 4Q259 II, 14). 2Q23 Apocryphal Prophecy is extremely fragmentary, but in addition to the collocation אבן פנת (I, 6) it contains the word מסלה, as in Isa 40:3. פנה occurs in line 21 of 1QH XVI, 17-21 in the "watering" passage noted above, but it is difficult to determine its sense. See Hughes, *Scriptural Allusions*, 142.

44. Further indication of the double significance of פנות may be found in the headings in the "manifesto" section. 1QS VIII, 10b refers to the establishment of a foundation, בהכון אלה ביסוד היחד, and VIII, 20 refers to walking, ואלה המשפטים אשר ילכו בם. See also the echo of Isa 28:13 in CD IV, 19 (צו), within a pericope describing the "building of a sure house" (III, 19) and relocation by founders of the community (שבי ישראל היוצאים מארץ יהודה).

45. See also CD VI, 6; 4QpNah 3-4 I 8 (and Berrin, *The Pesher Nahum Scroll*, 176-92). The focus of this pericope is upon the role of the Interpreter in expounding the Torah in order to guide the people toward proper observance. Such practical textual interpretation is precisely the connotation of both reading (קרא) and expounding (דרש) at Qumran. See Paul Heger, "The Development of Qumran Law: Nistarot, Niglot and the Issue of 'Contemporization,'" *RevQ* 23 (2007): 167-206. For the importance of Torah study as a means to acquisition of knowledge with a particular sectarian slant, see, *inter alia*, Fishbane, "Use, Authority, and Interpretation," 345-47; Fraade, "Interpretive Authority," esp. 57; and "Looking for Legal Midrash at Qumran," in *Biblical Perspectives: Early Use and Interpretation of the Bible in Light of the Dead Sea Scrolls. Proceedings of the First International Symposium of the Orion Center for the Study of the Dead Sea Scrolls and Associated Literature, 12-14 May 1996*, ed. Michael E. Stone and Esther G. Chazon. STDJ 28 (Leiden: Brill, 1998), 64; Lawrence H. Schiffman, *The Halakhah at Qumran*. SJLA 16 (Leiden: Brill, 1975), though Johann Maier challenges the sense of דרש as expounding, in his "Early Jewish Biblical Interpretation in the Qumran Literature," in *Hebrew Bible/Old Testament: The History of Its Interpretation*, vol. 1.1: *Antiquity*, ed. Magne Sæbø (Göttingen: Vandenhoeck & Ruprecht, 1996), 108-29. The frequent designation of Scripture as "written" (כתוב) would also emphasize the significance of reading as a means of access to the divine word. Dimant sees *"midrash haTorah"* as a pesher identification of the word "wilderness" in the verse ("Not Exile in the Desert," 28-33). In my understanding, the wilderness functions as the temporal and geo-

these words in the citations here in 1QS cols. VIII-IX, I suggest that they contributed to the origin of the exegetical tradition attested in this pericope.[46] The significance of Torah instruction in 1QS VIII-IX is highlighted by comparison with the superficially similar use of Isa 40:3 in the New Testament with reference to the ministry of John the Baptist. In Isaiah, the Hebrew is best rendered as "a voice cries: 'In the wilderness, prepare the way of the Lord.'" 1QS follows this — the voice directs the addressee to perform the necessary task in the wilderness. In the New Testament, the implied punctuation is "a voice cries in the wilderness: 'prepare the way of the Lord,'" accommodating the identification of John as the one crying out in the wilderness.[47] The sources attest to a shared exegetical tradition, associating Isa 40:3 with community formation, withdrawal from the Jerusalem establishment, and revelatory preaching by a charismatic leader, but the Qumran pericope focuses on textual instruction (perhaps by taking קרא as "reading"), whereas the Synoptic Gospels are interested in baptism and exhortation to repentance and the fourth Gospel applies the verse to the role of John the Baptist as herald (קרא as "calling out").[48] Joseph Fitzmyer assesses the usages of Isa 40:3 in the NT and 1QS as "almost identical."[49] Alfred Leaney correctly points to differences between the scriptural em-

---

graphical location for the instruction of Torah — it represents the time of the dominion of Belial, during which the Yahad Community serves as an oasis.

46. For this phenomenon, see, e.g., Kister, "Biblical Phrases and Hidden Biblical Interpretations." He states, "exegesis can be reconstructed, even where the verses are not cited explicitly . . . through analysis of the biblical context" (29).

47. George J. Brooke, "Shared Intertextual Interpretations in the Dead Sea Scrolls and the New Testament," in Stone and Chazon, *Biblical Perspectives,* 35-57.

48. Matt 3:3; Mark 1:3; Luke 3:4-6; John 1:23. Although Fraade recognizes the significance of Torah study and biblical interpretation in the 1QS passage, he nonetheless links this with the "teaching ministry" of John the Baptist in the Gospels ("Interpretive Authority," 52). There may be an element of "teaching" in John's preaching as found in the Synoptic Gospels, but in the form in which the traditions have been preserved in the NT, there is no reference to textual study and certainly not to proper instruction in the Law. Cf. Matt 3:1-3: "In those days John the Baptist appeared in the wilderness of Judea, proclaiming, 'Repent, for the kingdom of heaven has come near.' This is the one of whom the prophet Isaiah spoke when he said, 'The voice of one crying out in the wilderness. . . .'" Mark 1:4-5: "John came, who baptized in the wilderness and preached the baptism of repentance unto remission of sins. And there went out unto him all the country of Judaea, and all they of Jerusalem. And they were baptized of him in the river Jordan, confessing their sins." Luke 3:3: "He went into all the country around the Jordan, preaching a baptism of repentance for the forgiveness of sins." John 1:7-8: "The same came for witness, that he might bear witness of the light, that all might believe through him. He was not the light, but came that he might bear witness of the light."

49. Fitzmyer, "The Use of Explicit Old Testament Quotations," 35. He is followed by Metso, *Textual Development,* 86.

ployment in these sources, but leans too far to the opposite pole, denying any influence or commonality beyond what he perceives as a "disregard" for the original meaning of the verse.[50] A more balanced view is that of Barnabas Lindars. He says of the *Community Rule*'s citation of Isa 40:3, paraphrase of Isa 42:1 (focusing on the term "Elect"), and allusion to Isa 28:16 ("precious corner-stone"): "In all three cases a testimony employed by the Qumran sect with reference to itself is used christologically by the Church; and the link between the two different kinds of interpretation is the common eschatological motive."[51]

In sum, the citation of Isa 40:3, like the other explicit citations in 1QS, is a reuse of a biblical verse, within an exegetical tradition, employing familiar tropes to suit the particular context of the community. In all of the cases of explicit citations in 1QS, we have seen wordplay between the verse and key sectarian terminology, as well as resonance with words in, or close to, the particular passage containing the citation. The main sectarian terms in play were רחק, חשב, פנות, דרך, דבר, and possibly קרא; some of these were technical terms, and some encapsulated common ancient Jewish motifs (such as walking on a path) that appear with a sectarian slant in Qumran writings. For חשב, פנות, דבר, רחק we also noted isolexism within the relevant pericope itself. We observed that in two instances, the original biblical context would have been a significant factor in the shaping of the reapplication of the prophecy — with respect to the rejection of arrogance and preparation for eschatological salvation; in the case of the legal citation, the connection to the biblical context was weaker, but still demonstrable.

Verbal Allusion

Chazon defines "allusion" as "an echoing [of] key expressions and motifs."[52] In this section, I examine allusion in a somewhat more narrow sense. I restrict the discussion to verbal allusion in 1QS, which I identify on the basis of the employment of distinctive biblical terminology. Distinctiveness may be a function of (1) the rarity of an individual word or form in Biblical Hebrew; (2) the rarity of a particular collocation of words in Biblical Hebrew, especially in unusual

---

50. Leaney, *The Rule of Qumran*, 222.

51. Barnabas Lindars, *New Testament Apologetic: The Doctrinal Significance of the Old Testament Quotations* (Philadelphia: Westminister Press, 1961), 278. Cf. Otto Betz, *Offenbarung und Schriftforschung in der Qumransekte* (Tübingen: Mohr, 1960), 155-58.

52. Cf. Hughes, *Scriptural Allusions*, 41-55. Hughes notes that allusion entails "an indication that the . . . (adoptive text) directs the reader to a particular interpretation of the adopted text" (53).

grammatical forms; or (3) the clustering of a specific root or collocation in a particular passage or pericope of the Hebrew Bible *("Leitworte")*.[53] In each case presented below, the meaning and context of the biblical source text is relevant to the meaning of the passage in 1QS. Full appreciation of the message of the sectarian text requires recognition of the source of the allusion and an understanding of its relevance.[54]

At times, the author of 1QS lifts whole phrases from the Hebrew Bible. These allusions could be viewed as quotations, albeit revised quotations without formulaic citation markers.[55] The adaptation of the biblical priestly blessing in 1QS II, 2-4 is one such example. Our composition also features this sort of quasi-citation of Deut 29:18 and Mic 6:8. In addition, elements from these latter verses recur throughout 1QS as "refrains." I will begin our discussion of allusion with these "unflagged revised citations" and derivative refrains.

Unflagged (Revised) Citation

Numbers 6:24-27 Our first example of an unflagged revised citation is the expansion of the priestly blessing of Num 6:24-27 in the liturgy of the covenant renewal at 1QS II, 2-4. Although there is no technical formulaic marker an-

---

53. Our criteria are somewhat looser than those of Hughes. Thus, her first example is "correspondence with a hapax legomenon" (53).

54. That is, the three stages outlined by Ziva Ben-Porat, "The Poetics of Literary Allusion," *PTL: A Journal for Descriptive Poetics and Theory of Literature* 1 (1976): 105-28 (here 110-11). As summarized by Sommer (*A Prophet Reads Scripture*, 15), "Ben-Porat identifies at least three and often four stages in the recognition of an allusion: noticing the marker, identifying the source, bringing the marked sign to bear on the interpretation of the sign which includes the marker, and also noting additional aspects of the source text which affect the reading of the alluding text generally."

55. Cf. Vermes: "The least structured of these lines of reasoning utilizes a whole verse or part of it without an introductory formula indicating the presence of a quotation. The biblical words become integral parts of the author's account, possibly in a retouched version, in order to fit their new context" ("Biblical Proof-Texts," 497). Dimant terms this sort of scriptural employment "implicit quotation" and employs quantity of verbal parallel as her criterion: "a phrase of at least three words, which stems from a specific recognizable biblical context" ("Use, Authority," 401). She distinguishes this from "allusion," defined as "a device for the simultaneous activation of two texts, using a special signal referring to the independent external text. These signals may consist of isolated terms, patterns and motifs taken from the text alluded to" (409-10, with reference to Ben-Porat, "The Poetics of Literary Allusion," 105-7). For our purposes, my criterion for classifying a verbal allusion is that there is an element of explicit reference, such that the allusion is flagged by the use of words from the original, but there is a lack of formal external marker.

nouncing the citation, it is flagged in a way by the identification of the text as a priestly blessing:

> Then the priests shall bless[56] all the men of God's lot who walk perfectly in all his ways, and say, *"May he bless you* with all good and *may he keep you* from all evil; may he *enlighten your* heart with insight for living, *may he favor you* with eternal knowledge. *May he lift up his* merciful *countenance toward you* for eternal *peace."*

The italicized portions of the text are the words taken from Num 6:24-27. In the continuation of this liturgy, the levitical curses, the dependence upon this biblical passage is more subtle, as discussed below. Here in the formula to be recited by the priests, the biblical base text remains mostly intact; this is a revised quotation,[57] supplemented by sectarian expansion. The brief expansion incorporates key sectarian concepts — walking in the ways of God, dualism, knowledge, eternity — which are also central motifs in the Treatise of Two Spirits in 1QS III, 13-IV, 26.[58] An examination of the liturgical settings for the priestly blessing in ancient Judaism is beyond the scope of this discussion, but there is cogent evidence that 1QS II, 2-4 is a sectarian adaptation of widespread exegetical interpretation and liturgical use of Num 6:24-27. As Bilha Nitzan observes, the passage shows "a fairly well-crystallized literary practice of composing poetic and ceremonial works around the priestly blessing found in the Torah."[59]

Deuteronomy 29:18 Deuteronomy 29:18 (Eng. 19) describes a situation in which an individual publicly commits to the national covenant with God, but

---

56. Cf. the divine command to Moses in Num 6:23: "Speak to Aaron and his sons, saying: 'thus shall you bless the children of Israel. Say to them. . . .'"

57. The omission of the Tetragrammaton is typical of Qumran writings, due to reverence for the divine name; the word "countenance" is omitted in one phrase, though its second occurrence is retained. On additional variants, see Bilha Nitzan, *Qumran Prayer and Religious Poetry.* STDJ 12 (Leiden: Brill, 1994), 148-53.

58. For a thorough treatment of the sectarian expansion of the biblical priestly blessing in 1QS, see Nitzan, *Qumran Prayer.* See also Shani L. Berrin, "Lemma/Pesher Correspondence in Pesher Nahum," in Schiffman, Tov, and VanderKam, *The Dead Sea Scrolls Fifty Years after Their Discovery,* 342-43.

59. Nitzan, *Qumran Prayer,* 170. On exegetical and liturgical traditions pertaining to Num 6:24-27, see Nitzan, *Qumran Prayer,* 145-71, and Appendix I, "The Priestly Blessing in the Tradition of Jewish Worship," 357-58. George J. Brooke emphasizes the importance of Scripture in these reworkings, noting "the support *('asmaktâ)* given [to the priestly blessing] by its expansion with texts or allusions to biblical texts"; *Exegesis at Qumran: 4QFlorilegium in Its Jewish Context.* JSOTSup 29 (Sheffield: JSOT, 1985), 295-301. See also Daniel K. Falk, *Daily, Sabbath, and Festival Prayers in the Dead Sea Scrolls.* STDJ 27 (Leiden Brill, 1998), 224-25.

inwardly determines not to accept divine authority. It reads "when he hears the words of this sworn covenant, he blesses himself in his heart, saying, 'I shall be safe, though I walk in the stubbornness of my heart.'"[60] This is cited nearly verbatim in 1QS 2:14.[61] Although there is no formula announcing the citation, there is no doubt of the biblical origin of the words.[62] The author of 1QS recontextualizes the verse, generalizing from the one-time covenant ceremony in Deuteronomy 29 to the annual sectarian covenant renewal of his own experience.[63] In his own time, as in the historical wilderness period, a particular warning must be articulated against those who would commit superficially to the covenant while remaining unfaithful in their hearts. The broad original biblical context is fully relevant, as is the general Deuteronomistic "flavor" of the phrase, but the locution has also begun to take on a (sectarian) life of its own.[64] Elements of this verse, particularly "stubbornness of the heart," are sprinkled

---

60. והיה בשמעו את־דברי האלה הזאת והתברך בלבבו לאמר שלום יהיה־לי כי בשררות לבי אלך למען ספות הרוה את־הצמאה.

61. "When he hears the words of this covenant, he blesses himself in his heart, saying "I shall be safe, though I walk in the stubbornness of my heart."

והיה בשומעו את דברי הברית הזות יתברך בלבבו לאמור שלום יהי לי כיא בשרירות לבי אלך ונספתה רוחו הצמאה עם הרווה לאין סליחה

The sectarian author adopts the language of the Deuteronomist with minor variations, including synonymous substitution (ברית rather than אלה, עם instead of את; this is also explicative — disambiguating the biblical particle, which may be taken as either preposition or object marker); grammatical adaptation (יתברך for והתברך; ונספתה rather than למען ספות); rearrangement of word order (רוה and צמאה), and the addition of the word "spirit," which is a key term in 1QS. The concluding phrase "without forgiveness" summarizes the subsequent verse in Deuteronomy: "and the Lord will never forgive him."

62. The word שרירות occurs in the Pentateuch only at Deut 29:18; the remaining biblical occurrences are derivative of the usage in Deuteronomy. The idiom "to walk in the stubbornness of one's heart" appears several times in Jeremiah (3:17; 7:24; 9:13; 11:8; 13:10; 16:12; 18:12; 23:17), and once in Ps 81:13.

63. It is likely that Fitzmyer would have considered this as an example of "modernization," "in which the Old Testament text, which originally had a reference to some event in the contemporary scene at the time it was written, nevertheless was vague enough to be applied to some new event in the history of the Qumran sect" ("The Use of Explicit Old Testament Quotations," 16). This would be in contrast to the class of "accommodation" to which he relegated the explicitly marked proof-texts we examined above.

64. Jan Joosten argues that both 1QS and 1QpHab V, 7 rely upon an exegetical tradition shared with LXX; "ונספתה רוחו הצמאה עם הרויה': על פירוש דברים כט 18 במגילות קומראן' [The Interpretation of Deut. 29:18 in the Qumran Scrolls]," *Meghillot* 3 (2005): 231-38. If this is the case, this would be another example of sectarian adoption and adaptation of a broad interpretive tradition.

throughout 1QS and also in CD.[65] Jacob Licht describes this as a sort of "slogan" — insiders' jargon that is used regularly, with minor variations.[66] Licht also points out that a number of the allusions to Deut 29:18 in the Qumran writings incorporate Num 15:39 as well.[67]

וְלֹא תָתֻרוּ אַחֲרֵי לְבַבְכֶם וְאַחֲרֵי עֵינֵיכֶם אֲשֶׁר־אַתֶּם זֹנִים אַחֲרֵיהֶם

1QH XII, 15
ועם שרירות לבם יתורו

1QS I, 6-7
ולוא ללכת עוד בשרירות לב אשמה ועיני זנות לעשות כול רע

1QS III, 3
ולא יצדק במתור שרירות לבו

1QS V, 4
אשר לוא ילך איש בשרירות לבו לתעות אחר לבבו ועיניהו ומחשבת יצרו[68]

CD II, 15-18
להתהלך תמים בכל דרכיו ולא לתור במחשבות יצר אשמה וע(י)ני זנות
בלכתם בשרירות לבם ...

CD III, 11-12
ויתורו אחרי שרירות לבם

See also [לבו יתר בשרירות] in the fragmentary 4Q487 1 II 3 Sapiential work B.

The multiple allusions to Deut 29:18 throughout 1QS and in CD, as well as in 1QH and 1QpHab, and the combination of elements from this verse with those from Num 15:39 point to a pervasive exegetical tradition. שרירות לב has become a meme for expressing concern about sincerity of commitment and au-

---

65. 1QS I, 6; II, 26; III, 3; V, 4; VII, 19, 24; IX, 10. CD II, 17; III, 5, and in more modified form, CD III, 11; VII, 8, 19; XIX, 20, 33; XX, 9, as well as 1QH XII, 15. See also 11QpHab XI, 14; 4Q390 1 12; 4Q393 3 5.

66. See Licht, *The Rule Scroll*, 26-27, and Appendix A. Not all of the "slogans" he notes are biblical in origin.

67. Licht, *The Rule Scroll*, p. 60, points out that *Targum Onqelos* renders Num 15:39 as ולא תטעון בתר הרהור לבכון, inserting the word *hirhur* which serves as the Aramaic equivalent of שרירות throughout biblical targum. Note that in CD VIII, 8 and IX, 21, although שרירות לב occurs without reference to Num 15:39, the phrase יד רמה is employed, a term indicating willful sin, derived from Num 15:30. Aharon Shemesh discusses the significance of Deuteronomy 29-30 and Num 15:30 as paradigms of exile and excision, respectively, which underlie the penal code of the Qumran Community ("Expulsion and Exclusion in the Community Rule and The Damascus Document," *DSD* 9 [2002]: 52-63). The linguistic overlap in these allusions supports his analysis.

68. On the use of the term יצר here as indicative of an exegetical tradition, see Leaney, *The Rule of Qumran*, 167.

thenticity of declared righteousness, employed in sectarian Qumran writings
with respect to dedication to the Community.

Micah 6:8   Like Deut 29:18, Mic 6:8 is reflected in 1QS in both extensive and
partial quotations. The biblical verse reads: "O mortal, what is good; and what
does the LORD require of you but to do justice, to love kindness, and to walk
humbly with your God?"[69] Substantial "unflagged revised quotations" appear
at 1QS V, 3-4[70] and VIII, 2.[71] The abbreviated allusions to the verse feature the
collocations אהבת חסד (at II, 24 and V, 24-25)[72] or הצנע לכת (IV, 5), both of
which occur in the Hebrew Bible only in Mic 6:8.

Although the biblical source is readily identifiable, the revisions in the citations of Micah are substantial and are of a strongly sectarian nature.[73] The
added words "truth" (II, 24; V, 3; V, 24; VIII, 2) and "righteousness" (II, 24; V, 3;
VIII, 2), as well as "humility" (II, 24; V, 3; V, 24) and *"yahad"* (II, 24; V, 3) are significant terms in the writings of the Community. The substitution of "in all
their ways" (V, 4) and "with one another" (II, 8) for biblical "with God" are
exegetical modifications, emphasizing community.

In the use of Micah, as in the use of Deut 29:18, the context of the biblical
source text is essential to its selection. Chapter 6 of Micah is a "covenant law-
suit." Its emphasis on proper behavior over sacrifice, in a covenantal context, is
particularly well-suited to the message of 1QS. The author of 1QS combines
biblical allusion with self-referential linguistic modifications in order to
recontextualize the verses from a specific historical setting concerning Israel as
a whole, to a more general ongoing situation pertaining to his Community.

Our final illustrations of unflagged citations in 1QS are not pervasive refrains, but single cases of legal exegesis, again reflecting more widespread interpretive traditions. These are the law requiring rebuke in 1QS V, 26-VI, 1, paraphrasing Lev 19:17, and the law prohibiting grudges and revenge in 1QS VII, 8-9,
employing Lev 19:18. The phrase in 1QS V, 26–6:1 is conventionally reconstructed
as 1QS[74]. ואל ישנאהו [בעור[ל/]ת[לבבו כיא ביומ( ) יוכיחנו ולוא ישא עליו עוון

---

69. הִגִּיד לְךָ אָדָם מַה־טּוֹב וּמָה־יְהוָה דּוֹרֵשׁ מִמְּךָ כִּי אִם־עֲשׂוֹת מִשְׁפָּט וְאַהֲבַת חֶסֶד וְהַצְנֵעַ
לֶכֶת עִם־אֱלֹהֶיךָ

70. "According to their order shall go forth the determination of the lot about everything
concerning Torah, property, and judgment, to do truth (in) unity, humility, righteousness, justice, merciful love, circumspectly walking in all their ways."

71. ". . . to perform truth, righteousness, justice, merciful love, and circumspect walking,
each one with his fellow."

72. See Licht, *The Rule Scroll*, Appendix A, 293.

73. Licht, *The Rule Scroll*, 293, calls the echoes in V, 3-4 "distant forms."

74. The biblical verse reads לֹא־תִשְׂנָא אֶת־אָחִיךָ בִּלְבָבֶךָ הוֹכֵחַ תּוֹכִיחַ אֶת־עֲמִיתֶךָ וְלֹא־תִשָּׂא
עָלָיו חֵטְא; cf. Metso, *Textual Development*, 83-84.

VII, 8-9 reads ואשר יטור לרעהו אשר לוא ^במשפט ונענש ששה חדשים שנה אחת וכן לנוקם לנפשו.⁷⁵ The application of these verses in sectarian regulations is found also in CD. There is an explicit citation of Lev 19:17 in CD IX, 6-8 and an allusion in VII, 2. Leviticus 19:18 is cited explicitly in CD IX, 2, and partially repeated, with an identification, in line 4.⁷⁶ Licht and Leaney note similar applications of these verses elsewhere in Second Temple writings.⁷⁷ I will address these cases further below, in the context of the variant formulation of these laws in Cave 4 parallels, with language less close to the biblical source texts.

At this juncture, let us turn to examples of verbal allusion that contain fewer words in common with the source text, but which are identified by the distinctiveness of particular words. We proceed according to the subcategories outlined above in the introduction to this section: rare words, rare collocations, and *Leitworte.*

A Distinctive, Infrequent Word   The word *nigleh/niglot* appears in 1QS I, 9; V, 9, 12; VIII, 1, 15; IX, 13, 19. The noun form of the *niphal* of גלה appears in the Hebrew Bible only at Deut 29:28: "The hidden things *(nistarot)* are to the LORD and the revealed things *(niglot)* are to us and to our sons, to do all the words of this Torah." The use of *nigleh* in 1QS reflects an exegetical tradition that has been incorporated into the language of the community.⁷⁸

A Distinctive, Infrequent, Collocation   The combination יד רמה, indicating a deliberate transgression, occurs at 1QS V, 12; VIII, 17, 22; IX, 1.⁷⁹ This term de-

---

75. "Whoever bears a grudge against his fellow unjustly, shall be punished (for) one year, and the same for one who takes any revenge for himself." Lev 19:18 reads לֹא תִקֹּם וְלֹא־תִטֹּר אֶת־בְּנֵי עַמֶּךָ וְאָהַבְתָּ לְרֵעֲךָ כָּמוֹךָ אֲנִי יְהוָה

76. Cf. the collocation of the roots נקם and נטר in CD VIII, 5, and the use of לנטור in CD VII, 2, לא לנטור מיום ליום, along with the requirement for rebuke, להוכיח איש את אחיהו כמצוה (with כמצוה probably functioning as a flag to the biblical allusion.)

77. Licht, *The Rule Scroll*, 136; Leaney, *The Rule of Qumran*, 178. Cf. Sir 19:12-16; *T. Gad* 6:4-7; Heb 3:13; and also Matt 18:15-17. Rabbinic parallels are discussed by Aharon Shemesh, "Rebuke, Warning, and the Obligation to Testify in the Judean Desert Writings and Rabbinic Halakha," *Tarbiz* 66 (1997): 149-68 [Hebrew].

78. See *"nistar/ot"* in 1QS V, 11; VIII, 11-12; XI, 6; CD III, 13-16. Cf. See S. Berrin Tzoref, "The 'Hidden' and the 'Revealed': Progressive Revelation of Law and Esoterica," *Meghillot* 7 (2009): 157-90; Heger, "The Development of Qumran Law"; Aharon Shemesh and Cana Werman, "Hidden Things and Their Revelation," *RevQ* 18 (1998): 409-27; Alex Jassen, "The Presentation of the Ancient Prophets as Lawgivers at Qumran," *JBL* 127 (2008): 329-32; Lawrence H. Schiffman, *The Halakha at Qumran*, 22-32.

79. Cf. CD VIII, 8 = XIX, 21; X, 3; XX, 30.

rives from Num 15:30.[80] The usage in the *Community Rule*, with respect to a deliberate offense punishable by expulsion from the Community, reflects a sectarian exegetical tradition adapting the sense of being "cut off from the midst of one's people" to indicate this severe sanction.[81]

The expression לעבור בברית occurs only once in the Hebrew Bible, at Deut 29:11, a chapter that is very influential in 1QS.[82] The collocation recurs at 1QS I, 16, 18, 20, 24; II, 10, and a shortened form with עבר alone occurs at II, 19, 20, 21. The biblical phrase is addressed inclusively to the nation of Israel; the *Rule* adopts this covenantal language for the Community's ceremony of induction and affirmation, emphasizing the literal sense of "passing before."[83]

The usage of the collocation ילך רכיל in 1QS VII, 17 and VII, 18 reflects exegetical traditions concerning Lev 19:16 לא תלך רכיל בעמיך. The passage in the *Community Rule* distinguishes between slander against an individual fellow member of the Community, which is punished by a year of exclusion from the pure communal food, and slander against the Community as a whole, for which the punishment is expulsion. The expression for the former case, והאיש אשר ילך רכיל ברעהו, reflects Jer 9:3 וכל־רע רכיל יהלך, which itself plays off the pentateuchal verse. The more serious latter violation resonates with the *Temple Scroll*'s regulation on the capital offense of treason.[84]

---

80. וְהַנֶּפֶשׁ אֲשֶׁר תַּעֲשֶׂה בְּיָד רָמָה מִן־הָאֶזְרָח־מִן וּמִן־הַגֵּר אֶת־יְהוָה הוּא מְגַדֵּף וְנִכְרְתָה הַנֶּפֶשׁ הַהִוא מִקֶּרֶב עַמָּהּ.

81. Cf. Aharon Shemesh, "Expulsion and Exclusion in the Community Rule and the Damascus Document," *DSD* 9 (2002): 44-74 (here 59-61); Gary A. Anderson, "Intentional and Unintentional Sin in the Dead Sea Scrolls," in *Pomegranates and Golden Bells: Studies in Biblical, Jewish, and Near Eastern Ritual, Law, and Literature in Honor of Jacob Milgrom*, ed. David P. Wright, David Noel Freedman, and Avi Hurvitz (Winona Lake: Eisenbrauns, 1995), 49-64.

82. See our discussion of 29:18 above; Cf. Metso, *Textual Development*, 141; Hans F. Fuhs, "עָבַר," *TDOT* 10:424-25. On the theological significance of Deut 29:9–30:11 for the *Damascus Document*, see Shemesh and Werman, "Hidden Things and Their Revelation," 409-27.

83. See Murphy, *Wealth in the Dead Sea Scrolls*, 127.

84. 11QT 64:6-8. Cf. Yigael Yadin, *The Temple Scroll* (Jerusalem: Israel Exploration Society, 1983), 1:420-21; 2:373. Shemesh discusses the relevance of the *Temple Scroll* passage for CD IX, 1-8, which, as noted above, reuses Lev 19:17-18 in formulating regulations concerning rebukes and grudges; "Scriptural Interpretations in the Damascus Document and Their Parallels in Rabbinic Midrash," in *The Damascus Document: A Centennial of Discovery: Proceedings of the Third International Symposium of the Orion Center for the Study of the Dead Sea Scrolls and Associated Literature, 4-8 February 1998*, ed. Joseph M. Baumgarten, Esther G. Chazon, and Avital Pinnock. STDJ 34 (Leiden: Brill, 2000), 161-75. Wernberg-Møller posits a creative exegetical basis for the tradition, such that the author of 1QS took the prepositional *bet* of the biblical בעמך, "do not walk round as a talebearer *in* thy people," to mean "*about* thy people"; "Some Reflections," 54.

A Distinctive Collocation Typical of a Specific Group of Texts The centrality of Deuteronomistic covenant language is evident in the use of a number of "Deuteronomistic phrases" in 1QS. In addition to some of the examples noted above, featuring unusual words, there are a number of occurrences in which stock Deuteronomistic phrases are employed in the composition.[85]

Thus, the phrase "to do what is good and right" in 1QS I, 2 calls to mind Deut 12:28, as well as 2 Chr 14:1; 31:20, and Deut 6:18 ("to do that which is right and good in the eyes of the LORD"). This may not be a precise intertextual "hyperlink" to a specific biblical passage, but it is allusive, rather than simply "free use" of biblical idiom; the specific covenantal and Deuteronomistic contexts of the biblical occurrences of the phrase are significant for the context of 1QS.[86]

The collocation "with all [one's] heart and all [one's] soul," found in 1QS V, 9, reflects Deuteronomistic language rooted in ancient Near Eastern covenant formulas, as demonstrated by Moshe Weinfeld.[87] Whether or not the author of 1QS was aware of the more universal usage of this collocation, his own access to the phrase will have been filtered through the usage in Deuteronomy (especially in the Shema at 6:5, but also 4:29; 10:12; 11:13; 13:4; 26:16; 30:2, 6, 10) and perhaps other Deuteronomistic contexts, such as Solomon's prayer at 1 Kgs 8:48 and Josiah's covenant in 2 Kgs 23:3, 25.

Devorah Dimant has demonstrated that the use of the *hitpa'el* of נדב in 1QS reflects an exegetical process that originated in the use of this form of the root in Chronicles and Ezra. In these contexts, התנדב, מתנדב designate donors of free-will offerings to the temple. The *Community Rule* "employs the same construction to describe the voluntary sacrifice of their own lives, brought by the members of the community to their temple-like congregation."[88]

---

85. Cf. Murphy's discussion of "the Deuteronomic flavor of 1QS 1:1–4:26"; *Wealth in the Dead Sea Scrolls,* 125-30; Wernberg-Møller, "Some Reflections," 41. In these cases, 1QS does not allude to a specific biblical text but reflects broad Deuteronomistic influence. We consider this "allusion" in the sense that in order to fully appreciate the passage in which the Deuteronomistic language is employed, the reader must recognize the source text(s) and bring an understanding of the original context and meaning to bear upon the passage in 1QS. See n. 55 above.

86. See Jassen, "The Presentation of the Ancient Prophets," 314; Moshe Weinfeld, *Deuteronomy 1–11.* AB 5 (New York: Doubleday, 1991), 347.

87. Weinfeld, *Deuteronomy 1–11,* 338, 351-52; *Deuteronomy and the Deuteronomic School,* 81, 334; "The Loyalty Oath in the Ancient Near East," in *Normative and Sectarian Judaism in the Second Temple Period.* LSTS 54 (London: T. & T. Clark, 2005), 2-44. See also CD XV, 10, 12.

88. Dimant, "The Volunteers in the 'Rule of the Community,'" 245.

Free Use: Idioms

There are occasions in which 1QS uses biblical expressions that do not seem to allude to any particular biblical context. For example, the term תשיג ידו in VII, 10 echoes biblical language about financial constraints, but does not seem intended to take the reader back to any biblical occurrences of the phrase. It is best understood either as an everyday sort of expression still in regular use in the author's own time or as an archaism intended to give a general biblical feel to the text. Similarly, ריח ניחוח in 1QS VIII, 9 is not an allusion to a particular biblical verse, but evokes general biblical usage of the phrase to describe a pleasing offering to the Lord, enhancing the depiction of the Community as the embodiment of the temple.[89]

The expression פן ישיאנו עוון אשמה in 1QS V, 14 echoes Lev 22:16 והשיאו אותם עון אשמה. Metso terms this "a proof-text," along with Exod 23:7, and states that it is "cited implicitly."[90] It is unclear whether this motive clause for separation from nonmembers of the Community indeed functions as textual support for the sectarian regulation. It may instead be simple "free use" of biblical language.[91]

---

89. Cf. Licht, *The Rule Scroll,* 171-74; for a discussion of the development of the term ניחוח in Second Temple writings, see Noam Mizrahi, "The Lexicon and Phraseology of the *Songs of the Sabbath Sacrifice*" (Diss., Hebrew University, 2008) [Hebrew].

90. Metso, *Textual Development,* 81.

91. If Lev 22:16 is in fact being invoked, the verse would be understood differently than in its original context. The biblical verse may be plausibly explained as expressing concern (a) that priestly negligence in guarding the sanctity of priestly food would cause the Israelites to bear sin or (b) that priestly negligence would cause the priests themselves to bear sin (as in 11QT 35:13-15). See Jacob Milgrom, *Leviticus 17–22.* AB 3A (New York: Doubleday, 2000), 1868-69. The allusive phrase here seems to indicate that the impure individual would cause the community member to bear sin. If there is an intentional reference to Leviticus 22, then the interpretive grounds would be the shared concern about mingling sacred foods and nonsacred individuals. Murphy supports the supposed dependence upon Leviticus 22 on the basis of the relatively uncommon form of ישיאנו (she notes that the only other *hiphil* of נשא is at 2 Sam 17:13; *Wealth in the Dead Sea Scrolls,* 143). Murphy sees this purported intertextuality as ironic, presumably because the biblical context sets boundaries between priests and laymen, whereas 1QS is concerned with determining which laity is permitted access to the Community's pure food. If textual dependence could be demonstrated, this would not be so much an ironic coincidence, as a deliberate extension of priestly attributes to the Yahad Community at large. On the "democratization of the priesthood" in the Second Temple era, see Martha Himmelfarb, *A Kingdom of Priests: Ancestry and Merit in Ancient Judaism* (Philadelphia: University of Pennsylvania Press, 2006).

Implicit Exegetical Paraphrase

The most difficult type of scriptural dependence to recognize involves paraphrastic exegetical adaptation of biblical language, without the external flag of citation formulas or the internal evidence of lexical distinctiveness.[92] Examples of such implicit, and mediated, exegetical expression in 1QS are the levitical curses in II, 4b-10 and two exegetical reflections of the Shema, in I, 11 and X, 10-14.

1. In the covenant ceremony, the priestly blessing of 1QS II, 1-4a, is followed by levitical curses against the men of the lot of Belial. As an antithetical expansion of the priestly blessing, the levitical curse is also a reworking of Num 6:24-26. Although this might not have been noticeable without the intermediary step of the sectarian priestly blessing, the biblical basis for the curse is clear.[93]

Priestly Blessing Num 6:24-26	Levitical Curse 1QS II, 5-9
May the LORD bless you	Cursed be you . . .
and keep you;	May he visit upon you destruction . . .
May the LORD shine (יאר) his face upon you,	Cursed be you (ארור) . . . darkness . . .
and be gracious to you;	May God not be gracious to you . . .
May the LORD lift up his countenance upon you,	May he lift up his angry countenance . . .
and give you peace	May there be no peace for you

The exegetical tradition of inversion of the priestly blessing is already attested in the Bible itself. Michael Fishbane describes Mal 1:6-2:9 as a "veritable contrapuntal inversion of the sound and sense of the priestly blessing."[94] The liturgical levitical curse in 1QS is a sectarian extension of this tradition. The actual lexical overlaps with Num 6:24-26 in this formula are not very impressive — "peace" and "lifting one's face" are hardly rare words or collocations; but these

92. It is conventional to use the term "implicit" to describe unflagged citations; these examples are "more implicit" in that they lack internal as well as formulaic markers. These are similar to what Kister has called "hidden interpretations"; see above, n. 46.

93. The table indicates the most straightforward antitheses. For a detailed discussion of the exegetical techniques employed in the full text of the reversal and expansion of the blessing, see Berrin, "Lemma/Pesher Correspondence," 343; J. A. Loader, "The Model of the Priestly Blessing in 1QS," *JSJ* 14 (1983): 11-17; Nitzan, *Qumran Prayer*, 125-39.

94. *Biblical Interpretation in Ancient Israel*, 332-34.

direct allusions supplement the additional factors of wordplay and context that point to the biblical origins of the formula employed for the sectarian curse.[95]

2. Above, I noted that the requirement to dedicate "all one's heart and all one's soul" is an allusion to the Shema, Deut 6:4-7, which itself derives from ancient Near Eastern covenantal language and came to be the quintessential affirmation of covenantal commitment in Judaism. Further employment of the Shema in the *Community Rule* has been identified in the stipulation that members of the Community must commit all their knowledge, energy, and wealth. 1QS I, 11-13 states:

> all those devoting themselves to his truth shall bring all their *knowledge*, and their *strength*, and their *property* into the Community of God in order to strengthen their *knowledge* by the truth of God's statutes, and discipline their *strength* according to the perfection of his ways, and all their *property* according to his righteous counsel.

1QS III, 3 says of the one who is to be excluded from the Community: "his *knowledge, strength,* and *property* shall not come into the Council of the Community." These paraphrases do not reuse the familiar biblical language, but the context and the combination of elements point to Deut 6:5, and particularly to exegetical traditions for this verse. "Knowledge" is a natural representation of the element "heart" in the biblical formula, in that the heart is the seat of the intellect in the Hebrew Bible. Weinfeld points to ancient exegesis of מאד as wealth and strength to account for these terms in the formula in 1QS.[96] It may be preferable to align the elements more symmetrically and to identify strength as an interpretation of נפש and wealth as an interpretation of מאד.[97] In either case,

---

95. On a structural, rather than lexical level, this liturgical ceremony derives from the blessings and curses in the biblical covenant ceremony of Deuteronomy 27-28.

96. Moshe Weinfeld, "The Covenant in Qumran," in *The Bible and the Dead Sea Scrolls: The Second Princeton Symposium on Judaism and Christian Origins,* ed. James H. Charlesworth (Waco: Baylor University Press, 2006), 59-69; "'They Should Bring All of Their Mind, All of Their Strength and All of Their Wealth into the Community of God' (1QS 1:12)," in *Bible Studies: Y. M Grinz in Memoriam,* ed. Benjamin Uffenheimer. Te'uda 2 (Tel Aviv: Tel Aviv University, 1982) 37-41 [Hebrew]. See Menahem Kister, "Some Observations on Vocabulary and Style in the Dead Sea Scrolls," in *Diggers at the Well: Proceedings of a Third International Symposium on the Hebrew of the Dead Sea Scrolls and Ben Sira,* ed. Takamitsu Muraoka and John F. Elwolde. STDJ 36 (Leiden: Brill, 2000), 137-59; Murphy, *Wealth in the Dead Sea Scrolls,* 120-25. The dependence upon the Shema here was already observed by Matthew Black, *The Scrolls and Christian Origins: Studies in the Jewish Background of the New Testament.* BJS 48 (Chico: Scholars, 1983 [1961]), 123.

97. The attempt at precise alignment is complicated by overlaps in the semantic ranges for some of the terms. Hebrew כח as well as חיל and Greek δύναμις, can denote either physical prowess or wealth, and similar confusion is possible for הון/און. נפש is at times associated with

1QS I, 11-13 is an exegetical paraphrase of a key biblical verse that is identifiable despite the absence of a verbal echo.

An additional allusion to the Shema can be detected in the prayer in col. X, in lines 10, 13-14. The roots שכב and קום are common ones, and their appearance together is quite natural. It is the context of 1QS col. X that allows us to identify the dependence upon Deuteronomy, even in line 10, which does not use any words from the biblical source text.

3. We noted above that Mic 6:8 serves as a refrain in 1QS: "O mortal, what is good; and what does the LORD require of you but to do justice, to love kindness, and to walk humbly with your God?"[98] The allusive phrases that we noted above derive from the second half of the verse, itemizing the desirable behavior of a member of the Community. I would suggest, though, that the prominence of this verse in our composition is actually rooted in the portion that is not cited in the composition, "what does the LORD require of you but." This phrase echoes Deut 10:12-13: "And now Israel, what *does the LORD your God ask of you but* to fear the LORD your God, to walk in all of his paths, and to love him and to serve the LORD your God with all your heart and all your soul? To observe the commandments of God and his statutes which I command you today for your good."[99] This verse from Deuteronomy includes the elements that we have seen recurring in 1QS — walking in the paths of God and covenantal devotion with

---

knowledge, like לב, or with emotions, but can also more generally indicate life force, which would suit the reference in 1QS to walking in paths of perfection, whether this is intended as an indication of moral or physical fortitude. See CD XIII, 11, "And everyone who joins his congregation, he should examine concerning his actions, his intelligence, his strength, his courage, and his wealth" (ויפקדהו למעשיו, ושוכלו וכוחו וגבורתו והונו).

An exegetical tradition that may also be at play in the use of Deut 6:5 in 1QS is the interpretation of whole-heartedness as requiring commitment with both of one's "inclinations" (יצר), the good and the evil, especially in light of the significance of Deut 29:18 noted above, and the treatise of the Two Spirits, if the latter is taken in the sense of "psychological dualism." See John R. Levison, "The Two Spirits in Qumran Theology," in *The Bible and the Dead Sea Scrolls*, vol. 2: *The Dead Sea Scrolls and the Qumran Community*, ed. James H. Charlesworth (Waco: Baylor University Press, 2006), 169-94.

98. הִגִּיד לְךָ אָדָם מַה־טּוֹב וּמָה־יְהוָה דּוֹרֵשׁ מִמְּךָ כִּי אִם־עֲשׂוֹת מִשְׁפָּט וְאַהֲבַת חֶסֶד וְהַצְנֵעַ לֶכֶת עִם־אֱלֹהֶיךָ.

99. Licht also sees 1QpHab VII, 10-12 "men of truth doers of Torah . . ." as echoing a "slogan" that he associates with the allusions to Micah; *The Rule Scroll*, Appendix 1, 293. If he is correct, then this would reflect an evolutionary process whereby the phrase "to do truth" originated in traditions associated with Mic 6:8. These traditions would have continued to leave a mark even upon texts that do not preserve explicit traces of the biblical source. Similarly, Licht describes 1QS I, 5 "to do truth, righteousness, and justice in the land" as "patterned on the biblical model" of Mic 6:8 (*The Rule Scroll*, 122), even though only the words "to do" and "justice" overlap.

all one's heart and soul. This is the response to the rhetorical question — what does God ask of the true devotee.

Micah repeats this rhetorical question, but with the term דרש, which is a significant term in Qumran texts; and the answer given in Micah is thus woven into the *Community Rule,* with sectarian embellishment.[100]

Conclusion

Our examination of the use of Scripture in 1QS highlights the following points:

1. 1QS features pervasive evidence not only of the use of Scripture itself, but also of the influence of exegetical traditions. There is particular overlap with interpretations preserved in CD, but there are also parallels to exegesis found in other compositions from Qumran and adaptations of traditions attested in other ancient Jewish and early Christian sources. The author of the *Community Rule* rereads his biblical source texts to accommodate his own message, but he does not wreak havoc on the original sense of the text in its biblical context. He recontextualizes the scriptural terms and concepts within his own sectarian system, reworking inherited conceptions and interpretations within his interpretive framework.

2. Deuteronomy is the most significant source for biblical allusions in the *Community Rule.* This is in keeping with the significance of this book throughout the Qumran corpus. Moreover, one area that was beyond the scope of this study is the influence of the Hebrew Bible on the *Serakhim* at the macrolevel; here too Deuteronomy is key. The very concept of a covenant ceremony and of a liturgy of curses and blessings involving priests and Levites derives from the final chapters of Deuteronomy.[101]

100. Note also that the root *drš* is employed to denote the seeking of God, and specifically the attempt to determine proper desirable conduct (see n. 45 above). In 2 Chr 14:3, 6 seeking God is paired with observance of the Torah and commandments, and with reward: "to seek (לדרוש) the LORD, the God of their fathers, and to do (לעשות) the Torah and commandment . . . 'for we sought the LORD our God. We sought him and he gave us respite on all sides.' They were successful in their building."

Cf. also 2 Chr 31:21: "in the Torah and command, to seek God with all his heart." If God seeks appropriate obedience, those who would be obedient must seek proper knowledge of God's laws and then act accordingly, in order to merit reward.

101. See Falk, *Daily, Sabbath, and Festival Prayers,* 219-26, on the covenant ceremony and esp. on the biblical basis and models for confession with blessings and curses. Cf. Friedrich Baumgärtel, "Zur Liturgie in der 'Sektenrolle' vom Toten Meer," *ZAW* 65 (1953): 263-65. Again, Deuteronomy 27-30 is the most prominent source, but additional textual and practical tradi-

3. Although identifying explicit lexical overlap is the easiest tool to use to detect dependence upon Scripture, it can sometimes be misleading, and should not be the only criterion for determining biblical influence. On the one hand, the occurrence of even a rare biblical term may simply reflect "free use" of biblical language without any connection to the context in which the term appears in the Hebrew Bible. On the other hand, we observed that the levitical curses that so clearly derive from Scripture feature only minimal distinctive lexical flagging to Num 6:24-27, and that there is no verbal overlap at all between the threefold expression of commitment derived from the Shema and that biblical source text. Again, macrolevel analysis strengthens this observation, as has most recently been shown by Aharon Shemesh.[102]

In light of this third point, there may be reason to reconsider the significance attributed to the presence or absence of explicit biblical allusion for the purpose of redaction criticism. Among Metso's arguments for dating 4QS earlier than 1QS is her observation that biblical citations appearing in 1QS are lacking in the parallel passages in manuscripts 4QS[b] and 4QS[d] from Cave 4.[103] Metso argues that the scriptural proof-texts of 1QS are later additions intended "to provide a theological justification of the regulations already in force in the community." Nitzan uses the same reasoning in dating 4Q280 prior to 1QS.[104]

---

tions are relevant as well. Metso, *Textual Development*, 113, mentions Ps 106:6; 1 Kgs 8:47; Jer 3:25; Dan 9:5; Num 6:24-26; Neh 8:6, and the similar ritual in 1QM XIII, 1-6.

102. Aharon Shemesh, "The Scriptural Background of the Penal Code in the Rule of the Community and Damascus Document," *DSD* 15 (2008): 191-224. It is not that lexical clues are irrelevant in his analysis. Rather, Shemesh's work demonstrates that when a text employs a source (or sources) by means of paraphrase, then the reader must be sensitive to such additional factors as structural parallels and context in order to discern the intertextuality. This point also emerges in his "4Q265 and the Status of the Book of Jubilees in the Yahad Community," *Zion* 73 (2008): 5-20 [Hebrew]; Eng. in *Enoch and the Mosaic Torah*, ed. Gabriele Boccaccini and Giovanni Ibba (Grand Rapids: Eerdmans, 2009), 247-60.

Similarly, though on a different scale, Metso observes concerning the presentation of the list of 26 cases in the penal code in 1QS VI, 24–VII, 25 that "the literary *Gattung* of the list is that of casuistic law which has its prototype in the Old Testament, especially in the Book of the Covenant (Exod 20:22-23:33)." She also points to the introductory formula ואלה המשפטים in Exod 21:1 and 1QS VI, 24 and notes that the use of אשר in 1QS to introduce each case differs from אם . . . ואם in Exodus, but is similar to usage of the relative particle at Deut 15:2, and notes that the use of וכן to link regulations, is similar to Deut 15:17; 20:15; 22:3, 26; *Textual Development*, 125.

103. Thus, *inter alia*, *Textual Development*, 144; and "Biblical Quotations," 86-91. Similarly, see now Alec J. Lucas, "Scripture Citations as an Internal Redactional Control: 1QS 5:1-20a and Its 4Q Parallels," *DSD* 17 (2010): 30-52.

104. Nitzan in *Qumran Cave 4: XX, Poetical and Liturgical Texts, Part 2*, ed. Esther Chazon

The claim is that later authors would insert biblical citations and more explicit allusions in order to bolster the authority of sectarian texts. This argument would make sense if a sectarian text developed independently of biblical tradition and was then later deemed to require a more authoritative imprimatur. The hypothesis would be less logical, however, if it can be shown that even those texts lacking explicit markers nonetheless derived from Scripture in the first place.[105] In many of the cases we have examined in this study, there is evidence in all versions of the *Community Rule* that biblical sources are being employed. It is not a question of whether the Bible is being used, but of how this use is packaged.[106] The claim that an "appeal to the Bible" reflects a bid for increased authority would have to be reformulated as an argument that more ex-

---

et al. DJD 29 (Oxford: Clarendon, 1999), 2-3, notes the parallel between 4Q280 and 1QS col. 2 and the partial parallel to 4QBerakhot[a] (4Q286; *Qumran Cave 4: VI, Poetical and Liturgical Texts, Part 1*, ed. Esther Chazon et al. DJD 11 [Oxford: Clarendon, 1998]; cf. 4QBer 1-2; 4Q285 8 [= 11Q14 1]), and discusses the relationship between the texts. Her rationale for suggesting that 4Q280 is the earliest version is that it is "the least developed of the three" with regard to liturgical, literary, and stylistic factors. Although it may not be necessary to view 4Q280 as posterior to 1QS, I disagree that it is "less developed" simply because it is shorter. 1QS seems to me to provide a necessary intermediate step between the biblical base text and the form of the expulsion curse found in 4Q280. Cf. the use of the biblical priestly blessing in 1QS b, where the use of biblical language is much more subtle than in 1QS itself and yet clearly a more highly developed "free use of the expanded pattern" of the biblical text; Nitzan, *Qumran Prayer*, 155-58.

105. Unfortunately, evaluation of this "chicken-and-egg" question tends to be subjective, and there is no definitive methodology for determining when proof-texts provide the biblical sources for a sectarian regulation and when they are offered as support for preexisting rules. E.g., Fishbane has argued that "rules or directives to the community are sometimes justified by nonlegal citations. These are clearly of a *post hoc* nature"; *Biblical Interpretation*, 349. It is possible, however, that a conception of the multivalence of Scripture would have enabled a Qumran sectarian to derive law from a biblical text, even by reading the text in a manner foreign to its original context. A related question is the relationship between sectarian rules and Torah law in the Qumran legal conception. Fraade maintains that the study of Bible and "mišpāṭ" were distinctive elements in a two-part curriculum at Qumran; "Interpretive Authority," 21-22. In contrast, Metso states that "the hypothesis that the Community would have made distinction between its own rules and the regulations of the Torah does not seem plausible"; "Biblical Quotations," 89. Regarding the citations of Exod 23:7 and Isa 2:22 in 1QS 5, Bernstein and Koyfman write: "On occasion, biblical verses are employed explicitly, with citation formulas, to justify regulations which we would probably describe as sectarian rules" (rather than Torah law); "The Interpretation of Biblical Law," 72 n. 28.

106. Of the three instances of explicit citation in 1QS, the references to Exod 23:7 and Isa 2:22 are absent in the parallel passages in 4QS[b] and 4QS[d]. The use of Isa 40:3 is found in both 4QS[b] and 4QS[d] (though only the second occurrence is preserved in the 4QS[b]; the parallel section to col. VIII is not extant). The explicit citation formula is lacking, but the pronominal identifier remains: "[in order to depart into the wilderness to prepare there the Way of truth. This is the study of the Tora]h." The allusion to Isa 28:16 פנת יקר also is found in the Cave 4 parallel.

plicit flagging reflects a bid for greater authority. Alternatively, the opposite hypothesis might be more plausible — that traces of a source text would be more likely to fade over time than to be artificially introduced.[107] If 1QS "connects the dots" that are discernible in 4QS[b] and 4QS[d], then it might be simpler to suppose that 1QS was the initial template from which the connecting lines were erased, rather than to propose that the scribe producing 1QS connected the dots. As we noted at the outset, questions of redaction have occupied a significant position in recent scholarship on the *Serakhim*. It is hoped that the foregoing analysis will be able to provide some contribution to that ongoing discussion, as well as to illuminate the phenomenon of the use of Scripture in the *Community Rule*.

BIBLIOGRAPHY

Alexander, Philip S., and Geza Vermes. *Qumran Cave 4. XIX: 4QSerekh Ha-Yaḥad and Two Related Texts*. DJD 26. Oxford: Clarendon, 1998.

Bernstein, Moshe J., and Shlomo A. Koyfman. "The Interpretation of Biblical Law in the Dead Sea Scrolls: Forms and Methods." In *Biblical Interpretation at Qumran*, ed. Matthias Henze. SDSSRL. Grand Rapids: Eerdmans, 2005, 61-87.

Brooke, George J. "Isaiah 40:3 and the Wilderness Community." In *New Qumran Texts and Studies: Proceedings of the First Meeting of the International Organization for Qumran Studies. Paris 1992*, ed. Brooke and Florentino García Martínez. STDJ 15. Leiden: Brill, 1994, 117-32.

Charlesworth, James H. ed. *Princeton Theological Seminary Dead Sea Scrolls Project*. Tübingen: Mohr/Louisville: Westminster/John Knox Press, 1991-.

Chazon, Esther G. "The Use of the Bible as a Key to Meaning in Psalms from Qumran." In *Emanuel: Studies in the Hebrew Bible, Septuagint and Dead Sea Scrolls in Honor of Emanuel Tov*, ed. Shalom M. Paul, Robert A. Kraft, Lawrence H. Schiffman, and Weston W. Fields. VTSup 94. Leiden: Brill, 2003, 85-96.

———. "Scripture and Prayer in 'The Words of the Luminaries.'" In *Prayers That Cite Scripture*, ed. James L. Kugel. Cambridge, Mass.: Harvard University Press, 2007, 25-41.

Dimant, Devorah. "Qumran Sectarian Literature." In *Jewish Writings of the Second Temple Period: Apocrypha, Pseudepigrapha, Qumran Sectarian Writings, Philo, Josephus*, ed. Michael E. Stone. CRINT 2.2. Assen: Van Gorcum and Minneapolis: Fortress, 1984. 483-550.

107. Thus, although the close paraphrase of Lev 19:17 found in 1QS V, 26–VI, 1 is lacking in the parallel passage in frag. 1 col. II of 4QS[d], the phrase להוכיח איש את רעהו does appear in line 4 of 4QS[d] frag. 1 col. II, parallel 1QS V, 25. Similarly, we have identified adaptations of Mic 6:8 in 1QS II, 24; V, 3-4, 24-25; IV, 5, and VIII, 2. In the parallel passage to 1QS V, 3-4, 4QS[d] frag. 1 I, 3 retains the allusion and the subsequent allusion to Deut 29:18, though it lacks the additions of the sectarian terms "truth" and יחד found in 1QS. In the parallel to 1QS V, 24-25, in frag. 1 II, 4, the words "truth" and "humility" are omitted in 4QS[d].

————. "Not Exile in the Desert but Exile in Spirit: The Pesher of Isa. 40:3 in the Rule of the Community." *Meghillot* 2 (2004): 21-36. [Hebrew]

Fishbane, Michael. *Biblical Interpretation in Ancient Israel.* Oxford: Clarendon, 1985.

————. "Use, Authority and Interpretation of Mikra at Qumran." In *Mikra: Text, Translation, Reading and Interpretation of the Hebrew Bible in Ancient Judaism and Early Christianity,* ed. Martin J. Mulder. CRINT 2.1. Assen: Van Gorcum and Philadelphia: Fortress, 1988, 339-77.

Fitzmyer, Joseph A. "The Use of Explicit Old Testament Quotations in Qumran Literature and in the New Testament." *NTS* 7 (1961): 297-333. Repr. in *Essays on the Semitic Background of the New Testament.* London: Chapman, 1971; BRS. Grand Rapids: Eerdmans and Livonia: Dove, 1997, 3-58.

Fraade, Steven D. "Interpretive Authority in the Studying Community of Qumran." *JJS* 144 (1993): 46-69.

Glessmer, Uwe. "The Otot-texts (4Q319) and the Problem of Intercalations in the Context of the 364-day Calendar." In *Qumranstudien: Vorträge und Beiträge der Teilnehmer des Qumranseminars auf dem internationalen Treffen der Society of Biblical Literature. Münster 1993,* ed. Heinz-Josef Fabry, Armin Lange, and Hermann Lichtenberger. Göttingen: Vandenhoeck & Ruprecht, 1996, 125-64.

Hughes, Julie A. *Scriptural Allusions and Exegesis in the Hodayot.* STDJ 59. Leiden: Brill, 2006.

Kister, Menahem. "Biblical Phrases and Hidden Biblical Interpretations and Pesharim." In *The Dead Sea Scrolls: Forty Years of Research,* ed. Devorah Dimant and Uriel Rappaport. STDJ 10. Leiden: Brill, 1992, 27-39.

Licht, Jacob. *The Rule Scroll — A Scroll from the Wilderness of Judaea — 1QS, 1QSa, 1QSb: Text, Introduction and Commentary.* Jerusalem: Mosad Biyalik, 1965. [Hebrew]

Metso, Sarianna. *The Textual Development of the Qumran Community Rule.* STDJ 21. Leiden: Brill 1997.

————. "The Use of Old Testament Quotations in the Qumran Community Rule." In *Qumran Between the Old and New Testaments,* ed. Frederick H. Cryer and Thomas L. Thompson. JSOTSup 290. Sheffield: Sheffield Academic, 1998, 217-31.

————. "Biblical Quotations in the Community Rule." In *The Bible as Book: The Hebrew Bible and the Judaean Desert Discoveries,* ed. Edward D. Herbert and Emanuel Tov. London: British Library, 2002, 81-92.

————. *The Serekh Texts.* CQS 9. LSTS 62. London: T. & T. Clark, 2007.

Murphy, Catherine M. *Wealth in the Dead Sea Scrolls and in the Qumran Community.* STDJ 40. Leiden: Brill, 2002.

Nitzan, Bilha. *Qumran Prayer and Religious Poetry.* STDJ 12. Leiden: Brill, 1994.

Talmon, Shemaryahu. "The 'Desert Motif' in the Bible and in Qumran Literature." In *Biblical Motifs, Origins and Transformations,* ed. Alexander Altmann. Philip L. Lown Institute of Advanced Judaic Studies, Studies and Texts 3. Cambridge, Mass.: Harvard University Press, 1966, 31-66.

Vermes, Geza. "Biblical Proof-Texts in Qumran Literature." *JSS* 34 (1989): 493-508.

Wernberg-Møller, Preben. "Some Reflections on the Biblical Material in the Manual of Discipline." *ST* 9 (1955): 40-66.

Prophetic Interpretation in the *Pesharim*

George J. Brooke

The written traditions of Israel and the ongoing religious experiences of the members of the movement who collected the library together in the various Qumran caves presented opportunities for several different kinds of interpretation. I have suggested in several places that it is not inappropriate to categorize such interpretation under five broad headings: legal interpretation, homiletic or parenetic interpretation, narrative interpretation, poetic or liturgical interpretation, and prophetic interpretation.[1] Each category has its particular characteristics but also shares much with what is ongoing in the other categories. The purpose of this chapter is to focus on the last of these categories, prophetic interpretation.

The title of this chapter is in part deliberately ambiguous. On the one hand, the label "Prophetic Interpretation" describes the content of the interpretation as being concerned with the prophetic literature, however that might be defined. The so-called continuous pesharim found in the Qumran caves are the most obvious examples of this prophetic interpretation, being explicit commentaries on running prophetic texts from Isaiah, the twelve Minor Prophets,

---

1. George J. Brooke, "Biblical Interpretation in the Qumran Scrolls and the New Testament," in *The Dead Sea Scrolls Fifty Years after their Discovery: Proceedings of the Jerusalem Congress, July 20-25, 1997*, ed. Lawrence H. Schiffman, Emanuel Tov, and James C. VanderKam (Jerusalem: Israel Exploration Society and Shrine of the Book, 2000), 60-73; repr. with minor revisions in *The Dead Sea Scrolls and the New Testament* (London: SPCK and Minneapolis: Fortress, 2005), 52-69; "Biblical Interpretation in the Wisdom Texts from Qumran," in *The Wisdom Texts from Qumran and the Development of Sapiential Thought*, ed. Charlotte Hempel, Armin Lange, and Hermann Lichtenberger. BETL 159 (Leuven: Peeters, 2002), 201-20; "Biblical Interpretation at Qumran," in *The Bible and the Dead Sea Scrolls*, vol. 1: *Scripture and the Scrolls*, ed. James H. Charlesworth. The Second Princeton Symposium on Judaism and Christian Origins (Waco: Baylor University Press, 2006), 287-319.

and the Psalms. On the other hand, "Prophetic Interpretation" describes the method of interpretation as itself having prophetic characteristics, characteristics that are continuous with the activities of the very same prophetic figures whose literature is the basis for the interpretation.[2] It is important to hold on to both these matters in order to appreciate most fully the nature of prophetic interpretation in the Qumran library.

The Content of Prophecy

What constitutes prophecy, and what texts and other phenomena might have been considered suitable to form the basis of prophetic interpretation?[3] All students of prophecy have an ongoing problem of definition at the outset.[4] Recent work on prophets and prophecy has resulted in a welcome and more integrated reading of a very wide range of evidence and a determination to set the whole breadth of what might be labelled "prophetic" within a framework that includes both ancient Near Eastern parallels for the prophets of the Hebrew Bible[5] and also the classical traditions of the Greco-Roman world for the late Second Temple period and the evidence of the New Testament.[6] This broad framework categorically undermines any viewpoint that prophecy had ceased in the late Second Temple period and is increasingly and appropriately

2. Cf. Armin Lange, "Interpretation als Offenbarung: Zum Verhältnis von Schriftauslegung und Offenbarung in apokalyptischer und nichtapokalyptischer Literatur," in *Wisdom and Apocalypticism in the Dead Sea Scrolls and in the Biblical Tradition,* ed. Florentino García Martínez. BETL 168 (Leuven: Peeters, 2003), 17-33.

3. General overviews of prophets and prophecy at Qumran include the following: Millar Burrows, "Prophets and Prophecy at Qumran," in *Israel's Prophetic Heritage,* ed. Bernhard W. Anderson and Walter Harrelson (New York: Harper, 1962), 223-32; James E. Bowley, "Prophets and Prophecy at Qumran," in *The Dead Sea Scrolls after Fifty Years,* ed. Peter W. Flint and James C. VanderKam (Leiden: Brill, 1999), 2:354-78; George J. Brooke, "Prophecy," in *EDSS,* 2:694-700.

4. This has been helpfully addressed by Lester L. Grabbe, "Poets, Scribes, or Preachers? The Reality of Prophecy in the Second Temple Period," in *Knowing the End from the Beginning: The Prophetic, the Apocalyptic and Their Relationships,* ed. Grabbe and Robert D. Haak. JSPSup 46 (London: T. & T. Clark, 2003), 192-215.

5. See, e.g., Martti Nissinen, ed., *Prophecy in Its Ancient Near Eastern Context: Mesopotamian, Biblical, and Arabian Perspectives.* SBLSymS 13 (Atlanta: SBL, 2000); "Das kritische Potential in der altorientalischen Prophetie," in *Propheten in Mari, Assyrien und Israel,* ed. Matthias Köckert and Nissinen. FRLANT 201 (Göttingen: Vandenhoeck & Ruprecht, 2003), 1-32.

6. See, e.g., the landmark study by David E. Aune, *Prophecy in Early Christianity and the Ancient Mediterranean World* (Grand Rapids: Eerdmans, 1983); also Ben Witherington III, *Jesus the Seer: The Progress of Prophecy* (Peabody: Hendrickson, 1999), esp. chs. 8-10.

becoming the contextual basis for the consideration of prophecy in the Dead Sea Scrolls.[7]

The nonbiblical compositions found in the Qumran caves seem to challenge and deconstruct such a broad approach by insisting on certain lines of inherited continuity; in other words, the movement that was responsible for collecting the Qumran library claims to have looked to the scriptural past for its appreciation of its own prophetic activity rather than to the phenomena of prophecy in the Greco-Roman world. Nevertheless, the broadening of the definition of prophecy discernible in recent scholarly work assists the analyst of the Qumran scrolls by permitting a wider range of data to be included than might previously have been allowed. So the study of prophetic interpretation in the Dead Sea Scrolls should consider the interpretation of all the means of divine communication that are hinted at in the scrolls: "the transmission and interpretation of dreams and visions (as in the Enoch literature and Daniel), the use of lots and priestly means of divination,[8] such as the Urim and Thummim,[9] the writing down of angelic discourse (such as in Jubilees), inspired interpretation of authoritative oracles (as in the pesharim), and the symbolic activity of the community as a whole and of its individual members."[10] This is too large a task for this present chapter, so I will focus mainly on the literary evidence for prophetic interpretation, beginning with the so-called paratextual rewritten prophets.[11]

---

7. See esp. Alex P. Jassen, *Mediating the Divine: Prophecy and Revelation in the Dead Sea Scrolls and Second Temple Judaism.* STDJ 68 (Leiden: Brill, 2007); Martti Nissinen, "Transmitting Divine Mysteries: The Prophetic Role of Wisdom Teachers in the Dead Sea Scrolls," in *Scripture in Transition: Essays on Septuagint, Hebrew Bible, and Dead Sea Scrolls in Honour of Raija Sollamo,* ed. Anssi Voitila and Jutta Jokiranta. JSJSup 126 (Leiden: Brill, 2008), 513-33.

8. Nissinen, "Transmitting Divine Mysteries," 526-27, has noted: "Sometimes, as in Mesopotamia or probably in the kingdom of Judah, it is possible to make a rather clear-cut distinction between (non-technical) prophetic and (technical) other kinds of divination, but this seems to be no longer the case in Second Temple Judaism where prophecy as a concept began to amalgamate with literary and scribal roles and activities." Whereas in some contexts it is possible to catalogue divinatory practices apart from prophetic activity, there seems to be no clear-cut line between these in the life of the Qumran community.

9. See the references to their use in 4QpIsa[d] (4Q164) I 5; 4QMysteries[a] (4Q299) 69 2; 4QApocryphon of Moses B[b] (4Q376) 1 I, 3.

10. Brooke, "Prophecy," 695.

11. The suitability of the label "paratextual" is open to discussion; if it is understood simply to describe the phenomenon of how one text can be set alongside another upon which it seems to depend, then it is an improvement on "rewritten Bible," "parabiblical," and "parascriptural," which imply that there was a Bible or clearly defined set of authoritative Scriptures alongside which the paratextual compositions are to be put. The term "paratextual" is not used here to refer to all the additional material in a printed book (from the title to the material on the back cover) in the sense determined very influentially by Gérard Genette, *Seuils* (Paris: Seuil, 1987), 7-

Types of Prophetic Interpretation

The Paratextual Rewritten Prophets[12]

In the centuries of the Second Temple period, during virtually the whole of which the prophetic canon (as we retrospectively label it) was being created, the prophetic books themselves were copied and passed on, sometimes in more than one edition, as is often pointed out in relation to the book of Jeremiah.[13] Those scribal transmission processes have interpretative features that are sometimes discernible not just in the variety of text forms for each prophetic composition, whether of a major or a minor sort, but also in the way in which the text is presented on any particular manuscript by a scribe or scribes. Sometimes, for example, the text of a prophetic work is written out with spaces between paragraphs or also, as in the case with 1QIsa^a and possibly 4QIsa^b, with marginal marks indicating units of text; in many instances these paragraph space dividers or marginal marks correspond with the way that the prophetic text is presented in the Masoretic tradition, but there are also many variations.[14]

Beyond those various forms of prophetic text and the manuscript paraphernalia to be observed in some form in every manuscript, the literary prophets also gave rise to a wide-ranging process of adaptation and implicit interpretation. For the literary prophets the most notable developments of their traditions are to be found in the remains of the so-called *Jeremiah Apocrypha* (A-C^a-f) and of *Pseudo-Ezekiel^a-d*.[15] Furthermore, in addition to the literary

---

19. On the possibility for rehabilitating the label "Rewritten Bible," but in a restricted way, see Moshe J. Bernstein, "'Rewritten Bible': A Generic Category Which Has Outlived Its Usefulness?" *Text* 22 (2005): 169-96.

12. For a general survey of the major manuscripts containing parabiblical prophetic compositions, see George J. Brooke, "Parabiblical Prophetic Narratives," in Flint and VanderKam, *The Dead Sea Scrolls After Fifty Years*, 1:271-301.

13. See Emanuel Tov, "The Literary History of the Book of Jeremiah in the Light of Its Textual History," in *Empirical Models for Biblical Criticism*, ed. Jeffrey H. Tigay (Philadelphia: University of Pennsylvania Press, 1985), 211-37; "The Jeremiah Scrolls from Qumran," *RevQ* 14 (1989): 189-206; Eugene Ulrich, *The Dead Sea Scrolls and the Origins of the Bible*. SDSSRL (Grand Rapids: Eerdmans, 1999), 69.

14. For detailed descriptions of scribal practices see Emanuel Tov, *Scribal Practices and Approaches Reflected in the Texts from the Judean Desert*. STDJ 54 (Leiden: Brill, 2004); in Appendix 8 (331-35) Tov lists some scribal features of the biblical manuscripts, including the books of the prophets. The sense divisions and marginal marks in 1QIsa^a are discussed in detail in Eugene Ulrich and Peter W. Flint, *Qumran Cave 1. II: The Isaiah Scrolls, Part 2: Introductions, Commentary, and Textual Variants*. DJD 32 (Oxford: Clarendon, 2010), 82-88.

15. These are described fully in Devorah Dimant, *Qumran Cave 4: XXI, Parabiblical Texts, Part 4: Pseudo-Prophetic Texts*. DJD 30 (Oxford: Clarendon, 2001).

prophets (Isaiah, Jeremiah, Ezekiel, and the Twelve), several scriptural figures were understood as prophets, some obviously so, such as Samuel, Elijah, and Elisha, and others less obviously so as well, such as Moses, David, and Daniel. In the Qumran library there are nonsectarian paratextual compositions that can be associated with all these "nonliterary" prophets that indicate that the authority of earlier revelation was recognized in subsequent generations through the need for it to be re-presented afresh in rewritten and reworked forms. By way of example, for Samuel there is the so-called *Vision of Samuel* (4Q160), for Elijah the papyrus *Paraphrase of Kings* (4Q382), for Elisha the *Apocryphon of Elisha* (4Q418a), for Moses the *Words of Moses* (1Q22) and works such as the *Apocryphon of Moses* (4Q375-77) as well as several other traditions, for David the *Apocryphon of David* (2Q22) and the *Apocryphon of Samuel-Kings* (6Q9), and for Daniel works such as the so-called *Pseudo-Daniel* (4Q243-45).

It is not necessary in this chapter to consider the whole range of nonsectarian and quasi-sectarian paratextual or rewritten compositions that are associated in one way or another with the towering prophetic figures of earlier generations. If the broadest definition of prophetic literature is presented as a starting point, then nearly all of the writings now contained in the Law and the Prophets, as well as the Psalms and Daniel, together with all their various rewritten forms would need to be included, either because they were deemed to have been revealed or because they were associated with a prophet, which may amount to much the same thing. In light of the nonbiblical nonsectarian compositions found in the Qumran library, it is clear that a broad definition like this would be clear grounds for saying that one of the most significant characteristics of the literary activity of Second Temple Judaism was its attention to prophecy, and not just prophecy as an interpretative activity of the past, but as a past activity continuous with present interpretative needs and practices.

For the paratextual prophetic texts in particular, like the *Jeremiah Apocrypha* or *Pseudo-Ezekiel,* several features need to be discussed in a general fashion to indicate at least some of the ways in which prophetic interpretation took place in the Second Temple period. To begin with, the very existence of the paratextual rewritten prophetic texts shows that the prophets themselves were understood as forward-looking. The paratextual prophetic rewritings reflect the view that if ever classical prophecy had been about forth-telling, in the Second Temple period it was more clearly perceived by some Jews at least as fore-telling.[16] If the classical literary prophets had been perceived as simply speaking

---

16. Perceived on other grounds, e.g., by John C. Trever, "The Qumran Teacher — Another Candidate?" in *Early Jewish and Christian Exegesis: Studies in Memory of William Hugh Brownlee,* ed. Craig A. Evans and William F. Stinespring. SBL Homage Series 10 (Atlanta: Scholars, 1987), 103.

to their own generations alone, then they might have been studied for some antiquarian reasons as in some way foundational for later generations, but not as having direct relevance. So it is the case that the narrative framework of parts of at least one form of the *Jeremiah Apocryphon* is Jeremiah adapted to fit the chronological framework of Jubilee periods, which is a feature of the kind of eschatological historiographical prophecy evident in later nonsectarian and sectarian texts like the book of *Jubilees* and 11QMelchizedek. Likewise, some of the oracles of Ezekiel are adapted for contemporary purposes: that concerning the dry bones of Ezekiel 37, originally certainly about the postexilic restoration of Israel, is adjusted in *Pseudo-Ezekiel* to speak of future eschatological events, such as the end-time resurrection of all individuals.

Second, it seems as if the full diversity of genres in which the prophetic literature had been presented was adopted and recast in the paratextual prophetic compositions. Narratives were expanded and reworked; oracles were adjusted and adapted; dialogues between the prophet and God were retold; speeches addressed to Israel or others were recast. The generic continuity of the rewritten compositions with what they rewrite is indicative of the way in which those who saw themselves as the heirs of the prophets also identified with them. Thus the interpretation of the prophetic Scriptures in these paratextual prophetic texts was "prophetic interpretation" in both senses outlined at the opening of this chapter. The force of the rewriting of "prophetic" genres in their own look-alike forms probably also influenced the way other rewritings took place, so that, for example, the rewriting of Genesis-Exodus in the book of *Jubilees* took the form of an angelic revelatory speech with explicit oracular characteristics, and the *Temple Scroll* is written in the form of a revelatory divine speech presented in the first person of the divine voice.[17]

So, third, the continuity strongly suggests not that the rewriting and reworking of earlier prophetic traditions is something new, but that it is something that goes to the heart of what has already been revealed in some way. Earlier authoritative traditions were already indicating this, most notably in the way in which within some prophetic compositions doublets were visible, showing how traditions could be reused and adapted. This third point indicates that there is no need for the rewritten forms explicitly to claim revelatory status for themselves. Such status was inherent in the original authoritative prophetic texts and was transmitted in some way in the relationship between the reworked composition and its base text. In this way the paratextual rewritten

17. On how paratextual Mosaic discourses of the Second Temple period carry the marks of prophecy and inspired interpretation, see Hindy Najman, *Seconding Sinai: The Development of Mosaic Discourse in Second Temple Judaism*. JSJSup 77 (Leiden: Brill, 2003), 16-40.

compositions should be viewed neither as replacing the compositions they rework nor as entirely secondary and interpretative.[18] The ongoing status of the base composition is discernible in that it alone is used by later explicit commentators; there is, for example, no commentary tradition on the *Jeremiah Apocrypha* or *Pseudo-Ezekiel,* other than their own redactional development, which is sometimes difficult to differentiate from the processes of scribal transmission. But the imitative character of the compositions like the *Jeremiah Apocrypha* and *Pseudo-Ezekiel* strongly suggests that their authors intended them to be continuous with the traditions of the prophets with whom they identify, as if they reveal their true significance for the contemporary generation.

Fourth, a feature of the paratextual prophetic rewritings, as in other rewritings, is the tendency towards specificity. Part of this seems to have resulted from the lack of a full appreciation for the original context or setting of the prophetic work being reworked, but part of it was indeed a belief that the prophetic texts were originally written to speak to contemporary circumstances and so could be glossed with clarificatory explanations to fit the views and circumstances of the rewriter. However, although there is this tendency towards a new specificity in the rewritten texts, so it also needs to be recalled that there is little or nothing in the paratextual prophetic texts that might be labelled as clearly sectarian.[19] Sectarian readings of prophetic texts are indeed to be found in several different forms of interpretation such as the pesharim, but not apparently in the paratextual rewritings.

In sum, the re-presentation of the prophetic books in rewritten, paratextual forms is an interpretative extension of those very books. Those responsible for the rewritings were being no more derivative and secondary than were the members of the prophetic schools who compiled the prophetic oracles together into literary collections in the first place. In such cases this work of compilation sometimes took several generations (as with Isaiah), and sometimes took several forms (as with Jeremiah), and sometimes both. The rewriting process shows that the prophets were understood by some Jews at least as foretelling matters that needed to be apprehended and appropriated by each new generation. From all these perspectives it is most appropriate to view these rewritings of the literary prophetic texts as themselves examples of ongoing prophetic activity, "prophetic interpretation" in both senses.

18. The same should be said for the Septuagint, in which the translators sometimes conformed the wording of the original prophetic oracles to their own outlook. See, e.g., the descriptions of this process in several instances by F. F. Bruce, "Prophetic Interpretation in the Septuagint," *BIOSCS* 12 (1979): 17-26.

19. Even the adjustment of the Jeremiah tradition to Jubilee periods is not a clear sectarian marker.

Some Other Implicit Interpretations of the Literary Prophets

The paratextual prophetic literature described briefly in the preceding section is an obvious category of interpretative extension of the prophetic texts. However, it is clear that the literary prophets are used interpretatively in several other ways in the Dead Sea Scrolls, especially the sectarian compositions. A striking use of Isa 58:13-14 can be found in the sectarian *Damascus Document* (CD XI, 16–XII, 2):

> No-one shall do work on Friday from the time when the sphere of the sun is distant from the gate (by) its (the sun's) diameter, for this is (the import of) that which He said, "Observe the Sabbath day to sanctify it (Deut 5:12)." And on the Sabbath day, no one shall speak a wicked or vain word. Let him not lend his neighbor anything. Let him not dispute about wealth or profit. *Let him not speak of things* (relating to) the work and the labor to be done the next morning. No-one shall walk about in the field *to do his desired labor on the Sabbath.* Let him not walk outside of his city more than a thousand cubits. No-one shall eat (anything) on the Sabbath day except that which has been prepared (in advance) or from that which is decaying in the field. Let him not drink or eat except if he is in the camp. On the road, if he goes down to wash let him drink where he stands, but let him not draw (water) into any vessel. Let him not send a foreigner *to do his desire on the Sabbath.*[20]

The phrases in italics come from Isaiah 58. Indeed, one scholar has suggested that this whole passage of extended Sabbath law is structured on this Isaianic passage, adapted and itself extended through various exegetical techniques.[21] Other scriptural passages are also alluded to,[22] but the point of this example is to see that a prophetic exhortation is used to justify a piece of legislation. Given that the movement behind this new legislation considered that all it was doing was presenting what God had made known to community members which had been hidden from the rest of Israel (CD III, 12-14), then this creative interpreta-

---

20. Trans. Lawrence H. Schiffman, *The Halakhah at Qumran.* SJLA 16 (Leiden: Brill, 1975), 84-104.

21. Eliezer Slomovic, "Toward an Understanding of the Exegesis in the Dead Sea Scrolls," *RevQ* 7 (1969): 11-13.

22. On some of the uses of Deuteronomy and Leviticus in this passage, see Michael Fishbane, "Interpretation of Mikra at Qumran," in *Mikra: Text, Translation, Reading and Interpretation of the Hebrew Bible in Ancient Judaism and Early Christianity,* ed. Martin Jan Mulder. CRINT 2.1 (Assen: Van Gorcum and Philadelphia: Fortress, 1988), 348-49, 368-69, 372. Fishbane supposes that Isaiah 58 could not have been used as a source from which new laws could be derived, but was used to justify legal practice *ex post facto.*

tion has a revelatory status and is once again "prophetic interpretation" in both senses of the phrase, interpretation of a prophetic text that has its own prophetic oracular status, here with a legal function.

A similar point can be observed in the use of Jeremiah in at least one part of the *Hodayot* (1QH^a VII, 21–VIII, 41). This is implicit prophetic interpretation in a hymnic or poetic context. Julie Hughes has provided a close reading of what she understands to be the central stanza of a dualistic community hymn (addressed to the Maskil).[23] She has suggested convincingly that the central stanza is enfolded in two verses, in each of which there are strong resonances of the prayer of Jeremiah in Jer 10:23:[24]

> 25And I, *I know (ydʿty)* by your understanding
> *that not (kyʾ lʾ)* by the hand of flesh [. . .]
> [and *not for*] *a human (lʾ lʾdm)* 26*his way (drkw)*
> *nor* can *a man (ʾnwš) direct his steps (lhkyn sʿdw).*
> But *I know (ʾdʿh)* that by your hand (is) the formation of every spirit
> [and all] its [works] 27you *destined (hkynwth)* before you created it.
> And how can anyone change your decrees?
> . . .
> 34And what then itself (is) flesh
> that it understands [these?
> And a formati]on of dust
> how *can it direct its steps (lhkyn sʿdw)*
> 35You, you have formed the spirit
> and its works you have *destined (hkynwth)* [from before eternity].
> And from you (is) the *way (drk)* of every living being (1QH^a VII, 25-35).

The central parts of this section of the poem, lines 27-33, also reflect in minor ways the language of Jer 10:23, but promote other scriptural motifs as well. Even in the two verses presented above it is possible to see allusions to additional scriptural texts such as Isa 45:9-12, in which God is likened to a potter and described as the former or fashioner of the created order, a metaphor that is developed at length also in Jer 18:1-12. Hughes has reckoned that there are also strong echoes of Zech 12:1: "Thus says the LORD, who stretched out the heavens and founded the earth and formed the human spirit within."[25] In fact, the

---

23. Julie A. Hughes, *Scriptural Allusions and Exegesis in the Hodayot.* STDJ 59 (Leiden: Brill, 2006), 63-95.

24. Jer 10:23: "I know *(ydʿty),* O LORD, that *(kyʾ lʾ)* the way *(drkw)* of human beings *(ʾdm)* is not in their control, that mortals as they walk *(lʾ lʾyš hlk)* cannot direct *(hkyn)* their steps *(sʿdw).*"

25. Hughes, *Scriptural Allusions,* 74. She also notes a number of phrases that overlap with parts of Job 12:9-10.

method of poetic interpretation is to present anthologies of allusions in which the fresh coordination of phraseology refreshes the original prophetic text and brings it, in a way through the inspiration of the poet, into the contemporary experience and reflection of the reader or hearer.

In the use of Jer 10:23 above, what is the more precise significance of the poet's rephrasing and interpretation? In a general way the poet is asserting with the earlier prophetic materials that people cannot plan their future circumstances since God rewards and punishes as he sees fit. But such a point of view is developed, Hughes has indicated neatly, by extending such divine purpose back before an individual's birth and in relation to a person's nature, not just one's circumstances.[26] Beyond this meditative reflection, especially on Jeremiah, the poet of the *Hodayot* seems to do at least two other things through the use of the prophetic allusions. First, by aligning himself with the prayer of Jeremiah, he indicates that he can pray like Jeremiah, modelling himself on the prophet of the past who was chosen before birth. So, second, he also seems to consider himself (and also his primary audience) as among those destined from before birth for divine favor. The use of Jer 10:23 elsewhere in the sectarian literature from the Qumran caves suggests that these ideas were well known and recognized.[27]

Explicit Interpretation as Prophecy

Coherence between Prophecy and Explicit Prophetic Interpretation The presence of rewritten or paratextual prophetic works has indicated that in the late Second Temple period the prophetic voice was held to be enduring and made present through a variety of means that were continuous with the production of the classic literary prophetic works. Generically, these rewritten compositions imitate the compositions they rewrite; like them they contain interpretative material that is not presented as secondary and derivative but as coherent with the divine communication received by the prophet. In addition, the implicit use of phrases and motifs from the literary prophets in the sectarian compositions found in the Qumran caves indicates that those compositions share something of the revelatory status of the prophetic sources, whether through extension in legal material or adaptation in poetic contexts.

It can be argued, in addition, that such coherence is also a feature of the ex-

---

26. Hughes, *Scriptural Allusions*, 79.

27. Hughes, *Scriptural Allusions*, 87-95, outlines the principal features of the use of Jer 10:23 in 1QS X, 5–XI, 22; 1QH^a XV, 29-36; and 1QH^a XII, 6–XIII, 6.

plicit interpretations of prophecy in sectarian compositions, notably in the running commentaries on prophetic texts, the pesharim,[28] but also in other forms of explicit commentary such as the so-called thematic pesharim[29] and the smaller explicit exegetical units, like the so-called Amos-Numbers midrash, to be found in compositions like the *Damascus Document*. Part of the discernment of divine purposes in the prophetic literature and the lives of the prophets depended upon suitable scriptural interpretation.[30] The varieties of such interpretation covered not just halakic matters, such as in the revelatory rewritten presentations of the book of *Jubilees* or the *Temple Scroll,* but insight into how God might be working his purposes out through the current circumstances of the community and the wider movement of which it was a part. The pesharim provided a mode of interpretation of unfulfilled prophetic texts of all kinds that demonstrated that the experiences of the Community were anticipated in the prophecies of previous generations.[31] Prophetic text and inspired exegetical interpretation are coherent with one another, so much so that the interpretation sometimes infected the presentation of the prophetic text and parts of the prophetic text bear frequent repetition in the interpretation.[32]

Prophetic Interpretation as Inspired: The Case of the Teacher In *Pesher Habakkuk,* a composition almost certainly from the late first century B.C.E., there is a well-known passage that clearly indicates that God was considered to be still revealing his mysteries for the first-century reader. Habakkuk 2:2, "That

28. The pesharim are best set out and made available in Maurya P. Horgan, *Pesharim: Qumran Interpretations of Biblical Books.* CBQMS 8 (Washington: Catholic Biblical Association, 1979); "Pesharim," in *The Dead Sea Scrolls: Hebrew, Aramaic, and Greek Texts with English Translations,* vol. 6B: *Pesharim, Other Commentaries, and Related Documents,* ed. James H. Charlesworth (Tübingen: Mohr Siebeck and Louisville: Westminster John Knox, 2002), 1-194.

29. On these, see, e.g., George J. Brooke, "Thematic Commentaries on Prophetic Scriptures," in *Biblical Interpretation at Qumran,* ed. Matthias Henze. SDSSRL (Grand Rapids: Eerdmans, 2005), 134-57.

30. Rebecca Gray, *Prophetic Figures in Late Second Temple Jewish Palestine: The Evidence from Josephus* (New York: Oxford University Press, 1993), 105-7, considers the similarities and differences between Josephus's Essene prophets and pesher interpretation at Qumran, noting in particular the similarities. If the sectarian movement is to be identified with the Essenes in one form or another, then it is worth noting that Josephus has several things to say about their competence, matching his own (*B.J.* 3:352), in predicting the future and in other matters, such as dream interpretation: *B.J.* 1:78-80; 2:113, 159; *Ant.* 13:311; 15:373-79; 17:346-48.

31. The most recent elaborate attempt to articulate not just the historical significance of the pesharim but what they might reveal of Qumran history is by James H. Charlesworth, *The Pesharim and Qumran History: Chaos or Consensus?* (Grand Rapids: Eerdmans, 2002).

32. As pointed out with regard to the use of variants for exegetical purposes by F. F. Bruce, *Biblical Exegesis in the Qumran Texts* (Grand Rapids: Eerdmans, 1959), 12-16.

he who reads may read it speedily," is understood as concerning "the Teacher of Righteousness, to whom God made known all the mysteries of his servants the prophets" (1QpHab VII, 4-5). *Pesher Habakkuk* is commonly understood to be just such a set of divinely inspired mysteries and equally inspired revealed interpretations. Few scholars would say that *Pesher Habakkuk* was intended to be read in its final form as a product of the Teacher of Righteousness, since it speaks about him in the third person, but it was almost certainly intended to contain inspired interpretations as if they had been divinely revealed to him.

Put another way, in the first century B.C.E. continuous pesharim it is declared that a century or more earlier their Teacher had stood in continuity with prophetic scriptural texts and exposed and expounded them in foundational and insightful ways. Just as earlier rewriting activity had both received authority from what it rewrote and gave authority to it, so the Teacher's interpretative activity was recalled as authoritative inasmuch as it demonstrated the authenticity of the divine voice contained in the prophetic oracles and exposed its message in an inspired manner. It is in this sense that Lawrence Schiffman, for example, can talk of "the notion in *Pesher Habakkuk* that God gave the teacher the gift of an almost prophetic message."[33]

What happens more precisely concerning the inspired Teacher in *Pesher Habakkuk*? Intriguingly, the exegete comes as close as he can to calling the Teacher a prophet, but he does not take that final actual step. There are seven occurrences of the title Teacher of Righteousness. (1) In 1QpHab I, 13 the context seems to be about conflict, possibly with the Wicked Priest, but the text is very fragmentary. (2) In 1QpHab II, 2 conflict features again in the interpretation of Hab 1:5, as the traitors with the Man of the Lie are described as those who have not obeyed the words of the Teacher of Righteousness from the mouth of God. This phraseology echoes that associated with Jeremiah (2 Chr 36:12) and seems indirectly to mark the Teacher out as functioning like a prophet, but the interpretation continues by talking of the traitors to the new covenant, insiders who have failed to recognize the interpretative authority of the Teacher.[34] (3) 1QpHab V, 10 refers to those who refused to speak out when the Teacher uttered a rebuke (a subjective genitive)[35] and did not help him

---

33. Lawrence H. Schiffman, *Reclaiming the Dead Sea Scrolls: The History of Judaism, the Background of Christianity, the Lost Library of Qumran* (Philadelphia: Jewish Publication Society, 1994), 120.

34. Dependence upon CD XX, 10-11; IX, 36-37 is not an impossibility.

35. William H. Brownlee, *The Midrash Pesher of Habakkuk*. SBLMS 24 (Missoula: Scholars, 1979), 93, understands the phrase *btwkht mwrh hṣdq* as "at the time of the reproof by the Teacher of Right" and comments that in this context the Teacher is "an inspired spokesman who is wholly right."

against the Man of the Lie, who had rejected the Law. Here is the possibility of seeing further prophetic activity in the rebuking of one's internal foes, though this is a term *(twkht)* used more for proverbial correction than for prophetic challenge.[36] (4) 1QpHab VII, 4 describes the Teacher as the one to whom God made known all the mysteries of his servants the prophets;[37] the Teacher is the inspired interpreter[38] and like Daniel, who merits the label prophet in a Qumran composition (4Q174 1-3, II,13), can reveal the secret, the *raz* (Dan 2:18, 19, 27, 30, 47; 4:6). "The Teacher's importance as the *prophetic* herald of the secrets of the end of days is also clearly related to another feature of his role, namely his soteriological function: it is through their fidelity towards the Teacher and his ways of interpreting God's Torah that the pious members of the community will be saved."[39] So (5) 1QpHab VIII, 3 speaks of the Teacher as an object of faith for those who do the Law;[40] here the emphasis is on the suffering of the followers,[41] and the role of the Teacher as providing a socially cohesive identity for the group is clear. (6) 1QpHab IX, 9 speaks of the affliction of the Wicked Priest for having offended the Teacher and the men of his council; again the Teacher seems to be represented primarily as a focus within the community. (7) Lastly, 1QpHab XI, 5 describes the pursuit of the Teacher by the Wicked Priest on the Teacher's Day of Atonement; this is a recollection of an outside threat associated with the Teacher. Predominantly in these references the Teacher serves as the focus of identity against the enemy within and the enemy without; some elements in that focus are described in ways that might in-

36. Those who prefer to understand an objective genitive here, namely that the phrase implies that the Teacher was rebuked or chastised, might still permit a prophetic understanding of the Teacher as one persecuted like the prophets. For all the several options and a detailed discussion of them, see Brownlee, *The Midrash Pesher of Habakkuk,* 93-94.

37. It is possible to see here something of the historicization of the parts of the *Hodayot* in which the speaker talks of his role in receiving revelation and interpreting knowledge and secrets; e.g., 1QH[a] X, 13; XII, 27-29; XV, 27.

38. As such it must be recognized that the interpretations which he may have been supposed to have given were "as much a matter of divine revelation as the oracle originally received by the prophet" (Brooke, "Prophecy," 699).

39. Håkan Ulfgard, "The Teacher of Righteousness, the History of the Qumran Community, and Our Understanding of the Jesus Movement: Texts, Theories and Trajectories," in *Qumran between the Old and New Testaments,* ed. Frederick H. Cryer and Thomas L. Thompson. JSOTSup 290 (Sheffield: Sheffield Academic, 1998), 328 (my emphasis).

40. Brownlee, *The Midrash Pesher of Habakkuk,* 129, has commented: "Like the prophets, the Qumrân Teacher interprets God's will, and one believes him while trusting in the LORD alone for salvation."

41. Brownlee, *The Midrash Pesher of Habakkuk,* 127, thought that such suffering might be understood in the light of Isa 53:11a. If so, then there might be a case to be made that the suffering of the Teacher's followers is itself a kind of prophetic imitation.

dicate that those reading the commentary would appreciate that he had had a status and function not unlike the prophets, as rebuker and interpreter, and as one persecuted. The exegete comes as close as he can to calling the Teacher a prophet, but he does not take that final actual step; this may be a mirror of the Qumran self-understanding that their interpretation was a continuation of inspired activity, but for some reason it was not labelled explicitly as prophecy.

The Prophetic Character of the Pesharim   Such inspired interpretations as are associated with the Teacher of Righteousness were undoubtedly considered to have a special status, which looks to all intents and purposes as if it is prophetic. With the paratextual rewritten prophetic texts, it was argued above that the rewritten texts were not intended to replace the works of the literary prophets that they reworked and whose authority they carried forward and claimed through the subsequent act of rewriting. So too it is most likely that the relationship of inspired interpretation to the prophecy being interpreted in the pesharim and other explicit commentaries, short and long, was not one in which the interpretation negated the original force of the prophet's words, but rather it endorsed them for the present. For example, Shani Berrin has precisely noted that "the words of the biblical prophet Nahum would have been perceived as applicable to Assyria, but as ultimately important because of their applicability to the end-time. They would make sense in regard to Assyria, but would matter in regard to the Community and its contemporaries. In this view, pesher does in fact presuppose an originally meaningful base-text."[42] Thus, as with the paratextual rewritten prophetic compositions, so the pesharim can be viewed as continuous with the prophetic texts they interpret and, as such, as a further form of prophecy in their own right. Intriguingly, the view of the prophetic text as "fore-telling" results in an exegetical application that is "forth-telling," related directly to the concerns of the contemporary audience.

Furthermore, there is an additional parallel between the prophetic character of the implicit interpretation of the rewritten paratextual prophetic compositions and the explicit inspired exegesis of the pesharim. It was noted above that prophetic figures beyond the literary prophets attracted rewritings, whether as adjusted sacred narratives, or as revelations of what was written on heavenly tablets, or as records of direct divine speeches. So too, pesher interpretation cannot be confined solely to the literary prophets, notably Isaiah and the Twelve, but also include a wide range of authoritative texts. The sectarian compositions found in the Qumran caves indicate that pesher can be applied to any

---

42. Shani Berrin, *The Pesher Nahum Scroll from Qumran: An Exegetical Study of 4Q169.* STDJ 53 (Leiden: Brill, 2004), 15-16.

unfulfilled blessing, curse, promise, or prophecy, whether in the literary prophets or in some other authoritative writing.

The continuity of the pesharim with the predictive prophetic texts of various kinds that they complete raises the question of what kind of prophetic revelation they may consist. The philological and formal comparisons of pesher strongly suggest that it is akin to dream interpretation; notably, the term is used in Daniel 2 and 4. But, more broadly, their revealed interpretation can also be set in a wider framework. After a careful analysis of various technical terms for revelation, Edward M. Cook has asked the following questions of the sectarians reflected in the scrolls from the eleven Qumran caves: "What exactly were they doing when they received revelation? Did they hear an audible voice, or did they see or hear figures in a vision, or in a dream? Did they experience trances, or see miracles, or what? The question is important, because they claimed to have a revelation that the rest of Israel did not have, and we must try to understand what made them think it was a revelation and why only they had it."[43] Cook continues by underlining that most of the terms connected with the special knowledge that is the repository of this special revelation are intellectual terms. The sectarian community members seem to be very reticent about their experience of the divine: they do not claim to have literally heard the voice of God or to have seen a supernatural vision as the prophets of old had done. Cook goes on to insist, rightly, that no sectarian, not even the Teacher of Righteousness, is credited with a new vision or audition. Cook's analysis permits us to envisage that both the continuity of the inspired exegetical sections of the pesharim with the scriptural texts they interpret and the discontinuity of prophetic experience can be characterized as an intellectual transformation of prophecy. As already implied, this intellectual transformation is associated in the collective memory of the sectarian movement with the Teacher of Righteousness.

The Exegetical Methodology of Pesher Interpretation   The chief characteristic of the exegetical methodology in the Qumran sectarian prophetic interpretation is atomistic identification. What the prophets declare in their oracles is identified with something in the interpreter's present or future. In fact, under the umbrella of sectarian prophetic interpretation comes a wide spectrum of materials. At one end there are the more obviously continuous pesharim in which the prophetic text is cited in small units and the content of various aspects of each cita-

43. Edward M. Cook, "What Did the Jews of Qumran Know about God and How Did They Know It? Revelation and God in the Dead Sea Scrolls," in *Judaism in Late Antiquity*, Pt. 5: *The Judaism of Qumran: A Systemic Reading of the Dead Sea Scrolls*, Vol. 2: *World View, Comparing Judaisms*, ed. Alan J. Avery-Peck, Jacob Neusner, and Bruce D. Chilton. HO 17 (Leiden: Brill, 2001), 7.

tion is given an identification; at the other end of prophetic interpretations are simple quotations of a single prophetic phrase followed by some kind of identification often made through the use of a pronoun. Most famous among the so-called continuous pesharim, partly because it is the best preserved and partly because it was amongst the first scrolls to come to light, is *Pesher Habakkuk*, already mentioned briefly above. Although it seems to be self-contained continuous running commentary on Habakkuk chapters 1–2, the interpretations given to the units of text also contain allusions to other scriptural passages. So, for example, the interpretation of Hab 1:17 ("Therefore their sword is ever drawn to massacre nations mercilessly") reads: "Interpreted this concerns the Kittim (there is the first identification) who cause many (there is the second identification) to perish by the sword — youths, grown men, the aged, women and children — and who even take no pity on the fruit of the womb." The last phrase is an implicit quotation of Isa 13:18, part of an oracle against Babylon, the place that is fittingly being identified metaphorically with the Kittim.

Though there are some explicit statements about the inspired character of the exegesis of the pesher, such that it can be likened to prophecy itself, in fact the interpretation of each prophetic extract is linked with the prophetic text itself through a whole range of exegetical techniques. My theological favorite in *Pesher Habakkuk* occurs in the very last pericope of interpretation. Habakkuk 2:19-20 is quoted: "Woe to him who says to wood, 'Awake,' and to dumb stone, 'Arise!' Can such a thing give guidance? Behold, it is covered with gold and silver but there is no spirit within it. But the Lord is in his holy temple: let all the earth be silent before him." The prophetic commentator provides the following by way of interpretation: "Interpreted, this concerns all the nations which serve stone and wood. But on the Day of Judgment, God will destroy from the earth all idolatrous and wicked men." Here some matters, such as "stone" and "wood," are taken over directly from the text of Habakkuk, but the neatness of the interpretation (somewhat surprisingly to the modern reader) rests in an anagram. The Hebrew for temple is *hykl* as cited in Hab 2:20; the Hebrew for "he will destroy" is *yklh*, the very same consonants. The meaning is thus clear: when God is in his temple, as he surely will be on the Day of Judgment, his presence is destruction for all idolatrous and wicked men. This is inspired exegesis, as neat as a crossword puzzle, but such exegetical practices are not uncommon in Jewish literature of the time, nor even in the New Testament (cf. Isa 11:1 in Matt 2:23).

Together with prophetic texts that all would acknowledge as such, prophetic interpretation is also applied in the same way to the Psalms and some other texts. 11QPs[a] XXVII, 11 comments that all of David's compositions were "written through prophecy which was given him from before the Most High."

Also considered prophetic are unfulfilled blessings and curses. So in *Commentary on Genesis A* (4Q252) columns IV-VI, the blessings of Jacob in Genesis 49 are given identifying interpretation. Perhaps this is particularly because in the text of Gen 49:1 Jacob calls his sons together and says "gather around that I may tell you what will happen in the latter days *(bĕ'ahărît hayyāmîm)*." In 4Q252 IV, 5 the standard formula using the term *pesher* is used, a single extant usage in this commentary that caused the original team of editors to label the whole text a pesher on Genesis. But in other parts of the interpretation, identification is done through the use of pronouns, such as "'the staff,' *it* is the covenant of kingship" (V, 2). This kind of prophetic exegesis can be seen in several sections of the *Damascus Document* as well as in texts like *11QMelchizedek*. Its key characteristic once again is atomistic identification, but the identification may depend on any of a whole range of interpretative techniques and on secondary texts — it is not arbitrary. Nor intriguingly for any one prophetic text does the same identification always have to be given. Furthermore, though the identification is precise, it is customarily elusive, expressed in terms of symbol and cipher so that it can outlast any possibility that it might not be right.

The Eschatological Worldview of the Qumran Community   As has already been indicated in passing, much of the inspired interpretation of prophetic texts is applied to the Community in its present experiences, and these experiences themselves are seen to be part of the latter days, the final period of history before God himself vindicates those he has chosen. Much has been written on the eschatology of the Qumran community. The view that the Qumran community understood itself to be living in the final period of history, however prolonged that might be, is clear from the sectarian interpretations in both the continuous and the thematic pesharim. Indeed, the overall eschatological perspective of the pesharim would seem to indicate that the Qumran community understood that its eschatological role had a prophetic character inasmuch as its ongoing life in the last days was the ultimate fulfilment of and continuity with the prophets of old.

In general, the persecutions of the sectarian movement by fellow Jews and the disturbances to it through the political and military interference of Gentiles were seen as signs of life in the latter days. In particular, the Qumran sectarian texts (e.g., 1QS IX, 11; 4Q175; 11QMelchizedek) also attest the imminent expectation of an eschatological prophet who would play a role in the messianic age.[44] This figure is apparently developed from Mal 3:1 and 3:24 (4:6), where he her-

---

44. Jassen, *Mediating the Divine,* 133-95, provides a detailed analysis of the eschatological prophet.

alds an event rather than the messiah(s), and is visible also in the nonsectarian 4Q558 (4QpapVision^bar) and 4Q521 (the so-called *Messianic Apocalypse*).[45] The presentation of the eschatological prophet in the form of Samaritan Exodus 20 in the sectarian 4Q175 strongly suggests that the role of the eschatological prophet was understood as in some way continuous with the activity of Moses himself; probably he was thought to be some kind of lawgiver. In 11QMelchizedek the prophet seems to function as a herald of the salvation of the righteous. None of these sectarian compositions is concerned to identify the Teacher of Righteousness with the eschatological prophet.

Conclusion

In this brief study of some aspects of prophecy and prophetic interpretation in the scrolls that have survived from the Qumran caves, I have argued three things among others.

First, although within the texts themselves the explicit talk of prophets, seers, and visionaries is largely confined to the figures of the past and the one prophet looked for in the future, in the Qumran library as a whole there is plenty of evidence that discloses how some Jews in the Second Temple period envisaged their activities as continuous with those of the prophets as they mediated the divine to their communities. The literary data from the Qumran caves is best understood predominantly as a continuation of earlier prophetic activity; prophecy did not cease in the early postexilic period. To be sure, the character of that activity evolved and within the sectarian movement reflected in the scrolls may have gone through an intellectual transformation, but the claims to divine revelation remain persistent in a variety of different literary genres.

Second, the scrolls from the Qumran caves contain a variety of implicit interpretations of the lives and writings of the prophets. In the writings from the pre-Qumran era, the paratextual rewritings of the prophets are the most dominant form of this implicit interpretation. In the sectarian compositions, the prophets are used in several additional and different ways, such as in providing the basis for extending the application of the law and in the inspired poetry of the *Hodayot*. These kinds of implicit interpretations are not simply attempts at describing the correct meaning of the original prophetic utterances, but they are in some way continuous with those utterances, either in indicating how the law might be put into practice, or in terms of providing prophetic identity for the poet, or an authoritative intertextual form and structure for his poetry.

45. The future prophet, possibly eschatological, is also to be seen in 1 Macc 4:42-46; 14:41.

Third, the sect's explicit interpretations of all kinds of unfulfilled prophecies can also be understood as prophetically continuous with the texts that are interpreted. These explicit interpretations take a number of forms, from running commentaries on a single sequential prophetic text to more thematically organized compositions or smaller units of interpretation within other compositions. Whatever the form, the exegesis, even though inspired, applies various techniques to link the new interpretation with the text upon which it depends, as the contents of that earlier text are identified atomistically with particular experiences of the community. In some of these explicit interpretations the claim to authority is made by associating them with the Teacher of Righteousness, who was understood to have behaved in many ways like a prophet, though he was never called one as such. Though the explicit exegesis was projected back onto the founding Teacher, actually it represented how the community wanted to understand its role in the eschatological period, in which Rome became increasingly dominant in everyday experience but in which it was believed Jerusalem would be purified and restored.

BIBLIOGRAPHY

Aune, David E. *Prophecy in Early Christianity and the Ancient Mediterranean World.* Grand Rapids: Eerdmans, 1983.

Barstad, Hans. "Prophecy at Qumran?" In *In the Last Days: On Jewish and Christian Apocalyptic and Its Period,* ed. Knud Jeppesen, Kirsten Nielsen, and Bent Rosendal. Aarhus: Aarhus University Press, 1994, 104-20.

Barton, John. *Oracles of God: Perceptions of Ancient Prophecy in Israel after the Exile.* London: Darton, Longman, and Todd, 1986.

Bernstein, Moshe J. "Interpretation of Scriptures." In *EDSS,* 1:376-83.

Berrin, Shani. *The Pesher Nahum Scroll from Qumran: An Exegetical Study of 4Q169.* STDJ 53. Leiden: Brill, 2004.

―――. "Qumran Pesharim." In *Biblical Interpretation at Qumran,* ed. Matthias Henze. SDSSRL. Grand Rapids: Eerdmans, 2005, 110-33.

Blenkinsopp, Joseph. *A History of Prophecy in Israel from the Settlement in the Land to the Hellenistic Period.* Philadelphia: Westminster, 1983.

Bowley, James E. "Prophets and Prophecy at Qumran." In *The Dead Sea Scrolls after Fifty Years: A Comprehensive Assessment,* ed. Peter W. Flint and James C. VanderKam. Leiden: Brill, 1999, 354-78.

Brooke, George J. "Parabiblical Prophetic Narratives." In Flint and VanderKam, *The Dead Sea Scrolls after Fifty Years,* 271-301.

―――. "Prophecy." In *EDSS,* 2:694-700.

―――. "Thematic Commentaries on Prophetic Scriptures." In *Biblical Interpretation at Qumran,* ed. Matthias Henze. SDSSRL. Grand Rapids: Eerdmans, 2005, 134-57.

―――. "Biblical Interpretation at Qumran." In *The Bible and the Dead Sea Scrolls,* vol. 1:

Scripture and the Scrolls, ed. James H. Charlesworth. The Second Princeton Symposium on Judaism and Christian Origins. Waco: Baylor University Press, 2006, 287-319.

———. "Prophecy and Prophets in the Dead Sea Scrolls: Looking Backwards and Forwards." In *Prophets, Prophecy, and Prophetic Texts in the Second Temple Period*, ed. Michael H. Floyd and Robert D. Haak. LHB/OTS 427. London: T. & T. Clark, 2006, 151-65.

Brownlee, William H. *The Midrash Pesher of Habakkuk*. SBLMS 24. Missoula: Scholars, 1979.

Burrows, Millar. "Prophets and Prophecy at Qumran." In *Israel's Prophetic Heritage*, ed. Bernhard W. Anderson and Walter Harrelson. New York: Harper, 1962, 223-32.

Charlesworth, James H. *The Pesharim and Qumran History: Chaos or Consensus?* Grand Rapids: Eerdmans, 2002.

Fishbane, Michael. "Use, Authority and Interpretation of Mikra at Qumran." In *Mikra: Text, Translation, Reading and Interpretation of the Hebrew Bible in Ancient Judaism and Early Christianity*, ed. Martin Jan Mulder. CRINT 2.1. Assen: Van Gorcum and Philadelphia: Fortress, 1988, 339-77.

Grabbe, Lester L. "Poets, Scribes, or Preachers? The Reality of Prophecy in the Second Temple Period." In *Knowing the End from the Beginning: The Prophetic, the Apocalyptic and Their Relationships*, ed. Grabbe and Robert D. Haak. JSPSup 46. London: T. & T. Clark, 2003, 192-215.

Gray, Rebecca. *Prophetic Figures in Late Second Temple Jewish Palestine: The Evidence from Josephus*. New York: Oxford University Press, 1993.

Horgan, Maurya P. *Pesharim: Qumran Interpretations of Biblical Books*. CBQMS 8. Washington: Catholic Biblical Association, 1979.

———. In *The Dead Sea Scrolls: Hebrew, Aramaic, and Greek Texts with English Translations*. Vol. 6B: *Pesharim, Other Commentaries, and Related Documents*, ed. James H. Charlesworth. Tübingen: Mohr Siebeck and Louisville: Westminster John Knox, 2002.

Jassen, Alex P. *Mediating the Divine: Prophecy and Revelation in the Dead Sea Scrolls and Second Temple Judaism*. STDJ 68. Leiden: Brill, 2007.

Jokiranta, Jutta. "Pesharim: A Mirror of Self-Understanding." In *Reading the Present in the Qumran Library: The Perception of the Contemporary by Means of Scriptural Interpretations*, ed. Kristin De Troyer and Armin Lange. SBLSymS 30. Atlanta: SBL, 2005.

Lange, Armin. "Reading the Decline of Prophecy." In De Troyer and Lange, *Reading the Present in the Qumran Library*, 181-91.

Najman, Hindy. *Seconding Sinai: The Development of Mosaic Discourse in Second Temple Judaism*. JSJSup 77. Leiden: Brill, 2003.

Nissinen, Martti. "Transmitting Divine Mysteries: The Prophetic Role of Wisdom Teachers in the Dead Sea Scrolls." In *Scripture in Transition: Essays on Septuagint, Hebrew Bible, and Dead Sea Scrolls in Honour of Raija Sollamo*, ed. Anssi Voitila and Jutta Jokiranta. JSJSup 126. Leiden: Brill, 2008, 513-33.

Ulrich, Eugene. *The Dead Sea Scrolls and the Origins of the Bible*. SDSSRL. Grand Rapids: Eerdmans, 1999.

Biblical Interpretation in the *Hodayot*

Sarah J. Tanzer

Moshe Bernstein, writing on the "Interpretation of Scriptures" in the *Encyclopedia of the Dead Sea Scrolls,* observed that we can categorize biblical interpretation in the Scrolls as having either a primary or secondary function in the literary genre in which it is found. It can be seen as the immediate goal in those works that we would label *pesher* or commentary and in texts broadly construed as "Rewritten Bible."[1] But, according to Bernstein, it would be wrong to ignore those texts in which biblical interpretation has a secondary function, "to overlook the very pervasive nature of biblical interpretation in the Qumran scrolls as a whole . . . (because) the Bible was not merely the object of study for the Qumranites, it pervaded their lives, prescribing both practice and belief."[2] The *Hodayot* are an excellent illustration of a genre in which biblical interpretation has a secondary function. But "secondary" should not be thought of as interchangeable with "less important." As poetry, they are far removed generically from commentaries, and yet, the importance of biblical interpretation in the *Hodayot* cannot be missed because of the dense use of biblical language and imagery. It is more difficult to describe exactly how biblical interpretation works in these poems.

Studies of biblical interpretation in the *Hodayot* are especially concentrated in the early period of Scrolls scholarship and in the last several years, with not so much in between. One can only speculate about the reasons for this. Though Svend Holm-Nielsen[3] (writing in 1960) and Günter Morawe[4] (writing in 1961)

---

1. Moshe J. Bernstein, "Interpretation of Scriptures," in *EDSS,* 1:378-79.

2. Bernstein, "Interpretation of Scriptures," 1:378.

3. Svend Holm-Nielsen, *Hodayot: Psalms from Qumran.* ATDan 2 (Aarhus: Universitetsforlaget, 1960).

4. Günter Morawe, *Aufbau und Abgrenzung der Loblieder von Qumrân: Studien zur Gattungsgeschichtlichen Einordnung der Hodajôth.* Theologische Arbeiten 16 (Berlin: Evangelische, 1961).

had already proposed that the *Hodayot* can be divided into two distinct groups, studies a few years later by Gert Jeremias,[5] Jürgen Becker,[6] and Heinz-Wolfgang Kuhn[7] set out the distinguishing features of the Hymns of the Teacher and the Hymns of the Community. Literary analysis of the *Hodayot* (typically in relation to these two categories) has dominated much of *Hodayot* scholarship ever since. It is also possible that the sheer density of biblical language and imagery in the *Hodayot* coupled with the absence of explicit biblical quotations was a discouraging factor for those interested in the issue of biblical interpretation. In this study I have excluded some of the earliest scholarship that either leaned toward a messianic interpretation of the *Hodayot* or over-exaggerated the biblical character of the *Hodayot* ("the text sounds virtually like a mosaic of Biblical phrases and quotations . . .").[8] Both are views that have been soundly disproven.

The Density of Biblical Language in the *Hodayot*

The density of biblical language in the *Hodayot* has been noted from the outset. Jean Carmignac, who restricted himself to "citations manifestes," without mentioning the numerous adaptations, usages, or allusions of all other sorts in the *Hodayot,* has produced an impressive thirty-three-page list of such "citations précises de l'Ancien Testament."[9] Of these, five to six pages each are devoted to citations from Psalms and Isaiah. Carmignac notes in his conclusions the heavy dependence on these two books of the Bible, while also cautioning readers away from earlier tendencies to see in the *Hodayot* messianic references similar to those in the New Testament. He points out that there are only six citations from the Servant Songs of Isaiah and that the predilection of the *Hodayot* for Isaiah 40–66 can be explained as an appreciation of its optimism (as compared with the pessimism of Jeremiah).[10] As for the Psalms, the *Hodayot* most often cite Psalms 31, 51, and 107. On the other hand, they do not focus on those psalms we consider messianic (e.g., Pss 2, 72, and 110), and despite five citations of Psalm

---

5. Gert Jeremias, *Der Lehrer der Gerechtigkeit.* SUNT 2 (Göttingen: Vandenhoeck & Ruprecht, 1963).

6. Jürgen Becker, *Das Heil Gottes: Heils-und Sündenbegriffe in den Qumrantexten und im Neuen Testament.* SUNT 3 (Göttingen: Vandenhoeck & Ruprecht, 1964).

7. Heinz-Wolfgang Kuhn, *Enderwartung und gegenwärtiges Heil: Untersuchungen zu den Gemeindeliedern von Qumran.* SUNT 4 (Göttingen: Vandenhoeck & Ruprecht, 1966).

8. Menahem Mansoor, *The Thanksgiving Hymns: Translated and Annotated with an Introduction.* STDJ 3 (Leiden: Brill and Grand Rapids: Eerdmans, 1961), 28.

9. Jean Carmignac, "Les Citations de L'Ancien Testament et Spécialement des Poèmes du Serviteur, dans les Hymnes de Qumran," *RevQ* 2 (1959-60): 357.

10. Carmignac, "Les Citations de L'Ancien Testament," 383.

22, the citations of that psalm do not highlight the physical suffering of the victim, instead focusing on his moral suffering and his final triumph.[11]

Holm-Nielsen offers, alongside his translation of the *Hodayot,* an exhaustively detailed set of reference notes to the possible use of biblical texts within each poem, which makes this the most thorough treatment of biblical interpretation in the *Hodayot.* In addition to referencing biblical syntax and vocabulary, for each poem he has summarized possible biblical allusions and quotations. He has done this systematically for the entire collection of *Hodayot.* In his overall conclusions about biblical usage, he has observed that the *Hodayot* are most interested in the portrayal of misery in psalms of complaint and psalms of thanksgiving.[12] He has also noticed that along with those psalms that were most used (e.g., Pss 22, 31, 42, 104, and 107), others (including the historical psalms, psalms about the temple and cult, and the psalms related directly to the person of the king) were not used at all.[13] Like Carmignac, Holm-Nielsen has identified Isaiah (especially chs. 40-55) as the other dominant biblical source for the *Hodayot,* while noting that there is no focus on the concept of the Servant of the Lord from these chapters.[14] But in addition to Isaiah, he has observed that in general the invective in the prophets (both major and minor) against adversaries and God's judgment upon them are often brought together in the *Hodayot* with the portrayals of enemies in the Psalms — all suggesting an application to the community. In particular, he singles out Jeremiah and Ezekiel, before going on to survey other biblical books. With all of this, Holm-Nielsen urges a certain degree of caution, reminding us that in many instances we may not even be seeing an "actual use of Scripture, even when there is complete agreement of words and phrases, stereotyped expressions, customary terminology, which may well have originated somewhere or other in the Old Testament, but which existed in the everyday language of the time."[15]

Preben Wernberg-Møller takes the opposite point of view, based on the evidence that he has gathered. "It appears that in a large number of cases the author(s) of the Hymns depended directly on the Hebrew of the Bible, either in its Massoretic form, or in some other slightly different form."[16] Like Carmignac, he concludes that the *Hodayot* depend most heavily on the Psalms and Isaiah.

---

11. Carmignac, "Les Citations de L'Ancien Testament," 392.

12. Holm-Nielsen, *Hodayot,* 308.

13. Holm-Nielsen, *Hodayot,* 309.

14. Holm-Nielsen, *Hodayot,* 310. He singles out the writings of André Dupont-Sommer for having perpetuated this false connection with the Servant Songs.

15. Holm-Nielsen, *Hodayot,* 302.

16. Preben Wernberg-Møller, "The Contribution of the Hodayot to Biblical Textual Criticism," *Text* 4 (1964): 134.

These early studies have provided the material for more recent character-izations of the use of biblical language in the *Hodayot*. Michael Fishbane writes about the dense reuse of biblical language as a model for language in the *Hodayot*, noting that the predominance of biblical language and form at Qumran supports the sectarian ideology that it alone is the true Israel.[17] Carol Newsom has observed the remarkable density and variety of intertextual allu-sion in the *Hodayot*. Given the enormity of the range, "it would be absurd to suggest that a single type of use or significance occurs in every instance."[18] She also points out that the *Hodayot* are not unique in this; it is a feature of the ma-jority of Second Temple writings, especially poetry. Julie Hughes's study con-firms the early observations about the extensive use of Isaiah and Psalms, as well as working out more carefully the key role of Ezekiel and Jeremiah. She has also suggested a possible explanation for the overlapping uses of biblical lan-guage among the diverse collection of *Hodayot*:

> Coincidences of language in certain compositions are due to their common concern with group identity. One of the ways that the group legitimized its identity was by appeal to Scripture. This would lead to a common stock of fundamental passages and associated exegesis by which the group defined itself.[19]

She accounts for other similarities in biblical imagery and language (e.g., plant imagery, creation, destiny) by assuming a similar common stock known from the wider nonsectarian literature.

The Diversity of *Hodayot*

Early on, Holm-Nielsen recognized the great diversity of these poems, conclud-ing that one cannot speak about uniformity of content and there is no evidence to suggest that they come from the same author or even the same time. Never-theless, he suggested that they could be divided into two groups, both of which reflect the existence of the Qumran community — but with different emphases

---

17. Michael Fishbane, "Use, Authority and Interpretation of Mikra at Qumran," in *Mikra: Text, Translation, Reading and Interpretation of the Hebrew Bible in Ancient Judaism and Early Christianity*. CRINT 2.1 (Assen: Van Gorcum and Philadelphia: Fortress, 1988), 356.

18. Carol A. Newsom, *The Self as Symbolic Space: Constructing Identity and Community at Qumran*. STDJ 52 (Leiden: Brill, 2004), 213.

19. Julie A. Hughes, *Scriptural Allusions and Exegesis in the Hodayot*. STDJ 59 (Leiden: Brill, 2006), 233.

("the state of the community in a more terminological way" and "the community's theological view of life").[20] He further differentiated the *Hodayot* based on the extent of their biblical content, noticing that those which formally resembled a mix of psalms of complaint and thanksgiving (e.g., 1QH^a X, 3-21, XI, 20-37, and XV, 9-28)[21] predominantly draw their quotations from Psalms and Isaiah or other biblical texts that agree in context and form of expression with these writings.[22] Holm-Nielsen identified a lively use of Scripture in an "instructional poem" in 1QH^a VII, 14-39. In another group of *Hodayot* that have as their focus the greatness of God (e.g., 1QH^a IX, 1–X, 4 and XV, 29-36), "the use of Scripture is much weaker, and more sparse still are the scriptural references in a group of poems about God's salvation for an elect within the community (e.g., 1QH^a XIX, 6-17 and XIX, 18-31)."[23] Those poems that Holm-Nielsen identifies as "partly psalms of thanksgiving, partly psalms of penitence, which are obviously related to the community,"[24] barely show any signs of the use of Scripture (e.g., 1QH^a VI, 34ff. and IV, 20ff.). He concluded that those poems that "had a close contact of a technical sort with the community" demonstrated a use of Scripture that was sporadic and haphazard, while those that concerned themselves with the experience of the individual made far more comprehensive use of Scripture.

This diversity of the *Hodayot*, both in their literary characteristics and in their use of Scripture, has been reconsidered in some of the most recent scholarship. Newsom has suggested that it may be time to revisit the longstanding classification of the *Hodayot* into Hymns of the Teacher and Hymns of the Community. Her work looks at what the *Hodayot do* in shaping sectarian consciousness, whether the one reciting them is an ordinary member of the community or a leader (the *Maskil* or *Mebaqqer*), pointing out that the "Hodayot clearly contain compositions representing the persona of the ordinary member and compositions explicitly associated with the Maskil."[25] Effectively, this shifts the focus away from the issue of historical authorship in looking at these diverse poems. Specifically, Newsom challenges Jeremias's argument that there is a group of *Hodayot* in which the speaker/author is the Teacher of Righteousness

---

20. Holm-Nielsen, *Hodayot,* 331.

21. For the sake of uniformity, all column numbers refer to the construction of the *Hodayot* found in *DJD* 40 (*Qumran Cave 1, 3: 1QHodayot^a, with Incorporation of 4QHodayot^{a-f} and 1QHodayot^b*, ed. Hartmut Stegemann with Eileen Schuller; trans. of texts by Carol Newsom [Oxford: Clarendon, 2008]).

22. Holm-Nielsen, *Hodayot,* 312-313.

23. Holm-Nielsen, *Hodayot,* 313.

24. Holm-Nielsen, *Hodayot,* 313.

25. Newsom, *The Self as Symbolic Space,* 299.

and that they reflect his historical experiences. Instead, she presents the hypothesis that there are "certain Hodayot in which the 'I' is distinguishable from the community and presents itself as having special responsibilities or leadership functions vis-à-vis other members of the community."[26] These "Hodayot of the leader" express a leadership myth and the role of the leader in a way that is generic for this sectarian community, rather than suggesting specific, historical incidents. They could have been used by any current leader of the community. Further, these *Hodayot* are not "simply compositions about a leader, whether historical or contemporary. They are themselves *acts* of leadership, verbal attempts to articulate a community through the self-presentation of the persona of the leader."[27] These *Hodayot* confer an identity on the leader at the same time that they are mapping out the appropriate social world for the sect.

Julie Hughes's careful study of biblical allusions and exegesis in the *Hodayot* concludes that the diversity of scriptural use lifts up the deficiency of the categories, Hymns of the Teacher and Hymns of the Community.[28] She suggests that we think of the *Hodayot* as an anthology that had a variety of backgrounds before being collected together.[29] The diversity is reflected in style, content, and the possible use of the different hymns within the community but also in the way that Scripture is used.[30] The biblical allusions in some poems are wordplays and double meanings; in others two allusions are conflated, combining their connotations. In addition to the more common structural allusions and shorthand notations, some poems use pointer or gnomic allusions and dialectical allusions. The repetition of key words or phrases is employed in a variety of ways in the different poems. At least one poem (1QH^a XVI, 5–XVII, 36) changes genre between its different sections, moving from *mashal* to lament, to a declaration of confidence. Other poems simply defy the stereotypes associated with these two categories. By way of example, Hughes points out a Community Hymn in 1QH^a VII, 21–VIII, ?,[31] which does not fit the lack of biblical allusions usually associated with the Hymns of the Community. Two other poems, 1QH^a XI, 6-19 and

---

26. Newsom, *The Self as Symbolic Space*, 287.

27. Newsom, *The Self as Symbolic Space*, 299.

28. Hughes, *Scriptural Allusions*, 232. Hughes (234) also finds compelling Newsom's argument about the Hymns of the Teacher, observing that while the speaker in such poems could have a special claim to uniqueness, subsequent leaders could also identify themselves with the speakers in these poems.

29. Hughes, *Scriptural Allusions*, 34 and 233.

30. Hughes, *Scriptural Allusions*, 232-33.

31. Whenever a question mark follows a Roman numeral in citing one of the *Hodayot*, it indicates that we do not know the exact line where the poem begins or (as in this case) where it ends.

1QHᵃ XI, 20-37, seem to interpret Psalm 18 eschatologically.[32] But they do not demonstrate either an individual or communal orientation, suggesting once again the inadequacy of the Teacher and Community categories. Hughes suggests that where there are similarities, these may be accounted for by a common exegetical tradition and a common concern for group identity: "One of the ways that the group legitimised its identity was by appeal to scripture. This would lead to a common stock of fundamental passages and associated exegesis by which the group defined itself."[33] Other similarities that have counterparts in nonsectarian literature (e.g., plant imagery, creation, destiny, etc.) likely reflect use of the wider nonsectarian literary heritage.

Formal Relationships between the *Hodayot* and Biblical Psalms

Already in the earliest period of research on the *Hodayot*, Holm-Nielsen offered two insights into the formal relationship between the *Hodayot* and biblical texts that are still being worked out today. First, he observed that the authors of the *Hodayot* did not have as their goal the authorization of their work as "canonical writing by use of the Old Testament, but rather the creation of original poetry in an Old Testament style, and by means of the use of the Old Testament in this poetry, the expression of the relationship between God and the community, and between God and the community's individual member."[34] What is intriguing here is the idea of creating original poetry, yet poetry that imitates biblical style. Millar Burrows had already noticed that the *Hodayot* combined elements similar to biblical psalms of complaint with the note of thanksgiving, concluding that the "prevailing tone, however, . . . is that of thanksgiving for deliverance."[35] Holm-Nielsen also observed the reliance of the *Hodayot* on biblical psalms of complaint and thanksgiving, drawing on the portrayals of misery in those psalms and linking them with thanksgiving for deliverance already given (even while the persecutions were still going on!). He pointed out that the chronological relationship between misery and thanksgiving in the *Hodayot* differs from the biblical psalms.[36] This he related to the community's understanding of its own saved existence in an evil world.

---

32. Hughes, *Scriptural Allusions,* 232-33.
33. Hughes, *Scriptural Allusions,* 233.
34. Holm-Nielsen, *Hodayot,* 305.
35. Millar Burrows, *More Light on the Dead Sea Scrolls* (New York: Viking, 1958), 380.
36. Holm-Nielsen, *Hodayot,* 308. Bonnie Kittel, picking up on this mix of thanksgiving and complaint, calls the *Hodayot* a "mixed form" and observes that the *Hodayot* are "rather different than their Old Testament counterparts"; *The Hymns of Qumran: Translation and Commentary.* SBLDS 50 (Chico: Scholars, 1981), 1.

More recent scholars have touched on the idea that the *Hodayot* are an imitation of the biblical compositions without working this out in a detailed way. Bonnie Kittel cautioned us against taking this idea too far, reminding us that while "imitation of biblical style and idiom was intended," these are original poetry with significant stylistic differences from biblical poems.[37] Fishbane, writing about the paraenetic sections of the *Damascus Document,* the *Hodayot,* and the discursive narrative of the *War Scroll,* observed that the dense reuse of biblical language in these manuscripts serves to produce a kind of new biblical composition.[38] George Brooke, while comparing biblical interpretation at Qumran and in the New Testament, noticed that at Qumran a key method of interpretation "involves the presentation of new material in a form which looks in most respects like that which is being interpreted."[39] About the *Hodayot* and other apocryphal psalms and liturgical texts from Qumran, he concludes that they are all to some extent an imitation of biblical genres of poetry, especially of the biblical Psalms.[40]

Newsom, writing about what the *Hodayot* do, especially how they form a sense of the self in the speaker, observes that

> the Hodayot are a fascinating recasting of traditional materials into a distinctively sectarian form that negotiates the transformation of a nonsectarian into a sectarian identity. Although the Hodayot borrow much from Israelite psalms, they change the syntax of religious speech. Whereas the Israelite thanksgiving psalm was correlated with the complaint psalm, at Qumran there are only thanksgivings. Lament motifs are used in the Hodayot, but those motifs are always contained within a structure of speech that begins "I thank you, O Lord" or "Blessed are you, because. . . ." Thus there is only one normative stance from which to speak.[41]

In this formation of the sectarian self, the *Hodayot* reaccentuate the language of the Psalms following certain modes of discourse. Most typical is the construction of the speaker's self in relation to God in which "the sectarian first speaks with the powerful voice of insight that he possesses as a gift from God and then

---

37. Kittel, *The Hymns of Qumran,* 49.

38. Fishbane, "Use, Authority and Interpretation," 356.

39. George J. Brooke, "Biblical Interpretation in the Qumran Scrolls and the New Testament," in *The Dead Sea Scrolls Fifty Years After Their Discovery: Proceedings of the Jerusalem Congress, July 20-25, 1997,* ed. Lawrence H. Schiffman, Emanuel Tov, and James C. VanderKam. Jerusalem: Israel Exploration Society and Shrine of the Book, Israel Museum, 2000, 69.

40. Brooke, "Biblical Interpretation," 67.

41. Carol A. Newsom, "Constructing 'We, You, and the Others' through Non-Polemical Discourse," in *Defining Identities: We, You, and the Other in the Dead Sea Scrolls,* ed. Florentino Garcia Martinez and Mladen Popović. STDJ 70 (Leiden: Brill, 2008), 19.

uses that insight to view his own human nothingness."[42] Newsom refers to this pattern as the cultivation of the "masochistic sublime."[43] One feature of it is that the knowledge which the speaker has been granted by God puts him in an exalted circle, and yet, almost immediately he is plunged into disgust at his own humanness. A second typical mode of discourse is the relation between the self and the human other:

> . . . these are characteristically highly emotional accounts of endangerment and deliverance. They build on motifs and language of biblical complaint and thanksgiving psalms, and yet the self they construct is distinctively different. His endangerment is grasped not merely as an individual crisis but an aspect of a comprehensive cosmic conflict. Moreover, he lacks the quality of agency that characterizes the self at prayer in the biblical Psalms. What gives the speaker a kind of active participation in the preordained drama is not moral agency but rather his understanding of the significance of the events and his ability to articulate them.[44]

This lack of moral agency alongside God's gracious redemption sets the *Hodayot* apart from the biblical Psalms, in which we often hear of the speaker's moral accomplishments.[45] In the repeated drama of endangerment and deliverance, the self of the *Hodayot* reinforces both a sense of being part of a sectarian community and an alienation from the human other.

Text Criticism

Early studies of the *Hodayot* were hopeful about their potential contribution to the enterprise of text criticism of the Bible. Carmignac opens his extensive study of biblical citations in the *Hodayot* optimistically by noting: "elle nous fournit de précieux renseignements sur l'état du texte biblique et sur l'histoire de son interprétation."[46] Menahem Mansoor, in his general introduction to

---

42. Newsom, *The Self as Symbolic Space,* 348. Cf. Newsom, "Constructing," 20. Heinz-Wolfgang Kuhn *(Enderwartung und gegenwärtiges Heil)* identified this feature of the Hymns of the Community as *Niedrigkeitsdoxologie.* John Strugnell suggested to me that it might be best expressed in English as "worm's praise" — since the lowly human being is often rhetorically compared to the worm.

43. Newsom, *The Self as Symbolic Space,* 348.

44. Newsom, *The Self as Symbolic Space,* 348.

45. For an example of this, see Newsom, "Constructing," 20.

46. Carmignac, "Les Citations de L'Ancien Testament," 357. His conclusions on the subject of text criticism are found on p. 391.

the *Hodayot*, proclaimed: "For the first time we are able to see at first hand some of the types of pre-massoretic Biblical texts which were current in Palestine just before and after the turn of the Christian era."[47] Wernberg-Møller examined the first three columns of Sukenik's edition of the *Hodayot* in detail to find the numerous biblical allusions and to discuss their recensional background.[48] Between Carmignac's lengthy listing of biblical citations from all the books of the Bible and Wernberg-Møller's further work and detailed recensional analysis, a foundation was established for later work on text criticism and biblical interpretation in the *Hodayot*. Wernberg-Møller admitted that there were several methodological problems in trying to do this work, including the physical appearance of the 1QH^a manuscript, the fact that there are very few quotations (more typically there are allusions), and that where there is a quotation it rarely extends beyond four words. Despite these and other cautions, he believed that "in a great many cases the recensional background can be established, and interesting observations may be made in the individual instances."[49]

John Elwolde, building on the contributions of Wernberg-Møller and Carmignac's rich list of biblical citations, has completed a study of how the *Hodayot* might be used to further the text criticism of Psalms 1–41. Elwolde hoped to identify and examine those uses of the Psalms in the *Hodayot* that occur in a slightly different form from that in the MT, those that might therefore be linked to one of the non-Masoretic traditions.[50] What he found in the *Hodayot* was an "envelopment of sectarian life and thought by 'the world of the Bible,'"[51] making text critical analysis more complicated for several reasons. The dependence on the Bible in the *Hodayot* (with their poetic and evocative character) was likely to have been "more unconscious than considered,"[52] more concerned with the biblical message and less with its exact wording, and as a result we are more likely to find recasting of biblical language rather than "exact correspondences between expressions in the Hodayot and their ultimate biblical sources."[53] Other reasons include the brevity (typically two to four words) of any quoted sequences, their adaptation in a way that often obscures their origins in the MT, and almost always the lack of a shared context between the bib-

47. Mansoor, *The Thanksgiving Hymns*, 31.

48. Cols. IX-XI in DJD 40.

49. Wernberg-Møller, "The Contribution of the Hodayot," 136.

50. John Elwolde, "The Hodayot's Use of the Psalter: Text-Critical Contributions (Book I)," in *Psalms and Prayers*, ed. Bob Becking and Eric Peels. OtSt 55 (Leiden: Brill, 2007), 85.

51. Elwolde, "The Hodayot's Use of the Psalter," 80.

52. Elwolde, "The Hodayot's Use of the Psalter," 80.

53. Elwolde, "The Hodayot's Use of the Psalter," 81.

lical source and its use in the *Hodayot*.[54] Elwolde's careful work has led him to conclude that only on rare occasions does the evidence from the *Hodayot* have a compelling bearing on a known text-critical issue (so far he has seen this simply where it supports the MT). Two further stumbling blocks emerged over the course of his study. First, while it is easy to see a connection between the wording of the *Hodayot* and the Psalms, it is very difficult to demonstrate that such a relationship actually existed. Second, even when there is distinctive enough wording to suggest a dependency of the *Hodayot* on the Psalms, there is typically not the corresponding versional evidence to support a variation from the MT in the *Hodayot* passage. This leaves one wondering "whether the Hodayot author has actually been influenced by a biblical text that was different from MT; or has manipulated, for literary or ideological reasons, the same text as the one that appears in the MT; or has simply produced a text for which he has not consciously relied on a biblical passage."[55] But, as he reminds us, these conclusions are tentative, as he has only looked at Book I of Psalms.

Classifying the Uses of Scripture in the *Hodayot*

"The variety of ways in which scripture is quoted, interpreted, invoked, echoed, and imitated is so great that it still exceeds every attempt to organize and classify it."[56] Classifying with precision the uses of Scripture in the *Hodayot* has been an issue from the start. Among the difficulties that plague such work are: the lack of citation formulas;[57] the tendency for there to be agreement with the biblical text in only a few words or a single word; language that is close but not exactly what we have in the MT and known versions; conflation of multiple biblical passages; and the use of language and imagery that is known to us from more than one biblical text. This can give the impression that biblical references in the *Hodayot* are "always embedded or woven into the text as a whole and their identification is always a matter of speculation."[58]

54. Elwolde, "The Hodayot's Use of the Psalter," 83.

55. Elwolde, "The Hodayot's Use of the Psalter," 107.

56. Newsom, *The Self as Symbolic Space,* 213. On p. 246, Newsom gives an example of this remarkable density in the poem found in the first half of col. XI, where within four lines there are no less than nine specific biblical allusions.

57. Holm-Nielsen (*Hodayot,* 302) has noted that only in one instance (1QH[a] IV, 24) is a reference made to God speaking through Moses, "but even then there is no question of an actual quotation, but at most of a paraphrased use of an Old Testament text."

58. Elwolde, "The Hodayot's Use of the Psalter," 80. Cf. Mathias Delcor (*Les Hymnes de Qumrân [Hodayot]: Texte hébreu, introduction, traduction, commentaire.* Paris: Letouzy et Ané, 1962, 30), about the subtlety of biblical allusions in the *Hodayot*.

Holm-Nielsen observed that it is often difficult to decide whether the author has taken the material directly from the Bible or whether he is simply employing language current in the community (e.g., "certain permanent phrases, stereotyped expressions, customary terminology"), which was originally drawn from the Bible.[59] He noted another difficulty around the issue of biblical context for the expressions or words used in the *Hodayot*. Sometimes the language is picked up, but nothing of the biblical context seems to be in view.[60] This makes it problematic to decipher what the author may have understood about the biblical text and how the use of that biblical text contributes to an understanding of that poem.[61] However, he also points out that there is no question that there are plenty of examples in the *Hodayot* in which biblical texts have been used on purpose and in such a way that it is clear that the authors had a particular understanding of them.

> These provide enlightenment about two things: firstly, they tell us something about the actual concept of the Scriptures held by the community where these psalms belonged — we obtain an impression of the way in which the community read the Old Testament, and of the way in which it wished it to be read; and secondly, they tell us something about the community's understanding of itself, and of its place in life as a fulfillment of those prophecies. . . .[62]

But even this deliberate use of biblical texts, Holm-Nielsen is quick to point out, is not a matter of actual quotations, but rather "a free and paraphrasing use" of a biblical expression or its context or, on innumerable occasions, expressions of a similar sort are combined from very different places in the Bible, creating a single sentence.

Kittel, while appreciative of Holm-Nielsen's thorough work, also leveled several critiques. First, he did not do an adequate job of defining or distinguishing between what he means by allusion, inspiration, or quotation in his analysis. "Although there would seem to be quite a difference between these terms, the usage of them is often fuzzy and rather subjective. What is often labeled a 'quotation' is the use of one or two words occurring in the same form somewhere in the OT."[63] Second, he has often been misled by a word or phrase into

---

59. Holm-Nielsen, *Hodayot*, 302-3.

60. Holm-Nielsen, *Hodayot*, 302: ". . . it soon becomes apparent that there is either no attention at all, or else only very little paid to the context in the Old Testament. . . ."

61. Holm-Nielsen, *Hodayot*, 303-04.

62. Holm-Nielsen, *Hodayot*, 304.

63. Kittel, *The Hymns of Qumran*, 14. This critique is detailed on p. 49 and is also addressed to Carmignac.

seeing a connection with a particular biblical text. "When a rather unusual Hebrew word appears in a hymn, he is inclined to see the hymn passage as 'inspired by,' or 'alluding to' the OT passage where a similar word or form is found, even though other OT passages are far closer in general content or even vocabulary than the one he has chosen."[64] Third, he has a low view of the creativity of the author(s) of the Hodayot and "leaves the impression that these psalms are indeed 'mosaics of Old Testament quotations.' "[65] While there is indeed a "fuzziness" in his poem-by-poem analysis,[66] and Kittel's other critiques are also fair in that context, Holm-Nielsen's broader conclusions about biblical usage in the Hodayot are cautious and very much aligned with Kittel's views. In fact, her conclusions about biblical vocabulary and contexts are very similar to Holm-Nielsen's.[67]

Kittel refined the discussion about classification by attempting to define the types of borrowings from the Bible that are found in the *Hodayot*.[68] She distinguished between "deliberate" and "free" usage of biblical expressions by setting the following criteria for a deliberate use: (1) the context of the expression is the same as in Old Testament usage, and it is not a frequently employed idiom; (2) the meaning is the same as in the Old Testament, and it is not frequently employed there; (3) it marks a literary form; (4) it is an Old Testament metaphor or simile characteristic of a certain type of imagery.[69] She also delimited the use of "quotation" by defining it as consisting of several words and appearing with only the slightest variations from the original. "Allusion" she defined as referring to a single passage, with the context, meaning, and idiom itself converging on one text or, where that convergence is incomplete, being reinforced by surrounding references to the same passage.[70]

Scholars writing in the last few years have begun to unravel some of the problems of classification of biblical interpretation associated with the *Hodayot*. Yair Hoffman has proposed that some biblical genres, namely, wisdom and psalms, "do not use explicit quotations following an international lit-

---

64. Kittel, *The Hymns of Qumran*, 14.

65. Kittel, *The Hymns of Qumran*, 48.

66. I find that the observations he makes in his poem-by-poem analysis, using terms such as "mosaic of biblical language" or "quotation," stand in direct contradiction to the observations he offers in his section on "The Use of the Old Testament in the Hodayot."

67. Kittel, *The Hymns of Qumran*, 52.

68. Kittel, *The Hymns of Qumran*, 50. Quotation or allusion is used to recall a *specific* passage; (2) biblical literary forms are imitated by use of standardized phrases; (3) biblical imagery and metaphor characteristic of certain types of literature can be identified; (4) many thoughts are expressed in a manner consistent with biblical language and terminology.

69. Kittel, *The Hymns of Qumran*, 50.

70. Kittel, *The Hymns of Qumran*, 51.

erary tradition."[71] This hypothesis may offer some insight into the lack of citation formulas and explicit quotations in the *Hodayot*. Newsom has explored the reaccentuation of biblical language in the *Hodayot* by taking a biblical word or phrase and "making it keep company with other words that lend their own meanings to it or by using it in statements or constructions that require it to take on new connotations."[72] This reaccentuation of biblical language plays a role in alienating the sectarian from the common moral concerns of late Second Temple Judaism, while reassuring him of the truth of his own knowledge and further securing his identity.[73] Esther Chazon, while assessing the transference of the biblical context by allusion, has identified four criteria to help gauge the extent of biblical context that is being accessed: (1) a clearly identifiable quotation or allusion to a specific biblical passage, establishing the link between the two texts; (2) an additional marker flagging that particular passage and making it virtually impossible for a person who is biblically literate to ignore; (3) the totality of intertextual allusions; (4) the degree of continuity with the biblical source in content, genre, and especially context — engaging the biblical context and importing it into the new composition, rather than severing the allusion in a way that inhibits the transference of biblical images, connotations, and context.[74]

Hughes's study of five *Hodayot* brings sustained attention to the issue of how we might best sort out categories of biblical usage in the *Hodayot*. Along the way, she offers some revised working definitions, after acknowledging that modern preconceptions often get in the way. She points out that "the concept of verbatim quotation is potentially anachronistic when applied to the ancient world, where texts were copied by hand with multiple minor variations."[75] Her definition of quotation is "a phrase which is marked, explicitly or implicitly, as referring to the words of a speaker who is not the implied speaker of the compositions. The identity of the referent may or may not be known. The words may or may not be quoted verbatim."[76] Quotations do not play a major role in the

---

71. Yair Hoffman, "The Technique of Quotation and Citation as an Interpretive Device," in *Creative Biblical Exegesis: Christian and Jewish Hermeneutics through the Centuries*, ed. Benjamin Uffenheimer and Henning Graf Reventlow. JSOTSup 59 (Sheffield: JSOT, 1988), 78.

72. Newsom, *The Self as Symbolic Space*, 267.

73. Newsom, *The Self as Symbolic Space*, 269.

74. Esther G. Chazon, "The Use of the Bible as a Key to Meaning in Psalms from Qumran," in *Emmanuel: Studies in the Hebrew Bible, Septuagint and Dead Sea Scrolls in Honor of Emmanuel Tov*, ed. Shalom M. Paul, Robert A. Kraft, Lawrence H. Schiffman, and Weston W. Fields. VTSup 94 (Leiden: Brill, 2003), 95-96.

75. Hughes, *Scriptural Allusions*, 43.

76. Hughes, *Scriptural Allusions*, 44.

Hodayot.[77] A second category defined by Hughes is idiom. Idioms are "expressions that are known to occur commonly in literature found at Qumran, scriptural or otherwise."[78] An example of an idiom is "creature of clay, kneaded with water," which with variations shows up repeatedly in the *Hodayot*. It is not a biblical phrase, though it does share similarities of language with Job 10:9; 33:6; Isa 29:16; and 41:25, and its content (though not most of its vocabulary) could be taken as an allusion to the account of the formation of man in Gen 2:7.[79] But the boundary between idiom and allusion is not always so clear. Hughes points to 1QH^a XX, 29-38, where "the expression 'creature of clay' is combined with others in a clear evocation of Gen 3:19."[80] In this case it functions as an allusion. A major difficulty with allusions is identifying specific cases. Hughes offers a working definition of an allusion as "a reference which is recognised by a reader as referring to a textual source, knowledge of which contributes to the meaning for the reader."[81] She attaches two criteria to this definition: (1) identifying the marker, the verbal similarity to a biblical passage; and (2) an indication that the poem directs the reader to a particular interpretation of the adopted biblical text.[82] It is important also to keep in mind the function of scriptural allusions: they give a sense of authority to the text, and they create a sense of solidarity (recognizing the allusion reinforces a sense of belonging to a particular community).[83]

Fishbane has pointed out that the rich biblical texture created by such allusive language lends authority to the community's self-understanding as the new Israel.[84] 1QH^a VII, 21–VIII, ? provides an example in which there are a number of biblical texts (Jer 10:23 and 12:3; Zech 12:1; Job 12:10; and Deut 28:46) clearly alluded to, meeting both Hughes's definition and the markers (specific passage and clear contextual links) that she has set out. There are other likely allusions where the markers are not so clear-cut.[85] Hughes then demonstrates how this poem may provide a meditation on Jeremiah 10–12, supported by other biblical allusions, and how it innovates on the ideas of Jeremiah.[86] For Hughes, it is important to begin with an analysis of the overall structure of each poem, and

---

77. Elwolde discusses the reasons why the Hodayot tend to recast biblical language, rather than reproduce the exact words; "Hodayot's Use of the Psalter," 81.

78. Hughes, *Scriptural Allusions*, 48.

79. Hughes, *Scriptural Allusions*, 46.

80. Hughes, *Scriptural Allusions*, 47.

81. Hughes, *Scriptural Allusions*, 52.

82. Hughes, *Scriptural Allusions*, 53.

83. Hughes, *Scriptural Allusions*, 54.

84. Fishbane, "Use, Authority and Interpretation," 357.

85. Hughes, *Scriptural Allusions*, 78.

86. Hughes, *Scriptural Allusions*, 79-95.

then to try to understand how allusions and other poetic devices function within the context of that poem as a whole. Because of the diversity of style and content among the *Hodayot,* it is crucial not only to look at how scriptural allusions may be functioning, but also to look for diverse poetic devices.[87]

Biblical Interpretation and What the *Hodayot* Do[88]

There are of course a variety of answers to the question, "How does biblical interpretation relate to what the *Hodayot* do?" Newsom noted that Hans Bardtke posed and tentatively answered this question more than fifty years ago, "when he suggested that the Hodayot be understood as a collection of spiritual exercises. Bardtke observed that the repetition of various forms and images and even of particular emotional patterns in the Hodayot served to shape the beliefs and religious affections of those who read them."[89] Elwolde offers his own perspective on this: "The sectaries' lives and conceptual worlds were completely infused by the Bible; they did not so much 'know' the Bible as 'live' it. The divine plan . . . together with the Scriptures . . . was taking shape through the life and work of the sectaries; through them, the biblical period and the Bible itself, was being extended into the present and future."[90] Michael Daise, after looking at creation motifs in 1QH^a XVI, concluded that in that poem the claim is being made that the Qumran community was the beneficiary or perhaps even the act of a new creation.[91]

Newsom's hypothesis is that the *Hodayot*

> may not have been simply a textual corpus, but perhaps a collection of models for oral performance. The repeated and even stereotypical set of topoi, motifs, concepts, and patterns of emotion that one finds in the Hodayot suggests that there was a communal understanding of the patterned way in which one should give thanks to God and describe one's experience and sense of identity.[92]

---

87. Hughes, *Scriptural Allusions,* 232-33.

88. This is an adaptation from Newsom's question (*The Self as Symbolic Space,* 191), "What do Hodayot do?"

89. Hans Bardtke, "Considérations sur les cantiques de Qumrân," *RB* 63 (1956): 231, quoted by Newsom, *The Self as Symbolic Space,* 191.

90. Elwolde, "The Hodayot's Use of the Psalter," 80-81.

91. Michael A. Daise, "Biblical Creation Motifs in the Qumran Hodayot," in Schiffman, Tov, and VanderKam, *The Dead Sea Scrolls Fifty Years After Their Discovery,* 304-5. This is more what the *Hodayot* say than what they do.

92. Newsom, *The Self as Symbolic Space,* 203.

The oral performance of the *Hodayot* served especially well in the formation of insiders from outsiders for this sectarian community, by cultivating a sense of "we" that is separate from "others." A voluntary sectarian community needed to be able "to detach members from their prior identities and offer them new ones."[93] This was all the more important for Qumran, because the sect existed as a marginal phenomenon alongside of non-Essene Second Temple Judaism, a coexistence that "implicitly called into question the plausibility of Essene life. The formation of an alternative subjectivity is part of the counter-discourse of the sect, that is, the way it challenges structures of meaning taken for granted in other Jewish communities."[94]

It is easy to understand how this phenomenon works where there is polemical language (e.g., "children of light and children of darkness"). However, Newsom has demonstrated that in the *Hodayot*, especially in the poems that an ordinary sectarian would have recited, it is often through the nonpolemical aspects of the discourse of the self that one finds a subtle program of estrangement of the speaker from the world outside the sect.

> The self who is formed in this way now has dispositions, desires, motivations, and behaviors that are incompatible with other discourses. The discourses that had previously formed a person's identity now appear inadequate. One ceases to feel at home in them or in the institutions founded on and supported by them.[95]

Through such a process, affinity is strengthened for the new group, while estrangement from the old is taking place. In the language of the *Hodayot*, the individual's knowledge of self "is grounded in a radical contrast between the self and God," but also in the contrast between the self and human others. He has no moral agency of his own; God has given him knowledge, but it is knowledge of his own human nothingness. He is at once a part of sinful humanity and the redeemed elect. "A person who recites such first-person prayers, for whom this becomes his own language becomes different from others outside the sect in a profound way."[96]

The *Hodayot* of the leader also support sectarian identity, but in a different

93. Newsom, *The Self as Symbolic Space*, 194.
94. Newsom, *The Self as Symbolic Space*, 194.
95. Newsom, *The Self as Symbolic Space*, 194.
96. Newsom, "Constructing," 20. Cf. Newsom, *The Self as Symbolic Space*, 269: "Once a person is steeped in the language of the Hodayot, then other languages are disclosed to be 'unspeakable.' They appear faulty and defective or shallow and superficial. . . . This alienation from other moral languages reassures the sectarian of the truth of his own knowledge and further secures his identity."

way. The *Hodayot* of the leader construct a figure who compels loyalty. "*Who* he is in relation to God, the community, and their opponents is at the heart of these self-presentations. Through this means they help negotiate problems of sectarian fractiousness, provide the community with an acceptable under-standing of acts of disaffection that might otherwise undermine confidence, and encourage sentiments of affinity with the leadership of the community."[97]

The process of affinity and estrangement through repeated recitation of the *Hodayot* involves a reaccentuation of biblical language and familiar idioms of prayer, worship, wisdom instruction, and cultic language. Implicit in this is the recognition that the Qumran community has a shared heritage of texts and traditions with dominant Judaism, even though they reject dominant Judaism's understanding of that heritage.[98] Through reaccenting "ordinary words, words traditionally important for self-representation, such as 'righteousness' or 'spirit' may be given a slightly different nuance by being associated with a dif-ferent range of terms or employed in unusual constructions. Emphases may be different."[99] It is the traditional elements that allow a person to enter into the discourse precisely because of "their familiarity and the value already attached to them."[100] Familiar language and imagery (as from biblical texts), from which it would be difficult to identify anything as unique, is transformed, given a dis-tinctive quality. Through this reaccentuation, "it is possible to create the sense that one is only now understanding the true meaning of words that had long been familiar and important."[101]

Conclusion

Biblical interpretation is pervasive in the *Hodayot,* even though it is not thought of as a primary function of their poetic genre. We have seen how early studies on the *Hodayot* have provided a rich foundation for more recent ones, even in instances where the results differ significantly. In the area of text criti-cism, early optimism has so far not been borne out, leading to the conclusion that it is rare to find an example in the *Hodayot* that has a compelling bearing

---

97. Newsom, *The Self as Symbolic Space,* 345.

98. Maxine L. Grossman, "Cultivating Identity: Textual Virtuosity and 'Insider' Status," in García Martínez and Popović, *Defining Identities,* 2. She suggests (10) that Scripture alluded to in Qumran texts such as the *Hodayot* and the interpretation given to it "can contribute to the development of an insider identity in ways that are dynamic and reinforcing."

99. Newsom, *The Self as Symbolic Space,* 195.

100. Newsom, *The Self as Symbolic Space,* 195.

101. Newsom, *The Self as Symbolic Space,* 195.

on text criticism. The density of biblical language and imagery in the *Hodayot* was recognized and related to specific biblical texts early, especially the prevalence of language from the Psalms and Isaiah, but also Jeremiah and Ezekiel. There was also the caution that even where words and phrases identical to those in the Bible are used in the *Hodayot*, they may not have been drawn directly from the Bible, but may instead reflect a common stock of everyday language in the Community. More recently, scholars have tried to sort out exactly how these often-used texts (Isaiah, Psalms, Jeremiah, and Ezekiel) have been utilised in individual *Hodayot*, how they relate to the development of identity within the Community, and whether or not the "biblical" language found in the *Hodayot* are part of a broader sectarian or nonsectarian stock of idioms. The diversity of *Hodayot*, their lack of uniform character (raising the possibility of different authors), and even a significant range in the usage of biblical language and imagery led to the conclusion that there were at least two groups of *Hodayot*. Contemporary studies have called for a reconsideration of these two categories (the Hymns of the Teacher and Hymns of the Community) because they do not adequately describe the diversity found in the *Hodayot*, and also because of their possible functions within the Community and their divergent uses of Scripture. Where there does seem to be a common exegetical tradition, this may be accounted for as a shared heritage with nonsectarian Judaism and by the common concern of the *Hodayot* with sectarian identity.

Scholars have long recognized the formal similarities between the *Hodayot* and the Psalms (the *Hodayot* are viewed as a mix of biblical psalms of thanksgiving and complaint, with thanksgiving dominating) and their differences (the *Hodayot* are original poetry). Recent scholarship has asked what this imitation of biblical psalms with a new content might be all about, how traditional motifs and language are used in a distinctive sectarian form, and how this reaccentuation of the language of the Psalms functions. In classifying the uses of Scripture in the *Hodayot*, scholars from the outset have noted the lack of explicit quotations, the possibility of idiomatic language, and the need to assess how much of the biblical context carries over into the *Hodayot*. While early studies struggled with issues of whether or not the use of biblical language was deliberate or free and provided basic definitions of "quotation" and "allusion," contemporary studies have brought precision to those categories (and also to "idiom") and to identifying more carefully how much of the biblical context is in view and how it contributes to the meaning of a poem. A most interesting development of contemporary scholarship is the change in thinking about how biblical interpretation relates to what the *Hodayot* do. The question, "what do the *Hodayot* do?" tended, in the past, to focus on the possible *Sitz im Leben* of the *Hodayot*. Now there is more emphasis on how familiar, biblical language has been reaccented in the *Hodayot* to serve in the formation of Qumran's sectarian identity.

BIBLIOGRAPHY

Bardtke, Hans. "Considérations sur les cantiques de Qumrân." *RB* 63 (1956): 220-33.

Becker, Jürgen. *Das Heil Gottes: Heils- und Sündenbegriffe in den Qumrantexten und im Neuen Testament.* SUNT 3. Göttingen: Vandenhoeck & Ruprecht, 1964.

Bernstein, Moshe J. "Interpretation of Scriptures." In *EDSS*, 1:376-83.

Brooke, George J. "Biblical Interpretation in the Qumran Scrolls and the New Testament." In *The Dead Sea Scrolls Fifty Years After Their Discovery: Proceedings of the Jerusalem Congress, July 20-25, 1997,* ed. Lawrence H. Schiffman, Emanuel Tov, and James C. VanderKam. Jerusalem: Israel Exploration Society and Shrine of the Book, 2000, 60-73.

Burrows, Millar. *More Light on the Dead Sea Scrolls: New Scrolls and New Interpretations, with Translations of Important Recent Discoveries.* New York: Viking, 1958.

Carmignac, Jean. "Les Citations de L'Ancien Testament et Spécialement des Poèmes du Serviteur, dans les Hymnes de Qumran." *RevQ* 2 (1959-1960): 357-94.

Chazon, Esther G. "The Use of the Bible as a Key to Meaning in Psalms from Qumran." In *Emanuel: Studies in the Hebrew Bible, Septuagint and Dead Sea Scrolls in Honor of Emanuel Tov,* ed. Shalom M. Paul, Robert A. Kraft, Lawrence H. Schiffman, and Weston W. Fields. VTSup 94. Leiden: Brill, 2003, 85-96.

Daise, Michael A. "Biblical Creation Motifs in the Qumran Hodayot." In Schiffman, Tov, and VanderKam, *The Dead Sea Scrolls Fifty Years After Their Discovery,* 293-305.

Delcor, Mathias. *Les Hymnes de Qumrân (Hodayot): Texte hébreu, introduction, traduction, commentaire.* Paris: Letouzy et Ané, 1962.

Elwolde, John. "The Hodayot's Use of the Psalter: Text-Critical Contributions (Book I)." In *Psalms and Prayers: Papers Read at the Joint Meeting of the Society of Old Testament Study and the Oudtestamentische Werkgezelschap in Nederland en Belgie, Apeldoorn. August 2006,* ed. Bob Becking and Eric Peels. OtSt 55. Leiden: Brill, 2007, 78-108.

Fishbane, Michael. "Use, Authority and Interpretation of Mikra at Qumran." In *Mikra: Text, Translation, Reading and Interpretation of the Hebrew Bible in Ancient Judaism and Early Christianity.* CRINT 2.1. Assen: Van Gorcum and Philadelphia: Fortress, 1988, 339-77.

Grossman, Maxine L. "Cultivating Identity: Textual Virtuosity and 'Insider' Status." In *Defining Identities: We, You, and the Other in the Dead Sea Scrolls,* ed. Florentino García Martínez and Mladen Popovic. STDJ 70. Leiden: Brill, 2008, 1-11.

Hoffman, Yair. "The Technique of Quotation and Citation as an Interpretive Device." In *Creative Biblical Exegesis: Christian and Jewish Hermeneutics through the Centuries,* ed. Benjamin Uffenheimer and Henning Graf Reventlow. JSOTSup 59. Sheffield: JSOT, 1988, 71-79.

Holm-Nielsen, Svend. *Hodayot: Psalms from Qumran.* ATDan 2. Aarhus: Universitetsforlaget, 1960.

Hughes, Julie A. *Scriptural Allusions and Exegesis in the Hodayot.* STDJ 59. Leiden: Brill, 2006.

Jeremias, Gert. *Der Lehrer der Gerechtigkeit.* SUNT 2. Göttingen: Vandenhoeck & Ruprecht, 1963.

Kittel, Bonnie. *The Hymns of Qumran: Translation and Commentary.* SBLDS 50. Chico: Scholars, 1981.

Kuhn, Heinz-Wolfgang. *Enderwartung und gegenwärtiges Heil: Untersuchungen zu den Gemeindeliedern von Qumran.* SUNT 4. Göttingen: Vandenhoeck & Ruprecht, 1966.

Mansoor, Menahem. *The Thanksgiving Hymns: Translated and Annotated with an Introduction.* STDJ 3. Leiden: Brill and Grand Rapids: Eerdmans, 1961.

Morawe, Günter. *Aufbau und Abgrenzung der Loblieder von Qumrân: Studien zur Gattungsgeschichtlichen Einordnung der Hodajôth.* Theologische Arbeiten 16. Berlin: Evangelische, 1961.

Newsom, Carol A. "The Case of the Blinking I: Discourse of the Self at Qumran." In *Discursive Formations: Ascetic Piety and the Interpretation of Early Christian Literature, Part 1,* ed. Vincent L. Wimbush. Semeia 57. Atlanta: SBL, 1992, 13-23.

———. *The Self as Symbolic Space: Constructing Identity and Community at Qumran.* STDJ 52. Leiden: Brill, 2004.

———. "Constructing 'We, You, and the Others' through Non-Polemical Discourse." In García Martínez and Popović, *Defining Identities,* 13-21.

Schultz, Richard L. *The Search for Quotation: Verbal Parallels in the Prophets.* JSOTSup 180. Sheffield: Sheffield Academic, 1999.

Stegemann, Hartmut, with Eileen Schuller. *Qumran Cave 1, 3: 1QHodayot*[a], *with Incorporation of 4QHodayot*[a-f] *and 1QHodayot*[b]. Trans. of texts by Carol Newsom. DJD 40. Oxford: Clarendon, 2008.

Wernberg-Møller, Preben. "The Contribution of the Hodayot to Biblical Textual Criticism." *Text* 4 (1964): 133-75.

PART 5

Apocalyptic Literature and Testaments

The Use of Scripture in the Book of Daniel

Matthias Henze

The apocalypse is a form of revelatory literature. Driven like no other genre of early Jewish writing by an intense longing for knowledge about the future, it extends itself beyond the confines of the commonly knowable to catch a glimpse of what lies on the other side of history. The focus is squarely on the future, the eschatological future — so much so that it is easy for the reader to overlook how much the apocalypse, its language and world view are anchored in Israel's past. While the concern for the eschaton is well pronounced and explicit, the connection with the past is, for the most part, implicit and expressed in the choice of literary genres, fictitious setting, and language, all at home in Israel's traditional writings. Apocalyptic authors write in the biblical idiom, particularly in the literary idioms of prophecy and wisdom. To uncover the inner workings of this peculiar genre of early Jewish literature therefore requires an appreciation not just for the apocalyptic conceptualization of the future but also for the apocalypse's indebtedness to Israel's literary past.[1]

As James Kugel has noted in his introduction to this volume, the book of Daniel is somewhat of an exception in the present collection in that it is part of the biblical canon. To inquire into the use of Scripture in Daniel is thus an exercise in inner-biblical interpretation. Since Daniel in its present form dates from the second century B.C.E., however, it fits well within the chronological borders of this Companion. Indeed, Daniel has become something of a *locus classicus* of

---

1. A pioneer in examining the use of Scripture in early Jewish apocalyptic literature was Lars Hartman, *Prophecy Interpreted: The Formation of Some Jewish Apocalyptic Texts and the Eschatological Discourse Mark 13 Par.* ConBNT 1 (Lund: Gleerup, 1966); and *Asking for a Meaning: A Study of 1 Enoch 1–5.* ConBNT 12 (Lund: Gleerup, 1979). More recently, George W. E. Nickelsburg, "Scripture in *1 Enoch* and *1 Enoch* as Scripture," in *Texts and Contexts: Biblical Texts in their Textual and Situational Contexts. Essays in Honor of Lars Hartman,* ed. Tord Fornberg and David Hellholm (Oslo: Scandinavian University Press, 1995), 333-54, with further bibliog.

inner-biblical exegesis. One of Daniel's celebrated attributes is that he can give the interpretation (פִּשְׁרָה; Dan 2:7, etc.) of divine mysteries. Also, the reworking of earlier Scripture is rather overt in Daniel. In chapter 9 Daniel reads of Jeremiah's prophecy regarding the Babylonian exile and in response to his prayer is told by Gabriel that the exile will in fact last seventy week-years. Biblical interpretation in the book of Daniel is not limited to chapter 9, however. Indeed, even the most cursory reader will notice how Daniel 9 with its Deuteronomic theology is the exception rather than the rule in this intriguing apocalypse and therefore can hardly serve as a model for Daniel's use of Scripture in general.

The present article has a double task. The first is of a textual nature. By looking at a few select examples of Daniel's interaction with Scripture, this essay seeks to convey a sense of the extent to which the authors of Daniel invoke, paraphrase, rework, and otherwise make use of Israel's sacred writings. The use of Scripture in Daniel is all-pervasive and operates on different levels simultaneously. The terrain is vast and rugged, and so we will need to be selective. I have chosen three text samples, each representative of different forms of Daniel's use of Scripture: Daniel 2 and the ways in which Daniel's service at the court mimics that of Joseph in Egypt; Daniel 7 and 8 and the process of *Fortschreibung,* the continuous process of composing by which successive authors adopt earlier materials and elaborate on them by composing new and independent, albeit closely related texts; and Daniel 10–12 and the use of prophecy in Daniel's final historical apocalypse.

The second task is methodological in nature. While only few modern interpreters will dispute the central influence of the received written tradition on the book of Daniel, it remains unclear how best to describe this use of Scripture, in Daniel or in early Jewish apocalypses in general, for that matter. A blanket term such as "biblical interpretation" is too vague — does "interpretation" mean the deliberate effort of B to *explain* A, or does any *influence* of A on B, however defined, imply that B "interprets" A? — and fails to capture the complex processes of adopting, reworking, and recontextualizing the earlier materials. The case of Daniel is, again, intriguing. Since its exegetical techniques anticipate similar ways of reading Scripture at Qumran, in the Apocrypha, the Old Testament Pseudepigrapha, and in rabbinic literature, methodological considerations about Daniel's use of Scripture will be immediately relevant for, and applicable to a much broader corpus of early Jewish literature and its engagement with the Hebrew Bible.

Daniel at the Court

We begin our inquiry into the use of Scripture in Daniel with chapter 2, the first of Daniel's court legends. The plot of the tale revolves around a number of set tropes and stock motifs, which, in various combinations, are well familiar from similar Jewish tales, such as the Joseph Novella, Ahiqar, Esther, Tobit, and 1 Esdras 3–4. They include the uneasy sleep of a central figure, the irritated monarch, a task impossible to solve, the helpless experts, the fury of the king (or, alternatively, of the premier courtier), the imperiled hero, the divine intervention that leads to a full reversal of events, and the exoneration and reward of the hero.[2]

Daniel 2, the story of Nebuchadnezzar's first dream, divides into five parts, each centered on a different aspect of the tale. In the first scene (vv. 1-12), the Babylonian monarch presents his diviners with the impossible task to interpret the dream he refuses to tell. The situation quickly deteriorates, so that by verse 12 the monarch is reduced to rage and commands the execution of all wise men. The second scene (vv. 13-23) introduces Daniel. The reader learns in the middle of the scene that "the mystery [of Nebuchadnezzar's dream] was revealed to Daniel" (v. 19), which effectively solves the problem, even though the actual resolution will have to wait for another twenty verses.[3] Daniel's song in praise of his God (vv. 20-23) ends the scene and divides the chapter into half. When Daniel appears before Nebuchadnezzar in the third scene (vv. 24-30), he again makes sure to give due credit to God "who reveals mysteries" (v. 28) before he actually relates the dream and gives its interpretation. The dream report and its

---

2. W. Lee Humphreys, "A Life-Style for Diaspora: A Study of the Tales of Esther and Daniel," *JBL* 92 (1973): 211-23; Susan Niditch and Robert Doran, "The Success Story of the Wise Courtier: A Formal Approach," *JBL* 96 (1977): 179-93; Lawrence M. Wills, *The Jew in the Court of the Foreign King*. HDR 26 (Minneapolis: Fortress, 1990), 81-83; George W. E. Nickelsburg, *Jewish Literature between the Bible and the Mishnah* (1981; 2nd ed. Minneapolis: Fortress, 2005), 17-19; Erich S. Gruen, "Embellishments and Inventions," in *Heritage and Hellenism: The Reinvention of Jewish Tradition* (Berkeley: University of California Press, 1998), 160-88; Matthias Henze, "The Narrative Frame of Daniel: A Literary Assessment," *JSJ* 32 (2001): 5-24; Karel van der Toorn, "Scholars at the Oriental Court: The Figure of Daniel against Its Mesopotamian Background," in *The Book of Daniel: Composition and Reception*, ed. John J. Collins and Peter W. Flint. VTSup 83 (Leiden: Brill, 2001), 1:37-54.

3. Louis F. Hartman and Alexander A. Di Lella, *The Book of Daniel*. AB 23 (Garden City: Doubleday, 1978), 139, argue that vv. 13-23 are a secondary intrusion: "One may therefore assume that the story once circulated in at least two variant accounts, which have been combined, not very smoothly, in the account as now given in ch. 2." Their view is quoted approvingly by Michael Segal, "From Joseph to Daniel: The Literary Development of the Narrative in Daniel 2," *VT* 59 (2009): 123-49, who goes so far as to find "most blatant [. . .] internal contradictions" (125).

allegorical interpretation in the fourth scene (vv. 31-35) center on the scheme of the four successive kingdoms, a schema of central importance for the composition of the book. In the final scene (vv. 46-49), Nebuchadnezzar acknowledges the superiority of Daniel's God and promptly converts to "the God of gods" (v. 47), while appointing Daniel and his comrades to high offices.[4]

Of the numerous parallels between the court tales in Daniel and other Jewish legends, the affinities with the Joseph Novella are particularly striking.[5] Both Joseph and Daniel are taken into exile against their will, though due to divine providence their exile eventually turns out to be a blessing. They are both handsome in appearance (Gen 39:6; Dan 1:4), and they are recognized by the foreign king for their unparalleled wisdom (Gen 41:39; Dan 1:4). Both quickly climb to become courtiers of the monarch: they are given new, non-Hebrew names (Gen 41:45; Dan 1:7), they are decorated with a chain around their neck (Gen 41:42; Dan 5:29), and they are appointed over the whole kingdom (Gen 41:40; Dan 2:48; 5:29; 6:3).

A close comparison of Genesis 40–41 and Daniel 2 helps to cast the parallels and differences between the two texts into sharper relief.[6] The stories begin when Pharaoh and Nebuchadnezzar have "troubled spirits" because of their dreams (וַתִּפָּעֶם רוּחוֹ, Gen 41:8; וַתִּתְפָּעֶם רוּחוֹ, Dan 2:1). Both call for "magicians" to interpret their dreams (Gen 41:8; Dan 2:2, 27). The list of helpless experts is longer in Daniel and their situation much more dire. The word for magicians in Gen 41:8, חַרְטֻמִּים, also appears in Dan 2:2 and is elsewhere attested only in Exodus 8 and 9. The situation is saved when a young exile from among the Israelites who has been in the king's custody for two years is found who can solve the riddle. A cupbearer and the "chief executioner" (רַב־טַבָּחַיָּא, Dan 2:14;

---

4. The focus of Daniel 2 lies neither with the court setting or the dream but with the repeated profession of God's authority, clearly articulated in Daniel's psalmic doxology in vv. 20-23 (cf. vv. 27-28) and then repeated by Nebuchadnezzar himself (v. 47). The dream episode and the conflict culminate in the monarch's solemn confession, and so the story as a whole is fundamentally a conversion story. Philip R. Davies, "Daniel Chapter Two," *JTS* 27 (1976): 392-401; George W. E. Nickelsburg, *Resurrection, Immortality, and Eternal Life in Intertestamental Judaism and Early Christianity.* 2nd ed. HTS 56 (Cambridge, Mass.: Harvard University Press, 2006), 68-78.

5. Donald B. Redford, *A Study of the Biblical Story of Joseph (Genesis 37-50).* VTSup 20 (Leiden: Brill, 1970), 94-100, 226. See also G. G. Labonté, "Genèse 41 et Daniel 2; question d'origine," in *The Book of Daniel in the Light of New Findings,* ed. A. S. van der Woude. BETL 106 (Leuven: Leuven University Press and Peeters, 1993), 271-84, who reaches the unlikely conclusion, "Il est donc possible que le texte de Dn 2 et l'histoire de Joseph, dont Gn 41, datent de la même périod de l'histoire d'Israël" (284).

6. André Lacocque, *The Book of Daniel* (Atlanta: John Knox, 1979), 35-37; John E. Goldingay, *Daniel.* WBC 30 (Dallas: Word, 1987), 42-43.

cf. שַׂר הַטַּבָּחִים, Gen 39:1) serve to connect Joseph and Daniel to the royal throne. Unlike the native magicians, the youth can provide an "interpretation." The crucial word, פְּשַׁר in Dan 2:4 et al. and פָּתַר in Gen 41:15, of the roots פתר/פשר, "interpret," is only attested in Genesis 40–41 and Daniel 2–7.[7] It turns out that both dreams involve numbers that relate to their hidden meanings: seven years of plenty followed by famine (Gen 41:25-36) and four successive kingdoms (Dan 2:36-45). The most potent parallel, however, is the emphatic assertion of both sages that it is not they but God who unlocks the mystery and provides the interpretation (Gen 40:8 and 41:16; Dan 2:28, 47). In the Joseph Novella, God appears to communicate with Joseph promptly and without delay. This is noticeably different from Daniel 2, where Daniel has to ask Nebuchadnezzar for more time (Dan 2:16; notice the contrast with 2:8, where the king explicitly denies the Babylonian sages any time!). The seer then withdraws to his quarters, informs his comrades of what is happening, and only that night the mystery is revealed to him (Dan 2:17-19). The doxology in vv. 20-23 has no parallel in the Joseph Novella. It makes a connection between God's sovereignty over history, the dominion of kings, and the wisdom of the sages.[8] Each story concludes with the promotion of the youth to the office of prime minister over the whole land (Gen 41:40; Dan 2:48).

The points of contact between Daniel 2 and Genesis 40–41 have largely to do with the plot line and dream motif. Other aspects of the story in Daniel draw from other texts in the Hebrew Bible, most prominently from Second Isaiah.[9] One of these aspects concerns the wisdom of Daniel and the helplessness of the Babylonian magicians. A central theme in Deutero-Isaiah is the contrast

---

7. Dan 2:4-7, 45; 4:3, 15-16; 5:12, 15-16, 26; 7:16; and Gen 40:8, 16, 22; 41:8, 12-13, 15. The same word, *pesher*, comes to denote a form of biblical interpretation peculiar to the Qumran library; see Shani Berrin, "Pesharim," in *EDSS*, 2:644-47; and "Qumran Pesharim," in *Biblical Interpretation at Qumran*, ed. Mathias Henze. SDSSRL (Grand Rapids: Eerdmans, 2005), 110-33, with further bibliog.

8. God's sovereignty over history is not only crucial for the dream interpretation Daniel is about to offer in this chapter, it anticipates the judgment scene of Antiochus in Dan 7:24-26, where God does in fact exercise his sovereignty. Given the connection between Dan 2:20-23 and 7:24-25, Segal, "From Joseph to Daniel," 147, asserts that the two texts were written at the same time: "I would tentatively suggest that the addition in 2:15-23 was composed simultaneously to the passage in Daniel 7, and was intended both to foreshadow and offer a contrast to Antiochus' problematic behavior in 7:24-25." In light of a prevalent tendency in Daniel 7–12 to pick up and elaborate further on central motifs in Daniel 1–6, a tendency we will discuss further below, it seems much more likely that the author of Daniel 7, who is writing at a later time, refers back to Daniel's psalm and thus creates a verbal bridge between the two halves of the book.

9. C. L. Seow, *Daniel*. Westminster Bible Companion (Louisville: Westminster John Knox, 2003), 35-49.

between the God of Israel, who is an unfailing source of wisdom and knowledge, and the Babylonian gods, who cannot help. The God of Israel reveals what is unknown only to his own prophets but leaves the Babylonians in the dark. It is the God of the exiles

> who frustrates the omens of liars,
> and who makes fools of diviners;
> who turns back the wise,
> and makes their knowledge foolish;
> who confirms the word of his servant,
> and fulfills the prediction of his messengers. (Isa 44:25-26a)

The God of Israel reveals to his own "what is in darkness" (אוֹצְרוֹת חֹשֶׁךְ, Isa 45:3; cf. יָדַע מָה בַחֲשׁוֹכָא, Dan 2:22) and, at the same time, exposes the foolishness of the diviners, who are left to their own devices. In the end, the nations will come to realize that there is no other god beside the God of Israel (Isa 45:14; 49:23; Dan 2:47).

As soon as Daniel has explained the meaning of the dream to Nebuchadnezzar, the king falls on his face and worships Daniel (Dan 2:46). This bizarre and seemingly exaggerated response seems awkward, not least because Daniel had just predicted the demise of the Babylonian kingdom. Also, the Gentile monarch reveres Daniel and even brings him offerings. Nebuchadnezzar's behavior becomes intelligible, however, when read in the context of Deutero-Isaiah's prophecy to the exiles. The prophet repeatedly predicts the prostration of foreign dignitaries to the Israelites: "Kings shall see and stand up, princes, and they shall prostrate themselves" (Isa 49:7a; also 45:13-14; 49:23; 60:6-7). Read in that light, Nebuchadnezzar's dramatic response is in fulfillment of Second Isaiah's prediction that Israel's oppressors will bow down before their captives.

The purpose of the dream is to announce to Nebuchadnezzar the succession of four world empires, here represented by the four metals of the statue. The making of idols out of the same materials is a frequent motif in Second Isaiah, where the description of the process is typically rather polemical (40:18-20; 41:6-7, 21-29; 44:9-20). The statue itself is, strictly speaking, not an idol, but it carries such connotations.[10] It is then demolished by a powerful stone and shattered into pieces.

> Then the iron, the clay, the bronze, the silver, and the gold, were all broken in pieces and became like the chaff of the summer threshing floors; and the

---

10. Ida Fröhlich, "Daniel 2 and Deutero-Isaiah," in van der Woude, *The Book of Daniel in the Light of New Findings*, 266-70.

wind carried them away, so that not a trace of them could be found. But the stone that struck the statue became a great mountain and filled the whole earth. (Dan 2:35)

The verse, the climax of Daniel's dream account, combines allusions to several passages in Isaiah. We already mentioned the building materials. After striking down the statue, the stone turns into a gigantic mountain that fills the entire earth. The motif is reminiscent of Isa 2:2/Mic 4:1, the prophecy regarding the temple mount that shall be raised above all hills in the end time. Note also Isa 11:9, the promise that the knowledge of God will fill the earth. "They will not hurt or destroy on all my holy mountain; for the earth will be full of the knowledge of the LORD as the waters cover the sea."[11] Like the prophecy in Isa 11:6-9, the mysterious stone cut from the mountain "not by hands" (Dan 2:45; 8:25) has traditionally been interpreted as a messianic prediction.[12] But the origin of the motif is less certain. It is reminiscent of the prophecy in Isa 41:15-16a that the mountains of Babylon will be crushed and scattered in the wind so that Israel can return home: "Now, I will make of you a threshing sledge, sharp, new, and having teeth; you shall thresh the mountains and crush them, and you shall make the hills like chaff. You shall winnow them and the wind shall carry them away, and the tempest shall scatter them." The allusion is significant: Nebuchadnezzar's dream harkens back to the promise once given to the exiles. The obstacles will be removed, foreign powers will be shattered and carried away like the chaff by the wind. The dream is thus a reappropriation of the exilic promise.[13]

For the authors of the tales in Daniel 2–6, the Scriptures provided much stimulus for imagination and creativity. Clearly these authors felt at ease to adopt and reshape generously what they had received. But exactly how are we to describe this process of adaptation and rewriting? André Lacocque asserts with confidence, "Everyone agrees that Dan. 2 is a midrash on Gen. 41."[14] The term

---

11. James A. Montgomery, *A Critical and Exegetical Commentary on the Book of Daniel*. ICC (Edinburgh: T. & T. Clark, 1927), 169.

12. Louis Ginzberg, *The Legends of the Jews* (1928; repr. Philadelphia: Jewish Publication Society, 1968), 6:415, n. 80; in the NT most explicitly in Luke 20:18, but see also Mark 12:10-11; Matt 21:42; 1 Pet 2:6-8; and Rom 9:33. John J. Collins, *Daniel*. Hermeneia (Minneapolis: Fortress, 1993), 171.

13. Seow, *Daniel*, 44. By emphasizing the prophetic background of the legends, I do not wish to minimize their sapiential elements. The case for Daniel as an example of "mantic" wisdom has been made effectively by Hans-Peter Müller in a series of articles, "Mantische Weisheit und Apokalyptik," in *Congress Volume, Uppsala, 1971*, ed. G. W. Anderson. VTSup 22 (Leiden: Brill, 1972), 268-93; and "Märchen, Legende und Enderwartung: Zum Verständnis des Buches Daniel," *VT* 26 (1976): 338-50.

14. Lacocque, *The Book of Daniel*, 36.

"midrash" has been used rather loosely by modern scholars, and unfortunately Lacocque stops short of telling us exactly what he means. If "midrash" describes an act of textual interpretation that seeks to shed light on the base text to render clear what is perceived to be obscure, then the term is clearly inappropriate in our case, since there is nothing to suggest that the purpose of Daniel 2 is to explain Genesis 41.[15] John Goldingay surmises that Daniel 2 was composed after, and in light of, the tales in chapters 3–6, and serves to introduce them, much like Daniel 1 introduces the collection of tales. Goldingay is mindful of the numerous echoes from other parts of Scripture as well and concludes, "A fuller way of describing its midrashic aspect, then, is to see it as a rereading of Dan 3–6 in the light of Gen 41, Isa 40–66, and other passages; or as a reaffirmation of the fundamental themes of Isa 40–66 on the basis of the stories told in chaps. 3–6."[16] Goldingay is right to place such emphasis on the numerous scriptural echoes in Daniel 2, but it is far from certain that our story was, in fact, composed after the other tales, as Goldingay would have it, let alone that its aim is to interpret them.

From the Court to the Visions

The book of Daniel consists of two parts, the tales about Daniel in chapters 1–6 and the apocalyptic visions received by Daniel in chapters 7–12. It is widely agreed that the tales well predate the visions and originally circulated independently, whereas the book of Daniel as we have it today reached its current form during the Maccabean Revolt (167-64 B.C.E.), the time when the visions were composed. The authors of the visions adopted the tales for their purposes and used them as a narrative prelude.[17]

Given this history of the gradual growth of the book of Daniel, it does not surprise to find the authors of the latter half of the book refer back to, and in-

15. Similarly Klaus Koch, *Daniel.* BKAT 22.2 (Neukirchen: Neukirchener, 1994), 123, responding to Lacocque: "So läßt sich von Midrasch nur dann reden, wenn man darunter nicht mehr versteht als ein erbauliches Plagiat." See also Montgomery, *Daniel*, 185.

16. Goldingay, *Daniel*, 38. More helpful is Goldingay's remark that "Joseph could be seen as a type of Daniel" (43).

17. The unity of the biblical book has been the subject of considerable debate. See, e.g., Harold H. Rowley, "The Unity of the Book of Daniel," in *The Servant of the Lord and Other Essays on the Old Testament* (Oxford: Blackwell, 1965), 249-80; Harold L. Ginsberg, *Studies in Daniel* (New York: Jewish Theological Seminary, 1948); Brevard S. Childs, *Introduction to the Old Testament as Scripture* (Philadelphia: Fortress, 1979), 611-23, esp. 613-21. While there can be little doubt that Daniel 1–6 and Daniel 7–12 are not the product of a single hand, the question remains what the legends of the first half of the book meant to the authors/redactors of the second half and how these authors/redactors adopted and reinterpreted them.

terpret, the material now contained in the former half. This is a peculiar, though hardly unique form of biblical exegesis, in which a group of tradents — who are at once the collectors and archivists of the legends, the authors of the visions, and the redactors of the book as a whole — preserved and at the same time rewrote the material they inherited. As a result, the book of Daniel is self-referential, in the sense that its final authors/redactors were also its earliest interpreters.

An obvious and much celebrated example of an inner-Danielic reference is the schema of the four kingdoms, which bridges the two halves of the book, as it is introduced in Daniel 2 and repeated in Daniel 7. The parallels between Daniel 2 and 7 are evident and can briefly be summarized: in each case the protagonist has a dream vision;[18] a divinely authorized interpreter explains that the vision is an allegory of the last phase of world history; this final segment of time is further divided into four consecutive world empires:[19] the first is the Babylonian Empire,[20] the second and third reigns are mentioned only in passing, and the fourth is again described in considerable detail in both chapters; after its demise, God will establish his eternal kingdom.[21] The latter may well imply the ultimate consummation of history, though the act of crossing the eschatological threshold is not made explicit in either text.

The two depictions of the four-kingdom schema diverge significantly in their portrayal of the fourth and final kingdom. Daniel 2 is content merely to note that iron and clay do not mix, a likely reference to the intermarriages of the Seleucids and the Ptolemies, without making any further judgment call (v. 43). Daniel 7, by contrast, dwells at considerable length on the cruel nature of the fourth empire. The arrogance of the Seleucid king Antiochus IV Epiphanes and his eschatological demise are the celebrated climax of the story. Daniel 7 reemploys the four-kingdom schema from Daniel 2 and brings it in line with contemporary events. Its purpose is to give comfort to those who suffer under Antiochus by showing that the last kingdom has, in fact, already been defeated and judgment has been passed, albeit at this point only in heaven. We

18. According to Dan 2:1, Nebuchadnezzar had several disturbing dreams, of which Daniel relates only one, while Dan 7:1 speaks of one dream and multiple visions.

19. Seow, *Daniel*, 100, notes that the four empires in Daniel 2 "do not appear to be consecutive kingdoms, because they all are crushed *together* (see 2:44)."

20. Dan 2:38; the description of the fourth beast in Dan 7:4 closely resembles the description of Nebuchadnezzar's bestial transformation in Dan 4:30(Eng. 4:33) (Aphrahat, *Of Wars; Lev. Rabba* 13.5).

21. Dan 2:44; 7:26-27. Daniel 7 carries obvious eschatological overtones, whereas in Daniel 2, which speaks of an everlasting kingdom established by God, this is not clear (*contra* Hartman and Di Lella, *The Book of Daniel*, 149-50).

can thus think of Daniel 7 as a historical recontextualization, or actualization, of the historical schema introduced in Daniel 2.

Chapters 7 and 8 present another case in which an author reconsidered earlier material and elaborated on it by composing a new, related text. It has long been recognized that Daniel 8 is an interpretive expansion of Daniel 7.[22] The two chapters, which are roughly of equal length, are related in several ways. Both contain symbolic visions, the last in the book of Daniel, in which bizarre animals symbolize the military power of world empires. And both chapters follow the same structure: an introduction with a date formula (Dan 7:1; 8:1-2); the vision report (7:2-15; 8:3-14); a dream interpretation offered by a member of the heavenly court (7:16-27; 8:15-26); and a brief conclusion that makes clear that Daniel remains disturbed, even to the point of falling ill, in spite of the interpretation he was offered (7:28; 8:27). The opening verse of chapter 8 makes the link with chapter 7 explicit: the vision occurred in close sequence only two years after the earlier one. The two chapters are also linked by verbal agreements, most importantly "the little horn" as a designation of Antiochus (7:8; 8:9) and "the holy ones" (7:18; 8:24).[23]

Daniel 7 and 8 cover the same historical periods from the exile to Antiochus, albeit from different angles and with different interpretive emphases. Daniel 7 is concerned primarily with the succession of empires: dominion will finally be taken away from Antiochus and be given to the Son of Man (7:13-14). In Daniel 8, by contrast, the empires form the backdrop and the focus is on Antiochus's sacrilegious behavior. Similarly, whereas in chapter 7 the author remains vague about the nature of the king's arrogance of speech (7:8, 11), chapter 8 lists as Antiochus's main offenses the suppression of the sacrifices and the desecration of the temple (8:11-12). The cessation of the temple sacrifices will last three and a half years according to Dan 7:25, and just over three years according to 8:14.[24] Both chapters see in Antiochus's anger towards the Jews an

22. E.g., Goldingay, *Daniel*, 206-7, who writes about Daniel 8, "The chapter supplements the vision of oppression and judgment contained in chap. 7. It reaffirms the promise of chap. 7, perhaps in the light of a worsening situation." Also Holger Gzella, *Cosmic Battle and Political Conflict: Studies in Verbal Syntax and Contextual Interpretation of Daniel 8*. BibOr 47 (Rome: Pontificio Istituto Biblico, 2003), 71-73.

23. Klaus Koch, "Vom profetischen zum apokalyptischen Visionsbericht," in *Apocalypticism in the Mediterranean World and the Near East*, ed. David Hellholm (Tübingen: Mohr Siebeck, 1983), 413-46; repr. *Vor der Wende der Zeiten: Beiträge zur apokalyptischen Literatur*, ed. Uwe Gleßmer and Martin Krause. Gesammelte Aufsätze 3 (Neukirchen: Neukirchener, 1996), 143-78; Luc Dequeker, "The 'Saints of the Most High' in Qumran and Daniel," in *Syntax and Meaning: Studies in Hebrew Syntax and Biblical Exegesis*, ed. C. J. Labuschagne et al. OtSt 18 (Leiden: Brill, 1973), 108-87; and Collins, *Daniel*, 313-17.

24. In Dan 8:13, Daniel overhears one angel ask another how long "the transgression that

offense against God (7:10, 25; 8:25), as well as an assault on the host of heaven (Dan 7:11-14; 8:10). However, the solution to the crisis is played out differently. At the center of Daniel 7 stands a heavenly throne room scene, in which judgment is passed on the Seleucid king, who is stripped of his power, put to death, and burned with fire (7:11). Daniel 8 merely mentions that the king will be broken, and "not by human hands" (8:25), meaning that it is God who will defeat the Gentile monarch. This seems rather vague compared to the more resolute prediction of Antiochus's end in 7:11-12.

It remains somewhat of an open question how best to describe the literary relationship between Daniel 7 and 8. As we have seen, the two chapters are clearly related. Daniel 8 gives the impression of a sequel to Daniel 7, yet at the same time there is no indication in chapter 8 of a sustained reading of chapter 7, meaning that the latter chapter does not interpret the former chapter as a whole. Daniel 8 adopts the schema of the four kingdoms, focuses on the last kingdom, and spells out in greater detail the nature of Antiochus's offenses. In doing so the author fills in several details (the second and third kingdom are now identified as Media and Persia in 8:20; and the *angelus interpres* is named Gabriel in 8:16) and makes explicit what was left unsaid or implicit in Daniel 7.[25] In short, Daniel's second vision reinforces and elaborates on his first.

The continuous process of composing, in which a scribe adopts earlier materials, such as a central idea or literary motif, and develops them further by composing a related text that then becomes part of the same book or even the same pericope has a close precedent in Israel's Scripture. The process is known among redaction critics as *Fortschreibung* ("successive development" or "prolongation"). It seeks to explain why particularly in the prophetic books we find successive literary units, in which the latter passage expands on the former by broadening its scope. This is different from assuming that individual text units were composed independently and only later grew together, in that the process of *Fortschreibung* assumes a deliberate, creative effort on the part of the redactors to continue to write within the tradition. The phenomenon of *Fortschreibung* was described by Walter Zimmerli in his commentary on Ezekiel: "Much more characteristic for many parts of the book is the distinctive process of 'development' of a section." He observes how a base text ("das Grundwort") has subsequently been broadened by certain additions, "which cannot be regarded simply as independent units of tradition and which have

---

makes desolate" (שֹׁמֵם הַפֶּשַׁע; cf. Isa 64:9[10]) is going to last. The wording anticipates the famed formula in Dan 9:27, "an abomination that desolates" (שִׁקּוּצִים מְשֹׁמֵם), a reference to the desecration of the temple. See also Dan 11:31; 12:11; 1 Macc 1:54; 6:7; 2 Macc 6:2.

25. Seow, *Daniel*, 118.

not therefore simply been added in a process of 'collection.' On the contrary, they undeniably follow in new directions the theme set in the basic oracle."[26] Zimmerli was motivated by his desire to salvage the biblical redactors from their reputation as mere technicians who worked somewhat mechanically and without much thought on individual text passages. Instead, Zimmerli thought of them as creative writers with their own sets of skills. In Daniel we are not talking about short text passages but about entire chapters, but the basic idea is the same. Daniel 8 responds to and reworks Daniel 7.

The process of *Fortschreibung* in Daniel anticipates a form of biblical interpretation used widely in early Judaism and commonly referred to as "rewritten Bible." The term is used loosely in scholarship to designate the retelling of a scriptural passage from an interpretive angle. Prominent texts included in this category are 4QReworked Pentateuch, the *Genesis Apocryphon,* and *Jubilees. Fortschreibung* and "rewritten Bible" are not the same, but it is helpful to think of the redactional processes that gave shape to the biblical text as antecedents of Jewish biblical interpretation of the late Second Temple period.[27]

We would be remiss, finally, not to mention that Daniel 8 also draws on Scripture, in particular on the prophetic tradition, and quite independently of Daniel 7. The descriptions of the circumstances of Daniel's vision in vv. 1-2 as well as of the epiphany in vv. 15-18 are reminiscent of the equivalent scenes in the book of Ezekiel: the date and setting (Dan 8:1-2 and Ezek 1:1-3), the visionary journey to the place of the vision (Dan 8:2 and Ezek 8:3), Daniel standing "by the river" (Dan 8:2 and Ezek 1:1-3), the angelic figure "having the appearance of a man" (Dan 8:15 and Ezek 8:2), the direct address "son of man" (Dan 8:17 and

---

26. Walter Zimmerli, *Ezekiel 1: A Commentary on the Book of the Prophet Ezekiel, Chapters 1-24.* Hermeneia (Philadelphia: Fortress, 1979), 69 (translation of *Ezechiel I.* BKAT XIII.1 [Neukirchen: Neukirchener, 1969], 106); and "Das Phänomen der 'Fortschreibung' im Buche Ezechiel," in *Prophecy: Essays Presented to Georg Fohrer on His Sixty-Fifth Birthday, 6 September 1980,* ed. J. A. Emerton. BZAW 150 (Berlin: de Gruyter, 1980), 174-91; also Reinhard G. Kratz, "Redaktionsgeschichte/Redaktionskritik I," in *TRE* 28 (1997): 375; Helmut Utzschneider and Stefan Ark Nitsche, *Arbeitsbuch literaturwissenschaftliche Bibelauslegung: Eine Methodenlehre zur Exegese des Alten Testaments* (Gütersloh: Kaiser, 2001), 187-212.

27. See Moshe J. Bernstein, "'Rewritten Bible': A Generic Category Which Has Outlived Its Usefulness?" *Text* 22 (2005): 169-96, for a survey of the different uses of the term since it was introduced by Geza Vermes in his classic "Biblical Midrash," in *The History of the Jewish People in the Age of Jesus Christ,* ed. Emil Schürer, rev. Vermes, Fergus Millar, and Martin Goodman (Edinburgh: T. & T. Clark, 1986), 3:308-41. See also George J. Brooke, "Between Authority and Canon: The Significance of Reworking the Bible for Understanding the Canonical Process," in *Reworking the Bible: Apocryphal and Related Texts from Qumran,* ed. Esther G. Chazon, Devorah Dimant, and Ronald A. Clements. STDJ 58 (Leiden: Brill, 2005), 85-104; and "Rewritten Bible," in *EDSS,* 2:777-81.

Ezek 2:1; 8:5, etc.), and Daniel's falling unto his face "into a trance" yet being lifted up by the angel (Dan 8:17-18 and Ezek 1:28–2:2, 3:23-24).[28] Furthermore, the arrogance of Antiochus is expressed in Dan 8:10 in mythological terms: the horn is growing as high as the host of heaven, causing some of the stars to fall to the ground to be trampled on. The same myth underlies the song in Isaiah 14 taunting the king of Babylon. The prophet mocks the fallen tyrant king, who wanted to raise his throne "above the stars of God" (Isa 14:13), with the words, "How you are fallen from heaven, O Day Star, son of Dawn!" (Isa 14:12).[29]

Daniel's Final Vision (Daniel 10–12)

We have seen thus far that the authors of Daniel's court tales and of his first two visions extensively reworked the older sources. It should come as no surprise that a Jewish text, whose primary objective it is to predict the demise of Antiochus's oppressive regime, employs language and theology at home in Israel's prophetic Scriptures. The case can nowhere be made more compellingly than with regard to Daniel 10–12, Daniel's final vision. Michael Fishbane's apt characterization of chapter 11 as "a text saturated with reworked passages from the pre-exilic prophets" can easily be broadened to apply to chapters 10-12 as a whole.[30]

A principal concern for the author(s) of Daniel's final vision, the most detailed in the book, is the tyrannical rule of Antiochus.[31] Antiochus's aggressive

---

28. Goldingay, *Daniel*, 202.

29. Joseph Blenkinsopp, *Opening the Sealed Book: Interpretations of the Book of Isaiah in Late Antiquity* (Grand Rapids: Eerdmans, 2006), 16: "This would suggest that the Daniel group read this chapter (Isa 14:3-23) as referring to the contemporary tyrant, a procedure familiar from the Qumran pesharim."

30. Michael Fishbane, "From Scribalism to Rabbinism: Perspectives on the Emergence of Classical Judaism," in *The Garments of Torah: Essays in Biblical Hermeneutics* (Bloomington: Indiana University Press, 1989), 69; see also his *Biblical Interpretation in Ancient Israel* (Oxford: Clarendon, 1985), 443-99, 506-24, the most extensive treatment of biblical interpretation in Daniel. There Fishbane calls Daniel 9–12 an "anthologizing of old prophetic pronouncements" and "a coherent formulation of an apocalyptic programme out of many earlier prophetic pronouncements" (515).

31. Victor Tcherikover, "Antiochus' Persecution of Judaism," in *Hellenistic Civilization and the Jews* (1959; repr. Peabody: Hendrickson, 1999), 175-203; Otto Mørkholm, *Antiochus IV of Syria* (Copenhagen: Gyldendal, 1966); Jürgen-Christian Lebram, "König Antiochus im Buch Daniel," *VT* 25 (1975): 737-72; Steven Weitzman, "Plotting Antiochus's Persecution," *JBL* 123 (2004): 219-34; and Hanan Eshel, "The Roots of the Hasmonean Revolt: The Reign of Antiochus IV," in *The Dead Sea Scrolls and the Hasmonean State*. SDSSRL (Grand Rapids: Eerdmans and Jerusalem: Yad Ben-Zvi, 2008), 13-27.

nature, his assault on the righteous of Israel, as well as the concomitant silence of God in the face of such evil all begged for an explanation. The explanation comes in the form of an extended *ex eventu* prophecy about the history of the Macedonian kingdom, beginning with the Persian kings, who are defeated by Alexander the Great (11:2-4). The narrative pace then slows down and the focus shifts to the history of the Ptolemies and the Seleucids and their dealings with Israel (11:5-39). The revelation culminates, finally, in an erroneous prediction of the death of Antiochus (11:40-45). The book's final section as a whole can be broken down into three main parts: the circumstantial introduction (10:1–11:1), the revelation report (11:2–12:4), and the conclusion (12:5-13). We find in the introduction and the revelation in particular that considerable exegetical attention is spent on explaining the nature of Antiochus's oppressive regime and the delay in its defeat. It will be helpful to examine a few examples in greater detail.

Daniel 10 is the narrative overture to the book's climactic conclusion. The purpose of the chapter is to inform the reader of the circumstances of the vision, to describe Daniel's preparatory rites that make him available for the encounter with the divine, and to relate his exchange with the angelic figure. Throughout the scene, Daniel's visionary experience is portrayed in overtly prophetic terms. Daniel does not emerge from this episode as a prophet in his own right, but the reader is nonetheless struck by the extent to which the author reaches back and uses the language of the prophetic call narrative, specifically that of Ezekiel (Ezekiel 1–3) and Isaiah (Isaiah 6), to tell his own story.[32] It was not the call *per se* but their visionary dimension that made these prophetic stories such fertile interpretive ground.

Chapter 10 opens with the remark that Daniel received understanding "in the vision" (בַּמַּרְאֶה, Dan 10:1), a phrase reminiscent of the introductory clauses to both Ezekiel's (מַרְאוֹת אֱלֹהִים, Ezek 1:1) and Isaiah's (וָאֶרְאֶה אֶת־אֲדֹנָי, Isa 6:1) inaugural visions.[33] Daniel's religious experience is thus firmly anchored in the prophetic tradition, and his role as the seer of the end time is cast in deliberately conventional language. Next we read of Daniel's ascetic practices that are intended to invoke further revelation (10:2-3). These are without parallel in either Ezekiel or Isaiah, where the epiphany appears spontaneous rather than induced. Daniel's ascetic discipline of fasting and abstaining from ointment over a period of three weeks is not unique but likely reflects a more common ritual practice of preparation for receiving a divine

---

32. Fishbane, "From Scribalism to Rabbinism," 68-69; Seow, *Daniel,* 157.

33. In addition, Isa 6:1; Ezek 1:1-3; and Dan 10:1 all include a chronological formula that dates the vision according to the life of a king.

revelation.[34] If so, it marks a postexilic shift in Israel's revelatory culture from spontaneity to *askesis*.

Ezekiel received his vision in the land of Chaldeans, while standing "by the river Chebar" (Ezek 1:3). Similarly, Daniel is "standing on the bank of the great river, that is, the Tigris" (Dan 10:4; cf. 8:2). Looking up, Daniel sees a heavenly figure of extraordinary appearance, with a fiery body and resounding voice.

> I looked up and saw a man (וָאֶרָא וְהִנֵּה אִישׁ־אֶחָד) clothed in linen, with a belt of gold from Uphaz around his waist. His body was like beryl (כְתַרְשִׁישׁ), his face like lightning (כְּמַרְאֵה בָרָק), his eyes like flaming torches (כְּלַפִּידֵי אֵשׁ), his arms and legs like the gleam of burnished bronze (כְּעֵין נְחֹשֶׁת קָלָל), and the sound of his words like the roar of a multitude. (Dan 10:5-6)

Almost every element in Daniel's description of the angel has a direct parallel in Ezekiel's encounter with the divine in Ezekiel 1. Daniel tells us that he saw "a man," whereas Ezekiel merely states that he saw "something like a man" (דְּמוּת כְּמַרְאֵה אָדָם, Ezek 1:26). Ezekiel then goes on to describe in lush details how this figure is engulfed in fire and girded at "the loins" (Ezek 1:27). Beneath the humanlike figure Ezekiel sees the divine throne chariot, whose wheels are "like the gleaming of beryl" (כְּעֵין תַּרְשִׁישׁ, Ezek 1:16). The throne is surrounded by creatures who constantly move "like a flash of lightning" (כְּמַרְאֵה הַבָּזָק, Ezek 1:14). In their midst Ezekiel sees something "like torches" (כְּמַרְאֵה הַלַּפִּדִים, Ezek 1:13), and their limbs are "like burnished bronze" (כְּעֵין נְחֹשֶׁת קָלָל, Ezek 1:7).[35]

Understandably, Daniel is stunned by what he sees and falls face first to the ground, but is then lifted up by the angel (Dan 10:9-10, 18), much like Ezekiel, who also falls unto his face following his vision but is told to stand up again (Ezek 1:28–2:1; again in 3:23). Throughout his visionary experience, Daniel

---

34. *T. Reuben* 1:9-10: "And after this, with determination of soul, for seven years I repented before the Lord: I did not drink wine or liquor; meat did not enter my mouth, and I did not eat any pleasurable food. Rather, I was mourning over my sin, since it was so great." Also *4 Ezra* 6:35; *2 Bar.* 5:7; 9:1; etc. And Montgomery, *Daniel*, 406-7.

35. The affinities between Ezekiel and Daniel, here and, as we saw above, in Daniel 8, are particularly intriguing and merit further thought. In the history of Israel's culture of divine revelation, both are transitional figures. Ezekiel's vision, particularly of God's presence, is heavily imbued with elements that later triggered much esoteric and mystical speculation about the heavenly realm, and Daniel's visions mark the transition from prophetic to apocalyptic eschatology; both books feature a prophet/seer at the beginning of the Babylonian captivity in exile; and a certain Danel/Daniel is mentioned by name in Ezek 14:14, together with Noah and Job, as exemplary righteous men, even though the reference is most likely not to biblical Daniel but to Dan-El in the Canaanite legend of Aqhat from Ugarit.

shows signs of great fatigue and awe and finds himself unable to speak. And so the angel touches him (Dan 10:10, 16, 18) to replenish his strength. Daniel remains speechless (נֶאֱלָמְתִּי, Dan 10:15), as Ezekiel is also "speechless" (נֶאֱלָמְתָּ, Ezek 3:26), and it is only after the angel touches his lips (נֹגֵעַ עַל־שְׂפָתָי, Dan 10:16) that Daniel is able to communicate, albeit only briefly. The touching of lips to open one's mouth is also a central motif in Isaiah's call narrative. There a seraph touches the prophet's mouth to purify it, so that Isaiah, absolved of his sins, can speak the words of God (וַיַּגַּע עַל־פִּי וַיֹּאמֶר הִנֵּה נָגַע זֶה עַל־שְׂפָתֶיךָ, Isa 6:7; cf. Ezek 2:8–3:3).[36]

To summarize our observations thus far, Ezekiel's and Isaiah's visions are antecedents of Daniel's similar encounter with the divine. The author of Daniel makes sure that Daniel's dialogue with the angel closely follows the similar experiences of his prophetic predecessors.[37] And yet, Daniel's is not a call narrative. There is no concise oracle here, no prophetic commissioning, and Daniel is not sent to the people to proclaim to them what God has decreed. Instead, he is told to "keep the words secret and the book sealed until the time of the end" (12:4), when what the angel has described will finally come true.

The narrative overture to Daniel's climactic vision (10:1–11:1) is followed by the revelation report that tells of the ruthless reign of Antiochus IV Epiphanes (11:2–12:4).[38] The review of past events, here cast as an *ex eventu* prophecy (11:2-39), continues and turns seamlessly into a true prediction of the end time and the resurrection of the dead (11:40–12:4). Both historical review and eschatological prediction are largely compilations of old prophetic oracles, pronounce-

36. George G. Nicol, "Isaiah's Vision and the Visions of Daniel," *VT* 29 (1979): 501-4, who finds in Daniel "a genuine reflection . . . on the Isaianic call tradition" (503). Whereas the touching of the lips as an act of cleansing that enables the prophet to speak is an element shared by Isaiah and Daniel, there is another parallel between the two stories that points in a different direction. Isaiah is famously commissioned to declare to the people their hardening and inability to understand. "Keep hearing, but do not understand!" (שִׁמְעוּ שָׁמוֹעַ וְאַל־תָּבִינוּ, Isa 6:9). In Daniel's case, it is not the people but the visionary who has to admit, "I heard but could not understand" (וַאֲנִי שָׁמַעְתִּי וְלֹא אָבִין, Dan 12:8). The prophet/seer himself remains perplexed in spite of the angelic interpretation!

37. For Fishbane, "From Scribalism to Rabbinism," 68-69, the story in Daniel 10 "serves to legitimate a receiver of exegetical truth *about* the older Prophecies." In Fishbane's reading, Daniel becomes a new type of prophetic figure, "a pneumatic exegete, guided by divine instruction into the true meaning of ancient oracles." We should observe, however, that Daniel never engages in any kind of exegesis in chs. 10–12. There is no ancient text to be interpreted here, so that Fishbane's claim (69) that Daniel receives some "exegetical illumination" that in turn becomes "a new mode of access to God for a new type of community" is without basis in the text. We will return to Fishbane's theses in the final section of this chapter.

38. Mathias Delcor, "L'Histoire selon le livre de Daniel, notamment au chapitre 11," in van der Woude, *The Book of Daniel in the Light of New Findings*, 365-86.

ments taken from different books in Scripture and reassembled here to tell the story of Antiochus and his imminent demise. Excerpts from the prophecies of Isaiah, Balaam, and Habakkuk in particular are reused to speak of Antiochus's military aggression, his humiliation, and the delay of his punishment.[39]

In Isa 10:20-27a, the poetic message of First Isaiah is briefly interrupted by a short prose section. This section in turn consists of two passages, each with an oracle of salvation (vv. 20-23 and 24-27). Both oracles contain a hopeful vision of the future, promising that God will relieve Israel from her oppression and deliver a remnant from total annihilation. The first oracle (Isa 10:20-23) speaks graphically of the destruction of the northern kingdom. In his anger, God has used Assyria as an instrument of judgment (see already in Isa 10:5-11). The level of destruction wrought by the Assyrians is nearly complete: "For the Lord GOD of hosts will make a full end (כִּי כָלָה וְנֶחֱרָצָה אֲדֹנָי יְהוִה צְבָאוֹת), as decreed, in all the earth" (Isa 10:23; also 28:22). The second oracle (Isa 10:24-27a), addressed to Judah, is an extension of the first. Even though the northern kingdom was destroyed by the Assyrians, Judah should not lose hope, because God's anger will be redirected away from Israel and towards Israel's enemies: "For in a very little while my indignation will come to an end (וְכָלָה זַעַם), and my anger will be directed to their destruction" (Isa 10:25).

The author of Daniel's final vision combines the wording of both Isaianic passages in his description of Antiochus's excessive arrogance: "The king shall act as he pleases. He shall exalt himself and consider himself greater than any god, and shall speak horrendous things against the God of gods. He shall prosper until the period of wrath is completed (וְהִצְלִיחַ עַד־כָּלָה זַעַם כִּי נֶחֱרָצָה נֶעֱשָׂתָה), for what is determined shall be done" (Dan 11:36). The same phraseology used in Isaiah for the destruction caused by the Assyrians is reused in Daniel for the abominable acts of the Syrian king. But why did the author of Daniel 11 choose Isaiah 10 of all oracles of doom? Even though we cannot be certain, the passages in Isaiah provide an important clue in this regard. They are linked together in that they both address the destiny of "the remnant of Israel" (שְׁאָר יִשְׂרָאֵל, Isa 10:20, a catchword that links this vision with what precedes in Isa 10:19). The role of Assyria as a divine tool is temporary only. Those who survive are the faithful community. They are not simply those who are left over but the righteous of God, constituted by their faith. Such overtones of hope for a quick end of the current calamity and the promise to the survivors, the faithful

---

39. On the following examples, see Fishbane, *Biblical Interpretation*, 489-92; Michael A. Knibb, "'You Are Indeed Wiser than Daniel': Reflections on the Character of the Book of Daniel," in van der Woude, *The Book of Daniel in the Light of New Findings*, 404-9; and "The Book of Daniel in Its Context," in Collins and Flint, *The Book of Daniel*, 1:17-18.

remnant, must have resonated well with the Jews who suffered under Antiochus's persecutions.[40]

In Num 24:15-25 we read of the fourth and climactic oracle of the seer Balaam son of Beor, whom Balak, king of Moab, hired to curse Israel. Balaam predicts the rise of a victorious king and the defeat of Israel's enemy neighbors and then, at the conclusion of his oracle, speaks of a naval invasion from Kittim: "But ships shall come from Kittim (וְצִים מִיַּד כִּתִּים) and shall afflict Asshur and Eber; and he also shall perish forever" (Num 24:24). As has long been noted, the oracle is quoted in Dan 11:30, the verse that relates how, during his siege of Alexandria, Antiochus was confronted by a Roman envoy and forced to withdraw from Egypt, a humiliating defeat that led to his attack on Jerusalem:[41] "For ships of Kittim shall come against him (וּבָאוּ בוֹ צִיִּים כִּתִּים), and he shall lose heart and withdraw. He shall be enraged and take action against the holy covenant. He shall turn back and pay heed to those who forsake the holy covenant" (Dan 11:30). It is difficult to discern exactly how the author of Daniel's final vision interpreted Balaam's oracle, though it is likely that the affliction of Asshur and Eber by the Kittim — in Daniel as well as in the Qumran pesharim, "Kittim" is a cipher for the Romans — was interpreted to refer to the Syrians and the eastern part of the Seleucid empire and the final clause in Num 24:24 ("and he also shall perish forever") as a reference to Antiochus specifically.[42]

---

40. Brevard S. Childs, *Isaiah*. OTL (Louisville: Westminster John Knox, 2001), 93-94, makes much of the fact that, in addition to using the exodus from Egypt as a primary interpretive motif (Isa 10:24), both passages in Isa 10:20-27 also interpret earlier *written* sections of Isaiah's prophecies: "The distinctive feature of these two passages lies in the widespread usage of texts from the earlier Isaianic corpus. . . . What is reflected in these passages is a serious wrestling with the substance of the Isaianic tradition, already in a largely written form, in an effort to interpret the content of the prophetic word in a changing context. The point is not that editors simply adjusted the tradition to meet new historical realities, but rather that the coercion of the authoritative biblical text itself pressed the believing community to explore the fuller meaning of the prophetic witness as an ongoing extension of divine revelation that guided its faith and practice." Daniel's vision in chs. 10-12 presents another extension of Isaiah's divine revelation and continues the process of "wrestling with the substance of the Isaianic tradition" that begins within First Isaiah. Daniel's interpretive community, too, is part of Isaiah's faithful remnant and recipient of the prophetic promise. Childs's fixation on the *written* Isaianic traditions is problematic, as it deliberately excludes any oral channels of transmission, which, as we are only beginning to appreciate, were immensely significant, but the point Childs makes is important. The reuse of Scripture often is an ongoing, multilayered and evolving process, roughly analogous to the growth of books such as Isaiah or *1 Enoch*, not merely a matter of promise and fulfillment.

41. H. Louis Ginsberg, "The Oldest Interpretation of the Suffering Servant," *VT* 3 (1953): 401; Tcherikover, *Hellenistic Civilization*, 185-86; Lacocque, *The Book of Daniel*, 228-29; Collins, *Daniel*, 384.

42. Knibb, "The Book of Daniel in Its Context," 18.

The *angelus interpres* predicts Antiochus's ultimate demise — but it has not yet occurred, and the persecutions are still raging on. The community faces a delay between the promise and its fulfillment, between Daniel's visions of Antiochus's death, beginning with the execution of the horn that speaks arrogantly in Daniel 7, and the violence that is happening on the ground. And so, in an effort to respond to, and to explain God's seeming inertness in the face of the community's suffering, the author invokes yet another earlier prophecy, this time from the prophet Habakkuk. Having complained repeatedly to God that, in spite of the oppression by an invader, God remains silent and does nothing to stop the violence (an apt situation for Daniel to quote!), the prophet Habakkuk now stands watch to wait for a response. In his response, God instructs Habakkuk to write down the next vision and to await its fulfillment.

> For there is still a vision for the appointed time; it speaks of the end, and does not lie. If it seems to tarry, wait for it; it will surely come, it will not delay. (Hab 2:3)

כִּי עוֹד חָזוֹן לַמּוֹעֵד וְיָפֵחַ לַקֵּץ וְלֹא יְכַזֵּב
אִם־יִתְמַהְמָהּ חַכֵּה־לוֹ כִּי־בֹא יָבֹא לֹא יְאַחֵר:

We hear clear echoes of Habakkuk's oracle no fewer than three times in Daniel's vision. In chapter 10 the interpreting angel explains to Daniel that he was sent to help him understand what is to happen in the end of time, "for there is a further vision for those days" (כִּי־עוֹד חָזוֹן לַיָּמִים, 10:14). In Dan 11:27-28 the angel "predicts" Antiochus's first campaign into Egypt and his encounter with Ptolemy Philometor. Their exchange of lies will not endure, however, "for there remains an end at the appointed time" (כִּי־עוֹד קֵץ לַמּוֹעֵד, 11:27; cf. 11:29). And similarly in Dan 11:35 the angel repeats the promise that the end of time has not yet been reached, "for there is still an interval until the time appointed" (עַד־עֵת קֵץ כִּי־עוֹד לַמּוֹעֵד).

Such repeated appeal to Habakkuk's oracle underscores its significance in Daniel's revelation as a source of consolation and assurance.[43] It seeks to convey that, since the ultimate defeat of Antiochus is part of the end time which has not yet arrived, the faithful are not to lose hope but should endure until "the time appointed."

Towards the end of Daniel's vision, one particular group is singled out for the critical role its members play in the drama of the end time. "The wise" (הַמַּשְׂכִּלִים) are mentioned a few times here, though we learn relatively little

---

43. Fishbane, *Biblical Interpretation,* 492. See also Dan 8:17, 19.

about them.[44] They first appear in Dan 11:33, where they are said to give under-standing to "the many" (יָבִינוּ לָרַבִּים). Using similar language, the angel explains a little bit later that the wise "lead many to righteousness" (מַצְדִּיקֵי הָרַבִּים, 12:3). We may assume that they were a group of religious instructors, who inspired oth-ers through their teachings. In spite of — or perhaps, because of — their special status, they are not immune to the persecutions, and some of them will fall and die (Dan 11:33-35). But their reward will be great: they will be raised from the dead, and they will "shine like the brightness of the sky . . . , like the stars forever and ever" (12:3).

It has long been recognized that the language here used to describe "the wise" is taken from the prophet Isaiah, and specifically, from the last Servant Song (Isa 52:13–53:12). The anonymous Servant is said in Isa 53:11 to render many righteous: "The righteous one, my servant, shall make many righteous" (יַצְדִּיק צַדִּיק עַבְדִּי לָרַבִּים). Even the root שכל, from which derives the desig-nation "the wise," is already attested in the opening words of the Servant Song, as H. L. Ginsberg noted: "So, my servant shall prosper" (הִנֵּה יַשְׂכִּיל עַבְדִּי, Isa 52:13).[45] This makes Daniel 11–12 the oldest known interpretation in which the servant figure is identified with a group.

The author of Daniel's vision has identified the suffering servant in Isaiah with "the wise" and the many of the Isaianic passage with the many of his own day. The identification gives meaning to their suffering and implies that the current period of persecution will be followed by their vindication. While "the wise" will receive their postmortem reward, the wicked will awaken "to shame and everlasting contempt" (לַחֲרָפוֹת לְדִרְאוֹן עוֹלָם, Dan 12:2). This language, too, is taken from the prophet Isaiah, in this case from the final prose oracle, which describes a gruesome scene in which the priests go out and "look at the dead bodies of the people who have rebelled against me . . . they shall be an ab-horrence to all flesh" (Isa 66:24). The word for "abhorrence" (דִּרְאוֹן) occurs only in these two texts in the Hebrew Bible, and in both cases the shame is thought to be everlasting. Daniel takes the eschatological passages in Isaiah to the next level, as it were, so that "Third Isaiah reads like a description of the time of the writing of Daniel."[46]

---

44. Montgomery, *Daniel*, 458; more recently, Charlotte Hempel, "*Maskil(im)* and *Rabbim: From Daniel to Qumran*," in *Biblical Traditions in Transmission: Essays in Honour of Michael A. Knibb*, ed. Hempel and Judith M. Lieu. JSJSup 111 (Leiden: Brill, 2006), 133-56, with further bibliog. Most scholars suppose that the final editors of the book of Daniel were among "the wise."

45. Ginsberg, "The Oldest Interpretation," 400-404; Fishbane, *Biblical Interpretation*, 493; Nickelsburg, *Resurrection, Immortality, and Eternal Life*, 23-43; Knibb, "'You Are Indeed Wiser,'" 406-7.

46. Nickelsburg, *Resurrection, Immortality, and Eternal Life*, 34.

The Use of Scripture in Daniel: A Methodological Outlook

In his study of inner-biblical interpretation, Michael Fishbane has provided a thorough analysis of Daniel's prevalent recourse to earlier scriptural passages.[47] Surveying a vast amount of biblical materials, Fishbane divides all of inner-biblical exegesis into four categories: scribal, legal, aggadic, and mantological exegesis. For Fishbane, Daniel is a prime example of the latter category, mantological exegesis, which he defines as "the study of material which is ominous or oracular in scope and content."[48] The assumption is that by the time of Daniel's composition, the late biblical period, the precise meaning of the ancient prophecies, much like that of oracles, visions, or omens, was no longer self-evident and in dire need of explanation. It could be that a prophecy had become obscure and hence needed to be interpreted, that it was found to have failed altogether, or that it simply needed to be brought in line with current historical events. Because of this oracularization of Scripture, the words of the prophets themselves now became the subject of considerable exegetical attention; they had to be decoded and, in a sense, translated so that they could be updated and reapplied to the current situation.

It is easy to see why Fishbane chose to classify Daniel under the rubric "mantological exegesis of dreams, visions, and omens." For one, like Joseph before him, Daniel is given the rare ability to interpret dreams. Fishbane stresses two aspects in particular, the ominous nature of the dreams and the fact that the report of Daniel's own dream is based on a written text (Dan 7:1, "Then he [Daniel] wrote down the dream."). The dream is first properly recorded and only then interpreted, stemma by stemma. Another reason for Fishbane to label Daniel's exegesis as "mantological" undoubtedly is the frequent use of the word "interpretation," פִּשְׁרָה, in Daniel.[49] In selecting his four principal categories, Fishbane was eager to establish an unbroken, organic connection between biblical and extrabiblical, specifically rabbinic exegesis. "Mantological exegesis" as a category was undoubtedly inspired by the Qumran pesharim, which are overtly mantological.[50] A third reason, finally, is Daniel 9, the story in which

---

47. *Biblical Interpretation,* 474-524.

48. *Biblical Interpretation,* 443. He explains further, "For introductory purposes and preliminary consideration, the various mantological genres may be subdivided into two basic types: dreams, visions, and omens — visual phenomena — on the one hand; and oracles-auditory phenomena — on the other."

49. See note 7 above.

50. Fishbane explicitly makes that connection (*Biblical Interpretation,* 447). See also James L. Kugel, "The Bible's Earliest Interpreters," *Proof* 7 (1987): 275-76: "'Mantological exegesis' was no doubt encouraged by such phenomena as Qumranic pesher."

Daniel inquires into Jeremiah's prophecy that the exile will last seventy years (Jer 25:11-12; 29:10). The chapter is of critical importance for Fishbane to establish Daniel as an exegete of the written, sacred prophecy of old.[51]

Fishbane has greatly raised our awareness of Daniel's thorough reworking of Israel's Scriptures. As a particular technique of explaining texts of oracular content through proper interpretation, Fishbane's model of "mantological exegesis" is enlightening and impressively consistent. As a model that seeks to explain Daniel's use of Scripture, however, it fails, in my opinion, rather drastically, and for several reasons. First, even the casual reader of the biblical book will notice how chapter 9 stands out from its context. It interrupts the sequence of Daniel's visions that begins in chapters 7 and 8 and continues in chapters 10-12. Daniel is not distressed in chapter 9, nor does he have a vision, and there is no angelic dream interpretation either. Most strikingly, Daniel's lengthy prayer is a penitential prayer, whose Deuteronomic theology is strangely at odds with its present, apocalyptic context.[52] To find in Daniel 9 a model for Daniel's "mantological exegesis," then, misses the obvious tension that exists between this chapter and its context.

Second, Fishbane rightly points out that God gave both Joseph and Daniel the ability to interpret dreams. But this is a motif in the biblical text — it says nothing about the way in which the biblical authors rework earlier passages from Scripture. Commenting on Daniel 10–11, for example, Fishbane claims that Daniel acts as "a new type of 'prophetic' figure — a pneumatic exegete, guided by divine instruction into the true meaning of ancient oracles."[53] But does he really? No biblical text is ever mentioned in chapters 10-12, and Daniel does not act as an interpreter. The biblical author's reworking of earlier material is altogether different from Daniel's acting as an inspired exegete (which, it turns out, he does not), and the two should not be confused.

51. Lester L. Grabbe, "The End of the Desolations of Jerusalem: From Jeremiah's 70 Years to Daniel's 70 Weeks of Years," in *Early Jewish and Christian Exegesis: Studies in Memory of William Hugh Brownlee*, ed. Craig A. Evans and William F. Stinespring. Homage Series 10 (Atlanta: Scholars, 1987), 67-72; and "The 70-Weeks Prophecy (Daniel 9:24-27) in Early Jewish Interpretation," in *The Quest for Context and Meaning: Studies in Biblical Intertextuality in Honor of James A. Sanders*, ed. Craig A. Evans and Shemaryahu Talmon. Biblical Interpretation Series 28 (Leiden: Brill, 1997), 595-611.

52. The presence of a Deuteronomic prayer surrounded by apocalyptic visions, as well as the obvious friction that ensues from this juxtaposition, raises the question of authorial/redactional intention. See Rodney A. Werline, "Prayer, Politics, and Social Vision in Daniel 9," in *Seeking the Favor of God*, vol. 2: *The Development of Penitential Prayer in Second Temple Judaism*, ed. Mark J. Boda, Daniel K. Falk, and Werline. SBLEJL 22 (Leiden: Brill, 2007; 2 vols.), 2:17-32; and Pieter M. Venter, "Daniel 9: A Penitential Prayer in Apocalyptic Garb," 2:33-49.

53. Fishibane, "From Scribalism to Rabbinism," 69.

Third, it is important to consider the implications of Fishbane's category "mantological exegesis" for how we think the authors of Daniel understood their scriptural base texts. The claim that the earlier passages from Scripture had become the equivalent of an oracular dream or a vision implies that the word of God had turned into an object, a written document, that had somehow become esoteric and was on the verge of losing its meaning and relevance. To save it from fading into obscurity, the sacred text needed to be decoded and its true meaning made intelligible again.[54] But what in the text of Daniel supports this notion that the received prophetic utterances had become obscure or unintelligible to the authors of Daniel, or that the sayings of the prophets were interpreted like an oracle or an omen? The textual evidence suggests otherwise.

Fishbane makes much of Daniel 9, where Daniel studies Jeremiah's prophecy. Unlike the visions, however, the text of Jeremiah is perfectly clear to him, as Daniel himself tells us plainly: "I, Daniel, *understood* (אֲנִי דָנִיֵּאל בִּינֹתִי; cf. 10:1, 14) in the books the number of years that, according to the word of the LORD to the prophet Jeremiah, must be fulfilled for the devastation of Jerusalem, namely seventy years" (Dan 9:2).[55] For Daniel there is nothing odd about Jeremiah's prophecy, and so he does not ask for an interpretation. It is precisely because he understands Jeremiah's promise of restoration (Jer 29:10-14) so well that Daniel responds in prayer.

What prompted the authors of Daniel to make such extensive use of the prophetic texts was not their feeling of a "cognitive dissonance"[56] between them and the sacred text, but — quite to the contrary! — the consonance they found between the prophetic proclamation and their own situation. "The wise," for example, did not use the language of Isaiah 53 and apply it to themselves in order to fill once again with fresh meaning what they considered an empty and esoteric epithet. The rather impressive reception history of the Servant Songs suggests that ancient interpreters, including "the wise" in the book of Daniel, found

---

54. Fishbane is rather explicit on this point: "The older divine word is sealed up; its meaning is beyond the natural ken of the faithful. Indeed, it is the very belief in the secret supernatural meaning of the old oracles which constitutes the faith of this group — and to which they are faithful. As in other instances, the *traditio* is a prolongation of the original divine *traditium*. Only now the overt meaning of this *traditium* has become covert, an esoteric symbol to be divined by agents of the divine. Hence, *traditio* is here both subversive and restorative: it subverts the meaning of the original text by transforming its exoteric content into an esoteric code, and thereby restores the *traditium* to a historical teaching"; *Biblical Interpretation*, 518.

55. Fishbane's rendering of the same verse is rather forced: "For example, it is said the Daniel 'searched' (בִּינֹתִי) the old books and found the old oracle (v. 2) whose comprehension eluded him"; *Biblical Interpretation*, 487-88.

56. *Biblical Interpretation*, 509 and 510.

nothing obscure about them. It was profoundly meaningful to them. By adopting the identity of the suffering servant, "the wise" make the powerful claim that their suffering has a vicarious quality, too, and eventually will be rewarded (Isa 53:12). Even though they have to suffer under Antiochus and some of them are certain to die, in the end they will be vindicated and glorified.

The reward for "the wise," as we have seen, will be that they will be counted among those who will rise from the dead at the end of time. The promise of the resurrection of the dead, placed towards the end of the book of Daniel as the climax of its apocalyptic promises, is articulated in a mere three verses (Dan 12:1-3). This brief passage, too, in the words of Jon Levenson, is "rich in intertextual resonances" and "looks back to multiple scriptural antecedents of its own."[57] Among them are the fourth Servant Song, the so-called Isaianic Apocalypse (esp. Isa 26:13-19), as well as Ezekiel's celebrated vision of the valley of dry bones (Ezekiel 37), in which the prophet uses the imagery of resurrection to convey the promise of Israel's full restoration. Levenson acknowledges, together with virtually all modern biblical scholars, that in Dan 12:1-3 we have the first transparent and indisputable prediction of the resurrection of the dead in the Hebrew Bible. But he is at pains to point out that, while the concrete belief in the resurrection may be an innovation of second-century B.C.E. Jews suffering under Antiochus, the language and symbolism in which this promise is couched are anything but new.

> Modern historians, researching the origin of the Jewish idea of resurrection, understandably think of it as an innovation and seek a situation of keen discontinuity in which it arose. This is not necessarily wrong, but it does underestimate the verbal particularity and the textual character of its appearance — points of greater significance to the ancient Jewish culture itself. Given the rich intertextual connections and dependence in which it is enveloped, the resurrection of the dead in Dan 12:1-3 may have seemed (at least to some sectors) much less innovative than it does to those who, ignoring its linguistic embedding, think of it as an *idea*. Much is lost when the resurrection of the dead is treated as a free-floating concept whose essence remains constant no matter what the culture in which it appears or to which it migrates. . . . In the case of Judaism from the Second Temple period onward, religious affirmations (even new ones) are so deeply embedded in the particularity of the scriptural language that efforts to disregard the latter in order to penetrate back to a core "idea" only lead us into grave misunderstanding.[58]

57. Jon D. Levenson, *Resurrection and the Restoration of Israel: The Ultimate Victory of the God of Life* (New Haven: Yale University Press, 2006), 201.

58. Levenson, *Resurrection and the Restoration*, 185.

The point is immediately relevant for our discussion, too. The literal expectation of the resurrection of the dead may be new in Daniel, but the language in which it is articulated is not. This passage, like many others we have looked at, is rich in biblical allusions. Its author reaches back to earlier texts, not because these passages had become unintelligible or obscure, let alone in order to explain them, but rather because they remained profoundly meaningful. They provided the author with language, even though there is no explicit citation of Scripture, here or elsewhere in the book. The book of Daniel positions itself prominently in the prophetic tradition. Its authors continue to speak in the prophetic idiom, and, by doing so, make a powerful claim to prophetic, that is, revelatory authority.[59]

This raises a number of questions students of inner- and early postbiblical interpretation will have to address with greater clarity. I name two. The first concerns the general question of how best to approach the material before us, biblical and extrabiblical. The modern division of ancient biblical exegesis into fixed categories — aggadic *vs.* mantological; allusion *vs.* quotation; etc. — introduced by Fishbane and since then developed further by several scholars of inner-biblical interpretation, necessarily implies an imposition of *our* categories onto the text, an imposition that will always seem arbitrary. Rather than organizing the material around our rubrics, we may be well advised to move away from these categories altogether. An alternative approach would be to reconstruct a history of early biblical interpretation in Second Temple Judaism.[60] Clearly, the ways in which the Bible was read underwent significant changes from the Persian to the Hellenistic to the Roman period. With the full publication of the Dead Sea Scrolls and an improved understanding of the apocryphal and early pseudepigraphic Jewish literature, we can now begin to describe some major trends and developments in Israel's use of Scripture from the Babylonian exile to the Mishnah. The book of Daniel occupies a prominent place, in that, as we have seen, it makes extensive use of Scripture and yet soon after its completion became the subject of extensive interpretation itself.[61] What is more, its

59. Daniel is firmly rooted in the prophetic tradition and, in more than one way, forms its direct extension. Our earliest sources clearly thought of Daniel as a prophet (4QFlor ii.3; Matt 24:15; *Ant.* 10.267-68); see Klaus Koch, "Is Daniel Also Among the Prophets?," *Int* 39 (1985): 117-30.

60. This was already suggested by Kugel, "The Bible's Earliest Interpreters," 276.

61. The colorful reception history of the book of Daniel has attracted significant attention over the last decade. See, e.g., Matthias Henze, *The Madness of King Nebuchadnezzar: The Ancient Near Eastern Origins and Early History of Interpretation of Daniel 4.* JSJSup 61 (Leiden: Brill, 1999); Mariano Delgado, Klaus Koch, and Edgar Marsch, eds., *Europa, Tausendjähriges Reich und Neue Welt: Zwei Jahrtausende Geschichte und Utopie in der Rezeption des Danielbuches.* Studien zur christlichen Religions- und Kulturgeschichte 1 (Freiburg: Universitätsverlag

exegetical practices anticipate similar ways of reading the Bible in postbiblical Jewish literature.

Second, we have seen in Daniel a dizzying array of ways in which the authors engage with the received tradition. The tradents of the early Daniel material were also its authors, its editors were also its interpreters, and the people whom we consider Daniel's final redactors, "the wise," were religious instructors during trying times. Similarly, the processes of textual composition, its *Fortschreibung,* transmission, and dissemination were complex and intertwined with one another. How exactly, then, are we to understand the interaction of these redactors/authors with Scripture? It seems obvious that their engagement with the received tradition went significantly beyond the mere reading and interpretation of some text passages handed down to them on ancient scrolls.

In recent years scholars from a growing number of fields across the humanities have come to understand the significance of orality and oral performance for the study of ancient literature. Students of the Second Temple and early rabbinic periods in particular are beginning to realize that the cultures that produced these texts were predominantly oral and that the literature we have inherited from them went through complex textual as well as oral processes of transmission and transformation.[62] Studies on Daniel have remained largely untouched by these new developments.[63] That Judaism of the late- and

---

and Stuttgart: Kohlhammer, 2003); Lorenzo DiTommaso, *The Book of Daniel and the Apocryphal Daniel Literature.* SVTP 20 (Leiden: Brill, 2005); Katharina Bracht and David S. du Toit, eds., *Die Geschichte der Daniel-Auslegung in Judentum, Christentum und Islam: Studien zur Kommentierung des Danielbuches in Literatur und Kunst.* BZAW 371 (Berlin: de Gruyter, 2007); Gerbern S. Oegema, "The Reception of the Book of Daniel (and Danielic Literature) in the Early Church," in *The Pseudepigrapha and Christian Origins: Essays from the Studiorum Novi Testamenti Societas,* ed. Oegema and James H. Charlesworth. Jewish and Christian Texts in Contexts and Related Studies 4 (London: T. & T. Clark, 2008), 243-52.

62. The secondary literature on orality has grown exponentially. The classic remains Albert B. Lord, *The Singer of Tales,* ed. Stephen Mitchell and Gregory Nagy. Harvard Studies in Comparative Literature (1965; 2nd ed. Cambridge, Mass.: Harvard University Press, 2000). See also John Miles Foley, *The Singer of Tales in Performance* (Bloomington: Indiana University Press, 1995); Steven D. Fraade, "Literary Composition and Oral Performance in Early Midrashim," *Oral Tradition* 14 (1999): 33-51; Martin S. Jaffee, *Torah in the Mouth: Writing and Oral Tradition in Palestinian Judaism, 200 BCE–400 CE* (New York: Oxford University Press, 2001); Richard A. Horsley, Jonathan A. Draper, and John Miles Foley, eds., *Performing the Gospel: Orality, Memory, and Mark. Essays Dedicated to Werner Kelber* (Minneapolis: Fortress, 2006); Elizabeth Shanks Alexander, *Transmitting Mishnah: The Shaping Influence of Oral Tradition* (Cambridge: Cambridge University Press, 2006).

63. The only exception of which I am aware is Edgar Kellenberger, "Textvarianten in den Daniel-Legenden als Zeugnisse mündlicher Tradierung?" in *XIII Congress of the International*

postbiblical periods was suffused with traditions that were communicated orally hardly needs to be pointed out. What is less clear, however, is which role the oral reception and transmission of Scripture played for the Bible's earliest interpreters, including the redactors/authors of Daniel.[64]

BIBLIOGRAPHY

Commentaries

Collins, John J. *Daniel: With an Introduction to Apocalyptic Literature.* FOTL 20. Grand Rapids: Eerdmans, 1984.

———. *Daniel.* Hermeneia. Minneapolis: Fortress, 1993.

Goldingay, John E. *Daniel.* WBC 30. Dallas: Word, 1987.

Hartman, Louis F., and Alexander A. Di Lella. *The Book of Daniel.* AB 23. Garden City: Doubleday, 1978.

Koch, Klaus. *Daniel.* BKAT 22. Neukirchen: Neukirchener, 1986-.

Lacoque, André. *The Book of Daniel.* Atlanta: John Knox, 1979.

Lebram, Jürgen-Christian. *Das Buch Daniel.* ZBK 23. Zürich: Theologischer, 1984.

Montgomery, James A. *A Critical and Exegetical Commentary on the Book of Daniel.* ICC. Edinburgh: T. & T. Clark, 1927.

Seow, C. L. *Daniel.* Westminster Bible Companion. Louisville: Westminster John Knox, 2003.

Monographs, Articles, and Reviews

Collins, John J., and Peter W. Flint, eds. *The Book of Daniel: Composition and Reception.* 2 vols. VTSup 83. Leiden: Brill, 2001.

Eshel, Hanan. *The Dead Sea Scrolls and the Hasmonean State.* SDSSRL. Grand Rapids: Eerdmans and Jerusalem: Yad Ben-Zvi, 2008.

Fishbane, Michael. *Biblical Interpretation in Ancient Israel.* Oxford: Clarendon, 1985.

———. "From Scribalism to Rabbinism: Perspectives on the Emergence of Classical Judaism." In *The Garments of Torah: Essays in Biblical Hermeneutics.* Bloomington: Indiana University Press, 1989, 64-78.

Fröhlich, Ida. "Daniel 2 and Deutero-Isaiah." In van der Woude, *The Book of Daniel in the Light of New Findings,* 266-70.

Ginsberg, H. Louis. *Studies in Daniel.* New York: Jewish Theological Seminary, 1948.

———. "The Oldest Interpretation of the Suffering Servant." *VT* 3 (1953): 400-404.

Grabbe, Lester L. "The End of the Desolations of Jerusalem: From Jeremiah's 70 Years to Daniel's 70 Weeks of Years." In *Early Jewish and Christian Exegesis: Studies in Memory*

Organization for Septuagint and Cognate Studies: Ljubljana, 2007, ed. Melvin K. H. Peters. SBLSCS 55 (Atlanta: SBL, 2008), 207-23.

64. I would like to thank Professors Shira Lander, Martin Rösel, and Michael Segal, as well as my doctoral student Daewoong Kim, for their most helpful critique of earlier versions of this essay.

of William Hugh Brownlee, ed. Craig A. Evans and William F. Stinespring. Homage Series 10. Atlanta: Scholars, 1987, 67-72.

————. "The 70-Weeks Prophecy (Daniel 9:24-27) in Early Jewish Interpretation." In *The Quest for Context and Meaning: Studies in Biblical Intertextuality in Honor of James A. Sanders,* ed. Craig A. Evans and Shemaryahu Talmon. Biblical Interpretation 28. Leiden: Brill, 1997, 595-611.

Gruen, Erich S. *Heritage and Hellenism: The Reinvention of Jewish Tradition.* Berkeley: University of California Press, 1998.

Hempel, Charlotte. "Maskil(im) and Rabbim: From Daniel to Qumran." In *Biblical Traditions in Transmission: Essays in Honour of Michael A. Knibb,* ed. Hempel and Judith M. Lieu. JSJSup 111. Leiden: Brill, 2006, 133-56.

Henze, Matthias. *The Madness of King Nebuchadnezzar: The Ancient Near Eastern Origins and Early History of Interpretation of Daniel 4.* JSJSup 61. Leiden: Brill, 1999.

————. "The Narrative Frame of Daniel: A Literary Assessment." *JSJ* 32 (2001): 5-24.

Humphreys, W. Lee. "A Life-Style for Diaspora: A Study of the Tales of Esther and Daniel." *JBL* 92 (1973): 211-23.

Kellenberger, Edgar. "Textvarianten in den Daniel-Legenden als Zeugnisse mündlicher Tradierung?" In *XIII Congress of the International Organization for Septuagint and Cognate Studies: Ljubljana, 2007,* ed. Melvin K. H. Peters. SBLSCS 55. Atlanta: SBL, 2008, 207-23.

Knibb, Michael A. "'You Are Indeed Wiser than Daniel': Reflections on the Character of the Book of Daniel." In van der Woude, *The Book of Daniel in the Light of New Findings,* 399-411.

————. "The Book of Daniel in Its Context." In Collins and Flint, *The Book of Daniel,* 1:16-35.

Koch, Klaus. "Is Daniel Also Among the Prophets?" *Int* 39 (1985): 117-30.

————. "Vom profetischen zum apokalyptischen Visionsbericht." In *Apocalypticism in the Mediterranean World and the Near East,* ed. David Hellholm. Tübingen: Mohr Siebeck, 1983, 413-46; repr. *Vor der Wende der Zeiten: Beiträge zur apokalyptischen Literatur,* ed. Uwe Gleßmer and Martin Krause. Gesammelte Aufsätze 3. Neukirchen: Neukirchener, 1996, 143-78.

Kratz, Reinhard Gregor. *Translatio Imperii: Untersuchungen zu den aramäischen Danielerzählungen und ihrem theologiegeschichtlichen Umfeld.* WMANT 63. Neukirchen-Vluyn: Neukirchener, 1991.

Kugel, James L. "The Bible's Earliest Interpreters." *Proof* 7 (1987): 269-83.

Levenson, Jon D. *Resurrection and the Restoration of Israel: The Ultimate Victory of the God of Life.* New Haven: Yale University Press, 2006.

Nickelsburg, George W. E. *Jewish Literature between the Bible and the Mishnah.* 1981; 2nd ed. Minneapolis: Fortress, 2005.

Nicol, George. "Isaiah's Vision and the Visions of Daniel." *VT* 29 (1979): 501-4.

Rowley, Harold H. "The Unity of the Book of Daniel." In *The Servant of the Lord and Other Essays on the Old Testament.* Oxford: Blackwell, 1965, 249-80.

Segal, Michael. "From Joseph to Daniel: The Literary Development of the Narrative in Daniel 2." *VT* 59 (2009): 123-49.

Ulrich, Eugene C. "The Text of Daniel in the Qumran Scrolls." In Collins and Flint, *The Book of Daniel*, 573-85.

Wills, Lawrence M. *The Jew in the Court of the Foreign King: Ancient Jewish Court Legends.* HDR 26. Minneapolis: Fortress, 1990.

Woude, A. S. van der, ed. *The Book of Daniel in the Light of New Findings.* BETL 106. Leuven: Leuven University Press, 1993.

How to Make Sense of Pseudonymous Attribution: The Cases of 4 *Ezra* and 2 *Baruch*

Hindy Najman (with Itamar Manoff and Eva Mroczek)

This essay examines two texts, 4 *Ezra* and 2 *Baruch,* written shortly after the destruction of the Second Temple. The essay answers the following questions: Why are these texts attributed to ideal figures from the past? Why do they turn to traditions specifically about the figures Ezra and Baruch? What effect does this sort of attribution have on the earlier and contemporaneous literary tradition from which these texts draw?

Linked Traditions and Transmission

The ancient traditions about Ezra and Baruch are extremely diverse. This diversity is already reflected in the arrangement and editing of the biblical materials regarding these figures as well as in later Jewish and Christian traditions that continue to invoke and reuse these materials.[1] 4 *Ezra* and 2 *Baruch* are dated to the

---

1. On Ezra traditions, see e.g., Robert A. Kraft, "'Ezra' Materials in Judaism and Christianity," in *ANRW,* 2.19.1, 119-36; Theodore A. Bergren, "Ezra and Nehemiah Square Off in the Apocrypha and Pseudepigrapha," in *Biblical Figures Outside the Bible,* ed. Michael E. Stone and Bergren (Harrisburg: Trinity Press International, 1998), 340-65; Michael E. Stone, "An Introduction to the Esdras Writings," in *Apocrypha, Pseudepigrapha, and Armenian Studies: Collected Papers,* vol. 1: *Apocrypha, Pseudepigrapha, and Dead Sea Scrolls.* OLA 144 (Leuven: Peeters, 2006), 305-20. The Baruch literature is surveyed by J. Edward Wright, "Baruch: His Evolution from Scribe to Apocalyptic Seer," *Biblical Figures Outside the Bible,* 264-89, and his popular study, *Baruch Ben Neriah: From Biblical Scribe to Apocalyptic Seer* (Columbia; University of South Carolina Press, 2003).

Many thanks to my students, Nathalie Lacoste, Nicole Hilton, and Brauna Doidge, who helped with editing and assisted in the preparation of the bibliography. I also want to thank Paul Franks and Sol Goldberg for their suggestions and incisive comments.

end of the first century c.e. and have been regarded as closely related since the earliest comparative studies.[2] Most scholars assume a close textual relationship, even if, as Michael Stone notes, "the direction of the dependence is very difficult to determine."[3] *4 Ezra* and *2 Baruch,* moreover, appear together in a single Syriac manuscript.[4] In addition, the main figure in each work is from the biblical exilic past and is said to be responding to the destruction of the First Temple, a literary setting that resonated with communities living in the reality of post-70 destruction.[5] This essay highlights some deep affinities between these texts, especially in their renewal of older traditions and their representations of biblical protagonists for postdestruction audiences (post 586 B.C.E. and post 70 C.E.).

4 Ezra

4 Ezra was originally composed in Hebrew or Aramaic. While the Semitic original is now lost,[6] the text survived because it was widely disseminated in Chris-

---

2. Robert H. Charles, "II Baruch, or the Syriac Apocalypse of Baruch," in *APOT,* 2:476-77; Klaus Berger, with Gabriele Fassbeck and Heiner Reinhard, *Synopse des Vierten Buches Esra und der Syrischen Baruch-Apokalypse.* Texte und Arbeiten zum neutestamentlichen Zeitalter 8 (Tübingen: Francke, 1992).

3. Michael E. Stone, *Fourth Ezra: A Commentary on the Book of Fourth Ezra.* Hermeneia (Minneapolis: Augsburg Fortress, 1990), 39; see also Gwendolyn B. Sayler, *Have the Promises Failed? A Literary Analysis of 2 Baruch.* SBLDS 72 (Chico: Scholars, 1984), 106.

4. Stone, *Fourth Ezra,* 6. The Codex Ambrosianus (7a1), dated to the sixth or seventh century c.e., is the only manuscript that contains the entire *Syriac Apocalypse of Baruch.* See Albertus F. J. Klijn, "2 (Syriac Apocalypse of) Baruch," in *OTP,* 1:616; Mark F. Whitters, *The Epistle of Second Baruch: A Study in Form and Message.* JSPSup 42 (London: Sheffield Academic, 2003), 4.

5. Even though the *terminus ad quem* of both texts is debated, their composition is usually dated after the destruction of the Second Temple in 70 C.E. For an analysis of the internal debate, see Stone, *Fourth Ezra.* For an evaluation of the research regarding the dating of *2 Baruch,* see Sayler, *Have the Promises Failed?,* 104-10. On the postdestruction social context of the works, see Bruce W. Longenecker, "Locating 4 Ezra: A Consideration of Its Social Setting and Functions," *JSJ* 28 (1997): 271-93; Philip F. Esler, "The Social Function of 4 Ezra," *JSNT* 53 (1994): 99-123; and J. Edward Wright, "The Social Setting of the Syriac Apocalypse of Baruch," *JSP* 16 (1997): 81-96. For historical and literary context, as well as thematic links between the works, see also John J. Collins, "After the Fall: 4 Ezra, 2 Baruch, and the Apocalypse of Abraham," in *The Apocalyptic Imagination: An Introduction to Jewish Apocalyptic Literature.* 2nd ed. BRS (Grand Rapids: Eerdmans and Livonia: Dove, 1998), 194-232.

6. On the original language of the text, see among others Joshua Bloch, "The Esra Apocalypse: Was It Written in Hebrew, Greek or Aramaic?" *JQR* 48 (1958): 279-94; Stone, *Fourth Ezra,* 10-11; Stanisław Medala, "The Original Language of 4 Esdras," in *Intertestamental Essays in Honour of Józef Tadeusz Milik,* ed. Zdzisław J. Kapera. Qumranica Mogilanensia 6 (Kraków: Enigma, 1992), 313-26.

tian circles.[7] The extent of its dissemination is evident from the abundant tertiary and quaternary translations — Syriac and Latin, but also Ethiopic, Armenian, and Arabic, with fragments in Coptic and Georgian as well — that stem from a secondary Greek edition, which is extant only in a few quotations and one papyrus fragment (POxy1010) that preserves 15:57-59.[8] Extensive work has been done to reconstruct the Greek version of *4 Ezra*. The result of this work is an elaborate model describing the evolution of the text through its translations[9] and demonstrating a significant Christian influence.[10]

The Latin tradition of *4 Ezra* presents an interesting and complex case of textual transmission. As a result of this long process, *4 Ezra* is associated with two additional texts, namely *5* and *6 Ezra*, which appear respectively as chapters 1–2 and 15-16 in the Latin text.[11] These works have traditionally been described as Christian additions to the original nucleus of *4 Ezra*, but this position has been rethought and there are now more nuanced discussions of the religious context for *2 Baruch* and *4 Ezra*. For example, Robert Kraft has questioned the traditional identification of *5 Ezra* as a Christian text,[12] and, more recently, John Marshall has argued that *6 Ezra* should be understood as a product of a Jewish author from Asia Minor.[13]

While these much needed reevaluations of the text destabilize existing as-

---

7. On the transmission and use of such works by Christians, see the essays collected in James C. VanderKam and William Adler, eds., *The Jewish Apocalyptic Heritage in Early Christianity.* CRINT 3.4 (Assen: Van Gorcum and Minneapolis: Fortress, 1996).

8. Stone, *Fourth Ezra,* 1-9; Bruce M. Metzger, "The Fourth Book of Ezra," in *OTP,* 1:518-19.

9. Stone, *Fourth Ezra,* 3; Theodore A. Bergren, "Christian Influence on the Transmission History of 4, 5, and 6 Ezra," in VanderKam and Adler, *The Jewish Apocalyptic Heritage in Early Christianity,* 102-27, 105; Robert A. Kraft, "Towards Assessing the Latin Text of '5 Ezra': The Christian Connection," in *Christians Among Jews and Gentiles: Essays in Honor of Krister Stendahl on His Sixty-fifth Birthday,* ed. George W. E. Nickelsburg and George W. MacRae (Philadelphia: Fortress, 1986), 158-69.

10. Bergren, "Christian Influence," 107-13.

11. Bergren, "Christian Influence," 113-20, 127. See also Albertus F. J. Klijn, *Die Esra-Apokalypse (IV. Esra): Nach dem lateinischen Text unter Benutzung der anderen Versionen übersetzt und herausgegeben.* GCS (Berlin: Akademie, 1992).

12. In "Towards Assessing the Latin Text of '5 Ezra,'" Kraft addresses the question of 5 Ezra's "Christianity": "Unless we assume that whenever words and phrases that occur in 'biblical' writings are also found elsewhere, the extra-biblical uses must be derivative, there is no way to determine whether a writing such as 5 Ezra is dependent on scriptural texts, is used by scriptural texts, or independently reflects the same sort of language that also appears in scriptural texts. In general, the parallels between 5 Ezra and early Christian literature are not sufficiently characteristic of Christian interests and activities to be persuasive" (165-66).

13. John W. Marshall, "6 Ezra and Apocalyptic Judaism in Asia Minor," paper presented at the Seminar for Culture and Religion in Antiquity, University of Toronto, February 9, 2009.

sumptions about religious provenance, other approaches to the transmission history of such materials might be more illuminating. Instead of categorizing these texts in terms that still follow the established dichotomy between "Jewish" and "Christian" traditions, we might ask different kinds of questions: How do these texts expand older materials? What connection do these older materials have to the biblical figure of Ezra or to traditions tied to him? What common concepts and traditions do these Ezra traditions share with the texts attributed to another scribal-prophetic figure, Baruch?

2 Baruch

The whole of 2 *Baruch* is extant in one Syriac manuscript datable to the sixth or seventh century.[14] The epistle which appears at the end of the work is preserved in some Syriac manuscripts.[15] There is also a full Arabic version translated from the Syriac.[16] The surviving versions of 2 *Baruch*, like the surviving versions of 4 *Ezra*, are secondary or tertiary translations. A Syriac manuscript claims a Greek version as its *Vorlage*, and scholars believe that the Greek text was translated from a Hebrew — or at the very least a Semitic, i.e., Hebrew or Aramaic — original.[17] The transmission histories of 4 *Ezra* and 2 *Baruch*, then, seem to have followed a similar trajectory. Like the Ezra materials, Baruch literature shows Christian influence, including striking parallels with early Christian literature, e.g., the New Testament.[18] The consensus, however, is that the *Apocalypse of Baruch* was composed by a Jewish author living in the land of Israel soon after the destruction of the Second Temple.[19]

14. See Sven Dedering, "Apocalypse of Baruch," in *The Old Testament in Syriac, according to the Peshiṭta Version* 4.3 (Leiden: Brill, 1973); Robert H. Charles, *The Apocalypse of Baruch Translated from the Syriac* (London: Black, 1896); Klijn, "2 (Syriac Apocalypse of) Baruch"; Pierre-Maurice Bogaert, *L'Apocalypse de Baruch: Introduction, Traduction du Syriaque et Commentaire*. 2 vols. SC 144-45 (Paris: Cerf, 1969).

15. On these manuscript witnesses, see Whitters, *The Epistle of Second Baruch*, 13, and Klijn's "Introduction," in *OTP*, 1:616.

16. Fred Leemhuis, Albertus F. J. Klijn, G. J. H. van Gelder, eds., *The Arabic Text of the Apocalypse of Baruch: Edited and Translated with a Parallel Translation of the Syriac Text* (Leiden: Brill, 1986).

17. Albertus F. J. Klijn, "The Sources and Redaction of the Syriac Apocalypse of Baruch," *JSJ* 1 (1970) 65-76.

18. See, among others, Bogaert, *L'Apocalypse de Baruch*, 1:477; and Sayler, *Have the Promises Failed?*, 159.

19. Rivka Nir, *The Destruction of Jerusalem and the Idea of Redemption in the Syriac Apocalypse of Baruch*. SBLEJL 20 (Atlanta: SBL, 2003), argues that the work is best understood in the context of early Christian traditions, despite its lack of obviously "Christian" content. Nir's

Traditions associated with the figure of Baruch multiplied: in addition to the apocryphal book of *Baruch,* we also have a Greek apocalypse, *3 Baruch,*[20] which features heavenly ascent, as well as *4 Baruch* or *Paraleipomena Ieremiou,* which is found in Greek and Ethiopic.[21] Preserved by Christians, these works exist in various versions, are the product of long processes of composition and revision, and have complex interrelationships with one another that resist categorization and that make them resistant to stemma diagrams. Rather than trying to pin down these relationships or to sift through the Jewish and Christian layers of the texts, this essay seeks to illuminate the nature of the religious-literary tradition to which these texts belong by asking how these authors drew on their earlier traditions and what made Baruch such a productive figure for the development of these biblical interpretations.

In the remainder of this essay, the focus will be on how the texts of *4 Ezra* and *2 Baruch* engage with the concepts that they inherit and transform. I focus on three overlapping concepts — or rather, clusters of concepts — that are prominent in both works: the relation between prophecy and scribalism; the journey of the sage (Ezra or Baruch) from the despair of loss and destruction to divine vision and even to the reassumption of the role of leader (e.g., lawgiver or prophet); and the varied functions of pseudepigraphic attribution. An examination of these clusters reveals the deep affinities not only between the two textual traditions, but also between the intellectual milieus and the religious concerns of the communities in which they were produced, received, and transmitted.

Scribes and Prophets

4 Ezra

Already in the earliest biblical Ezra materials, one finds a complex figure who is represented in very complicated texts from a variety of different historical peri-

---

work points out the intimate interconnectedness of the two traditions and reminds us that lack of obvious Christian references does not automatically make a work Jewish, but her distancing of the work from Jewish traditions is not ultimately convincing; see Matthias Henze's review of the work, in *JSP* 15 (2006): 145-48.

20. See Daniel C. Harlow, *The Greek Apocalypse of Baruch (3 Baruch) in Hellenistic Judaism and Early Christianity.* SVTP 12 (Leiden: Brill, 1996).

21. See Robert Kraft and Ann-Elizabeth Purintun, eds., *Paraleipomena Jeremiou.* SBLTT 1 (Missoula: Scholars, 1972); Jean Riaud, ed., *Les Paralipomènes du Prophète Jérémie: Présentation, texte original, traduction et commentaires* (Angers: Université Catholique de l'Ouest, 1994); and a new edition by Jens Herzer, *4 Baruch (Paraleipomena Jeremiou).* SBLWGRW 22 (Atlanta: SBL, 2005). Herzer concludes (xxxvi) that Greek was the original language of composition, although a Semitic original has also been proposed.

ods, both exilic and postexilic. Ezra is portrayed as a priest, a scribe, and a political leader who brings the Torah of Moses to the returning exiles, reads it and interprets it publicly, deals with legal crises, and completes the rebuilding of the temple.[22] The many aspects of Ezra's character suggested by his different roles and his various accomplishments are expanded in later Jewish traditions. Rabbinic sources describe Ezra as a second Moses: "Ezra was sufficiently worthy that the Torah could have been given through him if Moses had not preceded him" (*t. Sanh.* 4.4). This emphasizes Ezra's importance for the correct interpretation of Mosaic law (see Ezra 7:10; Neh. 8:1) and reflects a view of Ezra as an authoritative figure who has the authority of a prophet and is a precursor to the rabbinic sage. Moreover, rabbinic depictions of Ezra attribute to him important scribal activities, such as writing Psalms (*Song Rab.* 4.9) and restoring the Torah to its "original Mosaic" Assyrian characters (e.g., *b. Sanh.* 21b).[23]

4 Ezra is a significant example of an early, noncanonical (or extrabiblical) text that incorporates and combines many previous "Ezrean" and other prophetic (e.g., Mosaic, Jeremianic, and Danielic) traditions into a single pseudonymous figure. In *4 Ezra,* we find references to Ezra as an ideal scribe and teacher who is able to impart divine wisdom to his people:

> Therefore write all these things that you have seen in a book, and put it in a hidden place; and you shall teach them to the wise among your people, whose hearts you know are able to comprehend and keep these secrets. (*4 Ezra* 12:37-38)[24]

In this passage, which concludes the "eagle vision," Ezra is instructed to write down his revelation and its correct interpretation in a book and to teach it to the wise. Ezra's scribal activity thus preserves divine revelation and wisdom, which his esoteric writing transmits to the next generation of wise men.[25]

Ezra's roles as scribe and teacher are closely intertwined with "all these things that" he "has seen," and so with his prophetic status. In *4 Ezra* 12:42, he is addressed as a prophet explicitly by the people, who are anxious for his guid-

---

22. Kraft notes that the biblical accounts that depict Ezra reflect different, sometimes inconsistent understandings of this figure, and this diversity in the biblical materials corresponds to different understandings in later traditions; "'Ezra' Materials in Judaism and Christianity," 124.

23. See Najman, "Ezra: Introduction," in *The Jewish Study Bible,* ed. Adele Berlin and Marc Zvi Brettler (Oxford: Oxford University Press, 1999), 1666-71, see esp. 1669.

24. Translations of *4 Ezra* are from Metzger, *OTP.*

25. See Michael A. Knibb, "Apocalyptic and Wisdom in 4 Ezra," *JSJ* 13 (1983): 56-74. Knibb shows how *4 Ezra* links apocalyptic revelation with the idea of wisdom. The author views apocalyptic writings, including his own, to be restricted to a small circle of the wise: "the apocalypses were in some sense seen as a form of wisdom, at any rate they contain wisdom" (64).

ance and leadership: "For of all the prophets you alone are left to us, like a cluster of grapes from the vintage, and like a lamp in a dark place, and like a haven for a ship saved from a storm." Ezra, an apocalyptic seer and recipient of divine revelation, is for the first time in the text identified as a prophet, for here he plays another role by becoming a mediator between God and the people,[26] a role that the angel of God fulfilled in previous visions in 4 Ezra.[27]

The process in which Ezra's scribal and prophetic roles are fused culminates in chapter 14, where he is likened to Moses and receives direct revelation from God:

> Then he [God] said to me, "I revealed myself in a bush and spoke to Moses when my people were in bondage in Egypt; and I sent him and led my people out of Egypt; and I led him up on Mount Sinai. . . . I kept him with me many days; and I told him many wondrous things, and showed him the secrets of the times, and declared to him the end of the times. Then I commanded him, saying: 'These words you shall publish openly, and these you shall keep secret.' And now I say to you: 'Lay up in your heart the signs that I have shown you, the dreams that you have seen and the interpretations that you have heard; for you shall be taken up from among men, and henceforth you shall live with my Son and with those who are like you, until the times are ended.'" (14:3)

In order to fulfill God's commands, Ezra must convey the signs, dreams, and visions he has experienced throughout his journey, along with their proper interpretation. Hence the experience of revelation is followed by the task of dictation, i.e., by Ezra's speaking and the scribes' writing:

> And on the next day, behold, a voice called me, saying, "Ezra, open your mouth and drink what I give you to drink." Then I opened my mouth, and behold, a full cup was offered to me; it was full of something like water, but its color was like fire. I took it and drank; and when I had drunk it, my heart poured forth understanding, and wisdom increased in my breast, for my spirit retained its memory; and my mouth was opened, and was no longer closed. And the Most High gave understanding to the five men, and by turns they wrote what was dictated, in characters which they did not know. They sat forty days, and wrote during the daytime, and ate their bread at night. As for me, I spoke in the daytime and was not silent at night. So during the forty days ninety-four books were written. (14:38-44)

26. Stone, *Fourth Ezra*, 376.
27. Stone, *Fourth Ezra*, 376-77.

In this scene, highly reminiscent of Ezekiel's eating of the scroll (Ezek 2:8–3:3),[28] revelation is manifested through an ecstatic act of scribalism. The functions of the "scribe," "prophet," and "lawgiver" are therefore not separate here; instead, these functions, each of which names a traditional model of religious exemplarity, come together in a single exemplary figure. By amalgamating in Ezra the different virtues of the scribe, the teacher, and the prophet, the text renders an exemplary figure who restores both the exoteric and esoteric teachings of Mosaic Law,[29] a figure who recovers a Utopian past while creating a way for the post-70 community to deal with the harsh reality of destruction, and who personifies how a dire crisis can become a possibility for divine revelation.[30]

2 Baruch

2 Baruch offers another perspective on the conceptual and institutional connections between the prophet and the scribe. Whereas in *4 Ezra* scribalism and prophecy are linked, in *2 Baruch* they are dissociated. The distinction between these two roles is suggested by comparing Baruch of *2 Baruch* with his biblical predecessor. Baruch ben Neriah appears in the book of Jeremiah, which describes him first and foremost as a scribe and as a companion to the prophet:[31] Baruch is involved in a legal transaction on behalf of Jeremiah (Jer 32:12-16), commits Jeremiah's oracles to writing (Jer 36:4), and reads them in the court of King Jehoiakim (Jer 36:10). But, notwithstanding his importance to the Jeremiah narrative, there is in the Jeremianic traditions no evidence of Baruch's prophetic activity. Thus the figure of Baruch in *2 Baruch* illustrates a significant

---

28. Knibb, "Apocalyptic and Wisdom in 4 Ezra," 63.

29. On *4 Ezra's* conception of law in its historical context, see Stefan Beyerle, "Du bist kein Richter über den Herrn (4 Esra 7,19): Zur Konzeption von Gesetz und Gericht in 4. Esrabuch," in *Recht und Ethos im Alten Testament — Gestalt und Wirkung: Festschrift für Horst Seebass zum 65. Geburtstag*, ed. Beyerle, Günter Mayer, and Hans Strauss (Neukirchen-Vluyn: Neukirchener, 1999), 315-37.

30. See Hindy Najman, "How Should We Contextualize Pseudepigrapha? Imitation and Emulation in 4 Ezra," in *Flores Florentino: Dead Sea Scrolls and Other Early Jewish Studies in Honour of Florentino García Martínez*, ed. Anthony Hilhorst, Émile Puech, and Eibert J. C. Tigchelaar. JSJSup 122 (Leiden: Brill, 2007), 529-36.

31. The existence of a historical scribe named Baruch ben Neriah has been corroborated by the finding of a seal bearing the name "Berekhyahu son of Neriyahu, the scribe." See Matthias Henze, "From Jeremiah to Baruch: Pseudepigraphy in the Syriac Apocalypse of Baruch," in *Biblical Traditions in Transmission: Essays in Honor of Michael A. Knibb*, ed. Charlotte Hempel and Judith M. Lieu. JSJSup 111 (Leiden: Brill, 2006), 157-77, esp. 162. On Baruch's early scribal role, see, e.g., Wright, "Baruch: His Evolution," and *Baruch Ben Neriah*, 1-39.

departure from his biblical antecedent. Baruch experiences visions, is a charismatic leader, and converses regularly and directly with God. In addition, the fact that he is never identified as a "scribe" and is hardly involved in any significant scribal activity perhaps confirms the fullness of his transition into the prophetic role.[32]

Moreover, coinciding with Baruch's centrality in the narrative is Jeremiah's relative insignificance. In fact, Jeremiah is essentially *removed* from the setting at an early stage:

> And it happened after seven days that the word of God came to me and said to me: "Tell Jeremiah to go away in order to support the captives unto Babylon. You, however, stay here in the desolation of Zion and I shall show you after these days what will happen at the end of days." And I spoke to Jeremiah as the Lord commanded me. (2 *Bar.* 10:1-4)[33]

This passage from 2 *Baruch* reverses the biblical roles of Jeremiah and Baruch: God speaks directly to Baruch, who in turn delivers the divine instructions to Jeremiah. From the outset, Baruch assumes the status formerly assigned to the prophet.

The tradition that understands Baruch as Jeremiah's successor may derive from a particular passage in the book of Jeremiah, in which Jeremiah addresses a prophecy of salvation to Baruch:

> The word which the prophet Jeremiah spoke to Baruch son of Neriah, when he was writing these words in a scroll at Jeremiah's dictation, in the fourth year of King Jehoiakim son of Josiah of Judah: Thus said the LORD, the God of Israel, concerning you, Baruch: You say, "Woe is me! The LORD has added grief to my pain. I am worn out with groaning, and I have found no rest." Thus shall you speak to him: "Thus said the LORD: I am going to overthrow what I have built, and uproot what I have planted — this applies to the whole land. And do you expect great things for yourself? Don't expect them. For I am going to bring disaster upon all flesh — declares the LORD — but I will at least grant you your life in all the places where you may go." (Jeremiah 45)[34]

While the Masoretic Text of Jeremiah situates this oracle before the oracles against the nations in chapters 46–51, the Greek version of Jeremiah places the oracle to Baruch at the end of the narrative. This narrative arrangement sup-

32. Henze, "From Jeremiah to Baruch," 165-66.
33. Translations of 2 *Baruch* are from Klijn, *OTP.*
34. JPS translation.

ports an interpretation that Jeremiah's role is transferred to Baruch[35] and might therefore even provide us with a glimpse of the origin of a tradition that understood Baruch not only as Jeremiah's amanuensis, but also as his prophetic successor.

Whether or not Jeremiah 45 directly inspired the author of *2 Baruch,* the figure of Baruch in the latter narrative is a full-fledged prophet. Indeed, like Ezra in *4 Ezra,* Baruch in *2 Baruch* is conceived as a second Moses, to whom the text often likens Baruch implicitly and explicitly.[36] The decision to elevate Baruch to a prophetic status comparable to that of Moses is charged with symbolic significance: prophets may come and go, but the institution of prophecy continues. And it continues, *2 Baruch* suggests, because the scribe Baruch attains exemplary status and assumes the characteristics of the prophet Jeremiah.

Transformation and Revelation

4 Ezra

As mentioned above, when Ezra reaches the pinnacle of his journey in an ecstatic moment of revelation, he restores the Torah of Moses and also receives and copies seventy esoteric books that are to be transmitted to "the wise among your people" (*4 Ezra* 14:47). *Fourth Ezra* thus concludes with a reenactment of the Sinai revelation, linking Ezra with the prophetic archetype of Moses in a literary move that invokes traditions about Ezra as a restorer of the Torah and as a leader like Moses (cf. Neh 8:1-8). This exalted status is achieved only after Ezra undergoes a tumultuous transformation that requires his withdrawal from the community to a deserted, unbuilt space. Just as Zion is destroyed, so Ezra must experience his own near destruction in an isolated, meditative, deathlike state.[37] Only after this process can he empathize fully with Zion's destruction, offer consolation, and proceed toward his own emergence as exemplary leader for the present and future community. Over the course of these seven difficult and, at times, traumatic visions, the text of *4 Ezra* becomes a kind of instruction

---

35. Wright, "Baruch: His Evolution," 266-67.

36. Wright, "Baruch: His Evolution," 272; Henze, "From Jeremiah to Baruch," 169; and "Torah and Eschatology in the *Syriac Apocalypse of Baruch,*" in *The Significance of Sinai: Traditions About Sinai and Divine Revelation in Judaism and Christianity,* ed. George J. Brooke, Hindy Najman, and Loren T. Stuckenbruck (Leiden: Brill, 2008), 201-15.

37. Najman, "Between Heaven and Earth: Liminal Visions in *4 Ezra,*" in *Other Worlds and Their Relation to This World: Early Jewish and Ancient Christian Traditions,* ed. Tobias Nicklas et al. JSJSup 142 (Leiden: Brill, 2010), 107-18.

manual for the overcoming of destruction, the achievement of readiness for divine communication, and, finally, the attainment of wisdom.[38]

The frequent use of "wisdom terminology," especially in the seventh and final vision of *4 Ezra*, has been discussed by Michael Knibb. The transmission of esoteric knowledge to the "wise" in this vision indicates that the text is "a product of learned study intended for a learned audience."[39]

The need for knowledge and understanding recurs over the span of Ezra's seven visions. Ezra, however, is not pursuing knowledge about anything knowable; he wants instead to comprehend the incomprehensible:

> I have seen how you endure those who sin, and have spared those who wickedly have destroyed your people, and have preserved your enemies, and have not shown to anyone how your way may be comprehended. Are the deeds of Babylon better than those of Zion? Or has another nation known you besides Israel? Or what tribes have so believed your covenants as these tribes of Jacob? Yet their reward has not appeared and their labor has borne no fruit. For I have traveled widely among the nations and have seen that they abound in wealth, though they are unmindful of your commandments. (*4 Ezra* 3:30-33)

Not unlike Job, Ezra begins by questioning the logic of God's actions and by attempting to grasp through mere human reason the meaning of destruction, an approach repeated in each of the first three visions. But this path does not lead to wisdom, as the angel makes clear: "Your understanding has utterly failed regarding this world, and do you think you can comprehend the way of the Most High?" (4:1-2). His futile attempts to understand something beyond human reason leave Ezra on the verge of complete despair: "It would be better for us not to be here than to come here and live in ungodliness, and to suffer and not understand why" (4:12). The limitations of human understanding are emphasized time and time again in the first three visions. Ezra must surrender his old dispositions and ways of reasoning because, paradoxically, one can gain true knowledge only by admitting one's inability to grasp the divine.[40]

---

38. Najman, "Between Heaven and Earth."

39. Knibb, "Apocalyptic and Wisdom in 4 Ezra," 72; see also Stone's discussion on understanding and inspiration in *Fourth Ezra*, 119-24. On this theme, see also Daniel J. Harrington, "Wisdom and Apocalyptic in 4QInstruction and 4 Ezra," in *Wisdom and Apocalypticism in the Dead Sea Scrolls and in the Biblical Tradition*, ed. Florentino García Martínez. BETL 168 (Leuven: Leuven University Press and Dudley: Peeters, 2003), 345-55.

40. Isolde Andrews, "Being Open to the Vision: A Study from Fourth Ezra," *Literature and Theology* 12 (1998): 231-41.

Renunciation of human understanding is an extremely painful experience for Ezra. He expresses this difficulty immediately after his vision of the grieving woman who transforms into Zion:

> Then I was afraid, and cried with a loud voice and said, "Where is the angel Uriel, who came to me at first? For it was he who brought me into this overpowering bewilderment; my end has become corruption, and my prayer a reproach. As I was speaking these words, behold, the angel who had come to me at first came to me, and he looked upon me; and behold, I lay there like a corpse and I was deprived of my understanding. (10:27-30)

Ezra's advance towards wisdom necessitates his purification from human prejudices and conventions; he will comprehend destruction only after he recognizes the limits of human reason.

It is Ezra's surrender to God's inscrutability that makes it possible for him to receive revelation. At the beginning of the fourth vision, after staying in a deserted plain and sustaining himself with the flowers of the field, Ezra recounts: "And my mouth was opened, and I began to speak before the Most High" (9:28). This opening of the mouth depicts Ezra's speech as a passive rather than an active state; it is as if, in his liminal, deathlike condition, words are not spoken by him, but rather extracted from him by an external force. The motif is intensified in 14:40-41, when Ezra drinks the cup of divine wisdom:

> And I took it and drank; and when I had drunk it, my heart poured forth understanding, and wisdom increased in my breast, for my spirit retained its memory; and my mouth was opened, and was no longer closed.

Ezra becomes a vessel for God's wisdom, and his mouth becomes a portal from which knowledge comes forth. This transformation involves a metaphorical emptying that enables the entry of God's revelation, which will later be externalized again as it is presented to the community.[41] Hence, in the sixth vision, Ezra's old knowledge has been discarded and divine wisdom can be received; his transformation is complete:

---

41. In this context it is interesting to note the idea of human beings as vessels for the incorruptible law, as seen in *4 Ezra* 9:34-37:

> And behold, it is the rule that, when the ground has received seed . . . and when it happens that what was sown or what was launched or what was put in is destroyed, they are destroyed, but the things that held them remain; yet with us it has not been so. For we who have received the Law and sinned will perish, as well as our heart which received it; the Law, however, does not perish but remains in its glory.

> And you alone have been enlightened about this, because you have forsaken your own ways and have applied yourself to mine, and have searched out my law; for you have devoted your life to wisdom, and called understanding your mother. Therefore I have shown you this, for there is a reward laid up with the Most High. And after three more days I will tell you other things, and explain weighty and wondrous matters to you. (13:53-56)

As the visions progress, then, Ezra is engaged in two interdependent processes: on the one hand, he is reduced to a marginal state in which he nevertheless retains his mental capacity and physical integrity; on the other hand, as Ezra is emptied of his old self, his visions become more and more vivid until they reach a climax in chapter 14. Ezra's reaction to these intensifying revelatory experiences moves from surrender and receptivity to his own enactment of the wisdom he gains: stripped of his human attributes, Ezra can participate in the transmission of divine revelation.

After the first three visions, Ezra recognizes that the divine tradition of Mosaic Torah is immutable and eternal. This recognition is essential to his transformation into a prophet. For Ezra must accept both the fact of the destruction of the temple and the charge he has been given to console the remnant, a role that he cannot play without overcoming his own personal sense of loss.[42] The turning point in Ezra's capacity to mourn occurs when he consoles the grieving woman:

> Do not say that, but let yourself be persuaded because of the troubles of Zion, and be consoled because of the sorrow of Jerusalem. For you see that our sanctuary has been laid waste, our altar thrown down, our temple destroyed; our harp has been laid low, our song has been silenced, and our rejoicing has been ended. . . . Therefore shake off your great sadness and lay aside your many sorrows, so that the Mighty One may be merciful to you again, and the Most High may give you rest, a relief from your troubles. (10:20-24)

In that moment of lament, a new Ezra emerges: full of compassion, insight, and acceptance of the divine punishment of destruction. Thus the ability to mourn is acknowledged as an achievement worthy of reward:

> And behold, you saw her likeness, how she mourned for her son, and you began to console her for what had happened. For now the Most High, seeing that you are sincerely grieved and profoundly distressed for her, has shown you the brightness of her glory, and the loveliness of her beauty. (10:49-50)

---

42. For more on this dramatic conversion see Najman, "Between Heaven and Earth."

Once Ezra not only sees but also responds compassionately to the likeness of the mourning woman, he is afforded a vision of her splendor as well as her sadness: the grieving woman is transformed into Zion before his eyes.[43]

This capacity to empathize with and comfort the distressed serves Ezra well when he receives the interpretation of the fifth vision. After the people implore him not to forsake them now that "of all the prophets [he] alone [is] left to us" (12:42), Ezra answers appropriately with a prophetic address, speaking on behalf of God, just as the angel did in previous visions:[44]

> Take courage, O Israel; and do not be sorrowful, O house of Jacob; for the Most High has you in remembrance, and the Mighty One has not forgotten you in your struggle. As for me, I have neither forsaken you nor withdrawn from you; but I have come to this place to pray on account of the desolation of Zion and to seek mercy on account of the humiliation of our sanctuary. (12:46-49)

Ezra's prophetic status here follows from the enactment of his newly acquired knowledge. Able at last to identify with the destruction of Zion, Ezra is prepared to console the people.

At this point, Ezra has fully evolved into a prophetic, divinely-inspired leader — a new Moses. He is committed to the restoration of divine law (14:19-22), encourages the people with an address (vv. 27-35), and commences the final enactment of revelation in this text: the production and re-creation of the Law in the form of sacred writing (vv. 37-48).[45] Ezra has now managed to overcome his despair and to offer solace to the community. He is truly exemplary: his incredible transformation offers as a model for a devastated community.

2 Baruch

Like Ezra of *4 Ezra*, Baruch of *2 Baruch* faces the breakdown of human understanding in the face of catastrophe;[46] and like that Ezra, this Baruch travels a

---

43. On this transformation, see Edith McEwan Humphrey, *The Ladies and the Cities: Transformation and Apocalyptic Identity in Joseph and Aseneth, 4 Ezra, the Apocalypse and the Shepherd of Hermas.* JSPSup 17 (Sheffield: Sheffield Academic, 1995); and Michael E. Stone, "The City in 4 Ezra," *JBL* 126 (2007): 402-7.

44. Stone, *Fourth Ezra*, 376-77.

45. Further on this motif, see Geert Hallbäck, "The Fall of Zion and the Revelation of the Law: An Interpretation of 4 Ezra," *SJOT* 6 (1992): 263-92.

46. See Nir, *The Destruction of Jerusalem*; and Jesús María Asurmendi, "Baruch: Causes, Effects and Remedies for a Disaster," in *History and Identity: How Israel's Later Authors Viewed Its Earlier History*, ed. Núria Calduch-Benages and Jan Liesen (Berlin: de Gruyter, 2005), 187-200.

path to understanding and consolation that takes him through Jobian protest and Jeremianic lament, through barren spaces and liminal states. But, whereas Ezra's compassion for the mourning woman is the pinnacle of his transformation, Baruch's anticipatory grief for Zion's impending destruction occurs near the beginning of the narrative.[47] Having sent Jeremiah away to Babylon, Baruch sits by the doors of the temple and fasts for seven days — one of four such fasts in the work. Ritual fasting and expression of profound sorrow for Zion prepare Baruch for revelation and exemplary leadership status.

As Baruch's expression of grief ends, a voice from heaven calls to him:

> Stand upon your feet, Baruch, and hear the word of the mighty God. Because you have been astonished at that which has befallen Zion, you will surely be preserved until the end of times to be for a testimony. (2 Bar. 13:2)

The term "testimony" is typically used to describe texts, particularly Torah (e.g., Deuteronomy 31; Isaiah 8; and *Jub.* 1:1);[48] here, it serves to designate Baruch as a witness.

Yet Baruch has not yet experienced divine revelation and insight into the future. This will occur only once he removes himself from the community and fasts:

> "Go away and sanctify yourself for seven days and do not eat bread and do not drink water and do not speak to anybody. And after this time come to this place, and I shall reveal myself to you. . . ." . . . I went from there and sat in the valley of Kidron in a cave of the earth and sanctified myself there and ate no bread, but I was not hungry; I drank no water, but I was not thirsty. (2 Bar. 20:5–21:1)

Baruch, whose fasting leaves him very weak (21:26), is given strength from heaven (22:1) as he begins to speak directly with God. Baruch's future dream visions come to him as he is sitting on the ruins of the destroyed temple. Much

---

47. This feminization of Zion as a suffering mother is, of course, another parallel with *4 Ezra*. For themes of the feminine in both books, see Deiana Giovanni, "Miti di origine, miti di caduta e presenza del femminino nel 4 Esdra e nel 2 *Baruch*," *RStB* 6 (1994): 141-52. On the feminine in *4 Ezra*, see Luzia Sutter Rehmann, "Das Vierte Esrabuch," in *Kompendium Feministische Bibelauslegung*, ed. Luise Schottroff, Marie-Theres Wacker, Claudia Janssen, and Beate Wehn (Gütersloh: Kaiser, 1998), 450-58.

48. On writing and testimony, see Hindy Najman, "The Symbolic Significance of Writing in Ancient Judaism," in *The Idea of Biblical Interpretation: Essays in Honor of James L. Kugel*, ed. Najman and Judith H. Newman, JSJSup 83 (Leiden: Brill, 2004), 139-73, esp. 145-46; and Hugh G. M. Williamson, "On Writing and Witnesses," in *The Book Called Isaiah: Deutero-Isaiah's Role in Composition and Redaction* (Oxford: Clarendon, 1994), 94-115.

like Ezra, Baruch receives divine insight only under the conditions of being in a place bereft of humanly built structures. Only in that space can Baruch (or Ezra) receive revelation. His physical strength now diminished through fasts, laments, and prayers, Baruch is filled with new insight and understanding from God.

Baruch becomes an exemplar who combines divine insight and revelation with being a Sage who lives in accordance with the Torah of Moses and Wisdom.[49] Once again, any attempt to classify the text as "apocalypse" or "wisdom" is unhelpful because wisdom, apocalyptic, and Torah discourse are inextricably interwoven. Consider, for example, the explanation of what will happen to the righteous and the wicked at the appointed time:

> As for the glory of those who proved to be righteous on account of my law, those who possessed intelligence in their life, and those who planted the root of wisdom in their heart — their splendor will then be glorified by transformations, and the shape of their face will be changed in the light of their beauty so that they may acquire and receive the undying world which is promised to them. Therefore, especially they who will then come will be sad, because they despised my Law and stopped their ears lest they hear wisdom and receive intelligence. . . . Miracles, however, will appear at their own time to those who are saved because of their works and for whom the Law is now a hope, and intelligence, expectation, and wisdom, a trust. For they shall see that world which is now invisible to them, and they will see a time which is now hidden to them. (51:3-8)

2 Baruch integrates "the call to observe Torah" with "the eschatological zeal of Jewish apocalypticism," as the author accepts that wisdom, understanding and knowledge are revealed to Moses on Sinai along with the Law (e.g., 59:7).[50] This intertwined tradition is embodied by the composite figure of Baruch — the sage, the new Moses, and the apocalyptic visionary, all in one.

As described above, essential to Ezra's spiritual transformation in *4 Ezra* is learning how to lament and to console his devastated community, for it is the acquisition of this capacity that enables him to become a leader. The narrative of *2 Baruch* focuses less on a dramatic journey of conversion than on a sus-

---

49. See, e.g., Wright, *Baruch ben Neriah*, 52-62.

50. Henze, "Torah and Eschatology," 210, argues that in this way, "our author seeks to overcome the sectarian divisions that had increasingly plagued second temple Judaism," calling *2 Baruch* "an inclusive text that seeks to rid apocalyptic literature of its sectarian stigma." Henze contrasts this inclusiveness with *4 Ezra*'s set of secret books, accessible only to the few, where wisdom, understanding and knowledge are to be found (*4 Ezra* 14:46-47).

tained series of dialogues and visions in which Baruch steadily comprehends the meaning of destruction, God's future plan for Israel, and his own leadership role.[51] Baruch progresses from despair to divine insight, but, perhaps most importantly, he endures a necessary period of "mental reorientation and religious reconstruction"[52] in becoming a teacher who can transform his devastated people. He is told explicitly: "You, therefore, admonish the people as much as you can. For this is our work. For, when you instruct them, you will make them alive" (2 *Bar.* 45:1-2). The insight that Baruch receives, in other words, is meant to be externalized, passed on to his community, to which he reports three times. The three public addresses "nicely reflect the development of his own leadership and of his thoughts about what should happen after his death"[53] — that is, an evolution of the sense that the Torah is the people's one imperishable hope.

Each time Baruch leaves his people after an address, they fear that he is abandoning them. In the first such scene, Baruch tells them that his absence is only temporary while he seeks further enlightenment (34:1). In the second instance, he reassures them that they will never want for a leader who is a "sage" and a "son of Torah" even after he is gone (46:4). Finally, in the third, the people despair that "the shepherds of Israel have perished, and the lamps which gave light are extinguished, and the fountains from which we used to drink have withheld their streams. Now we have been left in the darkness . . ." (77:13-14). This time, Baruch responds:

> Shepherds and lamps and fountains came from the Law and when we go away, the Law will abide. If you, therefore, look upon the Law and are intent upon wisdom, then the lamp will not be wanting and the shepherd will not give way and the fountains will not dry up. (77:15-16)

The people's fear of abandonment, of being disoriented, is relieved by the guarantee of a future that is oriented by Torah,[54] a guarantee that serves as the heart of Baruch's letter, which comes at the end of the work:[55]

> The righteous have been assembled, and the prophets are sleeping. Also we have left our land, and Zion has been taken away from us, and we have nothing now apart from the Mighty One and his Law. Therefore, if we direct and

51. See Collins, *Apocalyptic Imagination*, 213-14, on this difference between the personal narratives in the two texts.

52. Henze, "Torah and Eschatology," 201.

53. Henze, "Torah and Eschatology," 213.

54. Henze, "Torah and Eschatology," 213.

55. On the letter specifically, see Whitters, *The Epistle of Second Baruch;* and "Testament and Canon in the Letter of Second Baruch (2 Baruch 78–87)," *JSP* 12 (2001): 149-63.

dispose our hearts, we shall receive everything which we lost again by many times. (85:3-4)

As this passage shows, Baruch's letter suggests a means of "reorientation" and "reconstruction" in the face of catastrophe. That means is Law.

In both *2 Baruch* and *4 Ezra*, then, the culmination of the hero's visionary journey is the reestablishment of the Torah.[56] But there are differences, too. In *4 Ezra*, Torah is reestablished with Ezra's rewriting of the Scriptures; in *2 Baruch*, conversely, only a letter is written. Moreover, whereas *4 Ezra* distinguishes esoteric from exoteric Scriptures, no division between public and secret books occurs in *2 Baruch*. This latter difference may reflect the dissimilar social origins of the two works. Henze argues that, in contrast to *4 Ezra*, which sets up a division between those few who can access the seventy esoteric books and the many who can only know the twenty-four public ones, *2 Baruch* is *not* a "sectarian" work, that is, not the product of a marginalized group in opposition to some "mainstream" tradition, but rather an "inclusive" work concerned for the well-being of all Israel.[57] But whether or not we interpret this difference as a firm sign of sectarian or nonsectarian origin, we can say for certain that both works participate in larger intellectual traditions about the conditions for revelation and hope in a time of catastrophe. Like Ezra, Baruch becomes a new Moses, restoring the Torah as the community's unique path and establishing optimism for a future without a temple. The restoration of Torah can happen only when Baruch, the exemplary sage and seer, has been transformed through prayer, lament, fasting, and separation from human society. For only then can he communicate his visions to his people. Instructions for a new life are revealed, literally, on the ruins of the old.

The Nature of Pseudepigraphy and the Effacement of Self

The final section of this essay will focus on pseudepigraphic attribution, an issue closely linked to the exemplary, scribal-prophetic roles of the central figure

56. Michel Desjardins, "Law in *2 Baruch* and *4 Ezra*," *SR* 14 (1985): 25-37; and Henze, "Torah and Eschatology."

57. See Henze's discussion of this as a key aspect of *2 Baruch*, where there are no "insiders" or "outsiders" — rather, the author of the text "repeatedly shows his sincere concern for the well being of Israel as a whole"; "Torah and Eschatology," 209. Based on this and other factors, Henze convincingly argues that this particular apocalyptic text did not arise from a marginalized or disenfranchised group in opposition to some "mainstream" tradition, a model that has long been considered a central feature of apocalyptic literature.

of each text. The pseudepigraphy of ancient texts is typically examined through the lens of modern conceptions of authorship. However, this can lead one to an inadequate understanding of the literary device as mere "false attribution" or "pious fraud."[58] An alternative is to consider the notion of *a discourse tied to a founder:* a practice of ascribing texts to an ideal figure, in order not only to authorize the texts in question but also to restore the figure's authentic teachings. In *Seconding Sinai,* the prime example was discourse tied to Moses.

Thus, when what we might call a "new" law — perhaps even what we might regard as a significant "amendment" of older law — is characterized as the Law of Moses, this is not to imply that it is to be found within the actual words of a historical individual called Moses. It is rather to say that the implementation of the law in question would enable Israel to return to the authoritative teaching associated with the prophetic status of Moses.[59]

Seen in these terms, pseudonymous attribution is a literary device that engages, elaborates on, and reinterprets a tradition. This is the case with the use of pseudonymous attribution in *4 Ezra* and *2 Baruch,* which may be regarded as in participating with discourses tied to Ezra and Baruch respectively.

The choice of protagonists in *4 Ezra* and *2 Baruch* is highly deliberate, for the names Ezra and Baruch invoke rich traditions. Ezra, restorer of Mosaic Law and leader of returning exiles, is a figure associated with the hope and recovery of the Second Temple. Baruch, the biblical scribe and companion of Jeremiah, is thought to be a successor of Jeremiah and his prophecy in the aftermath of destruction. But the figures to which these texts are attributed do not remain static. The expansion of the Ezra and Baruch traditions begins with their direct engagement with destruction and exile. *4 Ezra,* for instance, begins by situating its narrative in a postdestruction context:

> In the thirtieth year after the destruction of our city, I, Salathiel, who am also called Ezra, was in Babylon. I was troubled as I lay on my bed, and my thoughts welled up in my heart, because I saw the desolation of Zion and the wealth of those who lived in Babylon. (*4 Ezra* 3:1-2)

This passage is often used as evidence for the dating of *4 Ezra* to ca. 100 C.E.[60] But there is another important element at play here besides a possible cryptic reference to the date of composition. By situating Ezra in exile and describing him as a witness of destruction, the author immediately *expands* Ezra's figure;

58. See Hindy Najman, *Seconding Sinai: The Development of Mosaic Discourse in Second Temple Judaism.* JSJSup 77 (Leiden: Brill, 2003), 4-5.

59. Najman, *Seconding Sinai,* 13.

60. See Stone, *Fourth Ezra,* 9-10.

the narrative starts not in the moment of restoration, but in the midst of disaster and despair. This setting is the backdrop for Ezra's journey and the starting point for his transformation into a figure that, in the seventh vision, eventually achieves the restoration of Mosaic Law. In the course of explaining the process Ezra had to undergo in order to become a leading figure and bearer of restoration, the author of *4 Ezra* weaves new interpretation together with traditional material.

Similarly, the author of *2 Baruch* places Baruch *at the moment of destruction:*

> Now it happened on the following day that, behold, an army of the Chaldeans surrounded the city. And in the evening I, Baruch, left the people, went outside, and set myself by an oak. And I was grieving over Zion and sighed because of the captivity which had come upon the people. And behold, suddenly a strong spirit lifted me and carried me above the wall of Jerusalem. And I saw, and behold, there were standing four angels at the four corners of the city, each of them with a burning torch in his hands. (*2 Bar.* 6:1-4)

This experience transforms Baruch, granting him prophetic authority and a divine promise to remain until the end of times.[61] Later on, Jeremiah is instructed to accompany the captives of the people to Babylon (10:2-3) while Baruch stays at the site of destruction where he receives visions of the ruins of Zion. This Baruch, who remains with the remnant, becomes a model leader in a time of despair. By assuming and emulating such figures as Baruch and Ezra in pseudepigraphic attribution, the writers of these texts *become* these characters, insofar as they — like the heroes they invoke — struggle to recover a perfect, holy, and idealized past in the face of destruction.[62] Baruch and Ezra provide models for the attainment of perfection and the overcoming of hardships. The extant traditions associated with these figures confer on them their exemplary status,

---

61. *2 Bar.* 13:3: "Because you have been astonished at that which has befallen Zion, you will surely be preserved until the end of times to be for a testimony."

62. Najman, "How Should We Contextualize Pseudepigrapha?," 530. However, as John Collins has argued, this is not a straightforward process of identification; "The Idea of Election in 4 Ezra," *JSQ* 16 (2009) 83-96. Collins writes that Ezra "is evoked here as an authoritative spokesperson, to serve as the mouthpiece for the agonized reflections of the author. [But] [i]t would be too simple to regard Ezra as the author's alter ego. There is, after all, another authoritative voice in these dialogues, that of the archangel Uriel. The tension between these two voices is one of the most intriguing features of this book" (83). This tension between authoritative voices reflects the conflicted ways authors and communities negotiated a postdestruction reality. For more about the polyvocal nature of these texts, see the ensuing discussion of the imitation of other biblical figures.

but at the same time these traditions are deepened and modified to fit the context of the postdestruction communities that produced and used the texts.

Besides the pseudepigraphic attribution of the whole text to a sage who is to be emulated, another layer of exemplarity operates in *4 Ezra* and *2 Baruch:* the protagonist's emulation of other exemplary figures. There is, in other words, a double layer of exemplary emulation and interpretation. Old traditions are engaged, both by the anonymous writer, who emulates an ancient figure by writing *as* that figure, and by the text's protagonist, who imitates still other ancient figures by taking on their roles and characteristics. In *4 Ezra,* for example, Ezra is portrayed as imitating various exemplars, such as Jeremiah, Daniel, and Moses.[63] Ezra's imitation of these other figures associates their outstanding features with him, and as he proceeds through a series of visions he accumulates the knowledge and wisdom of these exemplars. The imitation of other ideal figures thus not only transforms the protagonist of *4 Ezra,* but also expands the Ezrean tradition itself, which consequently incorporates Jeremianic, Danielic, and Mosaic discourses.

This process of imitation, then, becomes an *interpretation* of older traditions through the figure of Ezra. In the fifth vision, Ezra imitates Daniel insofar as he receives apocalyptic visions:

> He said to me, "This is the interpretation of this vision which you have seen: The eagle which you saw coming up from the sea is the fourth kingdom which appeared in a vision to your brother Daniel. But it was not explained to him as I now explain or have explained it to you." (*4 Ezra* 12:10-12)

This explicit reference to Daniel and to the four kingdoms that appear in Dan 7:7 is significant for a number of reasons. The author is interpreting an older tradition that pertains to a different political setting by reimagining it in a setting relevant to his own time. The nature of this political reinterpretation has led scholars to use it as evidence for the dating of the text.[64] But there is another important aspect that should be noticed here: it is not only the anonymous author of *4 Ezra* who engages in this rereading of the Danielic text; Ezra himself also explicitly interprets an older tradition. Daniel is called Ezra's "brother," indicating an affinity between the two figures. By letting "Ezra" acknowledge Daniel's vision, the text aligns the two chronologically and conceptually, thus conceptualizing them as members of a historical and religious succession.

---

63. Najman, "How Should We Contextualize Pseudepigrapha?," 533.

64. Stone, *Fourth Ezra*, 10; for a discussion of the Eagle Vision and the dating of 4 Ezra, see Lorenzo DiTommaso, "Dating the Eagle Vision of 4 Ezra: A New Look at an Old Theory," *JSP* 20 (1999): 3-38.

A similar reference to the four kingdoms can be found in 2 *Baruch*, albeit without the explicit mention of Daniel (2 *Bar.* 39:1-8). This allusion is as fascinating and complex as the one in 4 *Ezra*. With it, the author of 2 *Baruch* gives the chronological sequence relating these two literary figures, Baruch and Daniel, a new significance: the earlier is understood here not only as preceding but also as anticipating the later, which thus in turn becomes the fulfillment of the earlier.

For 2 *Baruch*, as for 4 *Ezra*, Moses is a key model for the protagonist to imitate. Baruch, we have seen, is transformed into a prophet who, because in direct contact with God, is able to lead and inspire the people; 2 *Baruch* contains, accordingly, many explicit and implicit references to Moses and Mosaic traditions.[65] A striking example appears when Ramiel announces Baruch's death, which recalls Moses' death in Deuteronomy 34:[66]

> You will surely depart from this world, nevertheless not to death but to be kept unto (the end) of times. Therefore, go up to the top of this mountain, and all countries of this earth will pass before you, as well as the likeness of the inhabited world, and the top of the mountains, and the depths of the valleys, and the depths of the seas, and the number of rivers, so that you may see that which you leave and whither you go. This will happen after forty days. Go, therefore, now during these days and instruct the people as much as you can . . . (2 *Bar.* 76:2-5)

The comparison to Moses contributes greatly to the re-creation of Baruch as a prophetic figure and serves to confer authority upon the text.[67]

As prophetic-scribal figures and community leaders, both Baruch and Ezra take on Mosaic characteristics in the course of their transformations, and this relation to the figure of Moses raises an important question. To what extent are 2 *Baruch* and 4 *Ezra*, which are clearly not pseudepigraphically attributed to Moses, nevertheless participating in Mosaic discourse? And if they are, is their authority conferred primarily by this association with Moses, perhaps rendering Ezra and Baruch secondary to the figure of Moses? This relationship to Mosaic discourse is complex and deserves separate treatment. A few comments can, nevertheless, be made in this regard. 4 *Ezra*'s and 2 *Baruch*'s engagement in Mosaic tradition should be examined through the authors' treatment of Mosaic Law and its preservation in the context of destruction, issues central to both texts. The affiliation with Moses serves as a potent strategy for reassuring the validity of the Law at a time of political and spiritual disarray.

65. Wright, "Baruch: His Evolution," 272; Henze, "From Jeremiah to Baruch," 169.
66. Sayler, *Have the Promises Failed?*, 97.
67. Henze, "From Jeremiah to Baruch," 169.

Furthermore, the comparisons to Moses are examples of imitation, but not identification. Baruch and Ezra do not become Moses to the effacement of their own identities; rather, they are repeatedly likened to Moses while remaining (transformed and composite versions of) themselves.[68] For example, Baruch's ability to perform Mosaic intercession on behalf of the people contrasts with the figure of Jeremiah and serves to enhance ideas of succession and supersession.[69] Likewise, Ezra's affinity with Moses in *4 Ezra* is informed by existing traditions already depicting him as a second Moses (e.g., Neh 8:1-8) so that, by the time of the text's composition, the link to Moses might have already been intrinsically Ezrean.

Conclusion

The intertwined traditions of *4 Ezra* and *2 Baruch,* with their inscrutable history of Jewish and Christian transmission and translation, do not lend themselves well to the type of historical analysis that is concerned with questions of geographical, religious, and chronological provenance. But there are other kinds of questions worth asking. Attention to the way their authors worked to expand older traditions and transform ancient heroes reveals features of these texts that tell us something meaningful about the communities who produced and used them: their shared conceptions of prophecy, scribalism, and revelation; their deep concern with spiritual transformation and community survival in the wake of disaster; and their creative deployment of ancient textual heritage as living, vibrant discourses for their own time. By placing Baruch and Ezra in new contexts, the writers are able to expand the traditions with which these figures are associated and to make these figures meaningful and relevant in a broader historical and religious context. Furthermore, in imitating still other ideal figures from the past, the writers interpret and adapt their sacred traditions, once as writers of texts produced in a post-70 reality and once as the ideal figures they are emulating.

BIBLIOGRAPHY

4 Ezra
Andrews, Isolde. "Being Open to the Vision: A Study from Fourth Ezra." *Literature and Theology* 12 (1998): 231-41.

68. Henze, "From Jeremiah to Baruch," 169.
69. Henze, "From Jeremiah to Baruch," 170.

Berger, Klaus, with Gabriele Fassbeck and Heiner Reinhard. *Synopse des Vierten Buches Esra und der Syrischen Baruch-Apokalypse.* Texte und Arbeiten zum neutestamentlichen Zeitalter 8. Tübingen: Francke, 1992.

Bergren, Theodore A. "Christian Influence on the Transmission History of 4, 5, and 6 Ezra." In *The Jewish Apocalyptic Heritage in Early Christianity,* ed. James C. VanderKam and William Adler. Assen: Van Gorcum and Minneapolis: Fortress, 1996, 102-27.

―――. "Ezra and Nehemiah Square Off in the Apocrypha and Pseudepigrapha." In *Biblical Figures Outside the Bible,* edited by Michael E. Stone and Bergren. Harrisburg: Trinity Press International, 1998, 340-65.

Beyerle, Stefan. "'Du bist kein Richter über dem Herrn' (4 Esr 7,19): zur Konzeption von Gesetz und Gericht im 4. Esrabuch." In *Recht und Ethos im Alten Testament — Gestalt und Wirkung: Festschrift für Horst Seebass zum 65. Geburtstag,* ed. Beyerle, Günter Mayer, and Hans Strauss (Neukirchen-Vluyn: Neukirchener, 1999), 315-37.

Bloch, Joshua. "The Ezra-Apocalypse: Was It Written in Hebrew, Greek or Aramaic?" *JQR* 48 (1958): 279-94.

Choi, Richard P. "The Intra-Jewish Dialogue in 4 Ezra 3:1–9:25." *AUSS* 41 (2003): 237-54.

Collins, John J. "After the Fall: 4 Ezra, 2 Baruch, and the Apocalypse of Abraham." In *The Apocalyptic Imagination: An Introduction to Jewish Apocalyptic Literature.* 2nd ed. BRS. Grand Rapids: Eerdmans and Livonia: Dove, 1998, 194-232.

―――. "The Idea of Election in 4 Ezra." *JSQ* 16 (2009): 83-96.

Cook, Joan E. "Creation in 4 Ezra: The Biblical Theme in Support of Theodicy." In *Creation in the Biblical Traditions,* ed. Richard J. Clifford and John J. Collins. CBQMS 24. Washington: Catholic Biblical Association, 1992, 129-39.

Del Verme, Marcello. "Sui rapporti tra 2Baruc e 4Ezra." *Orpheus* 24 (2003): 30-54.

DiTommaso, Lorenzo. "Dating the Eagle Vision of 4 Ezra: A New Look at an Old Theory." *JSP* 20 (1999): 3-38.

Esler, Philip F. "The Social Function of 4 Ezra." *JSNT* 53 (1994): 99-123.

Flannery Dailey, Frances. "Non-Linear Time in Apocalyptic Texts: The Spiral Model." In *SBLSP 1999.* Atlanta: Scholars, 1999, 231-45.

García Martínez, Florentino. "Le IVe Esdras et les MSS de Qumrân." In *Rashi, 1040-1990: Hommage à Ephraim E. Urbach,* ed. Gabrielle Sed-Rajana. Congrès européen des Études juives. Paris: Cerf, 1993, 81-90.

―――. "Traditions Common to 4 Ezra and the Dead Sea Scrolls." In *Qumranica Minora,* ed. García Martínez and Eibert J. C. Tigchelaar. STDJ 63. Leiden: Brill, 2007, 1:153-87.

Hallbäck, Geert. "The Fall of Zion and the Revelation of the Law: An Interpretation of 4 Ezra." *SJOT* 6 (1992): 263-92.

Harrington, Daniel J. "The 'Holy Land' in Pseudo-Philo, 4 Ezra, and 2 Baruch." In *Emanuel: Studies in Hebrew Bible, Septuagint, and Dead Sea Scrolls in Honor of Emanuel Tov,* ed. Shalom M. Paul, Robert A. Kraft, Lawrence H. Schiffman, and Weston W. Fields. VTSup 94. Leiden: Brill, 2003, 661-72.

―――. "Wisdom and Apocalyptic in 4QInstruction and 4Ezra." In *Wisdom and Apocalypticism in the Dead Sea Scrolls and in the Biblical Tradition,* ed. Florentino García Martínez. BETL 68. Leuven: Leuven University Press; Paris and Dudley: Peeters, 2003, 343-55.

Hayman, Allison P. "The 'Man from the Sea' in 4 Ezra 13." *JJS* 49 (1998): 1-16.

Hofmann, Norbert J. "Rezeption des Dtn im Buch Tobit, in der Assumptio Mosis und im 4. Esrabuch." In *Das Deuteronomium,* ed. Georg Braulik. ÖBS 23. Frankfurt: Lang, 2003, 311-42.

Humphrey, Edith McEwan. *The Ladies and the Cities: Transformation and Apocalyptic Identity in Joseph and Aseneth, 4 Ezra, the Apocalypse and The Shepherd of Hermas.* JSPSup 17. Sheffield: Sheffield Academic, 1995.

Klijn, Albertus F. J. *Die Esra-Apokalypse (IV. Esra): Nach dem lateinischen Text unter Benutzung der anderen Versionen übersetzt und herausgegeben.* GCS. Berlin: Akademie, 1992.

Knibb, Michael A. "Apocalyptic and Wisdom in 4 Ezra." *JSJ* 13 (1983): 56-74.

Kraft, Robert A. "Ezra Materials in Judaism and Christianity." In *ANRW,* 2.19.1 (1979), 119-36.

———. "Towards Assessing the Latin Text of '5 Ezra': The Christian Connection." In *Christians among Jews and Gentiles: Essays in Honor of Krister Stendahl on His Sixty-fifth Birthday,* ed. George W. MacRae, and George W. E. Nickelsburg. Philadelphia: Fortress, 1986, 158-69.

Lichtenberger, Hermann. "Zion and the Destruction of the Temple in 4 Ezra 9–10." In *Gemeinde ohne Tempel/Community without Temple: Zur Substituierung und Transformation des Jerusalemer Tempels und seines Kults im Alten Testament, antiken Judentum und frühen Christentum,* ed. Beate Ego, Kathrin Ehlers, Armin Lange, and Peter Pilhofer. WUNT 118. Tübingen: Mohr Siebeck, 1999, 239-49.

Longenecker, Bruce W. *2 Esdras.* Guides to Apocrypha and Pseudepigrapha. Sheffield: Sheffield Academic, 1995.

———. "Locating 4 Ezra: A Consideration of Its Social Setting and Functions." *JSJ* 28 (1997): 271-93.

Macholz, Christian. "Die Entstehung des hebräischen Bibelkanons nach 4 Esra 14." In *Die Hebräische Bibel und ihre zweifache Nachgeschichte: Festschrift für Rolf Rendtorff zum 65. Geburtstag,* ed. Erhard Blum, Macholz, and Ekkehard W. Stegemann. Neukirchen-Vluyn: Neukirchener, 1990, 379-91.

Marshall, John W. "6 Ezra and Apocalyptic Judaism in Asia Minor." Paper presented at Seminar for Culture and Religion in Antiquity, University of Toronto, February 9, 2009.

Medala, Stanisław. "Le 'Quatrième livre d'Esdras' et les textes qoumrâniens." *Mogilany 1989* 2 (1991): 197-207.

———. "The Original Language of 4 Esdras." In *Intertestamental Essays in Honour of Józef Tadeusz Milik,* ed. Zdzisław J. Kapera. *Qumranica Mogilanensia* 6. Kraków: Enigma, 1992.

Metzger, Bruce M. "The Fourth Book of Ezra." In *OTP,* 1:517-59.

Muñoz, Domingo León. "Universalidad de la salvación en la apocalíptica (Daniel, 4 de Esdras y 2 de Baruc)." *RevistB* 56 (1994): 129-48.

Najman, Hindy. "Ezra: Introduction." In *The Jewish Study Bible,* ed. Adele Berlin and Marc Zvi Brettler. Oxford: Oxford University Press, 1999, 1666-71.

———. "How Should We Contextualize Pseudepigrapha? Imitation and Emulation in 4 Ezra." In *Flores Florentino: Dead Sea Scrolls and Other Early Jewish Studies in Honour* of *Florentino García Martínez,* ed. Anthony Hilhorst, Émile Puech, and Eibert Tigchelaar. JSJSup 122. Leiden: Brill, 2007, 529-36.

————. "Between Heaven and Earth: Liminal Visions in 4 Ezra." In *Other Worlds and Their Relation to This World: Early Jewish and Ancient Christian Traditions,* ed. Tobias Nicklas et al. JSJSup 142. Leiden: Brill, 2010, 107-18.

Nuvolone, Flavio G. "Apocalypse d'Esdras Grecque et Latine, Rapports et Rhétorique." *Apocrypha* 7 (1996): 81-108.

————. "L'Initiation prophétique dans l'apocalypse grecque d'Esdras: Essai d'analyse et de reconstruction." *FZPhTh* 44 (1997): 408-44.

————. "Vision d'Esdras." In *Ecrits apocryphes chrétiens,* ed. François Bovon and Pierre Geoltrain. Bibliothèque de la Pléiade 442. Paris: Gallimard, 1997, 593-632.

Schmid, Konrad. "Esras Begegnung mit Zion: Die Deutung der Zerstörung Jerusalems im 4. Esrabuch und das Problem des 'bösen Herzens.'" *JSJ* 29 (1998): 261-77.

Stone, Michael E. *A Textual Commentary on the Armenian Version of IV Ezra.* SBLSCS 34. Atlanta: Scholars, 1990.

————. *Fourth Ezra: A Commentary on the Book of Fourth Ezra.* Hermeneia. Minneapolis: Fortress, 1990.

————. "Esdras, Second Book of." *Anchor Bible Dictionary* 2:611-14. Edited by David N. Freedman. New York: Doubleday, 1992.

————. "The Concept of the Messiah in IV Ezra." In *Apocrypha, Pseudepigrapha, and Armenian Studies: Collected Papers.* Vol. 1: *Apocrypha, Pseudepigrapha, and Dead Sea Scrolls.* OLA 144. Leuven: Peeters, 2006, 321-38.

————. "An Introduction to the Esdras Writings." In *Apocrypha, Pseudepigrapha, and Dead Sea Scrolls,* 305-20.

————. "On Reading an Apocalypse." In *Apocrypha, Pseudepigrapha, and Dead Sea Scrolls,* 339-52.

————. "A Reconsideration of Apocalyptic Visions." In *Apocrypha, Pseudepigrapha, and Dead Sea Scrolls,* 353-66.

————. "The City in 4 Ezra." *JBL* 126 (2007): 402-7.

Sutter Rehmann, Luzia. "Das Vierte Esrabuch." In *Kompendium Feministische Bibelauslegung,* ed. Luise Schottroff, Marie-Theres Wacker, Claudia Janssen, and Beate Wehn. Gütersloh: Kaiser, 1998, 450-58.

2 Baruch

Asurmendi, Jesús María. "Baruch: Causes, Effects and Remedies for a Disaster." In *History and Identity: How Israel's Later Authors Viewed Its Earlier History,* ed. Núria Calduch-Benages and Jan Liesen. Berlin: de Gruyter, 2005, 187-200.

Berger, Klaus, with Gabriele Fassbeck and Heiner Reinhard. *Synopse des Vierten Buches Esra und der Syrischen Baruch-Apokalypse.* Tübingen: Francke, 1992.

Bogaert, Pierre-Maurice. *L'Apocalypse de Baruch: Introduction, Traduction du Syriaque et Commentaire.* 2 vols. SC 144-45. Paris: Cerf, 1969.

————. "Le Livre Deutérocanonique de Baruch dans la Liturgie Romaine." In *Mélanges liturgiques offerts au R. P. Dom Bernard Botte à l'occasion du cinquantième anniversaire de son ordination sacerdotale (4 juin 1972).* Louvain: Abbaye du César, 1972, 31-48.

————. "Le Nom de Baruch dans la Littérature Pseudépigraphique: L'Apocalypse

Syriaque et le Livre Deutérocanonique." In *La Literature Juive entre Tenach et Mishnah: Quelques Problèmes,* ed. W. C. Van Unnik. RechBib 9. Leiden: Brill, 1974, 56-72.

———. "Le personnage de Baruch et l'histoire du livre de Jérémie: Aux origines du livre de Baruch." *BIOSCS* 7 (1974): 19-21.

———. "Les Apocalypses contemporaines de Baruch, d'Esdras et de Jean." In *L'Apocalypse johannique et l'Apocalyptique dans le Nouveau Testament,* ed. Jan Lambrecht. BETL 53. Leuven: Leuven University Press, 1980, 47-68.

———. "De Baruch à Jérémie: Les Deux Rédactions Conservées du Livre de Jérémie." In *Le Livre de Jérémie: Le Prophète et son Milieu, les Oracles et leur Transmission.* BETL 54. Leuven: Leuven University Press, 1981, 168-73.

———. "Le personnage de Baruch et l'histoire du livre de Jérémie: Aux origines du livre deutérocanonique de Baruch." In *Papers Presented to the Fifth International Congress on Biblical Studies Held at Oxford, 1973,* ed. Elizabeth A. Livingstone. SE 7. TUGAL 126. Berlin: Akademie, 1982, 73-81.

Brockington, Leonard H. "The Syriac Apocalypse of Baruch." In *The Apocryphal Old Testament,* ed. Hedley Fredrick Davis Sparks. Oxford: Clarendon, 1984, 835-95.

Carroll, Robert P. *Jeremiah.* OTL. Philadelphia: Westminster, 1986.

Ceriani, Antonio Maria. "Apocalypsis Baruch Syriace." In *Monumenta Sacra et Profana ex codicibus praesertim Bibliothecae Ambrosianae,* 1.2. Milan: Bibliotheca Ambrosiana, 1866, 73-98.

———. *Translatio syra Pescitto Veteris Testamenti ex codice Ambrosiano.* Milan: Mediolani, 1876.

Charles, Robert H. *The Apocalypse of Baruch Translated from the Syriac.* London: Black, 1896.

———. "II Baruch, or the Syriac Apocalypse of Baruch." In *APOT,* 2:470-526.

Clemen, Carl. "Die Zusammensetzung des Buches Henoch, der Apokalypse des Baruch und des vierten Buches Esra." *TSK* 11 (1898): 211-46.

Dedering, Sven. "Apocalypse of Baruch." In *The Old Testament in Syriac.* Leiden: Brill, 1973.

Desjardins, Michel. "Law in 2Baruch and 4Ezra." *SR* 14 (1985): 25-37.

Ego, Beate. "Review of Rivka Nir, *The Destruction of Jerusalem and the Idea of Redemption in the Syriac Apocalypse of Baruch.*" *ZAW* 116 (2004): 470.

Giovanni, Deiana. "Miti di origine, miti di caduta e presenza del femminino nel 4 Esdra e nel 2 Baruch." *RStB* 6 (1994): 141-52.

Hadot, Jean. "La Datation de l'Apocalypse Syriaque de Baruch." *Sem* 15 (1965): 79-95.

———. "Le Problème de l'Apocalypse Syriaque de Baruch d'après un Ouvrage Récent." *Sem* 20 (1970): 59-76.

Harlow, Daniel C. *The Greek Apocalypse of Baruch (3 Baruch) in Hellenistic Judaism and Early Christianity.* SVTP 12. Leiden: Brill, 1996.

Henze, Matthias. "Review of Rivka Nir, *The Destruction of Jerusalem and the Idea of Redemption in the Syriac Apocalypse of Baruch.*" *JSP* 15 (2006): 145-48.

———. "From Jeremiah to Baruch: Pseudepigraphy in the Syriac Apocalypse of Baruch." In *Biblical Traditions in Transmission: Essays in Honor of Michael A. Knibb,* ed. Charlotte Hempel and Judith M. Lieu. JSJSup 111. Leiden: Brill, 2006, 157-77.

———. "Qoheleth and the Syriac Apocalypse of Baruch." *VT* 58 (2008): 28-43.

———. "Torah and Eschatology in the Syriac Apocalypse of Baruch." In *The Significance* of Sinai: Traditions About Sinai and Divine Revelation in Judaism and Christianity, ed. George J. Brooke, Hindy Najman, and Loren T. Stuckenbruck. Leiden: Brill, 2008, 201-15.

Klijn, Albertus F. J. "The Sources and Redaction of the Syriac Apocalypse of Baruch." *JJS* 1 (1970): 65-76.

———. "2 (Syriac Apocalypse of) Baruch: A New Introduction and Translation." In *OTP*, 1:615-52.

———. "Recent Developments in the Study of the Syriac Apocalypse of Baruch." *JSP* 4 (1989): 3-17.

———. "The Character of the Arabic Version of the Apocalypse of Baruch." In *Jüdische Schriften in ihrem antik-jüdischen und urchristlichen Kontext*, ed. Hermann Lichtenberger and Gerbern S. Oegema. Studien zu den Jüdischen Schriften aus hellenistisch-römischer Zeit 1. Gütersloh: Gütersloher, 2002, 204-8.

Laato, Antti. "The Apocalypse of the Syriac Baruch and the Date of the End." *JSP* 18 (1998): 39-46.

Langen, Joseph. *De Apocalypsi Baruch Anno Superiori Primum Edita: Commentation.* Freiburg: Herder, 1867.

Leemhuis, Fred. "The Arabic Version of the Apocalypse of Baruch: A Christian Text?" *JSP* 4 (1989): 19-26.

———, Albertus F. J. Klijn, and G. J. H. van Gelder. *The Arabic Text of the Apocalypse of Baruch: Edited and Translated with a Parallel Translation of the Syriac Text.* Leiden: Brill, 1986.

Leuenberger, Martin. "Ort und Funktion der Wolkenvision und ihrer Deutung in der syrischen Baruchapokalypse." *JSS* 36 (2005): 206-46.

Murphy, Frederick J. *The Structure and Meaning of Second Baruch.* SBLDS 78. Atlanta: Scholars, 1985.

———. "2 Baruch and the Romans." *JBL* 104 (1985): 663-69.

———. "Sapiential Elements in the Syriac Apocalypse of Baruch." *JQR* 76 (1986): 311-27.

———. "The Temple in the Syriac Apocalypse of Baruch." *JBL* 106 (1987): 671-83.

Nir, Rivka. *The Destruction of Jerusalem and the Idea of Redemption in the Syriac Apocalypse of Baruch.* SBLEJL 20. Atlanta: SBL, 2003.

Riaud, Jean. *Les Paralipomènes du Prophète Jérémie: Présentation, Texte Original, Traduction et Commentaires.* Angers: Université Catholique de l'Ouest, 1994.

Sayler, Gwendolyn B. "2 Baruch: A Story of Grief and Consolation," *SBLSP 1982.* Chico: Scholars, 1982, 485-500.

———. *Have the Promises Failed? A Literary Analysis of 2 Baruch.* SBLDS 72. Chico: Scholars, 1984.

Speyer, W. "Baruch." *JAC* 17 (1974): 185-90.

Whitters, Mark F. "Testament and Canon in the Letter of Second Baruch (2 Baruch 78–87)." *JSP* 12 (2001): 149-63.

———. *The Epistle of Second Baruch: A Study in Form and Message.* JSPSup 42. London: Sheffield Academic, 2003.

Willett, Tom W. *Eschatology in the Theodicies of 2 Baruch and 4 Ezra.* JSPSup 4. Sheffield: JSOT, 1989.

Williamson, Hugh G. M. "On Writing and Witnesses." In *The Book Called Isaiah: Deutero-Isaiah's Role in Composition and Redaction*. Oxford: Clarendon, 1994, 94-115.

Wright, J. Edward. "The Social Setting of the Syriac Apocalypse of Baruch." *JSP* 16 (1997): 81-96.

———. "Baruch: His Evolution from Scribe to Apocalyptic Seer." In Michael E. Stone and Theodore A. Bergren, *Biblical Figures Outside the Bible*. Harrisburg: Trinity Press International, 1998, 264-89.

———. *Baruch Ben Neriah: From Biblical Scribe to Apocalyptic Seer*. Columbia: University of South Carolina Press, 2003.

The *Testaments of the Twelve Patriarchs:* A Not-So-Ambiguous Witness to Early Jewish Interpretive Practices

Robert Kugler

Some might see the inclusion of a chapter on the *Testaments of the Twelve Patriarchs* in a volume addressing early Jewish interpretation of the Hebrew Scriptures to be a fool's errand. No one denies that the *Testaments* in their existing form are the work of early Christians, and even those who argue that there was once a complete collection of Jewish testaments cannot agree on such a composition's contents and aim. That is to say, virtually all scholarship on the *Testaments* seems to render them an ambiguous witness to Jewish interpretive practices at best. Indeed, some would even say that considering the *Testaments* in this volume risks wrongly assigning Christian interpretive practices to Jews of Greco-Roman antiquity.

Of course, that is not the view I take. Quite the contrary: as the following survey of the *Testaments'* contents, genre, main themes, and research history proves — the essay is also meant to offer a serviceable introduction to the *Testaments* in general — the Hebrew Scriptures are the *Testaments'* root and stalk, and the interpretation of those Scriptures was the stock in trade of their authors. Moreover, as the final section of the essay shows, whatever their origin and no matter how ambiguous their testimony, the interpretive strategies the *Testaments* exhibit were common to Jews and Christians alike in Greco-Roman antiquity, and they evince myriad specific exegetical motifs that depend on the Hebrew Bible.[1]

---

1. The following section distills Robert A. Kugler, *The Testaments of the Twelve Patriarchs.* GAP (Sheffield: Sheffield Academic, 2001), 11-40.

Contents, Genre, and Main Themes

Contents

The *Testaments of the Twelve Patriarchs* present the fictional valedictory speeches of the sons of Jacob. They include an introduction followed by biography, exhortation, and prediction. They conclude with the patriarch's death and burial.

Standard Introduction   Each testament begins by announcing that it is a copy of the patriarch's final words spoken as death drew near and his family gathered around him. Next comes the patriarch's direct command to his children to heed his instructions. Some testaments preserve additional or contradictory elements in the introduction (e.g., when he spoke the patriarch was in sound health [*T. Levi* 1:2; *T. Naph.* 1:2a; *T. Ash.* 1:2]; some of his brothers were present [*T. Reu.* 1:4]; the testament was delivered at a banquet [*T. Naph.* 1:2b]).

Biography and Moral Exhortation   Following the introduction each testament usually presents three parts: an autobiographical account, moral exhortation, and eschatological predictions. The autobiographical accounts engender the themes of the ethical sections. The autobiographies entail the most obvious and concentrated evidence of the *Testaments'* dependence on Hebrew Scripture interpretation. For seven patriarchs their autobiographies derive from explicit exegesis of the book of Genesis, whether it be of as much as a full episode or as little as a single comment. The remaining five autobiographies are also "exegetically derived," but in subtler fashion, as the following survey demonstrates.

1. Reuben's autobiography makes a full story of the single-verse account of his sexual transgression with Bilhah, his father's concubine, in Gen 35:22. On the basis of that expanded biblical narrative he encourages his children to avoid the pitfalls of youthful foolishness, impurity, and attachment to the beauty of women (*T. Reu.* 2:1–6:4).
2. Simeon warns against envy that engendered his desire to kill Joseph and that led in part to Joseph's imprisonment in Egypt (*T. Sim.* 2:2–5:3). Oddly, the author makes nothing of Simeon's most prominent action in Genesis, his partnership with Levi in overthrowing Shechem (Genesis 34). It is likely instead that the author of the testament plays peremptorily on Simeon's unique role as a brother seized by Joseph on the brothers' trip to Egypt (Gen 42:24). This would not be surprising inasmuch as the *Testaments* of-

ten seem to have the full record of a patriarch's experiences, and even of his descendants, in mind in telling the story of his actions at the sale of Joseph (e.g., Dan; see below).

3. Levi can borrow on two aspects of the Bible's account of him in telling his story: his slaughter of the Shechemites after the rape of Dinah (Genesis 34) and his unique role as the ancestor of all priests (e.g., Deut 33:8-11). Thus his ethical exhortations remind his children of his zeal for the Lord's law and call upon his descendants to know and keep the law with similar intensity (implying a great deal about the authors' views on the central role of the priesthood; *T. Levi* 2:1–9:14; 11:1–13:9).

4. Judah uses his autobiographical account to explain how he mistook his own daughter-in-law, Tamar, as a (cultic?) prostitute when she used a deception to gain her rights as the widow of his sons (Genesis 38). He explains his indiscretion — and his failure to recognize his own daughter-in-law — as the result of his greed, impure desires, and fondness for alcohol. To avoid being similarly blinded to reality and making analogous errors, Judah encourages his children to be temperate and pure (*T. Jud.* 2:1–20:5).

5. Issachar's is the first autobiography to demonstrate certain dependence on the Septuagint. Where the Masoretic Text records Jacob's view that as a donkey might be satisfied with a life of forced labor so would be Issachar, the Septuagint has Jacob say that Issachar sought always the good and that upon pausing among the lots he determined that the land was productive and thus gave himself to farming (Gen 49:14-15 LXX). The testament's autobiography builds from this, with Issachar extolling the uncomplicated life of the farmer tilling the soil. Thus his ethical exhortation likewise commends the "simplicity" of his occupation to his children as the root of other good character traits he exhibited in life (*T. Iss.* 1:2–5:3; 7:1-7).

6. Zebulun's autobiography also rests on the Septuagint version of Jacob's deathbed blessing for the patriarch. Revising Jacob's prediction in the Masoretic Text that Zebulun's settlement at the edge of the sea will make him a harbor, the Septuagint decrees that he will dwell coastally and as a consequence take up with ships (Gen 49:13 LXX). Zebulun's autobiography builds on this modest suggestion in the Septuagint to say that he became a "simple" fisherman, whose ordinariness of life enabled him to be compassionate (in particular) toward Joseph. On this basis he encourages in his children a similar commitment to merciful warmheartedness borne of simplicity in lifestyle (*T. Zeb.* 1:4–9:4).

7. Dan says that his envy (like Simeon's) nurtured his desire to kill Joseph and led him to falsehood, and so he warns his children with his ethical exhortation against jealousy and deceit (*T. Dan* 1:3–5:3). While there appears at

first sight to be only the slimmest and most remote evidence for this self-description in the Hebrew Bible — Jacob argues that Dan will be like a roadside viper that strikes at the heels of horses to make their riders fall (Gen 49:17) — we shall see in the concluding section of this essay that Dan's descendant, Samson, is echoed richly in Dan's autobiography, and in the former we find quite enough evidence of jealousy, deceit, and a violent spirit in the line of Dan.

8. As with Dan, the biblical account of Naphtali is especially thin broth for a later author penning an autobiography for the patriarch. At first glance it seems likely that the author of the testament agreed entirely and chose simply to fabricate from thin air Naphtali's virtue as a swift runner who took pleasure in using his natural speed as the family's messenger; on this basis, Naphtali encourages his children likewise to live in harmony with natural order and goodness (*T. Naph.* 1:5–3:5; 8:4-10). However, a closer look at the single reference to Naphtali beyond the account of his conception and naming (Gen 30:8) reveals the likely exegetical basis for his natural runner's biography: Jacob's cryptic judgment that he is a "doe let loose" (Gen 49:21) perhaps conjured the image of a man who was by nature a swift runner.

9. Genesis 37:2 indicates that Joseph brought to Jacob a bad report regarding the sons of Zilpah and Bilhah. Gad's autobiography reveals the content of that report when he tells his children that he became angry with Joseph because he falsely told their father that the sons of Zilpah and Bilhah were eating the lambs of the flock. Gad goes on, though, to reveal that his rage backfired on him; so he pleads with his children to control their tempers (*T. Gad* 1:2–7:7).

10. Asher describes his single-minded effort to keep God's law to introduce a discourse on double- and single-mindedness and an exhortation to always choose the latter (*T. Ash.* 1:3–6:6). At first sight it is difficult to see a biblical basis for this, but one possibility is an "echo of the echoes" of the etymology for his name (Leah's happiness at his birth; Gen 30:13). For example, Ps 1:1 declares happy the person who chooses the path of righteousness and observation of the law of the Lord over that of sinners and the wicked (see also, for example, Ps 32:2; Isa 56:2).

11. Joseph exhorts his children to lead lives of chastity, endurance, and care for others. His grounds for arguing this position include the positive outcomes of his resistance to the lascivious advances of Potiphar's wife (Gen 39:6b-18), his patience in the face of imprisonment in Pharaoh's jails (39:19–40:23), and his mercy for his traitorous brothers in the wake of his father's death (50:20): even if his chastity vis-à-vis Potiphar's wife could not save him from prison, it established the value of practicing the virtue of self-

restraint; even if the baker forgot him in prison, his endurance there prepared him for his release to a new life of leading Egypt through its darkest
hour; and because he foreswore the pleasure of revenge on his brothers, his
mercy for them ensured the existence of the people who would become Israel in the promised land (*T. Jos.* 1:3–18:4).

12. Expanding on Joseph's merciful and emotional reception of his formerly
treacherous brothers in Gen 45:14-15, Benjamin depicts Joseph as entirely
forgiving of their actions in selling him to the Ishmaelites. Marveling thus
at Joseph's mercy, Benjamin praises him as a good man with a good mind,
whom Benjamin's children should emulate (*T. Benj.* 1:2–8:3).

To summarize the contents of the autobiographies, over half of the patriarchs' accounts depend explicitly on passages in Genesis (e.g., Reuben [Gen
35:22]; Levi [Genesis 34]; Judah [Genesis 38]; Issachar [Gen 49:14-15 LXX];
Zebulun [Gen 49:13]; Gad [Gen 37:2]; Joseph [Gen 39:6b-18]). The remaining
five also grow from the seedbed of the Hebrew Bible, but less explicitly so (Simeon, Dan, Naphtali, Asher, and Benjamin).

As for the moral exhortation sections, they all agree that right action,
whether it is to avoid a vice or embrace a virtue, is reducible to the terms of a
typical early Jewish summary of biblical law, the twofold commandment to love
God and one's neighbor (Lev 19:18; Deut 6:5; cf. Luke 10:27 and parallels; *T. Zeb.*
5:1; *T. Benj.* 5:3). This is equated in turn with pleasing God and opposing Beliar
(e.g., *T. Levi* 18:12; *T. Iss.* 7:7; *T. Zeb.* 9:8; *T. Dan* 5:1; *T. Naph.* 2:6; *T. Benj.* 6:1) and
heeding traditional Greco-Roman vices (e.g., πορνεία and φιλαργυρία [*T. Jud.*
18:2]) and virtues (e.g., ἁπλότης [*T. Iss.* 4:1]; εγκράτεια [*T. Iss.* 2:1; *T. Naph.* 8:8]).
Thus even as they move into the arena of early Jewish moral imagination and
its introduction of Beliar (Belial) as an agent of evil and the world of Greco-
Roman morality with its focus on vices and virtues, the ethical sections remain
fundamentally rooted in the resources of the Hebrew Scriptures.

Eschatology   After exhorting their children the patriarchs predict their descendants' futures. The patriarchs draw from several sources, all of which are
also rooted in exegesis of the Hebrew Bible. Enoch is the most popular source
for eschatological insight (*T. Sim.* 5:4; *T. Levi* 10:5; 14:1; 16:1; *T. Jud.* 18:1; *T. Naph.*
4:1; *T. Benj.* 9:1), and unsurprisingly so: he is renowned in early Judaism as a
seer, thanks to his heavenly ascent described in Gen 5:24 (*1 Enoch*; *Jubilees* 4,
etc.). But the patriarchs also cite the fathers (*T. Levi* 10:1), the fathers' writings
(*T. Zeb.* 9:5), and heavenly tablets (*T. Ash.* 7:5). The first and third of these
sources are common tropes in early Jewish exegesis that attribute to the ancestors special wisdom about humanity. The fathers can include Abraham, Isaac,

and Jacob, as well as some of the antediluvian figures (e.g., Abraham learned Hebrew from God [*Jub.* 12:26]; Isaac possessed before the existence of the office all knowledge necessary for priests [*ALD* 11–56]; Noah wrote a "book concerning the blood" [*ALD* 57]) and the "heavenly tablets" are the written form on which such information was often recorded and seen by heavenly travelers (e.g., 1 *En.* 103:2; 106:19).

The future-oriented passages come in several genres, all of which may also be traced back to the Hebrew Scriptures.[2] Sin-Exile-Return (S.E.R.) sections generally describe the future sins of the patriarchs' descendants, the tribes' exile among the Gentiles as punishment for their sin, and God's restoration of the tribes. The S.E.R. pattern is thoroughly rooted in the Hebrew Bible: see, for example, Ezekiel and other prophetic works for book-length expressions of the pattern; see also Deut 29:18–30:10; 1 Kgs 8:46-53 as briefer manifestations. S.E.R. passages include *T. Levi* 10; 14–15; 16; *T. Jud.* 18:1; 23; *T. Iss.* 6; *T. Zeb.* 9:5-7, 9; *T. Dan* 5:4a, 6-9; *T. Naph.* 4:1-3, 5; *T. Gad* 8:2; *T. Ash.* 7:2-3, 5-7; *T. Benj.* 9:1-2; the *Testaments of Reuben, Simeon,* and *Joseph* lack S.E.R. passages.[3]

A second kind of eschatological text, the Levi-Judah (L.J.) passage, is also rooted in the Hebrew Scriptures. These passages build from Gen 49:8-10; Num 24:17; Deut 33:8-11; Mal 2:4-7, and other classic texts for the traditions associated with the origins of Davidic messianism and a renewed priesthood from the line of Levi. In particular, the L.J. passages bemoan the descendants' rebellion against Levi's and Judah's descendants (*T. Reu.* 6:5-7; *T. Sim.* 5:4-6) and the certain defeat to follow (cf. *T. Dan* 5:4; *T. Gad* 8:2), but they also look forward to the descendants' loyalty and obedience to the tribes of Levi and Judah out of respect for their special biblical roles in providing priests, kings, and the messiah of Israel. L.J. passages include *T. Reu.* 6:5–7:8, 10-12; *T. Levi* 2:11; *T. Sim.* 5:4-6; 7:1-2; *T. Jud.* 21:1-6a; *T. Iss.* 5:7-8a; *T. Dan* 5:4, 6-7, 10; *T. Naph.* 8:2; *T. Gad* 8:1-2; *T. Jos.* 19:6; the *Testaments of Zebulun, Asher,* and *Benjamin* lack L.J. passages.[4]

Ideal savior passages are closely related to the messianic L.J. passages and depend on many of the same Hebrew Scripture texts, but they almost universally may be said to refer to Jesus (*T. Levi* 18; *T. Jud.* 24; *T. Zeb.* 9:8; *T. Dan* 5:10-13). *T. Levi* 18 anticipates a new high priest who will succeed the old failed priesthood: he will exemplify the best of the line of Levi, be free from its corruption, and bring salvation to his people. *T. Judah* 24 foresees a redeemer king from the line of Judah. *T. Zebulun* 9:8 describes a redeemer who will liberate

2. Marinus de Jonge, *The Testaments of the Twelve Patriarchs: A Study of Their Text, Composition, and Origin* (Assen: Van Gorcum, 1953).

3. Harm W. Hollander and Marinus de Jonge, *The Testaments of the Twelve Patriarchs: A Commentary.* SVTP 8 (Leiden: Brill, 1985), 39-41, 53-56.

4. Hollander and de Jonge, *The Testaments of the Twelve Patriarchs,* 40-41, 56-61.

those in captivity to Beliar, and *T. Dan* 5:10-13 designates that savior as from "the tribe of Judah and Levi." Notably, even these plainly Christian compositions rely on the classic texts of the Hebrew Scriptures that foretell savior kings and priests (see preceding paragraph).

A final group of future-oriented passages announces that the patriarch will be resurrected to rule over his tribe at the second coming of the Messiah (*T. Sim.* 6:7; *T. Levi* 18:14; *T. Jud.* 25; *T. Zeb.* 10:1-4; *T. Benj.* 10:6-10). While the concept of the rule of the resurrected is alien to the Hebrew Bible, even these passages connect themselves to the Scriptures by embracing in the resurrection all the sons of Jacob, *and* Abraham, Isaac, and Jacob, Enoch, Noah, and Shem, and any whose observance of the law or acceptance of Jesus as Messiah made them righteous.

Altogether the future-oriented passages predict the future of the patriarchs' descendants up to the coming of Jesus — their successes and failures, their righteousness and sins; they foretell the tribes' rebellion against the descendants of Levi (priests) and Judah (kings) and against the savior who will come from those two tribes, even as they admonish obedience to the two tribes and to the Messiah; they predict that Israel and especially the tribe of Levi will reject the Messiah; they say that then the messiah will turn away from Israel to the Gentiles and Israel will sporadically keep the commandments in the period between the first advent of the Messiah and his second coming; lastly, they predict that the Messiah will come again to complete God's plan of salvation for Israel, to redeem those who have kept the law and/or believe in Jesus Christ as Messiah.[5]

Concluding Elements   The patriarch concludes his speech, instructs his children on tending to his remains, and dies, and the text remarks that the patriarch's children followed his burial instructions (e.g., *T. Jud.* 26).

Genre

Scholars define a testament by formal literary characteristics and by content. The literary hallmark is a narrative framework that includes the testator's introduction, in which he gathers family or friends to give his near-death speech, and a conclusion that narrates the speaker's death.[6] The necessary content var-

5. Marinus de Jonge, "The Future of Israel in the Testaments of the Twelve Patriarchs," *JSJ* 17 (1986): 196-211.

6. John J. Collins, "Testaments," in *Jewish Writings of the Second Temple Period: Apocrypha, Pseudepigrapha, Qumran Sectarian Writings, Philo, Josephus,* ed. Michael E. Stone. CRINT 2.2 (Assen: Van Gorcum and Philadelphia: Fortress, 1984), 325-55.

ies in scholarly opinion. For some the *sine qua non* is parenesis;[7] others insist that prophetic or apocalyptic speeches, familiar from the Hebrew Bible, typify testaments;[8] and still others say that testaments merge parenesis and apocalyptic.[9] Our survey of the *Testaments'* contents proves that they meet the formal and all the content standards for a testamentary work.

Clearly, though, Jews and Christians recognized the formal genre, while the content standards are incontestably modern, scholarly constructs. And it is no wonder, since the *Testaments* are modeled on the biblical farewell discourses (e.g., Jacob [Genesis 49], Moses [Deuteronomy 33], and David [1 Chronicles 28–29]).[10] Those speeches conditioned ancient audiences to expect from the *Testaments* the patriarchs' accurate predictions of their descendants' future (e.g., Jacob on Judah in Gen 49:8-12, or Moses on Levi in Deut 33:8-11): the *Testaments* certainly meet this standard too; e.g., *T. Jud.* 21:6–22:2a unerringly foretells Judah's descendants' failure at kingship, and *T. Levi* 16:3 foretokens priestly complicity in Jesus' death.

The Christian form of the *Testaments* also moves beyond the boundaries of the farewell discourse to exceed predictions of the speakers' future and the audience's past by announcing the audience's future as well with the promise of Jesus' second coming to offer a final chance for redemption on Christian terms (e.g., *T. Levi* 16:5; *T. Ash.* 7:7). Thus, whatever their possible pre-Christian form, the *Testaments* became at the hands of their Christian redactors-composers "apocalyptic" farewell discourses encouraging readers to accept Jesus as a messiah. In spite of the Christian origin of the specific instance of it, this specialized genre is also rooted in the Hebrew Bible: the Daniel traditions are the quintessential expressions of apocalyptic narratives, and the farewell discourses, as noted above, are known above all from the speeches of Jacob and Moses. It is the marriage of these two Hebrew Scriptures genres that produced the Christian-authored eschatological speeches of the patriarchs.

7. Klaus Baltzer, *Das Bundesformular*. WMANT 4 (Neukirchen-Vluyn: Neukirchener, 1960; Eng. *The Covenant Formulary* [Philadelphia: Fortress, 1971]); Eckhard von Nordheim, *Die Lehre der Alten*, vol. 1: *Das Testament als Literaturgattung im Judentum der hellenistisch-römischen Zeit*. ALGHJ 13 (Leiden: Brill, 1980).

8. Johannes Munck, "Discours d'adieu dans le Nouveau Testament et dans la littérature biblique," in *Aux sources de la tradition chrétienne: mélanges offerts à M. Maurice Goguel à l'occasion de son soixante-dixième anniversaire* (Neuchâtel: Delachaux and Paris: Nestlé, 1950), 155-70.

9. A. B. Kolenkow, "The Genre Testament and Forecasts of the Future in the Hellenistic Jewish Milieu," *JSJ* 6 (1975): 57-71.

10. Enric Cortès, *Los discursos de adíos de Gn 49 a Jn 13–17* (Barcelona: Herder, 1976).

Main Themes

It is simplest to describe the main themes of the *Testaments'* ethics and eschatology: they urge modes of being and doing that determine one's fate in the age to come.[11] In this, too, the *Testaments* draw on the resources of the Hebrew Bible in large and small ways.

Indeed, even though there is abundant evidence that the *Testaments'* ethical sections were designed to appeal to Jewish, Christian, and pagan audiences alike, they depend first and foremost on a Hebrew Scripture interpretive trope of the era, the double commandment to love God (Deut 6:5) and neighbor (Lev 19:18). This double commandment is made an equivalent to the patriarchs' teaching on the virtuous life in *T. Iss.* 5:2; 7:6-7; *T. Dan* 5:2-3; *T. Gad* 4:1-2; *T. Jos.* 11:1; *T. Benj.* 3:1-3 (see also *T. Reu.* 6:8-9; *T. Sim.* 5:2).[12] Patriarchal moral instruction is identified in turn with Hellenistic ethical norms: heeding the Greco-Roman virtues and vices equates favorably with keeping the double commandment, conducting oneself as the patriarchs instructed, *and* following the ways of the Messiah.[13] Thus self-control (σώφρων, σωφρωσύνη) with respect to sexuality, or one's lack of it (πορνεία), informs Reuben's, Judah's, and Joseph's biographical accounts (*T. Reu.* 1:6; 3:3; 4:6-7; 6:1; *T. Jud.* 13:3; 14:2-3; 15:2; 18:2; *T. Jos.* 3–8). Envy (φθόνος) occupies Simeon's attention (*T. Sim.* 2:13; 3:1-2, 4, 6; 4:5, 7; 6:2). Arrogance (ὑπερήφανος) is a focus of Levi's discourse (*T. Levi* 17:1). Stories of valor (ἀνδρεῖος) dominate Judah's autobiographical recollections (*T. Jud.* 15:6), but lust (ἐπιθυμία, πορνεία) and greed (φιλαργυρία) becloud his reputation (*T. Jud.* 13:2; 14:1, 3; 16:1; 18:2; 19:1). Compassion (εὐσπλαγχνία, σπλαγχνίζομαι) and mercy (ἔλεος) characterize Zebulun (*T. Zeb.* 4:2; 5:1, 3-4; 6:4; 7:1-2, 3; 8:1-4, 6; 9:8).

---

11. P. Hartmut Ascherman, "Die paränetischen Formen der 'Testamente der zwölf Patriarchen' und ihr Nachwirken in der frühchristlichen Mahnung" (Diss., Humboldt-Universität-Berlin, 1955); Howard C. Kee, "The Ethical Dimensions of the Testaments of the XII as a Clue to Provenance," *NTS* 24 (1978): 259-70; Harm W. Hollander, *Joseph as an Ethical Model in the Testaments of the Twelve Patriarchs.* SVTP 6 (Leiden: Brill, 1981); Katell Berthelot, "Les parénèses de la charité dans les *Testaments des douze patriarches*," *MScRel* 60 (2003): 23-40.

12. Fulfilling the double commandment supersedes the specifics of biblical law. Marinus de Jonge, "The Pre-Mosaic Servants of God in the Testaments of the Twelve Patriarchs and in the Writings of Justin and Irenaeus," *VC* 39 (1985): 157-70; cf. H. Dixon Slingerland, "The Nature of *Nomos* (Law) with the *Testaments of the Twelve Patriarchs*," *JBL* 105 (1986): 39-48; and a reply by de Jonge, "Die Paränese in den Schriften des Neuen Testaments und in den Testamenten der Zwölf Patriarchen," in *Neues Testament und Ethik*, ed. Helmut Merklein (Freiburg: Herder, 1989), 538-50, esp. 549-50.

13. Hans D. Betz, *Galatians: A Commentary on Paul's Letter to the Churches in Galatia.* Hermeneia (Philadelphia: Fortress, 1979), 281-83, lists pagan, Jewish, and Christian uses of the vice and virtue lists.

Anger (θυμός) and hatred (μῖσος) consume Dan and Gad (*T. Dan* 1:3, 8; 2:1-2, 4; 3:1, 4-5; 4:1-3, 6-7; 5:1; 6:8; *T. Gad* 1:9; 2:2; 3:2-3; 4:1, 5-7; 5:1-4; 6:1-3; 7:7). Coherence with the natural order (τάξις φύσεως) is Naphtali's concern (*T. Naph.* 3:4-5). And the foundational Hellenistic virtue of simplicity (ἁπλότης) and vice of impurity (πορνεία) are the overarching themes of many patriarchs' moral discourse. But all of these are connected, root and stalk, with the double commandment and its deployment in the words of the patriarchs. Notably, in this way the virtual absence of moral instruction from the biblical patriarchs is remedied first with the resources of the biblical law (Lev 19:18; Deut 6:5) *and* with the resources of Greco-Roman morality. One can hardly imagine a larger-scale reinterpretation of the biblical record.

Mingling freely with this basic brew of ingredients from the Hebrew Scriptures and Greco-Roman moral teaching are many echoes of Greco-Roman, Christian, and Hellenistic-Jewish texts dealing in the vices and virtues of Hellenistic moral philosophy. A few examples suffice. *T. Judah* 18:4 reflects Eccl 4:8 LXX, on the negative power of impurity and greed.[14] Concern for the weak and needy in Job 30:25; 31:17, 39 LXX appears in *T. Iss.* 7:5.[15] The claim in *T. Naph.* 2:3 that God precisely measured all of creation's works echoes Wis 11:20. Rachel's self-control (ἐγκράτεια) regarding sexuality in *T. Iss.* 2:1 (cf. *T. Naph.* 8:8) parallels the standard Greco-Roman view on sexual moderation (cf. Musonius Rufus, *Fragments* 13A-B; Philo, *Creation* 161; *Prelim. Studies* 12; *Abraham* 137, 248-9; Justin, *Apology* 1.29).[16] Greek, Jewish, and Christian thought promotes the encompassing virtue of simplicity (ἁπλότης).[17] And Reuben's reliance on conscience (συνείδησις) echoes a common Hellenistic topos (*T. Reu.* 4:3; cf. Wis 17:10; Josephus, *Ant.* 2.52).[18]

In the ethical sections the *Testaments* also participate in a wider tradition in early Jewish exegesis of overlooking Joseph's peculiarly unsavory or insalubrious traits in the biblical story to valorize him as a hero of the faith (see, for example, *Joseph and Aseneth*; Philo, *Joseph*; Artapanus 2:4). The *Testaments* minimize or ignore entirely his churlish behavior toward the sons of Zilpah and Bilhah (Gen 37:2); his marriage to the daughter of a priest in service to an Egyptian god (41:45); his monopolistic policies aimed at ensuring Egypt's wealth

14. Hollander and de Jonge, *The Testaments of the Twelve Patriarchs*, 217.

15. Hollander and de Jonge, *The Testaments of the Twelve Patriarchs*, 251.

16. Marinus de Jonge, "Rachel's Virtuous Behavior in the *Testament of Issachar*," in *Greeks, Romans, and Christians: Essays in Honor of Abraham J. Malherbe*, ed. David Balch, Everett Ferguson, and Wayne Meeks (Minneapolis: Fortress, 1990), 340-52.

17. Joseph Amstutz, *ΑΠΛΟΤΗΣ: Eine begriffsgeschichtliche Studie zum jüdisch-christlichen Griechisch*. Theophaneia 19 (Bonn: Hanstein, 1968), 64-85.

18. Hollander and de Jonge, *The Testaments of the Twelve Patriarchs*, 100.

during the years of famine (41:46-57); and his ambiguous treatment of his brothers upon their repeated arrivals in Egypt for food (Genesis 42-45). In comparison, his generous moments are highlighted instead (Gen 45:1-15). Indeed, all but the *Testaments of Issachar* and *Asher* recall Joseph's sexual self-restraint, emotional equilibrium in the midst of triumph and tribulation, compassion and mercy even for his enemies, and lack of envy, anger, and vengefulness against those who wronged him. The *Testament of Benjamin* even foregoes Benjamin's biographical details in favor of a eulogy for Joseph as the quintessential good man (ἀγαθός ἀνήρ) with a good mind (ἀγαθὴ διάνοια) who achieved what the patriarchs, Greco-Roman society, and God's twofold commandment demand of one (*T. Benjamin* 4–5). The *Testaments* complete their idealization of Joseph by making him a type of Jesus as savior and morally correct actor (*T. Levi* 16:3; cf. *T. Zeb.* 2:2; 3:3; *T. Gad* 2:3; *T. Benj.* 3:8).[19]

The eschatological sections of the *Testaments* follow naturally from the biographical-ethical portions, and while they go beyond them in their Christian form, they too depend first and foremost on the Hebrew Scriptures, as we saw above. Echoing simple Deuteronomic theological traditions, the patriarchs predict that when the tribes heed their forefathers' advice they fare well (*T. Sim.* 6:2-4), but when they ignore the patriarchs' instructions they are punished (*T. Sim.* 5:4-6). Recalling myriad Hebrew Scripture traditions that hearken to the need to avoid evil and its temptations (see especially the Psalter; e.g., Pss 34:13-14, 21; 97:10), the *Testaments* argue that doing well depends on fleeing from Beliar to God's care (*T. Sim.* 2:4-6); conversely, remaining under Beliar's sway is to remain ensnared in vices (*T. Iss.* 6:1). Christian elements do appear when the patriarchs predict that their descendants will fail to heed their advice, accede to Beliar's influence, and rebel against the tribes of Judah and Levi (*T. Reu.* 6:5-8; *T. Sim.* 5:4-6), and even against the Messiah (*T. Levi* 10:1-5; 14:1-8). The tribes will appear doomed, but Israel's God will intervene through a savior who will destroy the power of Beliar and his spirits (*T. Levi* 18:12; *T. Jud.* 25:3; *T. Zeb.* 9:8; *T. Dan* 5:10-11) and offer salvation even to those who fail to attain virtue through heeding the patriarchs' advice and keeping the double commandment at his second coming (*T. Levi* 16:5; *T. Ash.* 7:7).

A Brief History of Research

The chief focus of research on the *Testaments of the Twelve Patriarchs* has been to determine their Jewish and/or Christian origin. This quest has engendered a

---

19. Aubrey W. Argyle, "Joseph the Patriarch in Patristic Teaching," *ExpTim* 67 (1956): 199-201.

number of research focuses, including text, source, form, and tradition criticism of the *Testaments*. Save textual criticism, all of these separate approaches strengthen this essay's simple contention that the *Testaments* are first and foremost exemplars of biblical interpretation: the *sources* they depend on, reproduce, and expand are all in one way or another part of interpretive trajectories that begin with the Hebrew Scriptures; the vast majority of *forms* they deploy are known from the Jewish Bible; and virtually all of the *traditions* they call upon can be linked to the Tanak.[20]

Textual Criticism

Fourteen Greek manuscripts of the *Testaments* dating from the tenth to the eighteenth centuries C.E. divide into two manuscript families. Manuscripts of family I are the oldest available witnesses, and comparing a few of them (mss. *bk*) with texts from family II permits critical reconstruction of an archetype.[21] There are also Armenian, Slavonic, Serbian, and Latin versions of the *Testaments*. All but the Latin, Robert Grosseteste's 1242 translation from the Greek manuscript *b*, belong to family II.[22] Only the Armenian text continues to be used as a potential resource for reconstructing an archetype, and with little success.[23] On this evidence Marinus de Jonge and his Leiden colleagues have concluded that the earliest attainable text of the *Testaments* is little younger than the ninth century C.E., and that text-critical efforts do not provide access to a pre-Christian form of the *Testaments*.[24]

20. For fuller treatments of research history, see Kugler, *The Testaments of the Twelve Patriarchs*, 11-41, *passim;* H. Dixon Slingerland, *The Testaments of the Twelve Patriarchs: A Critical History of Research*. SBLMS 21 (Missoula: Scholars, 1977); Jarl Henning Ulrichsen, *Die Grundschrift der Testamente der Zwölf Patriarchen: Eine Untersuchung zu Umfang, Inhalt und Eigenart der ursprünglichen Schrift*. Acta Universitatis Upsaliensis, Historia Religionum 10 (Stockholm: Almqvist & Wiksell, 1991), 15-20; for the earlier period, see Henrik J. de Jonge, "Die Patriarchentestamente von Roger Bacon bis Richard Simon," in *Studies on the Testaments of the Twelve Patriarchs: Text and Interpretation*, ed. Marinus de Jonge. SVTP 3 (Leiden: Brill, 1975), 3-42.

21. Henrik J. de Jonge, "The Earliest Traceable Stage of the Textual Tradition of the Testaments of the Twelve Patriarchs," in Marinus de Jonge, *Studies on the Testaments of the Twelve Patriarchs*, 63-86.

22. Marinus de Jonge, "Robert Grosseteste and the Testaments of the Twelve Patriarchs," *JTS* N.S. 42 (1991): 115-25.

23. For more on the translations, see the introductory section in Marinus de Jonge, *The Testaments of the Twelve Patriarchs: A Critical Edition of the Greek Text*. PVTG 1.2 (Leiden: Brill, 1978).

24. Quotations of the *Testaments* in the works of early Christian writers such as Origen, *Homilies on Joshua* 15.6; Jerome, *Homilies on the Psalms* 61 (Psalm 15) are text-critically insignifi-

Source Criticism

While attempts to use the various Jewish works that provide material parallel with or similar to what appears in the *Testaments* as proof of a pre-Christian form of the work as a whole have universally failed, they have demonstrated time and again that there were Jewish sources for the Christian composition, sources that were themselves exegetical reflections on the Hebrew Scriptures.

Some late Hebrew texts similar to the speeches of Judah and Naphtali are thought to hint at pre-Christian, Semitic language precursors of the Greek *Testaments*. Hebrew *T. Naphtali* 2–6 gives two visions like *T. Naphtali* 2–5, and Hebrew *T. Naph.* 10:5-7 describes the human body's organization as evidence of God's ordered creation as does *T. Naph.* 2:8. *Midrash Wayissa'u* (cf. the later *Chronicles of Jerahmeel*) recalls a war against the Amorites similar to that related in *T. Judah* 3–7 (cf. *Jub.* 34:1-9). The uncertain provenance of the two Hebrew works, though, makes them poor help in constructing Semitic originals of the *Testaments of Judah* and *Naphtali*, let alone in arguing for a complete, pre-Christian *Testaments*.[25] That having been said, the two sources do prove the dependence of the *Testaments* on earlier Jewish interpretive developments of the respective patriarchs' stories.

While Dead Sea Scrolls texts related to the *Testament* are old enough to be counted plausibly as Semitic-language precursors to the Greek text, *in toto* the evidence is also insufficient to prove the existence of a full Hebrew (or Aramaic) *Testaments;* we may only surmise that the author(s) of the Greek *Testaments* had various source materials that were part of the larger pool of exegetical traditions, some of which appear at Qumran. Least helpful in this regard are tiny fragments of 4Q538 that echo the story of Jacob's sons' second trip to Joseph in *T. Jud.* 12:11-12 (cf. Gen 43:1–45:10; *Jub.* 43:1-13), and 4Q539 1 and 2, which may reflect *T. Jos.* 14:4-5 (frag. 1) and 15:1–17:2 (frag. 2).[26] More certain is the link between 4Q215 1:2-5 and *T. Naph.* 1:11-12, both accounts of Bilhah's birth and genealogy.[27]

---

cant. The *Testaments'* original language also provokes curiosity; see Robert H. Charles, *The Greek Versions of the Testaments of the Twelve Patriarchs: Edited from Nine MSS* (London: Oxford University Press, 1908); Anders Hultgård, *L'Eschatologie des Testaments des Douze Patriarches,* vol. 2: *Composition de l'ouvrage, textes et traductions.* Acta Universitatis Upsaliensis, Historia Religionum 7 (Stockholm: Almqvist & Wiksell, 1981), 164-87.

25. For the Hebrew *Testament of Naphtali* and *Midrash Wayissa'u* in translation, see Hollander and de Jonge, *The Testaments of the Twelve Patriarchs,* 416-56.

26. Joseph T. Milik, "Écrits préesséniens de Qumrân; d'Hénoch à Amram," in *Qumrân: Sa piété, sa théologie et son milieu,* ed. M. Delcor. BETL 46 (Paris: Duculot, 1978), 97-101.

27. George Brooke et al., *Qumran Cave 4: XVII, Parabiblical Texts, Part 3.* DJD 22 (Oxford: Clarendon, 1996), 73-82; G. Wilhelm Nebe, "Qumranica I: Zu unveröffentlichten Handschriften aus Höhle 4 von Qumran," *ZAW* 106 (1994): 307-22.

By contrast there is a great deal of Qumran evidence for an early, Aramaic source for the *Testament of Levi*. A single manuscript from Cave 1 and six from Cave 4 give Aramaic texts parallel to parts of *T. Levi* 8–9; 11–14, as well as biographical, prayer, and wisdom speech texts unknown from the Greek *Testament*.[28] Two large fragments of an early medieval manuscript from the Cairo Geniza that preserve Aramaic parallels for *T. Levi* 6–7; 8-9; 11-13 supplement the Qumran texts.[29] Additionally, supplements to the Greek *Testament of Levi* in the Mount Athos manuscript of the *Testaments* at *T. Levi* 2:3; 5:2; and 18:2 parallel portions of the Qumran manuscripts and the Cairo Geniza fragments.[30] The debate over the precise relationships among these various textual witnesses is complex and cannot be summarized here. It is enough to say that even the most optimistic attempts to tie these Aramaic and Greek materials to the Greek *Testament of Levi* do nothing to argue for a complete, pre-Christian form of the *Testaments*.[31] But once more we do find evidence in such source material for the *Testaments'* fundamentally exegetical character: the Levi materials elaborate a narrative and interpretive thread that runs from before Genesis 34 and continues to 49:5-7, the story of Levi and the Shechemites and Jacob's curse of Levi in his deathbed speech, and the *Testament of Levi* embraces and converts for its own use that same thread.

Form Criticism

Form criticism has also been used to pursue pre-Christian *Testaments*. Does the Greek work reflect the use of distinctively Jewish and/or Christian genres and subgenres? Here too the evidence is inconclusive as to the *Testaments'* origin, but it is abundant for their reliance on interpretive traditions rooted in the Hebrew Scriptures.

As we have seen above, the *Testaments* rely on the biblical farewell discourse

28. 1Q21: Dominique Barthélemy and J. T. Milik, *Qumran Cave 1*. DJD 1 (Oxford: Clarendon, 1955), 87-91; 4Q213-214b: DJD 22, 1-71; the manuscripts date from the Hasmonean to early Herodian periods.

29. Robert H. Charles and Arthur Cowley, "An Early Source of the Testaments of the Patriarchs," *JQR* 19 (1907): 566-83; H. L. Pass and J. Arendzen, "Fragment of an Aramaic Text of the Testament of Levi," *JQR* 12 (1890-1900): 651-61.

30. For the most recent critical edition of the Levi resources, see Henryk Drawnel, *An Aramaic Wisdom Text from Qumran: A New Interpretation of the Levi Document*. JSJSup 86 (Leiden: Brill, 2004); see also Robert A. Kugler, *From Patriarch to Priest: The Levi-Priestly Tradition from Aramaic Levi to Testament of Levi*. SBLEJL 9 (Atlanta: Scholars, 1996).

31. Drawnel, *An Aramaic Wisdom Text*, 4-11, provides an up-to-date summary of scholarship.

genre, but they also give it an apocalyptic bent by predicting their recipients' future, and it is a genre that both Christians and Jews would have appreciated, even in its apocalyptic expression.[32] The *Testaments* have also been compared with the "covenant formulary," a speech that states covenantal obligations and motivates the audience to keep them by rehearsing God's wondrous deeds in history and/or through blessings and curses (cf. Daniel 9; Nehemiah 9; Bar 1:5–3:8; 3 Macc 2:2-20; Tob 3:1-6).[33] However, the ebb and flow of the *Testaments'* narrative limits this comparison's usefulness, and the exhortations in the *Testaments* pay little of the heed the comparative texts give to the law.

The variety of subgenres in the *Testaments* also disappoints searchers for pre-Christian *Testaments*, but they are a treasure trove of evidence for the work's interpretive character. The subgenres in the biographical sections — synagogue homilies (*T. Judah* 13–17), hymns (*T. Sim.* 6:2-7), visions (*T. Levi* 2:5–5:7; *T. Naph.* 5–6; 7), prayers (*T. Levi* 4:2), instructions (*T. Levi* 9), battle accounts (*T. Jud.* 3–7), seriatim memoirs (*T. Levi* 11; *T. Jud.* 2), paronomasia (*T. Iss.* 1:3-15; *T. Zeb.* 1:2-3), etiologies (*T. Zeb.* 6:1-3), and Rewritten Bible texts (*T. Levi* 6:3–7:4; *T. Jos.* 3:1–9:5; 11:2–16:6) — were familiar to Jews and Christians from the Hebrew and Greek Scriptures as well as from myriad other turn-of-the-era Jewish, Christian, and Hellenistic texts. Likewise, subgenres within the parenetical sections of the *Testaments* resonated equally well with Christian and Jewish authors and recipients: various forms of exhortation can be traced back to the wisdom books of the Septuagint, but also to non-Jewish Hellenistic authors such as Musonius (first century C.E.).[34] Likewise, the popular-philosophic diatribe, known as early as the third century B.C.E. (e.g., Teles), turns up in the *Testaments'* hortatory sections, but would also have been equally well known among Jews and Christians.[35] And the subgenres that Marinus de Jonge identified within the future-oriented sections of the *Testaments* affiliate well with material shared widely among Jews and Christians, including Deuteronomic recitations of history[36] and prophetic oracles of indictment and judgment (e.g., Amos 7:16-17), admonitory speeches (e.g., Jer 25:3-6), promises of salvation (Isa 41:8-13), and announcements of deliverers (e.g., Jer 23:1-8).

---

32. Cf. *T. Job; T. Moses;* 4QVisions of Amram[a-f] (4Q543), Émile Puech, *Qumrân Grotte 4: XXII, Textes araméens, première partie: 4Q529-549.* DJD 31 (Oxford: Clarenson, 2001), 289-318; 4QTestament of Kohath (4Q542), DJD 31, 257-82.

33. Baltzer, *Das Bundesformular/The Covenant Formulary.*

34. See Hollander, *Joseph as an Ethical Model,* 11.

35. Hollander, *Joseph as an Ethical Model,* 12.

36. Odil Hannes Steck, *Israel und das gewaltsame Geschick der Propheten: Untersuchungen zur Überlieferung des deuteronomischen Geschichtsbildes im Alten Testament, Spätjudentum und Urchristentum.* WMANT 23 (Neukirchen-Vluyn: Neukirchener, 1969).

Tradition Criticism

Making connections among the *Testaments* and the broader traditions evinced in Jewish texts has also been used to posit a pre-Christian form of the *Testaments*.[37] But this endeavor more than any other undercuts such efforts: it turns out that the *Testaments* echo traditions found across the widest possible spectrum of thought in Greco-Roman antiquity, making it virtually impossible to get behind the received form of *Testaments*. Fragments of Jewish Pseudepigrapha and rabbinic folklore populate the *Testaments*, especially in the biographical sections: compare *T. Reu.* 3:9–4:5 and *Jub.* 33:9-20 on Reuben and Bilhah (Gen 35:22); *T. Iss.* 1:3–2:5 and *Gen. Rab.* 72.3, 5 on the mandrakes-for-sex story (Gen 30:14-16).[38] But the *Testaments* also rely on the rhetoric, content, and thought of the Septuagint, the Scriptures for many early Jews *and* Christians (e.g., the Septuagint explains patriarchs' names and professions [*T. Jud.* 1:3; *T. Iss.* 1:15; *T. Zeb.* 1:3; *T. Naph.* 1:6; *T. Benj.* 1:6]; the wisdom and psalms of the Septuagint supply hortatory material [*T. Jud.* 18:4 and Eccl 4:8; *T. Iss.* 7:5 and Job 31:17, 39; *T. Naph.* 2:3 and Wis 11:20]).[39] Their connections to the New Testament are many (e.g., *T. Jud.* 24:1-2; Matt 3:16; Mark 1:10 on a messiah who sees the heavens open over him; *T. Reu.* 5:5; 1 Cor 6:18a on sexual indiscretion),[40] and they resonate with the thought world and literature of the early Christian church.[41] The connections between the *Testaments* and Cynic-Stoic philosophy are also well known (e.g., *T. Reu.* 2:3-8 and Stoic notions of what motivates human action according to Aetius 4.21.1-4; Philo, *QG* 1.75).[42] In any case, like source- and form-critical efforts to isolate a pre-Christian *Testaments of the Twelve Patriarchs*, we see as a result of the tradition-critical efforts along the same lines that the *Testaments* are founded chiefly on biblical interpretation.

37. E.g., P. Macky, "The Importance of the Teaching on God, Evil, and Eschatology for Dating the Testaments of the Twelve Patriarchs" (Diss., Princeton Theological Seminary, 1969).

38. James L. Kugel, *Traditions of the Bible: A Guide to the Bible as It Was at the Start of the Common Era* (Cambridge, Mass.: Harvard University Press, 1998).

39. Max Küchler, *Frühjüdische Weisheitstraditionen*. OBO 26 (Freiburg: Universitätsverlag, 1979); von Nordheim, *Die Lehre der Alten*, 1.

40. Brian S. Rosner, "A Possible Quotation of Test. Reuben 5.5 in 1 Corinthians 6.18A," *JTS* 43 (1992): 123-27; Aubrey W. Argyle, "The Influence of the Testaments of the Twelve Patriarchs on the New Testament," *ExpTim* 63 (1952): 256-58.

41. Hollander and de Jonge, *The Testaments of the Twelve Patriarchs*, 67-82; Marinus de Jonge, "Hippolytus' 'Benediction of Isaac, Jacob and Moses' and the Testaments of the Twelve Patriarchs," *Bijdr* 46 (1985): 245-60.

42. Kee, "Ethical Dimensions of the Testaments," *passim*; Hollander, *Joseph as Ethical Model, passim*.

The Origin of the Testaments

For all of the foregoing, there is no shortage of scholarship positing an original Jewish *Testaments*. I survey only the major contributors to this endeavor.[43]

In 1884 F. Schnapp resurrected the 1698 hypothesis of Joannes Ernestus Grabe that the *Testaments* were a Jewish composition later redacted by Christians. Schnapp posited parenesis as the first stage, inclusion of apocalyptic elements as the second stage, and Christian additions to the eschatological material as the third phase.[44] Robert H. Charles argued that pro-Levi *Testaments* originated during the reign of John Hyrcanus to express Pharisaic support for the Hasmoneans; the same Pharisaic group added anti-Levite texts around the middle of the first century B.C.E. to express dissatisfaction with the Hasmoneans; Christian additions were made after the turn of the era.[45] Jürgen Becker argued that a late-third-century B.C.E. Hellenistic-Jewish author created the *Testaments* as moral exhortation, and later Hellenistic-Jewish circles added synagogue homiletical material, the L.J. and S.E.R. passages, and still other apocalyptic and messianic passages; last came Christian additions.[46] Anders Hultgård theorized that a Levi-apocryphon attested in the Aramaic Levi materials expressed the views of a third-century B.C.E. Jerusalem Levitical-priestly group; it was gradually edited until the first century B.C.E., and around the turn of the era a separate Jewish group expanded the apocryphon to make its views more universalistic (e.g., the ideal savior passages in *T. Levi* 18; *T. Jud.* 24); Christians redacted the *Testaments* in the second century C.E.[47] Jarl H. Ulrichsen posited a Jewish parenetical *Grundschrift* that used Joseph as an ideal figure (ca. 200 B.C.E.); Jewish prophetic and eschatological-apocalyptic material was added to it between 160 and 100/63 B.C.E., and further Hebrew or Aramaic material of varied character accrued until the first century C.E., when the

43. Kugler, *The Testaments of the Twelve Patriarchs*, 31-38.

44. Joannes Ernestus Grabe, *Spicilegium SS. Patrum ut et Haereticorum, seculi post Christum natum I. II. & III.* 2 vols. (Oxford: E Theatro Sheldoniano, 1698); F. Schnapp, *Die Testamente der zwölf Patriarchen untersucht* (Halle: Niemeyer, 1884).

45. Robert H. Charles, *The Testaments of the Twelve Patriarchs: Translated from the Editor's Greek Text* (London: Oxford University Press, 1908).

46. Jürgen Becker, *Untersuchungen zur Entstehungsgeschichte der Testamente der Zwölf Patriarchen.* AGJU 8 (Leiden: Brill, 1970); and *Unterweisung in lehrhafter Form.* JSHRZ 3 (Gütersloh: Mohn, 1974).

47. Anders Hultgård, *L'Eschatologie des Testaments des Douze Patriarches,* vol. 1: *Interprétation des textes.* Acta Universitatis Upsaliensis, Historia Religionum 6 (Stockholm: Almqvist & Wiksell, 1977); *L'Eschatologie,* vol. 2; and "The Ideal 'Levite,' the Davidic Messiah, and the Saviour Priest in the Testaments of the Twelve Patriarchs," in *Ideal Figures in Ancient Judaism,* ed. John J. Collins and George W. E. Nickelsburg. SBLSCS 12 (Chico: Scholars), 93-110.

whole work was translated into Greek; Christian elements were added in the second century C.E.[48] James Kugel has argued in a different way that Jewish authors composed the *Testaments*. He points out that many of the exegetical motifs in the *Testaments* are explicable only as attempts to solve exegetical puzzles engendered by inconcinnities in the Hebrew Scriptures, a concern ostensibly typical especially of Jewish writers.[49] For our purposes it is worth noting that virtually all of these perspectives on the *Testaments*' purpose fundamentally view them as offspring of Hebrew Scripture interpretation.

Appearing at first to stand in contrast to the last observation, Marinus de Jonge holds that the *Testaments* are essentially a Christian composition.[50] In 1953 he argued on text-, source-, form-, and redaction-critical grounds that a pre-Christian form of the *Testaments* could not be reconstructed. He assigned them to a non-Palestinian "ordinary Christian" of the late second or early third century C.E. In the light of the Dead Sea Scrolls evidence de Jonge does accept the notion that, although they are in their present form a Christian work, the *Testaments* underwent a long compositional history that included a lengthy period during which some of them developed in Jewish circles. But he has never withdrawn his assertion that there is no getting behind the text of the *Testaments* to some pre-Christian, Jewish *Vorlage*: textual, literary, and form criticism do not establish a pre-Christian form of the *Testaments,* and traditio-historical criticism is too speculative and beset with the evidentiary problems described above. Thus for de Jonge, the Christian work only may be investigated. Through numerous publications de Jonge has made significant headway in that endeavor: he sees them as parenetical Christian compositions dedicated on one hand to instructing Christians in proper conduct through the instruc-

---

48. Ulrichsen, *Die Grundschrift der Testamente der Zwölf Patriarchen.*

49. James L. Kugel, "The Story of Dinah in the *Testament of Levi*," *HTR* 85 (1992): 1-34; "Levi's Elevation to the Priesthood in Second Temple Writings," *HTR* 86 (1993): 1-64; and "Reuben's Sin with Bilhah in the *Testament of Reuben*," in *Pomegranates and Golden Bells: Studies in Biblical, Jewish, and Near Eastern Ritual, Law, and Literature in Honor of Jacob Milgrom*, ed. David P. Wright, David Noel Freedman, and Avi Hurvitz (Winona Lake: Eisenbrauns, 1995), 525-54; and *Traditions of the Bible, ad loc.*

The *Testaments* have also been associated with the authors of the Dead Sea Scrolls; see André Dupont-Sommer, *Nouveaux Aperçus sur les Manuscrits de la Mer Morte* (Paris: Maisonneuve, 1953); Marc Philonenko, *Les interpolations chrétiennes des Testaments des Douze Patriarches et les manuscrits de Qoumrân* (Paris: Presses universitaires de France, 1960). The Essene identification fails inasmuch as the scrolls are preoccupied with details of the law that the *Testaments* virtually ignore.

50. For full bibliog. and his most recent statements on the topic, see Marinus de Jonge, *Pseudepigrapha of the Old Testament as Part of Christian Literature: The Case of the Testaments of the Twelve Patriarchs and the Greek Life of Adama and Eve.* SVTP 18 (Leiden: Brill, 2003).

tion of the Old Testament patriarchs, and on the other hand to using the same testimony to achieve Israel's salvation.[51] That said, it is impossible to separate de Jonge entirely from the scholars surveyed above: like them, he understands that the *Testaments* in any form are fundamentally exegetical and interpretive works inasmuch as they build from and develop the traditions of the Hebrew Scriptures at every turn; for his money, they happen to do so as a Christian composition from the start.

The Testaments of the Twelve Patriarchs and Early Jewish Biblical Interpretation: Further Proof of their Common Horizons

Notwithstanding the fact that de Jonge's decision to eschew the quest for their pre-Christian form seems a most reliable approach to addressing the *Testaments,* the foregoing survey of the *Testaments'* contents, genre, main themes, and research history has repeatedly demonstrated their essentially interpretive nature: we cannot speak of the *Testaments* without speaking of the interpretation of the Hebrew Scriptures. For that reason, one of the most profitable ways of studying the *Testaments* — tracing out more precisely their relationship to the root and stalk of the biblical tradition — remains a largely open avenue of research (but see Kugel above). Indeed, while obvious connections between the *Testaments* and the Hebrew Scriptures are known (see above), many more subtle echoes and readings of the Jewish Bible remain to be uncovered. I offer a few possibilities here.

The *Testaments* share with many other Jewish and Christian works one obvious overarching interpretive strategy: capitalizing on the emerging authority of the Hebrew Scriptures by invoking key figures in them to make fresh claims regarding the nature of being human in relationship with Israel's God. Other Jewish testaments prove this point (e.g., *Testament of Job; Testament of Moses; Testament of Abraham*), as do a host of other nontestamentary texts (e.g., *1 Enoch; Jubilees; Psalms of Solomon; Joseph and Aseneth*). And even if it is somewhat oblique, Christian gospels telling the story of Jesus and other non-narrative works that deploy his memory make a similar move (e.g., Jesus the fulfillment of promises to David and Abraham and the New Moses in Matt 1:1-2; 5:27-28; Jesus the ideal high priest in Heb 8:1; 9:11; Jesus and Melchizedek in Hebrews 7).

---

51. De Jonge, *Pseudepigrapha of the Old Testament,* 71-177; and bibliog.; see also *Jewish Eschatology, Early Christian Christology, and the Testaments of the Twelve Patriarchs: Collected Essays of Marinus de Jonge.* NovTSup 63 (Leiden: Brill, 1991), for many of the essays cited here.

Early Jewish and Christian interpretive texts also share the *Testaments'* specific strategies for exploiting the nascent authority of the Hebrew Scriptures and their key figures to make fresh theological arguments. To mention the two most routine strategies, developing and redeploying existing and nascent genres such as we see in the *Testaments* (e.g., deathbed speeches [Genesis 49; Deuteronomy 33], the Sin-Exile-Return formulary [Ezekiel; Deut 29:18–30:10; 1 Kgs 8:46-53]) is typical of other Jewish Pseudepigrapha (e.g., *Prayer of Manasseh; Psalms of Solomon*) as it is of early Christian writings (e.g., Israelite historiography in Luke-Acts; apocalypse in *Shepherd of Hermas*). Likewise, rewriting and repackaging the content of the Hebrew Scriptures to make new claims is a widely shared practice: we see it repeatedly in the *Testaments* (and most clearly in the *Testament of Levi,* which depends on a retelling and expansion of Genesis 34; cf. *T. Levi* 6:3–7:4), in Jewish Pseudepigrapha (cf. Genesis 1 to Exodus 14 and *Jubilees*), and in early Christian texts (cf. Exod 34:29-35 and Matt 17:1-8; Mark 9:2-8; Luke 9:28-36).

James Kugel has uncovered many of the exegetical motifs populating the *Testaments* that we also find in Jewish and Christian works of Greco-Roman antiquity.[52] What can be added to Kugel's perspective, though, are further, perhaps genuinely unique instances in the *Testaments* "echoing" biblical images through exegetical motifs.[53] I close by citing only a few from the valedictory addresses of Simeon and Dan as evidence of the rich vein that may remain to be mined in the *Testaments.*[54]

In *T. Sim.* 2:8, 12 Simeon says that God delivered Joseph "from my hands" (ἐκ τῶν χειρῶν μου), and that in recompense for his evil intentions God afflicted his right hand for seven days (ἡ χείρ μου ἡ δεξιὰ ἡμίξηρος ἦν ἐπὶ ἡμέρας ἑπτά). Hollander and de Jonge say that the disability is typical of the *Testaments'* view of punishment for sinful actions: according to *T. Gad* 5:10, one is afflicted in the organ that transgresses.[55] Likewise, they suggest that if Simeon acted against Joseph to kill him he would have used his hands to do so. There

52. See bibliog. in n. 49 above; see also Bruce Fisk, "One Good Story Deserves Another: The Hermeneutics of Invoking Secondary Biblical Episodes in the Narratives of Pseudo-Philo and the *Testaments* of the *Twelve Patriarchs,*" in *The Interpretation of Scripture in Early Judaism and Christianity: Studies in Language and Tradition,* ed. Craig A. Evans. JSPSup 33. SSEJC 7 (Sheffield: Sheffield Academic, 2000), 217-38.

53. On "echoing," see Richard B. Hays, *Echoes of Scripture in the Letters of Paul* (New Haven: Yale University Press, 1989); John Hollander, *The Figure of Echo: A Mode of Allusion in Milton and After* (Berkeley: University of California Press, 1981).

54. For these and other examples, see Kugler, *The Testaments of the Twelve Patriarchs,* 88-99.

55. De Jonge, *Critical Edition,* 114; see *T. Reu.* 1:7 (a sexual predator is plagued in the loins) and *T. Gad* 5:10 (Gad's liver is beset with illness because he set it against Joseph).

is a problem, though. As in the case of Gad's transgression, Simeon's sin was also seated in his liver ("and I set my liver against him to kill him," 2:7), and he never lifted a hand against his brother; moreover, he later reports that his liver pained him as a result of his anger against Joseph (4:1). Hence the afflicted hand seems superfluous, at least until one remembers Saul, who had already been ghosted into the Simeon narrative by the references to an evil spirit that afflicts one with envy (cf. *T. Sim.* 2:7b [πνεῦμα τοῦ ζήλου] and 1 Sam 19:9 [πνεῦμα θεοῦ πονηρὸν]). In 1 Sam 19:9-10, where Saul's spirit-induced envy is described, we hear that because of his emotions he tried to skewer David with a spear that is pointedly described as resting "in his hand" (ἐν τῇ χειρὶ αὐτοῦ; 19:9); but David was unharmed, because Saul missed and David escaped (cf. 1 Sam 18:12 MT, where the Hebrew text preserves material not included in the LXX; there David was spared כִּי־הָיָה יְהוָה עִמּוֹ וּמֵעִם שָׁאוּל סָר). So like Saul, Simeon's hand was denied its natural action because of his ill intent, and like David, Joseph escaped.

The *Testament of Dan* offers further instances of this more subtle Scripture exegesis. The testament dwells on the anger Dan felt toward his brother Joseph. Because the Bible reveals so little about the patriarch, the testament's authors resorted to bits of Scripture relating to the descendants of Dan to tell his story, and there are few Danites more famous than Samson; so it is not surprising that the principal figure echoed in this testament is that well-known judge.

In a general sense the theme of the testament recalls Samson. He was, like his forefather Dan in the testament's account, afflicted with an irrational anger. The Bible speaks explicitly about his rage after he lost his riddle-based bet with the Philistine men of Timnah (Judg 14:12-20). Judges 14:19 LXX uses the verb θυμόω to acknowledge that Samson's anger (ὀργή) at losing the bet drove him to act rashly in his attack on innocent Ashkelon. He even admits that he was not entirely just when he says about a second round of mischief against Philistia that "this time" he will be without blame (15:3). The implication is that Samson exercised poor judgment in his actions in the earlier incident. Likewise, the testament recounts Dan's unjust and senseless anger against Joseph. His jealousy drove him to plan violence that, without God's protection of Joseph, would have terminated his brother's line.

Another text provides a much more specific allusion to Samson. Anticipating his descendants' future, Dan says that they will "act impurely with the women of the lawless ones" (*T. Dan* 5:5). The behavior implied by Dan's exhortation is clearly intercourse with non-Israelites. While such unions are addressed already in *T. Levi* 9:10; *T. Jud.* 13:7; 14:6, this reference seems to come from nowhere. Isaac's insistence that Levi not marry a Gentile probably comes from the Levi tradition evident in the Aramaic source material, and the concern for marriage with non-Jews is natural in the *Testament of Judah,* preoccupied as it is with the difficulties that women — particularly non-Israelite women — engender for men. But in *T. Dan* 5:5 there is seemingly no context for the comment; it comes suddenly as a future sin of Dan's descendants, one that seems unrelated to his own history. Thus one is driven outside of the story world to locate a reason for Dan's claim against his children, and we need look no further than Samson. Judges 14:1–15:20 tells the story of his fateful marriage to the Philistine woman in Timnah; 16:1-3 recounts the tale of his encounter with the prostitute at Gaza and the locals' attempt on that occasion to destroy him; and of course, there is the story of his marriage to the "flirt" Deliliah, whose name would indicate her non-Israelite birth (although the valley of Sorek could have been the home of Gentiles or Israelites).

Lastly, there is also a very specific echo of Scripture in the testament that reflects the authors' level of sophistication in this regard. In 1:8 Dan notes that it was a spirit of anger that tried to convince him to "suck out Joseph as a leopard sucks out a lamb." The whole comment is peculiar, let alone the use of ἐκμύζαω, "to suck out,"[56] but the reference to a leopard and a lamb in one phrase is unmistakable: it recalls, and suggests, the near reversal of the messianic prediction passage of Isa 11:1-9, making this an oblique Joseph-as-type-of-Jesus passage.

Conclusion

There should be little lingering doubt about the *Testaments'* testimony to the interpretive practices of Jews of Greco-Roman antiquity. Their contents, genre, and themes bear witness to the Hebrew Scriptures as their root and stalk, and the history of research devoted to them since the late seventeenth century further demonstrates their rightful place among the Jewish Pseudepigrapha that rely on exegesis of the Hebrew Bible. The *Testaments of the Twelve Patriarchs,* Christian or Jewish in their original form, are undeniably and first and foremost the product of exegesis and interpretation of the Hebrew Bible.

BIBLIOGRAPHY

Becker, Jürgen. *Untersuchungen zur Entstehungsgeschichte der Testamente der Zwölf Patriarchen.* AGJU 8. Leiden: Brill, 1970.
———. *Unterweisung in lehrhafter Form.* JSHRZ 3. Gütersloh: Mohn, 1974.

---

56. See Charles, *The Testaments of the Twelve Patriarchs,* 124, for a suggested alternative reading that would allow one to translate the word as "crush."

Braun, F.-M. "Les Testaments des XII Patriarches et le problème de leur origine." *RB* 67 (1960): 516-49.

Burchard, Christoph. "Zur armenischen Überlieferung der Testamente der zwölf Patriarchen." In Eltester, *Studien zu den Testamenten der Zwölf Patriarchen*, 1-29.

Charles, Robert H. *The Greek Versions of the Testaments of the Twelve Patriarchs: Edited from Nine MSS.* London: Oxford University Press, 1908.

———. *The Testaments of the Twelve Patriarchs: Translated from the Editor's Greek Text.* London: Oxford University Press, 1908.

Collins, John J. "Testaments." In *Jewish Writings of the Second Temple Period: Apocrypha, Pseudepigrapha, Qumran, Sectarian Writings, Philo, Josephus*, ed. Michael E. Stone. CRINT 2.2. Assen: Van Gorcum and Minneapolis: Fortress, 1984, 325-55.

Dupont-Sommer, André. *Nouveaux Aperçus sur les Manuscrits de la Mer Morte.* Paris: Maisonneuve, 1960.

Eltester, Walther, ed. *Studien zu den Testamenten der Zwölf Patriarchen: Christoph Burchard, Jacob Jervell, Johannes Thomas.* ZNW 36. Berlin: Töpelmann, 1969.

Eppel, Robert. *Le Piétisme Juif dans les Testaments de Douze Patriarches.* Paris: Alcan, 1930.

Grabe, Joannes Ernestus. *Spicilegium SS. Patrum ut et Haereticorum, seculi post Christum natum I. II. & III.* 2 vols. Oxford: E theatro Sheldoniano, 1698.

Haupt, Detlev. "Das Testament des Levi: Untersuchungen zu seiner Entstehung und Überlieferungsgeschichte." Diss., Halle-Wittenberg, 1969.

Hollander, Harm W. *Joseph as an Ethical Model in the Testaments of the Twelve Patriarchs.* SVTP 6. Leiden: Brill, 1981.

Hollander, Harm W., and Marinus de Jonge. *The Testaments of the Twelve Patriarchs: A Commentary.* SVTP 8. Leiden: Brill, 1985.

Hultgård, Anders. *L'Eschatologie des Testaments des Douze Patriarches.* Vol. 1: *Interprétation des texts.* Acta Universitatis Upsaliensis, Historia Religionum 6. Stockholm: Almqvist & Wiksell, 1977.

———. *L'Eschatologie des Testaments des Douze Patriarches.* Vol. 2: *Composition de l'ouvrage, textes et traductions.* Acta Universitatis Upsaliensis, Historia Religionum 7. Stockholm: Almqvist & Wiksell, 1981.

Jonge, Henrik J. de. "The Earliest Traceable Stage of the Textual Tradition of the Testaments of the Twelve Patriarchs." In Marinus de Jonge, *Studies on the Testaments of the Twelve Patriarchs*, 63-86.

———. "Die Patriarchentestamente von Roger Bacon bis Richard Simon." In Marinus de Jonge, *Studies on the Testaments of the Twelve Patriarchs*, 3-42.

Jonge, Marinus de. *The Testaments of the Twelve Patriarchs: A Study of Their Text, Composition, and Origin.* Assen: Van Gorcum, 1953.

———. *The Testaments of the Twelve Patriarchs: A Critical Edition of the Greek Text.* PVTG 1.2. Leiden: Brill, 1975.

———. *Jewish Eschatology, Early Christian Christology, and the Testaments of the Twelve Patriarchs: Collected Essays of Marinus de Jonge.* NovTSup 63. Leiden: Brill, 1991.

———. *Pseudepigrapha of the Old Testament as Part of Christian Literature: The Case of the Testaments of the Twelve Patriarchs and the Greek Life of Adam and Eve.* SVTP 18. Leiden: Brill, 2003.

————, ed. *Studies on the Testaments of the Twelve Patriarchs: Text and Interpretation.* SVTP 3. Leiden: Brill, 1975.

Kugler, Robert A. *From Patriarch to Priest: The Levi-Priestly Tradition from Aramaic Levi to Testament of Levi.* SBLEJL 9. Atlanta: Scholars, 1996.

————. *The Testaments of the Twelve Patriarchs.* GAP. Sheffield: Sheffield Academic, 2001.

Nordheim, Eckhard von. *Die Lehre der Alten.* Vol. 1: *Das Testament als Literaturgattung im Judentum der hellenistisch-römischen Zeit.* ALGHJ 13. Leiden: Brill, 1980.

Philonenko, Marc. *Les interpolations chrétiennes des Testaments des Douze Patriarches et les manuscrits de Qoumrân.* Paris: Presses universitaires de France, 1960.

Schnapp, F. *Die Testamente der zwölf Patriarchen untersucht.* Halle: Niemeyer, 1884.

Slingerland, H. Dixon. *The Testaments of the Twelve Patriarchs: A Critical History of Research.* SBLMS 21. Missoula: Scholars, 1977.

Thomas, Johannes. "Aktuelles im Zeugnis der zwölf Väter." In Eltester, *Studien zu den Testamenten der zwölf Patriarchen,* 62-150.

Ulrichsen, Jarl Henning. *Die Grundschrift der Testamente der Zwölf Patriarchen: Eine Untersuchung zu Umfang, Inhalt und Eigenart der ursprünglichen Schrift.* Acta Universitatis Upsaliensis, Historia Religionum 10. Stockholm: Almqvist & Wiksell, 1991.

PART 6

WISDOM LITERATURE

Biblical Interpretation in the Book of Ben Sira

Benjamin G. Wright III

Ben Sira and "The Bible"

The book of Ben Sira stands caught in the middle of scholarly discussions about the development of the Hebrew Bible and the process of canonization. I do not intend to try to resolve any of those matters here, but some discussion is germane to any attempt to talk about "biblical interpretation" in Sirach. Moreover, the literature on these matters in Ben Sira is immense, and I will only highlight a selection of scholarly studies in this introductory section.

Traditionally, scholars have invoked Ben Sira as evidence for which books of what later became the Hebrew Bible were "canonical" in the early part of the second century B.C.E. The usual method has been to look for which books Ben Sira quoted or alluded to. If he "knew" books that ended up in the canon, so the reasoning goes, then they must have been authoritative, and probably canonical, by his time. Books he did not know were probably not authoritative, and hence not canonical. This approach to canon stems, at least in part, from some early assessments of Sirach that followed the discovery of the Hebrew manuscripts, such as that of Solomon Schechter and Charles Taylor, who damn Ben Sira with faint praise, when they write that he was "not entirely devoid of original ideas" because he was "a conscious imitator both as to form and as to matter, his chief model being the Book of Proverbs."[1] Of course, Ben Sira's presumed lack of originality depended on his supposed reliance on the Hebrew Bible. Schechter and Taylor provide an extensive list of passages that they presume proves "that there can be no reasonable doubt that they were either suggested to him by or directly copied from the Scriptures."[2]

---

1. Solomon Schechter and Charles Taylor, *The Wisdom of Ben Sira* (Cambridge: Cambridge University Press, 1899), 12-13.

2. Schechter and Taylor, *The Wisdom of Ben Sira,* 13. For other studies that use this method,

In 1967, John G. Snaith criticized views such as these.[3] He concluded, "The amount of Ben Sira's conscious literary quotation from the Hebrew Bible has been much over-estimated through lack of detailed investigation into each alleged instance."[4] Even though Snaith effectively critiques the way that scholars had tried to determine the extent of Ben Sira's biblical canon, he also falls into the trap of being bound by canonical boundaries and categories. All in all, however, Snaith offers a timely warning about adopting Schechter's and Taylor's simplistic viewpoints.

The prologue to the Greek translation raises the specter of canonical categories as well. Ben Sira's grandson, who translated the book, notes that his grandfather had an intimate familiarity with "the Law and the Prophets and the other ancestral books" (9–10), a remark that many scholars have taken to refer to the existence of a Jewish tripartite canon in this period.[5] Without doubt, the grandson recognizes that the traditional literature of Israel could be placed into categories — and "Law" likely refers to the Pentateuch — but the use of the term "canon," or even "biblical," in any strong sense to describe them injects unnecessary assumptions about their bounded and fixed natures.[6]

Recently, Robert Kraft has questioned the extent to which we can speak about the interpretation of "scriptures" in early Judaism.[7] Kraft distinguishes between two different attitudes, "scripture consciousness" and "canonical consciousness":

> Furthermore, it is not always clear what would constitute firm evidence of 'scripture consciousness' — that is, special reverential attitudes towards the localization and preservation of traditional authoritative materials in fixed written format. We are not speaking here of reverence to traditional law and/

---

see Andreas Eberharter, *Der Kanon des Alten Testaments zur Zeit des ben Sira.* ATA 3.3 (Münster: Aschendorff, 1911); and Jan L. Koole, "Die Bibel des Ben-Sira," *OtSt* 14 (1965): 374-96.

3. John G. Snaith, "Biblical Quotations in the Hebrew of Ecclesiasticus," *JTS* 18 (1967): 1-12.

4. Snaith, "Biblical Quotations," 11.

5. All translations of the Greek come from Albert Pietersma and Benjamin G. Wright, eds., *A New English Translation of the Septuagint and Other Greek Translations Traditionally Included Under That Title* (New York: Oxford University Press, 2007). Other translations come from the NRSV.

6. For a penetrating look at the idea of a tripartite canon at the time of Ben Sira, see John Barton, *Oracles of God: Perceptions of Ancient Prophecy in Israel After the Exile* (London: Darton, Longman, and Todd, 1986); and more recently his article "The Significance of a Fixed Canon of the Hebrew Bible," in *Hebrew Bible/Old Testament: The History of Its Interpretation,* vol. 1: *From the Beginnings to the Middle Ages (Until 1300),* Part 1: *Antiquity,* ed. Magne Sæbø (Göttingen: Vandenhoeck & Ruprecht, 1996), 67-83.

7. Robert A. Kraft, "Scripture and Canon in Jewish Apocrypha and Pseudepigrapha," in Sæbø, *Hebrew Bible/Old Testament,* 1.1:199-216.

or laws, or of its/their formulation as 'covenant,' or of familiarity with certain traditional stories or hymns/prayers or phrases that we find as part of what has come to be known as 'Jewish Scriptures' (Hebrew Bible, TaNaKh, OT, etc.). The 'scriptural consciousness' question focuses on the extent to which authoritative law and/or tradition has come to be explicitly associated with identifiable books and writings, or perhaps vice versa.

A further stage in this attempt to understand the development of text-related ideas of authority could be called 'canon consciousness.' Under what circumstances and in what formulations does the awareness of authoritative writings ('Scripture consciousness') come to exhibit itself in terms of collections (extension) and even a limited collection (exclusion) of writing invested with special authority (canonical consciousness)?[8]

So, Kraft maintains, when we find reverence for law or covenant in early Jewish literature, we cannot jump to the conclusion that it reflects either Scripture or canonical consciousness, nor does evidence that an author knows "personal names and stories and phrases" that *we* know from biblical materials indicate that the author was consciously dependent on "*written* sources that were at that time considered *authoritative*"[9] — that is, we cannot simply assume so without any confirming evidence. As for Sirach, Kraft notes that even though the grandson refers to three categories, the book itself contains no explicit references to scriptural passages, although in 24:23 Wisdom is embodied in "the book of the covenant of the Most High God," which is equated with "a law that Moses commanded us." The Praise of the Ancestors (chs. 44-50) invokes specific names and stories mentioned in biblical books. On the basis of this evidence, Kraft concludes that Sirach is one of a number of early Jewish texts for which there existed "a core 'canon' of sorts . . . in the form of the Mosaic book(s)." For Sirach, however, "[t]here is no indication in the prologue . . . that its vague list of three categories represented a closed collection. How the translator related his grandfather's 'instruction and wisdom' to the aforementioned books is not clear, nor how the grandfather himself might have viewed these issues."[10]

Ben Sira and Interpretation

Raising doubts about the nature of what is "biblical" or "canonical" for Ben Sira has a direct impact on what we look for when we try to identify biblical "inter-

8. Kraft, "Scripture and Canon," 200-201.
9. Kraft, "Scripture and Canon," 203.
10. Kraft, "Scripture and Canon," 211.

pretation." I am not suggesting that Ben Sira did not have textual sources at his disposal. Indeed, there is evidence of textuality throughout the book, and in some cases one finds intertextual connections with books that became "biblical."[11] Part of Ben Sira's scribal education must have encompassed learning, perhaps even memorizing, the inherited texts of Israel's past.[12] Some of these works had a religious authority or "scripture consciousness" for Ben Sira, most clearly seen in "the book of the covenant of the Most High God, a Law that Moses commanded us" (24:23). Outside of his statements about the "Law," though, Ben Sira does not indicate what authority any work might have had for him, especially since he does not introduce texts with citation formulae or some other explicit reference.

Three factors bear on any attempt to understand what constitutes biblical "interpretation" in Ben Sira. First, Ben Sira employed textual sources that influenced his work, and one can often map close intertextual relationships with his sources. Even if we bracket the Praise of the Ancestors from the rest of the book (see below), we encounter passages reminiscent of the Israelite literary tradition that might have played a critical role in Ben Sira's teaching. For this reason, James Kugel has called sages like Ben Sira and the author of the Wisdom of Solomon "transitional figures," since they are wisdom teachers in the traditional manner of the sages who produced Proverbs or Job, but in addition they now look to the Israelite literary heritage for inquiring into wisdom.[13] Moreover, the beginnings of biblical interpretation are found in wisdom, and Torah has become "part of the wisdom corpus."[14]

But to recognize that Ben Sira viewed Torah as part of the "wisdom corpus" does not tell the whole story. Torah, probably inherited in written form (but along with oral traditions and other sources?), indeed became a source of wisdom, but not the only one. In Sirach at least two other more traditional

11. For more detail on the arguments in this short section, see my paper, "The Use and Interpretation of Biblical Traditions in Ben Sira's Praise of the Ancestors," in *Studies in the Book of Ben Sira, Papers of the Third International Conference on the Deuterocanonical Books, Shime'on Centre, Pápa, Hungary, 18-20 May 2006*, ed. Géza Xeravits and József Zsengellér. JSJSup 127 (Leiden: Brill, 2008), 183-207.

12. For a study of ancient scribal education, see David M. Carr, *Writing on the Tablet of the Heart: Origins of Scripture and Literature* (Oxford: Oxford University Press, 2005).

13. James Kugel, "Ancient Biblical Interpretation and the Biblical Sage," in *Studies in Ancient Midrash* (Cambridge, Mass.: Harvard University Press, 2001), 1-26 (here 12). Of course, Kugel wants to use the term "Scripture," which, he claims, has become by the period of Sirach and Wisdom of Solomon "God's great book of instruction" and "the written record of the one true God's own teachings" (both quotes, 12). As I have already indicated, I am not as sure that we can talk about "Scripture" in such concrete ways when discussing Ben Sira.

14. Kugel, "Ancient Biblical Interpretation," 24.

sources play a role: (1) the wisdom of the sages, which was handed down orally and to which Ben Sira refers often, and (2) observation of the natural world, particularly meditation on the nature of creation. Ben Sira mines all these resources for wisdom that will prepare his students to lead good and productive lives in faithfulness to God. So, in his sources and his instruction, we encounter both orality and textuality. The oral nature of the educational process is central to Ben Sira's pedagogy — so, for example, his frequent admonitions for his students to *hear* what he has to *say*, such as, "Listen to me, your father, O child" (3:1). The goal of Ben Sira's instruction is not to exegete Scripture (whatever "Scripture" might look like) but to proffer Wisdom, which "becomes known through speech" (4:24). And yet, he *writes* his teaching as a legacy for subsequent generations: "Instruction and understanding and knowledge I have written in this book. . . . Happy are those who concern themselves with these things, and those who lay them to heart will be wise" (50:27-28). Ben Sira views his teaching as a legacy, a contribution to wisdom, and he transforms what he draws from his sources in significant ways.

Second, Ben Sira tries to construct a world for his students to inhabit. In a recent study of Qumran texts, Carol Newsom has argued that the *Serekh Hayaḥad* and the *Hodayot* work to form a sectarian identity among the members of the Qumran community. The discourse in these two texts "creates a figured world and self identity, thereby critically engaging other forms of contemporary Judaism."[15] As part of that larger conversation, Newsom points out the ubiquity of what she terms "biblicizing language and genres in Second Temple literature," where biblical language "both facilitates and authorizes their [i.e., Jewish works of the period] speech but at the same time dominates it. . . . The new compositions seek both to share in the cultural authority of scripture but also in some way to co-opt it."[16] I think that Ben Sira evinces this same concern. He wants to create a "figured world" for his disciples as they hear and absorb his teaching, and his use of "biblical" language and texts, as we will see, co-opts them and authorizes his own construction of the world and his students' place in it. In this light, we should not be surprised by the absence of citation formulae or other direct quotation of the texts that he interprets. Although direct citation can function in the ways that Newsom suggests, the texts that Ben Sira employs play supporting roles to his main character, his own wisdom teaching.

Third, in order for Ben Sira's adaptations of these traditional Israelite texts to serve his broader pedagogical purposes, he needed a strategy for conferring

---

15. Carol Newsom, *The Self as Symbolic Space: Constructing Identity and Community at Qumran*. STDJ 52 (Leiden: Brill, 2004), 21.

16. Newsom, *The Self as Symbolic Space*, 5-6.

authority on his interpretations, particularly since he does not distinguish between something identified as "Scripture" and his own use of it. He recognizes "the Law of the Most High" as a distinct and authoritative, although to us vague, category, but in the end *his* teaching must be authoritative. Hindy Najman has questioned the extent to which, in the Second Temple period, we can distinguish sharply "between the *transmission* and the *interpretation* of biblical traditions."[17] She describes the appearance in some Second Temple texts of what she calls "a discourse tied to a founder," in which "to rework an earlier text is to update, interpret, and develop the content of that text in a way that one claims to be an authentic expression of the law already accepted as authoritatively Mosaic."[18] This legitimating strategy fits into the larger framework of Second Temple conceptions of authority, "which always demanded roots in the pre-exilic past."[19] Whereas Najman has applied her notion of discourse tied to a founder primarily to making sense of the phenomenon of pseudepigraphy and of the practice of "rewriting" Scripture, so prevalent in Second Temple literature, it also elucidates the motives of an author like Ben Sira, where the "scriptural" text is so thoroughly submerged in and incorporated into a sage's teaching.

Even though Ben Sira connects the authority of his instruction to his personal authority as a sage by attaching his name to his book (which may say something about his views on the place of the sage in his social world), he also grounds his interpretations in even more ancient and authoritative sources. In the Praise of the Ancestors, which culminates in the glorious description of Simon II, the high priest appears as a constituent in a list of selected figures from Israel's past. In Simon the royal and the priestly coalesce, and Ben Sira praises both his priestly and kingly deeds.[20] In order to construct his ideal priest-ruler, however, Ben Sira fixes Simon's social, religious, and political activities within

---

17. Hindy Najman, *Seconding Sinai: The Development of Mosaic Discourse in Second Temple Judaism.* JSJSup 77 (Leiden: Brill, 2003), 8.

18. Najman, *Seconding Sinai*, 13.

19. Najman, *Seconding Sinai*, 14.

20. On the Praise of the Ancestors in general, see Burton Mack, *Wisdom and the Hebrew Epic: Ben Sira's Hymn in Praise of the Fathers* (Chicago: University of Chicago Press, 1985); and Thomas R. Lee, *Studies in the Form of Sirach 44–50.* SBLDS 75 (Atlanta: Scholars, 1986). On Simon as the ideal priest-ruler, see Martha Himmelfarb, "The Wisdom of the Scribe, the Wisdom of the Priest, and the Wisdom of the King According to Ben Sira," in *For a Later Generation: The Transformation of Tradition in Israel, Early Judaism and Early Christianity*, ed. Randal A. Argall, Beverly A. Bow, and Rodney A. Werline (Harrisburg: Trinity Press International, 2000), 89-99; and Benjamin G. Wright, "Ben Sira on Kings and Kingship," in *Jewish Perspectives on Hellenistic Rulers*, ed. Tessa Rajak et al. Hellenistic Culture and Society 50 (Berkeley: University of California Press, 2007), 76-91.

the framework of and as the logical conclusion to the actions and offices of the Israelite heroes that precede him.

The discourse of chapter 24 provides a more comprehensive strategy for conferring authority on Ben Sira's instruction. God sends Wisdom to the temple in Jerusalem where she ministers before him (vv. 8-11). Wisdom calls out to whoever would respond, and verses 19-22 transition to the critical verse 23 in which Ben Sira claims that Wisdom is embodied in the Torah. Ben Sira then describes the Law using fluvial metaphors, referring to the Pishon, Tigris, Euphrates, Jordan, Nile, and Gihon rivers. The Pishon and Gihon bracket this section, evoking the presence of Wisdom at creation, but more immediately forming a segue back to the connection of Wisdom and creation (vv. 28-29): "The first man did not complete knowing her [i.e., Wisdom], and so the last one did not track her out, for her thought was filled from the sea, and her counsel from the great abyss." The Law, then, can be compared to rivers, and Wisdom to the sea. Ben Sira continues with his water metaphors in verses 30-31, but now comparing his teaching to a canal that becomes a river and then a sea. Thus, Ben Sira's instruction flows directly into Wisdom and perhaps becomes identical with it. And if this metaphorical watershed does not make the point well enough, Ben Sira compares his teaching to prophecy (vv. 32-33). At the conclusion, his teaching becomes a conduit for anyone seeking Wisdom: "See that I have not toiled for myself alone, but for all who seek it (or, 'her') out." The authority for Ben Sira's teaching and interpretations of Israelite literature derives from a primordial source, Wisdom herself, who was with God in the beginning and who infuses the Torah. Ben Sira has direct access to her and hence to the heart of Torah. Moreover, since the person who single-mindedly pursues Wisdom can possess her, Ben Sira not only authorizes his own teaching, he also legitimates the entire enterprise of the sage.[21]

For Sirach, then, I use the word "interpretation" to indicate the ways in which he adapted and incorporated material from his sources — the literature of his national and ethnic heritage (whether or not he had any "canonical consciousness") — in order to construct his teachings. In some cases the way that Ben Sira employs his sources allows us to conclude that he interpreted a particular text, but in others it is impossible to pin down any specific text on which he might have depended. Rather than operating as an imitator or an exegete of Scripture, Ben Sira employed, manipulated, and performed the texts in the ser-

---

21. For more detail on Ben Sira's authorizing strategies, see my paper "Jubilees, Sirach, and Sapiential Tradition," given at the Fourth International Enoch Seminar, July 9-12, 2007, in *Enoch and the Mosaic Torah*, ed. Gabriele Boccaccini and Giovanni Ibba (Grand Rapids: Eerdmans, 2009), 116-30.

vice of his own pedagogy, which he understood as participating in the authority of Lady Wisdom herself. Of course, Wisdom is not only present in the Torah; the sages who sought her passed wisdom down to later generations, and since Wisdom was present at creation, she can be apprehended in nature as well. So, whereas I do not think that Ben Sira necessarily intended to elevate his interpretations to the level of Mosaic Torah, as we see, for example, in *Jubilees,* his authority-conferring strategies legitimate the various sources of the sages' teaching, sources that he has taken, shaped, and molded and that he "will pour out like prophecy" for his students.

Recent Studies on Ben Sira and Biblical Interpretation

Two recent studies have tried to establish that Ben Sira had a "canonical consciousness" while at the same time showing how he interpreted the texts.[22] In his book *Wisdom as a Hermeneutical Construct,* Gerald Sheppard argues that in some early Jewish works "wisdom became a theological category associated with an understanding of canon which formed a perspective from which to interpret Torah and prophetic traditions. In this sense wisdom became a hermeneutical construct for interpreting sacred scripture."[23] His parade example is Ben Sira. Sheppard's argument relies on two problematic positions, however: (1) Ben Sira used fixed and stable written texts that were part of a corpus that he regarded as sacred Scripture; and (2) the Greek and Syriac translations are reliable witnesses to the original Hebrew so that reconstructions based on them reflect accurately what Ben Sira wrote.[24] Sheppard concludes about his case studies (which include Bar 3:8–4:4):

> The case studies undertaken have confirmed the existence of recurring wisdom interpretations of *fixed* OT traditions in the post-exilic period. Fortu-

22. In a third study, Lester L. Grabbe, "The Law, the Prophets, and the Rest: The State of the Bible in Pre-Maccabean Times," *DSD* 13 (2006): 319-38, also argues for a canon of Scripture based on Ben Sira, but he does not deal with interpretation.

23. Gerald T. Sheppard, *Wisdom as a Hermeneutical Construct: A Study in the Sapientializing of the Old Testament.* BZAW 151 (Berlin: de Gruyter, 1980), 13.

24. Sheppard's latter assumption brings into relief a recurring problem with Ben Sira, the complicated nature of the extant textual witnesses. Sheppard, e.g., examines Ben Sira, 24:3-29 and 16:24–17:14, passages for which no Hebrew survives. Numerous problems attend the surviving texts of Sirach. Particularly difficult is our ability to make confident reconstructions based on the daughter versions, as I have tried to show in a study of some aspects of the Greek translator's approach to the Hebrew text; Benjamin G. Wright, *No Small Difference: Sirach's Relationship to Its Hebrew Parent Text.* SBLSCS 26 (Atlanta: Scholars, 1989).

nately, because of the *advanced stage of OT canonization* at the time of Ben Sira and the writer of Bar. 3:9–4:4, it is possible for the modern scholar to achieve relatively objective literary control in describing such phenomena. By recalling the original OT context of these references to *fixed* narrative and prophetic traditions, the nature of interpretation can frequently be measured as a function of the literary changes in the post-exilic re-application of the biblical material. . . . [T]he case studies provide ample evidence of a desire to prove exegetically that the Torah and the prophetic writings inform and anticipate the concerns of the biblical wisdom traditions.[25] (emphases mine)

The italicized portions of the quotation above reveal that, for Sheppard, "canon" indicates first a stable textual tradition, one that we can know and against which we can measure Ben Sira's use of it, and second, a set of books that is delimited and closed, which enables one to separate the interpretation from its source and indirectly to construct the outlines of what the canon was. His analysis of the two passages from Sirach invokes a veritable pastiche of biblical words and phrases that reminds one of Schechter's and Taylor's lists. One textual example will suffice here. Sheppard concludes that Sir 17:11-14

illustrates the arranging of several phrases of individual passages from different texts which relate the giving of the Law at Sinai. For example, the covenant is called "Law of Life" which is "set before them" (cf. Dt. 4:44). As at Sinai too, the people "beheld his glorious majesty" (cf. Ex. 24:16-17) and "heard his glorious voice" (Ex. 19:19, 20; Dt. 4:12; 5:4; 30:2, 10, 20). Although this language shows fidelity to the very words of the sacred tradition, the entire epitomization far exceeds the witness of a single text or tradition and encompasses the larger context of the related Scripture taken as a whole.[26]

This plethora of biblical references creates the impression that Ben Sira had practically all of Hebrew Scripture at his disposal and that he did a sophisticated cut-and-paste job, picking and choosing from a range of texts that he had before him.[27] As a result, even a general statement, such as "when God created his works" (16:26a), becomes an allusion to specific verses from the biblical text. Not only does this method "over-estimate" (to recall Snaith's term) the "biblical citations" in Sirach, it also minimizes Ben Sira's own inter-

25. Sheppard, *Wisdom as a Hermeneutical Construct*, 100. For more on this text, see below.

26. Sheppard, *Wisdom as a Hermeneutical Construct*, 104.

27. Although in this example, the texts that Sheppard cites are from the Pentateuch, for other verses in ch. 24 he argues that Ben Sira draws on Joshua, Jeremiah, Psalms, 2 Samuel, among others.

pretive creativity, originality, and claims to authority, even if, as Sheppard claims, Ben Sira's interpretation might "exceed the witness of a single text or tradition."

Yet, if one decouples Sheppard's tight connection between wisdom and a canon of Scripture, one can still see how wisdom functions as a *theological* category that transcends traditional "wisdom" and acts as a lens through which Ben Sira views the Israelite traditions that he inherited. Let me take just one of Sheppard's textual examples, Sir 24:15, "Like cinnamon and camel's thorn for spices and like choice myrrh I gave forth a fragrance, like galbanum and onycha and stacte and like the vapor of frankincense in a tent." Sheppard argues that by drawing his vocabulary from Exod 30:23, 34, and 36, Ben Sira shows that "even these exotic implements of the cult pertain to Wisdom."[28] In the service of this argument, he offers (1) a comparative diagram of the Greek texts of Sirach and the LXX of Exodus and (2) parallel citations of M. H. Segal's reconstruction of the Hebrew with Exodus.[29] But one does not have to invoke the specific vocabulary of Exodus 30 to conclude that Ben Sira brings cult within the orbit of Wisdom (and thus employs Wisdom as a theological construct, even if it is not narrowly hermeneutical in Sheppard's terms). If we compare the two passages thoroughly and not simply highlight their common elements, the "spices" (ἀρώματα) of Sirach are ἡδύσματα in Exodus, Exodus notably lacks Sirach's "camel's thorn" as one of the spices used in the temple, the "perfume" (εὐωδία) of Sirach is the adjective "sweet-smelling" (εὐώδης) in Exodus, and the "tent" of Sirach is the "tent of witness" in Exodus. When the evidence is considered *in toto* (even assuming with Sheppard that the Greek gives some access to the Hebrew), I doubt that Ben Sira excerpted Exodus here, even though he shares the primary aromatic substances used in the temple. Of course, he knows their names. Is there a canonical *text* here that we can separate from an *interpretation?* I doubt it. Does Ben Sira claim that Wisdom has a connection to the cult? Absolutely. Wisdom functions strategically in Ben Sira as a theological construct, a framework for understanding the world, including the temple cult and the "Law of the Most High." That Wisdom functions as a "hermeneutical construct," a principle for interpreting a fixed canon of Scripture, I find dubious, however.

In his article, "Canon and Scripture in the Book of Ben Sira," Pancratius C. Beentjes also argues for a canon of Scripture in Ben Sira, but when considering

28. Sheppard, *Wisdom as a Hermeneutical Construct,* 59.

29. I will not enter into an extended critique here of the problem of making reconstructions of the Hebrew from the daughter versions (primarily the Greek). Sheppard offers no discussion of *how* Segal reconstructed this passage, for example. As I have demonstrated, such reconstructions can be very problematic. See Wright, *No Small Difference,* 236-49.

individual passages, Beentjes is more circumspect than Sheppard.[30] Beentjes isolates three different uses of "scripture": (1) passages with "introductory formulae"; (2) "inverted quotations"; and (3) "structural uses" of scripture. Although I agree with Beentjes that Ben Sira sometimes has specific texts in mind, I do not think that such cases demonstrate Ben Sira's idea of a canon (use does not equal canonicity), and I think that Beentjes overestimates the number of places that we can identify specific scriptural passages. I will look at a couple of examples.

Beentjes argues that of the seven occurrences of the Hebrew interrogative הֲלֹא, four serve as markers of reference to Scripture, one of which is Sir 38:5, "Was not water made sweet with a tree in order that its power might be known?" In its context, this verse provides an example of the healing properties of medicines. Certainly this question reminds one of the episode at Marah in which Moses throws a piece of wood into bitter water to make it drinkable (see Exod 15:23-25). Yet, to say that הֲלֹא constitutes an introductory formula to a scriptural reference assumes that Ben Sira was pointing the reader to a canonical text and that he did not know it from another source or in another form. The language of this passage is not specific enough to identify Ben Sira's immediate source as Exodus, however.

As an example of "inverted" quotations of Scripture, that is, a place in Sirach where Scripture "has been quoted in a reversed order,"[31] Beentjes proposes Sir 20:5, "There is one who is silent and is thought to be wise, and there is one who is hated due to much talking,"[32] and Prov 17:28, "Even a fool who is silent will be thought wise; closing his lips, he (will be thought) understanding." Sirach 20:5a and Prov 17:28a share three words: (1) "one who is silent" (מחריש), (2) the verb חשב in the niphal, and (3) the adjective "wise" (חכם).[33] Sirach has the words in the order 1-2-3 and Proverbs has 1-3-2, thus the "inverted" aspect of the clause. Granting the similarity of the thought and the use of common language, must we consider this a quotation of Proverbs? When we compare the two clauses, we discover that Ben Sira is more coy about the subject, "one who is," which differs from the explicit "fool" of Proverbs. If we read Ben Sira as a direct quote of Proverbs, then the subject of the clause will be a fool.[34] Yet,

---

30. Published originally in Sæbø, *Hebrew Bible/Old Testament*, 591-605; repr. in Pancratius C. Beentjes, *"Happy the One Who Meditates on Wisdom" (SIR. 14,20): Collected Essays on the Book of Ben Sira.* CBET 43 (Leuven: Peeters, 2006), 169-86 (all references will be to the latter publication).

31. Beentjes, "Canon and Scripture," 177.

32. The translation is based on Ms C.

33. Missing in Ms C, but the likely reading.

34. This is also how Patrick W. Skehan and Alexander Di Lella read the verse; *The Wisdom of Ben Sira.* AB 39 (New York: Doubleday, 1987), 300.

both Sir 20:6 and 7 contrast the wise person who knows when to speak and the fool who does not. In that light, 20:5 might be construed to mean that the wise person will keep silent and be thought wise, whereas the fool will talk and be hated. By this reading, Sirach turns Proverbs on its head. Rather than a formal quotation of Proverbs, I think that this verse reflects of a common wisdom motif, which both Proverbs and Ben Sira employ in very similar terms, and I am not convinced that examples such as this constitute evidence for Ben Sira's "interpretation" of a "biblical" text.

"Biblical" Interpretation in Ben Sira

Even so, I do think that we can investigate how Ben Sira understood and appropriated the Israelite literary heritage. I say "appropriate," since given Ben Sira's notion of his own authority as a sage and the expectation that the sage will creatively manipulate his inherited traditions, the word "interpretation" might not be the most apt one. In this section, I will look at several passages that illustrate some different possibilities for understanding what Ben Sira did with the texts that he inherited.[35] I will focus on examples whose traditions can be found in the Pentateuch, since Ben Sira almost certainly considered these traditions to be authoritative and "scriptural."[36]

One difficulty confronts anyone working with Ben Sira — the problematic state of the text. According to the translator's prologue, Ben Sira's grandson translated the book from Hebrew into Greek. Eventually the Greek (and later Syriac and Latin) became the primary texts of transmission, and the Hebrew text fell into obscurity, only to be rediscovered in the Cairo Geniza in six fragmentary medieval manuscripts, all of which contain numerous difficulties. Another fragmentary manuscript containing Sir 39:27–44:17 came to light at Masada, which confirmed that the Geniza manuscripts *in their essentials* reflected the Hebrew of Ben Sira. At present about two-thirds of the book survives in Hebrew.[37] Along with the Greek, an important translation from Hebrew was made into Syriac, al-

---

35. The term "text" in this context does not have to mean something written. I only mean some form of tradition that is transmitted in a relatively consistent form.

36. I do not mean, however, that Ben Sira necessarily had a compilation of five fixed books in a fixed order, as comprises the Pentateuch now. Ben Sira does, of course, show familiarity with traditions that we find in other books that became part of the Hebrew Bible. For Ben Sira's relationship with Proverbs and other Jewish wisdom, see Jack T. Sanders, *Ben Sira and Demotic Wisdom.* SBLMS 28 (Chico: Scholars, 1983), 4-24.

37. For a detailed discussion of the extant texts of Ben Sira, see Skehan and Di Lella, *The Wisdom of Ben Sira,* 51-62.

though the Greek translation arguably remains the most significant witness to the text of Ben Sira. Unfortunately, the Greek translation was executed in such a way that using it to reconstruct the Hebrew original is fraught with difficulty. This situation must be kept in mind when we consider any passage for which no Hebrew survives. Additionally, where the Hebrew manuscripts overlap, we sometimes find that the text of one manuscript resembles a biblical text, and another does not. For example, in 15:14 Geniza ms B reads הוא מראש ברא אדם; Ms A and the margin of B have אלהים מבראשית ברא אדם, a text that corresponds to the MT of Gen 1:1. The Greek, αὐτὸς ἐξ ἀρχῆς ἐποίησεν ἄνθρωπον, suggests that ms B preserves the correct Hebrew and that the text in mss A and B (mg) has been harmonized to Genesis. So, in this verse Ben Sira alludes to the creation story but does not cite Genesis. Cases like this one alert us that during the process of transmission some passages, perhaps preserved in only a single manuscript, might have been brought into conformity with Scripture.

Ben Sira appropriated the Israelite literary heritage in a variety of ways. I will not say much about the use of wisdom proverbs here, since Ben Sira uses wisdom traditions and proverbs to accomplish many of the same goals as a work like Proverbs — that is, to inculcate values and to teach his students how to behave in order to live a successful life, pleasing to God. We find throughout Sirach familiar and conventional wisdom topics, such as speech, friends, women, and money. But Ben Sira goes well beyond offering proverbial advice for living a good life. He also draws other types of material into his teaching, particularly narrative and legal traditions, that help him to make a point or to provide a moral example or to speculate about the nature of God and creation or to praise heroes from Israel's past. Let us turn to some examples.

Sirach 16:6-10 God's Judgment and "Historical" Sinners

> 6In an assembly of sinners a fire is kindled,
>   and in a disobedient nation wrath blazes up.
> 7He did not forgive the princes of old
>   who rebelled in their might.
> 8He did not spare the neighbors of Lot
>   whom he loathed due to their arrogance.
> 9He showed no pity on the doomed nation,
>   on those dispossessed because of their sins;
> 10or on the six hundred thousand people on foot
>   who assembled in their stubbornness.

These verses allude to more extensive narratives that serve as "historical" examples introducing a short poem in which Ben Sira asserts that although God is merciful, he will not hesitate to punish wickedness, that "everyone receives according to his or her deeds" (vv. 11-14). Ben Sira expects that his audience will know the stories, which illustrate his point that since God punished these ancient sinners who were disobedient, rebellious, sinful, and stubborn, he would punish contemporary sinners.[38]

In verse 6 the phrase "in an assembly of sinners" alludes to the rebellion of Korah, which concludes with 250 men consumed by fire (Numbers 16). Ben Sira refers to the same episode in Sir 45:18-19, there too highlighting fire as the means of God's punishment. Verse 7 refers to events also narrated in Gen 6:1-4 and in the Enochic literature, the legend of the illicit union between the "daughters of men" and the "sons of God" that in the biblical text provides the rationale for the flood. For this verse, Ben Sira's Hebrew does not correspond to Genesis. Most importantly, the biblical text has הנפלים, "the Nephilim," who were גברים, "heroes/mighty men." Both mss A and B call them נסיכי קדם, "princes of old."[39] Ben Sira and the MT also differ in the rest of the verse. For Ben Sira, God refuses to forgive the "princes of old" because they "rebelled in their might." Although he does not state it explicitly, Ben Sira intimates that this rebellion instigated the flood, an assessment that is much closer to the Enochic literature than to Genesis. Curiously, in his praise of Noah in 44:17-18, Ben Sira does not ascribe any cause to the disaster.

In verse 8, Ben Sira offers a summary of the destruction of Sodom and Gomorrah. But as in verse 7, the vocabulary does not recall any specific biblical language. Ben Sira claims that God did not spare the inhabitants of the cities because of their arrogance (גאוה), a trait not attributed to them in Genesis. One biblical text, however, does include arrogance as part of the reason that God destroyed Sodom and Gomorrah. In an indictment of Jerusalem, Ezek 16:49-50 says, "This was the guilt of your sister Sodom: she and her daughters had pride (גאון), excess of food, and prosperous ease, but did not aid the poor

38. Throughout this section, mss A, B and B(mg) have almost identical texts, and Ben Sira's Hebrew does not appear very much in doubt. The Greek translation represents the Hebrew relatively closely.

39. On the Greek side, the translator of Genesis rendered both Hebrew terms by γίγας, "giant." The grandson also used γίγας to render נסיכי. The identification of the mighty ones as giants hints that Ben Sira's grandson might have known the Septuagint version of Genesis or the development of the story of the Watchers in early Judaism (or both?), especially in light of its widespread currency in Jewish literature outside of the Septuagint (so, e.g., "giants" occurs in 1 En. 7:1-3; Jub. 5:1; Wis 14:6; and Bar 3:26). Since there is every reason to think that נסיכי was what Ben Sira wrote, the Greek probably reflects exegesis of Ben Sira's Hebrew text.

and needy. They were haughty (תגבהינה) and did abominable things before me; therefore I removed them when I saw it." This evidence suggests that Ben Sira's version of the story already attributed a reason for the destruction, one also known to the author of Ezekiel 16.[40]

Verse 9 singles out the "doomed nation" that was dispossessed because of its "sins," a probable reference to the Canaanites whom God expelled so that the Israelites could settle the land. Ben Sira employs a general and inclusive term, whereas the biblical narratives condemn the Canaanites for a host of sinful practices, including idolatry (see Exod 23:23-33; 34:11-16; Deut 7:1-6) and various types of divination (Deut 18:9-14). Finally, verse 10 condemns the "six hundred thousand people on foot, who assembled in their stubbornness," a clear reference to the number of people who gathered to enter the land but who opposed God and were not allowed to enter because of their disobedience.

Ben Sira invokes these ancient examples of sin, disobedience, rebellion, arrogance, stubbornness, and God's response to them, in order to establish that God will bring punishment on the wicked, all the while showing mercy to the godly. These verses provide no unambiguous evidence that Ben Sira drew his examples from biblical texts. He does not use any language in verses 7 and 8 that would unequivocally demonstrate a connection with Genesis. The most we can say is that Ben Sira is alluding to events that Genesis also narrates. He might know versions of the story that blame the flood on the princes'/giants'/Watchers' rebelliousness, and it is possible, given the popularity of the story, that Ben Sira encountered the rebellion of the princes of old in some source other than Genesis. The same holds true for his allusion to Sodom and Gomorrah. Ben Sira's story about the destruction of the cities already had embedded within it an interpretive tradition that pinpointed arrogance as a reason for their demise.

Sirach 17:1-12 On the Origins of Humanity

1The Lord created a human being out of earth,
    and he returned him into it again.
2He gave them days in number and a fixed time,
    and he gave them authority over the things upon it.
3He clothed them in a strength like himself,[41]
    and in his image he made them.

---

40. This seems a more likely scenario than claiming that Ben Sira here incorporated Ezekiel into his epitome of Sodom and Gomorrah's destruction.

41. Another possible way to read this last phrase is: "a strength that is fitting for them."

4He placed the fear of him upon all flesh,
  even to have dominion over beasts and birds.
6Deliberation and a tongue and eyes,
  ears and a heart for thinking he gave them.
7With knowledge of understanding he filled them,
  and good things and bad he showed to them.
8He put the fear of him upon their hearts,
  to show them the majesty of his works.
10And they shall praise a name of holiness
9 in order to recount the majesties of his works.
11He set before them knowledge,
  and a law of life he allotted to them.
12A perpetual covenant he established with them,
  and his judgments he showed to them.[42]

These eleven verses are jam-packed with Ben Sira's understandings of the creation of humankind, and it would be impossible to explicate them fully here.[43] In this passage it is virtually impossible to escape the conclusion that Ben Sira knew some form of the accounts in Genesis 1–2, although he freely intermixes the two stories, and that he shares some interpretive approaches to them with other early Jewish texts.

No Hebrew survives, and even though the Greek demonstrates little connection with the biblical text, the passage displays several significant features of the Genesis creation story. (1) Creation "in the image" (v. 3),[44] (2) creation "out of earth" (v. 1), (3) return to the earth (v. 1), and (4) dominion "over the beasts and birds" (vv. 2 and 4) all suggest that Ben Sira was interpreting some form of the Genesis account and that he knew both creation stories, since themes (1) and (4) belong to Genesis 1 and (2) and (3) come from Genesis 2.

What Ben Sira does with those accounts is fascinating, however. He ignores one prominent and central feature of the Genesis Adam and Eve story, and he provides an explanation for one enigmatic text. Verses 1-2 establish the human condition. Humans originate from and return to earth, and they only live a

42. No Hebrew is extant for this section, and vv. 5, 8c, and 11c all belong to the so-called expanded Greek II version of Sirach and are not part of the original text.

43. For a full discussion of Ben Sira's views on the creation of humans, see John R. Levison, *Portraits of Adam in Early Judaism: From Sirach to 2 Baruch.* JSPSup 1 (Sheffield: JSOT, 1988), 33-48; and John J. Collins, "Before the Fall: The Earliest Interpretations of Adam and Eve," in *The Idea of Biblical Interpretation: Essays in Honor of James L. Kugel,* ed. Hindy Najman and Judith H. Newman. JSJSup 83 (Leiden: Brill, 2004), 293-308.

44. The phrase "in his image" of v. 3 reflects the LXX of Gen 1:26 "in our image" with only a difference in the pronoun.

fixed time. This second condition, a limited life span allotted by God, seems to be Ben Sira's understanding of the way God *intended* human life to operate. Of course, according to Genesis, the introduction of death into the world was an aberration, a consequence for disobeying God's order not to eat of the tree of the knowledge of good and evil. For Ben Sira, by contrast, death was part of God's divine intention all along, whether humans obeyed or not.[45]

Two passages elsewhere in the book support this reading. In 14:17, Ben Sira comments on human life, particularly that one should enjoy oneself. He remarks that in Hades there are no luxuries and "[a]ll flesh grows old like a garment, and the eternal (עולם/αἰῶνος) decree is, 'You shall surely die (גוע יגועו/ θανάτῳ ἀποθανῇ).'" Possibly in the background here is Gen 2:17, but the Hebrew verb in Ben Sira differs from Genesis, although both employ the Hebrew infinitive absolute.[46] The word "eternal/of old" conditions the entire statement, however. Is Ben Sira harking back to the command of God in the garden, which was disobeyed by the first pair, or is he noting that the divine decree has been *eternal* that death should come to humans? Sirach 33:14-15 might push us in the latter direction. In a short two bicola, Ben Sira comments on the structure of the created order. He observes, "Good is the opposite of evil, and life the opposite of death. . . . Look at the works of the Most High; they come in pairs, one the opposite of the other." Here Ben Sira argues that everything in the cosmos has its complementary opposite and that God created the world this way. The implication is that, just as life has been from the beginning, so has death.[47]

Ben Sira also ruminates on how human beings could be created in the image of God. But what is that image? Kugel has argued cogently that verses 4, 6-7 contain Ben Sira's answer.[48] God endows humans with authority or dominion over the animals, perhaps in an analogous way that God has dominion over humans. This notion brackets the reference to the image in verses 2-4: authority-power-*image*-fear of them (humans)-dominion. Verses 6 and 7 follow up with

45. This point is made by Collins, "Before the Fall," 296, where he cites James L. Kugel, *The Traditions of the Bible* (Cambridge, Mass.: Harvard University Press, 1998), 127.

46. Genesis 3:3 might also come into play, since it uses the verb גוע, though without an infinitive absolute.

47. Collins ("Before the Fall," 296) brings Sir 41:4 as evidence of "the view that humanity was always meant to be mortal," but I am not convinced that this is the point of the passage. One passage in Sirach, 25:24 could be construed as blaming Eve for death: "From a woman is the beginning of iniquity, and because of her we all die." Several considerations might mitigate this interpretation, but the verse is certainly reminiscent of what became the standard view. For the details, see Collins, "Before the Fall," 297-98; and John R. Levison, "Is Eve to Blame? A Contextual Analysis of Sirach 25:24," *CBQ* 47 (1985): 617-23 (cited in Collins, n. 18).

48. James L. Kugel, "Some Instances of Biblical Interpretation in the Hymns and Wisdom Writings of Qumran," in *Studies in Ancient Midrash*, 155-69; on the image of God, see 162-65.

the claim that God also gave human beings the ability to deliberate and think (v. 6) and God filled them with "knowledge of understanding," showing them "good things and bad."[49] Kugel notes that other ancient Jewish texts construe this same combination as the image of God. In this connection he points to 4Q303, 4Q504, the Wisdom of Solomon, and 2 *Enoch*.[50]

We see here two important features of Ben Sira's approach to his sources. Although we can be relatively sure that Ben Sira had some form of the Genesis creation story, remarkably, he does not appear constrained by any potential authority it might have for interpreting it. Not only does he summarize large portions of the story in a short clause, he ignores a central feature of Genesis in favor of an alternative view. His willingness to do this complicates how we understand the nature of the authority of texts that he holds to be scriptural. It also highlights the importance of the strategies that Ben Sira uses to confer authority on his views. After all, if for whatever reason death as a consequence for disobedience and humanity's acquisition of the knowledge of good and evil as the benefit of that transgression were not palatable to Ben Sira, he offers his alternative on his own authority as a sage.

Sirach 19:13-17 Relations with Friends and Neighbors

13Question a friend; perhaps he didn't,
    and if he did something, lest perchance he add [to it].
14Question your fellow; perhaps he didn't say,
    and if he has said, lest he repeat.
15Question a friend, for oftentimes it becomes slander,
    and do not believe every word.
16There exists one who slips, and it is not intentional —
    and who has not sinned with his tongue?
17Question your fellow before threatening,
    and give a place to the law of the Most High.

The previous two texts showed how Ben Sira could employ the Hebrew narrative tradition in his wisdom book. Yet, even though he never explicitly quotes from it, Ben Sira refers throughout his book to the "Law" or the "Law of the Most High," and there is no doubt that Ben Sira knew the Israelite legal tradi-

---

49. Here probably intending good and evil. The reference to good and evil also indicates that the idea that humans achieved such gifts through disobedience might not be palatable to Ben Sira.

50. Kugel, "Some Instances of Biblical Interpretation," 162, 165.

tion. In this vein, scholars have noted the possible relationship between Sir 19:13-14 and Lev 19:17 on reproof of kin or neighbor: "You shall not hate in your heart anyone of your kin; you shall reprove (הוכח תוכיח), or you will incur guilt yourself." Kugel has argued, based on the use of the infinitive absolute in Leviticus, that Ben Sira's double reference to questioning friend and neighbor in 19:13-14 shows that "Ben Sira deduced that the law actually envisaged two separate acts of reproval, one before any offense is committed, as a warning, and a second — should the first fail — to prevent any repetition."[51] As verse 17 indicates, Ben Sira connects questioning/reproving (ἐλέγχω) a friend (φίλος) or fellow (or, "neighbor," πλήσιος) with having consideration for the Law.[52]

Sirach 19:13-17 actually forms a short self-contained poem that follows a section on self-control (18:30–19:12) and that precedes a poem on wisdom and wickedness beginning in 19:20, which has questioning/reproving as a subtheme (20:1-2). The emphasis on reproof comes from the preceding verses, 19:8-12, where Ben Sira encourages his students not to repeat things that they hear: "Have you heard a word? Let it perish with you. Be brave! It will never make you burst. . . . An arrow stuck in a thigh of flesh, so is a word in the gut of a foolish person" (vv. 10, 12). In verses 13-17, Ben Sira alternates between reproving a friend and a neighbor so that he refers to each twice. In each case, the admonishment to question friend or neighbor arises out of the idea of not disclosing what one has heard. So, if one hears something about a friend or neighbor, ask about it. Maybe it is not true; if it is, there is the opportunity for correction. By this reading, Kugel's close mapping of Sir 19:13-14 onto Lev 19:17 does not pan out, since the verse really does not enjoin two separate warnings, but rather two possible responses when confronting someone about rumors. Ben Sira continues the same emphasis in verses 15-17. Question a friend, because the things one hears, if they are repeated, can turn to slander. Question a neighbor before "threatening" in consideration of the Law. Even if a close mapping of Sirach on Leviticus is not assured, is Ben Sira here interpreting the Leviticus admonition?

Answering this question is more complex than simply juxtaposing Leviticus and Sirach, particularly since by the time of Ben Sira guardianship of the Israelite literary tradition had come under the purview of the scribe/sage.[53] Not

51. Kugel, "Ancient Biblical Interpretation," 21. Skehan and Di Lella, *Wisdom of Ben Sira*, 289, call v. 17 "an allusion to Lev 19:17."

52. The passage is not extant in Hebrew. The Greek verb only occurs in 31:31 with a Hebrew equivalent. There the Hebrew verb is יכח, the same verb used in Lev 19:17 for the act of questioning or reproving.

53. I think that this is the larger point that both Kugel ("Ancient Biblical Interpretation") and Sheppard *(Wisdom as a Hermeneutical Construct)* are trying to make, even though I do not share their confidence about the shape and scope of "Scripture" in this period.

only was the narrative tradition grist for the sapiential mill, so was the legal tradition. Although Lev 19:17 is the only place in the specifically legal material in
the Pentateuch that uses the verb יכח, the notion of reproof (also with the noun
תוכחת) occurs as a frequent topic of wisdom advice, as in Proverbs (see, for example, 9:7-8 [verb]; 5:12; 10:17; 12:1; 13:18; 15:5, 10, 32 [with the noun]). With respect to Ben Sira's interpretation, to what degree is his advice about questioning
friends and neighbors filtered through the lens of sapiential tradition? The
question becomes a bit more pressing, since Lev 19:17 sits in a series of legal obligations to fellow Israelites, all articulated in the form of negative imperatives.
Furthermore, this section ends with the famous injunction to love neighbor as
self, an injunction with which Ben Sira does nothing in this context. Ben Sira's
specific reference to the "Law of the Most High" leads me to suspect that he had
some particular injunction in mind, but the significant point is that Ben Sira
appropriated a legal prescription that regulated behavior between Israelites and
transformed it into sage advice about how one should handle rumors and in-
nuendos when one hears them.

Given the nature of the development of the biblical text, the way the role of
the scribe/sage was developing in this period, and Ben Sira's individual agendas,
I am not sanguine about making general statements concerning Ben Sira's use
of biblical material and his interpretations of it.[54] Each passage requires investigation to see what Ben Sira's source(s) might have been and what he did with
them. Ben Sira relies on several sources of "wisdom," and the Israelite literary
tradition is only one of them. The passages I examined above demonstrate
above all that Ben Sira does not simply reproduce his sources. He manipulates,
transforms, and otherwise shapes them to fit his own agenda, even if at times
what he produces looks to us to contravene what he found there.

Praise of the Ancestors (Sirach 44–50)

I now turn to chapters 44–50, which have a different character from the rest of
Sirach. As we saw above, when Ben Sira depends on the Israelite literary tradition in the first forty-three chapters, he incorporates the texts into his own wisdom teaching. Narrative "history" becomes moral example, and legal prescription turns into practical advice about social relations. Although there are plenty

---

54. On the roles and function of the scribe/sage in this period, see Richard A. Horsley and
Patrick Tiller, "Ben Sira and the Sociology of the Second Temple," in *Second Temple Studies III:
Studies in Politics, Class, and Material Culture*, ed. Philip R. Davies and John M. Halligan.
JSOTSup 340 (Sheffield: Sheffield Academic, 2002), 74-107.

of connections between the Praise and the earlier chapters, chapters 44–50 do not have the formal character of wisdom teaching; that is, they are not composed of proverbial wisdom, either speculative or practical. In contrast to the way that he folded his sources into his proverbial wisdom, in the Praise Ben Sira extols a series of named heroes from the Israelite past leading up to his praise of the high priest Simon II (ch. 50). For each of the exemplary figures that he selects, Ben Sira includes plenty of specifics about them that virtually cry out for comparison with the parallel traditions included in the Hebrew Bible.[55] Even so, Ben Sira does not simply borrow or reproduce traditions about these men; he adapts them to his own purposes. One short example will illustrate the point.

Second in Ben Sira's list of ancient worthies is Noah in 44:17-18:[56]

> 17Noah was found perfect and righteous;
> > in a time of destruction he was the continuator;
> > therefore, a remnant was left on the earth,
> > and by a covenant the flood ceased.
> 18An eternal sign was established with him,
> > in order never again to destroy all flesh.

The Hebrew and Greek of these two verses are relatively unproblematic, and any differences between the two are explained without much difficulty. The textual evidence of these verses confirms that Ben Sira almost certainly knew the story of Noah from Genesis. The two adjectives, "perfect and righteous" in v. 17a, are the same as in Gen 6:9. Verse 17b represents Ben Sira's interpretive summary of the flood story, to which I will return. In 17c, Ben Sira plays with the vocabulary of the Noah story to achieve a clever interpretation. Genesis 7:23 relates that "Only Noah was left (יִשָּׁאֶר), and those with him on the ark." Ben Sira deftly recalls that sentence using the Hebrew הָיָה שְׁאֵרִית, "there was a remnant." Using the noun שְׁאֵרִית rather than the verb creates a parallel with the Hebrew תַּחֲלִיף, "continuator," in 17b. Since Noah was the continuator, the one who enabled humanity to survive the flood, he and his family formed a rem-

---

55. The form and purpose of the Praise are still not completely clear. For discussions of form and purpose, see esp. Lee, *Studies in the Form of Sirach 44–50;* and Mack, *Wisdom and the Hebrew Epic.*

56. Some scholars argue that the reference to Enoch in 44:16 does not belong there, which would make Noah first in the list. My own view is that Enoch stood at the head of Ben Sira's list. Rather than following the NRSV, I have provided my own, more literal translation of the Hebrew, so that the salient issues of Ben Sira's interpretation are more transparent. The treatment of Noah here is an abridged version of my discussion in "The Use and Interpretation of Biblical Traditions."

nant. It is hard to know for sure, but since Noah was faithful in the midst of a lawless generation, prophetic notions that a remnant that continues to be faithful to God will be preserved in the midst of Israel might also have influenced Ben Sira.

Verses 17d and 18 summarize the result of the flood story. Ben Sira uses the same Hebrew word for "flood" as in Genesis, but that is no surprise. In verse 17d Ben Sira refers to God making the flood cease via "a covenant." In Genesis, however, there are actually two covenants: in 6:18 God assures Noah that he, his family, and the animals will survive the flood, and in 9:8-17 God promises, with the rainbow as a sign, never again to destroy the earth via a deluge. It is not clear whether Ben Sira invokes both promises or only the second. The covenant of Sir 44:17d might allude to the first one, except that Ben Sira reports the fulfillment, not the promise. Or, alternatively and more likely, Ben Sira is referring to the rainbow, which is the "eternal sign" that God "establishes" with Noah. Interestingly, in Genesis it is the *covenant,* not the rainbow, that is called "eternal." The rainbow is its sign. If the covenant of 17d refers to the rainbow, Ben Sira has just the reverse. Ben Sira also uses the verb נכרת, the technical term for making a covenant, in conjunction with the rainbow and thereby reinforces the covenantal nature of the sign in the sky. Thus, Ben Sira makes the flood cease through a covenant, which God assures by establishing an eternal sign with Noah — a slight rearrangement of the Genesis narrative. Finally, verse 18b almost reproduces the end of Gen 9:15: "and the waters shall never again become a flood to destroy all flesh (לשחת כל־בשׂר)." Ben Sira writes, "in order never again to destroy all flesh (לבלתי השחית כל בשׂר)."

So, in a scant two verses, Ben Sira summarizes the major elements of the biblical Noah story. Throughout he alerts his reader to the exact features of the narrative that interest him by employing important vocabulary drawn from Genesis. Yet even the one place that offers us Ben Sira's major interpretive understanding of the story, 44:17b in which Noah is credited with continuing the human race, gets qualified immediately in 17c with phraseology drawn from the biblical account. Noah as remnant constitutes Noah as continuator. The survival of humanity after the flood leads for Ben Sira directly to God's selection of Abraham, whose legacy is both covenant and blessing. Ben Sira both summarizes *and* interprets the biblical story while maintaining literary contact with it.

Concluding Remarks

Ben Sira wrote at a time when we might expect that he would have access to "biblical" books. Whether they counted as "Bible" for him is another matter.

Simple use of a text does not communicate much about its authority, only its availability. Even traditions that originated in works that Ben Sira probably regarded as sacred he was willing to manipulate to his own instructional ends. We also need to guard against connecting any allusion or mention of something that we now know as biblical with Ben Sira's use of a biblical book. So, although Sir 16:7 alludes to some form of the myth that we find in Gen 6:1-4, the short scope of Ben Sira's reference and the distinct differences between it and the biblical text should instill caution about claiming that Ben Sira was using Genesis. In his account of Noah, Ben Sira probably knew the Genesis account. When it comes to the "biblical" part of "biblical interpretation" in Sirach, Ben Sira demonstrates what Kraft calls a "scripture consciousness" rather than a "canonical consciousness." Perhaps the Mosaic Torah formed a canon for him (in whole or in part), but it is not clear that Ben Sira had an exclusivistic view of those works. That is, while certain texts make up the "book of the covenant of the Most High God" and Ben Sira holds them in high regard, I am not convinced that he would have drawn *only* from them. Whether or not he used the Mosaic Torah *exclusively* determines how we can talk about biblical interpretation in the book. If we think that Ben Sira would have used only the Mosaic Torah in 16:7-10, then these verses demonstrate something of how he interpreted the biblical texts. If he drew from other "nonbiblical" sources for these stories, then we know much less about his interpretive strategies.

When we think about the "interpretation" part of our phrase, one thing is clear: Ben Sira had pedagogical goals, and he filtered these traditions through a sapiential lens that pulled them into the orbit of his instruction. Sometimes his views about the world might cause him to shape a text in a way that contradicted parts of his received tradition. So, even though it looks as if Ben Sira uses the Genesis creation account, he does not see death as a consequence of the disobedience of the first human pair, and he remains silent about the origin of death as Genesis constructs it. Did Ben Sira ignore this feature of Genesis because it did not comport with his views of how God created the world or with his understanding of human nature? Unfortunately, it is impossible to know the answer to that question.

One issue that Ben Sira's interpretive methods highlight is how he understood the instruction into which he worked his traditions and interpretations of them. The water metaphors of chapter 24 are instructive. On the one hand, Ben Sira's identification of himself with a canal, which becomes a river and a sea, rhetorically claims the authority of Lady Wisdom for his instruction. But in that same passage, he departs from the metaphorical to the explicit claim: "I will again pour out teaching like prophecy, and I will leave it behind for generations of eternity" (v. 33). The "pouring out" retains the linguistic and metaphorical connection to Wisdom, but Ben Sira also frames himself as one who speaks for God, whose utterances will last through time. I am not certain what exact status Ben Sira claims for himself here, but one could read this verse as Ben Sira donning the mantle of the prophets to whom God spoke directly. His use of simile might mitigate such a reading, however. Elsewhere in the book, he notes that the pious wisdom teacher will achieve a name that "will live through all generations" (39:9), a similar legacy to that of 24:33. At the very least, Ben Sira views his own teaching as authoritative, and he has employed conferring strategies to legitimate it in the eyes of his students to whom he addresses it.

The Wisdom of Ben Sira will continue to occupy a place of importance in any conversation that focuses on the history of the Hebrew Bible and its interpretation. Whatever we conclude about Ben Sira with respect to both of these matters, one thing seems sure. We do not find in this second-century B.C.E. teacher a hack who was "entirely devoid of original ideas." In this book we encounter a sage who has confidence both in his access to the sea of Wisdom, who was "in the beginning" and who is embodied in Torah, and in the authoritative status and lasting legacy of his instruction. In this respect, Ben Sira reminds me of Rashid Khalifa, the father of Haroun in Salman Rushdie's deceptively simple tale, *Haroun and the Sea of Stories*. When Rushdie's young protagonist asks Rashid where his captivating stories come from, his father replies: "From the great Story Sea. I drink the warm Story Waters and then I feel full of steam. . . . [The Water] comes out of an invisible Tap installed by one of the Water Genies. You have to be a subscriber."[57]

BIBLIOGRAPHY

Barton, John. *Oracles of God: Perceptions of Ancient Prophecy in Israel after the Exile*. London: Darton, Longman and Todd, 1986.

———. "The Significance of a Fixed Canon of the Hebrew Bible." In Sæbø, *Hebrew Bible/ Old Testament*, 1.1:67-83.

Beentjes, Pancratius C. "Canon and Scripture in the Book of Ben Sira (Jesus Sirach/ Ecclesiasticus)." In *"Happy the One Who Meditates on Wisdom" (SIR. 14,20): Collected Essays on the Book of Ben Sira*. CBET 43. Leuven: Peeters, 2006, 169-86.

Carr, David M. *Writing on the Tablet of the Heart*. Oxford: Oxford University Press, 2005.

Collins, John J. "Before the Fall: The Earliest Interpretations of Adam and Eve." In *The Idea of Biblical Interpretaion: Essays in Honor of James L. Kugel*, ed. Hindy Najman and Judith H. Newman. JSJSup 83. Leiden: Brill, 2004, 293-308.

Eberharter, Andreas. *Der Kanon des Alten Testaments zur Zeit des Ben Sira*. ATA 3.3. Münster: Aschendorff, 1911.

---

57. Salman Rushdie, *Haroun and the Sea of Stories* (New York: Granta, 1990), 17.

Grabbe, Lester L. "The Law, the Prophets, and the Rest: The State of the Bible in Pre-Maccabean Times." *DSD* 13 (2006): 319-38.

Himmelfarb, Martha. "The Wisdom of the Scribe, the Wisdom of the Priest, and the Wisdom of the King According to Ben Sira." In *For a Later Generation: The Transformation of Tradition in Israel, Early Judaism and Early Christianity,* ed. Randal A. Argall, Beverly A. Bow, and Rodney A. Werline. Harrisburg: Trinity Press International, 2000, 89-99.

Horsley, Richard A., and Patrick Tiller. "Ben Sira and the Sociology of the Second Temple." In *Second Temple Studies III: Studies in Politics, Class, and Material Culture,* ed. Philip R. Davies and John M. Halligan. JSOTSup 340. Sheffield: Sheffield Academic, 2002, 74-107.

Koole, Jan L. "Die Bibel des Ben-Sira." *OtSt* 14 (1965): 374-96.

Kraft, Robert A. "Scripture and Canon in the Apocrypha and Pseudepigrapha." in Sæbø, *Hebrew Bible/Old Testament,* 1.1: 199-216.

Kugel, James L. "Ancient Biblical Interpretation and the Biblical Sage." In *Studies in Ancient Midrash,* 1-26.

———. "Some Instances of Biblical Interpretation in the Hymns and Wisdom Writings of Qumran." In *Studies in Ancient Midrash,* 155-69.

Kugel, James L., ed. *Studies in Ancient Midrash.* Cambridge, Mass.: Harvard University Press, 2001.

Lee, Thomas R. *Studies in the Form of Sirach 44–50.* SBLDS 75. Atlanta: Scholars, 1986.

Levison, John R. "Is Eve to Blame? A Contextual Analysis of Sirach 25:24." *CBQ* 47 (1985): 617-23.

———. *Portraits of Adam in Early Judaism: From Sirach to 2 Baruch.* JSPSup 1. Sheffield: JSOT, 1988.

Najman, Hindy. *Seconding Sinai: The Development of Mosaic Discourse in Second Temple Judaism.* JSJSup 77. Leiden: Brill, 2003.

Newsom, Carol A. *The Self as Symbolic Space: Constructing Identity and Community at Qumran.* STDJ 52. Leiden: Brill, 2004.

Sæbø, Magne. *Hebrew Bible/Old Testament: The History of Its Interpretation.* Vol. 1: *From the Beginnings to the Middle Ages (until 1300).* Pt. 1: *Antiquity.* Göttingen: Vandenhoeck & Ruprecht, 1996.

Sanders, Jack T. *Ben Sira and Demotic Wisdom.* SBLMS 28. Chico: Scholars, 1983.

Schechter, Solomon, and Charles Taylor. *The Wisdom of Ben Sira: Portions of the Book of Ecclesiasticus from Hebrew Manuscripts in the Cairo Genizah Collection.* Cambridge: Cambridge University Press, 1899.

Sheppard, Gerald T. *Wisdom as a Hermeneutical Construct: A Study in the Sapientialization of the Old Testament.* BZAW 151. Berlin: de Gruyter, 1980.

Skehan, Patrick W., and Alexander A. Di Lella. *The Wisdom of Ben Sira.* AB 39. New York: Doubleday, 1987.

Snaith, John G. "Biblical Quotations in the Hebrew of Ecclesiasticus." *JTS* 8 (1967): 1-12.

Wright, Benjamin G. "Ben Sira on Kings and Kingship." In *Jewish Perspectives on Hellenistic Rulers,* ed. Tessa Rajak et al. Hellenistic Culture and Society 50. Berkeley: University of California Press, 2007, 76-91.

————. *No Small Difference: Sirach's Relationship to Its Hebrew Parent Text.* SBLSCS 26. Atlanta: Scholars, 1989.

————. "The Use and Interpretation of Biblical Traditions in Ben Sira's Praise of the Ancestors." In *Studies in the Book of Ben Sira: Papers of the Third International Conference on the Deuterocanonical Books, Shime'on Centre, Pápa, Hungary, 18-20 May 2006*, ed. Géza Xeravits and József Zsengellér. JSJSup 127. Leiden: Brill, 2008, 183-207.

————. "Jubilees, Sirach, and Sapiential Tradition." In *Enoch and the Mosaic Torah*, ed. Gabriele Boccaccini and Giovanni Ibba. Grand Rapids: Eerdmans, 2009, 116-30.

Pseudo-Solomon and His Scripture: Biblical Interpretation in the Wisdom of Solomon

Peter Enns

The question of Pseudo-Solomon's use of Scripture is a multifaceted one and can, therefore, be addressed on multiple levels. One such level pertains to the presence of allusions and echoes to biblical themes, episodes, and perhaps passages. These phenomena are certainly worthy of attention in a volume such as this and will be addressed briefly below. Still, allusions and echoes are a step away from what would conventionally be referred to as biblical *interpretation.* As I see it, the presence of allusions or echoes is certainly important for understanding the central role Scripture played for Pseudo-Solomon's declaration of Jewish self-definition during the Second Temple period. It is not, however, so much a topic of hermeneutical interest as it is an indication of how the author's biblical orientation is transformed by and applied to his Hellenistic context — more precisely, a transformation to which Pseudo-Solomon is both heir as well as a major contributor.

More pertinent to matters of interpretative interest, which will form the lion's share of this essay, are those occurrences where biblical themes and figures are deliberately engaged by Pseudo-Solomon, which we see in a focused fashion in chapters 10–19, with his rehearsal of Israel's salvation history in 10:1-14 (Adam to Joseph) and then his appeal to the exodus and wilderness traditions from 10:15-19:21. Yet, here too, Pseudo-Solomon's engagement of Scripture is not simply cut out of whole cloth. Rather, it is informed by exegetical conventions and interpretive traditions of his particular historical context that had gained currency by the time Pseudo-Solomon composed his work.[1] To be sure,

---

1. As with much of ancient literature, it is very difficult to pin down with any degree of certainty when the Wisdom of Solomon was written. A date somewhere between 100 B.C.E. and 50 C.E. is a broadly accepted opinion. More precisely, David Winston has argued persuasively for a date during the reign of Roman Emperor Gaius Caligula (37-41 C.E.); *The Wisdom of Solomon,*

what the author says about Scripture is a function of a number of factors, including his general philosophical/intellectual climate[2] and cultural/political factors. Nevertheless, how Pseudo-Solomon handled his Scripture in his Hellenistic context, pressed in by Roman persecution (see 2:12–5:14), is not so much determined by these factors. Rather, they are the concrete historical realities to which Pseudo-Solomon will now apply and adapt scriptural teaching for the benefit of his readers.

This raises two related questions. First, what bearing does the context of persecution into which Pseudo-Solomon is writing have for our understanding his approach to biblical interpretation? In brief, it seems to suggest that his purpose was not so much to explore Scripture, as one might in the shelter of one's study, but to bring Scripture to bear on people living in very difficult circumstances. As we will see at various points below, the author's brief allusions to existing interpretive traditions in a work focused on encouraging a persecuted readership suggests how firmly entrenched these traditions had become. His purpose, in other words, was to encourage his readers biblically not to set them on a clever interpretive adventure. This leads to our second question: What constitutes the "scriptural teaching" that Pseudo-Solomon is so intent on bringing before his beleaguered readers? It is not simply the words of Scripture, considered privately, nor is it simply what is written. Rather, Pseudo-Solomon's Scripture was a Scripture as it had come to be understood by interpretive communities that preceded him. In other words, what Pseudo-Solomon understands Scripture to say and how he goes about mining its riches have, not entirely but to a certain extent, already been worked out for him, irrespective of the remarkable intellectual and spiritual energy he poured into his work. Pseudo-Solomon's Bible is an "interpreted Bible," the impact of which is so deeply engrained that his exposition of Scripture betrays both interpretive traditions and techniques that reveal perhaps more of his conditioned understanding of Scripture than of Scripture itself. In other words, Pseudo-Solomon's appeal to Scripture is often actually an appeal to "Scripture plus," not as a deliberate attempt to showcase his learning, but as an incidental indication of what he understood Scripture actu-

---

AB 43 (Garden City: Doubleday, 1979), 22-25. His reasons are essentially threefold: (1) The cataclysmic event of the destruction of the Jerusalem temple in 70 C.E. is neither mentioned nor alluded to in the book. In fact, in 3:14 and 9:8 its existence is assumed. (2) The Wisdom of Solomon indicates a clear undercurrent of strong persecution (see 2:12-5:14), which is consistent with Caligula's reign of terror. (3) The author's vocabulary consists of a significant number of words and usages, some associated with Middle Platonic philosophy, that are unattested elsewhere before the first century C.E.

2. See Winston's extended discussion of Pseudo-Solomon's religious ideas and how they reflect Middle Platonism; *The Wisdom of Solomon*, 25-63.

ally to mean. For this reason, when our topic concerns biblical interpretation by Pseudo-Solomon, our focus must be to try to understand what he is doing in the context of the interpretive traditions and exegetical methods that were current in his Second Temple hermeneutical milieu.

One final introductory matter concerns the overall structure of the book. Pseudo-Solomon's engagement with Israel's history is absent in chapters 1–9 but is persistent in chapters 10-19. This seems to be structurally significant. There are, to be sure, numerous schemes for dividing the Wisdom of Solomon into smaller, logical, units, all of which enjoy a certain degree of persuasiveness.[3] My preference is to make a clear division at 9:18, regardless of what smaller divisions are certainly present in chapters 1–9.[4] One of the themes of these chapters is Pseudo-Solomon's appeal to his readers to follow wisdom amid trying circumstances. He makes his appeal by employing certain rhetorical conventions[5] and by echoing biblical themes. His argument is amply summarized in the final verse of part 1, Wis 9:18: "And thus the paths of those on earth were set right, and people were taught what pleases you, and were saved by wisdom." What follows in

---

3. Wisdom is typically divided into two or three sections, although there is no clear consensus on where the divisions are to be made. Advocates of a three-part approach include Paul Heinisch, who divides the book: 1:1-5:23, 6:1-9:18, and 10:1-19:22; *Das Buch der Weisheit*. EHAT 24 (Münster: Aschendorff, 1912), xiv; see also Harold van Broekhoven, "Wisdom and World: The Functions of Wisdom Imagery in Sirach, Pseudo-Solomon and Colossians" (Diss., Boston University, 1988), 87. Winston's scheme is a bit different: 1:1-6:21, 6:22-10:21, 11-19; *The Wisdom of Solomon*, 9-12. Bruce M. Metzger is one of many who have argued for a two-part division: 1:1-9:18 and 10:1-19:22; *An Introduction to the Apocrypha* (New York: Oxford University Press, 1957), 68-73, and it is his division that I accept. Addison G. Wright likewise has a two-part division but makes the division at 11:2 rather than 10:1; "The Structure of the Book of Wisdom," *Bib* 48 (1967): 165-84.

4. Chs. 1–9 can be divided into two main sections. Chs. 1–6 deal largely with death, persecution, immortality, and the eventual prosecution of the unrighteous by the righteous after death. Chs. 7–9 offer a more abstract or philosophical treatise of the nature of wisdom, its surpassing greatness, and Solomon's quest for wisdom. As further indication of a division at 10:1, one can appeal to Pseudo-Solomon's use of vocabulary in part 2 that echoes similar usage in part 1; see Peter Enns, *Exodus Retold: Ancient Exegesis of the Departure from Egypt in Wis 10:15-21 and 19:1-9*. HSM 57 (Atlanta: Scholars, 1997), 155-68. What these verbal correspondences suggest is that Israel's enemies, whether Egypt (part 2) or a current political regime (part 1), are both subject to Wisdom's sovereignty, that God's people, past and present, will be delivered. A similar argument has been made previously by James M. Reese, although his focus was on demonstrating the authorial unity of the book; *Hellenistic Influence on the Book of Wisdom and Its Consequences*. AnBib 41 (Rome: Biblical Institute, 1970), 122-52. Reese argues for the book's unity on the basis of words and phrases that appear in both chs. 10–19 and chs. 1–9, what he calls "flashbacks." Reese's work is a fuller version of a similar view put forth earlier by Georg Ziener, *Die theologische Begriffssprache im Buche der Weisheit* (Bonn: Hanstein, 1956), 95-96.

5. Winston, *The Wisdom of Solmon*, 14-18.

chapters 10–19 is a *further explication of this affirmation,* but now made on the basis of personified Wisdom's presence in concrete figures and episodes in Israel's history. The focus, in other words, shifts from, let us say, a philosophical/ rhetorical appeal (with Scripture echoed at various junctures) to an appeal to Scripture itself, i.e., to a historical/rhetorical strategy.

It is in these chapters that we find Pseudo-Solomon to be most intentional in bringing the biblical message to his readers while at the same time providing a window to the state of biblical interpretation at his time. But before looking a bit more closely at his interpretive activity in the second half of the book, we will first review briefly how otherwise the Hebrew Bible plays a role in Pseudo-Solomon's work.

The Presence of the Hebrew Bible in the Wisdom of Solomon

The author's adoption of a Solomonic persona (seen, for example, in 9:7-8 in his claim to have received the command to build the temple) and his self-evident biblical orientation would lead us to expect an interaction with biblical passages and themes, whether direct or indirect. There has been a fair amount of scholarly thought given to this phenomenon. One of the more widely discussed issues is the degree to which Pseudo-Solomon makes use of the book of Isaiah. There is little question that Isaiah plays an important role in Pseudo-Solomon's exposition of the current crisis before him. For example, Wisdom 1–6, with its theme of the persecution and triumph of the righteous, seems to echo the fourth Servant Song of Isa 52:13–53:12, and perhaps Isaiah 13-14 as well.[6] Likewise, Pseudo-Solomon's idol polemic in 13:11-19 (see also 15:10) seems quite reminiscent of Isa 44:9-20.[7] Also worth mentioning are Wis 2:12a and LXX Isa 3:10; Wis 3:14 and Isa

6. Maurice Gilbert, "Wisdom of Solomon in Scripture," in *Hebrew Bible/Old Testament: The History of Its Interpretation,* vol. 1: *From the Beginnings to the Middle Ages (Until 1300),* Part 2: *The Middle Ages,* ed. Magne Sæbø (Göttingen: Vandenhoeck & Ruprecht, 1996), 609; John J. Collins, *Jewish Wisdom in the Hellenistic Age.* OTL (Louisville: Westminster John Knox, 1997), 184. M. Jack Suggs makes a case for the dependence of Wis 2:10 through ch. 5 as based on the fourth Servant Song but considers Wis 3:15–4:15 to be of dubious dependence on Isaiah; "Wisdom of Solomon 2:10–5: A Homily Based on the Fourth Servant Song," *JBL* 76 (1957): 29. Pancratius C. Beentjes argues, conversely, for the literary integrity of Wis 3:1–4:19 vis-à-vis the fourth Servant Song; "Wisdom of Solomon 3,1–4,19 and the Book of Isaiah," in *Studies in the Book of Isaiah: Festschrift Willem A. M. Beuken,* ed. J. van Ruiten and M. Vervenne. BETL 132 (Leuven: Leuven University Press, 1997), 413-20.

7. See Gilbert, "Wisdom of Solomon in Scripture," 613, although he is somewhat reluctant to make a full commitment: "The portrait of the idolatrous woodcutter (Wis 13:11-19) is partly inspired by Isa 44:9-20."

56:2, 4-5; Wis 5:17-20 and Isa 59:16-17.[8] When Wisdom of Solomon is considered as a whole, especially with the dominance of the exodus theme (see below), it is little surprise that so much of Isaiah cited is from those sections that pertain to Israel's captivity in Babylon. Clearly a major theme for Pseudo-Solomon is God's rescue of his righteous people, and he employs the pertinent portions of Scripture to make his point.

There is much ground to cover, beyond Isaiah, concerning potential allusions to Scripture in the Wisdom of Solomon, and space does not permit a fuller treatment.[9] There is one particularly interesting example, however, that does not yet seem to have been given its due attention, and outlining it here briefly may help further to illustrate the pervasiveness of Scripture in the Wisdom of Solomon. This concerns Wis 1:16–2:11 and whether Pseudo-Solomon's comments here are an attempt to counter Qoheleth's skepticism concerning death (e.g., Eccl 3:18-21; 6:12). Maurice Gilbert cautions that "it is impossible to demonstrate any allusion to Qohelet, even though the message of Wisdom concerning immortality offers an answer to both the fears of Qohelet and the anxiety of Job."[10] Just below he refers to the "surprising . . . absence of Qohelet" in the Wisdom of Solomon.[11] "Demonstration" is, of course, impossible at any rate in the absence of an explicit citation by the author, but this alone should not deter us from seeing if some link between the two can be discerned. Moreover, much of the interpretive substance of ancient interpreters is found precisely in allusions and echoes of biblical material, not explicit citations, and so a closer look seems justified. Further, the fact that the Wisdom of Solomon is so richly influenced by Scripture — which we have glimpsed above and will see in greater detail below — suggests that similarities between Wis 1:16–2:11 and portions of Ecclesiastes may be more than superficial. Gilbert's observations are not to be taken lightly, but it nevertheless seems that Pseudo-Solomon's reflections resound with strong echoes of Qoheleth's complaints, and indeed seem geared toward countering Qoheleth's pessimism.[12]

8. Gilbert, "Wisdom of Solomon in Scripture," 608-9; Collins, *Jewish Wisdom in the Hellenistic Age*, 192, 215. On the penultimate example, Collins notes that Pseudo-Solomon's decision to avoid the reference to Sabbaths in Isa 56:4-5 and speak rather of unlawfulness and wickedness indicates Pseudo-Solomon's strategy of applying what was particular to the universal.

9. Gilbert, "Wisdom of Solomon in Scripture," gives a helpful overview of many of the important issues, and his discussion includes the Wisdom of Solomon and Genesis, Psalms, canonical wisdom books, and other portions of Scripture. See also Lester L. Grabbe, *Wisdom of Solomon*. GAP 3 (Sheffield: Sheffield Academic, 1997), 39-46.

10. Gilbert, "Wisdom of Solomon in Scripture," 616.

11. Gilbert, "Wisdom of Solomon in Scripture," 617.

12. See also William Horbury, who sees portions of the Wisdom of Solomon as an "attack on the powerful who deny the after-life," as we see in Ecclesiastes; "The Christian Use and the

We must bear in mind that Qohelet's preoccupation with death, as that which ultimately renders life absurd (הֶבֶל),[13] i.e., without profit (יִתְרוֹן), fits hand in glove with his apparent complete skepticism concerning the afterlife, portrayed so clearly in 3:18-21.

> I said in my heart with regard to human beings that God is testing them to show that they are but animals. For the fate of humans and the fate of animals is the same; as one dies, so dies the other. They all have the same breath, and humans have no advantage over the animals; for all is vanity [הֶבֶל]. All go to one place; all are from the dust, and all turn to dust again. Who knows whether the human spirit goers upward and the spirit of animals goes downward to the earth?

Such a view may be juxtaposed to that of Pseudo-Solomon, who gives prominence to the afterlife. In fact, through much of the first six chapters of the book, immortality is portrayed as the promised final end of all those who follow the path of wisdom.[14] For example, 3:4-8 outlines the otherworldly benefits of the righteous who, though currently undergoing suffering and persecution, will ultimately "receive great good":

> For though in the sight of others they were punished,
> their hope is full of immortality.
> Having been disciplined a little,
> they will receive great good,
> because God tested them and found them worthy of himself. . . .
> In the time of their visitation they will shine forth,

Jewish Origins of the Wisdom Tradition," in *Wisdom in Ancient Israel: Essays in Honour of J. A. Emerton,* ed. John Day, Robert P. Gordon, and H. G. M. Williamson (Cambridge: Cambridge University Press, 1995), 195.

13. My understanding of *hebel* as "absurd" follows the observations of Michael V. Fox; *A Time to Tear Down and a Time to Build Up: A Rereading of Ecclesiastes* (Grand Rapids: Eerdmans, 1999), 139.

14. An excellent study on death and immortality in Wisdom of Solomon is Michael Kolarcik, *The Ambiguity of Death in the Book of Wisdom 1-6: A Study of Literary Structure and Interpretation.* AnBib 127 (Rome: Pontifical Biblical Institute, 1991). Other studies include: Yehoshua Amir, "The Figure of Death in the 'Book of Wisdom,'" *JJS* 30 (1979); 154-78 (repr. in *Studien zum antiken Judentum.* BEATAJ 2 [Frankfurt am Main: Lang, 1985]); John J. Collins, "The Root of Immortality: Death in the Context of Jewish Wisdom," *HTR* 71 (1980): 177-92; Roland E. Murphy, "'To Know Your Might Is the Root of Immortality' (Wis 15,3)," *CBQ* 25 (1963): 88-93; R. J. Taylor, "The Eschatological Meaning of Life and Death in the Book of Wisdom," *ETL* 42 (1966): 72-137; John P. Weisengoff, "Death and Immortality in the Book of Wisdom," *CBQ* 3 (1941): 104-33.

and will run like sparks through the stubble.
They will govern nations and rule over peoples,
and the Lord will reign over them forever.

There is really nothing comparable to this in OT wisdom literature, where the focus is more on mastery of this life than on attainment of the life to come.

But more to the point, it seems quite suggestive to me not only that Wis 1:16–2:11 stands in stark contrast to Qoheleth's statements (of which Pseudo-Solomon must certainly have been aware) but that some conscious interaction on Pseudo-Solomon's part is a reasonable conclusion to draw. Particularly striking is Wis 2:1, which appears to echo and critique the negative attitude of Eccl 3:18-21, "They reasoned unsoundly, saying to themselves, 'Short and sorrowful is our life, and there is no remedy when a life comes to its end, and no one knows to return from Hades.'" Pseudo-Solomon is too knowledgeable of his Scripture, too deliberate in his exposition, to think that he himself would not have perceived some echo of Ecclesiastes in his own words. And Qoheleth's skepticism toward death and the afterlife will not do for Pseudo-Solomon, who is addressing readers living in a context of persecution. For Pseudo-Solomon, wisdom is not merely a means to attaining mastery of this life, but the proper means to attaining the all-important life to come. Those who do not share this perspective he calls "ungodly." His words, in effect, are an attempt to apply the wisdom ideal to a situation that the biblical wisdom tradition either did not address or, as we see in Ecclesiastes, did not address adequately for this later context.[15]

The importance Pseudo-Solomon places on the afterlife can be seen in yet another way, and this will help us to see more clearly the bold way in which he represents a tradition that transforms biblical wisdom. In the first half of the book, he twice refers to death as ἔξοδος, in 3:2 and 7:6. The "exodus" mentioned in 3:2 refers to the faithful who die at the hands of tormentors. In 7:6, the word is used to describe the death of all people. Although it is generally ill-advised to load too much significance in individual words, in this case the description of death as an "exodus" is very striking in view of the Wisdom of Solomon as a whole, where chapters 10-19 have as a main focus Israel's exodus from Egypt and wilderness period. With this in view, we can now turn our attention to Pseudo-Solomon's interpretation of Israel's salvation history, which is focused in the second half of the book.

---

15. A thought–provoking study of the concept of death in Ecclesiastes is Shannon Burkes, *Death in Qoheleth and Egyptian Biographies of the Late Period.* SBLDS 170 (Atlanta: SBL, 2002).

Second Temple Interpretative Traditions in Wisdom 10–19

In Wis 10–19, Pseudo-Solomon begins to recount personified Wisdom's acts of deliverance throughout Israel's history, focusing in particular on Israel's exodus from Egypt and subsequent wandering in the wilderness. In the light of Pseudo-Solomon's practical focus on encouraging his readers to face death, one begins to see a possible motive behind not only his reference to death as an "exodus" in chapters 3 and 7, but also his choice of Israel's exodus experience as one of the primary themes of chapters 10-19. Israel's exodus, her passage from death to life, as it were, is presented by Pseudo-Solomon as the prime biblical portrait of what Wisdom is doing *now* in the lives of these persecuted Alexandrian Jews — in their own passage from death to life, their own exodus. In other words, Pseudo-Solomon's treatment of death and the afterlife in the first half of the book is a recontextualizion of the exodus of the Bible; it is his attempt to apply the lessons from Israel's history to the daily trials and struggles of a people who were asking hard questions and looking to God for answers. Whereas Israel's wisdom tradition, represented in Proverbs and to a lesser extent in Job, often emphasizes the lessons to be learned from the created order and observations of human behavior, Pseudo-Solomon, like his predecessor Ben Sira (Sirach 44–50), finds lessons to be learned from interacting with God's past dealings with Israel. In short, the sage's job description now includes the exegesis of Scripture.[16]

Although it is certainly true that in his use of Scripture Pseudo-Solomon focuses on the complex of events surrounding the exodus, we must also take note that the biblical material from which he draws his lessons is much broader. His application of Israel's history actually begins in Wis 10:1-14, where he relates the well-known stories of Adam, Cain, Noah, Abraham, Lot, Jacob, and Joseph. He follows with a brief exposition of the exodus itself (10:15-21; see also 19:1-9)[17]

---

16. The increased importance of the written word in Second Temple Judaism, and therefore exegesis of Scripture as a means of continuing the divine-human discourse in the absence of classical prophecy, is succinctly discussed in James L. Kugel and Rowan A. Greer, *Early Biblical Interpretation*. LEC 3 (Philadelphia: Westminster, 1986), esp. 13-106. The issue is also amply summarized by Michael Fishbane: "[S]cripture has become the vehicle of new revelations, and exegesis the means of new access to the divine will. Thus, complementing the divine revelation now embodied in a written Torah, the sage seeks from God the grace of an *ongoing revelation* through the words of scripture itself — as mediated *through exegesis*"; "From Scribalism to Rabbinism: Perspectives on the Emergence of Classical Judaism," in *The Sage in Israel and the Ancient Near East*, ed. John G. Gammie and Leo G. Perdue (Winona Lake: Eisenbrauns, 1990), 442-43 (emphasis original).

17. On Pseudo-Solomon's interpretation of the exodus, see Enns, *Exodus Retold*. For a valuable study that takes a different angle on a number of issues, see Samuel Cheon, *The Exodus*

and the wilderness period (11:1-14). The remainder of the book moves back and forth between a number of issues centering on the exodus and God's treatment of the Israelites in contrast to his treatment of the Egyptians.[18]

To help us see more clearly the manner in which Pseudo-Solomon handles his Scripture, it may be useful to highlight at the outset four general principles of interpretation we see at work in his book.

1. Pseudo-Solomon appeals to Israel's history to show the workings of divine justice.

Despite the present appearance of things — which includes the unjust suffering and death of people well before their time (e.g., 4:7-8) — Pseudo-Solomon is absolutely convinced about the existence of an underlying plan of God that will

---

Story in the Wisdom of Solomon: A Study in Biblical Interpretation. JSPSup 23 (Sheffield: Sheffield Academic, 1997). Another study, broader in scope, is Udo Schwenk-Bressler, *Sapientia Salomonis als ein Beispiel frühjüdischer Textauslegung: die Auslegung des Buches Genesis, Exodus 1–15 und Teilen der Wüstentradition in Sap 10–19.* BEATAJ 32 (Frankfurt am Main: Lang, 1993).

18. This is seen in the following thematic outline of 10:15–19:22:
1. *Exodus:* 10:15-21; 19:1-9
2. *Wilderness:* 11:1-14; 19:10-12
3. *Plagues:*
   a. 11:15-20 (animals)
      11:21–12:2: God's strength and mercy
      12:3-11: Canaan shown mercy [Conquest]
      12:12-22: moral: God does as he pleases
   b. 12:23-27 (animals)
      13:1-9: nature worship is "excusable"
      13:10–15:17: man-made idols (wood and clay)
      [14:1-7: the wood of Noah's ark contrasted to the wood of idols]
   c. 19:13-21 (darkness)
4. *Egypt and the plagues contrasted to Israel and the wilderness:*
   a. 15:18–16:4 and 19:10-12: Egypt is plagued by animals, but Israel receives quail in the desert.
      [16:5-14: but when Israel is plagued by animals in the desert, they are quickly delivered.]
   b. 16:15-29: Egypt is plagued by heavenly elements (rains, hail, storms), but Israel receives manna.
   c. 17:1–18:4: Egypt is plagued by darkness, but Israel has the pillar to guide them through the desert
   d. 18:5-25: Egypt is plagued by death of the firstborn. Israel, too, is plagued by death in the desert, but only for a short while. (It is interesting to note that in his effort to maintain the plague/wilderness contrast, Pseudo-Solomon does not contrast the death of the Egyptian firstborn to the deliverance of Israel's firstborn from Pharaoh's decree as he does in 19:4-5.)

right all wrongs. This conviction is clearly communicated in the closing verses of each of the book's two halves.

> Who has learned your counsel,
> unless you have given wisdom
> and sent your holy spirit from on high?
> And thus the paths of those on earth were set right,
> and people were taught what pleases you,
> and were saved by wisdom. (9:17-18)

> For in everything [κατὰ πάντα], O Lord,
> you have exalted and glorified your people,
> and you have not neglected to help them at all times and in all places
>   [ἐν παντὶ καιρῷ καὶ τόπῳ]. (19:22)

These verses remind the faithful that God never neglects his people. It matters little what the circumstances are; he is with them "in everything." Nor is God's saving power relegated to a bygone era; he is with his people "at all times." And God's saving power knows no boundary; he is with his people "in all places," even in death, as chapters 1–6 so eloquently describe.

2. Biblical characters are presented as models of virtue.

The heroic persons of the Bible are viewed by Pseudo-Solomon as examples for the faithful of his own day; as such, it will not do to present these figures from the past in any way other than the ideal.[19] This is clearly seen in the historical review of Wisdom 10. For example, Pseudo-Solomon hardly mentions Adam's troubles (10:1-2). Instead, Adam is simply described as the "first-formed father of the world" who was "delivered . . . from his transgression" and given "strength to rule all things." Likewise, in 10:5 Abraham is simply a "righteous man." In the incident of the binding of Isaac, the author neglects to mention Abraham's earlier doubts about God's commitment to give him and Sarah a son in their old age (Gen 17:17-18).

The same holds true for Pseudo-Solomon's presentation of Lot and Jacob: they are models of absolute virtue, whereas the biblical narratives paint a more nuanced portrait. For instance, although Lot's "righteousness" (Wis 10:6) has a clear biblical warrant in light of Abraham's persistence in pleading with the angels (Gen 18:16-33), this remains a selective reading of the story of Genesis as a whole, given Lot's own choice to settle in the disreputable "cities of the plain"

---

19. John J. Collins and George W. E. Nickelsburg, eds., *Ideal Figures in Ancient Israel: Profiles and Paradigms.* SBLSCS 12 (Chico: Scholars, 1980).

(Gen 13:10-13). Likewise, Rebekah and Jacob's deceit of Isaac (Genesis 27) ought to have raised an eyebrow. But again, Pseudo-Solomon's Jacob is not guilty of any wrongdoing. He is, as are the others, simply "righteous" (Wis 10:10).

It is no surprise, therefore, that Pseudo-Solomon does not mention Moses' near fatal slip-up on the way from Midian (Exod 4:18-26), nor his disobedience at Meribah (Num 20:7-12) and his subsequent exclusion from Canaan. For Pseudo-Solomon, Moses is simply a "servant of the Lord" into whose soul Wisdom "entered" (Wis 10:16). Moreover, those he brings out of Egypt are no longer a people prone to doubt and rebellion but "a holy people and blameless race" (10:15). In all of this, Pseudo-Solomon's hortatory purpose is clear: he seeks to find in these figures a biblical precedent for the circumstances he is addressing.

3. The biblical characters in the Wisdom of Solomon are anonymous.

A glance at Wis 10:1-21, for example, will show that these figures are described by means of episodes in their biblical stories rather than by their names. Their names are avoided because who they were in the past is of little importance; what matters is what they represent now as models of wise conduct. To put it another way, these biblical figures have become democratized and as such become more generalized models of conduct for times, places, and people beyond the confines of the original events. For Pseudo-Solomon, the word of God must speak clearly to the present, stressful situation. As James Kugel puts it (commenting on a similar "catalog of heroes" in Sir 44-50), "These once-real people have become, essentially, *lessons,* whose importance can be captured in a line or two."[20]

4. Of significance concerning Pseudo-Solomon's exposition of Israel's history is the extent to which his own understanding of that history is influenced by interpretive traditions that preceded him.

One need only glance at the opening verses of chapter 10 to see that Pseudo-Solomon does not relate the content of the biblical narratives in a straightforward manner. Rather, he regularly includes elements that are not actually found in the corresponding biblical narratives but that reflect Second Temple interpretive traditions and exegetical techniques. Pseudo-Solomon is most certainly an interpreter of Scripture in that he brings Scripture to bear, deliberately, creatively, intelligently, on his present circumstances. But more than that, the Wisdom of Solomon not only reveals to us Pseudo-Solomon the *interpreter,* i.e., *his* exegetical method. We also see captured in his words a glimpse of what consti-

---

20. Kugel and Greer, *Early Biblical Interpretation,* 49.

tuted proper biblical *understanding* for Pseudo-Solomon and his readers. Pseudo-Solomon was heir to an interpreted Bible, and much of what he said about Scripture was not his own creation but the fruit of previous exegetical activity with which he was evidently quite familiar.

A question worth posing is to what extent, if at all, Pseudo-Solomon was conscious that he was in fact incorporating these "traditions" into the sacred text. No definitive answer can be given, but I would venture to suggest that these traditions had simply come to be a part of what constituted a proper biblical understanding for Pseudo-Solomon and the people for whom he wrote. It is not at all clear, therefore, to what extent Pseudo-Solomon was interacting explicitly with past exegetical activity when he wrote his book. It is more likely, in my opinion, that he was simply doing his best to bring "proper" biblical understanding to bear on his current situation. In this sense, Geza Vermes's observation on the manner in which exegetical traditions are incorporated into the *Genesis Apocryphon,* the expansive retelling of portions of Genesis found among the Dead Sea Scrolls, is apt:

The author never attempts to introduce unrelated or extraneous matter. His technique is simple and he exercises no scholarly learning, no exegetical virtuosity, no play on words. His intention is to explain the biblical text, and this he does either by bringing together various passages of Genesis or by illustrating a verse with the help of an appropriate story. The resulting work is certainly one of the jewels of midrashic exegesis, and the best illustration yet available of the primitive haggadah and of the unbiased rewriting of the Bible.[21]

Vermes's insight is largely applicable not only to the Wisdom of Solomon, as the examples below will illustrate, but to numerous Second Temple and early rabbinic works that bear clear marks of working with an understanding of Scripture that is informed by previous exegetical activity. Specific instances are far too numerous, and therefore unnecessary, to catalog, but are famously included throughout such works as: *Jubilees, L.A.B.,* Qumran pesher commentaries, Targums (notably *Pseudo-Jonathan* and *Neofiti*), Josephus's *Antiquities of the Jews,* various of Philo's works, *Mekilta,* Sirach 44–50, and the New Testament (e.g., Acts 7 and Hebrews 11).[22] Our focus, however, is on the Wisdom of

---

21. Geza Vermes, *Scripture and Tradition in Judaism: Haggadic Studies,* 2nd rev. ed. StPB 4 (Leiden: Brill, 1973), 126.

22. Discerning the nature of biblical interpretation in these and other texts has produced, quite understandably, a considerable volume of literature. The present volume treats some of these texts, and these discussions will suffice to round out the issue a bit more. Some scholars whose work I have found to be most helpful include: Gary A. Anderson, *The Genesis of Perfection: Adam and Eve in Jewish and Christian Imagination* (Louisville: Westminster John Knox, 2001);

Solomon, and we now turn our attention to five examples of Pseudo-Solomon's engagement of Scripture in chapters 10–19.

Abraham Was a Contemporary of the Tower of Babel Episode

One example of Pseudo-Solomon's incorporation (again, whether deliberate or not cannot be clearly determined) of a particular interpretive tradition is found in Wis 10:5, where Pseudo-Solomon juxtaposes the story of Abraham the patriarch and the account of the tower of Babel:

> Wisdom also, when the nations in wicked agreement
> had been put to confusion,
> recognized the righteous man [Abraham]
> and preserved him blameless before God.

To be "put to confusion" is a clear allusion to the tower of Babel story.[23] Hence, what is meant here is that Abraham's resistance to the building effort, as he was guided by Wisdom, is what "preserved him blameless before God." That Pseudo-Solomon would thus connect Abraham and the tower of Babel seems curious in that Abraham is not mentioned at all in the biblical tower narrative: his name does not appear until Gen 11:26, purportedly several hundred years after the Babel incident. This displacement of Abraham is not unique to Pseudo-

---

"The Interpretation of the Purification Offering (חטאת) in the *Temple Scroll* (11QTemple) and Rabbinic Literature," *JBL* 111 (1992): 17-35; Renée Bloch, "Midrash," *DBSup* 5 (1950), 1263-81; repr. in *Approaches to Ancient Judaism: Theory and Practice*, vol. 1, ed. William Scott Green. BJS 1 (Missoula: Scholars, 1978), 29–50; James H. Charlesworth, ed., *OTP*; Collins and Nickelsburg, *Ideal Figures in Ancient Israel*; David Daube, "Alexandrian Methods of Interpretation and the Rabbis," in *Festschrift Hans Lewald* (Basel: Helbing and Lichtenhahn, 1953), 27-44; repr. in *Essays in Greco-Roman and Related Talmudic Literature*, ed. Henry A. Fischel (New York: Ktav, 1977), 165-82; "Rabbinic Methods of Interpretation and Hellenistic Rhetoric," *HUCA* 22 (1949): 239-64; Devorah Dimant, "Use and Interpretation of Mikra in the Apocrypha and Pseudepigrapha," in *Mikra: Reading, Translation and Interpretation of the Hebrew Bible in Ancient Judaism and Early Christianity*, ed. Martin Jan Mulder. CRINT 2.1 (Assen: Van Gorcum and Philadelphia: Fortress, 1990), 379-419; Maurice Gilbert, "Sagesse de Salomon," in *DBSup* 60 (1986), 58-119; "Wisdom Literature," in *Jewish Writings of the Second Temple Period*, ed. Michael E. Stone. CRINT 2.2 (Assen: Van Gorcum and Philadelphia: Fortress, 1984), 283-324; James L. Kugel, *In Potiphar's House: The Interpretive Life of Biblical Texts* (San Francisco: HarperSanFrancisco, 1990); *The Ladder of Jacob: Ancient Interpretations of the Biblical Story of Jacob and His Children* (Princeton: Princeton University Press, 2006); Vermes, *Scripture and Tradition in Judaism*; Jacob Weingreen, *From Bible to Mishna: The Continuity of Tradition* (Manchester: Manchester University Press, 1976).

23. See LXX Gen 11:7, 9, where the same Greek root is used for "confusion" (συγχέω).

Solomon, however, but is also reflected in the somewhat contemporary text, Pseudo-Philo's *Book of Biblical Antiquities* 6-7, where the author expounds at length on Abraham's resistance to the tower-building project.[24]

It might be tempting at this juncture to suggest some direction of influence between these texts, but that is neither fruitful nor necessary. The sheer brevity, the "matter-of-factness" of Pseudo-Solomon's remark is an indication that the tradition was well known and needed no explanation. It is unlikely that Pseudo-Solomon's passing remark has generated the fuller version in *L.A.B.* 6-7, since the brevity of Pseudo-Solomon's comment certainly attests to the tradition's well-established existence. However, this "as-we-all-know" quality of Pseudo-Solomon's remark likewise suggests that *L.A.B.* 6-7 can hardly be the lone source of Wis 10:5. It seems more reasonable to suggest that the relative dating of these two texts is not the most pressing issue at hand, for settling the matter of dating would not in any way be determinative for suggesting some direction of direct influence. Rather, it is more logical — and less ambitious — to posit that these texts are only indirectly related somehow, and that the simple presence of both is an indication that an "Abraham and the tower" tradition formed part of a Second Temple body of interpretive traditions, as Kugel and others have so persistently argued.[25]

How such a tradition arose in the first place is matter of some speculation (a process Kugel refers to as "reverse engineering").[26] Still, it is reasonable to posit that the connection between Abraham and the tower narrative, however odd to us, served some purpose for ancient interpreters, perhaps to explain oddities in other narratives. In Josh 24:2, for example, it is stated that Terah and his sons Abraham and Nahor worshiped other gods in Mesopotamia before

---

24. In his expansive retelling of the Genesis narrative, Pseudo-Philo has Abraham and eleven others actively resist the effort to build the tower; as a result, they are threatened with death by fire if they do not recant (*L.A.B.* 6:1-5). The group is given a seven-day respite to decide, and during this time they have an opportunity to escape (6:6-10). Abraham alone refuses to flee, trusting rather in God's justice (6:11-12). God delivers him from a fiery fate by causing a great earthquake (6:15-18). This, however, does not deter the builders from trying once again to construct a tower to reach up to heaven. This time God punishes them by confusing their language (7:1-5).

25. E.g., *In Potiphar's House*; *The Ladder of Jacob*. In addition to *L.A.B.* 6-7, this tradition also appears in rabbinic literature (e.g., *Gen. Rab.* 38:13; 44:13). Geza Vermes discusses the tradition in some length; *Scripture and Tradition in Judaism*, 85-90. See also George W. E. Nickelsburg, "Good and Bad Leaders in Pseudo-Philo's *Liber Antiquitatum Biblicarum*," in Collins and Nickelsburg, *Ideal Figures in Ancient Israel*, 51-52. Here, too, the question of the direct dependence of these rabbinic texts on *L.A.B.* 6-7 (and less likely on Wis 10:5) is of little interest to me. Rather, these rabbinic texts are later developments and articulations of an older, well-established tradition, already attested in *L.A.B.* 6-7 and Wis 10:5.

26. Kugel, *In Potiphar's House*, 251-53.

they left for Haran. Such a curious (and troubling) comment is made even more so by virtue of the complete absence of such a notion in the Genesis narrative itself. Early interpreters, perhaps in their attempt to construct a story to explain this inconsistency, and to exonerate their father Abraham, may have created this interpretative tradition, making Abraham not merely a resident among idolatrous people but, more specifically, an actual contemporary of the tower of Babel episode, who successfully resisted their idolatrous behavior and thus was preserved "blameless," as Pseudo-Solomon puts it. This would also help explain why it is that Abraham specifically was called by God and given the inestimable honor of being the one through whom God would make a "great nation" and in whom "all the families of the earth shall be blessed" (Gen 12:2-3): he showed himself worthy in Babel.

Two other passages in Genesis, working in tandem, may have lent further support for justifying such an interpretation. First, in Gen 15:7 God tells Abraham that he has taken him out of "Ur of the Chaldeans." Given that the name Ur is a homonym for one of the Hebrew words for fire (אוּר; see Isa 31:9; 50:11), this verse can be read as a cryptic reference to Abraham's having been delivered from some sort of Chaldean conflagration. Second, ancient interpreters linked this fire of the Chaldeans to the very fire used to burn the bricks for the tower of Babel in Gen 11:3, a connection made explicit in *L.A.B.* 6:16-17.

While such exegetical maneuvering may seem far-fetched for contemporary readers, it is crucial to remember that Pseudo-Solomon is not the only one to make Abraham a contemporary of the tower story. Once again, it is the fact that Pseudo-Solomon alludes to this tradition so briefly (when compared to the more detailed explanation in *L.A.B.*) that suggests that, already in his day, the tradition was well known and so needed no special introduction, reminder, or defense. It formed part of Pseudo-Solomon's repertoire of biblical knowledge, and so found its way into his homily.

The Sodomites Were Guilty of Inhospitality

A second example of Pseudo-Solomon's exposition of Scripture is found in Wis 19:13-17. Here Pseudo-Solomon describes the Egyptians as particularly inhospitable, ungrateful hosts to the Israelites: they received the Israelites only to turn right around and enslave them. This much is self-evident, but he adds a curious comment in v. 14: "Others had refused to receive strangers when they came to them." Who were these "others"? We find out in verse 17, where we read that the Egyptians were punished for their treatment of the Israelites by "loss of sight — just as were those at the door of the righteous man," which refers to the Sodom and Gomorrah episode. Hence, we see another example of Pseudo-Solomon linking two seemingly unconnected events: the "loss of sight" is an allusion to the ninth plague (Exod 10:22-23); and "those at the door of the righteous man" are those who came to the house of Lot (the "righteous") demanding he hand his guests over to them and whom the angels struck blind (Gen 19:11).

This connection may or may not be one forged intentionally by Pseudo-Solomon himself. The two episodes have similar themes and may have struck him or any informed reader as important to point out. But what may be more interesting to note, especially for contemporary readers, is that Pseudo-Solomon adduces the story of Sodom's destruction to buttress his condemnation of Egypt's *inhospitality*, which indicates that he, at least on one level, understands the sin of Sodom as essentially a refusal "to receive strangers." Pseudo-Solomon is not alone in this view. We see this tradition reflected in *Ant.* 1.194, where Josephus regards the sin of the Sodomites as inhospitality, dislike of foreigners, and arrogance. Similarly, this tradition may be reflected in the Synoptic Gospels (Matt 10:11-15; Luke 10:8-12), where Jesus instructs his disciples to shake the dust from their feet from any town that does not receive them, noting that "it will be more tolerable for Sodom and Gomorrah on the day of judgment than for that town" (Matt 10:15).[27] It would seem reasonable to conclude that the Sodom and Gomorrah story is adduced as an object lesson for inhospitality because inhospitality was seen as the sin of Sodom and Gomorrah.

It may be that Ezek 16:49-50 played some role in the development of this tradition. There the inhabitants of Sodom are condemned, at least in part, because they "had pride, excess of food, and prosperous ease, but did not aid the poor and needy." What seems to be highlighted here is the Sodomites' mistreatment of other people, not their sexual misconduct (although the latter is certainly not excluded). At any rate, Pseudo-Solomon's casual reference to Sodom's inhospitality is hardly his own innovation; it reveals the extent to which his own understanding of this episode was shaped by his interpretive environment.

---

27. Sirach 16:8 and 3 Macc 2:5 may also reflect this motif: both condemn the Sodomites for their "arrogance" (ὑπερηφανία). See also Rev 11:8, where Sodom is mentioned in the context of a city's inhabitants' refusal to bury the bodies of the "two witnesses." Interestingly, Rev 11:8 refers to the city in question figuratively as "Sodom and Egypt," thus drawing a connection between the two as does Pseudo-Solomon. Apparently for the writer of the Apocalypse, both Sodom and Egypt are worthy paradigms for the mistreatment of the two strangers in Rev 11:7-10. Hebrews 13:1-2 also seems to refer to the Sodom episode in the context of entertaining strangers.

Who Is Responsible for Causing the Flood?

In Wis 14:6, Pseudo-Solomon seems to place the blame for the flood on "arrogant giants," no doubt alluding to the very difficult reference in Gen 6:1-4 to the "sons of God" who consorted with the "daughters of humans" and the reference to the Nephilim in v. 4, those giants known to us from Num 13:33 and Deut 2:10-11. No clear connection is made between the offspring of divine/human cohabitation and the Nephilim in Gen 6:1-4. Moreover, the explicit cause for the flood is given in v. 5, the "wickedness of humankind." Even though causal connections are not made explicit in Genesis 6, the fact that verses 1-4 are followed by verse 5 could suggest that *some* lesson was waiting to be drawn from this juxtaposition. (We saw a similar issue above with the proximity of the tower of Babel narrative and Abraham's call.) The answer seems to be found in connecting the cause of the flood in verse 5 to what was addressed in verses 1-4, which is precisely what we find in Wis 14:6. What is of particular interest to us is that the same or similar sentiment is also found in 3 Macc 2:4; Sir 16:7; Bar 3:26-28; 1 En. 6:2; and *Jub.* 5:1-11. Pseudo-Solomon's understanding of the cause of the flood is not the result of his own exegetical ingenuity but a well-documented interpretive tradition of his day.[28]

An added twist is seen in Wis 10:4, where Pseudo-Solomon seems to offer an alternate interpretation: the blame for the flood is placed on Cain (". . . the earth was flooded because of him [Cain] . . ."). This raises two questions: how can Cain be blamed for an event long after he was gone, and why does Pseudo-Solomon offer two different explanations for the cause of the flood? With respect to the first question, blaming Cain for the flood provides an account for the *human* wickedness referred to in Gen 6:5, since no other act of human wickedness is recounted in the previous chapters. This is not to suggest that Cain alone is the cause of the flood, but that his act of murdering his brother was a primary instigator of the flood, which is hinted at in *T. Adam* 3:5: "A flood is coming and will wash the whole earth because of the daughters of Cain, your [Seth's] brother, who killed your brother Abel."[29]

---

28. See Jack P. Lewis, *A Study of the Interpretation of Noah and the Flood in Jewish and Christian Literature* (Leiden: Brill, 1968), 17-19; Winston, *The Wisdom of Solomon,* 267; Chrysostome Larcher, *Le Livre de la Sagesse, ou, La Sagesse de Salomon.* EBib 1 (Paris: Gabalda, 1983), 3:797. Gerald T. Sheppard discusses Bar 3:26-28 at length in *Wisdom as a Hermeneutical Construct: A Study of the Sapientializing of the Old Testament.* BZAW 151 (Berlin: de Gruyter, 1980), 85-90. More recently, see the work of Loren T. Stuckenbruck, who focuses on the interpretation of Gen 6:1-4 in 1 *Enoch* and *Jubilees;* "The Origins of Evil in Jewish Apocalyptic Tradition: The Interpretation of Genesis 6:1-4 in the Second and Third Centuries B.C.E.," in *The Fall of the Angels,* ed. Christoph Auffarth and Stuckenbruck (Leiden: Brill, 2002), 87-118.

29. On this tradition, see James L. Kugel, *Traditions of the Bible: A Guide to the Bible As It*

The answer to the second question is a bit more conjectural. I would suggest that Pseudo-Solomon's incorporation of both interpretive traditions hints not only at the diversity of interpretive traditions to which he was exposed but also underscores the degree to which his incorporation of these traditions is not necessarily a deliberate exegetical decision. Similarly, this phenomenon lends credence to the notion that these exegetical traditions were not clearly (if at all) marked off from the biblical texts being retold. The line between text and commentary was blurred. This is what we often find in Second Temple midrashic texts, when biblical events are retold again and again by different authors with some of the same interpretive embellishments, which Kugel refers to as the "legendizing" of midrash.[30] In this sense, Pseudo-Solomon's statements about the Bible can be seen, at least to a certain extent, as valuable witnesses, not so much to how he himself "handled" Scripture (i.e., his own exegetical method), but to exegetical traditions that must have been current in his day and that influenced his understanding of Scripture.

The Israelites Were "Paid" for Leaving Egypt

As noted above, much of Wisdom 10–19 concerns the exodus and wilderness periods, a topic that begins in 10:15. Two examples of Pseudo-Solomon's handling of the exodus vis-à-vis Second Temple interpretive traditions will be considered here. The first is Wis 10:17, where Pseudo-Solomon describes Israel leaving Egypt with "the reward of their labors." This phrase offers a different interpretation of events from that given in the Exodus account, where the Israelites are said to "plunder" (MT נצל; LXX σκυλεύω) the Egyptians (Exod 12:36; cf. 3:21-22; 11:2). Pseudo-Solomon's comment is representative of a well-documented apologetic interpretive tradition aimed at responding to accusations that plundering was a less than holy activity for such a supposedly holy people.[31] After all, only thieves "plunder." Pseudo-Solomon's re-

---

Was at the Start of the Common Era (Cambridge, Mass.: Harvard University Press, 1998), 172. Kugel continues to discuss reasons why, if Cain were so culpable, so much time would pass between that act and God's punishment (173-90). Kugel also references a related and popular ancient tradition in which Cain actually perishes in the flood (166).

30. James L. Kugel, "Two Introductions to Midrash," *Proof* 3 (1983): 131-55, esp. 151; repr. *Midrash and Literature,* ed. Geoffrey H. Hartman and Sanford Budick (New Haven: Yale University Press, 1986), 77-103.

31. Winston, *The Wisdom of Solomon,* 220. This interpretive tradition is quite early, appearing in *Jub.* 48:18 (early second century B.C.E.), Philo's *Moses* 1.141 (around the turn of the Common Era), and Ezekiel the Tragedian's *Exagoge* 162–66 (late second century B.C.E.).

sponse is that the "plundering" was in fact a just payment for years of slavery to the Egyptians.

It is worth noting here, once again, how Pseudo-Solomon's comment does not seem to be of his own making. In fact, in the flow of chapter 10 it hardly adds anything of immediate importance to the overall purpose of that section, namely, to describe how Wisdom has been with God's people from the beginning. Yet, and as we have seen above, this is precisely why taking note of the presence of such an interpretive tradition is of importance for our understanding of Second Temple hermeneutics. The presence of such incidental remarks in an otherwise highly intentional piece of literature suggests that the interpretive traditions to which Pseudo-Solomon referred had by his time become sufficiently attached to the biblical account so to require no explanation. In other words, they represented proper and commonly-accepted views on what the Bible "says."

The Egyptians Were Cast onto the Shore of the Red Sea

The second exodus tradition to be considered is found in Wis 10:19-20. Pseudo-Solomon's comment on the Egyptians' death at the Red Sea is an unmistakable witness to a popular exegetical tradition (e.g., Philo's *Moses* 2.225). He says that Wisdom "cast them [the Egyptians] up from the depth of the sea. Therefore the righteous plundered the ungodly." Pseudo-Solomon's comment here is fascinating in its brevity and invites us to offer some explanation. Many commentators compare Pseudo-Solomon's handling of the above episode with *Targum Pseudo-Jonathan* to Exod 15:12, which tells of a protracted debate between the sea and the land in which each refuses to accept the Egyptian dead, lest God's wrath be upon it.[32] The sea, not wanting to incur God's wrath, casts them onto the shore for all to see. Only after God promises that there will be no repercussions does the land swallow the dead.

This interpretative tradition seems to be a clever attempt to reconcile several apparently contradictory passages in the biblical narrative. How is it that the dead Egyptians could be plainly seen by the Israelites on the shore (Exod

---

32. Joseph Reider, *The Book of Wisdom* (New York: Harper, 1957), 139; Ernest G. Clarke, *Targum Pseudo-Jonathan of the Pentateuch: Text and Concordance* (Hoboken: Ktav, 1984), 72; Winston, *The Wisdom of Solomon*, 221; Carl L. W. Grimm, *Kurtzgefasstes exegetisches Handbuch zu den Apokryphen des Alten Testaments*, 6th ed. (Leipzig: Hirzel, 1860), 203; A. T. S. Goodrick, *The Book of Wisdom* (New York: Macmillan, 1913), 327; Larcher, *Le Livre de la Sagesse*, 2:644-45; William J. Deane, *The Book of Wisdom* (Oxford: Clarendon, 1881), 167. See also *Pirqe R. El.* 42; *b. Pesaḥ.* 118b.

14:30), while elsewhere they are said to have sunk "like a stone" (15:5) or "like lead" (15:10) in the sea, and then been "swallowed" by the earth (15:12)? Of course, one could easily envision that first the Egyptians drowned (sunk like stone or lead) and then later their lifeless bodies washed up on shore in plain view. To be "swallowed" by the earth is not a subsequent event, but simply an idiom meaning that they died. There really is nothing of a problematic nature in these passages. But early interpreters reasoned differently. For the Egyptians to be seen on the shore in Exod 14:30 *after* they had sunk in the sea, they must have been cast up again after they had drowned. Whether or not Pseudo-Solomon has this fuller targumic tradition consciously in mind is impossible to tell. Nevertheless, we see again that his own apparently unique interpretation of what the Bible says must be viewed in the broader context of how other exegetes — both contemporaries and precursors — were handling Scripture.[33]

Conclusion

The above examples help to illustrate the increasing importance of biblical interpretation during the Second Temple period and to sketch the broader context within which to view the interpretive activity seen in the Wisdom of Solomon. It appears that Pseudo-Solomon's strategy was to present the biblical data in such a way as to make all Scripture speak more clearly to the ever-changing situations of the readers. This is why he portrays the heroes of Israel's past in black-and-white categories: they have become models of virtue. This is also why these heroes have become nameless figures: the past is dehistoricized in an effort to bring it more forcefully into the present.[34] This is not to say that Pseudo-Solomon treats the historical events themselves lightly. In calling upon this "dehistoricized" past — one that does not emphasize the particulars of the events — Pseudo-Solomon is simply telling his readers that the God of Israel is still with them, that who they are now amid the changing fortunes of history must be seen in light of the never-changing God who has never failed to deliver

33. We might also mention here the significance of "therefore" at the beginning of Wis 10:20. The Egyptians being cast onto the shore is what made it possible for the Israelites to plunder the Egyptians, thus addressing another unanswered detail of the biblical narrative: whence did the Israelites get the weapons to wage war against the Amalekites in Exod 17:8-16?

34. Collins argues that the universalism afforded by anonymity allows Pseudo-Solomon's words to apply to the enemies of his day, namely the Alexandrians and Romans; *Jewish Wisdom in the Hellenistic Age,* 218-19. In my view, Pseudo-Solomon's intentionality in this regard makes his casual inclusion of ancient Jewish interpretive traditions appear even more intended, and so all the more intriguing.

the faithful who have gone before (again, see 9:18 and 19:22 cited above). Idealizing the past does not obliterate history but makes it transportable. For Pseudo-Solomon, therefore, the idealized past is the only proper backdrop for viewing one's present, historical situation. It is the solid rock that stands high above the ebb and flow of their contemporary struggle. And, according to our author, it is Wisdom herself who has been God's active agent throughout Israel's history, bringing the godly through trying times. His readers, therefore, are exhorted to seek (Wis 6:12-16), honor (6:21), pray for (7:7), love (8:2), and befriend (8:18) her. Acquiring Wisdom now is the key to the present, for it is Wisdom who has been active throughout Israel's past.

Pseudo-Solomon's portrayal of Wisdom as the primary player in Israel's history naturally leads to placing such an understanding of Wisdom in the general context of the Second Temple period. We see already in Proverbs 8 the personification of Wisdom, who has some special status in creation, either as the first of God's creations (Prov 8:22),[35] or at least as being present at creation (Prov 8:30; cf. 3:19). Proverbs 8 is one of the few expressions (and certainly the clearest) of the personification of Wisdom in the Old Testament (see also Job 28; Proverbs 1, 9). But the reticence with which the Old Testament speaks of personified Wisdom may be what motivated early interpreters to find out more about her. Hence, the nature of personified Wisdom takes on added importance in postbiblical times. Specifically, there is a well-documented postbiblical tendency to equate the concept of Wisdom with Torah. A well-known, and early, example is Sir 24:1-29.[36] For Ben Sira, Torah is the source of wisdom, a point he makes unequivocally clear in Sir 24:23-29. Wisdom is the first of God's creations existing from eternity to eternity (24:9; also 1:4, 9).[37] She then is said to make her dwell-

---

35. The root קנה in Prov 8:22 could also suggest "beget" or "acquire."

36. For a study of wisdom and law in Ben Sira, intertestamental literature, the Dead Sea Scrolls, and the Apostle Paul, see Eckhard J. Schnabel, *Law and Wisdom from Ben Sira to Paul: A Tradition History Enquiry into the Relation of Law, Wisdom, and Ethics.* WUNT ser. 2, 16 (Tübingen: Mohr Siebeck, 1985). See also Robert L. Wilken, ed., *Aspects of Wisdom in Judaism and Early Christianity* (Notre Dame: University of Notre Dame Press, 1975); Joseph Blenkinsopp, *Wisdom and Law in the Old Testament: The Ordering of Life in Israel and Early Judaism* (Oxford: Oxford University Press, 1983); Gabriele Boccaccini, *Middle Judaism: Jewish Thought, 300 B.C.E. to 200 C.E.* (Minneapolis: Fortress, 1991), 81-99; and Winston, *The Wisdom of Solomon,* 33-38. Many rabbinic passages assume the equation of Torah and Wisdom while referring specifically to Prov 8:22: e.g., *Mek. Shir.* 9:123, which cites Prov 8:22 as a proof-text that Torah is a possession of God. See also *Gen. Rab.* 1:4; 11:3; 19:1; *Cant. Rab.* 5:11.

37. Ben Sira certainly models his discussion of wisdom after Proverbs 8; Patrick W. Skehan, "Structures in Poems in Wisdom: Proverbs 8 and Sirach 24," *CBQ* 41 (1979): 365-79. In contrast to Ben Sira, however, Pseudo-Solomon presents wisdom as having a role in the act of creation itself (Wis 7:22; 8:4, 6).

ing in Israel (24:8-11) and then "takes root" among God's people and grows tall and flourishes (24:12-17). What distinguishes Sir 24:1-29 from Wis 10:1-21 is that Pseudo-Solomon deals with specific instances of Wisdom's participation in Israel's history, whereas Ben Sira mentions only her presence at creation and gives a muted nod to her presence in Israel.[38] But this distinction pertains only to Sir 24:1-29, for Ben Sira turns to the topic of wisdom's participation in Israel's history in great detail in chapters 44–50, where the author recounts the deeds of "famous men" (44:1) whose lives stand as permanent examples of righteous lives, righteous because they exemplify the wisdom ideal (see 44:2-6).[39]

The larger interpretive point to be illustrated in the Wisdom of Solomon, particularly the second half of the book, is that Scripture, specifically Torah, has become the depository of wisdom. The role of wisdom, as Gerald Sheppard puts it, has moved from "mundane advice to wisdom's recital of her participation in Israel's traditions."[40] In wisdom books like Proverbs, Job, and Ecclesiastes, we find scarcely a single, clear scriptural allusion. Starting with Ben Sira and Wisdom of Solomon, however, we see books of wisdom that are steeped through and through with references to biblical figures and events. This fact does not make these two books any less a part of the wisdom genre. Rather, it is the nature of wisdom itself that has shifted. Whereas the sages of the Hebrew Bible were concerned with observing patterns in the created order as the basis for godly conduct — "exegeting the world," so to speak — Ben Sira and Pseudo-Solomon were concerned with observing the nature of God's activity by exegeting the Book: the sage's focus of attention now includes Scripture. The Wisdom of Solomon, therefore, is not simply a commentary on Scripture but a search for wisdom, a search for God's overarching, eternal plan, revealed by a careful, sagely reading of Scripture. God's eternal wisdom is to be learned from the Bible, for it is Scripture that is the depository of wisdom.

We can see, therefore, why biblical interpretation gained such importance in

38. Hence, Jack T. Sanders's observation that "the author of the Wisdom of Solomon . . . seems to make a more deliberate attempt than do other sages of the second-temple period to accommodate the Mosaic Torah to the sapiential tradition"; "When Sacred Canopies Collide: The Reception of the Torah of Moses in the Wisdom Literature of the Second-Temple Period," *JSJ* 32 (2001): 129.

39. In this context one thinks, too, of the catalog of heroes in Hebrews 11. Armin Schmitt cites a number of examples of *historische Beispielreihen* in antiquity, including biblical, apocryphal, pseudepigraphal, Hellenistic, and classical Greek literature; "Struktur, Herkunft und Bedeutung der Beispielreihe in Weish 10," *BZ* 21 (1977): 1-22. See also Collins, *Jewish Wisdom in the Hellenistic Age*, 213-17; Leong Cheng Michael Phua, "The Wise Kings of Judah according to Ben Sira: A Study in Second Temple Use of Biblical Interpretation" (Diss., Westminster Theological Seminary, 2008).

40. Sheppard, *Wisdom as a Hermeneutical Construct*, 6.

the Second Temple period. Simply stated, Scripture is God's wisdom. It is rich in meaning and invites — even demands — that one search for that meaning. It is little wonder, then, that the exegetical traditions witnessed to in the Wisdom of Solomon came to be so closely associated with the biblical text. Scripture must be properly interpreted in order for it to serve as a guide for living. A biblical passage is of little use if its meaning is unclear. But when it is "interpreted," its meaning becomes clear. These interpretive traditions are more than entertaining embellishments. They are the fruit of sagely activity that treated the Bible as a gift from God for a standard of faith and conduct with, at least for Pseudo-Solomon, eternal consequences. It is wisdom that is contained, yet hidden, in the text. It is to meet the challenge of bringing God's wisdom to God's people that biblical interpretation became a wisdom activity in the Second Temple period, and the Wisdom of Solomon remains a vital link to this important development.

BIBLIOGRAPHY

Cheon, Samuel. *The Exodus Story in the Wisdom of Solomon: A Study in Biblical Interpretation.* JSPSup 23. Sheffield: Sheffield Academic, 1997.

Collins, John J. *Jewish Wisdom in the Hellenistic Age.* OTL. Louisville: Westminster John Knox, 1997.

Collins, John J., and George W. E. Nickelsburg, eds. *Ideal Figures in Ancient Judaism: Profiles and Paradigms.* SBLSCS 12. Chico: Scholars, 1980.

Enns, Peter. *Exodus Retold: Ancient Exegesis of the Departure from Egypt in Wis 10:15-21 and 19:1-9.* HSM 57. Atlanta: Scholars, 1997.

———. "A Retelling of the Song at the Sea in Wis 10,20-21." *Bib* 76 (1995): 1-24; repr. *The Function of Scripture in Early Jewish and Christian Tradition,* ed. Craig A. Evans and James A. Sanders. JSNTSup 154. SSEJC 6. Sheffield: Sheffield Academic, 1998, 142-65.

Georgi, Dieter. *Weisheit Salomos.* JSHRZ 3.4. Gütersloh: Gütersloher, 1980.

Gilbert, Maurice. "Wisdom of Solomon." Pp. 301-13 in *Jewish Writings of the Second Temple Period: Apocrypha, Pseudepigrapha, Qumran Sectarian Writings, Philo, Josephus.* Edited by Michael Stone. CRINT, 2.2. Assen: Van Gorcum; Minneapolis: Fortress Press, 1984.

———. "Wisdom of Solomon in Scripture." In *Hebrew Bible/Old Testament: The History of Its Interpretation.* Vol. 1: *From the Beginnings to the Middle Ages (Until 1300).* Part 2: *The Middle Ages,* ed. Magne Sæbø. Göttingen: Vandenhoeck & Ruprecht, 2000, 606-17.

Grabbe, Lester L. *Wisdom of Solomon.* GAP 3. Sheffield: Sheffield Academic, 1997.

Kolarcik, Michael. *The Ambiguity of Death in the Book of Wisdom 1-6: A Study of Literary Structure and Interpretation.* AnBib 127. Rome: Pontifical Biblical Institute, 1991.

Kugel, James L. *In Potiphar's House: The Interpretive Life of Biblical Texts.* San Francisco: HarperCollins, 1990.

———. *The Ladder of Jacob: Ancient Interpretations of the Biblical Story of Jacob and His Children.* Princeton: Princeton University Press, 2006.

―――. *Traditions of the Bible: A Guide to the Bible as It Was at the Start of the Common Era*. Cambridge, Mass.: Harvard University Press, 1998.

―――. "Two Introductions to Midrash." *Proof* 3 (1983): 131-55; repr. *Midrash and Literature*, ed. Geoffrey H. Hartman and Sanford Budick. New Haven: Yale University Press, 1986, 77-103.

Kugel, James L., and Rowan A. Greer. *Early Biblical Interpretation*. LEC 3. Philadelphia: Westminster, 1986.

Larcher, Chrysostome. *Études sur le Livre de la Sagesse*. EBib. Paris: Gabalda, 1969.

―――. *Le Livre de la Sagesse, ou, La Sagesse de Salomon*. 3 vols. Paris: Gabalda, 1983-85.

Lillie, Betty J. "A History of Scholarship on the Wisdom of Solomon from the Nineteenth Century to Our Time." Diss., Hebrew Union College, 1982.

Reese, James M. *Hellenistic Influence on the Book of Wisdom and Its Consequences*. AnBib 41. Rome: Biblical Institute, 1970.

Reider, Joseph. *The Book of Wisdom*. New York: Harper, 1957.

Rooden, Peter T. van. "Die antike Elementarlehre und der Aufbau von Sapientia Salomonis 11–19." In *Tradition and Re-interpretation in Jewish and Early Christian Literature: Essays in Honour of Jürgen C. H. Lebram*, ed. Jan W. van Henten et al. StPB 36. Leiden: Brill, 1986, 81-96.

Schaberg, Jane. "Major Midrashic Traditions in Wisdom 1,1–6,25." *JSJ* 13 (1982): 75-101.

Schmitt, Armin. "Struktur, Herkunft und Bedeutung der Beispielreihe in Weish 10." *BZ* 21 (1977): 1-22.

―――. *Das Buch der Weisheit: Ein Kommentar*. Würzburg: Echter, 1986.

Schwenk-Bressler, Udo. *Sapientia Salomonis als ein Beispiel frühjüdischer Textauslegung: Die Auslegung des Buches Genesis, Exodus 1–15 und Teilen der Wüstentradition in Sap 10–19*. BEATAJ 32. Frankfurt am Main: Lang, 1993.

Sheppard, Gerald T. *Wisdom as a Hermeneutical Construct: A Study in the Sapientialization of the Old Testament*. BZAW 151. Berlin: de Gruyter, 1980.

Skehan, Patrick W. "Isaias and the Teaching of the Book of Wisdom." *CBQ* 2 (1940): 289-99; repr. *Studies in Israelite Poetry and Wisdom*, 163-71.

―――. "The Text and Structure of the Book of Wisdom," *Traditio* 3 (1945): 1-12; repr. *Studies in Israelite Poetry and Wisdom*, 132-36.

―――. "Borrowings from the Psalms in the Book of Wisdom." *CBQ* 10 (1948): 384-97; repr. *Studies in Israelite Poetry and Wisdom*, 149-62.

―――. "The Literary Relationship of the Book of Wisdom to Earlier Wisdom Writings." In *Studies in Israelite Poetry and Wisdom*, 172-236.

―――. *Studies in Israelite Poetry and Wisdom*. CBQMS 1. Washington: Catholic Biblical Association, 1971.

Stein, Edmund. "Ein jüdisch-hellenistischer Midrash über den Auszug aus Ägypten." *MGWJ* 78 (1934): 558-75.

Stuckenbruck, Loren T. "The Origins of Evil in Jewish Apocalyptic Tradition: The Interpretation of Genesis 6:1-4 in the Second and Third Centuries B.C.E." In *The Fall of the Angels*, ed. Christoph Auffarth and Stuckenbruck. Leiden: Brill, 2002, 87-118.

Winston, David. *The Wisdom of Solomon*. AB 43. Garden City: Doubleday, 1979.

Wright, Addison G. "The Structure of the Book of Wisdom." *Bib* 48 (1967): 165-84.

―――. "The Structure of Wisdom 11–19." *CBQ* 27 (1965): 28-34.

PART 7

HELLENISTIC JUDAISM

The Interpreter of Moses:
Philo of Alexandria and the Biblical Text

Gregory E. Sterling

In a remarkable autobiographical statement Philo of Alexandria lamented a change in his circumstances that had affected his life's work: "There was once a time when I had leisure for philosophy and the contemplation of the cosmos and the things in it, when I enjoyed the beautiful, dearly loved, and truly blessed life of the mind. . . ." Alas, these days had disappeared: "But the most troublesome of evils, good-hating envy, was lying in wait for me. It suddenly fell on me and did not cease dragging me down forcefully until it had cast me down into the great sea of civil concerns." He was probably referring to the pogrom that had broken out at the visit of Agrippa I to Alexandria and his subsequent role in the embassy to Gaius.[1] Yet not all was lost: "Look at me. I dare not only read the sacred explanations of Moses, but also in my love of knowledge peer into each to unfold and reveal the things that are not known to the many."[2]

Philo's passion for reading and explaining Scripture was genuine. He was the most prolific commentator on Moses among Second Temple Jewish authors.[3] While he also wrote apologetic and philosophical works that cited Hellenistic authors rather than Moses, commenting on the Pentateuch was his life's

---

1. Philo wrote *Flaccus* and *Embassy* in connection with these events. His role in the embassy is repeatedly mentioned in testimonia about him, e.g., Josephus, *Ant.* 18.258; Eusebius, *Hist. eccl.* 2.5.6; *Chron.* 204, 214; Jerome, *Vir. ill.* 11. Erwin R. Goodenough thought that this referred to Philo's role in a judicial capacity, e.g., in the senate. See "Philo and Public Life," *JEA* 12 (1926): 77-79.

2. Philo, *Spec. Laws* 3.1-6. The citations are from 1, 3, and 6. All translations are my own.

3. The most important works that have pointed out Philo's fundamental task as an exegete are Valentin Nikiprowetzky, *Le commentaire de l'Écriture chez Philon d'Alexandrie.* ALGHJ 11 (Leiden: Brill, 1977); and Peder Borgen, *Philo of Alexandria: An Exegete for His Time.* NovTSup 86 (Leiden: Brill, 1997; repr. Atlanta: SBL, 2005).

work.[4] The centrality of the Scriptures in his treatises raises at least three major issues: how did he use the Scriptures in his commentaries, what was the extent of the texts he considered sacred, and what was the text of his Greek Bible.

Philo's Use of the Scriptures in His Commentaries

Philo wrote more than seventy treatises. Christians preserved about two-thirds of these.[5] He organized his commentaries into three major series: *Questions and Answers on Genesis and Exodus,* the Allegorical Commentary, and the Exposition of the Law. His use of the Scriptures varies in each of the series.[6]

Questions and Answers on Genesis and Exodus

The Questions and Answers on Genesis and Exodus have come down to us in a rather literal sixth-century Armenian translation[7] and some Greek fragments.[8]

4. For summaries of the Philonic corpus, see Jenny Morris, "The Jewish Philosopher Philo," in Emil Schürer, *The History of the Jewish People in the Age of Jesus Christ,* rev. Geza Vermes, Fergus Millar, and Martin Goodman (Edinburgh: T. & T. Clark, 1973-87), 3.2:819-70; and James R. Royse, "The Works of Philo," in *The Cambridge Companion to Philo,* ed. Adam Kamesar (Cambridge: Cambridge University Press, 2009), 32-64.

5. On the preservation of Philo's corpus, see David T. Runia, *Philo in Early Christian Literature: A Survey.* CRINT 3.3 (Assen: Van Gorcum and Minneapolis: Fortress, 1993), 16-31.

6. For recent treatments of Philo's exegetical techniques, see Daniel I. Brewer, *Techniques and Assumptions in Jewish Exegesis before 70 C.E.* TSAJ 30 (Tübingen: Mohr Siebeck, 1992), 198-213; Folker Siegert, "Early Jewish Interpretation in a Hellenistic Style," in *Hebrew Bible/Old Testament: The History of Its Interpretation,* Vol. 1: *From the Beginnings to the Middle Ages (Until 1300),* Part 1: *Antiquity,* ed. Magne Sæbø (Göttingen: Vandenhoeck & Ruprecht, 1996), 162-88; and Adam Kamesar, "Biblical Interpretation in Philo," in *The Cambridge Companion to Philo,* 65-91.

7. The only edition of the Armenian is J. B. Aucher, *Judaei paralipomena Armena (Libri videlicet quottuor In Genesin, libri duo In Exodum, sermo unus De Sampsone, alter De Jona, tertius De tribus angelis Abraamo apparentibus): Opera hactenus inedita (Ex Armena versione antiquissima ab ipso originali textu Graeco ad verbum stricte exequuta saeculo v. nunc primum in Latium fideliter translata)* (Venice: Lazarus, 1826). Aucher provided a Latin translation. English speakers have access to Philo most easily through Francis Henry Colson, George Herbert Whitaker, and Ralph Marcus, eds., *Philo.* 10 vols. and 2 supplementary vols. LCL (Cambridge, Mass.: Harvard University Press, 1929-62); hereafter abbreviated PLCL. *The Questions and Answers* are translated in the two supplementary volumes.

8. Françoise Petit, *Quaestiones in Genesim et in Exodum: Fragmenta graeca.* Les Œuvres de Philon d'Alexandrie 33 (Paris: Cerf, 1978). See also James R. Royse, "Further Greek Fragments of Philo's *Quaestiones,*" in *Nourished with Peace: Studies in Hellenistic Judaism in Memory of Samuel Sandmel,* ed. Frederick E. Greenspahn, Earle Hilgert, and Burton L. Mack (Chico: Scholars, 1984), 143-53; and "Philo's *Quaestiones in Exodum* 1.6," in *Both Literal and Allegorical: Studies in*

As is the case for each of the three commentary series, some of the works have been lost: the Armenian preserves four books for Genesis and two for Exodus, although these probably represent parts of an original six books on Genesis and six on Exodus.[9] The works provide a running commentary on Gen 2:4–28:9 and Exod 12:2–28:24 (with gaps). The commentary is cast in the form of questions and answers. They stand in the literary tradition that began with Aristotle's *Homeric Problems* and became commonplace in philosophical circles, e.g., Plutarch's *Platonic Questions*. Previous Jewish authors such as Demetrius (frags. 2 and 5) and Aristobulus (frag. 2) had used the format, but Philo is the first known Jewish author to cast a full-scale commentary in a zetematic form.

The Jewish exegete cast each unit in two elements: the question and the answer. The questions typically begin with a standard interrogative such as διὰ τί ("why") or τί ἐστιν ("what is"). These are typically followed by a quotation from the biblical text. The occasion for the question is an issue posed by the text or a philosophical issue that impinges on the text. In a couple of cases, a secondary text is cited — but this is unusual. The answer moves on two levels: the literal and the figurative or allegorical. Philo listed the options in a way that reminds a reader of a modern commentary that offers possible readings for a text. He often included a reference to the biblical text and in approximately 10 percent of the answers cited a secondary lemma, although he did not develop these extensively.[10]

An example of how the Alexandrian handled the biblical text in this commentary will illustrate his practice. Philo was bothered by the idiom θανάτῳ ἀποθανεῖσθε in Gen 2:17 that renders the Hebrew infinitive absolute literally (מות תמות). In the commentary he asked: "What is the meaning of 'You will die by death'?" (Gen 2:17). He gave a philosophical response: "The death of worthy people is the beginning of another life. For life is double: there is one with corruptible body and there is another without body (that is) incorruptible." The reference to twofold death drew from a philosophical tradition that reached back to Heraclitus, who was the first to posit the death of the soul. Philo made the reference clear as he continued: "So then the evil person alone dies by death even while he breathes, before he is buried as though he did not preserve for himself any spark at all of the true life — and this is outstanding character." He contrasted the virtuous person: "But the decent and worthy person does not die

---

Philo of Alexandria's Questions and Answers on Genesis and Exodus, ed. David M. Hay. BJS 232 (Atlanta: Scholars, 1991), 17-27.

9. I have followed the analysis of James R. Royse, "The Original Structure of Philo's *Quaestiones*," *SPhil* 4 (1976-77): 41-78; and "Philo's Division of His Works into Books," *SPhA* 13 (2001): 76-85.

10. On the secondary lemmata in the QGE, see David T. Runia, "Secondary Texts in Philo's *Quaestiones*," in Hay, *Both Literal and Allegorical*, 47-79.

by death, but after living long, expires to eternity, that is to say that he is carried to eternal life."[11] It is thus possible to die a death that has nothing to do with physical death; it is the moral death of the soul. In this way, Philo was able to make sense of the Hebrew idiom that made little sense in Greek.[12]

The character of a commentary that offers brief responses and lists options in those responses suggests that it was for beginning students, perhaps students in a school Philo operated.[13] The questions and answers would have given them an orientation to the biblical text.

The Allegorical Commentary

The second major commentary that Philo wrote is his longest and most famous. We call it the Allegorical Commentary, although the title is not original to Philo but was taken from some of the initial treatises in the commentary. Eusebius was the first to have called these treatises by this name, and it has endured in the tradition.[14] Nineteen treatises[15] and a fragment of another have come down to us.[16] We know of twelve others that have been lost.[17] They are

11. Philo, *QG* 1.16.

12. On the philosophical background and Philo's appropriation of it, see Dieter Zeller, "The Life and Death of the Soul in Philo of Alexandria: The Use and Origin of a Metaphor," *SPhA* 7 (1995): 19-56; John T. Conroy, Jr., "'The Wages of Sin Is Death': The Death of the Soul in Greek, Second Temple Jewish, and Early Christian Authors" (Diss., Notre Dame, 2008); and Emma Wasserman, *The Death of the Soul in Romans 7: Sin, Death, and the Law in Light of Hellenistic Moral Psychology*. WUNT ser. 2, 256 (Tübingen: Mohr Siebeck, 2008).

13. On this possibility, see Gregory E. Sterling, "'The School of Sacred Laws': The Social Setting of Philo's Treatises," *VC* 53 (1999): 148-64.

14. Eusebius, *Hist. eccl.* 2.18.1; Origen, *Comm. Matt.* 17:17; *Cels.* 4.51; Photius, *Bibliotheca* col. 103.

15. Philo, *Alleg. Interp.* 1 (from *Alleg. Interp.* 1-2), 3; *Cherubim, Sacrifices, Worse, Posterity, Giants,* and *Unchangeable* (originally one treatise but now two), *Agriculture, Planting, Drunkenness* 1; *Sobriety, Confusion, Migration, Heir, Prelim. Studies, Flight, Names, Dreams* 2 and 3 (= *Dreams* 1 and 2). The standard critical edition is Leopold Cohn, Paul Wendland, Sigofred Reiter, and Ioannes Leisegang, eds., *Philonis Alexandrini opera quae supersunt.* 7 vols. (Berlin: Reimer, 1896-1930; 2nd ed., Berlin: Gruyter, 1962). Hereafter abbreviated PCW. An English translation is available in PLCL.

16. *On God (De Deo)* is preserved in an Armenian fragment. See Folker Siegert, *Philon von Alexandrien, Über die Gottesbezeichnung "wohltätig verzehrendes Feuer" (De Deo): Rückübersetzung des Fragments aus dem Armenischen, deutsche Übersetzung und Kommentar.* WUNT 46 (Tübingen: Mohr, 1988); and "The Philonian Fragment *De Deo*: First English Translation," *SPhA* 10 (1998): 1-13.

17. Some of these can be posited by lacunae, others by references to them: Gen 1:1-31 is missing (see Thomas H. Tobin, "The Beginning of Philo's *Legum Allegoriae*," *SPhA* 12 [2000]:

more similar in form to some of the commentaries in the philosophical tradition than to any other form of commentary, especially to the anonymous *Theaetetus Commentary,* Plutarch's *On the Generation of the Soul in the Timaeus,* and Porphyry's *On the Cave of Nymphs.*[18] There is, however, a basic difference between these individual commentaries and the thirty-two treatises in the Allegorical Commentary: Philo linked all of his treatises together into a unified whole.

The unity of the series is directly tied to the biblical text: they form a running commentary on Gen 2:1–17:22. If we add the fragment *On God,* coverage extends to Gen 18:2. The treatises *On Dreams* interpret later texts in Genesis and do not form a direct continuation. The unity of the treatises is confirmed by another feature of these treatises. The fourth-century B.C.E. historian Ephorus oriented readers of his thirty-volume universal history by providing secondary prefaces at the beginning of books.[19] Later authors such as Diodorus Siculus[20] and Josephus followed the practice.[21] Philo did as well: he wrote secondary prefaces for at least six of the treatises in this commentary.[22] For example, he opened *On Planting* with these words: "In the former book (ἐν μὲν τῷ προτέρῳ βιβλίῳ) we discussed the matters pertaining to general agricultural skills, at least what was appropriate to it. In this book we will explain (ἐν δὲ τούτῳ . . . ἀποδώσομεν) — as best we can — the particular skill of tending vines."[23] Philo set the stage for this preface in the final words of the preceding treatise: "Let us speak in turn about his skill in cultivating plants."[24] The connection between the two led Eusebius to speak of two works *Concerning Agriculture.*[25] The reference to "this book" in the opening of *On Agriculture* made it clear that the two

---

29-43); Gen 3:1b-8a is missing (= *Alleg. Interp.* 2); Gen 3:20-23 is missing (= "Alleg. Interp." 4; see also *Sacrifices* 51); Gen 4:5-7 is missing.

18. For a brief overview of scholarship on the study of the structure of the treatises in the Allegorical Commentary, see David T. Runia, "The Structure of Philo's Allegorical Treatise *De agricultura,*" *SPhA* 22 (2010): 87-109.

19. Ephorus, *FGrH* 70.

20. All of the extant books have full prefaces except for 2, 3, and 11. Many of the partially preserved books also have secondary prefaces. For Diodorus's practice, see Kenneth S. Sacks, "The Lesser Prooemia of Diodorus Siculus," *Hermes* 110 (1982): 434-43; and *Diodorus Siculus and the First Century* (Princeton: Princeton University Press, 1990), 9-22.

21. Josephus, *Ant.* 8.1; 13.1; 14.1; 15.1; 20.1. For an analysis, see Gregory E. Sterling, *Historiography and Self-definition: Josephos, Luke-Acts and Apologetic Historiography.* NovTSup 64 (Leiden: Brill, 1992), 247-48.

22. Philo, *Planting* 1; *Drunkenness* 1; *Sobriety* 1; *Heir* 1; *Flight* 2; *Dreams* 1.1.

23. Philo, *Planting* 1.

24. Philo, *Agriculture* 181.

25. Eusebius, *Hist. eccl.* 2.18.2. See also Eusebius, *Praep. ev.* 7.13.3-4; and Jerome, *Vir. ill.* 11.

treatises were individual units of a larger whole that the author thought of as a unity rather than a collection of discrete essays.

The biblical text also played a pivotal role within the internal structure of each treatise. Philo always worked from a primary lemma (a citation or a paraphrase of the biblical text), just as he did in the *Questions and Answers*. However, he often commented at great length on a lemma. For example, the treatises *On Agriculture, On Planting, and Drunkenness* 1 cover Gen 9:20a; 9:20b; 9:21, respectively. He worked through the text by citing a word or phrase and commenting on it before repeating the process with a subsequent word or phrase. He expanded his treatment of each word or phrase by introducing secondary and tertiary biblical lemmata. While he incorporated some secondary texts in the *Questions and Answers*, they were infrequent and minor, whereas they appear routinely and play a significant role in the Allegorical Commentary. He joined secondary lemmata to the primary lemma largely through wordplays or through thematic treatments. For example, Philo cited Gen 9:24 as the primary lemma in *On Sobriety*: "Noah *sobered up* from the wine and knew what his *younger son* had done to him."[26] He began with a treatment of *sobriety* (§§1-5) and then moved to *"younger son"* (§§6-29), where he introduced a series of secondary lemmata. He set up his discussion by suggesting that young does not refer to chronological years as much as it refers to character (§6). This led him to a series of individuals who were called young in the biblical text, but more with respect to character than to years (§§7-15). These include Ishmael, who was a παιδίον, in contrast to Isaac, who represented fully-developed virtue (Gen 21:14-16; see §§7-9), the "children" (τέκνα) of Israel, who were foolish (Deut 32:4-6; §§10-11); Rachel, who was shapely in body and was therefore younger (νεώτερα) than Leah, who was beauty of soul (§12); and Joseph, who was the champion of the powers of the body and was therefore the "young" (νέος [Gen 37:2]) or the "youngest" (νεώτατος [Gen 49:22]) of Jacob's sons (§§13-15). In contrast, those who are older are praised (§§16-20): Abraham (Gen 24:1; see §§17-18) and the seventy elders (Num 11:16; see §§19-20). Philo concluded his discussion of the "younger son" by providing an analysis of a text that offered a contrast: the law of honoring the firstborn, even if he is born of a "hated" wife rather than a wife that one loves (Deut 21:15-17; see §§21-29). The younger son is from the beloved wife, who represents pleasure, while the older son is from the hated wife, or prudence (§§21-25). This led him to mention the famous stories of Jacob and Esau, since Jacob was younger in years but older in virtue (§26), and Jacob's blessing of Joseph's sons, where the ancestor gave the greater blessing to Ephraim, who was younger in years but older in virtue than Manasseh

---

26. Philo, *Sobriety* 1.

(Gen 48:13-14; see §§27-29). The commentator made the case by drawing on the etymologies for the names of each and then connecting the etymology with a larger issue. So in this case, he associated Ephraim ("fruit-bearing") with "memory" and Manasseh (from "forgetfulness") with "recall." Memory is better than recall, since the latter presumes forgetfulness.[27] Philo has thus built a commentary on the basis of the contrast between "young" and "old" by giving them a moral interpretation.

The complex nature of the exegesis in the Allegorical Commentary and its focus on the figurative or allegorical interpretation of the text suggest that it may have been intended for advanced students in Philo's school or other Jewish exegetes.

Exposition of the Law

The third and final commentary of Philo was a series of treatises that we call the Exposition of the Law. We have twelve[28] of fifteen treatises.[29]

Unlike *The Questions and Answers* and the Allegorical Commentary that were restricted to the first two books of the Pentateuch (at least what has come down to us), the Exposition is Philo's attempt to explain the entire Pentateuch. Philo summarized his plan for the Exposition in three different texts.[30] The last is the fullest and most mature. He opened with a statement that set out his understanding of the different parts of the Pentateuch: "There are three types of oracles (given) through the prophet Moses: the first is the creation of the cosmos, the second is historical, and the third is legislative." In his two other programmatic statements he had envisioned two parts. In this statement he separated creation out as a distinct category and made the ancestors the historical part. The fuller nature of this statement indicates that he wrote it toward the end of his work on the Exposition, after his thinking about the nature of the Pentateuch was fully mature — the treatise is the final treatise in the Exposition. Philo continued by expanding his treatment of the legislative part: "Of the legislative, one part consists of a general subject, the other consists of the com-

27. On Philo's etymologies see David T. Runia, "Etymology as an Allegorical Technique in Philo of Alexandria," *SPhA* 16 (2004): 101-21.

28. Philo, *Moses* 1 and 2; *Creation; Abraham; Joseph; Decalogue; Spec. Laws* 1, 2, 3, 4; *Virtues; Rewards.* The standard critical edition is PCW. The text with an English translation can be found in PLCL.

29. The three lost treatises are *Isaac* (see *Joseph* 1); *Jacob* (see *Joseph* 1); and *Passions* (see *Alleg. Interp.* 3.139).

30. Philo, *Abraham* 2-5; *Moses* 2.45-47; *Rewards* 1-3.

mandments of specific laws." He unpacked the distinction between general subject and specific laws based on the medium through which the laws came: "On the one hand there are the ten heads, which are said to have been delivered not through an interpreter but, formed in the height of the atmosphere, are rational articulation. On the other hand, the particular laws were delivered through the prophet." He has in mind the distinction between the Ten Words set out in *On the Decalogue* and the use of the Ten Commandments as headings for specific laws in *On the Special Laws*. With his understanding of the Exposition set out, he moved to standard secondary preface language: "I have gone through all of these as was opportune in the preceding treatises (ἐν ταῖς προτέραις συντάξεσι), and in addition, the virtues that he allots to peace and war" — a reference to *On the Virtues* — "I now pursue in sequence the rewards set out for the good and the punishments for the evil."[31] The scope of the work thus coincides with the entire Pentateuch: it began with creation in Genesis 1 *(Creation)* and extended to the blessings and curses in Moses' final speech in Deuteronomy *(Rewards)*. The unity of the treatises as a single work is confirmed by the secondary prefaces that open every treatise except *Creation,* for which we would not expect a secondary preface since it is the first treatise.[32]

There is, however, an important exception. The *Life of Moses* 1–2 does not fit into either the plan that Philo outlined or the sequence of treatises linked by secondary prefaces. At the same time, it has a clear relationship with the treatises in the Exposition of the Law. It provides one of the three summaries of the plan for the Exposition.[33] Futher, Philo alluded back to it on two different occasions in the final treatises of the Exposition. The first is in *On the Virtues:* "The things that he did from his early years to old age for the attention and care of each person and for all people have been shown earlier in two treatises that I wrote about the life of Moses (δεδήλωται πρότερον ἐν δυσὶ συντάξεσιν, ἃς ἀνέγραψα περὶ τοῦ βίου Μωυσέως)."[34] Philo again referred to the *Life of Moses* in the next treatise, *On Rewards and Punishments:* "All the virtues are virgins, but the one of the greatest beauty, the leading place — as if in a dance — is piety with which the theologian Moses was especially filled and for which, along with other virtues that are mentioned in the writings about his life (ἐν ταῖς γραφεῖσι περὶ τοῦ κατ' αὐτὸν βίου), he obtained four special roles: king, legislator, prophet, and high priest."[35] The roles are an echo of Philo's outline of Moses' life at the outset of the

31. Philo, *Rewards* 1-3.
32. Philo, *Abraham* 1-6; *Joseph* 1; *Decalogue* 1; *Spec. Laws* 1.1; 2.1; 3.7; 4.1, 132-35 (for *Virtues*); *Rewards* 1-3.
33. Philo, *Moses* 2.45-47.
34. Philo, *Virtues* 52.
35. Philo, *Rewards* 53.

second book.[36] The explicit reference to the work in *On the Virtues* and *On Rewards and Punishments* makes it clear that Philo wrote *The Life of Moses* prior to these works. The fact that the two treatises are part of the Exposition suggests that he may have written *The Life of Moses* at approximately the same time that he wrote the Exposition. How should we explain the apparent independence of the *Life of Moses* and yet its unambiguous ties to the Exposition? Albert Geljon suggested that the work was an introductory philosophical bios, written to introduce the reader to Moses' works in much the same way that Porphyry's *Life of Plotinus* introduced the *Enneads*.[37] This works particularly well if we think of it as an introduction to the Exposition of the Law.

How does the biblical text function within the Exposition? It functions differently in the Exposition than it did in the *Questions and Answers* and the Allegorical Commentary. In those two series, Philo cited the text and commented on it. One of the surprising features of the Exposition is that Philo rarely cited biblical lemmata. For example, in the treatise *On the Creation of the Cosmos* he only cited the biblical text verbatim six times.[38] He occasionally paraphrased the text, but most commonly wove individual words or phrases into his exposition.[39] His standard handling of the text is to summarize the account and to comment on his summary. For example, in *The Life of Abraham*, Philo summarized an event in the ancestor's life within his exposition at the literal level and then offered an allegorical interpretation. The first is the call of Abraham. He summarized it and Abraham's obedience in §§60-67 and then offered an allegorical interpretation in §§68-88. The second story he selected was Abraham's trip to Egypt and Pharaoh's incorporation of Sarah into his harem. Once again, he summarized the story at the literal level (§§89-98) and then offered an allegorical interpretation (§§99-106). This is his standard procedure for the exposition of Abraham and Joseph.

The fact that Philo summarized the biblical narrative led Peder Borgen to call Philo's treatment of the biblical text "rewritten Bible."[40] He argued that the best parallels for Philo's handling of the biblical text in the Exposition of the Law are *Jubilees*, the *Genesis Apocryphon*, Pseudo-Philo's *Library of Biblical An-*

---

36. Philo, *Moses* 2.3.

37. Albert C. Geljon, *Philonic Exegesis in Gregory of Nyssa's De vita Moysis*. BJS 333. SPhM 5 (Providence: Brown Judaic Studies, 2002), 7-46.

38. Gen 1:1 in *Creation* 26; Gen 1:2 in *Creation* 32; Gen 1:26 in *Creation* 72; Gen 2:4-5 in *Creation* 129; Gen 2:6 in *Creation* 131, 133; and Gen 2:7 in *Creation* 134-35, 139.

39. For an analysis, see David T. Runia, *Philo of Alexandria*, On the Creation of the Cosmos according to Moses: *Introduction, Translation and Commentary*. PAC 1 (Leiden: Brill, 2001), 10-17.

40. Borgen, *Philo of Alexandria*, 46-79, esp. 63-79.

tiquities, and Josephus's *Jewish Antiquities*. All of the works summarize the biblical text in the chronological framework provided by the biblical narrative. However, there is a significant difference between Philo's handling of the text and that of his compatriots: he added a layer of commentary at the figurative or allegorical level that they did not. For this reason, I think that it would be preferable to say that Philo appropriated the tradition of rewriting the text in the Exposition but used it as a technique within the commentary tradition. If this is correct, the Exposition is not rewritten Scripture, but a commentary that uses the technique of rewritten Scripture to summarize the text rather than to cite it as Philo had done in the other two commentary series.

The difference in the handling of Scripture hints that the implied audience of the Exposition of the Law is different than the audiences of the *Questions and Answers* and the Allegorical Commentary. In this case, it is likely that Philo was reaching out to a wider audience, probably the entire Jewish community or perhaps any interested reader.

The Extent of Philo's Scriptures

The scope of Philo's commentaries raises an important question: what was the extent of his Scriptures? It would be a mistake to ask about his canon, since this is a later Christian construct. We can, however, ask which books he considered Scripture. Philo's commentaries were on the Pentateuch, and more particularly on Genesis. There is no evidence that he wrote separate commentaries on a prophet or the Psalms as we find at Qumran.[41] His commentaries are restricted to the Pentateuch. But what about his secondary or tertiary citations within the commentaries? Does he draw from works beyond the Pentateuch? The following table on page 425 will answer this question.[42] Even a cursory glance at the table indicates the extent of Philo's concentration on the Pentateuch. He cited or alluded to the Pentateuch 8,215 times. In contrast, he cited or alluded to the remainder of the books that we recognize as Scripture 204 times plus 43 citations or allusions to Deuterocanonical works. This means that he cited or al-

---

41. Isaiah (4QpIsa^a [4Q161]; 4QpIsa^b [4Q162]; 4QpIsa^c [4Q163]; 4QpIsa^d [4Q164]; 4QpIsa^e [4Q165]); Hosea (4QpHos^a [4Q166]; 4QpHos^b [4Q167]); Micah (1QpMic = 1Q14); Nahum (4QpNah [4Q169]); Habbakuk (1QpHab); Zephaniah (1QpZeph [1Q15]; 4QpZeph [4Q170]); Psalms (1QpPs [1Q16]; 4QpPs^a [4Q171]; 4QpPs^b [4Q173]). For an analysis of these, see Maurya P. Horgan, *Pesharim: Qumran Interpretations of Biblical Books*. CBQMS 8 (Washington: Catholic Biblical Association, 1979). There was a commentary on Genesis at Qumran (4Q252).

42. The numbers are based on the references in Jean Allenbach et al., eds., *Biblia patristica*. Supplement: *Philon d'Alexandrie* (Paris: Centre national de la recherche scientifique, 1982).

Citations or Echoes of Scripture in Philo

Biblical Text	Number of Citations or Echoes
Genesis	4,303
Exodus	1,755
Leviticus	737
Numbers	586
Deuteronomy	834
Joshua	4
Judges	4
1 Samuel	24
1 Kings	9
2 Kings	2
Isaiah	24
Jeremiah	18
Ezekiel	7
Hosea	7
Zechariah	2
Psalms	50
Job	8
Proverbs	30
Ecclesiastes	2
Esther	1
1 Chronicles	10
2 Chronicles	2
Wisdom	32
Sirach	11

luded to the Pentateuch over forty times more frequently than other books. If we restrict our analysis to citations, we find that of the 1,161 citations of the biblical text in Philo, only forty-one or 3.5 percent are from outside the Pentateuch.[43] If we reverse the perspective and work from the biblical text back to Philo's treatments rather than from Philo's citations or echoes back to the biblical text, we discover that he cited or referred to 24.5 percent of the verses in the Pentateuch versus 0.5 percent of the verses outside the Pentateuch.[44] No matter

43. Helmut Burkhardt, *Die Inspiration heiliger Schriften bei Philo von Alexandrien* (Giessen: Brunnen, 1988; 2nd ed. 1992), 134.

44. So Beate Zuber, "Die 'Geschichts' — Traditionen der alttestamentlichen 'Königszeit': — z.B. als literarischer Niederschlag einer historischen Auseinandersetzung mit der Herodes-

how we approach the question, there is no doubt that Philo concentrated on the Pentateuch.

How did he view the texts beyond the Pentateuch? It is important to ask about the texts, since Philo called a number of people "sacred" or "divine."[45] The question was not whether a person might understand God, but whether Philo attributed divine status to texts outside the Pentateuch. There are at least four texts that deserve mention. In the defense of the Jewish people that he probably prepared in his role as an ambassador of the Jewish people following the pogrom of 38 C.E.,[46] Philo wrote: "This is the account of the exodus. But when they entered this land, how they were established and possessed the land is indicated in their sacred records (ἐν ταῖς ἱεραῖς ἀναγραφαῖς)."[47] The statement indicates that he considered Joshua to be part of the Jews' "sacred records." Similarly, he says "For this reason the greatest of the kings and prophets, Samuel — as the sacred account says (ὡς ὁ ἱερὸς λόγος φησίν) — 'will not drink wine or strong drink as long as he lives'" (1 Sam 1:11).[48] The introduction makes it clear that Philo considered 1 Samuel sacred. He said something similar of Isaiah. He wrote: "It is not permitted for any worthless person to rejoice, as it is sung in prophetic words: 'It is not for the impious to rejoice, said God'" (Isa 48:22). He explained: "For the saying is in fact a divine oracle that the life of every wretch is gloomy, sad, and full of bad luck, even if he manages to have a smile on his face."[49] It is clear that Philo believed that Isaiah contained divine oracles. Even more intriguing than these introductions to citations is his description of the Therapeutae. He wrote: "In each residence there is a sacred room that is called a consecrated place or dedicated room, in which they alone celebrate the rites of the mysteries of the sacred life." He then explained what they had in these dedicated spaces: "They take in nothing — neither drink, nor food, nor any of the necessities that address the needs of the body — but the

---

Dynastie zu lessen?" in *Landgabe: Festschrift für Jan Heller zum 70. Geburtstag*, ed. Martin Prudký (Prague: Oikúmené and Kampen: Kok Pharos, 1995), 133-72, esp. 145-47.

45. E.g., he called the Pythagoreans "the most sacred band of Pythagoreans" (τὸν τῶν Πυθαγορείων ἱερώτατον θίασον) in *Good Person* 2 and Plato "most sacred" (κατὰ τὸν ἱερώτατον Πλάτωνα) in *Good Person* 13.

46. On the setting of the *Hypothetica*, see Gregory E. Sterling, "Philo and the Logic of Apologetics: An Analysis of the *Hypothetica*," in *The Society of Biblical Studies 1990 Seminar Papers*, ed. David J. Lull. SBLSP 29 (Atlanta: Scholars, 1990), 412-30; and the essays in the special section on the *Hypothetica* in *SPhA* 22 (2010), esp. those by Michael Cover, "Reconceptualizing Conquest: Colonial Narratives and Philo's Roman Accuser in the *Hypothetica*," 183-208; and Dulcinea Boesenberg, "Philo's Descriptions of Jewish Sabbath Practice," 143-64.

47. Philo, *Hypothetica* 8.6.5.

48. Philo, *Drunkenness* 143.

49. Philo, *Names* 169.

laws, the oracles delivered by the prophets, the psalms, and the other works by which knowledge and piety may be increased and perfected."[50] The reference to the laws, oracles, and psalms has suggested to some that Philo knew a threefold division of sacred Jewish texts.[51] However, we should keep two things in mind. First, Philo added a fourth category, "and the other works by which knowledge and piety may be increased and perfected." While he left the contents of this category unspecified, it should make us question whether he thought of a threefold canon. Second, he was describing a specific group. While he projected onto the group some of his own ideas, we should not immediately assume that the Therapeutae represented Philo or Judaism more broadly.[52]

What should we make of this evidence? Philo knew sacred books beyond the Pentateuch.[53] However, we should remember that he only wrote commentaries on the Pentateuch and subordinated other texts into his interpretations of the Pentateuch. Thus while he recognized sacred texts beyond the Pentateuch, the Pentateuch was *de facto* his Scriptures; at least it had a status that no other texts had. Perhaps we could say that he had a "canon within the canon" as long as we recognize that he did not have a "canon."

The Text of Philo's Scriptures

If the extent of Philo's Bible is debatable, the nature of the text that he read is problematic. While there have been a few defenders of his knowledge of Hebrew, the majority of Philonists believe that Philo used only a Greek text.[54] The issue is the nature of his text. Philo would lead us to believe that there was a uniform text in his time. He described the process of the Greek translation of the Hebrew Scriptures on the island of Pharos in these words: "They situated

50. Philo, *Contempl. Life* 25.

51. E.g., Roger Beckwith, *The Old Testament Canon of the New Testament Church and Its Background in Early Judaism* (Grand Rapids: Eerdmans, 1985), 117-18.

52. David M. Hay, "Things Philo Said and Did Not Say about the Therapeutae," in *Society of Biblical Literature 1992 Seminar Papers,* ed. Eugene H. Lovering, Jr. SBLSP 31 (Atlanta: Society of Biblical Literature, 1992), 673-83, provides a helpful perspective on the use of *Contempl. Life.*

53. For a treatment of the Psalms see David T. Runia, "Philo's Reading of the Psalms," *SPhA* 13 (2001): 102-21.

54. Harry Austryn Wolfson, *Philo: Foundations of Religious Philosophy in Judaism, Christianity, and Islam* (Cambridge, Mass.: Harvard University Press, 1947), 1:88-90, argued that Philo knew Hebrew. This has been widely rejected. The strongest evidence consists of the etymologies; however, Lester L. Grabbe has demonstrated that Philo probably had access to onomastic lists that offered the etymologies; *Etymology in Early Jewish Interpretation: The Hebrew Names in Philo.* BJS 115 (Atlanta: Scholars, 1988).

themselves in a removed spot, with nothing present except the elements of nature — earth, water, air, heaven — whose origin they were about to expound
first in the sacred narrative, since the beginning of the laws consists of the account of the creation of the cosmos." In such a locale, "they became inspired, as
if they were possessed by God, and set out not some one thing and others
something else, but all wrote the same nouns and verbs, as if a prompter were
invisibly whispering to each." Philo expressed his surprise at this verbal agreement since Greek is capable of multiple expressions for the same thought. "It is
said that this did not happen with our legislation, but the proper words were
matched with the proper words, the Greek with the Chaldean, since they harmonized especially well with the things that they signified."[55] While this idealic
picture of a uniform text makes for good press, it does not comport with reality.[56] The differences between Philo's citations and the major manuscripts of
the LXX are proof that the situation was much more complex.

There have been several explanations of the variations between Philo's text
and the manuscripts of the LXX. First, most scholars who worked on Philo at
the outset of the critical study of his corpus believed that he used the LXX.
Thomas Mangey, who compiled the first critical edition of Philo, wrote: "*Philo
ubique sequitur LXX.*"[57] Variations were relatively minor and were part of the
natural process of copying.[58] Second, an anonymous reviewer of Mangey's edition offered an alternative explanation. The reviewer suggested that Philo followed a different text than the LXX or that someone redacted his biblical text in
light of Aquila's verison.[59] This suggestion won significant support in the debates that surrounded the preparations for the *editio major* of Philo's works. A
number of scholars argued that Philo's variants were closer to the Hebrew and
constituted the oldest known form of the Greek Bible.[60] Third, the editors of

55. Philo, *Moses* 2.37-38.

56. For a concise summary of the modern debate over the origins and the revisions of the
LXX, see Emanuel Tov, "The Septuagint," in *Mikra: Text, Translation, Reading and Interpretation
of the Hebrew Bible in Ancient Judaism and Early Christianity,* ed. Martin Jan Mulder. CRINT 2.1
(Assen: Van Gorcum and Philadelphia: Fortress, 1988), 161-88.

57. Thomas Mangey, cited by Peter Katz, *Philo's Bible: The Aberrant Text of Bible Quotations
in Some Philonic Writings and Its Place in the Textual History of the Greek Bible* (Cambridge:
Cambridge University Press, 1950), 128.

58. Carl Siegfried, "Philo und der überlieferte Text der LXX," *ZWT* 16 (1873): 217-38, 411-28,
522-40; and Henry Barclay Swete, *An Introduction to the Old Testament in Greek.* 2nd ed., rev.
Richard Rusden Ottley (Cambridge: Cambridge University Press, 1914; repr. New York: Ktav,
1968), 372-76.

59. *Bibliothèque Raisonnée des Ouvrages des Savans de l'Europe* 32 (1744): 299-309. The review is summarized by Katz, *Philo's Bible,* 127-29.

60. The most important representatives are Eberhard Nestle, "Zur Rekonstruktion der

Philo's works, Paul Wendland and Leopold Cohn, differed. They thought that Philo's text had been corrected by later hands that moved the text closer to a literal translation of the Hebrew, a view that was championed by Peter Katz, later known as Peter Walters.[61] Fourth, in recent years, James Royse has pointed out a number of places where the variations appear to be deliberate choices made by Philo, although he has not developed a full theory for the text.[62]

The issue is complex and involves a number of factors. The four major complications are these. First, in some cases the manuscript tradition for the biblical text in Philo is split among the families of manuscripts. So, for example, MSS UFL have a pronounced tendency to offer more literal readings than MAP that offer a more literary reading. We thus have to compare more than one set of readings to the manuscripts of the LXX in an effort to reconstruct Philo's own biblical text. Second, we also need to take into consideration the fact that Philo often repeated the language of the biblical text, but not the exact wording — or at least the wording does not agree in the manuscripts. In the Allegorical Commentary he cited the full biblical text at the outset of his exposition and then repeated each phrase as he worked through the text. We have to take both sets of readings into account. Third, we can not assume that the same scribes preserved all of Philo's treatises. We have to work treatise by treatise. Fourth, as we have seen, Philo cited the biblical text in two different commentary series: the *Questions and Answers on Genesis and Exodus* and the Allegorical Commentary. Since the *Questions and Answers on Genesis and Exodus* are primarily preserved in Armenian and the treatises in the Allegorical Commentary in Greek,

---

Septuaginta," *Phil* 58 (1899): 121-31; "Zur neuen Philo-Aufgabe," *Phil* 59 (1900): 256-71; and "Zur neuen Philo-Aufgabe: Eine Replik," *Phil* 60 (1901): 271-76; August Schröder, "De Philonis Alexandrini Vetere Testamento" (Diss., Gryphiae, 1907); Paul Kahle, "Untersuchungen zur Geschichte des Pentateuchtextes," *TSK* 88 (1915): 399-439, esp. 420-23; and *The Cairo Geniza*, 2nd ed. (Oxford: Blackwell,), 247-49. George E. Howard, "The 'Aberrant' Text of Philo's Quotations Reconsidered," *HUCA* 44 (1973): 197-209, argued that some of the aberrant readings belonged to Philo's text.

61. Paul Wendland, "Zu Philo's Schrift *de posteritate Caini* (Nebst Bemerkungen zur Rekonstruktion der Septuaginta)," *Phil* 57 (1898): 248-88, esp. 284-87; Leopold Cohn and Paul Wendland, "Zur neuen Philo-Ausgabe: Eine Erwiederung," *Phil* 59 (1900): 521-36, esp. 525, and 532-36; Peter Katz, "Das Problem des Urtextes der Septuaginta," *TZ* 5 (1949): 1-24; *Philo's Bible;* and "Septuagintal Studies in the Mid-Century: Their Links with the Past and Their Present Tendencies," in *The Background of the New Testament and Its Eschatology in Honor of Charles Harold Dodd*, ed. W. D. Davies and David Daube (Cambridge: Cambridge University Press, 1956), 205-8.

62. James R. Royse, "Some Observations on the Biblical Text in Philo's *De Agricultura*," *SPhA* 22 (2010): 111-29. See also "The Text of Philo's *Legum Allegoriae*," *SPhA* 12 (2000): 1-28; "The Text of Philo's *De virtutibus*," *SPhA* 18 (2006): 73-101; and "The Text of Philo's *De Abrahamo*," *SPhA* 20 (2008): 151-65.

it is difficult to make precise comparisons without Greek fragments for the *Questions and Answers.*

With these caveats in mind, we turn to some examples to illustrate the nature of the material. The first are the series of statements about "eating" from Gen 3:14-19.

Gen 3:14
MT: ועפר תאכל
LXX: καὶ γῆν φάγῃ
Philo: καὶ γῆν φάγεσαι

Gen 3:18
MT: ואכלת את עשׂב השׂדה
LXX: καὶ φάγῃ τὸν χόρτον τοῦ ἀγροῦ
Philo: καὶ φάγεσαι τὸν χόρτον τοῦ ἀγροῦ

Gen 3:19
MT: תאכל לחם
LXX: φάγῃ τὸν ἄρτον σου
Philo: φάγεσαι τὸν ἄρτον σου

We should also consider Gen 2:16.[63]

Gen 2:16
MT: מכל עץ הגן אכל תאכל
LXX: ἀπὸ παντὸς ξύλου τοῦ ἐν τῷ παραδείσῳ βρώσει φάγῃ
Philo (MAP): ἀπὸ παντὸς ξύλου τοῦ ἐν τῷ παραδείσῳ βρώσει φάγῃ
Philo (UFL): ἀπὸ παντὸς ξύλου τοῦ ἐν τῷ παραδείσῳ φάγεσαι

There is a clear pattern among the Greek translations. The LXX used the aorist subjunctive (φάγῃ), while the MSS of Philo used the future indicative (φάγεσαι): UFL in 2:16 and the MSS of *Alleg. interp.* 3 in Gen 3:14, 18, 19. We might question whether the future indicative rather than the aorist subjunctive is the reading in Philo, except that it also appears in the exposition of Gen 3:14 at a significant remove from the citation of the lemma. The exception to this is the MAP family of MSS that reads the aorist subjunctive in Gen 2:16. The Philonic MSS that read the future indicative are the only Greek MSS that have this reading, with the exception of a single minuscule for the LXX of Gen

---

63. The Philonic MSS also differ in 2:17, where MAP use the plural οὐ φάγεσθε ἀπ' αὐτοῦ and φάγητε, while UFL use the singular οὐ φάγεσαι and φάγῃ. Philo is insistent on the plural in his exposition (*Alleg. interp.* 1.101), which makes the text certain.

3:18.[64] The future indicative is closer to the Hebrew imperfect than the aorist subjunctive.[65] These considerations led Katz to argue that φάγεσαι was one of the marks of a later effort to bring Philo's MSS more into line with a literal rendering of the text.[66]

A second example is perhaps even clearer.

Gen 15:18

MT: ביום ההוא כרת יהוה את אברם ברית

LXX: ἐν τῇ ἡμέρᾳ ἐκείνῃ διέθετο κύριος τῷ Ἀβρὰμ διαθήκην

Philo (Papyrus): ἐν τῇ ἡμέρᾳ ἐκείνῃ διέθετο κύριος τῷ Ἀβρὰμ (διαθή)κην

Philo (Codices): ἐν τῇ ἡμέρᾳ ἐκείνῃ συνέθετο κύριος τῷ Ἀβρὰμ συνθήκην

The LXX and papyrus use the cognates διέθετο and διαθήκην to refer to the covenant that God made with Abram. The codices use the cognates συνέθετο and συνθήκην. The last noun only translates ברית one time in the LXX;[67] the standard and normative translation is διαθήκη. On the other hand, συνθήκη was the standard word for covenant in Greek. Most importantly, it was favored by Symmachus and Aquila.[68] This suggests that the codices have altered the earlier LXX usage to bring it more into line with standard Greek usage.

While two examples are hardly sufficient to illustrate all of the issues involved in this question, these indicate a pattern that supports the view of Katz. It does appear that in some cases — each treatise should be studied independently — scribes altered the readings of Philo's text to bring them more into line with a literal translation of the Pentateuch. This means that the version of the Greek Bible that Philo knew was probably more polished than the version in some of the manuscripts, although we must always remember that Philo may have modified the text himself.

---

64. 129 has φάγεσαι in Gen 3:18.

65. Genesis 3:18 has the perfect, but it is converted with a waw consecutive that continues the imperfect in the preceding clause (תצמיח).

66. Katz, *Philo's Bible*, 14-15, 82-83. He argued that it was a borrowing from Aquila.

67. 4 Kgdms 17:15.

68. John William Wevers, *Notes on the Greek Text of Genesis*. SBLSCS 35 (Atlanta: Scholars, 1993), 86.

Conclusions

In his preface to *On the Creation of the Cosmos* Philo wrote: "No one — whether poet or prose author — is capable of adequately celebrating the beauty of the ideas in the account of the creation of the cosmos." This is an unusual introduction. It was a commonplace for ancient authors in the Greek world to claim that they were in a special position that enabled them to write their account. Philo denied this in the case of his *Hexameron*. He explained, "For they transcend speech and hearing since they are greater and more august than can be adapted to the sense-perceptible organs of any mortal." In spite of the transcendent nature of the ideas, he will make the attempt: "We will not however keep silent, but for the sake of the God-beloved author we will dare to speak beyond our capacity."[69] While Philo's hyperbole was calculated, the spirit behind his statement was genuine. He devoted his life to interpreting Moses. The result is one of the largest corpuses that has come down to us from the Greek world: only Aristotle and Plutarch have larger corpuses. It was a monumental effort. While Philo recognized that other thinkers could be inspired and other Jewish texts were sacred, Moses was his "God loved" author who wrote the definitive statement about God. Every other author was measured by Moses, even the authors of sacred texts within Judaism. For this reason, Philo wrote his three series of commentaries on the Pentateuch.

Within the Pentateuch he had a special affinity for Genesis: half of the treatises in the *Questions and Answers* are devoted to Genesis, all of the treatises in the Allegorical Commentary are dedicated to Genesis, and four of the fifteen treatises or 27 percent in the Exposition of the Law address texts in Genesis. This means that forty-two of the fifty-nine treatises or 81 percent of the treatises in the three-commentary series are dedicated to Genesis. The concentration on Genesis is also evident if we consider Philo's citations and echoes of Scripture. Of the 8,462 citations and echoes of Scripture in Philo, 4,303 or 51 percent are from Genesis. However we measure his writings, Genesis was the book to which he devoted more attention than any other.

Why? One of the major factors is probably that the ancestors naturally lent themselves to Philo's allegory of the soul. In the first Life that we have from Philo, he set out his understanding of the Pentateuch. He thought that it had two components. The first was creation: "We have described accurately — as best as possible — the manner in which the cosmos was set in order in the preceding treatise (διὰ τῆς προτέρας συντάξεως)" — a clear allusion to *On the Creation of the Cosmos*. The second component was the law: "But since it is neces-

---

69. Philo, *Creation* 4.

sary to examine the laws in proper sequence, we will postpone the individual laws as copies and examine the general laws as archetypes first." He explained what he meant by the general laws or archetypes: "These are men who lived blamelessly and well, whose virtues are inscribed in the holy Scriptures — not for their praise alone, but to urge the reader to pursue the same zeal." He then unpacked their relationship to the written law: "These men were embodied and rational laws whom he praised for two reasons. First, he wanted to show that the legislated ordinances are not out of harmony with nature" — a point that Philo will make in other connections as well; "second, that it does not require an enormous effort for those who want to live by the stipulated laws, since the ancestors made use of unwritten legislation with perfect ease before any of the individual laws were recorded." He concluded: "Someone could say that the enacted laws are nothing but memorials of the lives of the ancients setting out from antiquity the deeds and words they used."[70] The exemplary lives of the ancestors made them ideal for Philo's work: he wrote to demonstrate how humans can cultivate lives of virtue in their ascent to God.[71] This is probably the major reason why he concentrated on Genesis.

While Philo concentrated on Genesis, his scope of work was broader. Eusebius recognized the complexity of Philo's enterprise when he provided a catalogue of the works of Philo in the episcopal library of Caesarea. Eusebius summarized the Philonic enterprise in these words: "Philo was prolific in expression and broad in thought: he was lofty and elevated in his perspectives on the divine writings and wrote his exposition of the sacred works in varied and diverse ways."[72] The bishop was right.

BIBLIOGRAPHY

Allenbach, Jean, et al., eds. *Biblia patristica.* Supplement: *Philon d'Alexandrie.* Paris: Centre national de la recherche scientifique, 1982.

Borgen, Peder. *Philo of Alexandria: An Exegete for His Time.* NovTSup 86. Leiden: Brill, 1997; repr. Atlanta: SBL, 2005.

Brewer, Daniel I. *Techniques and Assumptions in Jewish Exegesis before 70 C.E.* TSAJ 30. Tübingen: Mohr Siebeck, 1992.

Cohn, Leopold, and Paul Wendland. "Zur neuen Philo-Ausgabe: Eine Erwiederung." *Phil* 59 (1900): 521-36.

Grabbe, Lester L. *Etymology in Early Jewish Interpretation: The Hebrew Names in Philo.* BJS 115. Atlanta: Scholars, 1988.

70. Philo, *Abraham* 2-5.
71. See the helpful analysis of Kamesar, "Biblical Interpretation in Philo," 85-91.
72. Eusebius, *Hist. eccl.* 2.18.1.

Howard, George E. "The 'Aberrant' Text of Philo's Quotations Reconsidered." *HUCA* 44 (1973): 197-209.

Kamesar, Adam. "Biblical Interpretation in Philo." In *The Cambridge Companion to Philo,* 65-91.

———, ed. *The Cambridge Companion to Philo.* Cambridge: Cambridge University Press, 2009.

Katz, Peter. *Philo's Bible: The Aberrant Text of Bible Quotations in Some Philonic Writings and Its Place in the Textual History of the Greek Bible.* Cambridge: Cambridge University Press, 1950.

———. "Septuagintal Studies in the Mid-Century: Their Links with the Past and Their Present Tendencies." In *The Background of the New Testament and Its Eschatology in Honor of Charles Harold Dodd,* ed. W. D. Davies and David Daube. Cambridge: Cambridge University Press, 1956, 176-208.

Morris, Jenny. "The Jewish Philosopher Philo." In Emil Schürer, *The History of the Jewish People in the Age of Jesus Christ,* rev. Geza Vemes, Fergus Millar, and Martin Goodman. Edinburgh: T. & T. Clark, 1987, 3.2: 819-70.

Nestle, Eberhard. "Zur Rekonstruktion der Septuaginta." *Phil* 58 (1899): 121-31.

———. "Zur neuen Philo-Aufgabe." *Phil* 59 (1900): 256-71.

———. "Zur neuen Philo-Aufgabe: Eine Replik." *Phil* 60 (1901): 271-76.

Niehoff, Maren R. *Jewish Exegesis and Homeric Scholarship in Alexandria.* Cambridge: Cambridge University Press, 2011.

Nikiprowetzky, Valentin. *Le commentaire de l'Écriture chez Philon d'Alexandrie.* ALGHJ 11. Leiden: Brill, 1977.

Petit, Françoise. *Quaestiones in Genesim et in Exodum: Fragmenta graeca.* Les Œuvres de Philon d'Alexandrie 33. Paris: Cerf, 1978.

Royse, James R. "The Works of Philo." In Kamesar, *The Cambridge Companion to Philo,* 32-64.

———. "Some Observations on the Biblical Text in Philo's *De agricultura*." *SPhA* 22 (2010): 111-29.

Runia, David T. "Secondary Texts in Philo's *Quaestiones*." In *Both Literal and Allegorical: Studies in Philo of Alexandria's* Questions and Answers on Genesis and Exodus, ed. David M. Hay. BJS 232. Atlanta: Scholars, 1991, 47-79.

———. *Philo in Early Christian Literature: A Survey.* CRINT 3.3. Assen: Van Gorcum and Minneapolis: Fortress, 1993.

———. *Philo of Alexandria,* On the Creation of the Cosmos according to Moses: *Introduction, Translation and Commentary.* PAC 1. Leiden: Brill, 2001.

———. "Philo's Reading of the Psalms." *SPhA* 13 (2001): 102-21.

———. "Etymology as an Allegorical Technique in Philo of Alexandria." *SPhA* 16 (2004): 101-21.

———. "The Structure of Philo's Allegorical Treatise *De agricultura*." *SPhA* 22 (2010): 87-109.

Siegert, Folker. "Early Jewish Interpretation in a Hellenistic Style." In *Hebrew Bible/Old Testament: The History of Its Interpretation.* Vol. 1: *From the Beginnings to the Middle Ages (Until 1300).* Part 1: *Antiquity,* ed. Magne Sæbø. Göttingen: Vandenhoeck & Ruprecht, 1996, 162-88.

Siegfried, Carl. "Philo und der überlieferte Text der LXX." *ZWT* 16 (1873): 217-38, 411-28, 522-40.

Sterling, Gregory E. "'The School of Sacred Laws': The Social Setting of Philo's Treatises." *VC* 53 (1999): 148-64.

Tobin, Thomas H. "The Beginning of Philo's *Legum Allegoriae*." *SPhA* 12 (2000): 29-43.

Wendland, Paul. "Zu Philo's Schrift *de posteritate Caini* (Nebst Bemerkungen zur Rekonstruktion der Septuaginta)." *Phil* 57 (1898): 248-88.

Wolfson, Harry Austryn. *Philo: Foundations of Religious Philosophy in Judaism, Christianity, and Islam*. 2 vols. Cambridge, Mass.: Harvard University Press, 1947.

Josephus's Biblical Interpretation

Zuleika Rodgers

One of the most prolific contemporary commentators on Josephus, Louis H. Feldman, notes that, "Second only perhaps to his significance as a historian is Josephus's importance for our knowledge of the text and interpretation of the Bible in the first century."[1] This is certainly reflected in the great amount of attention given to the examination of Josephus's biblical interpretation, with focused studies on sources — both biblical and nonbiblical — traditions, and techniques. In particular, his twenty-volume *Jewish Antiquities*, over half of which includes a type of biblical paraphrase, has been an invaluable source for the study of Scripture and its interpretation in early Judaism. The extensive bibliography devoted to the examination of Josephus's biblical interpretation testifies to the huge scholarly interest. Many of these studies, however, share a methodological assumption that has been challenged in recent decades. The traditional, or "classical," conception of Josephus considered him a compiler — and not always a careful one — of traditions and sources, and once Josephus's bias and agenda were revealed, this could be peeled away to reveal his sources (e.g., biblical text), or a true version of events (e.g., the revolt of 66-70 c.e.).[2]

---

1. Louis H. Feldman, "Use, Authority and Exegesis of Mikra in the Writings of Josephus," in *Mikra: Text, Translation, Reading and Interpretation of the Hebrew Bible in Ancient Judaism and Early Christianity,* ed. Martin Jan Mulder. CRINT 2.1 (Assen: Van Gorcum and Minneapolis: Fortress, 1988), 455-518 (here 455).

2. Per Bilde, *Flavius Josephus between Jerusalem and Rome: His Life, His Works and Their Importance.* JSPSup 2 (Sheffield: JSOT, 1988), 123-71, has produced a survey of trends in Josephan scholarship in which he categorizes the different methodological approaches as "classical" and "modern" conceptions of Josephus. A more recent review of scholarship appears in Steve Mason, "Introduction to the *Judean Antiquities,*" in *Flavius Josephus: Translation and Commentary,* Vol. 3: *Judean Antiquities 1–4* (Leiden: Brill, 2004), xiii-xxxv; and "Contradiction or Counterpoint? Josephus and Historical Method," *RRJ* 6 (2003): 186. For a wide range of es-

Attempts to understand Josephus as an author in control of both his sources and the historian's craft have characterzied modern Josephan studies, as has the focus on Josephus's immediate historical setting in Flavian Rome.[3] Furthermore, in light of this greater appreciation of the literary and historical contexts of his work, the question of Josephus's agenda in these works has also been reassessed. This has produced some startling rethinking about the author in relation to his social and political milieu. The reconception of Josephus's work and method will be the main consideration for our examination of Josephus's biblical interpretation, in full cognizance of the fact that there have been extraordinary contributions in the numerous studies of various aspects of Josephus's sources and interpretations.[4]

It is on the *Jewish Antiquities* that we mainly rely as our primary source for the interpretation of Scripture, and this biblical paraphrase is examined in terms of the text and its context, both literary — within the larger narrative — and historical. The *Jewish War* does not include substantial references to the Bible, but scholars have made assumptions regarding Josephus's knowledge of Scripture and traditions based on the text, and we offer an overview of the contributions of this scholarship to the wider debate. *Against Apion* is central to understanding Josephus's interpretative context, and we shall focus on what this work can reveal about Josephus's text and the process of its elucidation.

Jewish Antiquities: Text and Context

Text: Scope and Structure

The main source of Josephus's biblical interpretation is found in the first eleven books of his twenty-volume *Jewish Antiquities*. Here we find a loose, but extensive paraphrase of the story of the Hebrews from creation through the destruction of the first temple in Jerusalem (*Ant.* 10) to the restoration under Cyrus (*Ant.* 11).

---

says on the question of historical method, see Zuleika Rodgers, ed., *Making History: Josephus and Historical Method.* JSJSup 110 (Leiden: Brill, 2007).

3. For recent explorations, see Jonathan Edmondson, Steve Mason, and James Rives, eds., *Flavius Josephus and Flavian Rome* (Oxford: Oxford University Press, 2005); Joseph Sievers and Gaia Lembi, eds., *Josephus and Jewish History in Flavian Rome and Beyond.* JSJSup 104 (Leiden: Brill, 2005); Steve Mason, *Flavius Josephus: Translation and Commentary,* Vol. 9: *Life of Josephus* (Leiden: Brill, 2000), xix-xxi, xxxiv-l; and "Flavius Josephus in Flavian Rome: Reading on and Between the Lines," in *Flavian Rome,* ed. Anthony J. Boyle and William J. Dominik (Leiden: Brill, 2003), 559-89.

4. These studies are referenced in the relevant discussions.

The second part of the narrative focuses on the period of the Second Temple, Hasmonean rule (12–13), the Herodians (14–17), and Roman rule (18–20).

Content of Jewish Antiquities with Corresponding Biblical Sources for Ant. 1–11

- *Ant.* 1.26-346: Creation to the deaths of Isaac and Rebecca
    Genesis 1–35
- *Ant.* 2: From Jacob and Esau to the Exodus
    Genesis 36–48; Exodus 1–15
- *Ant.* 3: The Hebrews wandering in the desert and the giving of the Law at Sinai
    Exodus 16–40 with laws from Exodus, Leviticus, and Numbers
- *Ant.* 4: The forty-year period in the desert, from the rebellion against Moses to his death
    Numbers 14–36; Deuteronomy with material from Exodus, Leviticus, and Numbers
- *Ant.* 5: Conquest of Canaan under Joshua
    Joshua; Judges; Ruth; 1 Samuel 1–4
- *Ant.* 6: Clashes with the Philistines under the leadership of Samuel and Saul
    1 Samuel 5–31
- *Ant.* 7: Reign of David
    2 Samuel 1–24 and 1 Kings 1–2 combined with material from 1 Chronicles 1–29 and 2 Chronicles 2
- *Ant.* 8: Reign of Solomon and the division of the kingdoms
    1 Kings 2–22 with material from 2 Chronicles 1–18
- *Ant.* 9: From the death of Ahab to the fall of the northern kingdom
    2 Chronicles 19–31 with material from 1 Kings 22, 2 Kings 1–17, Jonah, Zechariah, and Nahum
- *Ant.* 10: Fall of the first temple
    2 Kings 18–24; 2 Chronicles 32–36; Isaiah 38–39; Ezekiel 12; Jeremiah 22–52; Daniel 1–8
- *Ant.* 11: From Cyrus to Alexander the Great
    1 Esdras; Nehemiah; Isaiah 44; Haggai and Zechariah; Esther
- *Ant.* 12: The death of Alexander the Great to the death of Judas Maccabaeus
- *Ant.* 13: John Hyrcanus to the death of Alexandra Salome
- *Ant.* 14: Roman rule and the rise of Herod the Great
- *Ant.* 15: Herod's conquest of Jerusalem and his building projects

- *Ant.* 16: Dedication of Herodian temple through Herod's relationship with Rome and his family
- *Ant.* 17: Herod's later years and the rule of Archelaus
- *Ant.* 18: Roman rule in Judea to death of Gaius
- *Ant.* 19: Claudius and Agrippa I; Jews in Alexandria
- *Ant.* 20: Death of Agrippa I, outbreak of rebellion in 66 C.E.

Scholars have attempted to illustrate the structural relationship between the two parts of *Jewish Antiquities:* the most obvious structural feature is the centerpoint created by the story of the destruction of the first temple in *Ant.* 10, where we also find a prediction (*Ant.* 10.79, 276) for its future destruction anticipating the account of the outbreak of the revolt in *Ant.* 20. Accordingly, *Ant.* 1–10 focuses on the First Temple period, and *Ant.* 11–20 charts the Second Temple period.[5] *Ant.* 10 is pivotal in that it describes the destruction of the first temple and predicts that of the second, and it points to and parallels *Ant.* 20. While this may provide a loose framework for the narrative, there have been numerous attempts to refine this further on both chronological and thematic grounds. Harold Attridge suggested that the second part of *Antiquities* be divided into three sections, which relate to later periods of Jewish history, but with the last section lacking a particular focus: *Ant.* 11–13; 14–17; and 18–20.[6] Per Bilde reworks this proposal, suggesting that the first half be divided between *Ant.* 1–5 and 6–10, corresponding first with Israel's existence outside the land and dominated by Moses' leadership, and second with their life in the land under the rule of the kings.[7] He concurs that *Ant.* 11–20 falls into three sections, and suggests that these are based on three phases of the second temple, from restoration to destruction. Furthermore, he sees a thematic link between *Ant.* 1–10 and 11–20, where the narrative cycle of Herod's reign in *Ant.* 14–17 is paralleled in the descriptions of other key figures (i.e., Abraham, Joseph, Moses, Samson, David, Esther, and Agrippa II). Steve Mason, in line with his compositional approach, has proposed that *Antiquities* is organized concentrically, with *Ant.* 10 acting as the fulcrum of the narrative, with the two halves of the work linked by consistent thematic concerns, and in particular, Josephus's interest in the issue of governance.[8]

---

5. This was noted early on by Henry St. John Thackeray, *Josephus, The Man and the Historian* (1928; repr. New York: Ktav, 1968).

6. Harold W. Attridge, "Josephus and His Works," in *Jewish Writings of the Second Temple Period: Apocrypha, Pseudepigrapha, Qumran Sectarian Writings, Philo, Josephus,* ed. Michael E. Stone. CRINT 2.2 (Assen: Van Gorcum and Philadelphia: Fortress, 1984), 213.

7. Bilde, *Flavius Josephus between Jerusalem and Rome,* 89-92.

8. Mason, "Introduction to the *Judean Antiquities*," xx-xxii.

Text: Sources

Biblical and Nonbiblical Text(s) As later discussions will indicate, Josephus thoroughly reworked his sources. While scholars refer to his *editorial* activity with regard to the biblical material, we must be clear that the debates concerning his reliance on a *Vorlage* or dependence on an interpretative tradition should not obscure his own contribution. This becomes clear when one turns to scholarship on the question of Josephus's biblical sources. The issue is beset by methodological difficulties about the nature of the source texts and how and for which volumes of the *Jewish Antiquities* Josephus used those sources.

A tentative consensus has emerged suggesting that he did not rely solely on one particular text but had at hand a Hebrew text, a Greek text, and possibly an Aramaic targum.[9] Book by book analysis certainly highlights the parallels, but the evidence very much points to the fact that Josephus freely adapted whatever sources were available to him.[10] Feldman offers an important insight when he notes that "it is hard, however, to prove at any given point what text Josephus is relying upon, inasmuch as he is usually paraphrasing rather than translating and since he is elaborating as well."[11] We shall offer some general remarks on the main issues, but for a detailed study of these issues the Brill Josephus project provides scholars with a word-for-word commentary, and it is here that updated detailed exposition and analysis can be found.[12]

9. A full discussion of the history of scholarship on this issue can be found in Harold W. Attridge, *The Interpretation of Biblical History in the* Antiquitates Judaicae *of Flavius Josephus*. HDR 7 (Missoula: Scholars, 1976); Feldman, "Use, Authority and Exegesis," 455-66. Classic works on the subject include: Heinrich Bloch, *Die Quellen des Flavius Josephus in seiner Archäologie* (Leipzig: Teubner, 1879; repr. Wiesbaden: Sändig, 1968); Justus von Destinon, *Die Quellen des Flavius Josephus*, vol. 1: *Die Quellen der Archäologie Buch XII–XVII = Jüd. Krieg Buch I.* (Kiel: Lipsius & Tischer, 1882); Gustav Hölscher, "Josephus" in PW 18 (1916): 1934-2000; Marcus Olitzki, *Flavius Josephus und die Halacha* (Berlin: Itzkowski, 1885); Salomo Rappaport, *Agada und Exegese bei Flavius Josephus* (Vienna: Alexander Kohut Memorial Foundation, 1930); Thackeray, *Josephus*, 75-99.

10. For an example of an analysis that recognizes Josephus's rewriting technique, see Thomas W. Franxman, *Genesis and the Jewish Antiquities of Flavius Josephus*. BibOr 35 (Rome: Biblical Institute Press, 1979).

11. Feldman, "Use, Authority and Exegesis," 457.

12. Of the *Jewish Antiquities*, volumes 1-10 have been published as *Flavius Josephus: Translation and Commentary*, ed. Steve Mason (Leiden: Brill, 2000-2007): Louis H. Feldman, Vol. 3: *Judean Antiquities Books 1–4* (2004); Christopher T. Begg and Paul Spilsbury, Vol. 5: *Judean Antiquities Books 8–10* (2005). These are also available online: http://pace.mcmaster.ca. For other close analyses of possible sources, see Christopher T. Begg, *Josephus' Account of the Early Divided Monarchy (AJ 8,212-420): Rewriting the Bible*. BETL 108 (Leuven: Leuven University Press, 1993);

There have been numerous analyses examining the particular form of the biblical text used for each book of the Bible. The main problem facing scholars is the uncertainty with regard to which forms of these texts were available to Josephus: where a case could be made for use of a Hebrew text, it would seem to diverge from the Masoretic Text, and where it is possible that a Greek text lies behind his paraphrase, scholars can see evidence of different LXX versions (B and L).[13]

Arguments in support of an underlying Hebrew text for Josephus's biblical paraphrase particularly focus on the Pentateuch.[14] Apart from the question of the form of that Hebrew text and its similarity with its Greek translation, there are some significant correlations with the LXX, and also Josephus tends to use the Greek forms of names.[15] Names and numbers, however, are too susceptible to editorial redaction both by the original author and in the manuscript tradition to constitute reliable evidence.[16] For Joshua, Judges, and Ruth, scholars have also suggested a Semitic source, and in particular it is here where they discern the use of an Aramaic targum. Those in support of a targumic source have identified particular parallels, especially in the cases of names and etymologies.[17] Scholars further suggest that the extensive elaborations and explanations of the targumic tradition would not only have appealed to Josephus by providing him with much of his material for *Ant.* 1–5, but a lost Aramaic translation may also have provided him with his narrative additions.[18] The case for his reli-

---

and *Josephus' Story of the Later Monarchy (AJ 9,1-10,185)*. BETL 145 (Leuven: Leuven University Press, 2000).

13. See esp. for 1 and 2 Samuel.

14. See Feldman, "Use, Authority and Exegesis," 456-57.

15. An examination of Josephus's rendering of biblical names in Genesis is found in Robert J. H. Shutt, *Studies in Josephus* (London: SPCK, 1961), 167-82. Étienne Nodet, *Le Pentateuque de Flavius Josèph* (Paris: Cerf, 1996), 27-29, has attempted to reconstruct the Hebrew text used by Josephus.

16. See Shaye J. D. Cohen, *Josephus in Galilee and Rome: His Vita and Development as a Historian* (Leiden: Brill, 1979), 33-36, n. 45, 38, on the unreliability of names and numbers.

17. For a list of relevant passages in *Antiquities* (including the Pentateuchal material) see Thackeray, *Josephus*, 81-82; Rappaport, *Agada und Exegese bei Flavius Josephus*, xxi-xxiv; Schalit, "Introduction," in *Namenwörterbuch zu Flavius Josephus* (Leiden: Brill, 1968), xxxi-xxxii; among the targumim, written in Josephus's mother-tongue, Feldman suggests that we find the closest counterpart for Josephus's paraphrase, and yet there remain significant divergences; "Use, Authority and Exegesis," 459-60.

18. Naomi G. Cohen, "Josephus and Scripture: Is Josephus's Treatment of the Scriptural Narrative Similar Throughout the *Antiquities* I–XI?" *JQR* 54 (1963-64): 311-32, distinguishes a looser, but more stylized, approach to source material in *Ant.* 1–5; see Feldman, "Use, Authority and Exegesis," for a summary of these views.

ance on written Aramaic sources remains inconclusive, and similarities may simply be due to the fact that Josephus was an Aramaic speaker.[19]

In the prologue to the *Jewish Antiquities,* Josephus cites the LXX as a forerunner to his own translation (*Ant.* 1.10-20), but while some scholars have concluded that his main source was a Greek translation, it is also clear that Josephus deviates from the LXX linguistically and stylistically. Improvement on the Greek style of the LXX or the avoidance of semitisms has been suggested as possible motivation for these changes, especially since he follows more closely the literary language of the Greek additions to 1 Esdras and Esther.[20] For Esdras, scholars have discerned a knowledge of the MT textual tradition, or something close to it, and again we find inconsistencies with numbers and names. Close examination of Josephus's rendering of 1 and 2 Samuel has given rise to a case for his using a Greek text that is closer to the proto-Lucianic version for 1 and 2 Samuel.[21]

For *Ant.* 12.241–13.214, there is consensus that while Josephus makes significant modifications to the story of the Maccabees and polishes the language, it is the Greek version that underlies his text.[22] Jeremiah and Daniel are important figures in the narratives of both the *Jewish War* and *Jewish Antiquities,* and they receive significant treatment by Josephus, yet it is unclear which text(s) he

19. Attridge, *The Interpretation of Biblical History,* 31-32; Cohen, *Josephus in Galilee and Rome,* 35-36, n. 45; and Feldman, "Use, Authority and Exegesis," 458-60.

20. Cohen, *Josephus in Galilee and Rome,* 42-43, on Josephus's text for and modification of 1 Esdras.

21. Eugene C. Ulrich, *The Qumran Text of Samuel and Josephus.* HSM 19 (Missoula: Scholars, 1978).

22. Detailed examinations of Josephus's use of 1 Maccabees with a focus on stylistic and linguistic features can be found in Bloch, *Die Quellen des Flavius Josephus,* 80-90, while a more recent study by Isaiah M. Gafni ("Josephus and I Maccabees," in *Josephus, the Bible and History,* ed. Louis H. Feldman and Gohei Hata [Leiden: Brill, 1989], 116-31) summarizes the main issues in the debate and assesses Josephus's reworking of the text; he concludes that the alterations are not adopted from an intermediary source. Cohen, *Josephus in Galilee and Rome,* 44-47, summarizes the significant changes made by Josephus.

23. The importance of both Jeremiah and Daniel for Josephus has been explored by Christopher T. Begg, "Daniel and Josephus: Tracing Connections," in *The Book of Daniel in Light of New Findings,* ed. A. S. van der Woude. BETL 106 (Leuven: University Press and Peters, 1993), 539-45; Shaye J. D. Cohen, "Josephus, Jeremiah, and Polybius," *History and Theory* 21 (1982): 366-81; David Daube, "Typology in Josephus," *JJS* 31 (1980): 18-36; David Satran, "Daniel: Seer, Prophet, Holy Man," in *Ideal Figures in Ancient Judaism: Profiles and Paradigms,* ed. John J. Collins and George W. E. Nickelsburg. SBLSCS 12 (Chico: Scholars, 1980), 33-48; Steve Mason, "Josephus, Daniel, and the Flavian House," in *Josephus and the History of the Greco-Roman Period: Essays in Memory of Morton Smith,* ed. Fausto Parente and Joseph Sievers. StPB 41 (Leiden: Brill, 1994), 161-91.

used.[23] The evidence is again complex, and there are echoes of MT, LXX, and targumic traditions as well as the possible incorporation of traditions that have not been transmitted in any surviving source.[24]

Josephus's interest in the canonical prophets is limited, although he identifies biblical characters as prophets where this is lacking in the Hebrew or LXX text or he adds emphasis to their role as a prophet by repeating this designation.[25]

In identifying the presence of these multiple textual traditions in the *Jewish Antiquities* scholars have revealed it to be a rich and extensive resource for the study of biblical texts in early Judaism. We have seen that the extrabiblical material in the narrative, as well as certain interpretative traditions, is paralleled in targumic sources, but many of these features can also be found in other Jewish sources from the Hellenistic and Roman period, in the contexts of "Rewritten" Bible, Jewish-Hellenistic historical writings, and rabbinic literature.

Among the texts traditionally classified as "rewritten" Bible, studies have revealed similar exegetical practices in Pseudo-Philo's *Biblical Antiquities, Jubilees,* and the *Genesis Apocryphon,* as well as the Samaritan *Asatir.*[26] Yet at the same time, Josephus's framework and interpretative technique for his biblical sources is very different from these works. There have also been a number of attempts to draw conclusions about Josephus's knowledge of rabbinic traditions, and in particular with regard to the development of midrashic traditions about biblical personalities.[27]

The fragments of the historical works of Eupolemus, Demetrius, Artapanus, and Ezekiel the Tragedian have yielded further evidence of some common traditions, which Josephus may have drawn on for his paraphrase of the Bible. In *Ant.* 1.240 he mentions Cleodamus Malchus, whom he knew through the work of Alexander Polyhistor, and in *Ag. Ap.* 1.218 he refers to Demetrius Phalereus, the "elder Philo," and Eupolemus. It is generally agreed that he was also familiar with these two latter authors from Alexander Polyhistor (or

24. See Christopher T. Begg and Paul Spilsbury, "Excursus: Josephus on Daniel (Judean Antiquities 10.186-281)," in Mason, *Flavius Josephus: Translation and Commentary,* Vol. 5: Judean Antiquities *Books 8–10 (Leiden: Brill, 2005),* 265-67.

25. Louis H. Feldman, "Prophets and Prophecy in Josephus," *JTS* 41 (1990): 419-21.

26. Louis H. Feldman, "Prolegomenon," in *The Biblical Antiquities of Philo,* ed. M. R. James (London: SPCK, 1917; repr. New York: Ktav, 1971), vii-clxix; and Moses Gaster, *The Asatir: The Samaritan Book of the "Secrets of Moses" Together with the Pitron or Samaritan Commentary and the Samaritan Story of the Death of Moses* (London: Royal Asiatic Society, 1927), 61-80, found parallels in *Antiquities* and the Samaritan *Asatir,* and proposed that they shared a common Palestinian source.

27. See the references for Louis H. Feldman's examination of Josephus's portraits of biblical personalities. See Paul Spilsbury, *The Image of the Jew in Flavius Josephus's Paraphrase of the Bible.* TSAJ 69 (Tübingen: Mohr Siebeck, 1998), 29, for a summary of scholarship.

through an intermediary document).[28] There has been considerable discussion about Josephus's familiarity with the works of Philo of Alexandria. Josephus mentions him by name in *Ant.* 18.259-60, and we find a number of exegetical similarities, especially with regard to allegorical interpretations (e.g., the symbolic interpretation of the tent, the priests' clothing, and the sacred vessels in *Ant.* 3.180-87).[29] The various studies, including those of the possible parallels between Philo's *Hypothetica* and the presentations of Moses and the Jewish constitution in *Ag. Ap.* 2, have not proved conclusively direct or indirect dependence (through an intermediary Alexandrian source) of Josephus on Philo.

The history of scholarship on Josephus's sources for his biblical texts has been marked by an attempt to get behind Josephus's reworking to identify the form of the texts that he utilized and the tradition within which Josephus worked, as well as to reveal something of the author's aims in the *Antiquities*. In some cases scholars have postulated dependence on sources that have not survived. Others have drawn attention to the fact that Josephus may have included oral traditions that he was familiar with from his Jerusalem education and priestly experience and then from the Diaspora communities during the later part of his life in Rome.[30]

On the whole, what emerges from these examinations is that Josephus is not reliant on one particular text or tradition, and he combined his sources to serve his own narrative interests. The *Antiquities* should not be considered "simply a sterile compilation of traditions" but rather a unique "personal contribution to that tradition."[31] The main methodological considerations must include an appreciation of the control that the author wields over his material; divergence from text traditions do not necessarily denote either an ignorance on the part of Josephus or omission for ideological reasons. Josephus's approach to the biblical texts and his incorporation of traditions must be under-

---

28. For a review of early scholarship, see Attridge, *The Interpretation of Biblical History*, 34-35; Ben Zion Wacholder, *Eupolemus: A Study of Judaeo-Greek Literature*. HUCM 3 (Cincinnati: Hebrew Union College Press, 1974), 52-57; John M. G. Barclay, *Against Apion*, vol. 10 of Mason, *Flavius Josephus: Translation and Commentary* (Leiden: Brill, 2007), 124 nn. 745, 746, and 747. Tessa Rajak, "Moses in Ethiopia: Legend and Literature," *JJS* 29 (1978): 111-22, notes one particular example of how the parallels between Artapanus and Josephus cannot provide conclusive evidence of a common source.

29. Louis H. Feldman, *Judean Antiquities Books 1–4*, 280, n. 474, on the interpretation of this passage with a particular view to Philo. See n. 86 below on Josephus's possible knowledge of Philo.

30. The debate about Josephus's use of oral and written material is summarized in Spilsbury, *The Image of the Jew*, 26-28.

31. Spilsbury, *The Image of the Jew*, 29.

stood within the larger narrative framework and without prior assumptions regarding his audience and agenda.[32] In the absence of conclusive evidence regarding his knowledge of a particular tradition, we cannot make assumptions about authorial choice. This authorial independence and creativity become evident on examination of the patterns, techniques, and themes in Josephus's narrative composition, which demonstrate that *Ant.* 1–11 is an integral part of the overall work and must be viewed as such.

Text: Josephus's Narrative Technique

The extensive debate about Josephus's sources for his biblical interpretation arises from the fact that he does not follow one particular text or interpretative tradition and that, as we shall see, he reworks those materials available to him for his narrative interests. He omits material, elaborates on his sources, offers explanations, and systemizes and supplements the narrative, while placing it within a larger narrative framework. In identifying the main features of these modifications, scholars have focused on uncovering a narrative technique, or lack thereof.[33] While there is some debate as to the consistency of the changes and Josephus's use of sources, there are some general points of agreement regarding his narrative technique. It has been noted that the order of the Bible is usually followed, but there is some significant reordering of the sequence of particular episodes, which has been understood as arising from his historiographical concern for thematic coherence.[34] This leads to a sytematization of narratives, where material on a particular theme is drawn together: for example, *Ant.* 7.46-129 brings together material on David from 2 Samuel, 1 Kings, and 1 and 2 Chronicles. This tendency is also clear with regard to the legal sections in *Ant.* 3 and 4, where material from Exodus, Leviticus, and Numbers is presented systematically. Another noted tendency in Josephus's narrative approach is the resolution of perceived problems such as contradictions, inconsistencies, chronological difficulties, and anthropomorphisms.[35]

The language and style of *Antiquities* have been the focus of much detailed

---

32. E.g., Feldman will often conclude that behind certain modifications, and in particular the hellenizations he identifies, were personal or national apologetics. For a critique of this approach, see Spilsbury, *The Image of the Jew,* 29–34.

33. For a critical view of Josephus's use of sources, see Cohen, *Josephus in Galilee and Rome,* 24–47: "Josephus was not a meticulous and attentive craftsman."

34. Cohen, *Josephus in Galilee and Rome,* 39-42, lists examples of this reordering for thematic purposes.

35. Feldman, "Use, Authority and Exegesis," 476-77, lists examples of this tendency.

research: in some cases the results have indicated that Josephus has diminished the rich language of a source; others have called attention to the improvements he makes to Greek sources (where necessary), his variation in vocabulary and terminology, and what is seen as his atticizing tendencies.[36] That Josephus seems to display a familiarity with classical Greek authors and the inclusion of stylistic and rhetorical devices (as well as certain motifs from Greco-Roman literature) might imply the use of assistants, a theory proposed by Thackeray, but one that has found little support.[37] The centrality of Greco-Roman culture for both the literary and thematic presentation in Josephus's *Antiquities* will be discussed in detail in the following section.

Josephus does offer a programmatic statement regarding his approach to the biblical material: "This narrative will, therefore, in due course, set forth the precise details of what is in the Scriptures according to its proper order. For I promised that I would do this throughout this treatise, neither adding nor omitting anything" (*Ant.* 1.17 [Feldman, Brill Josephus Project]), and he further restates this in *Ant.* 10.218 (see also *Ag. Ap.* 1.42; 2.291). Scholars have pointed out that among ancient historians, particularly those of Eastern origin, it is not uncommon to find claims regarding the faithful use of sources and the accurate transmission of traditions.[38] In this prologue, Josephus sets himself within the tradition of the LXX (*Ant.* 1.10-12), which also did not simply offer a translation, but included interpretation.[39] There is certainly no attempt to separate translation from commentary, to mark out the biblical text from the additions, or to justify omissions.

We have already noted that in the *Antiquities* the part of the text that is

---

36. André Pelletier, *Flavius Josèphe, adapteur de la lettre d'Aristée* (Paris: Klincksieck, 1962), has offered a detailed study of Josephus's use of the Letter of Aristeas, and he shows that Josephus thoroughly reworked the original language, diminishing certain features of the Greek in order to meet the atticizing tastes of his first-century Roman audience. Feldman, "Use, Authority and Exegesis," 482-85, provides examples of phrases in *Antiquities* reminiscent of classical authors.

37. Thackeray, *Josephus,* 100-124. *Contra* this theory, see Attridge, *The Interpretation of Biblical History,* 38-39; Tessa Rajak, *Josephus, The Historian and His Society* (London: Duckworth, 1983), 233-36; Feldman, "Use, Authority and Exegesis," 481-82.

38. Analyses of the terminology employed by Josephus for the act of translating demonstrates that his use of μεθερμηνεύω and ἑρμηνεύω (and related terms) expresses much more than translation (*Ant.* 1.5; 12.20; 12.48; 1.29; 12.39; 12.49; 12.108; 20.264) when referring to his own work or the production of the Septuagint. For further discussion, see Cohen, *Josephus in Galilee and Rome,* 24-31; and more recently Feldman, *Judean Antiquities Books 1–4,* 3-5, n. 4; Begg and Spilsbury, *Judean Antiquities Books 8–10,* 288-89, nn. 938, 939, and 940.

39. Louis H. Feldman, *Josephus's Interpretation of the Bible* (Berkeley: University of California Press, 1998), 44-46, has collected the various uses of these terms.

based on the Bible belongs within a larger historiographical context. It constitutes only part of the larger work, which just over halfway through takes up, and devotes almost as much space to, the later history of the Judeans, in particular Herodian and Roman rule. It is to this wider context, both narrative and historical, that we must look to understand Josephus's biblical interpretation.

Jewish Antiquities: Literary and Historical Context

Recent trends in Josephan studies have radically altered the way in which the relationships between the composite parts of the *Judean Antiquities* are understood. Whereas the traditional *Quellenkritik* approach could reveal certain dominant themes and tendencies, there is now a much greater appreciation of the importance of the literary and historical contexts in forming those interpretations.[40] Reading Josephus's works with a focus on the thematic and compositional aspects of the larger narrative, as well as situating him within his immediate cultural and social environment, can expose the dominant concerns and literary techniques of the author.

Thematic and Literary Context

Scholars concerned with the literary character of the *Antiquities* look to Josephus's own claims about the nature and form of his work, and in particular the programmatic statement in his prologue (*Ant.* 1.1-26): Josephus defines his work as an account of the "ancient history" (ἀρχαιολογία) and "constitution" (πολιτεία) of the Jewish nation (*Ant.* 1.5). This includes a survey of the events over five thousand years — wars, military leadership, and changes in governance (*Ant.* 1.13) — that will demonstrate that:

> those who comply with the will of God and do not venture to transgress laws that have been well enacted succeed in all things beyond belief and that happiness lies before them as a reward from God. But to the extent that they dissociate themselves from the scrupulous observance of these laws the practicable things become impracticable and whatever seemingly good thing they pursue with zeal turns into irremediable misfortunes. (*Ant.* 1.14 [Feldman, Brill Josephus Project])

---

40. Mason, "Introduction to the *Judean Antiquities*," xiv, on the main results of this trend of *Quellenkritik*.

This ancient history (*Ant.* 1.8 and *Ag. Ap.* 1.1), based on an accurate "translation" of the Hebrew writings, is dedicated to Epaphroditus and written for the
attention of the Greek-speaking world (*Ant.* 1.5, 12; 16.174; 20.262). The readers
are invited to evaluate the Jewish lawgiver (νομοθέτης), Moses, upon whose
wisdom and conception of the divine all is dependent (*Ant.* 1.18). Moses' conception of the divine has "shown that God possesses a virtue that is pure, that
human beings ought to try to participate in it, and he unrelentingly punishes
those who do not share these thoughts or believe in them" (*Ant.* 1.23 [Feldman,
Brill Josephus Project]).

The first major study that attempted to use Josephus's programmatic statement in the prologue to identify prevailing themes was that of Attridge. Chal-
lenging interpretations of Josephus's reworking of the Bible in *Ant.* 1–11 that did
not take into account its literary context, Attridge distinguishes two guiding interpretative themes: divine providence *(pronoia)* and a moralizing understanding of history.[41] The lessons of history — punishment for transgressors and reward for the righteous — and the evidence for God's care for humanity are
repeatedly illustrated in Josephus's narrative, and in particular in the speeches
attributed to biblical characters.[42] For example, the episodes of the Aqedah
(*Ant.* 1.222-31) and the exodus (*Ant.* 2.325-33) illustrate divine care for the righteous, while the perpetrators of the revolts against Moses (*Ant.* 4.14-56, 131-55)
are portrayed as transgressing ancestral laws and so bringing about disaster.
These themes are picked up in the second part of *Antiquities,* but especially
characterize the account of the Herodian dynasty:[43] ". . . Josephus now takes up
the career of Herod and his immediate successors to be in itself a prime example of divine providence at work and also an essential component in the provi-
dentially directed chain of events leading up to the destruction of Jerusalem by
the Romans."[44] This approach highlights the role of Josephus as author and indicates that his interpretation of the biblical narrative is guided principally by
thematic concerns.

The pervasive nature of Josephus's literary interests is further demonstrated by Feldman in his extensive examination of Josephus's portrayals of

41. Feldman, "Use, Authority and Exegesis," 499, notes the correspondence of this term in
Stoic philosophy, while Josephus's Moses is represented as a Stoic-type sage. Feldman also observes that Josephus highlights divine providence while at the same time diminishing divine activity in the narrative.

42. E.g., Moses' final speech to the Israelites in *Ant.* 4.185.

43. Attridge, *The Interpretation of Biblical History,* 67-144. The theme of divine providence,
while somewhat less significant, also appears in *Ant.* 11–13 (e.g., *Ant.* 11.169-71, 247, 268; 12.258,
259-61; 13.314).

44. Attridge, "Josephus and His Works," 220.

biblical characters, who are characterized as exhibiting the virtues that belong to the ideal Greco-Roman statesman.[45] Josephus's hellenized biblical personalities are of good birth, share extraordinary physical qualities, and demonstrate in their actions the four cardinal virtues (wisdom, courage, temperance, and justice), while fulfilling expectations of piety. Moses, as legislator, is central to this hellenized presentation and appears as "a Platonic-like philosopher-king." Paul Spilsbury's chronological examination of the biblical paraphrase has further exposed a consistent concern with the image of the Jew governing the narrative.[46] Most recently, Mason, in his introduction to the Brill translation and commentary of *Ant.* 1–4, has identified ethnographic, political, and philosophical themes that not only unite the composite sections of *Jewish Antiquities*, but also dominate the *Life* and *Against Apion*.[47]

The antiquity of the Jews and their culture is a central theme of *Antiquities*, and this ethnographic concern is evinced in the title of the work, its scope in tracing Jewish history from the moment of creation, and the emphasis on Jewish cultural independence. In *Ag. Ap.* 1:1, Josephus explicitly cites this theme:

> Through my treatise on Ancient History, most eminent Epaphroditus, I consider that, to those who will read it, I have made it sufficiently clear concerning our people, the Judeans, that it is extremely ancient and had its own original composition and how it inhabited the land that we now possess; for I composed in the Greek language a history covering 5,000 years, on the basis of our sacred books. (Barclay, Brill Josephus Project)

The Greeks and Romans placed great value on antiquity, and being able to provide proof of a long and distinguished national heritage was essential in that climate of cultural and ethnographic competition.[48] Josephus belonged to an Eastern tradition that sought to claim a place for its culture and institutions in the history of the nations. Gregory Sterling asserted that the *Jewish Antiquities* belongs within a genre that he identifies as "apologetic historiography"; this phenomenon developed among oriental priestly elites who produced accounts of their nations' history claiming to be based on their ancient rec-

---

45. These studies can be found reprinted in two volumes: Louis H. Feldman, *Josephus's Interpretation of the Bible;* and *Studies in Josephus's Rewritten Bible.* JSJSup 58 (Leiden: Brill, 1998).

46. Spilsbury, *The Image of the Jew,* esp. 217-30, for his conclusions.

47. Steve Mason, "Introduction," in *Life of Josephus,* xlvii-l; and "Introduction to the Judean Antiquities," xxiii-xxxiv.

48. Feldman, *Jew and Gentile in the Ancient World,* 177-200, on the Jewish concern with antiquity. See also Steve Mason, "The Greeks and the Distant Past in Josephus's *Judaean War,*" in *Antiquity in Antiquity: Jewish and Christian Pasts in the Greco-Roman World,* ed. Gregg Gardner and Kevin L. Osterloh. TSAJ 123 (Tübingen: Mohr Siebeck, 2008), 93-130.

ords.[49] Josephus portrays the Judean nation as culture-bearers who contributed to the development of Egyptian civilization, which was universally recognized as ancient by both Greeks and Romans. The proof for these claims is to be found in the sacred texts, where one can find not only the superior constitution of the Judeans but also predictions concerning the events of world history.[50] The hellenization of biblical characters is seen as serving a similar apologetic: Judean heroes are not only local, aside from displaying Greek values, but are of universal relevance.[51] This apologetic focus of the narrative is also perceived as implicitly responding to anti-Judean slanders, some of which were directly addressed in *Against Apion*.[52] The apologetic concern is also identified in the second half of *Jewish Antiquities*, where Josephus presents material in defense of the rights of Jewish communities in the Hellenistic kingdoms and the Roman Empire.[53]

The portrayal of biblical personalities is also characterized by political and philosophical reflections.[54] Mason's work in particular has demonstrated that Josephus's interest in the "constitution" as indicated in the prologue also thematically unifies the different parts of the *Jewish Antiquities*: central to the narrative framework of *Jewish Antiquities* is a reflection on good governance and justice that results in harmony (ἁρμονία) and happiness (εὐδαιμονία), the relationship between the character of the state and its individuals, and the virtues of the lawgiver and the ideal statesman.[55] Aside from specific passages where Josephus explicitly reflects on these issues, the whole narrative is constructed around demonstrating that where good governance is instituted, the nation prospers. The "aristocratic" Judean constitution is cast as one in which God alone rules through the agency of his priesthood, and when another form of

---

49. Gregory E. Sterling, *Historiography and Self-definition: Josephos, Luke-Acts, and Apologetic Historiography.* NovTSup 64 (Leiden: Brill, 1992). The works of Hecataeus, Manetho, and Berossus belong to this genre wherein native cultures attempted to establish their identity and cultural independence.

50. Tessa Rajak, "Josephus and the 'Archaeology' of the Jews," *JJS* (1982): 465-77. Besides tracing the similarities with these pagan historians, Rajak also notes that Josephus differed from them, as they had a variety of sources at their disposal but Josephus had to work in the *Antiquities* within the confines of the Bible, although he also made omissions and additions. *Ant.* 10.266-81; 11.1-3, 331-39.

51. E.g., Abraham teaches arithmetic and astrology to the Egyptians (*Ant.* 1.166-67).

52. Barclay, "Introduction," in *Against Apion*, xxxvi-xliv, reconstructs possible anti-Jewish slanders that might have been common in Flavian Rome and addressed in *Against Apion*.

53. E.g., *Ant.* 14.186, 266, 323; 16.162-73, 174-75. See Attridge, "Josephus and His Works," 225-26.

54. Mason, *Life of Josephus;* the character of the members of a society determines its worth, and so *Antiquities* describes the character of the heroes of Jewish history.

55. Moses, as the lawgiver (νομοθέτης) is responsible for this constitution.

governance is introduced, i.e., monarchy, it brings the inevitable problems associated with succession and absolute power. Throughout the narrative monarchy is correlated with tyranny and the corruption of society. Josephus's extensive coverage of Herod the Great in *Ant.* 14–17 considers at length the corrupt nature of this form of governance. This narrative, according to Mason, is carefully constructed to parallel Judean and Roman constitutional problems and to condemn autocratic monarchical style rule (*Ant.* 19.222-23).[56] Contiguous to the arguments regarding good governance are Josephus's moralizing statements about divine providence: lives and systems are assessed in moral terms, and this is a consistent theme in both halves of *Jewish Antiquities*.[57]

Earlier analyses of *Jewish Antiquities* had recognized this "nationalistic" interest; Richard Laqueur proposed that Josephus, between writing the pro-Roman propagandistic *Jewish War* and the patriotic pro-Jewish *Jewish Antiquities,* had undergone a change of heart, while Shaye Cohen contended that this later work supported the Pharisaic movement at Yavneh, providing a sort of recommendation for a Jewish and Roman audience.[58] Seth Schwartz supports this view: he reads the *Jewish War* as a pro-priestly document, while *Jewish Antiquities* is considered as representing a new prorabbinic position.[59]

These analyses have been critiqued, as new readings of *Jewish War* indicate that it did not function as pro-Roman propaganda nor do we have sufficient evidence to draw conclusions regarding Yavneh and the early rabbinic movement. Appreciation of *Jewish Antiquities* as a literary construction has provided scholars with a view of Josephus's pro-priestly presentation of the Jewish constitution, in spite of the criticism of individual priests as noted by Schwartz.

The underlying assumptions about the possible apologetic agenda for both *Jewish Antiquities* and *Against Apion* have been challenged, as scholars consider the literary and historical contexts of these works. It has been long recognized that, beyond the hellenizations and the theoretical interests, Josephus's literary models and techniques are Greco-Roman: "From the point of view of language, style, and form, Josephus belongs to the Greek and Hellenistic literature, and as

---

56. See Mason, "Introduction to the *Judean Antiquities*," xxxii-xxxiv.

57. Mason, "Introduction to the *Judean Antiquities*," xxxii-xxxiv, highlights this as an important aspect for understanding Josephus's presentation of Herod and his family in *Ant.* 14–20.

58. Richard Laqueur, *Der jüdische Historiker Flavius Josephus: Ein biographischer Versuch auf neuer quellenkritischer Grundlage* (Giessen: Münchow, 1920; repr. Darmstadt: Wissenschaftliche Buchgesellschaft, 1970), 52-56; Cohen, *Josephus in Galilee and Rome*, 232-42, for his conclusions. Steve Mason, *Flavius Josephus on the Pharisees: A Compositional-Critical Study.* StPB 39 (Leiden: Brill, 1991), analyzed the texts and concluded that there was no evidence to confirm that Josephus was pro-Pharisaic.

59. Seth Schwartz, *Josephus and Judaean Politics* (Leiden: Brill, 1990).

a writer he belongs to Greco-Roman historiography."[60] The hellenization of biblical personalities is also evident in the literary format of their presentation; a particularly important study by Martin Braun showed that Josephus introduced erotic and novelistic elements found in Greek novels.[61] Examination of his historiographical statements and other Greco-Roman literary features in the narrative has led to suggestions of a Greco-Roman model for *Jewish Antiquities*. Thackeray theorized that Josephus fashioned his *Jewish Antiquities* on Dionysius of Halicarnassus's twenty-volume *Roman Antiquities* (published in 7 B.C.E.) and in doing so made competing claims about Judean culture,[62] while we saw that Sterling identified it as belonging to an Eastern genre of apologetic historiography. Close comparison between the works of Dionysius and Josephus shows the parallels to be merely superficial and does not support Thackeray's hypothesis,[63] while Sterling's focus on *Jewish Antiquities* as an apologetic has been challenged on a literary and historical level. In his new translation and commentary on *Against Apion,* John Barclay questions such broad understanding of the term "apologetic" and its use for "*any form* of self-justification or explanation, whether addressed to outsiders or to one's own group . . .," and notes that the presence of apologetic motifs does not constitute an "apology."[64] The issue of Josephus's audience and historical context also challenges the apologetic conception of the work.

Clearly emerging among scholars today is the view that Josephus's *Jewish Antiquities* is a complex piece of work that draws on Greek and Roman literary and historiographical traditions for its form, language, and style, and on Judean sacred texts and history for its content, while addressing an audience familiar with and interested in political and philosophical discourse. While Josephus seems to be aware of a multitude of interpretative and exegetical traditions, we cannot ignore the authorial control that he wields and the narrative and conceptual frameworks in which he places that material — and the particular historical context in which he worked.

---

60. Bilde, *Flavius Josephus between Jerusalem and Rome,* 202.

61. Martin Braun, *Griechischer Roman und hellenistische Geschichtsschreibung* (Frankfurt: Klostermann, 1934), 108-9, examined these features as they appear in Josephus's version of the story of Joseph and Potiphar's wife (*Ant.* 2.39-59); and *History and Romance in Greco-Oriental Literature* (Oxford: Blackwell, 1938). For further analysis, see Horst R. Moehring, "Novelistic Elements in the Writings of Flavius Josephus" (Diss., Chicago, 1957).

62. Thackeray, *Josephus,* 56; Attridge, *The Interpretation of Biblical History,* 43-59; and "Josephus and His Works," 217, supports this view, as does David L. Balch, "Two Apologetic Encomia: Dionysius on Rome and Josephus on the Jews," *JSJ* 13 (1982): 102-22.

63. Rajak, "Josephus and the 'Archaeology' of the Jews," 466.

64. Barclay, "Introduction," xxxv.

Jewish Antiquities: Historical Context

In the recent commentaries by Barclay and Mason, the question of Josephus's audience has been reassessed. For *Against Apion,* Barclay has identified three levels of audience: the declared audience, the implied audience, and the intended audience. The first two can be identified from within the text, but the third can only be deduced from the historical and social context. The declared audience for *Antiquities* includes Epaphroditus and those in the Greek-speaking world who find it deserving of their attention (*Ant.* 1.5). There is some difficulty in the identification of Epaphroditus: he may have been a freedman of the Emperor Nero who was executed by Domitian in 95 C.E. or the Greek grammarian, M. Mettius Epaphroditus, who lived on into the time of Nerva.[65] The final book of *Antiquities* dates the conclusion of the work to the thirteenth year of the reign of Domitian and the fifty-sixth year of his own life, that is 93/94 C.E. (*Ant.* 20.267). The implied audience are Greek speakers, but Mason points out that this does not imply a non-Latin-speaking Roman audience, as most of the Roman elite had a Greek education and many Greek-speaking scholars resided in Rome at that time. Furthermore, it would have been unwise for Josephus to attempt Latin prose, and in the uncertain environment of Domitianic Rome, works in Greek were not treated with the same suspicion as those in Latin.[66] The unstable situation in Rome under Domitian led scholars to suggest that *Jewish Antiquities* was addressed to the Roman governing elite as a work of political apologetic. From the hellenizations and explanations, others see the main audience as being Greeks and Romans, with perhaps an occasional Jewish reader.[67]

Mason has suggested that the implied audience can be further deduced from the main themes of the narrative: Josephus's renunciation of autocratic forms of government and, in particular, monarchy's being influenced by the ideals of aristocratic Romans. He observes that Josephus's condemnation of autocratic rule would have resonated with his aristocratic Roman audience, espe-

---

65. Louis-Hugues Vincent, "Chronologie des Oeuvres de Josèphe," *RB* 8 (1911): 375-76, provides source material for these persons, but he does not conclusively identify Josephus's Epaphroditus with either one. Cohen, *Josephus in Galilee and Rome,* 174, argues that there is insufficient evidence to select one over the other, as does Mason, "Introduction," in *Life of Josephus,* xviii-xix. Rajak, *Josephus,* 223, opts for M. Mettius Epaphroditus, as does Schwartz, *Josephus and Judaean Politics,* 16-17.

66. Mason, "Introduction," in *Life of Josephus,* xviii-xix.

67. Elvira Migliario, "Per l'interpretazione dell' Autobiografia di Flavio Giuseppe," *Athenaeum* 69 (1981): 92-137, proposes that the main audience for all of Josephus's works was Jewish, but this view has not attracted support.

cially during the reign of Domitian. His focus on Herod's succession woes is paralleled in *Ant.* 18–19 with his treatment of the constitutional crisis in Rome occasioned by the imminent death of the emperor Tiberias.[68]

As for the intended audience, Mason suggests that we look for clues in the practices of ancient publication, where the process of writing was an essentially social affair with a limited final production. While Josephus might have hoped for a wide and sustained readership, "we should imagine book production in Josephus' context as driven by an author and his friends more than by the merits of a disembodied text. Writing was a personal and social activity issuing from the status *(auctoritas)* of the author and his friends."[69]

An audience taking on a twenty-volume history of the Judeans must have been interested and sympathetic, and while the text may address certain anti-Jewish slanders, enemies or critics would not search such a document for a rebuttal of their opinions.[70] In *Jewish Antiquities* 3 and 4, the laws themselves are set out in a way that a non-Jewish audience would easily access them,[71] but unlike in *Against Apion,* there is no real interest in proving the value of these laws to a Greek or Roman audience.[72] There seems to have been a long-standing interest in Rome in Judean culture, and those who attempted to follow this long and detailed history must have been among them. In this case, *Jewish Antiquities* is not simply an apologetic, but it rather functions "to provide a handbook of Judean law, history and culture for a Gentile audience in Rome that is keenly interested in Jewish matters."[73]

68. Mason, "Introduction," in *Life of Josephus,* xxxiv-xxxv.

69. Mason, "Introduction," in *Life of Josephus,* xvii-xviii.

70. On the attraction to Judean culture among Romans, see e.g., Shaye J. D. Cohen, "Respect for Judaism by Gentiles according to Josephus," *HTR* 80 (1987): 409-30; Louis H. Feldman, *Jew and Gentile in the Ancient World: Attitudes and Interactions from Alexander to Justinian* (Princeton: Princeton University Press, 1993); and "Reading Between the Lines: Appreciation of Judaism in Anti-Jewish Writers Cited in *Contra Apionem,*" in *Josephus's Contra Apionem: Studies in Its Character and Context with a Latin Concordance to the Portion Missing in Greek,* ed. Feldman and John R. Levison. AGJU 34 (Leiden: Brill, 1996), 250-69.

71. Mason, "Introduction," in *Life of Josephus,* xxiv-xxvi. Mason finds comparisons between the constitutional presentation in *Jewish Antiquities* and Cicero's *On the Republic* and *On the Laws.*

72. Barclay, *Against Apion,* 259, n. 620, on the difference between the presentation of the laws in *Against Apion* and *Jewish Antiquities* 3–4.

73. Steve Mason, "'Should Any Wish to Enquire Further' (*Ant.* 1.25): The Aim and Audience of Josephus's *Judean Antiquities/Life,*" in *Understanding Josephus: Seven Perspectives.* JSPSup 32 (Sheffield: Sheffield Academic, 1998), 64-103. Mason undertakes a reexamination of the aims and audience of *Jewish Antiquities,* as he deems the traditional interpretations deficient in that they do not take into account the social conditions in Rome in which Josephus wrote nor the internal indications in the *Antiquities.*

The movement towards understanding Josephus's authorial technique and the thematic and literary construction of the narrative has demanded that we reassess Josephus's biblical paraphrase in *Antiquities* 1–11. While contemporary and later texts and traditions may be identified, this text is mainly a witness to the creative impulses of a first-century Jewish priest living in Rome during the later years of the first century C.E.

Jewish War: Text and Context

The first of Josephus's works, *Jewish War,* offers a seven-book account of the Jewish revolt against Rome. Studies on *Jewish War* have focused on the literary and historiographical presentation of the events of the war, Josephus's own actions during that period, and the relationship between Rome and the Judeans. While some scholars cannot find any evidence of Josephus's knowledge of the Bible in *Jewish War,* others have noted the presence of a historiography rooted in the biblical traditions, as well as a knowledge of certain prophetic texts.

Schwartz has undertaken an examination of the biblical material in *Jewish War,* and he lays out what have been identified as references to the Bible in the narrative.[74] The main sustained reference to the biblical narrative appears in Josephus's speech during the siege of Jerusalem (*Ant.* 5.379-93). Here he uses examples from Israel's past to encourage the rebels to surrender. He includes accounts of the stories of Abraham, Sarah, and the Pharaoh (*Ant.* 5.379-81), the exodus (5.382-83), the rescuing of the ark from the Philistines (5.384-87), the destruction of Sennacherib's army (5.387-88), the restoration under Cyrus (5.389-91), and finally the downfall of Jerusalem under the Babylonians and Antiochus IV (5.391-95). The main issue regarding these episodes, and the other biblical references, is that they diverge significantly from the biblical account and often contradict the scriptural source.

Schwartz also identifies a priestly bias in his biblical interpretation in *Jewish War,* and he concludes that Josephus was only familiar with sections of the Bible. Even this paltry knowledge was not gained from a first-hand knowledge of the texts, but through the oral culture of the priesthood.[75]

Other scholars have deduced a familiarity with the Bible from Josephus's theological Deuteronomic understanding of history and the role of prophecy. The interpretation of the defeat by the Romans as divine punishment for the sins of the Jewish nation (e.g., *J. W.* 2.455; 5.19) and the focus on their transgres-

---

74. Schwartz, *Josephus and Judaean Politics,* 24-25.
75. Schwartz, *Josephus and Judaean Politics,* 24-35, 43-44.

sions (*J.W.* 2.454-56, 589; 4.314-18, 383-88) is a unifying narrative theme. The theme of the rise and fall of nations under divine supervision and the role of the prophetic voice permeate the account, and scholars have identified Jeremianic and Danielic influence, even if they do not appear in direct references.[76]

Josephan scholarship on *Jewish War* has also undergone a methodological shift. It is no longer an accepted conclusion that Josephus wrote this work either as Roman propaganda under Flavian patronage or in an attempt to argue the case for the priests among the Jewish elite.[77] The idea that Josephus underwent a conversion of sorts and latterly became a Jewish apologist or nationalist has been undermined in light of the close studies of the narratives of *War* and *Antiquities*, where many of the themes of the earlier work are present in his later history: divine providence and the role of prophets are two such themes.

The question of Josephus's knowledge of the Bible cannot easily be answered with regard to *War*. The narrative focus does not lend itself to extensive biblical references, and the meager examples we have can only confirm what we know about his interpretative method in *Antiquities*: that it is not dictated by text or tradition and it corresponds to the larger narrative interest of the work.

Against Apion: Text and Context

The final work in Josephus's corpus, *Against Apion*, also does not include biblical paraphrase, but it does offer further evidence related to his ideas on the status and interpretation of Scripture, the nature of the ancient Jewish writings, the role of prophecy in their formation, their preservation and interpretation, and the exposition of certain biblical laws.

Reflection on the writings (ἀναγραφαί) of the Judeans is set within the larger context of Josephus's claims regarding the age and accuracy of Judean records, in comparison with Greek civilization:[78]

76. Helgo Lindner, *Die Geschichtsauffassung des Flavius Josephus im Bellum Judaicum.* AGJU 12 (Leiden: Brill, 1972), 42-48; Cohen, "Josephus, Jeremiah, and Polybius," 366-81; Rebecca Gray, *Prophetic Figures in Late Second Temple Jewish Palestine: The Evidence from Josephus* (Oxford: Oxford University Press, 1993), 70-79; Mason, "Josephus, Daniel, and the Flavian House." Josephus compares his own appeals to the rebels at Jerusalem with Jeremiah's forewarning of destruction (*J.W.* 5.391-92).

77. Steve Mason, "Of Audience and Meaning: Reading Josephus's *Judean War* in the Context of a Flavian Audience," in *Josephus, Judea, and Christian Origins: Methods and Categories* (Peabody: Hendrickson, 2009), 45-68.

78. At *Ag. Ap.* 1.1-5, Josephus refers to those who doubt Judean antiquity because of the scarcity of external references.

But that our ancestors took the same, not to say still greater, care over the records as did those just mentioned, assigning this task to the chief-priests and prophets, and how this has been maintained with great precision down to our own time — and, if one should speak with greater boldness, will continue to be maintained — I shall try to indicate briefly. (*Ag. Ap.* 1.29 [Barclay, Brill Josephus Project])

He compares Judean record-keeping with that of the Babylonians and Egyptians (*Ant.* 1.28) and insists on the purity of stock and continuity of succession of the Judean priestly caste (*Ag. Ap.* 1.29-36), who protect and preserve these most precise (ακρίβεια) of national records. To further emphasize the trustworthiness of these records, he states:

Naturally, then, or rather necessarily, seeing that it is not open to anyone to write of their own accord, nor is there any disagreement present in what is written, but the prophets alone learned, by inspiration from God, what had happened in the distant and most ancient past and recorded plainly events in their own time just as they occurred among us, there are not thousands of books in disagreement and conflict with each other, but only twenty-two books, containing the record of all time, which are rightly trusted. Five of these are the books of Moses, which contain both the laws and the tradition from the birth of humanity up to his death; this is a period of a little less than 3,000 years. From the death of Moses until Artaxerxes, king of the Persians after Xerxes, the prophets after Moses wrote the history of what took place in their own times in thirteen books; the remaining four books contain hymns to God and instructions for people on life. (*Ag. Ap.* 1.37-40 [Barclay, Brill Josephus Project])

Josephus's comments within his defense of the antiquity of the Jews make substantial assertions regarding the nature of the Judean sacred records: unlike the scattered records of the Greeks, the activity of record-writing was limited to the prophets, who through divine inspiration were able to include matters that are beyond the limits of human knowledge. These are gathered in a single stable, authoritative, unified collection of twenty-two volumes, to which the Judean nation is wholly committed. The authority and status of this single collection is demonstrated by limiting the prophetic in current historiography: "From Artaxerxes up to our own time every event has been recorded, but this is not judged worthy of the same trust, since the exact line of succession of the prophets did not continue" (*Ag. Ap.* 1.41 [Barclay, Brill Josephus Project]). Barclay has noted that this dualistic historiography that clearly defines the records of the past from the present is a theme that is carried through from the *Jewish War* (*J.W.* 1.13-16).[79]

These comments have elicited much scholarly debate regarding the possible existence, as well as composition, of a canon, either bi- or tripartite at the end of the first century C.E. Notably, Josephus's text has been employed by those arguing for *and* against a closed canon, as well as in support of both a two- and a three-part collection. Increasingly, however, with the emphasis shifting towards the wider compositional context, there is some consensus that Josephus is witness to neither a bipartitie or tripartite canon.[80] Reading Josephus on his own terms rather than imposing external categories reveals that Josephus is not concerned with the question of a closed canon for a Pharisaic or rabbinic movement, but rather the discussion is historiographical: he makes a very distinctive claim about the authority of Judean Scriptures: they are unique because they were written by the prophets of the past, who have now come to an end and cannot be matched by contemporary histories.

We noted that certain prophetic motifs arose within Josephus's *Jewish Antiquities* and *Jewish War*. While Josephus does not set out a systematic presentation of prophecy, scholars have noted his careful use of language, and especially the appellation "prophets" for postbiblical seers.[81] In describing his own predictive abilities, Josephus assiduously avoids calling himself a prophet. In terms of his history-writing credentials, he qualifies by virtue of being a priest (*J.W.* 1.3; 3.352; *Life* 1–6; *Ag. Ap.* 1.54), as is the case with those who produced the LXX (*Ant.* 1.10-13). While biblical prophets share the ability to predict the future, all those who predict the future in Josephus's narrative are not deemed prophets.

Regarding the composition of these sections of thirteen and four books, Josephus does not itemize the constituent parts. From other evidence in Josephus's text, and in line with much scholarly opinion, Barclay proposes that the thirteen prophetic books are: Joshua, Judges + Ruth, Samuel, Kings, Isaiah, Jeremiah + Lamentations, Ezekiel, the Twelve, Chronicles, Ezra-Nehemiah, Daniel, Job, and Esther; the four include Psalms, Proverbs, Song of Songs, and Qoheleth (if Lamentations falls within the prophetic category).[82]

In spite of earlier attempts to show Josephus's interest in the Pharisees and/

---

79. Barclay, *Against Apion*, 30, n. 165.

80. Steve Mason, "Josephus and his Twenty-Two Book Canon," in *The Canon Debate*, ed. Lee Martin McDonald and James A. Sanders (Peabody: Hendrickson, 2002), 110-27, reviews the debate and suggests that the distinction between these three sections is based on genre.

81. See Joseph Blenkinsopp, "Prophecy and Priesthood in Josephus," *JJS* 25 (1974): 240-46; Feldman, "Prophets and Prophecy in Josephus," 405; Gray, *Prophetic Figures in Late Second Temple Jewish Palestine*, 23-26.

82. Barclay, *Against Apion*, 30, nn. 165 and 166.

or rabbinic movement, the special status of priests in Judean society has been recognized as a feature of all of Josephus's works.[83] The priests are linked not only with the preservation of the sacred texts, but they also are responsible for their interpretation. Josephus establishes his own historiographical credentials both as an eyewitness and as a priest:

> . . . the *Ancient History,* as I said, I translated from the sacred writings, being a priest by ancestry and steeped in the philosophy contained in those writings; and I wrote the history of the war having been personally involved in many events, an eyewitness of most of them, and not in the slightest deficient in my knowledge of anything that was said or done." (*Ag. Ap.* 1.54 [Barclay, Brill Josephus Project])

Josephus's focus on the status of the priesthood is linked not only with his own self-presentation and as biblical interpreter, but is central to his construction of Judean identity. We have seen how in the *Jewish Antiquities* the biblical para-phrase is informed by a concern for governance with priestly aristocracy as the ideal constitution (*Ant.* 3.188; 4.223-34; 4.304; 6.36).[84]

The Judean constitution is revisited in an encomium in *Against Apion* 2.145-286, where Josephus formulates the "aristocracy" of *Antiquities* as a "the-ocracy" (θεοκρατία). The different articulation of the constitution and its con-stituent laws in *Jewish Antiquities* and *Against Apion* has given rise to much dis-cussion about Josephus's sources, especially regarding the diverging interpretations of biblical law. In line with earlier trends in research, it has been proposed that *Against Apion* was largely a compilation of Judean sources from Alexandria.[85] The presence of *hapax legomena* (240 according to Barclay), the inclusion of new legal material (and its arrangement), as well as some clear par-allels with Hellenistic Jewish texts such as Pseudo-Phocylides and Philo's *Moses* 2 and *Hypothetica* could support this conjecture.[86] But again, recent studies

---

83. On the place of the priesthood in *Antiquities* and *Against Apion,* see Zuleika Rodgers, "Monarchy vs. Priesthood: Josephus, Justus of Tiberias, and Agrippa II," in *A Wandering Gali-lean: Essays in Honour of Seán Freyne,* ed. Rodgers, Margaret Daly-Denton, and Anne Fitzpatrick-McKinley. JSJSup 132 (Leiden: Brill, 2009), 173-84.

84. Positive views of priestly aristocracy are combined with a critique of monarchy. *Ant.* 6.33, 39, 60-61, 89; 262-68; 13.300-301; 14.41-42; 19.222-23.

85. See Barclay's review of the debate in "Appendix 5: The Sources of the Apologetic Enco-mium," in *Against Apion,* 353-61.

86. On Josephus's possible indebtedness to Philo, see Attridge, *The Interpretation of Biblical History,* 36; George P. Carras, "Philo's Hypothetica and Josephus's Contra Apionem and the Question of Sources," in *SBLSP* 1990, ed. David J. Lull (Atlanta: Scholars, 1990), 431-50. Also more recently, Barclay, "Appendix 5," 353-61.

that are sensitive to Josephus's narrative techniques and interests challenge this view: while it may be the case that Josephus was influenced by these sources, and others that are not extant, "he appears to have adapted and supplemented his inheritance in his own hand."[87] Again we must appreciate that Josephus chose those sources and set them within a particular and distinct form. The literary and historical contexts are essential for gaining an insight into that process; themes explored in the *Jewish War,* and in particular in *Jewish Antiquities,* are worked through again in *Against Apion,* but in a way that is more appropriate to the genre and literary interests.[88] And audience matters: there may indeed be echoes of Jewish traditions, but it is employed to communicate a message relevant to its cultural and political setting: "although the Judeans in this treatise are not simply 'Romans' from another place, they are at least partly represented in ways that a Roman audience would both understand and applaud."[89]

Conclusion

That Josephus had access to diverse sources — oral and written, and possibly in a number of languages — as well as to rich interpretative traditions is clear from our survey of the relevant texts. For scholars of Scripture and its interpretation in the first century C.E., Josephus's texts present an impossibly rich resource, full of allusions, citations, and resonances, but to draw conclusions about those texts and their sources without full consideration of the literary and historical contexts and the creative contribution of the author is methodologically unsound and can only distort the evidence.

BIBLIOGRAPHY
Attridge, Harold W. *The Interpretation of Biblical History in the Antiquitates Judaicae of Flavius Josephus.* HDR 7. Missoula: Scholars, 1976.
———. "Josephus and His Works." In *Jewish Writings of the Second Temple Period: Apocrypha, Pseudepigrapha, Qumran Sectarian Writings, Philo, Josephus,* ed. Michael E. Stone. CRINT 2.2. Assen: Van Gorcum and Minneapolis: Fortress, 1984, 185-232.
Balch, David L. "Two Apologetic Encomia: Dionysius on Rome and Josephus on the Jews." *JSJ* 13 (1982): 102-22.
Barclay, John M. G. *Against Apion.* Vol. 10 of Mason, *Flavius Josephus: Translation and Commentary.* Leiden: Brill, 2007.

87. Barclay, "Introduction," xxiv.

88. See Barclay, "Introduction," xxii-xxvi, on the place of *Against Apion* in Josephus's literary career.

89. Barclay, "Appendix 6: Judaism in Roman Dress?" in *Against Apion,* 369.

Begg, Christopher T. "Daniel and Josephus: Tracing Connections." In *The Book of Daniel in Light of New Findings*, ed. Adam S. van der Woude. BETL 106. Leuven: University Press and Peters, 1993, 539-45.

———. *Josephus' Account of the Early Divided Monarchy (AJ 8,212-420): Rewriting the Bible*. BETL 108. Leuven: Leuven University Press, 1993.

———. *Josephus' Story of the Later Monarchy (AJ 9,1-10,185)*. BETL 145. Leuven: Leuven University Press, 2000.

Begg, Christopher T., and Paul Spilsbury. *Judean Antiquities Books 8–10*. Vol. 5 of Mason, *Flavius Josephus: Translation and Commentary*. Leiden: Brill, 2005.

Bilde, Per. *Flavius Josephus between Jerusalem and Rome: His Life, His Works and Their Importance*. JSPSup 2. Sheffield: JSOT, 1988.

———. "*Contra Apionem* 1.28-56: An Essay on Josephus' View of His Own Work in the Context of the Jewish Canon." In Feldman and Levison, *Josephus's Contra Apionem*, 94-114.

Blenkinsopp, Joseph. "Prophecy and Priesthood in Josephus." *JJS* 25 (1974): 239-62.

Bloch, Heinrich. *Die Quellen des Flavius Josephus in seiner Archäologie*. Leipzig: Teubner, 1879; repr. Wiesbaden: Sändig, 1968.

Borgen, Peder. *Philo of Alexandria: An Exegete for His Time*. NovTSup 86. Leiden: Brill, 1997; repr. Atlanta: SBL, 2005.

Braun, Martin. *Griechischer Roman und hellenistische Geschichtsschreibung*. Frankfurt: Klostermann, 1934.

———. *History and Romance in Greco-Oriental Literature*. Oxford: Blackwell, 1938.

Carras, George P. "Philo's *Hypothetica* and Josephus's *Contra Apionem* and the Question of Sources." In *SBLSP* 1990, ed. David J. Lull. Atlanta: Scholars, 1990, 431-50.

Cohen, Naomi G. "Josephus and Scripture: Is Josephus's Treatment of the Scriptural Narrative Similar throughout the *Antiquities* I–XI?" *JQR* 54 (1964): 311-32.

Cohen, Shaye J. D. *Josephus in Galilee and Rome: His Vita and Development as a Historian*. Leiden: Brill, 1979.

———. "Josephus, Jeremiah, and Polybius." *History and Theory* 21 (1982): 366-81.

———. "Respect for Judaism by Gentiles according to Josephus." *HTR* 80 (1987): 409-30.

Daube, David. "Typology in Josephus." *JJS* 31 (1980): 18-36.

Destinon, Justus von. *Die Quellen des Flavius Josephus*. Vol. 1: *Die Quellen der Archäologie Buch XII–XVII = Jüd. Krieg Buch I*. Kiel: Lipsius & Tischer, 1882.

Edmondson, Jonathan, Steve Mason, and Jonathan Rives, eds. *Flavius Josephus and Flavian Rome*. Oxford: Oxford University Press, 2005.

Feldman, Louis H. "Prolegomenon." In *The Biblical Antiquities of Philo*, ed. Montague R. James. London: SPCK, 1917; repr., New York: Ktav, 1971, vii-clxix.

———. *Josephus and Modern Scholarship, 1937-1980*. Berlin: de Gruyter, 1984.

———. "Use, Authority and Exegesis of Mikra in the Writings of Josephus." In *Mikra: Text, Translation, Reading and Interpretation of the Hebrew Bible in Ancient Judaism and Early Christianity*, ed. Martin Jan Mulder. CRINT 2.1. Assen: Van Gorcum and Philadelphia: Fortress, 1988, 455-518.

———. "Prophets and Prophecy in Josephus." *JTS* 41 (1990): 386-422.

———. *Jew and Gentile in the Ancient World: Attitudes and Interactions from Alexander to Justinian*. Princeton: Princeton University Press, 1993.

————. "Reading Between the Lines: Appreciation of Judaism in Anti-Jewish Writers Cited in *Contra Apionem*." In *Josephus's Contra Apionem: Studies in Its Character and Context with a Latin Concordance to the Portion Missing in Greek,* ed. Feldman and John R. Levison. AGJU 34. Leiden: Brill, 1996.

————. *Josephus's Interpretation of the Bible.* Berkeley: University of California Press, 1998.

————. *Studies in Josephus's Rewritten Bible.* JSJSup 58. Leiden: Brill, 1998.

————. *Judean Antiquities Books 1–4.* Vol. 3 of Mason, *Flavius Josephus: Translation and Commentary.* Leiden: Brill, 2004.

Feldman, Louis H., and Gohei Hata, eds. *Josephus, the Bible and History.* Leiden: Brill, 1989.

Feldman, Louis H., and John R. Levison, eds. *Josephus's Contra Apionem: Studies in Its Character and Context with a Latin Concordance to the Portion Missing in Greek.* AGJU 34. Leiden: Brill, 1996.

Feldman, Louis H., and Heinz Schreckenberg. *Josephus: A Supplementary Bibliography.* New York: Garland, 1986.

Franxman, Thomas W. *Genesis and the Jewish Antiquities of Flavius Josephus.* BibOr 35. Rome: Biblical Institute Press, 1979.

Gafni, Isaiah. "Josephus and I Maccabees." In Feldman and Hata, *Josephus, the Bible and History,* 116-31.

Gaster, Moses. *The Asatir: The Samaritan Book of the "Secrets of Moses" Together with the Pitron or Samaritan Commentary and the Samaritan Story of the Death of Moses.* London: Royal Asiatic Society, 1927.

Gray, Rebecca. *Prophetic Figures in Late Second Temple Jewish Palestine: The Evidence from Josephus.* New York: Oxford University Press, 1993.

Hölscher, Gustav. "Josephus." In PW, 18 (1916): 1934-2000.

Krieger, Klaus-Stefan. *Geschichtsschreibung als Apologetik bei Flavius Josephus.* TANZ 9. Tübingen: Francke, 1994.

Laqueur, Richard. *Der jüdische Historiker Flavius Josephus: Ein biographischer Versuch auf neuer quellenkritischer Grundlage.* Giessen: Münchow, 1920; repr. Darmstadt: Wissenschaftliche Buchgesellschaft, 1970.

Leiman, Sid Z. "Josephus and the Canon of the Bible." In Feldman and Hata, *Josephus, the Bible and History,* 50-58.

Lindner, Helgo. *Die Geschichtsauffassung des Flavius Josephus im Bellum Judaicum.* AGJU 12. Leiden: Brill, 1972.

Mason, Steve. *Flavius Josephus on the Pharisees: A Compositional-Critical Study.* StPB 39. Leiden: Brill, 1991.

————. "Josephus, Daniel, and the Flavian House." In *Josephus and the History of the Greco-Roman Period: Essays in Memory of Morton Smith,* ed. Fausto Parente and Joseph Sievers. StPB 41. Leiden: Brill, 1994, 161-91.

————. "'Should Any Wish to Enquire Further' (*Ant.* 1.25): The Aim and Audience of Josephus's *Judean Antiquities/Life.*" In *Understanding Josephus: Seven Perspectives.* JSPSup 32. Sheffield: Sheffield Academic, 1998, 64-103.

————. *Life of Josephus.* Vol. 9 of *Flavius Josephus: Translation and Commentary.* Leiden: Brill, 2000.

————. "Josephus and His Twenty-Two Book Canon." In *The Canon Debate,* ed. Lee Martin McDonald and James A. Sanders. Peabody: Hendrickson, 2002, 110-27.

————. "Flavius Josephus in Flavian Rome: Reading on and between the Lines." In *Flavian Rome: Culture, Image, Text,* ed. Anthony J. Boyle and William J. Dominik. Leiden: Brill, 2003, 559-89.

————. "Contradiction or Counterpoint? Josephus and Historical Method." *RRJ* 6 (2003): 145-88.

————. "Introduction to the *Judean Antiquities.*" In *Flavius Josephus: Translation and Commentary,* Vol. 3: *Judean Antiquities 1–4* (2004), xiii-xxxv.

————. "Of Audience and Meaning: Reading Josephus's Bellum Judaicum in the Context of a Flavian Audience." In *Josephus and Jewish History in Flavian Rome and Beyond,* ed. Joseph Sievers and Gaia Lembi. JSJSup 104. Leiden: Brill, 2005, 71-100.

————. "The Greeks and the Distant Past in Josephus's *Judaean War.*" In *Antiquity in Antiquity: Jewish and Christian Pasts in the Greco-Roman World,* ed. Gregg Gardner and Kevin L. Osterloh. TSAJ 123. Tübingen: Mohr Siebeck, 2008, 93-130.

————. "Of Audience and Meaning: Reading Josephus's *Judean War* in the Context of a Flavian Audience." In *Josephus, Judea, and Christian Origins: Methods and Categories.* Peabody: Hendrickson, 2009, 45-68.

————, ed. *Flavius Josephus: Translation and Commentary.* 10 vols. Leiden: Brill, 2000-2007.

Migliario, Elvira. "Per l'interpretazione dell' Autobiografia di Flavio Giuseppe." *Athenaeum* 69 (1981): 92-137.

Moehring, Horst R. "Novelistic Elements in the Writings of Flavius Josephus." Diss., Chicago, 1957.

Nodet, Étienne. *Le Pentateuque de Josèphe.* Paris: Cerf, 1996.

Olitzki, Marcus. *Flavius Josephus und die Halacha.* Berlin: Itzkowski, 1885.

Pelletier, André. *Flavius Josèphe, adapteur de la lettre d'Aristée.* Paris: Klincksieck, 1962.

Rajak, Tessa. "Moses in Ethiopia: Legend and Literature." *JJS* 29 (1978): 111-22.

————. "Josephus and the 'Archaeology' of the Jews." *JJS* (1982): 465-77.

————. *Josephus, The Historian and His Society.* London: Duckworth, 1983.

Rappaport, Salomo. *Agada und Exegese bei Flavius Josephus.* Vienna: Alexander Kohut Memorial Foundation, 1930.

Rodgers, Zuleika. "Monarchy vs. Priesthood: Josephus, Justus of Tiberius, and Agrippa II." In *A Wandering Galilean: Essays in Honour of Seán Freyne,* ed. Rodgers, Margaret Daly-Denton, and Anne Fitzpatrick-McKinley. JSJSup 132. Leiden: Brill, 2009, 173-84.

————, ed. *Making History: Josephus and Historical Method.* JSJSup 110. Leiden: Brill, 2007.

Satran, David. "Daniel: Seer, Prophet, Holy Man." In *Ideal Figures in Ancient Judaism: Profiles and Paradigms,* ed. John J. Collins and George W. E. Nickelsburg. SBLSCS 12. Chico: Scholars, 1980, 33-48.

Schalit, Abraham. *Namenwörterbuch zu Flavius Josephus.* Leiden: Brill, 1968.

Schwartz, Seth. *Josephus and Judaean Politics.* Leiden: Brill, 1990.

Shutt, Robert J. H. *Studies in Josephus.* London: SPCK, 1961.

Sievers, Joseph, and Gaia Lembi, eds. *Josephus and Jewish History in Flavian Rome and Beyond.* JSJSup 104. Leiden: Brill, 2005.

Spilsbury, Paul. "*Contra Apionem* and *Antiquitates Judaicae:* Points of Contact." In Feldman and Levison, *Josephus's Contra Apionem,* 348-68.

————. *The Image of the Jew in Flavius Josephus's Paraphrase of the Bible*. TSAJ 69. Tübingen: Mohr Siebeck, 1998.

Sterling, Gregory E. *Historiography and Self-Definition: Josephos, Luke-Acts, and Apologetic Historiography*. NovTSup 64. Leiden: Brill, 1992.

Thackeray, Henry St. John. *Josephus, The Man and the Historian*. 1928; repr. New York: Ktav, 1968.

Ulrich, Eugene C. *The Qumran Text of Samuel and Josephus*. HSM 19. Missoula: Scholars, 1978.

Vincent, Louis-Hugues. "Chronologie des Oeuvres de Josèphe." *RB* 9 (1911): 366-83.

Wacholder, Ben Zion. *Eupolemus: A Study of Judaeo-Greek Literature*. HUCM 3. Cincinnati: Hebrew Union College Press, 1974.

PART 8

BIBLICAL INTERPRETATION IN ANTIQUITY

Biblical Exegesis and Interpretations from Qumran to the Rabbis

Aharon Shemesh

An examination of the Qumran scrolls clearly demonstrates that their authors invested a lot of time and thoughtful effort in the study of the Holy Scriptures and in their interpretation. This essay has two aims. First, I wish to elucidate the various types of Qumranic interpretations in general and, in particular, those that consider halakah. Second, I will try to sketch the developmental process of the creation of commentaries on the Bible from Qumran to rabbinic literature, with special attention to the literary genres and the interpretative techniques that are employed therein.

This investigation involves a number of complex methodological problems. At its center is the definition of the term "interpretation." In order to simplify this analysis, I will begin with those works that openly state that they are interpretations. These I will call "explicit interpretations." In the second part of the article I proceed to discuss what I term "implicit interpretations." My basic claim is that in not a few cases we may, through a careful linguistic and literary analysis of a given halakic text, arrive at a better understanding of the exegetical process that led to its creation, even though the text does not present itself as an interpretation of the biblical text.

Explicit Interpretations

Pesher and Midrash

Of the explicit interpretations found in Qumran, the most prominent one is the pesher — a type of literature unique to the Dead See Scrolls. No less than fifteen compositions of this type were found in the caverns by Qumran. These compositions are well-organized interpretations of defined biblical text units.[1] The name "pesher" is derived from the texts' construction. Each unit of these texts begins by quoting a biblical verse (lemma) and then is followed by its explication. The explication is signaled by the phrase "its pesher (interpretation) concerns . . . ," or "the pesher of the matter is . . ." All pesharim deal with prophetic biblical texts, and they interpret them as referring to their authors' own time or to the eschaton. The theological assumption that lies behind the pesharim is the belief that their authors had the special ability to extrapolate the secrets and historical information that are embedded in the words of the prophets, who themselves were unaware of them. Thus, *Pesher Habakkuk* states: "And as for what he says 'That he who reads may read it speedily,' its interpretation concerns the Teacher of Righteousness, to whom God has made known all the mysteries of the words of his servants the prophets" (1QpHab VI, 3-5). In fact, *Pesher Habakkuk* mentions elsewhere this concept even more explicitly, though only in a negative context. On the verse, "Look among the nations, observe well and be utterly astounded: for a work is being wrought in your days which you would not believe if it were told" (Hab 1:5), the scroll states: "The interpretation of the word concerns the traitors in the last days. They are violators of the covenant who will not believe when they hear all that is going to happen to the final generation, from the mouth of the Priest whom God has placed within the Community, to foretell the fulfillment of all the words of his servants, the prophets, by means of whom God has declared all that is going to happen to his people Israel" (1QpHab II, 5-10). Here we learn that the secret content of the words of the prophets that the Teacher of Righteousness reveals, using his ability to interpret them, concerns the future: "all that is going to happen to his people Israel." Moreover, the author explicitly calls this activity of the Teacher of Righteousness "to interpret."

The repeated use of the linguistic terminology "its pesher concerns" and "the pesher of the matter is" to present the interpretation of the prophetic vision in these compositions has led their modern editors to subsume them all under the general title "pesharim." Specific interpretations bear the titles *Pesher Nahum, Pesher Habakkuk,* and the like. Thus the word "pesher" is now used as descriptive of this unique literary genre.[2] However, in my opinion, the

1. I am referring here to the scrolls designated by scholars as "continuous pesharim." There are also "thematic pesharim." These compositions, though they share the same genre, differ from the "continuous pesharim" in that they are arranged topically rather than according to the sequence of the biblical text. They are 4Q174 *(Florilegium)* and 11Q13 *(Melchizedek)*.

2. See, e.g., Shani Berrin, "Qumran Pesharim," in *Biblical Interpretation at Qumran,* ed. Matthias Henze. SDSSRL (Grand Rapids: Eerdmans, 2005), 110-33. The various suggestions that have been given for the word's linguistic origins and its etymology were influenced also from

facts lead to a different conclusion. The very works that use the word "pesher" to describe themselves do not fit the genre designated pesher by scholars. 4Q180, first published by John Allegro,[3] begins as follows: "Pesher concerning the periods made by God, (each) Period in order to terminate [all that is] and all that will be." Here the author introduces the subject of his work and specifically declares it to be "a pesher." The same formula is repeated in line 7, where a new paragraph begins with the words "[And] a pesher concerning Azaz'el and the angels wh[o went unto the daughters of man]."[4] Notwithstanding this terminology, Devorah Dimant has argued that this pesher does not belong to the same type of composition as the pesharim on the prophetic books. Even though it shares a deterministic outlook and vocabulary, which is common in the scrolls of Qumran, its interpretations nevertheless focus on the dim past rather than the present or future like other pesharim.[5] More importantly, and contrary to the other pesharim, this author does not interpret a specific text, but rather dwells on the subject matter at hand. In the first case, the pesher is primarily interested in the "periods" of the dawn of humanity: "for all the periods of their dominion. This is the order of the son[s of Noah, from Shem to Abraham un]til he begot Isaac; the ten generations" (lines 4-5). And in the second case it deals with the tradition of Azaz'el and the angels who mingled with the daughters of men.

It is more plausible to argue that the authors of the Qumran scrolls used to name their interpretations of the Prophets "midrash." See the following quotation from 4Q174 (4QFlorilegium): "Midrash of 'Blessed the man who does not walk in their counsel of the wicked.' The interpretation of the matter [. . .]" (1-2 I, 14). Although the content of the pesher is no longer extant, it clearly comments on the first verse of the book of Psalms. Its interpretation opens with the expected language: "Its pesher is. . . ." Most importantly for our purposes, the entire section begins with the words, "Midrash of 'Blessed is the man. . . .'" With these words, the author informs the reader that he is about to present an interpretation of a verse in Psalms, which he presents with the word "midrash." It may even be that the author is quoting from a composition that he had before him. Indeed, we find the word "midrash" used to describe a type of composition elsewhere as well. Unlike other scrolls, 4Q249 has a note scribbled across its

---

the fact that it is widely used in prophetic contexts. Bilha Nitzan, *Megilat Pesher Habakkuk* (Jerusalem: Mosad Bialik, 1986), 21-33 [Hebrew].

3. John M. Allegro with A. A. Anderson, *Qumrân Cave 4: I (4Q158-4Q186)*. DJD 5 (Oxford: Clarendon, 1968), 77-80.

4. The translation is from Devorah Dimant, "The 'Pesher on the Periods' (4Q180) and 4Q181," *IOS* 9 (1979): 77-102.

5. Dimant, "The 'Pesher on the Periods,'" 91-92.

backside. The note states: "Midrash of the Book of Moses."[6] Such a note placed where it must be a description of the contents of the scroll, similar to the quotation from *Florilegium:* "Midrash of 'Blessed the man. . . .'" On the basis of the evidence, we must conclude that the use of the word "pesher" as a term to describe a type, or genre, of literature is not accurate. Rather, we should adopt the description of the authors of the scrolls themselves, who called their interpretations of Scripture "midrash." This term, "midrash," is also used as a description of the interpretations of other parts of the Holy Scriptures, and it is not unique to interpretations in which the prophetic vision is applied to the commentator's own day.[7]

In fact, even the use of phrases such as "the pesher of the matter is" and "its interpretation is" is not limited to interpretations of the prophetic books, which the author relates to the present or to an eschatological future. At least two examples testify to this. A section in 4Q159 mentions the word "pesher" twice. Moshe Bernstein suggests the following partial reconstruction of fragment 5:

> [When they ang]ered God and died. The interpretation of the matter
> the sons of Le[vi]
> in judgment. And what he says
> when Moses took [the Tent and set it outside of the camp and all those
> who would seek God] will go there. Interpretation of the m[atter (פשר
> הדבר)
> to exp]ound the Law in distress and[8]

According to this reconstruction, the passage considers the consequences of the event of the golden calf. The reference to the sons of Levi in this context reflects their role in the killing of the people who worshipped the calf (Exod 32:26-28), while the mentioning of Moses' removal of the tent of meeting to a place outside the camp is taken from the verse, "and whoever sought the Lord would go out to the tent of meeting" (Exod 33:7). The last two lines interpret the last few

---

6. Joseph Baumgarten et al., *Qumran Cave 4: XXV, Halakhic Texts.* DJD 35 (Oxford: Clarendon, 1999), 7; see also the introduction, 1.

7. For a general discussion of the use of the verb דרש in the scrolls, see Steven D. Fraade, "Looking for Legal Midrash at Qumran," in *Biblical Perspectives: Early Use and Interpretation of the Bible in Light of the Dead Sea Scrolls,* ed. Michael E. Stone and Esther G. Chazon. STDJ 28 (Leiden: Brill, 1998), 59-79, and the bibliog. listed in n. 1.

8. Moshe J. Bernstein, "4Q159 Fragment 5 and the 'Desert Theology' of the Qumran Sect," in *Emanuel: Studies in the Hebrew Bible, Septuagint and Dead Sea Scrolls in Honor of Emanuel Tov,* ed. Shalom M. Paul, Robert A. Kraft, Lawrence H. Schiffman, and Weston W. Fields. VTSup 94 (Leiden: Brill, 2003), 43-56.

words of the verse: "*pesher hadabar* [. . .] to expound the Law in distress," etc. According to Bernstein, the Yahad's use of Moses' leaving the camp is meant to bolster its ideological seclusion in the desert. In this vein, he explains the use of the term "pesher" to refer to an actualization of a past biblical event. While Bernstein's interpretation is acceptable, it should be admitted that one can find no clue in the text itself (or what is left of it) to attest to its being the subject of a pesher (either about the present reality of the sect or about the eschatological future). We may, therefore, conclude that the meaning of the words פשר הדבר/ *pesher hadabar* can only mean "the interpretation of the matter" or "its interpretation is."

The second example further clarifies my argument. The following passage comes from a composition that interprets select parts of the book of Genesis (4Q252).

> Blessings of Jacob: "Reuben, you are my first-born and the first-fruits of my manhood, pre-eminent in stature and pre-eminent in strength; you seethe like water; you shall not enjoy supremacy. You mounted your father's bed; then you defiled it, he had lain in it "Its interpretation (פשרו): That he re-proved him, because he lay with Bilhah, his concubine. And, he said: "You are my first-born" [. . .] Reuben is the first-fruits[9]

After the superscription "Jacob's blessings," the scroll apparently presents the interpretation of Jacob's blessings to each of his sons before his death, although the extant fragments contain only parts of the blessing to Reuben and Judah. The passage dealing with Reuben's blessing forms an organized interpretation. It opens with a lemma (a quotation of the interpreted verse) and a statement about the verse's subject: "That he reproved him, because he lay with Bilhah, his concubine." Following this, a detailed interpretation is given on each part of the verse. Two sections have survived here: "And, he said: 'You are my first-born,'" followed by "Reuben is the first-fruits," an obvious interpretation of the words ראשית אוני. The author employs the word פשרו to establish that the subject of the legacy to Reuben is an admonishment for his act with Bilhah. Clearly this pesher has nothing to do with the author's own day, nor does it contain any eschatological reference to the future end time. Rather, it is a simple interpretation that explains the reason why Jacob admonished Reuben at a time when he was expected to bless him.[10]

---

9. 4Q252 (4QCommentary Genesis A) 5 IV, 4-7; George Brooke et al., *Qumran Cave 4: XVII, Parabiblical Texts, Part 3*. DJD 22 (Oxford: Clarendon, 1996).

10. Admittedly, the scroll's interpretation of Judah's blessing contains classical sectarian es-chatological elements. The scroll explains the biblical words of Gen 49:10: "The 'Ruler' (מחוקק)

The Exegetical Formula "for A is B"

I now wish to focus the discussion on the interpretative formula that is used in the last passage of 4Q252, which was quoted in the paragraph above. In his interpretation of the words "Reuben, you are my first-born, first-fruits of my manhood," the author is saying that "Reuben is the first." Probably the sentence is cut off at the end. However, for our purposes, the key point here is the formula "A equals (is) B." This formula is ubiquitous in the pesharim. A good example that demonstrates how it functions is provided in *Pesher Habakkuk*. The pesher deals with the explanation of the verse, "For the lawlessness against Lebanon shall cover you, the destruction of beasts shall overwhelm you, for crimes against men and wrongs against lands, against cities and all their inhabitants" (Hab 2:17).

> The interpretation of the passage (פשר הדבר) concerns the Wicked Priest — to pay him his due inasmuch as he dealt wickedly with the poor ones; for "Lebanon" is the council of the community, and the "beasts" are the simple ones of Judah, those who observe the Law — whom God will sentence to complete destruction because he plotted to destroy completely the poor ones. (1QpHab XII, 2-6)[11]

The general subject of this homily is the Wicked Priest: God will repay him and give him his just reward for plotting to destroy the poor completely. I am interested here in two particular interpretations included in the pesher: "for 'Lebanon' is the council of the community" and "the 'beasts' are [the simple ones] of Judah." The author explains to the reader that biblical "Lebanon" is identical to the council of the Community and that the "beasts" symbolize the people of Judah. The earliest use of this exegetical formula "for A is B" can be found in Isa 9:14: "The elder and honorable man is the head; and the prophet that teaches lies, he is the tail," which translates the preceding verses: "Therefore, the LORD cut off from Israel, head and tail, branch and rush, in one day."[12]

This formula is not unique to the pesharim. Indeed, it is employed by other

---

is the covenant of the kingdom, and the [thou]sands of Israel are the 'standards' until the arrival of the righteous messiah, scion of David, for to him and his seed was given the covenant of the kingdom of his people for eternal generations" (4Q252 6 V, 2-4). Furthermore, in line 5 the "men of the community" (אנשי היחד) are mentioned. Surprisingly, the introductory formula פשר הדבר ("its interpretation") is missing here.

11. Maurya P. Horgan, *Pesharim: Qumran Interpretations of Biblical Books.* CBQMS 8 (Washington: Catholic Biblical Association, 1979), 20.

12. Moshe H. Goshen-Gottstein, "Hebrew Syntax and the History of the Bible Text," *Text* 8 (1973): 100-106.

scrolls to interpret biblical verses, and it is used in halakic contexts as well. Several of these instances can be found in 4Q251 *(Midrash Mishpatim)*.[13]

In the first lines of fragment 9 (1-3) it is written:

[Let no man eat grain, wi]ne, or oil unless [he gave the priest] their first-fruits. And let no man delay the (offering) of the first-fruits and the must (מלאה), for [wine and oil] is the first of the must, [and] the grain is the *dema'a.*

The first halakah prohibits the consumption of the new crop before the firstfruits gift is given to the priest. Therefore, stresses the second halakah, the owner should not withhold the gifts but promptly give them to the priest. The ruling in this passage is based on Exod 22:28, "You shall not delay to offer the first of thy must (מלאתך), and of thy *dema'a* (דמעך)." The author explains the relation between his halakic formulation and the verse in the following sentence: "for [the wine and oil] is the first of the must and the grain is the *dema'a.*" As the meaning of the biblical מלאה and דמע is obscure, the author replaced these terms in his halakic statement, the first with "wine and oil" and the second with "grain." The author's interpretation of the verse reveals his assumption that the reader of his day will not understand its meaning, therefore he translates them: 'for [the wine and oil] is the first of the מלאה and the grain is the דמע." Note that this is the exact same formula of "for A is B," which we found in the pesharim above. However, unlike the pesher that interprets and actualizes the words of the prophet, this scroll provides a straightforward interpretation that merely replaces a difficult word with a known and clearer word. Notice that, in fact, the text that is being interpreted is not the biblical verse. Rather, it is the first halakah: "one must not eat grain, wine, and oil." The author is not arguing that מלאה (which is mentioned in the verse) is wine and oil and that the דמע (also mentioned in the verse) is the grain. Instead, he explains that the wine and oil mentioned in the halakah are equivalent to the biblical מלאה and the grain to the דמע.

In light of this finding, I have suggested a reconstruction of another passage of 4Q251 in a similar fashion.[14] Only a few words have survived from fragment 13. According to my reconstruction, this is a revision of Exod 21:22-25 and its interpretation. Here is the passage and its reconstruction:

01 [if a man deals a blow to
02 a pregnant woman and her children are aborted, but (other) harm does not occur

---

13. See Aharon Shemesh, "4Q251: *Midrash Mishpatim,*" DSD 12 (2005): 280-302.
14. Shemesh, "4Q251: *Midrash Mishpatim.*"

1 he is to be fined as im[posed for him by her spous]e,

but 2 he is to give it (only) according to ass[essment. For the assessment

i]s (by) reckoning (]כי הבקשה הי[א פלילים).

3 But if harm should occur, then you are to give life in plac]e of life

The Torah states: "When men fight, and one of them pushes a pregnant woman and a miscarriage results, but no other harm ensues, the one responsible shall surely be fined as the woman's husband may demand of him, the payment to be based on reckoning (ונתן בפלילים). But if other damage ensues, the penalty shall be life for life, eye for eye, tooth for tooth, hand for hand, foot for foot, burn for burn, wound for wound, bruise for bruise" (Exod 21:22-25). Like its counterpart in the Bible, the scroll's rewritten version of these verses begins with a description of the incident: a pregnant woman is hurt. Then it rules in two possible scenarios: in the event of no further harm and in the event that other harm ensues. The author includes a linguistic comment in the rewriting of the verses — "For בקשה is פלילים." Such a comment is necessary given that the word פלילים is truly rare and difficult to explain. Semantically, the word בקשה ("request") in our scroll should be interpreted as "inquiry and examination," as in the verse "The matter was investigated (ויבוקש הדבר) and found to be so" (Esth 2:23). Using these guidelines, the author explains that the compensation promised by the Torah ("shall surely be fined as the woman's husband may demand of him") should be preceded "by a request," after inquiry and examination. Just as we saw in the previous example, the author does not interpret the biblical word פלילים, but rather focuses on the word "request" (בקשה), which is used in the halakah. The author seeks to clarify that this word, which he assumes is clear to his readers, is the interpretation/translation of the biblical word (פלילים).

The "for A is B" interpretative formula that characterized the interpretation of the scrolls is also used by the sages in their halakic (legal) midrashim, though in its negative mirrored structure: "אין א אלא ב" (best translated as "A is none but B"). In rabbinic literature (as in the example cited above from *Pesher Habakkuk*), the first word of the formula "A" is a biblical quote, and the second word "B" is its translation. Saul Lieberman considers this formula to be the basic structure of midrash. Its role in exegesis is "to explain the *realia* and to render the rare and difficult terms in a simpler Hebrew, or, sometimes, in Aramaic."[15] Indeed, one can find a parallel to our second example (כי הבקשה היא פלילים) in rabbinic literature. A baraita in the *Mekilta* (the tannaitic legal

15. Saul Lieberman, *Hellenism in Jewish Palestine: Studies in the Literary Transmission, Beliefs and Manners of Palestine in the I Century* B.C.E.–IV *Century* C.E. Texts and Studies of the Jewish Theological Seminary of America 18 (New York: Jewish Theological Seminary, 1950), 48.

midrash to Exodus) states as follow: "'According as the woman's husband may impose on him.' Does this mean whatever he pleases? But it says: 'The payment to be based on *pelilim*,' and *pelilim* means judges, as it says: 'In our enemies' own estimation *(pelilim)*' (Deut 32:31). And it also says: 'If a man sins against a man, the Lord shall judge him (ופללו אלוהים)'" (1 Sam 2:25).[16] I am not claiming that there is a literary connection between the version that appears in the scrolls and that which appears in the midrash. However, I do believe that the comparison demonstrates that the scrolls attest to the first stages of fixed interpretative formulas pertaining to halakic matters that would later become *midot*, or standard hermeneutical principles, in rabbinic midrashim.

Explanations for difficult words in markedly legal contexts can be found in a unique section among the remains of the *Damascus Document* from Cave 4. This section is a nearly continuous interpretation of Leviticus 13, which discusses the instructions given to the priest that enable him to determine whether various types of lepers are pure or impure. Like its biblical counterpart, the scroll also begins with the case of leprosy of the skin and then continues with cases of leprosy of the head and the beard. As we might expect, the paragraph quotes the first verse of the chapter: "When a man has on the skin of his body a swelling or a scab or a bright spot, and it becomes an infection of leprosy on the skin of his body. . . ." The interpretation immediately follows: "a swelling is שומה ('tumor'), and the rash (ספחת) is a blow by wood or stone, or any wound" (4Q272 1 I, 1-2).[17] This verse is truly difficult. Throughout history, commentators have deliberated over the identification of the three afflictions that are mentioned: שאת *(se'et),* ספחת *(sapahat),* and בהרת *(baheret).*[18] The scroll's author clarifies the matter by substituting a commonly understood word for an unclear word. According to the restoration that is suggested here, the scroll's translation of the biblical word שאת is exactly the same as that found in the ancient targumim, *Neofiti, Pseudo-Jonathan,* and the *Samaritan* — all three replace the word with שומה. Similarly, all three translate the word ספחת as קליפי, which, apparently, means a wound scab. I believe the author has this in mind when he interprets the phrase "a blow by wood or stone or any wound," that is, the scab that develops from the injury that looks like [an addition] — ספחת on the skin.

It is astonishing to see just how structurally similar this section in the scroll is to the sages' homily on the verse, notwithstanding the fact that their interpre-

---

16. *Mekilta Nezikin* 8. A similar explanation was provided by *Onkelos* and *Pseudo-Jonathan,* who translated בפלילים ונתן :דיניא מימר על דיתן.

17. The translation reflects the new and improved readings of Prof. Elisha Qimron in the new edition he is preparing of the *Damascus Document.*

18. Jacob Milgrom, *Leviticus 1–16.* AB 3 (New York: Doubleday, 1991), 773-75.

tation is different. We read in *Sifra,* the Tannaitic legal midrash on Leviticus (*Neg.* 1.1):

> "*Se'et*" is *se'et,* "*baheret*" is *baheret*
> "*Sapaḥat*" is secondary to *baheret,* מראה עמוק ("that which looks deep")
> — secondary to *se'et*

Like the scroll, the midrash explains each of the details in the verse one by one. The explanation seems odd because in both of its first sections the midrash merely repeats the biblical text. However, its meaning is clear in light of the following Mishnah in tractate *Nega'im* (1:1), "The sights of *Nega'im* — two that are four — the *Baheret,* strong as snow, and in its weaker form (lit., 'secondary to it') it looks like the whitewash of the temple, and the *Se'et* that looks like an egg's membrane, and in its weaker form (lit., 'secondary to it') as a white wood, words of Rabbi Meir. And the Sages say the *Se'et* looks like white wood, and in its weaker form it looks like an egg's membrane." The Mishnah clarifies that both forms of the key afflictions are the *Baheret* and the *Se'et,* while the *Sapaḥat* is nothing but a weaker form of the *Baheret.*

The *Damascus Document* continues the description of the halakot that consider diagnosing leprosy in accordance with the biblical text. However, its author adds a theological or medical explanation of the disease to the Torah's instructions. According to the text, leprosy develops as a result of "the spirit that comes and takes hold of the artery, and the blood returns upwards and downwards," and its cure is reached when "the spirit of life goes up and down, and the flesh has grown until the blood returns to the artery" (4Q272 1 I, 2-8).

One of the symptoms of leprosy that is described in the Torah is that black hair turns yellow. The scroll explains this characteristic with a botanical parable: "For it is like a plant under which there is a worm which cuts its root so that its fruit turns pale" (lines 16-17).[19] In addition, it adds a rationale for another biblical command. The Torah commands the leper to shave his hair, except for the area of the scale (Lev 13:33). This is how this case is explained in the *Damascus Document:* "And what he said, 'The priest shall order them to shave their flesh head, but not to shave their ringworm,' it is so that the priest can count the dead with living hairs and see whether living hairs have been added to the dead ones during the seven days, then he is impure; but if living hairs have not been added to the dead ones and the artery is full of blood, and the spirit of life goes up and down through it, that disease is healed" (4Q266 6 I, 8-13).

---

19. Joseph M. Baumgarten, "The 4Q Zadokite Fragments on Skin Disease," *JJS* 41 (1990): 153-65.

Complex Interpretations

Apparently, there are a good number of "explicit" interpretations of biblical instructions pertaining to halakah in the scrolls. Nevertheless, all the examples dealt with to this point are very simple in their form and content. The "A is B" formula explanations are merely a translation, a replacement of a difficult biblical word with another one better understood by the readers. None of the examples we have presented thus far contain complex interpretations similar to the ones that characterize rabbinic halakic midrashim. In other words, they do not detail and reveal the processes and deliberations of their interpretations and lack the dialectic nature of the later rabbinic midrash, which I define as "complex interpretation." Such interpretations are rare in the scrolls, though not completely absent. The examples that we will consider here are indeed exceptional. However, the few cases in which the authors of the scrolls reveal their interpretative methodology and reflect on how they arrived at their unique halakic positions are of great value. Once elucidated, it is but a short step to determine the interpretative stages that lie behind many other halakic rules, which henceforth have remained unclear. Two illuminating examples can be found in 4QMMT (the *Halakhic Letter*).

The following passage has been preserved in an especially poor state, and despite the reconstruction efforts of its editors, it remains very difficult to comprehend. Notwithstanding the difficulty, the subject of this passage is clear enough: the passage discusses where and how far from the temple one can slaughter a beast for the purpose of eating it, without offering it in the temple as a *shlemim* ("well-being") sacrifice.

> [And concerning] that it is written: [if a person slaughters inside the camp, or slaughters] outside the camp cattle or sheep or goat: for [. . . in the northern part of the camp]. And we are of the opinion that the sanctuary [is the "tent of meeting"] and that Jerusalem is the "camp," and that "outside the camp" [is outside Jerusalem], that is the encampment of their settlements. It is "outside the c[amp" where one should . . . the purification-offering and] take out the ashes of [the] altar and bu[rn the purification-offering. For Jerusalem] is the place which [he has chosen] from among all the tribes [of Israel . . .]. (B 27-33)

The starting point for this discussion is the verses quoted at the beginning of the passage. "If anyone of the house of Israel slaughters an ox or sheep or goat in the camp, or does so outside the camp and does not bring it to the entrance of the tent of meeting to present it as an offering to the LORD before the LORD's tabernacle, bloodguilt shall be imputed to that man" (Lev 17:3-4). The simple meaning of this command is that one may not eat meat unless it is *shlemim* meat that was slaughtered in the tent of meeting. The author's opponents did not follow this command, because they believed that the Torah intended to limit this law's efficacy to the period of the Israelites' wanderings in the desert. In their view, once the Israelites entered the land of Israel and built the temple in God's chosen site, God permitted them to slaughter animals for eating purposes at any place (Deut 12:20-32).

Clearly, the author of MMT is signaling his disagreement with this interpretation. In his view, the limitations on slaughtering animals for eating purposes remain even in the land of Israel. Specifically, he argues that the halakah in Leviticus ought to be implemented in the land of Israel. He clarifies: "We think that the temple [is the tent of meeting] and Jerusalem is a camp and outside the camp [is outside of Jerusalem]." Therefore one must not slaughter for the purposes of eating in any place that is equivalent to "the camp" or "outside the camp." Not only does the author present his interpretation of the Levitical verse, he goes further to prove it and to substantiate the veracity of his interpretation. As some scholars have noted, the sentence "and] take out the ashes of [the] altar and bu[rn the purification-offering" sets out to prove that the meaning of "outside the camp" in Leviticus means "outside of Jerusalem." The author derives this from other places in the Pentateuch where the term "outside the camp" appears. In Lev 6:4, the Torah commands about the serving priest: "He shall then take off his vestments and put on other vestments and carry the ashes outside the camp to a clean place." This is the same place in which the Torah commands to burn different parts of certain sacrifices. Such are, for example, the remains of the *ḥaṭṭ'at* ("sin offering") the high priest should bring in case he sins unintentionally. The Torah commands that "all the rest of the bull he shall carry to a clean place outside the camp to the ash heap and burn it up in a wood fire; it shall be burned on the ash heap" (Lev 4:12). In this case, so argues the author of MMT, everyone agrees that the ashes are to be poured outside of Jerusalem. This is therefore a proof that "outside the camp" equals "outside Jerusalem."[20] Such interpretative claims, which are based on a comparison of different commands in the Torah and which clarify one subject with the assistance of another, are found commonly in the halakic midrashim of the rabbis.

Here is a second example from 4QMMT:

And concerning the practice of illegal marriage that exists among the people: (this practice exists) despite their being so[ns] of holy [seed], as is written,

---

20. David Henshke, "The Holiness of Jerusalem: Between the Rabbis and the Sectarian Law," *Tarbiz* 67 (1998): 5-28. [Hebrew]

Israel is holy. And concerning his (i.e., Israel's) [clean ani]mal, it is written that one must not let it mate with another species; and concerning his clothes [it is written that they should not] be of mixed stuff; and he must not sow his field and vine[yard with mixed specie]s. Because they (Israel) are holy, and the sons of Aaron are [most holy.] But you know that some of the priests and [the laity mingle with each other, and they] unite with each other and pollute the [holy] seed [as well as] their own [seed] with women whom they are forbidden to marry. (B 75-82)

In this passage, the author complains about a certain type of mixed marriage common among the priests, which he deems forbidden and which he opposes.[21] To justify his halakic point of view, the author uses a sort of *kal vachomer*:[22] if the Torah forbids mating pure beasts with impure ones, wearing *shatnez*, and seeding the field and the vineyard with hybrid seeds, how much more should this apply to the sons of Aaron, who are the holiest ones. Therefore, they must not marry these women lest they contaminate the holy line. Perhaps the very need to use *kal vachomer* supports Qimron's and Strugnell's arguments that the kind of mixed marriage being debated in this passage is marriage between priests and their daughters with other Israelites rather than marriages between Jews and Gentiles. Otherwise, the author would not have required the principle of *kal vachomer*. Instead, he could have quoted verses from the Torah that forbid it (such as Exod 34:15-16). Clearly, the need to use *kal vachomer* arose from the Bible's failure to prohibit intermarriage between priests and nonpriests. This seems to have been the halakic position of the priestly sects, whereas this passage teaches us that the rest of the people as well as some of the priests were not strict about it.

Another interesting example attesting to complex interpretation in halakic matters can be found in the *Damascus Document*. In the following paragraph, the author blames the "builders of the barrier," who are the enemies of the Yahad, because they are sinning in several halakic matters. One of these is the following:

And they marry each his brothers' or sisters' daughters, but Moses said: "To your mother's sister you may not draw near, for she is your mother's near re-

---

21. Elisha Qimron and John Strugnell, eds., *Qumran Cave 4: V, Miqṣat Ma'aśe ha-Torah*. DJD 10 (Oxford: Clarendon, 1994), 55, are of the view that MMT condemns the marriage of priests with nonpriests. Joseph Baumgarten ("The 4Q Zadokite Fragments"), on the other hand, believes that the subject here is intermarriage between Jews and non-Jews. See my discussion further below.

22. This is an *a fortiori* inference, one of the classical hermeneutical principles of rabbinic exegesis.

lation." Now the precept of incest is written from the point of view of males, but the same (law) applies to women, so if a brother's daughter uncovers the nakedness of the brother of her father, it is a (forbidden) close relationship. (CD V, 9-11)

The author of the *Damascus Document* objects to the custom of his opponents that allows a man to marry the daughter of a brother or a sister. He claims that such marriages are forbidden and that they are included among the forbidden marriages between relatives that are clearly banned in the Torah. One of the bans prohibits marrying one's aunt: "Do not uncover the nakedness of your mother's sister, for she is your mother's flesh" (Lev 18:13). The author casts the interpretative principle that leads to the prohibition of marrying the daughter of one's brother or sister as follows: "The precept of incest is written from the point of view of males, but the same (law) applies to women." In other words, although the Torah formulated its ban as if it was speaking to a man, one still must apply the ban to women as well. Thus, just as the Torah banned a man from marrying his mother's sister, so also a woman is banned from marrying her father's brother. Since this is the same case as that of a man marrying his brother's daughter, such pairing is prohibited according to the Torah. As I have demonstrated elsewhere, the above argument is not merely an *ad hoc* local claim but was an interpretative principle in the halakah of Qumran.[23]

Intermediate Summary

To this point, we have shown that the most characteristic interpretations of Qumranic literature are indeed those known as pesharim. These works provide continuous interpretations of long textual units. As we have shown above, halakic compositions also include exegetical passages. However, these interpretations are isolated in nature and thus do not provide consistent interpretations of entire chapters, let alone of entire books. Both Menahem Kister and Steven Fraade have considered this fact and have offered different (though not necessarily contradicting) explanations.[24] Kister believes that the phenomenon stems from the gradual transition from the biblical to the postbiblical era.

---

23. Aharon Shemesh, *Punishments and Sins: From Scripture to the Rabbis* (Jerusalem: Magnes, 2003), 16-17. [Hebrew]

24. Fraade, "Looking for Legal Midrash at Qumran"; Menahem Kister, "A Common Heritage: Biblical Interpretation at Qumran and Its Implications," in Stone and Chazon, *Biblical Perspectives*, 101-11.

The development of a formal interpretation to Scripture is linked to the process of dissociation from the biblical world, since creating interpretation requires the author to situate himself outside of the world of the interpreted text. The pesharim were developed first, since they were not explanations of the biblical text itself, but rather an attempt to discover the applied reality of the prophecy in the present or the eschaton. Over time, interpretations of the prophetic texts and biblical poetry began to be developed. However, there was no parallel production of interpretations of the biblical prose or of the Torah's halakic portions until the creation of the midrash in the rabbinic period. Fraade, on the other hand, argues that the lack of midrash halakah in Qumran is intentional. Even in places where it is clear that the sect's halakah stems from biblical exegesis, the sect's authors consistently avoided presenting it as such and hid from the reader both the way in which they derived the halakah from the text and the fact that the halakah is a result of their study of the biblical text. The reason for this is ideological. It stems from the sect's belief that the authority of the new halakot — the ones that are called "hidden" — derives from divine revelation, as opposed to the view of the sages, who developed the concept of Oral Torah and emphasized the power of interpretation as the source for halakah.

Our discussion here joins and supports Fraade's explanation. Above, I presented a few examples of explicit halakic dialectical give-and-take in the scrolls. All of these examples, which lay out their interpretative logic, share one thing in common: they are found in polemical contexts. There is a good reason for this: Qumran writers do not tend to reveal their exegetical considerations when speaking to their own community members. Doing so would undermine their authority and encourage their audience to suggest alternative competing explanations. Rather, the halakah is presented as a religious imperative, something over which there can be no deliberation. However, it is quite another matter to convince someone who not only does not accept one's authority but has one's own interpretation that is different and which contains its own rationale. Here, the only way to convince the other party is to lay bare the interpretative principles that lie behind one's interpretation. Not surprisingly, then, such complex interpretations only appear in polemical works, where the sect is arguing with other groups. 4QMMT is a prime example of a polemical work in which we find complex interpretations. Its author contrasts his own halakic positions with those of his opponents and attempts to persuade the reader of the correctness of his method. The same applies to the example quoted above from the *Damascus Document*. It is located in the admonition part of the composition, and its context is explicitly polemical as it is directed against the Pharisees, "the Builders of the barrier."

Implicit Interpretations

General Observations

It appears, then, that most of the halakic material in the scrolls does not present itself explicitly as an interpretation of the biblical text. Nevertheless, given what we have demonstrated thus far about the interpretative practices of the Qumran authors, it behooves us to attempt to extract the exegetical techniques and interpretative strategies of these authors even in cases where they are not presented as interpretations. This I call "implicit interpretations."

There are two main styles of halakic writing in the literature of Qumran: the abstract halakic style that is typical of many sections of the *Damascus Document* and the rewritten Bible style most prominently found in the *Temple Scroll*.[25] With regard to the rewritten Bible style, the writer's exegetical technique is nearly identical to its literary genre. Bernstein has discerned some of the exegetical activities of these authors. When rewriting the Bible, the author chooses the material he seeks to revise, reorganizes it, adds to it, deletes other parts, and replaces some words with others.[26] In addition, we must add the main practice that is used in the *Temple Scroll* for halakic matters, which is collecting material regarding a specific subject from all of its attestations in the Torah into one text, while resolving and reconciling the contradictions and differences that exist between the various passages. A good example for the *Temple Scroll*'s technique is its presentation of the Deuteronomic law permitting those living at a distance from the temple to slaughter sheep and cattle for consumption (Deuteronomy 12). To the biblical injunction, the *Temple Scroll* adds the obligation to cover the blood with dust (LIII, 4-8). This is taken from Lev 17:13, where it relates to a captured bird or wild animal. The Deuteronomic verse, on the other hand, speaks of consuming cattle. The *Temple Scroll*'s incorporation of Leviticus's command to "cover it with dust" into the Deuteronomic halakah extends this obligation to cattle as well. Yigal Yadin termed this practice "harmonization,"[27] while Jacob Milgrom preferred to call it "homogenization."[28]

---

25. The use of rewritten Bible as a genre is not restricted to Qumran literature. Flavius Josephus's account of Moses' constitution in his *Antiquities* is also essentially a rewritten Bible. For a phenomenological discussion of the rewritten bible phenomenon, see Hindy Najman, *Seconding Sinai: The Development of Mosaic Discourse in Second Temple Judaism.* JSJSup 77 (Leiden: Brill, 2003).

26. Moshe Bernstein, "Interpretation of Scriptures," in *EDSS*, 1:376-83 (here 379).

27. Yigael Yadin, *The Temple Scroll* (Jerusalem: Israel Exploration Society, 1977), 1:74-75.

28. Jacob Milgrom, "The Qumran Cult: Its Exegetical Principles," in *Temple Scroll Studies*, ed. George J. Brooke. JSPSup 7 (Sheffield: Sheffield Academic, 1989), 165-80.

All of this is achieved without changing the basic structure of the biblical text. Moreover, the rewritten text never reveals itself as such; it always presents itself as the authoritative (biblical) text, never as an interpretation that refers to another text.

As for the halakic compositions written in the other genre, that of the *Damascus Document,* the gap between these and Scripture is so vast that many scholars have argued that one of these scrolls' defining characteristics is their disassociation from the biblical text. Nonetheless, it is quite obvious that the majority of the halakic details in the scrolls are based on their authors' reading and interpretations of Scripture. Much scholarly effort is invested in uncovering the biblical exegetical process that lay behind these rulings. Thus for example, Louis Ginzberg has argued that the *Damascus Document's* condemnation of his opponents' practice of לקחת שתי נשים בחייהם ("taking two wives in their lives," CD IV, 20-21) is the result of his interpretation to the biblical prohibition (Lev 18:18) "ואשה אל אחותה לא תקח לצרר לגלות ערותה עליה בחייה" ("and you shall not take a woman as a rival wife to her sister, uncovering her nakedness while her sister is yet alive"). The author of CD read the word אחותה ("her sister") as referring not to her biological sister but to any other woman. "Such reading is linguistically quite possible and indeed occurs in Scripture several times with this meaning, e.g. Exod. 26:5, 6, 17."[29]

It should be stressed at this point that the Qumranic writers themselves provide no clues as to the exegetical process whereby the halakic details were derived. Even if scholars can provisionally reconstruct the exegetical process, in any event, as presented, the intent of the halakah as stated is to establish its existence rather than to reveal to the reader how it was created. That is to say, the scrolls are not meant to, and do not function as a commentary.

Scrolls' Organization as Commentary

Having said all the above, I wish now to present an interesting literary phenomenon found in not a few compositions from Qumran that has a strong exegetical aspect. In two articles published in recent years, I have shown that some of the scrolls are organized according to the sequence of textual units in the Torah, notwithstanding the fact that their language is nonbiblical and their style mimics that of abstract halakot.[30] Examples of this type include, in my

29. Louis Ginzberg, *An Unknown Jewish Sect* (New York: Jewish Theological Seminary, 1976; German ed. New York, 1922), 19.

30. "4Q251: *Midrash Mishpatim,*" *DSD* 12 (2005): 280-302; "The Scriptural Background of

opinion, 4Q251 (4QHalakhah[a]), as well as the sect's Penal Code, which appears in the *Rule of the Community* (1QS 6:24–7:25) and in the *Damascus Document*.[31] Recognizing this phenomenon may be the key to uncovering the interpretative background of a number of the halakot in the scrolls. I will here present but one example to support my contention.

The Penal Code of the Qumran sectarians is a list comprising thirty or so sins along with their punishments. Some differences exist between the two versions of the Penal Code in the *Damascus Document* and in the *Rule of the Community* regarding the duration of the punitive period of exclusion associated with specific sins, but otherwise they are nearly identical. The sins listed and the order in which they appear are also identical. This fact suggests that the ordering and grouping of sins and punishments are not random and that the rationale behind them should be investigated. In my article mentioned above, I argued that the Penal Code is based on three biblical pericopes that deal with the holiness of the people of Israel and their dwelling place.[32] Violators of these laws endanger the holiness of the community and therefore need to be excluded. In other words, the Penal Code is actually the Yahad's self-manifestation of being the holy congregation. Here I wish to concentrate on one section of the Penal Code. Clauses 19-23 of the Penal Code comprise a unit in and of itself that deals with the issue of modesty. Three of the clauses (the first, middle, and last) deal with a case of a person who walks entirely or partially naked.

1. And whoever walks about naked in front of his fellow, without needing to, shall be punished for three months.
2. And the person who spits in the course of a meeting of the Many shall be punished thirty days.
3. And whoever takes out his "hand" from under his clothes, or if these are rags which allow his nakedness to be seen, he will be punished thirty days.
4. And whoever guffaws improperly and makes his voice to be heard shall be punished thirty days.
5. And whoever takes his left hand out (of his garment) to gesticulate with it (while speaking) shall be punished ten days. (1QS, VII, 12-16)

What is the connection between walking nude and spitting in the course of the meeting of the Many, or the ban on laughing out loud? The answer lies in the bib-

---

the Penal Code in The Rule of the Community and Damascus Document," *DSD* 15 (2008): 191-224.

31. Joseph M. Baumgarten et al., eds., *Qumran Cave 4: XIII, The Damascus Document (4Q266-273)*. DJD 18 (Oxford: Clarendon, 1996), 76-77 (on 4Q270) and 162-63 (on 4Q266).

32. "The Scriptural Background of the Penal Code."

lical background of the list. It is my opinion that this series of prohibitions is based on the sect's interpretation of Deut 23:11-15. The Torah commands that someone who has nocturnal emission must leave the camp and also that anyone who needs to relieve himself should do it outside the camp. The rationale for these two injunctions is found in v. 15. "Since the LORD your God moves about in your camp, to protect you, and to deliver your enemies to you; let your camp be holy, let him not find anything unseemly among you (ולא יראה בך ערות דבר) and turn away from you." Undoubtedly the authors of the penal code saw the phrase ולא יראה בך ערות דבר as the source for the offenses in this group of provisions. Josephus's description of the care taken by the Essenes not to expose their skin to the sun while relieving themselves indicates that they interpreted this injunction literally: namely, as a prohibition against exposing their nakedness.[33] Thus, the source of the clauses dealing with exposing one's body in the Penal Code is this biblical passage. No wonder the Yahad read these verses concerning the holiness of the camp as referring to their own dwelling place. They saw themselves as the holy congregation, coined their residence "the holy camp," and described מושב הרבים ("the meeting sessions of the Many") as the place where the "holy angels are in their council."[34] If we recognize that these verses from Deuteronomy are the source of the sections in the Penal Code, we can explain (with the help of the following midrash) the inclusion of clause 20 about "spitting at the meeting of the Many" in this unit rather than in the one before it, which deals with procedures of these meetings, where we might have expected it to appear. The phrase "so the camp is to be holy" is interpreted in the *Sifre*, the legal Midrash to Deuteronomy, as follows: "'let your camp be holy' — make it holy. Hence the Sages have said: One should not enter the Temple Mount carrying his staff, sandals, purse, or even the dust upon his feet" (*Sifre Deuteronomy* 258). The word "hence" (מכאן אמרו) in the midrash refers to *m. Ber.* 9:5, where this injunction concludes with the following addition: "And one should not use [the Temple Mount] for a shortcut." And spitting [there likewise is forbidden, as is proven by an argument] *a minori ad majus* (מקל וחומר). Apparently, like the homilist of this midrash, the editor of the Penal Code had a similar tradition that connected the ban on spitting in the holy place to the verse "let your camp be holy," with which the other clauses that deal with seeing the genitalia are connected — "let him not find anything unseemly among you." Thus, we have identified the reason the author intuitively included this clause within the framework of this group of

---

33. *J.W.* 2.8.9 (2.148-49).

34. CD, XV, 15-18; 1QSa II, 8-9. For other aspects of this conception, see Aharon Shemesh, "'The Holy Angels are in their Council': The Exclusion of Deformed Persons from Holy Places in Qumranic and Rabbinic Literature," *DSD* 4 (1997): 179-206.

bans that are derived from the same verses, and not in the previous unit that deals with appropriate behavior during the meeting of the Many.

The Implicit Midrash: Between the Scrolls and the Mishnah

The example that we have discussed here and others that I discussed elsewhere[35] teach us that, at times, texts, which at first seem to be entirely disassociated from the Bible, are actually structured on the basis of a whole set of continuous biblical verses. This discovery allows us to understand better the way in which the authors of the scrolls interpreted these verses. It was the associations generated by these verses in the minds of the scrolls' authors that dictated the concoction of laws that were molded into a homogenous unit. This phenomenon is even more interesting in light of the fact that these texts usually do not mention the verses on which they are based. This means that at least in some cases, such as the Penal Code, the laws were indeed created in different contexts and only later were brought together and reorganized by the current authors. Apparently, the authors of the scrolls memorized the biblical text and could recall it at will. Thus, it served them as a natural framework upon which they could hang and accordingly arrange the interpretative and legal materials that the sect created and that touched upon these topics.

Similar literary and interpretative phenomena can be found later in Tannaitic literature. More widely known and simpler in form are an array of paragraphs in the Mishnah that follow the sequence of a passage in the Torah (though they do not constitute a midrash). The most famous of these are chapters 8–9 of tractate *Soṭah*. This text discusses setting out to war according to Deuteronomy 20 and the ceremony of the decapitated heifer (עגלה ערופה), required by the Torah in Deuteronomy 21 in cases where a dead body is found and the murderer is not known. More interesting is the similarity between the Qumranic examples that we discussed here and two mishnaic units, which I depict as mishnaic formulations of midrashim that either existed but did not survive or never even existed in the literary form of midrash.

The first of these cases is *m. Mak.* 2:1. The Mishnah refers to the biblical law that states if a man kills unintentionally he should flee to one of the cities of refuge and stay there until the high priest dies (Num 35:28):

---

35. Above note 30; and Aharon Shemesh, "Scriptural Interpretations in the Damascus Document and their Parallels in Rabbinic Midrash," in *The Damascus Document: A Centennial of Discovery. Proceedings of the Third International Symposium of the Orion Center for the Study of the Dead Sea Scrolls and Associated Literature, 4-8 February 1998*, ed. Joseph M. Baumgarten, Esther G. Chazon, and Avital Pinnick. STDJ 34 (Leiden: Brill, 2000), 161-75.

These are they who go into exile [to the Cities of Refuge]: one that slays a human being unintentionally.

(If) he was rolling down [the cement on a roof] with a roller and it fell down on someone and killed him,

or he was lowering a cask and it fell on somebody and killed him,

or he was descending by a ladder and he fell down on some person and killed him, then he flees into exile; but if he was drawing up with a roller, and it fell down on a man and killed him, or if he was drawing [water] with a cask and the rope parted and it fell on someone and killed him, or if he was ascending by a ladder, and he fell down and killed somebody, then he does not have to escape into exile. This is the general principle: in every case [where the mishap occurred] in the course of descent, he must go into exile, but when not in the course of a descent, he need not flee into exile.

The Mishnah demonstrates the rule that any person who kills in the course of descent shall be exiled, and if he kills somebody in the course of ascent he shall not be exiled. The passage uses three examples. These examples were not simply fabricated by the Tannaitic sages. Rather, they are based on the passage concerning unintentional killing that is found in Numbers 35. The Torah describes the case as follows: "But if he pushed him without malice aforethought or hurled any object (כלי, lit., "vessel") at him unintentionally, or inadvertently dropped upon him any deadly object of stone, and death resulted — though he was not an enemy of his and did not seek his harm — in such cases the assembly shall decide between the slayer and the blood-avenger." In my opinion, the three examples in the Mishnah are based on the above description. The case of rolling down with a roller is the example that the Mishnah chose for the case of a person who killed someone using a stone mentioned in the Torah. The cask mentioned in the Mishnah is an example for a "vessel" (כלי) that is mentioned in the verse, whereas a person who falls from a ladder is compared to a person who was pushed by his friend without malice, meaning that he killed him using his body (and not any other object). Realizing that the Mishnah is based on these verses is key to understanding the rule: "In every case [where the mishap occurred] in the course of descent, he must go into exile, but when not in the course of a descent, he need not flee into exile." It is important to note that, as opposed to the description of the intentional murderer whom the Torah describes (Num 35:16-21) as "striking" his friend, with a tool or by hand, the verbs the Torah uses to describe the actions of the unintentional killer are "pushing," "dropping," or "falling." What is common in all of these cases is that the victim eventually dies, not from the blow of the murderer, but from the weight of the object that fell on him or from the impact of his body hitting the ground when he is pushed from a high place. The sages understood that you could attribute the death to the killer and force him to run to a sanctuary, only if the case occurred while descending. The implication is that the heavy object fell or rolled in the direction in which the killer directed it. However, when the event happens while ascending (such as in a case of a person who pulls a cement block with a roller uphill from below and the rope to which it is connected is torn, and it falls in the opposite direction and kills), the person does not have to be exiled, because he did not cause his friend's death. Rather, this case is considered to be an unfortunate incident, and thus he (the "killer") bears no responsibility for the death.

The other example constitutes the first part of chapter 3 of tractate *Makkot*. This is a list, the content of which I have analyzed in depth elsewhere, that delineates who should be flogged.[36] I have found that the Mishnah's list of those who should be flogged is similar to the Qumran Penal Code, in that it consists of three sublists: the first deals with forbidden sexual relationships; the second deals with forbidden foods; and the third includes the ban on damaging the body (such as scratching on the dead and creating a tattoo). The lists are summations of all the different references to the relevant bans in the Torah and do not relate to a specific passage. Nevertheless, they are not detached entirely from their biblical sources, and they follow faithfully the order and the style of the texts. For example, one can point to the group of incest, which is punished by כרת ("excision"). This list is essentially a mishnaic version of a midrash that collected incest prohibitions derived from Leviticus 18 and 20. The list consists primarily of chapter 18. However, further prohibitions from chapter 20 have been added to it. Indeed, it is chapter 18 that contains the general warning of the punishment of excision for all those who transgress the bans contained on the list.

In conclusion, we have seen that both rabbinic literature and the Qumran scrolls use the Torah as the natural and central basis around which interpretations and halakic traditions are woven. This is true even in cases where the formulations themselves are not related to the biblical text. Revealing these structures may help not only to understand these texts but also to trace the origins of the interpretative and midrashic traditions of their authors.

---

36. Shemesh, *Punishments and Sins*, 178-204.

BIBLIOGRAPHY

Bernstein, Moshe J., and Shlomo A. Koyfman. "The Interpretation of Biblical Law in the Dead Sea Scrolls: Forms and Methods." In *Biblical Interpretation at Qumran,* ed. Matthias Henze. SDSSRL. Grand Rapids: Eerdmans, 2005, 61-87.

Kahana, Menahem. "The Halakhic Midrashim." In *The Literature of the Sages.* Part 2: *Midrash and Targum, Liturgy, Poetry, Mysticism, Contracts, Inscriptions, Ancient Science and the Languages of Rabbinic Literature,* ed. Shmuel Safrai. CRINT 2.3. Assen: Van Gorcum and Philadelphia: Fortress, 2006, 3-105.

Kister, Menahem. "Some Aspects of Qumranic Halakhah. In *The Madrid Qumran Congress: Proceedings of the International Congress on the Dead Sea Scrolls, March 1991,* ed. Julio Trebolle Barrera and Luis Vegas Montaner. Leiden: Brill, 1992, 2:571-88.

Segal, Michael. "Between Bible and Rewritten Bible." In *Biblical Interpretation at Qumran,* ed. Matthias Henze. SDSSRL. Grand Rapids: Eerdmans, 2005, 10-28.

Shemesh, Aharon. *Halakhah in the Making: The Development of Jewish Law from Qumran to the Rabbis.* Berkeley: University of California Press, 2009.

Shemesh, Aharon, and Cana Werman. "Halakhah at Qumran: Genre and Authority." *DSD* 10 (2003): 104-29.

Strack, Hermann L., and Günter Stemberger. "Rabbinical Hermeneutics." In *Introduction to the Talmud and Midrash,* trans. and ed. Markus Bockmuehl. 2nd ed. Minneapolis: Fortress, 1996, 15-130.

An extensive list of bibliog. may be found in Moshe J. Bernstein, "Interpretation of Scriptures." In *EDSS,* 1:376-83.

Contributors

Moshe J. Bernstein
Professor of Bible
Yeshiva University

George J. Brooke
Rylands Professor of Biblical Criticism and Exegesis
University of Manchester

Edward M. Cook
Associate Professor of Semitic Languages
Catholic University of America

Peter Enns
Landsdale, PA

Matthias Henze
Associate Professor of Religious Studies
Rice University

Howard Jacobson
Professor Emeritus, Department of Classics
University of Illinois at Urbana–Champaign

James L. Kugel
Professor of Hebrew Bible
Bar Ilan University

Robert Kugler
Professor of Christian Studies
Lewis & Clark College

490

HINDY NAJMAN
Associate Professor of Religious Studies
Yale University

ZULEIKA RODGERS
Lecturer in Jewish Studies
Trinity College Dublin

MARTIN RÖSEL
Professor of Old Testament
University of Rostock

JACQUES VAN RUITEN
Associate Professor of Old Testament Studies and Early Jewish Literature
University of Groningen

AHARON SHEMESH
Professor, Talmud Department
Bar Ilan University

GREGORY E. STERLING
Professor of Theology
University of Notre Dame

SARAH J. TANZER
Professor of New Testament and Early Judaism
McCormick Theological Seminary

SHANI TZOREF
Dead Sea Scrolls Project
Israel Antiquities Authority

BENJAMIN G. WRIGHT III
Professor of Religious Studies
Lehigh University

YAIR ZAKOVITCH
Professor of Hebrew Bible
The Hebrew University of Jerusalem

Bibliography

Adler, William. "Abraham and the Burning of the Temple of Idols: Jubilees' Traditions in Christian Chronography." *JQR* 77 (1986-87): 95-11.

Aejmelaeus, Anneli. "Translation Technique and the Intention of the Translator." In *VII Congress of the International Organization for Septuagint and Cognate Studies, Leuven 1989*, ed. Claude E. Cox. SBLSCS 31. Atlanta: Scholars, 1991, 23-36.

Aichele, George, and Gary A. Phillips, eds. *Intertextuality and the Bible*. Semeia 69-70. Atlanta: SBL, 1995.

Albani, Matthias, Jörg Frey, and Armin Lange, eds. *Studies in the Book of Jubilees*. TSAJ 65. Tübingen: Mohr Siebeck, 1997.

Albeck, Chanoch. *Das Buch der Jubiläen und die Halacha*. Berlin: Scholem, 1930.

Alexander, Philip S. "Retelling the Old Testament." In *It Is Written — Scripture Citing Scripture: Essays in Honour of Barnabas Lindars*, ed. D. A. Carson and H. G. M. Williamson. Cambridge: Cambridge University Press, 1988.

———. "Targum, Targumim." *ABD*, 6:320-31.

———. *The Targum of Canticles*. ArBib 17A. Collegeville: Liturgical, 2003.

Alexander, Philip S., and Geza Vermes. *Qumran Cave 4. XIX: 4QSerekh Ha-Yaḥad and Two Related Texts*. DJD 26. Oxford: Clarendon, 1998.

Allenbach, Jean, et al., eds. *Biblia patristica*. Supplement: *Philon d'Alexandrie*. Paris: Centre national de la recherche scientifique, 1982.

Amihay, Aryeh, and Daniel A. Machiela. "Traditions of the Birth of Noah." In Stone, Amihay, and Hillel, *Noah and His Book(s)*, 53-69.

Anderson, Gary A. "The Interpretation of Genesis 1:1 in the Targums." *CBQ* 52 (1990): 21-29.

———. "The Life of Adam and Eve." *HUCA* 63 (1992): 1-38.

Andrews, Isolde. "Being Open to the Vision: A Study from Fourth Ezra." *Literature and Theology* 12 (1998): 231-41.

Aptowitzer, Victor. "Asenath, the Wife of Joseph: A Haggadic Literary-Historical Study." *HUCA* 1 (1924): 239-306.

Asurmendi, Jesús María. "Baruch: Causes, Effects and Remedies for a Disaster." In *History *and Identity: How Israel's Later Authors Viewed Its Earlier History,* ed. Núria Calduch-Benages and Jan Liesen. Berlin: de Gruyter, 2005, 187-200.

Attridge, Harold W. *The Interpretation of Biblical History in the* Antiquitates Judaicae *of Flavius Josephus.* HDR 7. Missoula: Scholars, 1976.

———. "Josephus and His Works." In Stone, *Jewish Writings of the Second Temple Period,* 185-232.

Aune, David E. *Prophecy in Early Christianity and the Ancient Mediterranean World.* Grand Rapids: Eerdmans, 1983.

Avigad, Nahman, and Yigael Yadin. *A Genesis Apocryphon: A Scroll from the Wilderness of Judaea.* Jerusalem: Magnes and Heikhal ha-Sefer, 1956.

Baker, Cynthia. "Pseudo-Philo and the Transformation of Jephthah's Daughter." In *Anti-Covenant,* ed. Mieke Bal. JSOTSup 81. Sheffield: Almond, 1989, 195-209.

Balch, David L. "Two Apologetic Encomia: Dionysius on Rome and Josephus on the Jews." *JSJ* 13 (1982): 102-22.

Barclay, John M. G. *Against Apion.* Vol. 10 of Mason, *Flavius Josephus: Translation and Commentary.* Leiden: Brill, 2007.

Bardtke, Hans. "Considérations sur les cantiques de Qumrân." *RB* 63 (1956): 220-33.

Barr, James. *The Typology of Literalism in Ancient Biblical Translations.* NAWG, Phil.-Hist. Kl. 11. Göttingen: Vandenhoeck & Ruprecht, 1979.

———. *Holy Scripture: Canon, Authority, Criticism.* Philadelphia: Westminster, 1983.

———. "Did the Greek Pentateuch Really Serve as a Dictionary for the Translation of the Later Books?" In *Hamlet on a Hill: Semitic and Greek Studies Presented to Professor T. Muraoka,* ed. Martin F. J. Basten and W. Th. van Peursen. OLA 118. Leuven: Peeters, 2003, 523-43.

Barstad, Hans. "Prophecy at Qumran?" In *In the Last Days: On Jewish and Christian Apocalyptic and Its Period,* ed. Knud Jeppesen, Kirsten Nielsen, and Bent Rosendal. Aarhus: Aarhus University Press, 1994, 104-20.

Barton, John. *Oracles of God: Perceptions of Ancient Prophecy in Israel after the Exile.* London: Darton, Longman, and Todd, 1986.

———. "The Significance of a Fixed Canon of the Hebrew Bible." In Sæbø, *Hebrew Bible/Old Testament,* 1.1:67-83.

Bauckham, Richard. "The Liber Antiquitatum Biblicarum of Pseudo-Philo and the Gospels as 'Midrash.'" In *Gospel Perspectives,* vol. 3: *Studies in Midrash and Historiography,* ed. R. T. France and David Wenham. Sheffield: JSOT, 1983, 33-76.

Baumgarten, Joseph M. *Studies in Qumran Law.* SJLA 24. Leiden: Brill, 1977.

———. "The 4Q Zadokite Fragments on Skin Disease." *JJS* 41 (1990): 153-65.

Baumgarten, Joseph M., et al. *Qumran Cave 4: XIII, The Damascus Document (4Q266-273).* DJD 18. Oxford: Clarendon, 1996.

Beattie, D. R. G., and J. Stanley McIvor. *The Targum of Ruth and The Targum of Chronicles.* ArBib 19. Collegeville: Liturgical, 1993.

Beck, John A. *Translators as Storytellers: A Study in Septuagint Translation Technique.* Studies in Biblical Literature 25. New York: Lang, 2000.

Becker, Jürgen. *Das Heil Gottes: Heils- und Sündenbegriffe in den Qumrantexten und im Neuen Testament.* SUNT 3. Göttingen: Vandenhoeck & Ruprecht, 1964.

———. *Untersuchungen zur Entstehungsgeschichte der Testamente der Zwölf Patriarchen.* AGJU 8. Leiden: Brill, 1970.

———. *Unterweisung in lehrhafter Form.* JSHRZ 3. Gütersloh: Mohn, 1974.

Beentjes, Pancratius C. "Canon and Scripture in the Book of Ben Sira (Jesus Sirach/ Ecclesiasticus)." In *"Happy the One Who Meditates on Wisdom" (SIR. 14,20): Collected Essays on the Book of Ben Sira.* CBET 43. Leuven: Peeters, 2006, 169-86.

Begg, Christopher T. "Daniel and Josephus: Tracing Connections." In *The Book of Daniel in Light of New Findings,* ed. Adam S. van der Woude. BETL 106. Leuven: University Press and Peters, 1993, 539-45.

———. *Josephus' Account of the Early Divided Monarchy (AJ 8,212-420): Rewriting the Bible.* BETL 108. Leuven: Leuven University Press, 1993.

———. "The Massacre of the Priests of Nob in Josephus and Pseudo-Philo." *EstBib* 55 (1997): 171-98.

———. *Josephus' Story of the Later Monarchy (AJ 9,1-10,185).* BETL 145. Leuven: Leuven University Press, 2000.

Begg, Christopher T., and Paul Spilsbury. *Judean Antiquities Books 8–10.* Vol. 5 of Mason, *Flavius Josephus: Translation and Commentary.* Leiden: Brill, 2005.

Belkin, Samuel. *The Midrash of Philo.* New York: Yeshiva University Press, 1989. [Hebrew]

Berger, Klaus. *Das Buch der Jubiläen.* JSHRZ 5.3. Gütersloh: Gütersloher, 1981.

Berger, Klaus, with Gabriele Fassbeck and Heiner Reinhard. *Synopse des Vierten Buches Esra und der Syrischen Baruch-Apokalypse.* Texte und Arbeiten zum neutestamentlichen Zeitalter 8. Tübingen: Francke, 1992.

Bergren, Theodore A. "Christian Influence on the Transmission History of 4, 5, and 6 Ezra." In *The Jewish Apocalyptic Heritage in Early Christianity,* ed. James C. VanderKam and William Adler. Assen: Van Gorcum and Minneapolis: Fortress, 1996, 102-27.

———. "Ezra and Nehemiah Square Off in the Apocrypha and Pseudepigrapha." In Stone and Bergren, *Biblical Figures Outside the Bible,* 340-65.

Bernstein, Moshe J. "Re-arrangement, Anticipation and Harmonization as Exegetical Features in the Genesis Apocryphon." *DSD* 3 (1996): 37-57.

———. "Noah and the Flood at Qumran." In *The Provo International Conference on the Dead Sea Scrolls: Technological Innovations, New Texts, and Reformulated Issues,* ed. Donald W. Parry and Eugene Ulrich. STDJ 30. Leiden: Brill, 1999, 199-231.

———. "Interpretation of Scriptures." In *EDSS,* 1:376-83.

———. "4Q159 Fragment 5 and the 'Desert Theology' of the Qumran Sect." In Paul, Kraft, Schiffman, and Fields, *Emanuel,* 43-56.

———. "From the Watchers to the Flood: Story and Exegesis in the Early Columns of the *Genesis Apocryphon.*" In Chazon, Dimant, and Clements, *Reworking the Bible,* 39-63.

———. "'Rewritten Bible': A Generic Category Which Has Outlived Its Usefulness?" *Text* 22 (2005): 169-96.

———. "Divine Titles and Epithets and the Sources of the Genesis Apocryphon." *JBL* 128 (2009): 291-310.

———. "Is the Genesis Apocryphon a Unity? What Sort of Unity Were You Looking For?" *Aramaic Studies* 8 (2010): 107-34.

—————. "The Genre(s) of the Genesis Apocryphon." In Berthelot and Stökl Ben Ezra, *Aramaica Qumranica*, 317-38.

—————. "The Genesis Apocryphon and the Aramaic Targumim Revisited." In *The Dead Sea Scrolls in Context: Integrating the Dead Sea Scrolls in the Study of Ancient Texts, Languages, and Cultures.* Edited by Armin Lange, Emanuel Tov, and Matthias Weigold. VTSup 140. Leiden: Brill, 2011, 2:651-71.

Bernstein, Moshe J., and Shlomo A. Koyfman. "The Interpretation of Biblical Law in the Dead Sea Scrolls: Forms and Methods." In Henze, *Biblical Interpretation at Qumran*, 61-87.

Berrin, Shani. *The Pesher Nahum Scroll from Qumran: An Exegetical Study of 4Q169.* STDJ 53. Leiden: Brill, 2004.

—————. "Qumran Pesharim." In Henze, *Biblical Interpretation at Qumran*, 110-33.

Berthelot, Katell, and Daniel Stökl Ben Ezra, eds. *Aramaica Qumranica: The Aix-en-Provence Colloquium on the Aramaic Dead Sea Scrolls.* STDJ 94. Leiden: Brill, 2010.

Beyerle, Stefan. "'Du bist kein Richter über dem Herrn' (4 Esr 7,19): Zur Konzeption von Gesetz und Gericht im 4. Esrabuch." In *Recht und Ethos im Alten Testament — Gestalt und Wirkung: Festschrift für Horst Seebass zum 65. Geburtstag,* ed. Beyerle, Günter Mayer, and Hans Strauss. Neukirchen-Vluyn: Neukirchener, 1999, 315-37.

La Bible d'Alexandrie. Vol. 1: *La Genèse, Traduction du texte grec de la Septane: Introduction et Notes par Marguerite Harl.* Paris: Cerf, 1986.

Bilde, Per. *Flavius Josephus between Jerusalem and Rome: His Life, His Works and Their Importance.* JSPSup 2. Sheffield: JSOT, 1988.

—————. "*Contra Apionem* 1.28-56: An Essay on Josephus' View of His Own Work in the Context of the Jewish Canon." In Feldman and Levison, *Josephus' Contra Apionem*, 94-114.

Blenkinsopp, Joseph. "Prophecy and Priesthood in Josephus." *JJS* 25 (1974): 239-62.

—————. *A History of Prophecy in Israel from the Settlement in the Land to the Hellenistic Period.* Philadelphia: Westminster, 1983.

Bloch, Heinrich. *Die Quellen des Flavius Josephus in seiner Archäologie.* Leipzig: Teubner, 1879; repr. Wiesbaden: Sändig, 1968.

Bloch, Joshua. "The Ezra-Apocalypse: Was it Written in Hebrew, Greek or Aramaic?" *JQR* 48 (1958): 279-94.

Bogaert, Pierre-Maurice. *L'Apocalypse de Baruch: Introduction, Traduction du Syriaque et Commentaire.* 2 vols. Paris: Cerf, 1969.

—————. "Le Livre Deutérocanonique de Baruch dans la Liturgie Romaine." In *Mélanges liturgiques offerts au R. P. Dom Bernard Botte à l'occasion du cinquantième anniversaire de son ordination sacerdotale (4 juin 1972).* Louvain: Abbaye du César, 1972, 31-48.

—————. "Le Nom de Baruch dans la Littérature Pseudépigraphique: L'Apocalypse Syriaque et le Livre Deutérocanonique." In *La Littérature Juive entre Tenach et Mishnah: Quelques Problèmes,* ed. W. C. Van Unnik. RechBib 9. Leiden: Brill, 1974, 56-72.

—————. "Le personage de Baruch et l'histoire du livre de Jérémie: Aux origines du livre de Baruch." *BIOSCS* 7 (1974): 19-21.

—————. "Les Apocalypses contemporaines de Baruch, d'Esdras et de Jean." In *L'Apocalypse johannique et l'Apocalyptique dans le Nouveau Testament,* ed. Jan Lambrecht. BETL 53. Leuven: Leuven University Press, 1980, 47-68.

————. "De Baruch à Jérémie: Les Deux Rédactions Conservées du Livre de Jérémie." In *Le Livre de Jérémie: Le Prophète et son Milieu, les Oracles et leur Transmission.* BETL 54. Leuven: Leuven University Press, 1981, 168-73.

————. "Le personage de Baruch et l'histoire du livre de Jérémie: Aux origines du livre deutérocanonique de Baruch." In *Papers Presented to the Fifth International Congress on Biblical Studies Held at Oxford, 1973,* ed. Elizabeth A. Livingstone. SE 7. TUGAL 126. Berlin: Akademie, 1982, 73-81.

Borgen, Peder. *Philo of Alexandria: An Exegete for His Time.* NovTSup 86. Leiden: Brill, 1997; repr. Atlanta: SBL, 2005.

Bowker, John. *The Targums and Rabbinic Literature.* London: Cambridge University Press, 1969.

Bowley, James E. "Prophets and Prophecy at Qumran." In Flint and VanderKam, *The Dead Sea Scrolls after Fifty Years,* 354-78.

Braun, F. C. "Les Testaments des XII Patriarches et le problème de leur origine." *RB* 67 (1960): 516-49.

Braun, Martin. *Griechischer Roman und hellenistische Geschichtsschreibung.* Frankfurt: Klostermann, 1934.

————. *History and Romance in Greco-Oriental Literature.* Oxford: Blackwell, 1938.

Brayford, Susan. *Genesis.* Septuagint Commentary Series. Leiden: Brill, 2007.

Brewer, Daniel I. *Techniques and Assumptions in Jewish Exegesis before 70 c.e.* TSAJ 30. Tübingen: Mohr Siebeck, 1992.

Brock, Sebastian P. "The Phenomenon of the Septuagint." *OtSt* 17 (1972): 11-36.

————. "Abraham and the Ravens: A Syriac Counterpart to Jubilees 11-12 and Its Implications." *JSJ* 9 (1978): 135-52.

————. "Aspects of Translation Technique in Antiquity." *GRBS* 20 (1979): 69-87.

Brock, Sebastian P., Charles T. Fritsch, and Sidney Jellicoe, comps. *A Classified Bibliography of the Septuagint.* ALGHJ 6. Leiden: Brill, 1973.

Brockington, Leonard H. "The Syriac Apocalypse of Baruch." In *The Apocryphal Old Testament,* ed. Hedley Fredrick Davis Sparks. Oxford: Clarendon, 1984, 835-95.

Brooke, George J. "Isaiah 40:3 and the Wilderness Community." In *New Qumran Texts and Studies: Proceedings of the First Meeting of the International Organization for Qumran Studies, Paris 1992,* ed. Brooke and Florentino García Martínez. STDJ 15. Leiden: Brill, 1994, 117-32.

————. "Parabiblical Prophetic Narratives." In Flint and VanderKam, *The Dead Sea Scrolls After Fifty Years,* 271-301.

————. "Prophecy." In *EDSS,* 2:694-700.

————. "Thematic Commentaries on Prophetic Scriptures." In Henze, *Biblical Interpretation at Qumran,* 134-57.

————. "Biblical Interpretation at Qumran." In *The Bible and the Dead Sea Scrolls,* vol. 1: *Scripture and the Scrolls,* ed. James H. Charlesworth. The Second Princeton Symposium on Judaism and Christian Origins. Waco: Baylor University Press, 2006, 287-319.

————. "Prophecy and Prophets in the Dead Sea Scrolls: Looking Backwards and Forwards." In *Prophets, Prophecy, and Prophetic Texts in the Second Temple Period,* ed. Michael H. Floyd and Robert D. Haak. LHB/OTS 427. London: T. & T. Clark, 2006, 151-65.

————. "The Place of Prophecy in Coming Out of Exile: The Case of the Dead Sea Scrolls." In Voitila and Jokiranta, *Scripture in Transition*, 535-50.

————, ed. *Temple Scroll Studies*. JSPSup 7. Sheffield: JSOT, 1989.

Brownlee, William H. *The Midrash Pesher of Habakkuk*. SBLMS 24. Missoula: Scholars, 1979.

Bruce, Frederick F. "The Earliest Old Testament Interpretation." *OtSt* 17 (1972): 37-52.

Burchard, Christoph. "Zur armenischen Überlieferung der Testamente der zwölf Patriarchen." In Eltester, *Studien zu den Testamenten der Zwölf Patriarchen*, 1-29.

Burnette-Bletsch, Rhonda. "At the Hands of a Woman: Rewriting Jael in Pseudo-Philo." *JSP* 17 (1998): 53-64.

Burrows, Millar. *More Light on the Dead Sea Scrolls: New Scrolls and New Interpretations, with Translations of Important Recent Discoveries*. New York: Viking, 1958.

————. "Prophets and Prophecy at Qumran." In *Israel's Prophetic Heritage*, ed. Bernhard W. Anderson and Walter Harrelson. New York: Harper, 1962, 223-32.

Campbell, Jonathan G. *The Use of Scripture in the Damascus Document 1-8, 1-20*. BZAW 228. Berlin: de Gruyter, 1995.

Carmignac, Jean. "Les Citations de L'Ancien Testament et Spécialement des Poèmes du Serviteur, dans les Hymnes de Qumran." *RevQ* 2 (1959-1960): 357-94.

Carr, David M. *Writing on the Tablet of the Heart*. Oxford: Oxford University Press, 2005.

Carras, George P. "Philo's *Hypothetica* and Josephus's *Contra Apionem* and the Question of Sources." In *SBLSP* 1990, ed. David J. Lull. Atlanta: Scholars, 1990, 431-50.

Carroll, Robert P. *Jeremiah*. OTL. Philadelphia: Westminster, 1986.

Cathcart, Kevin J., and Robert P. Gordon. *The Targum of the Minor Prophets*. ArBib 14. Wilmington: Glazier, 1989.

Ceriani, Antonio Maria. "Apocalypsis Baruch Syriace." In *Monumenta Sacra et Profana ex codicibus praesertim Bibliothecae Ambrosianae*, 1.2. Milan: Bibliotheca Ambrosiana, 1866, 73-98.

————. *Translatio syra Pescitto Veteris Testamenti ex codice Ambrosiano*. Milan: Mediolani, 1876.

Charles, Robert H. *The Ethiopic Version of the Hebrew Book of Jubilees*. Anecdota Oxoniensia 8. Oxford: Clarendon, 1895.

————. *The Apocalypse of Baruch Translated from the Syriac*. London: Black, 1896.

————. *The Greek Versions of the Testaments of the Twelve Patriarchs: Edited from Nine MSS*. London: Oxford University Press, 1908.

————. *The Testaments of the Twelve Patriarchs: Translated from the Editor's Greek Text*. London: Oxford University Press, 1908.

————. *The Book of Jubilees, or the Little Genesis: Translated from the Ethiopic Text*. London: SPCK, 1917.

————. "II Baruch, or the Syriac Apocalypse of Baruch." In *APOT*, 2:470-526.

Charlesworth, James H. *The Pesharim and Qumran History: Chaos or Consensus?* Grand Rapids: Eerdmans, 2002.

————, ed. *The Old Testament Pseudepigrapha*. 2 vols. Garden City: Doubleday, 1983-85.

————, ed. *Princeton Theological Seminary Dead Sea Scrolls Project*. Tübingen: Mohr and Louisville: Westminster John Knox, 1991-.

Chazon, Esther G. "The Use of the Bible as a Key to Meaning in Psalms from Qumran." In Paul, Kraft, Schiffman, and Fields, *Emanuel*, 85-96.

———. "Scripture and Prayer in 'The Words of the Luminaries.'" In *Prayers That Cite Scripture*, ed. James L. Kugel. Cambridge, Mass.: Harvard University Press, 2007, 25-41.

Chazon, Esther G., Devorah Dimant, and Ruth E. Clements, eds. *Reworking the Bible: Apocryphal and Related Texts at Qumran. Proceedings of a Joint Symposium by the Orion Center for the Study of the Dead Sea Scrolls and Associated Literature and the Hebrew University Institute for Advanced Studies Research Group on Qumran, 15-17 January, 2002.* STDJ 58. Leiden: Brill, 2005.

Cheon, Samuel. *The Exodus Story in the Wisdom of Solomon: A Study in Biblical Interpretation.* JSPSup 23. Sheffield: Sheffield Academic, 1997.

Chilton, Bruce D. *The Isaiah Targum.* ArBib 11. Wilmington: Glazier, 1987.

Choi, Richard P. "The Intra-Jewish Dialogue in 4 Ezra 3:1–9:25." *AUSS* 41 (2003): 237-54.

Clarke, Ernest G. *Targum Pseudo-Jonathan of the Pentateuch: Text and Concordance.* Hoboken: Ktav, 1984.

———. *Targum Pseudo-Jonathan: Deuteronomy.* ArBib 5B. Collegeville: Liturgical, 1995.

Clemen, Carl. "Die Zusammensetzung des Buches Henoch, der Apokalypse des Baruch und des vierten Buches Esra." *TSK* 11 (1898): 211-46.

Cohen, Naomi G. "Josephus and Scripture: Is Josephus's Treatment of the Scriptural Narrative Similar throughout the *Antiquities* I–XI?" *JQR* 54 (1964): 311-32.

Cohen, Shaye J. D. *Josephus in Galilee and Rome: His Vita and Development as a Historian.* Leiden: Brill, 1979.

———. "The Beauty of Flora and the Beauty of Sarai." *Helios* 8 (1981): 41-53.

———. "Josephus, Jeremiah, and Polybius." *History and Theory* 21 (1982): 366-81.

———. "Respect for Judaism by Gentiles according to Josephus." *HTR* 80 (1987): 409-30.

Cohn, Leopold. "An Apocryphal Work Ascribed to Philo of Alexandria." *JQR* 10 (1898): 277-332.

———. "Pseudo-Philo und Jerachmeel." In *Festschrift zum siebzigsten Geburtstage Jakob Guttmanns*, ed. Martin Philippson. Leipzig: Fock, 1915; repr. New York: Arno, 1980, 173-85.

Cohn, Leopold, and Paul Wendland. "Zur neuen Philo-Ausgabe: Eine Erwiederung." *Phil* 59 (1900): 521-36.

Collins, John J. *Daniel: With an Introduction to Apocalyptic Literature.* FOTL 20. Grand Rapids: Eerdmans, 1984.

———. "Testaments." In Stone, *Jewish Writings of the Second Temple Period*, 325-55.

———. *Daniel.* Hermeneia. Minneapolis: Fortress, 1993.

———. *Jewish Wisdom in the Hellenistic Age.* OTL. Louisville: Westminster John Knox, 1997.

———. "After the Fall: 4 Ezra, 2 Baruch, and the Apocalypse of Abraham." In *The Apocalyptic Imagination: An Introduction to Jewish Apocalyptic Literature.* 2nd ed. BRS. Grand Rapids: Eerdmans and Livonia: Dove, 1998, 194-232.

———. "Before the Fall: The Earliest Interpretations of Adam and Eve." In *The Idea of Biblical Interpretation: Essays in Honor of James L. Kugel*, ed. Hindy Najman and Judith H. Newman. JSJSup 83. Leiden: Brill, 2004, 293-308.

―――. "The Idea of Election in 4 Ezra." *JSQ* 16 (2009): 83-96.

Collins, John J., and Peter W. Flint, eds. *The Book of Daniel: Composition and Reception.* 2 vols. VTSup 83. Leiden: Brill, 2001.

Collins, John J., and George W. E. Nickelsburg, eds. *Ideal Figures in Ancient Judaism: Profiles and Paradigms.* SBLSCS 12. Chico: Scholars, 1980.

Comprehensive Aramaic Lexicon Targumic Studies Module. http://cal1.cn.huc.edu/targumstartpage.html.

Cook, Edward. *A Glossary of Targum Onkelos: According to Alexander Sperber's Edition.* Studies in the Aramaic Interpretation of Scripture 6. Leiden: Brill, 2008.

Cook, Joan E. "Creation in 4 Ezra: The Biblical Theme in Support of Theodicy." In *Creation in the Biblical Traditions,* ed. Richard J. Clifford and John J. Collins. CBQMS 24. Washington: Catholic Biblical Association, 1992, 129-39.

―――. "Exegesis in the Septuagint." *JNSL* 30 (2004): 1-19.

Crawford, Cory D. "On the Exegetical Function of the Abraham/Ravens Tradition in Jubilees 11." *HTR* 97 (2004): 91-97.

Crawford, Sidnie White. *Rewriting Scripture in Second Temple Times.* SDSSRL. Grand Rapids: Eerdmans, 2008.

Daise, Michael A. "Biblical Creation Motifs in the Qumran Hodayot." In *The Dead Sea Scrolls Fifty Years After Their Discovery: Proceedings of the Jerusalem Congress, July 20-25, 1997,* ed. Lawrence H. Schiffman, Emanuel Tov, and James C. VanderKam. Jerusalem: Israel Exploration Society and Shrine of the Book, 2000, 293-305.

Dalman, Gustaf. *Aramäisch-Neuhebräisches Handwörterbuch zu Targum, Talmud und Midrasch.* 1901; 2nd ed., Frankfurt: Kauffman, 1922.

Daube, David. "Typology in Josephus." *JJS* 31 (1980): 18-36.

Davenport, Gene L. *The Eschatology of the Book of Jubilees.* StPB 20. Leiden: Brill, 1971.

Dedering, Sven. "Apocalypse of Baruch." In *The Old Testament in Syriac, according to the Peshiṭta Version* 4.3. Leiden: Brill, 1973.

Dehandschutter, Boudewijn. "Le rêve dans l'Apocryphe de la Genèse." In *La littérature juive entre Tenach et Mischna: Quelques problèmes,* ed. Willem Cornelis van Unnik. RechBib 9. Leiden: Brill, 1974, 48-55.

Delcor, Mathias. *Les Hymnes de Qumrân (Hodayot): Texte hébreu, introduction, traduction, commentaire.* Paris: Letouzy et Ané, 1962.

Del Verme, Marcello. "Sui rapporti tra 2Baruc e 4Ezra." *Orpheus* 24 (2003): 30-54.

Desjardins, Michel. "Law in 2Baruch and 4Ezra." *SR* 14 (1985): 25-37.

Destinon, Justus von. *Die Quellen des Flavius Josephus.* Vol. 1: *Die Quellen der Archäologie Buch XII–XVII = Jüd. Krieg Buch I.* Kiel: Lipsius & Tischer, 1882.

De Troyer, Kristin, and Armin Lange, eds. *Reading the Present in the Qumran Library: The Perception of the Contemporary by Means of Scriptural Interpretations.* SBLSymS 30. Atlanta: SBL, 2005.

Dietzfelbinger, Christian. *Pseudo-Philo: Antiquitates Biblicae.* JSHRZ 2.2. Gütersloh: Gütersloher, 1975.

Diez Macho, Alejandro. *Targum palestinense Ms. de la Biblioteca vaticana.* 6 vols. Madrid and Barcelona: Consejo Superior de Investigaciones Cientificas, 1968-1979.

Dillmann, August. "Das Buch der Jubiläen oder die kleine Genesis." *JBW* 2 (1850): 230-56; 3 (1851): 1-96.

Dimant, Devorah. "The 'Pesher on the Periods' (4Q180) and 4Q181." *IOS* 9 (1979): 77-102.

―――. "Qumran Sectarian Literature." In Stone, *Jewish Writings of the Second Temple Period*, 483-550.

―――. "Use, Authority and Interpretation of Mikra in the Apocrypha and Pseudepigrapha." In Mulder, *Mikra*, 384-418.

―――. "Not Exile in the Desert but Exile in Spirit: The Pesher of Isa. 40:3 in the Rule of the Community." *Meghillot* 2 (2004): 21-36. [Hebrew]

Dines, Jennifer M. *The Septuagint*. London: T. & T. Clark, 2004.

DiTommaso, Lorenzo. "Dating the Eagle Vision of 4 Ezra: A New Look at an Old Theory." *JSP* 20 (1999): 3-38.

Dogniez, Cécile. *Bibliography of the Septuagint — Bibliographie de la Septante (1970-1993)*. VTSup 60. Leiden: Brill, 1995.

Dorival, Gilles. "Les phénomènes d'intertextualité dans le livre grec des Nombres." In ΚΑΤΑ ΤΟΥΣ Ο': *Selon Les Septante. Festschrift Marguerite Harl*, ed. Dorival and Olivier Munnich. Paris: Cerf, 1995, 253-85.

Dorival, Gilles, Marguerite Harl, and Olivier Munnich. *La Bible Grecque des Septante: Du Judaïsme Hellénistique au Christianisme Ancient*. Paris: Cerf, 1988.

Draisma, Sipke, ed. *Intertexuality in Biblical Writings: Essays in Honour of Bas van Iersel*. Kampen: Kok, 1989.

Dupont-Sommer, André. *Nouveaux Aperçus sur les Manuscrits de la Mer Morte*. Paris: Maisonneuve, 1960.

Eberharter, Andreas. *Der Kanon des Alten Testaments zur Zeit des Ben Sira*. ATA 3.3. Münster: Aschendorff, 1911.

Edmondson, Jonathan, Steve Mason, and Jonathan Rives, eds. *Flavius Josephus and Flavian Rome*. Oxford: Oxford University Press, 2005.

Ego, Beate. "Review of Rivka Nir, *The Destruction of Jerusalem and the Idea of Redemption in the Syriac Apocalypse of Baruch*." *ZAW* 116 (2004): 470.

Eltester, Walther, ed. *Studien zu den Testamenten der Zwölf Patriarchen: Christoph Burchard, Jacob Jervell, Johannes Thomas*. ZNW 36. Berlin: Töpelmann, 1969.

Elwolde, John. "The Hodayot's Use of the Psalter: Text-Critical Contributions (Book I)." In *Psalms and Prayers: Papers Read at the Joint Meeting of the Society of Old Testament Study and the Oudtestamentische Werkgezelschap in Nederland en Belgie, Apeldoorn. August 2006*, ed. Bob Becking and Eric Peels. OtSt 55. Leiden: Brill, 2007, 78-108.

Endres, John C. *Biblical Interpretation in the Book of Jubilees*. CBQMS 18. Washington: Catholic Biblical Association, 1987.

Enns, Peter. *Exodus Retold: Ancient Exegesis of the Departure from Egypt in Wis 10:15-21 and 19:1-9*. HSM 57. Atlanta: Scholars, 1997.

―――. "A Retelling of the Song at the Sea in Wis 10,20-21." *Bib* 76 (1995): 1-24; repr. *The Function of Scripture in Early Jewish and Christian Tradition*, ed. Craig A. Evans and James A. Sanders. JSNTSup 154. SSEJC 6. Sheffield: Sheffield Academic, 1998, 142-65.

Eppel, Robert. *Le Piétisme Juif dans les Testaments de Douze Patriarches*. Paris: Alcan, 1930.

Eshel, Esther. "Isaiah 11:15: A New Interpretation Based on the Genesis Apocryphon." *DSD* 13 (2006): 38-45.

―――. "The *imago mundi* of the *Genesis Apocryphon*." In *Heavenly Tablets: Interpretation*,

Identity and Tradition in Ancient Judaism, ed. Lynn LiDonnici and Andrea Lieber. JSJSup 119. Leiden: Brill, 2007, 111-31.

―――. "The Aramaic Levi Document, the Genesis Apocryphon, and Jubilees: A Study of Shared Traditions." In *Enoch and the Mosaic Torah: The Evidence of Jubilees,* ed. Gabriele Boccaccini and Giovanni Ibba. Grand Rapids: Eerdmans, 2009, 82-98.

―――. "The Dream Visions in the Noah Story of the Genesis Apocryphon and Related Texts." In *Northern Lights on the Dead Sea Scrolls: Proceedings of the Nordic Qumran Network 2003-2006,* ed. Anders Klostergaard Peterson et al. STDJ 80. Leiden: Brill, 2009, 41-61.

―――. The Genesis Apocryphon and Other Related Aramaic Texts from Qumran: The Birth of Noah." *Aramaica Qumranica,* 277-97.

―――. "The Noah Cycle in the Genesis Apocryphon." In Stone, Amihay, and Hillel, *Noah and His Book(s),* 77-95.

―――. "The Genesis Apocryphon: A Chain of Traditions." Paper presented at The Dead Sea Scrolls and Contemporary Culture: Celebrating 60 Years of Discovery, Israel Museum, Jerusalem, July 2008.

Eshel, Hanan. *The Dead Sea Scrolls and the Hasmonean State.* SDSSRL. Grand Rapids: Eerdmans and Jerusalem: Yad Ben-Zvi, 2008.

Esler, Philip F. "The Social Function of 4 Ezra." *JSNT* 53 (1994): 99-123.

Evans, Craig E. "The Genesis Apocryphon and the Rewritten Bible." *RevQ* 13 (1988): 153-65.

Evans, Craig E., and Shemaryahu Talmon, eds. *The Quest for Context and Meaning: Studies in Biblical Intertextuality in Honor of James A. Sanders.* Biblical Interpretation 28. Leiden: Brill, 1997.

Fabry, Heinz-Josef, and Dieter Böhler, eds. *Im Brennpunkt: Die Septuaginta.* Vol. 3: *Studien zur Theologie, Anthropologie, Ekklesiologie, Eschatologie und Liturgie der griechischen Bibel.* BWANT 174. Stuttgart: Kohlhammer, 2007.

Fabry, Heinz-Josef, Armin Lange, and Hermann Lichtenberger, eds. *Qumranstudien: Vorträge und Beiträge der Teilnehmer des Qumranseminars auf dem internationalen Treffen der Society of Biblical Literature, Münster, 25.-26. Juli 1993.* Göttingen: Vandenhoeck & Ruprecht, 1996.

Fabry, Heinz-Josef, and Ulrich Offerhaus, eds. *Im Brennpunkt: Die Septuaginta.* Vols. 1-2: *Studien zur Entstehung und Bedeutung der griechischen Bibel.* BWANT 153-61. Stuttgart: Kohlhammer, 2001-2004.

Falk, Daniel K. *The Parabiblical Texts: Strategies for Extending the Scriptures in the Dead Sea Scrolls.* CQS 8; LSTS 63. London: T. & T. Clark, 2007.

―――. "Divergence from Genesis in the *Genesis Apocryphon.*" In Parry et al., *Qumran Cave 1 Revisited,* 193-204.

Feldman, Louis H. "Prolegomenon." In James, *The Biblical Antiquities of Philo,* vii-cxix.

―――. *Josephus and Modern Scholarship, 1937-1980.* Berlin: de Gruyter, 1984.

―――. "Use, Authority and Exegesis of Mikra in the Writings of Josephus." In Mulder, *Mikra,* 455-518.

―――. "Prophets and Prophecy in Josephus." *JTS* 41 (1990): 386-422.

―――. *Jew and Gentile in the Ancient World: Attitudes and Interactions from Alexander to Justinian.* Princeton: Princeton University Press, 1993.

―――. "Reading Between the Lines: Appreciation of Judaism in Anti-Jewish Writers

Cited in *Contra Apionem.*" In *Josephus's* Contra Apionem: *Studies in Its Character and Context with a Latin Concordance to the Portion Missing in Greek,* ed. Feldman and John R. Levison. AGJU 34. Leiden: Brill, 1996.

———. *Josephus's Interpretation of the Bible.* Berkeley: University of California Press, 1998.

———. *Studies in Josephus's Rewritten Bible.* JSJSup 58. Leiden: Brill, 1998.

———. "The Destruction of Sodom and Gomorrah According to Philo, Pseudo-Philo and Josephus." *Hen* 23 (2001): 185-98.

———. "The Portrayal of Sihon and Og in Philo, Pseudo-Philo and Josephus." *JJS* 53 (2002): 264-72.

———. "The Plague of the First-Born Egyptians in Rabbinic Tradition, Philo, Pseudo-Philo and Josephus." *RB* 109 (2002): 403-21.

———. "The Portrayal of Phinehas by Philo, Pseudo-Philo, and Josephus." *JQR* 92 (2002): 315-45.

———. *Judean Antiquities Books 1–4.* Vol. 3 of Mason, *Flavius Josephus: Translation and Commentary.* Leiden: Brill, 2004.

Feldman, Louis H., and Gohei Hata, eds. *Josephus, the Bible and History.* Leiden: Brill, 1989.

Feldman, Louis H., and John R. Levison, eds. *Josephus'* Contra Apionem: *Studies in Its Character and Context with a Latin Concordance to the Portion Missing in Greek.* AGJU 34. Leiden: Brill, 1996.

Feldman, Louis H., and Heinz Schreckenberg. *Josephus: A Supplementary Bibliography.* New York: Garland, 1986.

Fernández Marcos, Natalio. *The Septuagint in Context: Introduction to the Greek Version of the Bible.* Trans. Wilfred G. E. Watson. Leiden: Brill, 2000.

Fewell, Danna N., ed. *Reading between Texts: Intertexuality and the Hebrew Bible.* Louisville: Westminster John Knox, 1992.

Fishbane, Michael. *Biblical Interpretation in Ancient Israel.* Oxford: Clarendon, 1985.

———. "Use, Authority and Interpretation of Mikra at Qumran." In Mulder, *Mikra,* 339-77.

———. "From Scribalism to Rabbinism: Perspectives on the Emergence of Classical Judaism." In *The Garments of Torah: Essays in Biblical Hermeneutics.* Bloomington: Indiana University Press, 1989, 64-78; repr. *The Sage in Israel and the Ancient Near East,* ed. John G. Gammie and Leo G. Perdue. Winona Lake: Eisenbrauns, 1990, 439-56.

Fisk, Bruce N. *Do You Not Remember? Scripture, Story and Exegesis in the Rewritten Bible of Pseudo-Philo.* JSPSup 37. Sheffield: Sheffield Academic, 2001.

Fitzmyer, Joseph A. "The Use of Explicit Old Testament Quotations in Qumran Literature and in the New Testament." *NTS* 7 (1961): 297-333; repr. *Essays on the Semitic Background of the New Testament.* London: Chapman, 1971; BRS. Grand Rapids: Eerdmans and Livonia: Dove, 1997, 3-58.

———. *The Genesis Apocryphon of Qumran Cave 1 (1Q20): A Commentary.* 3rd ed. BibOr 18B. Rome: Pontifical Biblical Institute, 2004.

Flannery Dailey, Frances. "Non-Linear Time in Apocalyptic Texts." In *SBLSP 1999.* Atlanta: Scholars, 1999, 231-45.

Flint, Peter W., and James C. VanderKam, eds. *The Dead Sea Scrolls after Fifty Years: A Comprehensive Assessment.* 2 vols. Leiden: Brill, 1999.

Forestell, J. Terence. *Targumic Traditions and the New Testament: An Annotated Bibliography with a New Testament Index.* Aramaic Studies 4. Chico: Scholars, 1979.

Fraade, Steven D. *Enosh and His Generation: Pre-Israelite Hero and History in Postbiblical Interpretation.* SBLMS 30. Chico: Scholars, 1984.

———. "Interpretive Authority in the Studying Community of Qumran." *JJS* 144 (1993): 46-69.

———. "Looking for Legal Midrash at Qumran." In Stone and Chazon, *Biblical Perspectives,* 59-79.

Franxman, Thomas W. *Genesis and the Jewish Antiquities of Flavius Josephus.* BibOr 35. Rome: Biblical Institute Press, 1979.

Frenkel, Yonah. *Darkhe ha-Aggadah veha-midrash.* Givataim: Yad la-talmud, 1991. [Hebrew]

Fröhlich, Ida. "Daniel 2 and Deutero-Isaiah." In van der Woude, *The Book of Daniel in the Light of New Findings,* 266-70.

Gafni, Isaiah. "Josephus and I Maccabees." In Feldman and Hata, *Josephus, the Bible and History,* 116-31.

García Martínez, Florentino. "Le IVe Esdras et les MSS de Qumrân." In *Rashi, 1040-1990: Hommage à Ephraim E. Urbach. Congrès européen des études juives,* ed. Gabrielle Sed-Rajana. Paris: Cerf, 1993, 81-90.

———. "Traditions Common to 4 Ezra and the Dead Sea Scrolls." In *Qumranica Minora,* ed. García Martínez and Eibert J. C. Tigchelaar. STDJ 63. Leiden: Brill, 2007, 1:153-87.

García Martínez, Florentino, and Mladen Popović, eds. *Defining Identities: We, You, and the Other in the Dead Sea Scrolls.* STDJ 70. Leiden: Brill, 2008.

García Martínez, Florentino, Eibert J. C. Tigchelaar, and Adam S. van der Woude, eds. "11QtargumJob." In *Qumran Cave 11: II, 11Q2-18, 11Q20-31.* DJD 23. Oxford: Clarendon, 1998, 79-180.

Gaster, Moses. *The Asatir: The Samaritan Book of the "Secrets of Moses" Together with the Pitron or Samaritan Commentary and the Samaritan Story of the Death of Moses.* London: Royal Asiatic Society, 1927.

Georgi, Dieter. *Weisheit Salomos.* JSHRZ 3.4. Gütersloh: Gütersloher, 1980.

Gevirtz, Marianne Luijken. "Abram's Dream in the Genesis Apocrypon: Its Motifs and Their Function." *Maarav* 8 (1992): 229-43.

Gilbert, Maurice. "Wisdom of Solomon." In Stone, *Jewish Writings of the Second Temple Period,* 301-13.

———. "Wisdom of Solomon in Scripture." In Sæbø, *Hebrew Bible/Old Testament,* 1.2 (2000): 606-17.

Ginsberg, Harold Louis. *Studies in Daniel.* New York: Jewish Theological Seminary, 1948.

———. "Daniel" (addition to entry). *Encyclopedia Mikra'it.* Jerusalem: Mosad Bialik, 1960, 2:949-52. [Hebrew]

———. "The Oldest Interpretation of the Suffering Servant." *VT* 3 (1953): 400-404.

Ginzberg, Louis. *Legends of the Jews.* 7 vols. Philadelphia: Jewish Publication Society, 1909-1938; repr. 2 vols., 2003.

———. *An Unknown Jewish Sect.* New York: Jewish Theological Seminary, 1976; German ed. New York, 1922.

Giovanni, Deiana. "Miti di origine, miti di caduta e presenza del femminino nel 4 Esdra e nel 2 Baruch." *RStB* 6 (1994): 141-52.

Glessmer, Uwe. "The Otot-texts (4Q319) and the Problem of Intercalations in the Context of the 364-day Calendar." In Fabry, Lange, and Lichtenberger, *Qumranstudien*, 125-64.

Goldingay, John E. *Daniel.* WBC 30. Dallas: Word, 1987.

Gooding, David W. "Two Possible Examples of Midrashic Interpretation in the Septuagint Exodus." In *Wort, Lied und Gottesspruch.* Vol. 1: *Beiträge zur Septuaginta. Festschrift Joseph Ziegler,* ed. Josef Schreiner. FB 1. Würzburg: Echter, 1972, 39-48.

Goshen-Gottstein, Moshe H. "Hebrew Syntax and the History of the Bible Text." *Text* 8 (1973): 100-106.

Grabbe, Lester L. "The End of the Desolations of Jerusalem: From Jeremiah's 70 Years to Daniel's 70 Weeks of Years." In *Early Jewish and Christian Exegesis: Studies in Memory of William Hugh Brownlee,* ed. Craig A. Evans and William F. Stinespring. Homage Series 10. Atlanta: Scholars, 1987, 67-72.

———. *Etymology in Early Jewish Interpretation: The Hebrew Names in Philo.* BJS 115. Atlanta: Scholars, 1988.

———. "The 70-Weeks Prophecy (Daniel 9:24-27) in Early Jewish Interpretation." In Evans and Talmon, *The Quest for Context and Meaning,* 595-611.

———. *Wisdom of Solomon.* GAP 3. Sheffield: Sheffield Academic, 1997.

———. "Poets, Scribes, or Preachers? The Reality of Prophecy in the Second Temple Period." In *Knowing the End from the Beginning: The Prophetic, the Apocalyptic and Their Relationships,* ed. Grabbe and Robert D. Haak. JSPSup 46. London: T. & T. Clark, 2003, 192-215.

———. "The Law, the Prophets, and the Rest: The State of the Bible in Pre-Maccabean Times." *DSD* 13 (2006): 319-38.

Grabe, Joannes Ernestus. *Spicilegium SS. Patrum ut et Haereticorum, seculi post Christum natum I. II. & III.* 2 vols. Oxford: E theatro Sheldoniano, 1698.

Gray, Rebecca. *Prophetic Figures in Late Second Temple Jewish Palestine: The Evidence from Josephus.* New York: Oxford University Press, 1993.

Greenfield, Jonas C., and Elisha Qimron. "The Genesis Apocryphon Col. XII." In *Studies in Qumran Aramaic,* ed. Takamitsu Muraoka. AbrNSup 3. Leuven: Peeters, 1992, 70-77.

Grelot, Pierre. "Le Livre des Jubilés et le Testament de Lévi." In *Mélanges Dominiques Barthélemy: Études bibliques offertes à l'occasion de son 60ᵉ anniversaire,* ed. Pierre Casetti, Othmar Keel, and Adrian Schenker. OBO 38. Göttingen, 1981, 109-31.

———. "De *l'Apocryphe de la Genèse* aux *Targoums:* sur Genèse 14,18-20." In Kapera, *Intertestamental Essays in Honour of Józef Tadeusz Milik,* 77-90.

Grossfeld, Bernard. *A Bibliography of Targum Literature.* Vols. 1-2: Cincinnati: Hebrew Union College Press, 1972-77; vol. 3: New York: Sepher-Hermon, 1990.

———. *The Targum Onqelos to Genesis.* ArBib 6. Wilmington: Glazier, 1988.

———. *The Targum Onqelos to Exodus.* ArBib 7. Wilmington: Glazier, 1988.

———. *The Targum Onqelos to Leviticus and the Targum Onqelos to Numbers.* ArBib 8. Wilmington: Glazier, 1988.

———. *The Targum Onqelos to Deuteronomy.* ArBib 9. Wilmington: Glazier, 1988.

———. *A Bibliography of Targum Literature.* Vol 3. New York: Sepher-Hermon, 1990.

———. *The Two Targums of Esther.* ArBib 18. Collegeville: Liturgical, 1991.

Grossman, Maxine L. "Cultivating Identity: Textual Virtuosity and 'Insider' Status." In García Martínez and Popović, *Defining Identities*, 1-11.

Grossman, Maxine L., ed. *Rediscovering the Dead Sea Scrolls: An Assessment of Old and New Approaches and Methods*. Grand Rapids: Eerdmans, 2010.

Gruen, Erich S. *Heritage and Hellenism: The Reinvention of Jewish Tradition*. Berkeley: University of California Press, 1998.

Hadot, Jean. "La Datation de l'Apocalypse Syriaque de Baruch." *Sem* 15 (1965): 79-95.

———. "Le Problème de l'Apocalypse Syriaque de Baruch d'après un Ouvrage Récent." *Sem* 20 (1970): 59-76.

Hallbäck, Geert. "The Fall of Zion and the Revelation of the Law: An Interpretation of 4 Ezra." *SJOT* 6 (1992): 263-92.

Halpern-Amaru, Betsy. *Rewriting the Bible: Land and Covenant in Post-biblical Jewish Literature*. Valley Forge: Trinity Press International, 1994.

———. *The Empowerment of Women in the Book of Jubilees*. JSJSup 60. Leiden: Brill, 1999.

———. "Burying the Fathers: Exegetical Strategies and Source Traditions in Jubilees 46." In Chazon, Dimant, and Clements, *Reworking the Bible*, 135-52.

Hanhart, Robert. "Die Septuaginta als Interpretation und Aktualisierung: Jesaja 9:1(8:23)-7(6)." In *Isaac Leo Seeligmann Volume: Essays on the Bible and the Ancient World*. Vol. 3: *Non-Hebrew Section*, ed. Alexander Rofé and Yair Zakovitch. Jerusalem: Rubenstein, 1983, 331-46.

———. "The Translation of the Septuagint in the Light of Earlier Tradition and Subsequent Influences." In *Septuagint, Scrolls and Cognate Writings: Papers Presented to the International Symposium on the Septuagint and Its Relations to the Dead Sea Scrolls and Other Writings, Manchester, 1990*, ed. George J. Brooke and Barnabas Lindars. SBLSCS 33. Atlanta: SBL, 1992, 339-79.

Hanneken, Todd Russell. "Angels and Demons in the Book of Jubilees and Contemporary Apocalypses." *Hen* 28 (2006): 11-25.

Harlow, Daniel C. *The Greek Apocalypse of Baruch (3 Baruch) in Hellenistic Judaism and Early Christianity*. SVTP 12. Leiden: Brill, 1996.

Harrington, Daniel J. "The Original Language of Pseudo-Philo's Liber Antiquitatum Biblicarum." *HTR* 63 (1970): 503-14.

———. "Pseudo-Philo." In *OTP*, 2:297-377.

———. "The 'Holy Land' in Pseudo-Philo, 4 Ezra, and 2 Baruch." In Paul, Kraft, Schiffman, and Fields, *Emanuel*, 661-72.

———. "Wisdom and Apocalyptic in 4QInstruction and 4Ezra." In *Wisdom and Apocalypticism in the Dead Sea Scrolls and in the Biblical Tradition*, ed. Florentino García Martínez. BETL 68. Leuven: Leuven University Press; Paris and Dudley: Peeters, 2003, 343-55.

Harrington, Daniel J., Jacques Cazeaux, Charles Perrot, and Pierre-Maurice Bogaert. *Pseudo-Philon: Les Antiquités Bibliques*. 2 vols. SC 229-30. Paris: Cerf, 1976.

Harrington, Daniel J., and Anthony J. Saldarini. *Targum Jonathan of the Former Prophets*. ArBib 10. Wilmington: Glazier, 1987.

Hartman, Louis F., and Alexander A. Di Lella. *The Book of Daniel*. AB 23. Garden City: Doubleday, 1978.

Haupt, Detlev. "Das Testament des Levi: Untersuchungen zu seiner Entstehung und Überlieferungsgeschichte." Diss., Halle-Wittenberg, 1969.

Hayman, Allison P. "The 'Man from the Sea' in 4 Ezra 13." *JJS* 49 (1998): 1-16.

Hayward, C. T. Robert. *The Targum of Jeremiah.* ArBib 12. Wilmington: Glazier, 1987.

———. "The Figure of Adam in Pseudo-Philo's Biblical Antiquities." *JSJ* 23 (1992): 1-20.

———, trans. *Saint Jerome's Hebrew Questions on Genesis.* Oxford: Clarendon, 1995.

Heinemann, Isaak. *Darkhe Ha-Agadah.* Jerusalem: Magnes, 1954; repr. 1970.

Hempel, Charlotte. "Maskil(im) and Rabbim: From Daniel to Qumran." In Hempel and Lieu, *Biblical Traditions in Transmission,* 133-56.

———. "Sources and Redaction in the Dead Sea Scrolls: The Growth of Ancient Texts." In Grossman, *Rediscovering the Dead Sea Scrolls,* 162-81.

Hempel, Charlotte, and Judith M. Lieu, eds. *Biblical Traditions in Transmission: Essays in Honour of Michael A. Knibb.* JSJSup 111. Leiden: Brill, 2006.

Hengel, Martin. *The Septuagint as Christian Scripture: Its Prehistory and the Problem of Its Canon.* OTS. London: T. & T. Clark, 2002.

Henshke, David. "The Holiness of Jerusalem: Between the Rabbis and the Sectarian Law." *Tarbiz* 67 (1998): 5-28. [Hebrew]

Henze, Matthias. *The Madness of King Nebuchadnezzar: The Ancient Near Eastern Origins and Early History of Interpretation of Daniel 4.* JSJSup 61. Leiden: Brill, 1999.

———. "The Narrative Frame of Daniel: A Literary Assessment." *JSJ* 32 (2001): 5-24.

———. "From Jeremiah to Baruch: Pseudepigraphy in the Syriac Apocalypse of Baruch." In Hempel and Lieu, *Biblical Traditions in Transmission,* 157-77.

———. "Review of Rivka Nir, *The Destruction of Jerusalem and the Idea of Redemption in the Syriac Apocalypse of Baruch.*" *JSP* 15 (2006): 145-48.

———. "Qoheleth and the Syriac Apocalypse of Baruch." *VT* 58 (2008): 28-43.

———. "Torah and Eschatology in the Syriac Apocalypse of Baruch." In *The Significance of Sinai: Traditions About Sinai and Divine Revelation in Judaism and Christianity,* ed. George J. Brooke, Hindy Najman, and Loren T. Stuckenbruck. Leiden: Brill, 2008, 201-15.

———. *Jewish Apocalypticism in Late First Century Israel: Reading Second Baruch in Context.* TSAJ 142. Tübingen: Mohr Siebeck, 2011.

———, ed. *Biblical Interpretation at Qumran.* SDSSRL. Grand Rapids: Eerdmans, 2005.

Hertzberg, Hans Wilhelm. "Die Nachgeschichte alttestamentlicher Texte innerhalb des Alten Testaments." *BZAW* 66 (1936): 110-21.

Hilhorst, Anthony, Émile Puech, and Eibert Tigchelaar, eds. *Flores Florentino: Dead Sea Scrolls and Other Early Jewish Studies in Honour of Florentino García Martínez.* Leiden: Brill, 2007.

Himmelfarb, Martha. "The Wisdom of the Scribe, the Wisdom of the Priest, and the Wisdom of the King According to Ben Sira." In *For a Later Generation: The Transformation of Tradition in Israel, Early Judaism and Early Christianity,* ed. Randal A. Argall, Beverly A. Bow, and Rodney A. Werline. Harrisburg: Trinity Press International, 2000, 89-99.

Hoek, Annewies van den. *Clement of Alexandria and His Use of Philo in the Stromateis: An Early Christian Reshaping of a Jewish Model.* VCSup 3. Leiden: Brill, 1988.

Hoffman, Yair. "The Technique of Quotation and Citation as an Interpretive Device." In

Creative Biblical Exegesis: Christian and Jewish Hermeneutics through the Centuries, ed. Benjamin Uffenheimer and Henning Graf Reventlow. JSOTSup 59. Sheffield: JSOT, 1988, 71-79.

Hofmann, Norbert J. "Rezeption des Dtn im Buch Tobit, in der Assumptio Mosis und im 4. Esrabuch." In *Das Deuteronomium,* ed. Georg Braulik. ÖBS 23. Frankfurt: Lang, 2003, 311-42.

Hollander, Harm W. *Joseph as an Ethical Model in the Testaments of the Twelve Patriarchs.* SVTP 6. Leiden: Brill, 1981.

Hollander, Harm W., and Marinus de Jonge. *The Testaments of the Twelve Patriarchs: A Commentary.* SVTP 8. Leiden: Brill, 1985.

Holm-Nielsen, Svend. *Hodayot: Psalms from Qumran.* ATDan 2. Aarhus: Universitetsforlaget, 1960.

Hölscher, Gustav. "Josephus." In PW, 18 (1916): 1934-2000.

Honigman, Sylvie. *The Septuagint and Homeric Scholarship in Alexandria: A Study in the Narrative of the Letter of Aristeas.* London: Routledge, 2003.

Horgan, Maurya P. *Pesharim: Qumran Interpretations of Biblical Books.* CBQMS 8. Washington: Catholic Biblical Association, 1979.

————. "Pesharim." In *The Dead Sea Scrolls: Hebrew, Aramaic, and Greek Texts with English Translations.* Vol. 6B: *Pesharim, Other Commentaries, and Related Documents,* ed. James H. Charlesworth. Tübingen: Mohr Siebeck and Louisville: Westminster John Knox, 2002.

Horsley, Richard A., and Patrick Tiller. "Ben Sira and the Sociology of the Second Temple." In *Second Temple Studies III: Studies in Politics, Class, and Material Culture,* ed. Philip R. Davies and John M. Halligan. JSOTSup 340. Sheffield: Sheffield Academic, 2002, 74-107.

Horst, Pieter W. van der. *Essays on the Jewish World of Early Christianity.* NTOA 14. Freiburg: Universitätsverlag, 1990.

Howard, George E. "The 'Aberrant' Text of Philo's Quotations Reconsidered." *HUCA* 44 (1973): 197-209.

Hughes, Julie A. *Scriptural Allusions and Exegesis in the Hodayot.* STDJ 59. Leiden: Brill, 2006.

Hultgård, Anders. *L'Eschatologie des Testaments des Douze Patriarches.* Vol. 1: *Interprétation des texts.* Acta Universitatis Upsaliensis, Historia Religionum 6. Stockholm: Almqvist & Wiksell, 1977.

————. *L'Eschatologie des Testaments des Douze Patriarches.* Vol. 2: *Composition de l'ouvrage, textes et traductions.* Acta Universitatis Upsaliensis, Historia Religionum 7. Stockholm: Almqvist & Wiksell, 1981.

Humphrey, Edith McEwan. *The Ladies and the Cities: Transformation and Apocalyptic Identity in Joseph and Aseneth, 4 Ezra, the Apocalypse and The Shepherd of Hermas.* JSPSup 17. Sheffield: Sheffield Academic, 1995.

Humphreys, W. Lee. "A Life-Style for Diaspora: A Study of the Tales of Esther and Daniel." *JBL* 92 (1973): 211-23.

Jacobson, Howard. "Marginalia to Pseudo-Philo Liber Antiquitatum Biblicarum and to the Chronicles of Jerahmeel." *REJ* 142 (1983): 455-59.

————. *A Commentary on Pseudo-Philo's Liber Antiquitatum Biblicarum, with Latin Text and English Translation.* AGJU 31. 2 vols. Leiden: Brill, 1996.

James, Montague R. *The Biblical Antiquities of Philo.* London: SPCK, 1917; repr. New York: Ktav, 1971.

Japhet, Sara. *The Ideology of the Book of Chronicles and Its Place in Biblical Thought.* BEATAJ 9. Frankfurt: Lang, 1989.

Jassen, Alex P. *Mediating the Divine: Prophecy and Revelation in the Dead Sea Scrolls and Second Temple Judaism.* STDJ 68. Leiden: Brill, 2007.

Jeremias, Gert. *Der Lehrer der Gerechtigkeit.* SUNT 2. Göttingen: Vandenhoeck & Ruprecht, 1963.

Jobes, Karen H., and Moises Silva. *Invitation to the Septuagint.* Grand Rapids: Baker, 2000.

Jokiranta, Jutta. "Pesharim: A Mirror of Self-Undersanding." In De Troyer and Lange, *Reading the Present in the Qumran Library,* 23-34.

Jonge, Henrik J. de. "The Earliest Traceable Stage of the Textual Tradition of the Testaments of the Twelve Patriarchs." In Marinus de Jonge, *Studies on the Testaments of the Twelve Patriarchs,* 63-86.

————. "Die Patriarchentestamente von Roger Bacon bis Richard Simon." In Marinus de Jonge, *Studies on the Testaments of the Twelve Patriarchs,* 3-42.

Jonge, Marinus de. *The Testaments of the Twelve Patriarchs: A Study of Their Text, Composition, and Origin.* Assen: Van Gorcum, 1953.

————. *The Testaments of the Twelve Patriarchs: A Critical Edition of the Greek Text.* PVTG 1.2. Leiden: Brill, 1975.

————. *Jewish Eschatology, Early Christian Christology, and the Testaments of the Twelve Patriarchs: Collected Essays of Marinus de Jonge.* NovTSup 63. Leiden: Brill, 1991.

————. *Pseudepigrapha of the Old Testament as Part of Christian Literature: The Case of the Testaments of the Twelve Patriarchs and the Greek Life of Adam and Eve.* SVTP 18. Leiden: Brill, 2003.

————, ed. *Studies on the Testaments of the Twelve Patriarchs: Text and Interpretation.* SVTP 3. Leiden: Brill, 1975.

Kahana, Menahem. "The Halakhic Midrashim." In *The Literature of the Sages.* Part 2: *Midrash and Targum, Liturgy, Poetry, Mysticism, Contracts, Inscriptions, Ancient Science and the Languages of Rabbinic Literature,* ed. Shmuel Safrai. CRINT 2.3. Assen: Van Gorcum and Philadelphia: Fortress, 2006, 3-105.

Kamesar, Adam. "Biblical Interpretation in Philo." In *The Cambridge Companion to Philo,* 65-91.

————, ed. *The Cambridge Companion to Philo.* Cambridge: Cambridge University Press, 2009.

Kapera, Zdzislaw J., ed. *Intertestamental Essays in Honour of Józef Tadeusz Milik.* Qumranica Mogilanensia 6. Kraków: Enigma, 1992.

Katz, Peter. *Philo's Bible: The Aberrant Text of Bible Quotations in Some Philonic Writings and Its Place in the Textual History of the Greek Bible.* Cambridge: Cambridge University Press, 1950.

————. "Septuagintal Studies in the Mid-Century: Their Links with the Past and Their Present Tendencies." In *The Background of the New Testament and Its Eschatology in*

Honor of Charles Harold Dodd, ed. W. D. Davies and David Daube. Cambridge: Cambridge University Press, 1956, 176-208.

Kellenberger, Edgar. "Textvarianten in den Daniel-Legenden als Zeugnisse mündlicher Tradierung?" In *XIII Congress of the International Organization for Septuagint and Cognate Studies: Ljubljana, 2007,* ed. Melvin K. H. Peters. SBLSCS 55. Atlanta: SBL, 2008, 207-23.

Kisch, Guido. *Pseudo-Philo's Liber Antiquitatum Biblicarum.* Notre Dame: University of Notre Dame Press, 1949.

Kister, Menahem. "Some Aspects of Qumranic Halakhah. In *The Madrid Qumran Congress: Proceedings of the International Congress on the Dead Sea Scrolls, March 1991,* ed. Julio Trebolle Barrera and Luis Vegas Montaner. Leiden: Brill, 1992, 2:571-88.

————. "Biblical Phrases and Hidden Biblical Interpretations and Pesharim." In *The Dead Sea Scrolls: Forty Years of Research,* ed. Devorah Dimant and Uriel Rappaport. STDJ 10. Leiden: Brill, 1992, 27-39.

————. "Observations on Aspects of Exegesis, Tradition, and Theology in Midrash, Pseudepigrapha, and Other Writings." In Reeves, *Tracing the Threads,* 1-34.

————. "A Common Heritage: Biblical Interpretation at Qumran and Its Implications." In Stone and Chazon, *Biblical Perspectives,* 101-11.

Kittel, Bonnie. *The Hymns of Qumran: Translation and Commentary.* SBLDS 50. Chico: Scholars, 1981.

Klein, Michael L. *Genizah Manuscripts of Palestinian Targums to the Pentateuch.* 2 vols. Cincinnati: Hebrew Union College Press, 1986.

Klijn, Albertus F. J. "The Sources and Redaction of the Syriac Apocalypse of Baruch." *JSJ* 1 (1970): 65-76.

————. "2 (Syriac Apocalypse of) Baruch: A New Introduction and Translation." In *OTP,* 1:615-52.

————. "Recent Developments in the Study of the Syriac Apocalypse of Baruch." *JSP* 4 (1989): 3-17.

————. *Die Esra-Apokalypse (IV. Esra): Nach dem lateinischen Text unter Benutzung der anderen Versionen übersetzt und herausgegeben.* GCS. Berlin: Akademie, 1992.

————. "The Character of the Arabic Version of the Apocalypse of Baruch." In Lichtenberger and Oegema, *Jüdische Schriften in ihrem antik-jüdischen und urchristlichen Kontext,* 204-8.

Knibb, Michael A. "Apocalyptic and Wisdom in 4 Ezra." *JSJ* 13 (1983): 56-74.

————. "Jubilees and the Origins of the Qumran Community." Inaugural Lecture, King's College. London, 1989.

————. "'You Are Indeed Wiser than Daniel': Reflections on the Character of the Book of Daniel." In van der Woude, *The Book of Daniel in the Light of New Findings,* 399-411.

————. "The Book of Daniel in Its Context." In Collins and Flint, *The Book of Daniel,* 1:16-35.

————, ed. *The Septuagint and Messianism.* BETL 195. Leuven: Peeters, 2006.

Knowles, Michael P. "Abram and the Birds in Jubilees 11: A Subtext for the Parable of the Sower?" *NTS* 41 (1995): 145-51.

Koch, Klaus. "Is Daniel Also Among the Prophets?" *Int* 39 (1985): 117-30.

————. *Daniel.* BKAT 22. Neukirchen: Neukirchener, 1986-.

————. "Vom profetischen zum apokalyptischen Visionsbericht." In *Apocalypticism in the Mediterranean World and the Near East,* ed. David Hellholm. Tübingen: Mohr Siebeck, 1983, 413-46; repr. *Vor der Wende der Zeiten: Beiträge zur apokalyptischen Literatur,* ed. Uwe Gleßmer and Martin Krause. Gesammelte Aufsätze 3. Neukirchen: Neukirchener, 1996, 143-78.

Kolarcik, Michael. *The Ambiguity of Death in the Book of Wisdom 1–6: A Study of Literary Structure and Interpretation.* AnBib 127. Rome: Pontifical Biblical Institute, 1991.

Kooij, Arie van der. "Perspectives on the Study of the Septuagint: Who Are the Translators?" In *Perspectives in the Study of the Old Testament and Early Judaism. Festschrift Adam S. van der Woude,* ed. Florentino García Martínez and Edward Noort. VTSup 73. Leiden: Brill, 1998, 214-29.

————. "The Septuagint of Isaiah: Translation and Interpretation." In *The Book of Isaiah — Le Livre d'Isaïe: Les Oracles et leurs Relectures, Unité et complexité de l'ouvrage,* ed. Jacques Vermeylen. BETL 81. Leuven: Peeters, 1989, 127-33.

Koole, Jan L. "Die Bibel des Ben-Sira." *OtSt* 14 (1965): 374-96.

Koskenniemi, Erkki. *The Old Testament Miracle-Workers in Early Judaism.* WUNT ser. 2, 206. Tübingen: Mohr Siebeck, 2005.

Kraft, Robert A. "Ezra Materials in Judaism and Christianity." In *ANRW,* 2.19.1 (1979), 119-36.

————. "Towards Assessing the Latin Text of '5 Ezra': The Christian Connection." In *Christians among Jews and Gentiles: Essays in Honor of Krister Stendahl on His Sixty-fifth Birthday,* ed. George W. MacRae and George W. E. Nickelsburg. Philadelphia: Fortress, 1986, 158-69.

————. "Scripture and Canon in the Apocrypha and Pseudepigrapha." In Sæbø, *Hebrew Bible/Old Testament,* 1.1:199-216.

Kratz, Reinhard Gregor. *Translatio Imperii: Untersuchungen zu den aramäischen Daniel-erzählungen und ihrem theologiegeschichtlichen Umfeld.* WMANT 63. Neukirchen-Vluyn: Neukirchener, 1991.

Kraus, Wolfgang, and R. Glenn Wooden, eds. *Septuagint Research: Issues and Challenges in the Study of the Greek Jewish Scriptures.* SBLSCS 53. Atlanta: SBL, 2006.

Krieger, Klaus-Stefan. *Geschichtsschreibung als Apologetik bei Flavius Josephus.* TANZ 9. Tübingen: Francke, 1994.

Kugel, James L. "Two Introductions to Midrash." *Proof* 3 (1983): 131-55; repr. *Midrash and Literature,* ed. Geoffrey H. Hartman and Sanford Budick. New Haven: Yale University Press, 1986, 77-103.

————. "The Bible's Earliest Interpreters." *Proof* 7 (1987): 269-83.

————. *In Potiphar's House: The Interpretive Life of Biblical Texts.* San Francisco: HarperSanFrancisco, 1990.

————. "Levi's Election to the Priesthood in Second Temple Writings." *HTR* 86 (1993): 1-64.

————. *Traditions of the Bible: A Guide to the Bible as It Was at the Start of the Common Era.* Cambridge, Mass.: Harvard University Press, 1998.

————. "Ancient Biblical Interpretation and the Biblical Sage." In *Studies in Ancient Midrash,* 1-26.

————. "Some Instances of Biblical Interpretation in the Hymns and Wisdom Writings of Qumran." In *Studies in Ancient Midrash,* 155-69.

————. *The Ladder of Jacob: Ancient Interpretations of the Biblical Story of Jacob and His Children.* Princeton: Princeton University Press, 2006.

————. "Which Is Older, Jubilees or the Genesis Apocryphon? An Exegetical Approach." In Roitman, Schiffman, and Tzoref, *The Dead Sea Scrolls and Contemporary Culture,* 257-94.

————, ed. *Studies in Ancient Midrash.* Cambridge, Mass.: Harvard University Press, 2001, 1-26.

Kugel, James L., and Rowan A. Greer. *Early Biblical Interpretation.* LEC 3. Philadelphia: Westminster, 1986.

Kugler, Robert A. *From Patriarch to Priest: The Levi-Priestly Tradition from Aramaic Levi to Testament of Levi.* SBLEJL 9. Atlanta: Scholars, 1996.

————. *The Testaments of the Twelve Patriarchs.* GAP. Sheffield: Sheffield Academic, 2001.

Kuhn, Heinz-Wolfgang. *Enderwartung und gegenwärtiges Heil: Untersuchungen zu den Gemeindeliedern von Qumran.* SUNT 4. Göttingen: Vandenhoeck & Ruprecht, 1966.

Kuiper, Gerald J. "A Study of the Relationship between A Genesis Apocryphon and the Pentateuchal Targumim in Genesis $14_{1\text{-}12}$." In *In Memoriam Paul Kahle,* ed. Matthew Black and Georg Fohrer. BZAW 103. Berlin: Töpelmann, 1968, 149-61.

Kutscher, Edward Y. "The Language of the Genesis Apocryphon: A Preliminary Study." In *Aspects of the Dead Sea Scrolls,* ed. Chaim Rabin and Yigael Yadin. ScrHier 4. Jerusalem: Magnes, 1958, 1-35.

Laato, Antti. "The Apocalypse of the Syriac Baruch and the Date of the End." *JSP* 18 (1998): 39-46.

Lacoque, André. *The Book of Daniel.* Atlanta: John Knox, 1979.

Lagarde, Paul de. *Hagiographa Chaldaice.* Leipzig, 1872; repr. Osnabrück: Zeller, 1967.

Lange, Armin. "1QGenAp XIX_{10}–XX_{32} as Paradigm of the Wisdom Didactic Narrative." In Fabry, Lange, and Lichtenberger, *Qumranstudien,* 191-204.

————. "Reading the Decline of Prophecy." In De Troyer and Lange, *Reading the Present in the Qumran Library,* 181-91.

Langen, Joseph. *De Apocalypsi Baruch Anno Superiori Primum Edita: Commentation.* Freiburg: Herder, 1867.

Laqueur, Richard. *Der jüdische Historiker Flavius Josephus: Ein biographischer Versuch auf neuer quellenkritischer Grundlage.* Giessen: Münchow, 1920; repr. Darmstadt: Wissenschaftliche Buchgesellschaft, 1970.

Larcher, Chrysostome. *Études sur le Livre de la Sagesse.* EBib. Paris: Gabalda, 1969.

————. *Le Livre de la Sagesse, ou, La Sagesse de Salomon.* 3 vols. Paris: Gabalda, 1983-85.

Lebram, Jürgen-Christian. *Das Buch Daniel.* ZBK 23. Zürich: Theologischer, 1984.

Le Déaut, Roger. *Targum du Pentateuque: Traduction des Deux Recensions Palestiniennes Complètes.* Vol. 1: *Genèse.* 2: *Exode et Lévitique.* 3: *Nombres.* 4: *Deutéronome.* SC. Paris: Cerf, 1978-1980.

————. "La Septante, un Targum?" In *Études sur le Judaïsme Hellénistique: Congrès de Strasbourg 1983,* ed. Raymond Kuntzmann and Jacques Schlosser. LD 119. Paris: Cerf, 1984, 147-95.

————. "The Targumim." In *CHJ,* 2:563-90.

Lee, Thomas R. *Studies in the Form of Sirach 44–50.* SBLDS 75. Atlanta: Scholars, 1986.

Leemhuis, Frerich. "The Arabic Version of the Apocalypse of Baruch: A Christian Text?" *JSP* 4 (1989): 19-26.

Leemhuis, Fred, Albertus F. J. Klijn, and G. J. H. van Gelder. *The Arabic Text of the Apocalypse of Baruch: Edited and Translated with a Parallel Translation of the Syriac Text.* Leiden: Brill, 1986.

Legrand, Thierry. "Exégèses targumiques et Techniques de Réécriture dans *l'Apocryphe de la Genèse* (1Qap Gen ar)." In Berthelot and Stökl Ben Ezra, *Aramaica Qumranica,* 225-52.

Lehmann, Manfred R. "1Q Genesis Apocryphon in the Light of the Targumim and Midrashim." *RevQ* 1 (1958-59): 249-63.

Leiman, Sid Z. *The Canonization of the Hebrew Scripture: The Talmudic and Midrashic Evidence.* Hamden: Archon, 1976; repr. 1991.

———. "Josephus and the Canon of the Bible." In Feldman and Hata, *Josephus, the Bible and History,* 50-58.

Leuenberger, Martin. "Ort und Funktion der Wolkenvision und ihrer Deutung in der syrischen Baruchapokalypse." *JSS* 36 (2005): 206-46.

Levenson, Jon D. *Resurrection and the Restoration of Israel: The Ultimate Victory of the God of Life.* New Haven: Yale University Press, 2006.

Levey, Samson H. *The Targum of Ezekiel.* ArBib 13. Wilmington: Glazier, 1987.

Levison, John R. "Is Eve to Blame? A Contextual Analysis of Sirach 25:24." *CBQ* 47 (1985): 617-23.

———. *Portraits of Adam in Early Judaism: From Sirach to 2 Baruch.* JSPSup 1. Sheffield: JSOT, 1988.

Levy, Jacob. *Chaldäisches Wörterbuch über die Targumim.* Leipzig: Baumgärtner, 1866; repr. Darmstadt: Melzer, 1966.

Lewis, Jack P. *A Study of the Interpretation of Noah and the Flood in Jewish and Christian Literature.* Leiden: Brill, 1968.

Licht, Jacob. *The Rule Scroll — A Scroll from the Wilderness of Judaea — 1QS, 1QSa, 1QSb: Text, Introduction and Commentary.* Jerusalem: Mosad Biyalik, 1965. [Hebrew]

Lichtenberger, Hermann. "Zion and the Destruction of the Temple in 4 Ezra 9–10." In *Gemeinde ohne Tempel/Community without Temple: Zur Substituierung und Transformation des Jerusalemer Tempels und seines Kults im Alten Testament, antiken Judentum und frühen Christentum,* ed. Beate Ego, Kathrin Ehlers, Armin Lange, and Peter Pilhofer. WUNT 118. Tübingen: Mohr Siebeck, 1999, 239-49.

Lichtenberger, Hermann, and Gerbern S. Oegema. *Jüdische Schriften in ihrem antikjüdischen und urchristlichen Kontext.* Studien zu den Jüdischen Schriften aus hellenistisch-römischer Zeit 1. Gütersloh: Gütersloher, 2002.

Lieberman, Saul. *Hellenism in Jewish Palestine: Studies in the Literary Transmission, Beliefs and Manners of Palestine in the I Century B.C.E.–IV Century C.E.* Texts and Studies of the Jewish Theological Seminary of America 18. New York: Jewish Theological Seminary, 1950.

Lillie, Betty J. "A History of Scholarship on the Wisdom of Solomon from the Nineteenth Century to Our Time." Diss., Hebrew Union College, 1982.

Lindner, Helgo. *Die Geschichtsauffassung des Flavius Josephus im Bellum Judaicum.* AGJU 12. Leiden: Brill, 1972.

Littmann, Enno. "Das Buch der Jubiläen." In *Die Apokryphen und Pseudepigraphen des Alten Testaments,* ed. Emil F. Kautzsch. Tübingen: Mohr, 1900, 2:31-119; repr. Darmstadt, 1975.

Longenecker, Bruce W. *Eschatology and the Covenant: A Comparison of 4 Ezra and Romans 1–11.* JSNTSup 57. Sheffield: JSOT, 1991.

———. *2 Esdras.* Guides to Apocrypha and Pseudepigrapha. Sheffield: Sheffield Academic, 1995.

———. "Locating 4 Ezra: A Consideration of Its Social Setting and Functions." *JSJ* 28 (1997): 271-93.

Louw, Theo A. W. van der. *Transformations in the Septuagint: Towards an Interaction of Septuagint Studies and Translation Studies.* CBET 47. Leuven: Peeters, 2007.

Lucas, Alec J. "Scripture Citations as an Internal Redactional Control: 1QS 5:1-20a and Its 4Q Parallels." *DSD* 17 (2010): 30-52.

Machiela, Daniel A. "'Each to his own inheritance': Geography as an Evaluative Tool in the Genesis Apocryphon." *DSD* 15 (2008): 50-66.

———. *The Dead Sea Genesis Apocryphon: A New Text and Translation with Introduction and Special Treatment of Columns 13-17.* STDJ 79. Leiden: Brill, 2009.

———. "Genesis Revealed: The Apocalyptic Apocryphon from Qumran Cave 1." In Parry et al., *Qumran Cave I Revisited,* 205-22.

Macholz, Christian. "Die Entstehung des hebräischen Bibelkanons nach 4 Esra 14." In *Die Hebräische Bibel und ihre zweifache Nachgeschichte: Festschrift für Rolf Rendtorff zum 65. Geburtstag,* ed. Erhard Blum, Macholz, and Ekkehard W. Stegemann. Neukirchen-Vluyn: Neukirchener, 1990, 379-91.

Maher, Michael. *Targum Pseudo-Jonathan: Genesis.* ArBib 1B. Wilmington: Glazier, 1992.

Mangan, Celine, John F. Healey, and Peter S. Knobel. *The Targum of Job, The Targum of Proverbs, The Targum of Qoheleth.* ArBib 15. Collegeville: Liturgical, 1991.

Mansoor, Menahem. *The Thanksgiving Hymns: Translated and Annotated with an Introduction.* STDJ 3. Leiden: Brill and Grand Rapids: Eerdmans, 1961.

Maori, Yeshayahu. *The Peshitta Version of the Pentateuch and Early Jewish Exegesis.* Jerusalem: Magnes, 1995. [Hebrew]

Marquis, Galen. "Explicit Literary Allusions in Biblical Historiography (The Pentateuch and Former Prophets)." Ph.D. diss., Hebrew University, 1999. [Hebrew]

Marshall, John W. "6 Ezra and Apocalyptic Judaism in Asia Minor." Paper presented at Seminar for Culture and Religion in Antiquity, University of Toronto, February 9, 2009.

Mason, Steve. *Flavius Josephus on the Pharisees: A Compositional-Critical Study.* StPB 39. Leiden: Brill, 1991.

———. "Josephus, Daniel, and the Flavian House." In *Josephus and the History of the Greco-Roman Period: Essays in Memory of Morton Smith,* ed. Fausto Parente and Joseph Sievers. StPB 41. Leiden: Brill, 1994, 161-91.

———. "'Should Any Wish to Enquire Further' (*Ant.* 1.25): The Aim and Audience of Josephus's *Judean Antiquities/Life.*" In *Understanding Josephus: Seven Perspectives.* JSPSup 32. Sheffield: Sheffield Academic, 1998, 64-103.

———. *Life of Josephus.* Vol. 9 of *Flavius Josephus: Translation and Commentary.* Leiden: Brill, 2000.

———. "Josephus and His Twenty-Two Book Canon." In *The Canon Debate,* ed. Lee Martin McDonald and James A. Sanders. Peabody: Hendrickson, 2002, 110-27.

———. "Flavius Josephus in Flavian Rome: Reading on and between the Lines." In *Flavian Rome: Culture, Image, Text,* ed. Anthony J. Boyle and William J. Dominik. Leiden: Brill, 2003, 559-89.

———. "Contradiction or Counterpoint? Josephus and Historical Method." *RRJ* 6 (2003): 145-88.

———. "Introduction to the *Judean Antiquities.*" In *Flavius Josephus: Translation and Commentary,* Vol. 3: *Judean Antiquities 1–4* (2004), xiii-xxxv.

———. "Of Audience and Meaning: Reading Josephus's Bellum Judaicum in the Context of a Flavian Audience." In *Josephus and Jewish History in Flavian Rome and Beyond,* ed. Joseph Sievers and Gaia Lembi. JSJSup 104. Leiden: Brill, 2005, 71-100.

———. "The Greeks and the Distant Past in Josephus's *Judaean War.*" In *Antiquity in Antiquity: Jewish and Christian Pasts in the Greco-Roman World,* ed. Gregg Gardner and Kevin L. Osterloh. TSAJ 123. Tübingen: Mohr Siebeck, 2008, 93-130.

———. "Of Audience and Meaning: Reading Josephus's *Judean War* in the Context of a Flavian Audience." In *Josephus, Judea, and Christian Origins: Methods and Categories.* Peabody: Hendrickson, 2009, 45-68.

———, ed. *Flavius Josephus: Translation and Commentary.* 10 vols. Leiden: Brill, 2000-2007.

McNamara, Martin. *The New Testament and the Palestinian Targum to the Pentateuch.* AnBib 27. Rome: Pontifical Biblical Institute, 1966.

———. *Targum Neofiti: Genesis.* ArBib 1A. Wilmington: Glazier, 1992.

———. *Targum Neofiti 1: Deuteronomy.* ArBib 5A. Collegeville: Liturgical, 1997.

———. "Interpretation of Scripture in the Targumim." In *A History of Biblical Interpretation,* vol. 1: *The Ancient Period,* ed. Alan J. Hauser and Duane F. Watson. Grand Rapids: Eerdmans, 2003, 167-97.

McNamara, Martin, and Ernest G. Clarke, *Targums Neofiti 1 and Pseudo-Jonathan: Numbers.* ArBib 4. Collegeville: Liturgical, 1995.

McNamara, Martin, and Michael Maher. *Targums Neofiti 1 and Pseudo-Jonathan: Exodus.* ArBib 2. Collegeville: Liturgical, 1994.

———. *Targums Neofiti 1 and Pseudo-Jonathan: Leviticus.* ArBib 3. Wilmington: Glazier, 1994.

Medala, Stanisław. "Le 'Quatrième livre d'Esdras' et les textes qoumrâniens." *Mogilany 1989* 2 (1991): 197-207.

———. "The Original Language of 4 Esdras." In Kapera, *Intertestamental Essays in Honour of Józef Tadeusz Milik,* 313-26.

Metso, Sarianna. *The Textual Development of the Qumran Community Rule.* STDJ 21. Leiden: Brill, 1997.

———. "The Use of Old Testament Quotations in the Qumran Community Rule." In *Qumran Between the Old and New Testaments,* ed. Frederick H. Cryer and Thomas L. Thompson. JSOTSup 290. Sheffield: Sheffield Academic, 1998, 217-31.

———. "Biblical Quotations in the Community Rule." In *The Bible as Book: The Hebrew*

Bible and the Judaean Desert Discoveries, ed. Edward D. Herbert and Emanuel Tov. London: British Library, 2002, 81-92.

————. *The Serekh Texts*. CQS 9. LSTS 62. London: T. & T. Clark, 2007.

Metzger, Bruce M. "The Fourth Book of Ezra." In *OTP*, 1:517-59.

Migliario, Elvira. "Per l'interpretazione dell' Autobiografia di Flavio Giuseppe." *Athenaeum* 69 (1981): 92-137.

Milgrom, Jacob. "The Qumran Cult: Its Exegetical Principles." In Brooke, *Temple Scroll Studies*, 165-80.

————. *Leviticus 1–16*. AB 3. New York: Doubleday, 1991.

Milik, Jósef T. "4Q Visions de Amram et une citation d'Origèn." *RB* (1972): 77-97.

————. "Targum du Lévitique," "Targum du Job." In *Qumrân grotte 4.II: I. Archéologie, II. Tefillin, Mezuzot et Targums (4Q128-4Q157)*, ed. Roland de Vaux and Jósef T. Milik. DJD 6. Oxford: Clarendon, 1977, 86-90.

Moehring, Horst R. "Novelistic Elements in the Writings of Flavius Josephus." Diss., Chicago, 1957.

Montgomery, James A. *A Critical and Exegetical Commentary on the Book of Daniel*. ICC. Edinburgh: T. & T. Clark, 1927.

Morawe, Günter. *Aufbau und Abgrenzung der Loblieder von Qumrân: Studien zur Gattungsgeschichtlichen Einordnung der Hodajôth*. Berlin: Evangelische, 1961.

Morgenstern, Matthew. "A New Clue to the Original Length of the Genesis Apocryphon." *JJS* 47 (1996): 345-47.

Morgenstern, Matthew, Elisha Qimron, and Daniel Sivan. "The Hitherto Unpublished Columns of the Genesis Apocryphon." *AbrN* 33 (1995): 30-54.

Morris, Jenny. "The Jewish Philosopher Philo." In Emil Schürer, *The History of the Jewish People in the Age of Jesus Christ*, rev. Geza Vermes, Fergus Millar, and Martin Goodman. Edinburgh: T. & T. Clark, 1987, 3.2: 819-70.

Müller, Karlheinz. "Die hebräische Sprache der Halacha als Textur der Schöpfung: Beobachtungen zum Verhältnis von Tora und Halacha im Buch der Jubiläen." In *Bibel in jüdischer und christlicher Tradition: Festschrift für Johann Maier zum 60. Geburtstag*, ed. Helmut Merklein, Müller, and Günter Stemberger. BBB 38. Frankfurt a/M: Hain, 1993, 157-76.

Müller, Mogens. *The First Bible of the Church: A Plea for the Septuagint*. JSOTSup 206. Copenhagen International Seminar 1. Sheffield: Sheffield Academic, 1996.

Mulder, Martin Jan, ed. *Mikra: Text, Translation, Reading and Interpretation of the Hebrew Bible in Ancient Judaism and Early Christianity*. CRINT 2.1. Assen: Van Gorcum and Philadelphia: Fortress, 1988.

Muñoz, Domingo León. "Universalidad de la salvación en la apocalíptica (Daniel, 4 de Esdras y 2 de Baruc)." *RevistB* 56 (1994): 129-48.

Muraoka, Takamitsu. "Notes on the Aramaic of the Genesis Apocryphon." *RevQ* 8 (1972): 7-51.

————. "Further Notes on the Aramaic of the 'Genesis Apocryphon." *RevQ* 16 (1993-95): 39-48.

Murphy, Catherine M. *Wealth in the Dead Sea Scrolls and in the Qumran Community*. STDJ 40. Leiden: Brill, 2002.

Murphy, Frederick J. *The Structure and Meaning of Second Baruch.* SBLDS 78. Atlanta: Scholars, 1985.

———. "2 Baruch and the Romans." *JBL* 104 (1985): 663-69.

———. "Sapiential Elements in the Syriac Apocalypse of Baruch." *JQR* 76 (1986): 311-27.

———. "The Temple in the Syriac Apocalypse of Baruch." *JBL* 106 (1987): 671-83.

———. *Pseudo-Philo: Rewriting the Bible.* New York: Oxford University Press, 1993.

Najman, Hindy. "Ezra: Introduction." In *The Jewish Study Bible,* ed. Adele Berlin and Marc Zvi Brettler. Oxford: Oxford University Press, 1999, 1666-71.

———. "Interpretation as Primordial Writing: Jubilees and Its Authority Conferring Strategies." *JSJ* 30 (1999): 379-410.

———. *Seconding Sinai: The Development of Mosaic Discourse in Second Temple Judaism.* JSJSup 77. Leiden: Brill, 2003.

———. "How Should We Contextualize Pseudepigrapha? Imitation and Emulation in 4 Ezra." In Hilhorst, Puech, and Tigchelaar, *Flores Florentino,* 529-36.

———. "Between Heaven and Earth: Liminal Visions in 4Ezra." In *Other Worlds and Their Relation to This World: Early Jewish and Ancient Christian Traditions,* ed. Tobias Nicklas et al. JSJSup 142. Leiden: Brill, 2010, 107-18.

———. *Past Renewals: Interpretative Authority, Renewed Revelation, and the Quest for Perfection in Jewish Antiquity.* JSJSup 53. Leiden: Brill, 2010.

Nestle, Eberhard. "Zur Rekonstruktion der Septuaginta." *Phil* 58 (1899): 121-31.

———. "Zur neuen Philo-Aufgabe." *Phil* 59 (1900): 256-71.

———. "Zur neuen Philo-Aufgabe: Eine Replik." *Phil* 60 (1901): 271-76.

Newman, Judith. *Praying by the Book: The Scripturalization of Prayer in Second Temple Judaism.* SBLEJL 14. Atlanta: Scholars, 1999.

Newsletter for Targumic and Cognate Studies. http://www.targum.info.

Newsom, Carol A. "The Case of the Blinking I: Discourse of the Self at Qumran." In *Discursive Formations: Ascetic Piety and the Interpretation of Early Christian Literature, Part 1,* ed. Vincent L. Wimbush. Semeia 57. Atlanta: SBL, 1992, 13-23.

———. *The Self as Symbolic Space: Constructing Identity and Community at Qumran.* STDJ 52. Leiden: Brill, 2004.

———. "Constructing 'We, You, and the Others' through Non-Polemical Discourse." In García Martínez and Popović, *Defining Identities,* 13-21.

Nickelsburg, George W. E. "Abraham the Convert: A Jewish Tradition and Its Use by the Apostle Paul." In Stone and Bergren, *Biblical Figures Outside the Bible,* 151-75.

———. "Patriarchs Who Worry about Their Wives: A Haggadic Tendency in the Genesis Apocryphon." In Stone and Chazon, *Biblical Perspectives,* 137-58.

———. *Jewish Literature between the Bible and the Mishnah.* 1981; 2nd ed. Minneapolis: Fortress, 2005.

Nicol, George. "Isaiah's Vision and the Visions of Daniel." *VT* 29 (1979): 501-4.

Niehoff, Maren R. *Jewish Exegesis and Homeric Scholarship in Alexandria.* Cambridge: Cambridge University Press, 2011.

Nikiprowetzky, Valentin. *Le commentaire de l'Écriture chez Philon d'Alexandrie.* ALGHJ 11. Leiden: Brill, 1977.

Nir, Rivka. *The Destruction of Jerusalem and the Idea of Redemption in the Syriac Apocalypse of Baruch.* SBLEJL 20. Atlanta: SBL, 2003.

Nissinen, Martti. "Transmitting Divine Mysteries: The Prophetic Role of Wisdom Teachers in the Dead Sea Scrolls." In Voitila and Jokiranta, *Scripture in Transition,* 513-33.

Nitzan, Bilha. *Megillat Pesher Habakkuk.* Jerusalem: Mosad Bialik, 1986. [Hebrew]

————. *Qumran Prayer and Religious Poetry.* STDJ 12. Leiden: Brill, 1994.

Nodet, Étienne. *Le Pentateuque de Josèphe.* Paris: Cerf, 1996.

Nordheim, Eckhard von. *Die Lehre der Alten.* Vol. 1: *Das Testament als Literaturgattung im Judentum der hellenistisch-römischen Zeit.* ALGHJ 13. Leiden: Brill, 1980.

Nuvolone, Flavio G. "Apocalypse d'Esdras Grecque et Latine, Rapports et Rhétorique." *Apocrypha* 7 (1996): 81-108.

————. "L'Initiation prophétique dans l'apocalypse grecque d'Esdras: Essai d'analyse et de reconstruction." *FZPhTh* 44 (1997): 408-44.

————. "Vision d'Esdras." In *Ecrits apocryphes chrétiens,* ed. François Bovon and Pierre Geoltrain. Bibliothèque de la Pléiade 442. Paris: Gallimard, 1997, 593-632.

Olitzki, Marcus. *Flavius Josephus und die Halacha.* Berlin: Itzkowski, 1885.

Olofsson, Staffan. *God Is My Rock: A Study of Translation Technique and Theological Exegesis in the Septuagint.* ConBOT 31. Stockholm: Almqvist & Wiksell, 1990.

Parry, Donald W., et al. *Qumran Cave 1 Revisited: Texts from Cave 1 Sixty Years after Their Discovery. Proceedings of the Sixth Meeting of the IOQS in Ljubljana.* STDJ 91. Leiden: Brill, 2010.

Paul, Shalom M., Robert A. Kraft, Lawrence H. Schiffman, and Weston W. Fields, eds. *Emanuel: Studies in the Hebrew Bible, Septuagint and Dead Sea Scrolls in Honor of Emanuel Tov.* VTSup 94. Leiden: Brill, 2003.

Pelletier, André. *Flavius Josèphe, adapteur de la lettre d'Aristée.* Paris: Klincksieck, 1962.

Peters, Dorothy. "The Recombination and Evolution of Noah Traditions as Found in the *Genesis Apocryphon* and *Jubilees:* The DNA of Fraternal Twins." In Parry et al., *Qumran Cave I Revisited,* 223-32.

Petit, Françoise. *Quaestiones in Genesim et in Exodum: Fragmenta graeca.* Les Œuvres de Philon d'Alexandrie 33. Paris: Cerf, 1978.

Philonenko, Marc. *Les interpolations chrétiennes des Testaments des Douze Patriarches et les manuscrits de Qoumrân.* Paris: Presses universitaires de France, 1960.

Pietersma, Albert. "A New Paradigm for Addressing Old Questions: The Relevance of the Interlinear Model for the Study of the Septuagint." In *Bible and Computer: The Stellenbosch AIBI-6 Conference: Proceedings of the Association Internationale Bible et Informatique,* ed. Johann Cook. Leiden: Brill, 2002, 337-64.

Polaski, D. C. "On Naming Tamar: Amran's Rhetoric and Women's Roles in Pseudo-Philo's *Liber Antiquitatum Biblicarum* 9." *JSP* 13 (1995): 79-99.

Qimron, Elisha, and John Strugnell, eds., *Qumran Cave 4: V, Miqṣat Ma'aśe ha-Torah.* DJD 10. Oxford: Clarendon, 1994.

Rajak, Tessa. "Moses in Ethiopia: Legend and Literature." *JJS* 29 (1978): 111-22.

————. "Josephus and the 'Archaeology' of the Jews." *JJS* (1982): 465-77.

————. *Josephus, The Historian and His Society.* London: Duckworth, 1983.

Rappaport, Salomo. *Agada und Exegese bei Flavius Josephus.* Vienna: Alexander Kohut Memorial Foundation, 1930.

Reed, Stephen A. "The Use of the First Person in the 'Genesis Apocryphon.'" In *Aramaic in*

Postbiblical Judaism and Early Christianity, ed. Eric M. Meyers and Paul V. M. Flesher. Winona Lake: Eisenbrauns, 2010, 193-215.

Reese, James M. *Hellenistic Influence on the Book of Wisdom and Its Consequences.* AnBib 41. Rome: Biblical Institute, 1970.

Reeves, John C., ed. *Tracing the Threads: Studies in the Vitality of the Jewish Pseudepigrapha.* SBLEJL 6. Atlanta: Scholars, 1994.

Reider, Joseph. *The Book of Wisdom.* New York: Harper, 1957.

Reinmuth, Eckart. *Pseudo-Philo und Lukas.* WUNT 74. Tübingen: Mohr Siebeck, 1994.

Riaud, Jean. *Les Paralipomènes du Prophète Jérémie: Présentation, Texte Original, Traduction et Commentaires.* Angers: Université Catholique de l'Ouest, 1994.

Riessler, Paul. *Altjüdisches Schrifttum ausserhalb der Bibel.* Augsburg: Filser, 1928.

Rodgers, Zuleika. "Monarchy vs. Priesthood: Josephus, Justus of Tiberius, and Agrippa II." In *A Wandering Galilean: Essays in Honour of Seán Freyne,* ed. Rodgers, Margaret Daly-Denton, and Anne Fitzpatrick-McKinley. JSJSup 132. Leiden: Brill, 2009, 173-84.

————, ed. *Making History: Josephus and Historical Method.* JSJSup 110. Leiden: Brill, 2007.

Rofé, Alexander. "The End of the Book of Joshua according to the Septuagint." *Hen* 4 (1982): 17-36.

Roitman, Adolfo. "The Traditions about Abraham's Early Life in the Book of Judith (5:6-9)." In *Things Revealed: Studies in Early Jewish and Christian Literature in Honor of Michael E. Stone,* ed. Esther G. Chazon, David Satran, and Ruth A. Clements. JSJSup 89. Leiden: Brill, 2004, 73-87.

Roitman, Adolfo D., Lawrence H. Schiffman, and Shani L. (Berrin) Tzoref, eds. *The Dead Sea Scrolls and Contemporary Culture: Proceedings of the International Conference held at the Israel Museum, Jerusalem (July 6-8, 2008).* STDJ 93. Leiden: Brill, 2010.

Rönsch, Hermann. *Das Buch der Jubiläen: oder, Die kleine Genesis; unter Beifügung des revidierten Textes der in der Ambrosiana aufgefundenen lateinischen Fragmente.* Leipzig: Fues, 1874; repr. Amsterdam: Rodopi, 1970.

Rooden, Peter T. van. "Die antike Elementarlehre und der Aufbau von Sapientia Salomonis 11–19." In *Tradition and Re-interpretation in Jewish and Early Christian Literature: Essays in Honour of Jürgen C. H. Lebram,* ed. Jan W. van Henten et al. StPB 36. Leiden: Brill, 1986, 81-96.

Rook, John. "The Names of the Wives from Adam to Abraham in the Book of Jubilees." *JSP* 7 (1990): 105-17.

Rösel, Martin. *Übersetzung als Vollendung der Auslegung: Studien zur Genesis-Septuaginta.* BZAW 223. Berlin: de Gruyter, 1994.

————. "The Text-Critical Value of the Genesis-Septuagint." *BIOSCS* 31 (1998): 62-70.

————. "The Septuagint-Version of the Book of Joshua." *SJOT* 16 (2002): 5-23.

————. "Towards a 'Theology of the Septuagint.'" In Kraus and Wooden, *Septuagint Research,* 239-52.

————. "The Reading and Translation of the Divine Name in the Masoretic Tradition and the Greek Pentateuch." *JSOT* 31 (2007): 411-28.

Royse, James R. "The Works of Philo." In Kamesar, *The Cambridge Companion to Philo,* 32-64.

————. "Some Observations on the Biblical Text in Philo's *De agricultura.*" *SPhA* 22 (2010): 111-29.

Rowley, Harold H. "The Unity of the Book of Daniel." In *The Servant of the Lord and Other Essays on the Old Testament*. Oxford: Blackwell, 1965, 249-80.

Ruiten, Jacques T. A. G. M. van. *Primaeval History Interpreted: The Rewriting of Genesis 1–11 in the Book of Jubilees*. JSJSup 66. Leiden: Brill, 2000.

————. "Abraham, Job and the Book of Jubilees: The Intertextual Relationship of Genesis 22:1-19, Job 1:1–2:13, and Jubilees 17:15–18:19." In *The Sacrifice of Isaac: The Aqedah (Genesis 22) and Its Interpretations*, ed. Ed Noort and Eibert Tigchelaar. TBN 7. Leiden: Brill, 2002, 58-85.

————. "Lot versus Abraham: The Interpretation of Genesis 18:1–19:38 in Jubilees 16:1-9." In *Sodom's Sin: Genesis 18–19 and Its Interpretation*, ed. Ed Noort and Eibert J. C. Tigchelaar. TBN 7. Leiden: Brill, 2004, 29-46.

————. "The Birth of Moses in Egypt according to the *Book of Jubilees* (*Jub* 47.1-9)." In *The Wisdom of Egypt: Jewish, Early Christian, and Gnostic Essays in Honour of Gerard P. Luttikhuizen*, ed. George H. van Kooten and Anthony Hilhorst. AGJU 59. Leiden: Brill, 2005, 43-66.

————. "Between Jacob's Death and Moses' Birth: The Intertextual Relationship between Genesis 50:15–Exodus 1:14 and *Jubilees* 46:1-16." In Hilhorst, Puech, and Tigchelaar, *Flores Florentino*, 467-89.

Runia, David T. *Exegesis and Philosophy: Studies on Philo of Alexandria*. Brookfield: Gower, 1990.

————. "Secondary Texts in Philo's *Quaestiones*." In *Both Literal and Allegorical: Studies in Philo of Alexandria's Questions and Answers on Genesis and Exodus*, ed. David M. Hay. BJS 232. Atlanta: Scholars, 1991, 47-79.

————. *Philo in Early Christian Literature: A Survey*. CRINT 3.3. Assen: Van Gorcum and Minneapolis: Fortress, 1993.

————. *Philo of Alexandria, On the Creation of the Cosmos according to Moses: Introduction, Translation and Commentary*. PAC 1. Leiden: Brill, 2001.

————. "Philo's Reading of the Psalms." *SPhA* 13 (2001): 102-21.

————. "Etymology as an Allegorical Technique in Philo of Alexandria." *SPhA* 16 (2004): 101-21.

————. "The Structure of Philo's Allegorical Treatise *De agricultura*." *SPhA* 22 (2010): 87-109.

Sacchi, Paolo. "Libro dei Giubilei." In *Apocrifi dell'Antico Testamento*, 1. Turin: Unione tipografico-editrice torinese, 1981, 179-411.

Sæbø, Magne. *Hebrew Bible/Old Testament: The History of Its Interpretation*. Vol. 1: *From the Beginnings to the Middle Ages (until 1300)*. Pt. 1: *Antiquity*. Pt. 2: *From the Renaissance to the Enlightenment*. Göttingen: Vandenhoeck & Ruprecht, 1996-.

Sanders, Jack T. *Ben Sira and Demotic Wisdom*. SBLMS 28. Chico: Scholars, 1983.

Sarna, Nahum. "Psalm 89: A Study in Inner Biblical Exegesis." In *Biblical and Other Studies*, ed. Alexander Altmann. Cambridge, Mass.: Harvard University Press, 1963, 29-46.

Satran, David. "Daniel: Seer, Prophet, Holy Man." In Collins and Nickelsburg, *Ideal Figures in Ancient Judaism*, 33-48.

Sayler, Gwendolyn B. "2 Baruch: A Story of Grief and Consolation." *SBLSP 1982*. Chico: Scholars, 1982, 485-500.

──────. *Have the Promises Failed? A Literary Analysis of 2 Baruch.* SBLDS 72. Chico: Scholars, 1984.

Schaberg, Jane. "Major Midrashic Traditions in Wisdom 1,1–6,25." *JSJ* 13 (1982): 75-101.

Schalit, Abaraham. *Namenwörterbuch zu Flavius Josephus.* Leiden: Brill, 1968.

Schaller, Berndt. "Gen. 1.2 im antiken Judentum: Untersuchungen über Verwendung und Deutung der Schöpfungsaussagen von Gen 1.2 im antiken Judentum." Diss., Göttingen, 1961.

Schaper, Joachim. *Eschatology in the Greek Psalter.* WUNT ser. 2, 76. Tübingen: Mohr Siebeck, 1995.

──────. "Der Septuaginta-Psalter: Interpretation, Aktualisierung und liturgische Verwendung der biblischen Psalmen im hellenistischen Judentum." In *Der Psalter in Judentum und Christentum,* ed. Erich Zenger. HBS 18. Freiburg: Herder, 1998, 165-83.

Schechter, Solomon, and Charles Taylor. *The Wisdom of Ben Sira: Portions of the Book of Ecclesiasticus from Hebrew Manuscripts in the Cairo Genizah Collection.* Cambridge: Cambridge University Press, 1899.

Schiffman, Lawrence H. *The Halakhah at Qumran.* SJLA 16. Leiden: Brill, 1975.

──────. *Sectarian Law in the Dead Sea Scrolls: Courts, Testimony, and the Penal Code.* BJS 33. Chico: Scholars, 1983.

Schmid, Konrad. "Esras Begegnung mit Zion: Die Deutung der Zerstörung Jerusalems im 4. Esrabuch und das Problem des 'bösen Herzens.'" *JSJ* 29 (1998): 261-77.

Schmitt, Armin. "Struktur, Herkunft und Bedeutung der Beispielreihe in Weish 10." *BZ* 21 (1977): 1-22.

──────. *Das Buch der Weisheit: Ein Kommentar.* Würzburg: Echter, 1986.

Schnapp, F. *Die Testamente der zwölf Patriarchen untersucht.* Halle: Niemeyer, 1884.

Schultz, Richard L. *The Search for Quotation: Verbal Parallels in the Prophets.* JSOTSup 180. Sheffield: Sheffield Academic, 1999.

Schwartz, Seth. *Josephus and Judaean Politics.* Leiden: Brill, 1990.

Schwarz, Eberhard. *Identität durch Abgrenzung: Abgrenzungsprozesse in Israel im 2. Vorchristlichen Jahrhundert und ihre traditionsgeschichtliche Voraussetzungen: Zugleich ein Beitrag zur Erforschung des Jubiläenbuches.* Europäische Hochschulschriften, ser. 23, 162. Frankfurt am Main: Lang, 1982.

Schwenk-Bressler, Udo. *Sapientia Salomonis als ein Beispiel frühjüdischer Textauslegung: Die Auslegung des Buches Genesis, Exodus 1–15 und Teilen der Wüstentradition in Sap 10–19.* BEATAJ 32. Frankfurt am Main: Lang, 1993.

Scott, James M. *Geography in Early Judaism and Christianity: The Book of Jubilees.* SNTSMS 113. Cambridge: Cambridge University Press, 2002.

──────. *On Earth as in Heaven: The Restoration of Sacred Time and Sacred Space in the Book of Jubilees.* JSJSup 91. Leiden: Brill, 2005.

Seeligmann, Isac Leo. "Voraussetzungen der Midraschexegese." *VTSup* 1 (1953): 150-81.

──────. *Gesammelte Studien zur Hebräischen Bibel/Isac Leo Seeligman,* ed. Erhard Blum. FAT 41. Tübingen: Mohr Siebeck, 2004.

──────. "Anfänge der Midraschexegese in der Chronik." In *Gesammelte Studien,* 31-54.

Segal, Michael. "Between Bible and Rewritten Bible." In Henze, *Biblical Interpretation at Qumran,* 10-28.

————. *The Book of Jubilees: Rewritten Bible, Redaction, Ideology and Theology.* JSJSup 117. Leiden: Brill, 2007.

————. "From Joseph to Daniel: The Literary Development of the Narrative in Daniel 2." *VT* 59 (2009): 123-49.

Seow, C. L. *Daniel.* Westminster Bible Companion. Louisville: Westminster John Knox, 2003.

Shemesh, Aharon. "'The Holy Angels are in their Council': The Exclusion of Deformed Persons from Holy Places in Qumranic and Rabbinic Literature." *DSD* 4 (1997): 179-206.

————. "Scriptural Interpretations in the Damascus Document and Their Parallels in Rabbinic Midrash." In *The Damascus Document: A Centennial of Discovery. Proceedings of the Third International Symposium of the Orion Center for the Study of the Dead Sea Scrolls and Associated Literature, 4-8 February 1998,* ed. Joseph M. Baumgarten, Esther G. Chazon, and Avital Pinnick. STDJ 34. Leiden: Brill, 2000, 161-75.

————. *Punishments and Sins: From Scripture to the Rabbis.* Jerusalem: Magnes, 2003. [Hebrew]

————. "4Q251: *Midrash Mishpatim.*" *DSD* 12 (2005): 280-302.

————. "The Scriptural Background of the Penal Code in The Rule of the Community and Damascus Document." *DSD* 15 (2008): 191-224.

————. *Halakhah in the Making: The Development of Jewish Law from Qumran to the Rabbis.* Berkeley: University of California Press, 2009.

Shemesh, Aharon, and Cana Werman. "Halakhah at Qumran: Genre and Authority." *DSD* 10 (2003): 104-29.

Sheppard, Gerald T. *Wisdom as a Hermeneutical Construct: A Study in the Sapientialization of the Old Testament.* BZAW 151. Berlin: de Gruyter, 1980.

Shinan, Avigdor. "The Development of a Rabbinic Aggadah: The Story of Doeg ben Yosef." *Maḥanaim* 7 (1984): 70-75. [Hebrew]

Shinan, Avigdor, and Yair Zakovitch. "Midrash on Scripture and Midrash within Scripture." *ScrHier* 31 (1986): 257-77.

Shutt, Robert J. H. *Studies in Josephus.* London: SPCK, 1961.

Sichardt, Johannes. *Philonis Iudaei Alexandrini Libri Antiquitatum, Quaestionum et Solutionum in Genesin.* Basel: Adamus Petrus, 1527.

Siegert, Folker. "Early Jewish Interpretation in a Hellenistic Style." In Sæbø, *Hebrew Bible/Old Testament,* 1.1, 162-88.

————. *Zwischen Hebräischer Bibel und Altem Testament: Eine Einführung in die Septuaginta.* MJS 9. Münster: Lit, 2001.

Siegfried, Carl. "Philo und der überlieferte Text der LXX." *ZWT* 16 (1873): 217-38, 411-28, 522-40.

Sievers, Joseph, and Gaia Lembi, eds. *Josephus and Jewish History in Flavian Rome and Beyond.* JSJSup 104. Leiden: Brill, 2005.

Skehan, Patrick W. "Isaias and the Teaching of the Book of Wisdom." *CBQ* 2 (1940): 289-99; repr. *Studies in Israelite Poetry and Wisdom,* 163-71.

————. "The Text and Structure of the Book of Wisdom." *Traditio* 3 (1945): 1-12; repr. *Studies in Israelite Poetry and Wisdom,* 132-36.

————. "Borrowings from the Psalms in the Book of Wisdom." *CBQ* 10 (1948): 384-97; repr. *Studies in Israelite Poetry and Wisdom*, 149-62.

————. "The Literary Relationship of the Book of Wisdom to Earlier Wisdom Writings." In *Studies in Israelite Poetry and Wisdom*, 172-236.

————. *Studies in Israelite Poetry and Wisdom*. CBQMS 1. Washington: Catholic Biblical Association, 1971.

Skehan, Patrick W., and Alexander A. Di Lella. *The Wisdom of Ben Sira*. AB 39. New York: Doubleday, 1987.

Slingerland, H. Dixon. *The Testaments of the Twelve Patriarchs: A Critical History of Research*. SBLMS 21. Missoula: Scholars, 1977.

Smits, Edmé R. "A Contribution to the History of Pseudo-Philo's Liber Antiquitatum Biblicarum in the Middle Ages." *JSJ* 23 (1992): 197-216.

Snaith, John G. "Biblical Quotations in the Hebrew of Ecclesiasticus." *JTS* 8 (1967): 1-12.

Sokoloff, Michael. *A Dictionary of Jewish Palestinian Aramaic of the Byzantine Period*. 1990; 2nd ed. Ramat-Gan: Bar-Ilan University Press and Baltimore: Johns Hopkins University Press, 2002.

Sommer, Benjamin D. *A Prophet Reads Scripture: Allusion in Isaiah 40–66*. Stanford: Stanford University Press, 1998.

Sperber, Alexander. *The Bible in Aramaic Based on Old Manuscripts and Printed Texts*. Vol. 1: *Targum Onkelos*; vol. 2: *Targum Jonathan to the Former Prophets*; vol. 3: *Targum Jonathan to the Latter Prophets*; vol. 4A: *Targums to Chronicles, Ruth, Song of Songs, Lamentations, Qoheleth, and Esther [first targum]*). Leiden: Brill, 1959.

Speyer, W. "Baruch." *JAC* 17 (1974): 185-90.

Spilsbury, Paul. "*Contra Apionem* and *Antiquitates Judaicae*: Points of Contact." In Feldman and Levison, *Josephus' Contra Apionem*, 348-68.

————. *The Image of the Jew in Flavius Josephus's Paraphrase of the Bible*. TSAJ 69. Tübingen: Mohr Siebeck, 1998.

Stec, David M. *The Targum of Psalms*. ArBib 16. Collegeville: Liturgical, 2004.

Stegemann, Hartmut, with Eileen Schuller. *Qumran Cave 1, 3: 1QHodayot^a, with Incorporation of 4QHodayot^{a-f} and 1QHodayot^b*. Trans. of texts by Carol Newsom. DJD 40. Oxford: Clarendon, 2008.

Stein, Edmund. "Ein jüdisch-hellenistischer Midrash über den Auszug aus Ägypten." *MGWJ* 78 (1934): 558-75.

Steiner, Richard C. "The Mountains of Ararat, Mount Lubar, and הר הקדם." *JJS* 42 (1991): 247-49.

————. "The Heading of the *Book of the Words of Noah* on a Fragment of the Genesis Apocryphon: New Light on a 'Lost' Work." *DSD* 2 (1995): 66-71.

Sterling, Gregory E. *Historiography and Self-Definition: Josephos, Luke-Acts, and Apologetic Historiography*. NovTSup 64. Leiden: Brill, 1992.

Stone, Michael E. *A Textual Commentary on the Armenian Version of IV Ezra*. SBLSCS 34. Atlanta: Scholars, 1990.

————. *Fourth Ezra: A Commentary on the Book of Fourth Ezra*. Hermeneia. Minneapolis: Fortress, 1990.

————. "Esdras, Second Book of." *ABD* 2:611-14.

————. "The Concept of the Messiah in IV Ezra." In *Apocrypha, Pseudepigrapha, and Dead Sea Scrolls,* 321-38.

————. "An Introduction to the Esdras Writings." In *Apocrypha, Pseudepigrapha, and Dead Sea Scrolls,* 305-20.

————. "On Reading an Apocalypse." In *Apocrypha, Pseudepigrapha, and Dead Sea Scrolls,* 339-52.

————. "A Reconsideration of Apocalyptic Visions." In *Apocrypha, Pseudepigrapha, and Dead Sea Scrolls,* 353-66.

————. "The Book(s) Attributed to Noah." *DSD* 13 (2006): 4-23.

————. "The City in 4 Ezra." *JBL* 126 (2007): 402-7.

————, ed. *Jewish Writings of the Second Temple Period: Apocrypha, Pseudepigrapha, Qumran Sectarian Writings, Philo, Josephus.* CRINT 2.2. Assen: Van Gorcum and Minneapolis: Fortress, 1984.

————, ed. *Apocrypha, Pseudepigrapha, and Armenian Studies: Collected Papers.* Vol. 1: *Apocrypha, Pseudepigrapha, and Dead Sea Scrolls.* OLA 144. Leuven: Peeters, 2006.

Stone, Michael E., Aryeh Amihay, and Vered Hillel, eds. *Noah and His Book(s).* SBLEJL 28. Atlanta: Society of Biblical Literature, 2010.

Stone, Michael E., and Theodore A. Bergren, eds. *Biblical Figures Outside the Bible.* Harrisburg: Trinity Press International, 1998.

Stone, Michael E., and Esther G. Chazon, eds. *Biblical Perspectives: Early Use and Interpretation of the Bible in the Light of the Dead Sea Scrolls: Proceedings of the First International Symposium of the Orion Center for the Study of the Dead Sea Scrolls and Associated Literature, 12-14 May 1996.* STDJ 28. Leiden: Brill, 1998.

Strack, Hermann L. and Günter Stemberger. "Rabbinical Hermeneutics." In *Introduction to the Talmud and Midrash,* trans. and ed. Markus Bockmuehl. 2nd ed. Minneapolis: Fortress, 1996, 15-130.

Stuckenbruck, Loren T. "The Origins of Evil in Jewish Apocalyptic Tradition: The Interpretation of Genesis 6:1-4 in the Second and Third Centuries B.C.E." In *The Fall of the Angels,* ed. Christoph Auffarth and Stuckenbruck. Leiden: Brill, 2002, 87-118.

————. "The Lamech Narrative in the Genesis Apocryphon (1QapGen) and Birth of Noah (4QEnoch^c ar): A Tradition-Historical Study." In Berthelot and Stökl Ben Ezra, *Aramaica Qumranica,* 253-71.

Sutter Rehmann, Luzia. "Das Vierte Esrabuch." In *Kompendium Feministische Bibelauslegung,* ed. Luise Schottroff, Marie-Theres Wacker, Claudia Janssen, and Beate Wehn. Gütersloh: Kaiser, 1998, 450-58.

Talmon, Shemaryahu. "The 'Desert Motif' in the Bible and in Qumran Literature." In *Biblical Motifs, Origins and Transformations,* ed. Alexander Altmann. Philip L. Lown Institute of Advanced Judaic Studies, Studies and Texts 3. Cambridge, Mass.: Harvard University Press, 1966, 31-66.

Tauberschmidt, Gerhard. *Secondary Parallelism: A Study of Translation Technique in LXX Proverbs.* Academia Biblica 15. Atlanta: SBL, 2004.

Thackeray, Henry St. John. *Josephus, The Man and the Historian.* 1928; repr. New York: Ktav, 1968.

Thomas, Johannes. "Aktuelles im Zeugnis der zwölf Väter." In Eltester, *Studien zu den Testamenten der zwölf Patriarchen,* 62-150.

Tobin, Thomas H. "The Beginning of Philo's *Legum Allegoriae*." *SPhA* 12 (2000): 29-43.

Tov, Emanuel. *The Text-Critical Use of the Septuagint in Biblical Research*. 2nd rev. ed. Jerusalem Biblical Studies 8. Jerusalem: Simor, 1997.

———. *The Greek and Hebrew Bible: Collected Essays on the Septuagint*. VTSup 72. Leiden: Brill, 1999.

Ulrich, Eugene C. *The Qumran Text of Samuel and Josephus*. HSM 19. Missoula: Scholars, 1978.

———. *The Dead Sea Scrolls and the Origins of the Bible*. SDSSRL. Grand Rapids: Eerdmans, 1999.

———. "The Text of Daniel in the Qumran Scrolls." In Collins and Flint, *The Book of Daniel*, 573-85.

Ulrich, Eugene, and Peter W. Flint. *Qumran Cave 1. II: The Isaiah Scrolls, Part 2: Introductions, Commentary, and Textual Variants*. DJD 32. Oxford: Clarendon, 2010.

Ulrichsen, Jarl Henning. *Die Grundschrift der Testamente der Zwölf Patriarchen: Eine Untersuchung zu Umfang, Inhalt und Eigenart der ursprünglichen Schrift*. Acta Universitatis Upsaliensis, Historia Religionum 10. Stockholm: Almqvist & Wiksell, 1991.

VanderKam, James C. "Textual Affinities of the Biblical Citations in the Genesis Apocryphon." *JBL* 97 (1978): 45-55.

———. "Enoch Traditions in Jubilees and Other Second-Century Sources." *SBLSP* 1 (1978): 229-51; repr. *From Revelation to Canon*, 305-31.

———. "The Poetry of 1QApGen, xx,2-8a." *RevQ* 10 (1979-1981): 57-66.

———. *The Book of Jubilees: A Critical Text*. 2 vols. CSCO 510-11. Scriptores Aethiopici 87-88. Leuven: Peeters, 1989.

———. "The Birth of Noah." In Kapera, *Intertestamental Essays in Honour of Józef Tadeusz Milik*, 213-31.

———. "Biblical Interpretation in 1 Enoch and Jubilees." In *The Pseudepigrapha and Early Biblical Interpretation*, ed. James H. Charlesworth and Craig A. Evans. JSPSup 14. Sheffield: Sheffield Academic, 1993, 96-125.

———. "Genesis 1 in Jubilees 2." *DSD* 1 (1994): 300-321.

———. "The Granddaughters and Grandsons of Noah." *RevQ* 16 (1994): 457-61.

———. "The *Aqedah*, Jubilees, and PseudoJubilees." In Evans and Talmon, *The Quest for Context and Meaning*, 241-61.

———. *Calendars in the Dead Sea Scrolls: Measuring Time*. The Literature of the Dead Sea Scrolls. London: Routledge, 1998.

———. *From Revelation to Canon: Studies in the Hebrew Bible and Second Temple Literature*. JSJSup 62. Leiden: Brill, 2000.

———. "Studies in the Chronology of the Book of Jubilees." In *From Revelation to Canon*, 522-44.

———. *An Introduction to Early Judaism*. Grand Rapids: Eerdmans, 2001.

———. "Questions of Canon Viewed through the Dead Sea Scrolls." *BBR* 11 (2001): 269-92.

———. *The Book of Jubilees*. Guides to Apocrypha and Pseudepigrapha. Sheffield: Sheffield Academic, 2001.

———. "The Scriptural Setting of the Book of Jubilees." *DSD* 13 (2006): 61-72.

Vermes, Geza. *Scripture and Tradition in Judaism: Haggadic Studies.* StPB 4. Leiden: Brill, 1961; 2nd rev. ed. 1973.

———. *Post-Biblical Jewish Studies.* SJLA 8. Leiden: Brill, 1975.

———. "Biblical Proof-Texts in Qumran Literature." *JSS* 34 (1989): 493-508.

Vincent, Louis-Hugues. "Chronologie des Oeuvres de Josèphe." *RB* 9 (1911): 366-83.

Voitila, Anssi, and Jutta Jokiranta, eds. *Scripture in Transition: Essays on Septuagint, Hebrew Bible, and Dead Sea Scrolls in Honour of Raija Sollamo.* JSJSup 126. Leiden: Brill, 2008.

Wacholder, Ben Zion. *Eupolemus: A Study of Judaeo-Greek Literature.* HUCM 3. Cincinnati: Hebrew Union College Press, 1974.

———. "Jubilees as the Super Canon: Torah-Admonition versus Torah-Commandment." In *Legal Texts and Legal Issues: Proceedings of the Second Meeting of the International Organization for Qumran Studies, Cambridge 1995, Published in Honour of Joseph M. Baumgarten,* ed. Moshe Bernstein, Florentino García Martínez, and John Kampen. STDJ 23. Leiden: Brill, 1997, 195-211.

Wadsworth, Michael. "Making and Interpreting Scripture." In *Ways of Reading the Bible.* Brighton: Harvester, 1981, 7-22.

Weigold, Matthias. "Aramaic *Wunderkind:* The Birth of Noah in the Aramaic Texts from Qumran." In Berthelot and Stökl Ben Ezra, *Aramaica Qumranica,* 299-315.

———. "One Voice or Many? The Identity of the Narrators in Noah's Birth Story (1QapGen 1-5.27) and in the 'Book of the Words of Noah' (1QapGen 5.29–18.23)." *Aramaic Studies* 8 (2010): 89-105.

Weingreen, Jacob. "Rabbinic-Type Glosses in the Old Testament." *JSS* 2 (1957): 149-62.

———. "Exposition in the Old Testament and in Rabbinic Literature." In *Promise and Fulfillment: Essays Presented to Professor S. H. Hooke,* ed. Frederick F. Bruce. Edinburgh: T. & T. Clark, 1963, 187-201.

———. "The Deuteronomic Legislator — A Proto Rabbinic Type." In *Proclamation and Presence: Old Testament Essays in Honour of Gwynne Henton Davies,* ed. John I. Durham and J. R. Porter. Richmond: John Knox, 1970; repr. 1983, 76-89.

Weitzman, Steve. "Why Did the Qumran Community Write in Hebrew?" *JAOS* 119 (1999): 35-45.

Wendland, Paul. "Zu Philo's Schrift *de posteritate Caini* (Nebst Bemerkungen zur Rekonstruktion der Septuaginta)." *Phil* 57 (1898): 248-88.

Werman, Cana. "Qumran and the Book of Noah." In *Pseudepigraphic Perspectives: The Apocrypha and Pseudepigrapha in Light of the Dead Sea Scrolls: Proceedings of the Second International Symposium of the Orion Center for the Study of the Dead Sea Scrolls and Associated Literature, 12-14 January 1997,* ed. Esther G. Chazon and Michael E. Stone. STDJ 31. Leiden: Brill, 1999, 171-81.

Wernberg-Møller, Preben. "Some Reflections on the Biblical Material in the Manual of Discipline." *ST* 9 (1955): 40-66.

———. "The Contribution of the Hodayot to Biblical Textual Criticism." *Text* 4 (1964): 133-75.

Wevers, John William. *Notes on the Greek Text of Exodus.* SBLSCS 35. Atlanta: Scholars, 1990.

———. "The Interpretative Character and Significance of the Septuagint Version." In Sæbø, *Hebrew Bible/Old Testament,* 1:1 (1996), 84-107.

Whitters, Mark F. "Testament and Canon in the Letter of Second Baruch (2 Baruch 78–87)." *JSP* 12 (2001): 149-63.

———. *The Epistle of Second Baruch: A Study in Form and Message.* JSPSup 42. London: Sheffield Academic, 2003.

Wiesenberg, Ernest. "The Jubilee of Jubilees." *RevQ* 3 (1961): 3-40.

Willett, Tom W. *Eschatology in the Theodicies of 2 Baruch and 4 Ezra.* JSPSup 4. Sheffield: JSOT, 1989.

Williamson, Hugh G. M. "On Writing and Witnesses." In *The Book Called Isaiah: Deutero-Isaiah's Role in Composition and Redaction.* Oxford: Clarendon, 1994, 94-115.

Wills, Lawrence M. *The Jew in the Court of the Foreign King: Ancient Jewish Court Legends.* HDR 26. Minneapolis: Fortress, 1990.

Winston, David. *The Wisdom of Solomon.* AB 43. Garden City: Doubleday, 1979.

Wolfson, Harry Austryn. *Philo: Foundations of Religious Philosophy in Judaism, Christianity, and Islam.* 2 vols. Cambridge, Mass.: Harvard University Press, 1947.

Woude, A. S. van der, ed. *The Book of Daniel in the Light of New Findings.* BETL 106. Leuven: Leuven University Press, 1993.

Wright, Addison G. "The Structure of Wisdom 11–19." *CBQ* 27 (1965): 28-34.

———. "The Structure of the Book of Wisdom." *Bib* 48 (1967): 165-84.

Wright, Benjamin G. *No Small Difference: Sirach's Relationship to Its Hebrew Parent Text.* SBLSCS 26. Atlanta: Scholars, 1989.

———. "Ben Sira on Kings and Kingship." In *Jewish Perspectives on Hellenistic Rulers,* ed. Tessa Rajak et al. Hellenistic Culture and Society 50. Berkeley: University of California Press, 2007, 76-91.

———. "The Use and Interpretation of Biblical Traditions in Ben Sira's Praise of the Ancestors." In *Studies in the Book of Ben Sira: Papers of the Third International Conference on the Deuterocanonical Books, Shime'on Centre, Pápa, Hungary, 18-20 May 2006,* ed. Géza Xeravits and József Zsengellér. JSJSup 127. Leiden: Brill, 2008, 183-207.

———. "Jubilees, Sirach, and Sapiential Tradition." In *Enoch and the Mosaic Torah,* ed. Gabriele Boccaccini and Giovanni Ibba. Grand Rapids: Eerdmans, 2009, 116-30.

Wright, J. Edward. "The Social Setting of the Syriac Apocalypse of Baruch." *JSP* 16 (1997): 81-96.

———. "Baruch: His Evolution from Scribe to Apocalyptic Seer." In Stone and Bergren, *Biblical Figures Outside the Bible,* 264-89.

———. *Baruch Ben Neriah: From Biblical Scribe to Apocalyptic Seer.* Columbia: University of South Carolina Press, 2003.

Yadin, Yigael, ed. *The Temple Scroll.* 3 vols. Jerusalem: Israel Exploration Society, 1977-1983.

Zakovitch, Yair. "The Synonymous Word and Synonymous Name in Name-Midrashim." *Shnaton: An Annual for Biblical and Ancient Near Eastern Studies* 2 (1977): 100-115.

———. "The Varied Faces of Inner-biblical Interpretation." *Tarbiz* 56 (1986): 136-43. [Hebrew]

———. *An Introduction to Inner-biblical Interpretation.* Even Yehudah: Rekhes, 1992. [Hebrew]

———. *Through the Looking Glass: Reflection Stories in the Bible.* Tel Aviv: ha-Kibuts ha-Me'uhad, 1995. [Hebrew]

———. "Juxtaposition in the Abraham Cycle." In *Pomegranates and Golden Bells: Studies* in Biblical, Jewish, and Near Eastern Ritual, Law, and Literature in Honor of Jacob Milgrom, ed. David P. Wright, David Noel Freedman, and Avi Hurvitz. Winona Lake: Eisenbrauns, 1995, 509-24.

―――. "Was It Not at His Hand the Sun Stopped? (Ben Sira 46:6): A Chapter in Literary Archaeology." In Tehillah le-Moshe: Biblical and Judaic Studies in Honor of Moshe Greenberg, ed. Mordechai Cogan, Barry L. Eichler, and Jeffrey H. Tigay. Winona Lake: Eisenbrauns, 1997, 107*-14*.

―――. "The Exodus from Ur of the Chaldeans: A Chapter in Literary Archaelogy." In Ki Baruch Hu: Ancient Near Eastern, Biblical, and Judaic Studies in Honor of Baruch A. Levine, ed. Robert Chazan, William W. Hallo, and Lawrence H. Schiffman. Winona Lake: Eisenbrauns, 1999, 429-39.

Index of Modern Authors

Index of Subjects

Index of Passages

9 780802 803887